GOVERNANCE OF THE CONSUMING PASSIONS
A HISTORY OF SUMPTUARY LAW

Also by the same author

FOUCAULT AND LAW (*with Gary Wickham*)
EXPLORATIONS IN LAW AND SOCIETY
READING DWORKIN CRITICALLY
MARX AND ENGELS ON LAW (*with Maureen Cain*)
THE SOCIOLOGICAL MOVEMENT IN LAW

Governance of the Consuming Passions

A History of Sumptuary Law

Alan Hunt
Professor, Department of Law and Sociology
Carleton University, Ottawa

St. Martin's Press
New York

GOVERNANCE OF THE CONSUMING PASSIONS

For information, address:

St. Martin's Press, Scholarly and Reference Division,
175 Fifth Avenue, New York, N.Y. 10010

First published in the United States of America in 1996

Printed in Great Britain

ISBN 0-312-12922-X

Library of Congress Cataloging-in-Publication Data
Hunt, Alan.
Governance of the consuming passions : a history of sumptuary law / Alan Hunt.
p. cm.
Includes bibliographical references and index.
ISBN 0-312-12922-X
1, Sumptuary laws—Europe—History. 2. Clothing and dress–
–Europe—Social aspects—History. 3. Police power—Europe—History.
I. Title.
KJC6066.S85H86 1996
340'.115—dc20 96-11857
CIP

Contents

List of Figures

List of Tables

Preface

ORIGINS OF THE PROJECT

Since the present book has provided me with the opportunity to roam outside my customary intellectual terrain I should give some account of how I came to undertake the present project. I had for some time been interested in the general question of the ways in which law does not work in isolation, but always in combination with other economic, political and social mechanisms. One strand of those inquiries led me to become involved in a reassessment of the implications of Foucault's treatment of the role of law in the advent of modernity (Hunt 1992). I became increasingly aware of a tension between Foucault's exciting treatment of discipline and a growing dissatisfaction with his characterization of the part played by law in the transition to modernity. He had a tendency to reduce his account of pre-modern law to a system of royal commands backed by the threat of force. This just seemed too simple. I found myself reading material on the role of law and government in the transition to modernity. I came across Marc Raeff's fascinating account of the 'well-ordered police state' in early modern Germany (Raeff 1983). It was here that I first encountered a brief reference to the existence of sumptuary laws. Despite a disciplinary background in law I was surprised to encounter a species of law whose existence I was not aware of.

My initial explorations in the field were intended merely to fill this gap. I discovered that the typical piece of sumptuary legislation imposed restrictions on the type of clothing that people could wear, usually by prohibiting named cloths or styles. There also existed many other varieties of sumptuary law, but restrictive dress codes will serve as my standard example. Not only did I discover that such laws had been widespread, but I found myself becoming more and more fascinated because they disclosed the existence of distinctive projects of governance whose unique character offered a potentially fertile context in which to explore how projects of governance came to be formed, pursued and subsequently changed or abandoned. The very distance between sumptuary law and more typically 'modern' forms of legal regulation seemed to be a distinct advantage.

As a result of this brief encounter with sumptuary law, I formulated a rather rough and ready hypothesis that tracking the history of this neglected form of pre-modern law would provide a potentially fruitful means of exploring some of the general characteristics of the part played by law in the transition to modernity. As I pushed my inquiries further back into medieval Europe on the trail of sumptuary law I make some interesting discoveries. In the first place it became clear that, although the orthodox modern legal histories barely mentioned the existence of sumptuary legislation, it existed in great volume and in considerable variety in many different cultures and civilizations.

One feature that stood out from the mass of scattered accounts of sumptuary law I gathered together was that, with only a few interesting exceptions, their authors treated the existence of sumptuary law with unrestrained condescension as if the very idea of regulating dress was absurd and doomed any law which so attempted to an early demise or subversion. Many of the detailed studies of national or local sumptuary regulation were produced in the late nineteenth or early twentieth centuries. They all took the Whiggish view that sumptuary laws were alien to modernity and their disappearance provided evidence of the advancing good sense of rulers who no longer thought it desirable to seek to regulate such 'private' matters as what people should wear. There was a brief rekindling of interest in sumptuary matters in the United States in the inter-war period when sharp controversies over Prohibition, the paradigm case of modern regulation of consumption, gave the issue contemporary relevance. It was opponents of Prohibition that invoked the analogy with sumptuary law to deride such intervention, both old and new; they were intent on showing that such efforts were misguided, doomed to failure and fundamentally repressive of important liberties.

In the main sumptuary laws have not received very sympathetic treatment. Yet the more I discovered about the range and scope of sumptuary regulation the more I became concerned to grapple with a series of questions that challenged this orthodox consensus. In the first place I wanted to address the question: what did the great investment of legislative and governmental energy signify? If, as all the commentators seem to agree, they were doomed to failure, why did so many legislators, rulers, administrators, judges and others continue to enact and reenact sumptuary provisions? The provisional context within which I posed these issues was that the existence of such regulatory projects could reveal something of the historical transformations of the processes of governance. This sense of the connection between regulation and governance is brilliantly captured by Proudhon:

> Being governed means being under police supervision, being inspected, spied upon, directed, buried under laws, regulated, hemmed in, indoctrinated, preached at, controlled, assessed, censored, commanded . . . noted, registered, captured, appraised, stamped, surveyed, evaluated, taxed, patented, licensed, authorized, recommended, admonished, prevented, reformed, aligned, and punished in every action, every transaction, every movement.
> (Proudhon, quoted Oestreich 1982:272)

THE TRACES OF THE SUMPTUARY PROJECTS

It became clear that if I were to get any further toward understanding sumptuary law it would be necessary to examine its specific forms and contents more closely. Why should anyone want to control the number of women mourners at an Athenian funeral? What was the significance of the preoccupation about how citizens dressed? Was this primarily a matter, as the label sumptuary suggests, of a concern to control consumption? It was clear that sumptuary discourse was closely linked to the medieval discourses surrounding 'luxury' which itself exhibited a close interweaving of economic and theological controversies. Yet this did not seem sufficient to account for the fact that although sumptuary law was directed against many aspects of consumption, from the number of guests who could be invited to weddings to the expenditure permitted on funerals, this did not seem to explain the most persistent feature of the sumptuary laws, namely the preoccupation with how people dressed.

While I will discuss the variety and diversity of the types of social objects and practices at which regulation was directed, it will be the attempt to regulate dress and other aspects of appearance that occupies the great bulk of this book. There existed a pervasive 'sumptuary ethic' that held that it is the right and proper function of government, whether of state, church, guild or household, to regulate the consumption, in general, and the dress, in particular, of the participants. The attempt to regulate dress was directed at the project of bringing social appearance under control. Most commentators were agreed that a central feature was the concern of social superiors to preserve exclusivity by monopolizing the right to wear furs, silks, velvets, brocades or whatever else was conceived as conferring sartorial advantage on those so entitled. This account seemed to provide a plausible approach to those contexts that corresponded to some version of the classical model of a rising bourgeoisie in competition with a declining feudal aristocracy. This account, however, fitted less comfortably with the enormous sumptuary productivity of the predominantly bourgeois urban communities, from the pre-Renaissance Italian city-states to the post-Reformation trading cities of Germany and the Low Countries. The nagging doubt grew that it was necessary to penetrate further into the significance of 'appearance' to understand its evident significance in a wide range of different social milieus. This concern with appearance led to the need to explore a range of connected conceptions, in particular those of 'social visibility' and 'social recognition', that in turn drew my attention to issues about the place of material culture within conflictual and competitive social relations and, in particular, with the experience of urbanization that formed the general context of the period of the highest density of sumptuary activity. If the significance of appearance were to be grasped, this would require a broader understanding of both the 'invention' of fashion and more importantly its social dynamic. This necessitated an engagement with the social history of fashion. These inquiries fanned out in a number of different directions, some of which took me into new and unfamiliar directions.

An obvious and striking feature of the great bulk of sumptuary law was that it was directed at conceptions and images of the social order. It was concerned with attempts to protect hierarchical conceptions of social relations, to resist some of the most directly visible manifestations of rising social groups challenging the incumbents of advantaged social positions. The great bulk of this competitive social activity occurred in contexts in which modern social classes were, at best, only in the process of formation.

Another striking feature of sumptuary legislation is the way in which it was gendered. Overwhelmingly the detailed provisions laid down specific rules for women and for men. The surprising feature was the changing gender-targeting of sumptuary law. In some periods sumptuary legislation was directed exclusively against women and was saturated with misogynistic discourses, while in other cases women's dress remained entirely unregulated and the provisions were directed exclusively against men. This distinctive manner in which sumptuary legislation was genderized offers an opportunity to track significant features of gender relations during the transition to modernity. Particularly challenging is the prevalence of misogynous ideology during a historical period in which, on the surface at least, women did not pose any apparent challenge to male privilege and domination. Yet perhaps there were underlying tensions in gender relations that explain the complex dynamic of the gender dimension of sumptuary law.

Sumptuary discourses were embedded in the primary role of religious ideologies which formed the dominant intellectual discourse throughout most of the long period of active sumptuary intervention. Sumptuary ideals frequently invoked theological rationales, expressed in terms of preoccupation with the sin of pride and the consequent moralization of luxury, but sumptuary legislation was distinctively secular. While some echoes of these theological roots find expression in ecclesiastical jurisdictions the typical agent of the sumptuary ethos was the well-to-do city burgher. Many commentators have suggested a link between the Reformation and sumptuary laws seeing some predisposition in the Protestant concern with the moral governance of the individual to regulate personal consumption. But it became clear that there was no sumptuary version of the 'Protestant ethic'. It even seemed likely that the reverse was the case; sumptuary laws were perhaps more common under Catholic rule. While it is true that Calvinists and other Puritan traditions held strong views on the connection between appearance and purity the trajectory of sumptuary law was barely ruffled by the Reformation. The volume and targets of sumptuary intervention remained largely unchanged. Only in the interesting exception of the utopian projects of the New England colonies were fresh attempts made to create a sumptuary regime expressive of both faith and hierarchy. Significantly it has been in the United States that the most significant modern sumptuary projects have occurred. Alongside the well-known case of the constitutional 'Prohibition' of alcohol in the inter-war period, there seems to be a greater predisposition than elsewhere to countenance legislative prohibitions on consumption.

The realization that the sumptuary impulse had not only survived the transition to modernity, but had persisted into the twentieth century, gave rise to the thought that perhaps the almost universal assumption that sumptuary law had died with the rise of modernity was itself an over-simplification. It was certainly true that there were few overtly sumptuary enactments in modern states, but it was also true that sumptuary laws were used to propel more or less authoritarian modernizing programmes in such countries as Turkey, Iran and Singapore. More significant was the suggestion that sumptuary regimes had not so much died, but had rather changed, shifting, for example, into the realm of private corporate legislation in the form of employers' dress and grooming codes. This in turn raised the question of whether more recent attempts at moral regulation, such as the currently controversial debate about the prohibition of pornography, should be regarded as having a strong sumptuary dimension.

In exploring the persistence of sumptuary law, and the suggestion that it might have migrated into the late twentieth century in changed form, created the risk of beginning to think that sumptuary laws were perhaps more significant than the available evidence could sustain. It is important to bear in mind that there seems to be little evidence that any sustained attempt was made to enforce the sumptuary laws. This fact must be understood in a context in which the general pattern of law enforcement was much more haphazard and episodic, marked by short bursts of intensive activity followed by long periods of relative quiescence. The machinery of administration and its personnel was very limited in comparison to the resources available to modern law enforcement. Indeed it became clear that the significance of much of the attempted sumptuary regulation itself made a significant contribution to the processes of state formation which would lay the basis for a more extensive and regularized pattern of law enforcement.

Early records of the enforcement of sumptuary laws are rare, especially when compared to other widespread 'street offences' such as begging and prostitution. Although rarely spoken of in these terms the sumptuary laws were paradigmatically 'street offences'; it was the visibility and display of consumption that was the very essence of the offence. These comparisons may not be the most pertinent for they rather miss the distinctive dimension that the typical sumptuary offender is likely to have been a more privileged and certainly more economically comfortable citizen than the 'dangerous classes' who were the targets of most street offences. There may be some merit in the analogy between sumptuary offences and today's motoring offences for it is precisely the ordinary, more-or-less respectable citizen who is the typical offender, and this must have been the case with sumptuary laws. The dynamic of their existence and their enforcement (or lack of it) stems from the fact that it was entirely normal and typical social behaviour which was criminalized, just as today it is the normal, respectable citizen who routinely and persistently commits motoring offences. Where sumptuary laws and motoring offences part company is with respect to their tactics of enforcement, the complex technical, administrative and other information techniques that are today available.

When account is taken of the patchy enforcement of the sumptuary rules we should beware of jumping too quickly to the conclusion that these offences were unimportant. We may surmise that the very existence of sumptuary laws provided some normative elements to the practices of appearance and self-presentation, but we will not be able to say much in this regard until we have a clearer picture of the variety of sumptuary provisions and their location within the wider practices of government.

A study of the range and breadth undertaken here inevitably renders itself a hostage to fortune, but it also gives rise to opportunities that narrower studies can less easily take advantage of. On the debit side I have strayed into fields in which I remain an amateur. I am particularly sensitive to the concern of historians that a study of this breadth can only skate over the surface of the rich materials touched upon and places too great a reliance upon secondary sources. I have avoided any attempt to evade these difficulties by constructing broad sociological models and hypotheses. I come away from this project with enormous respect for the historian's craft. I hope that I have not made my material sustain more than it is capable of carrying and of not covering up the unevenness of the material itself. Similarly difficulties have attended my encounter with a host of disciplinary specialisms. Encounters with elements of the theory of fashion, theological debates on luxury, developments in economic thought and countless other strands leave me feeling humbled by the recognition of how little one knows and hoping not to have done too much violence to the richness of these fields of study. My respect for the richness I discovered has not, however, inhibited me from intervening in fields of intellectual inquiry in which I am totally untutored.

The positive dimensions of a study of this breadth are that it creates the possibility of a cross-fertilization between the intellectual traditions on which it draws. The broad organizing framework in which the sumptuary laws have been explored is as an intriguing instance of projects of governance giving rise to diverse regulatory practices. In the course of this exploration I have attempted to understand the regulation of dress as an incidence of the interaction between consumption and the systems of production in which it is located; this approach is an example of an attempt by both sociologists and economic historians to take consumption seriously without counterposing consumption to production.

The focus on governance conceived as sets of concrete techniques of regulation has brought me into close proximity with two important intellectual traditions which remain surprisingly distant from each other; from sociologically oriented cultural studies I have attempted to link a study of the struggles surrounding the civilizing and distinguishing projects that traverse the long haul to modernity with the social historian's focus on the reform of popular culture. In so doing I have elaborated a view of the significance of the attempts to police social recognizability with other projects of governance that impinged upon the diversity of life in late medieval and early modern society as illustrated by the regulation of prostitution and the struggles over popular pastimes and recreations. The intersecting struggles over the regulation of labour and of idleness bring out the distinctive significance of social appearance in these processes. Sumptuary law emerges in this study, no longer as some faintly amusing aberration on the way to modernity, but as a component of the complex of discursive struggles and practical encounters that sharpen our understanding of the link between governance and culture.

This focus on the linkages between governance and the everyday culture of dress and appearance provides a way of connecting up with elements of the history of subjectivity. The concerns and anxieties that emerge during the expansion of commodity or consumption cultures bring to the surface the association between consumption and excitement and self-expression which underpins the investments, both economic and emotional, in the construction of self-presentation. At the same time it opens up an understanding of how these matters came to be constructed as proper and necessary targets of governmental concern and action.

SOME PROCEDURAL CONSIDERATIONS

There is no escape from the difficulties inherent in the terms used to identify the periodization of historical time. My approach has been to refuse any attempt to 'solve' such conflicts as those between 'feudal' and 'pre-industrial', 'capitalism' and the myriad alternates, or between 'economic' and 'socio-political' descriptive terms. At the risk of being eclectic I have used those terms which, in context, draw attention to the most relevant feature. The result is that I use different descriptive terms in different contexts. The only merit I can claim is that this undercuts the claims of any single set of categories to some theoretically privileged status. Particular difficulties arise with respect to the term 'class'. It is important to avoid over-extension of conceptualizations which draw on the language of class and class struggle. I try to hold this constraint in place by insisting that in so far as the conflict involved can usefully be thought of through the metaphor of class, it is with what may be called 'class struggle before classes' with which I will be dealing (Thompson 1978).

I employ the following historical periodization: (high) Middle Ages *c.* 1050–1300, late Middle Ages *c.* 1300–1550, Early Modern *c.* 1550–1800, Modern post–1800.

It should be noted that I intentionally use a singular gender-neutral 'their' as a possessive pronoun rather than 'his/her' and use the nouns 'person' and 'people' as my preferred contribution to the quest for a gender-neutral language.

I have used notes in an intentionally informal manner and this has been facilitated by the placing of most citations in the text. I have in some cases used notes for citations referring to statutes, proclamations and case references where to have included them in the text would be disruptive. Notes are used primarily for asides, comments, and conjectures, often as notes of topics and questions that might be followed up. This book has intentionally been left with many loose ends. Had it not been so it might never have been completed. More importantly it expresses my conviction about the necessarily unfinished nature of all worthwhile projects.

THE STRUCTURE OF THE WORK

Chapter 1 argues a case for the reopening of the sumptuary file and outlines some broad parameters of the sociology of governance within which this study is organized. I thought it necessary, given the lack of attention in both social and legal history to sumptuary laws, to offer in Chapter 2 an overview of the chronology of sumptuary regulation. Chapters 3 and 4 narrow the focus of attention to the paradigm form of sumptuary rules as projects for the regulation of appearance, setting these considerations against the phenomenon of fashion and conspicuous consumption and the interaction with the critiques of luxury and extravagance. Chapter 5 identifies a pervasive contradiction at the heart of all attempts to regulate appearance before moving on, in Chapter 6, to advance a general explanatory framework of sumptuary laws as attempts to stabilize social recognizability in the characteristically urban 'world of strangers'. Chapters 7 and 8 explore the urban context by focusing first on the connection between sumptuary projects and class relations and within the specific practices of the governance of cities. Chapters 9 and 10 explore the gendered dimension of sumptuary laws as components of 'gender wars' and their part in the pervasive misogynous discourses of late medieval and early modern societies. Chapter 11 explores sumptuary laws in their interaction within wider projects directed at the reform of popular culture. This theme is illustrated in a more concrete context in Chapter 12 which explores the history of English sumptuary legislation; attention is focused on the changing interconnections between these legislative and other projects of governance, in particular those directed at vagrancy and at the regulation of popular recreation.

Chapter 13 surveys the evidence regarding the enforcement of sumptuary laws. Chapter 14 traces the transformations in which distinctively sumptuary regulation became swallowed up by the rising discourses of protectionist economic governance that come to the fore in the early modern period. Chapter 15 challenges the view that sumptuary regulation actually died, and develops an argument that in the modern world the regulation of consumption persists, but becomes dispersed throughout a range of both public and private forms of governance. The conclusions developed stress the persistence of projects of governance of personal appearance and of private consumption. In so doing the view is defended that studies of legal forms of regulation need to be situated within the wider projects of governance, that is the economic, social and moral regulation in which legal regulation is embedded.

Acknowledgements

This project happened rather than being planned. It emerged from a long period of unstructured and unfocused reading. Thus my first thanks should go to the always helpful librarians at the Macodrum Library at Carleton University where the project began to take shape, at the British Library and the Senate House Library were most of the work was undertaken and to the Law Library of the University of Western Australia where many of the gaps were filled.

I owe a special thanks to the University of Western Australia and in particular to John Phillipps, Dean of the Law School, who provided the ideal sabbatical berth where the bulk of the text was written. Peter Goodrich provided a niche at Birkbeck College in London. Financial support from the Social Science and Humanities Research Council provided my first notebook computer which has changed the conditions of intellectual production more than I could have realized.

Most of all I am grateful to all those who gave generously of their time to talk, to pass on references, to read drafts and to offer encouragement. Jane Abray, Ros Allchin, Peter Goodrich, Peter Fitzpatrick, Judy Fudge, Catherine Kovesi-Killerby, Dave Lewis, Dag Lindström, Roger Matthews, Hans Mohr, Pat O'Malley, Louis Proksch, Trevor Purvis, Nikolas Rose, Derek Smith, Ceylan Tokluoglu-Cesur, John Tweedy, Mariana Valverde, Gary Wickham, Elizabeth Wilson and Tony Woodiwiss and the others I have unintentionally omitted, helped fuel and lubricate the process while deserving no blame for its result.

1

Why Study Sumptuary Law?

I. LOCATING SUMPTUARY LAW

Sumptuary laws came in many varieties. An English statute of 1336 required that:

> no man, of what state or condition soever he be, shall cause himself to be served in his house or elsewhere, at dinner, meal or supper, or at any other time, with more than two courses and each mess of two sorts of victuals at the utmost, be it Flesh or Fish, with the common sorts of pottage, without sawce or any sort of victuals . . . except only on the principal feasts of the year . . ., on which days every man may be served with three courses at the utmost, after the manner aforesaid.
>
> (10 Edw. III: st.3; SR 1: 278–79)

The preamble to a Nürnburg ordinance from 1657 complained:

> It is unfortunately an established fact that both men and womenfolk have, in utterly irresponsible manner, driven extravagance in dress and new styles to such shameful and wanton extremes that the different classes are barely to be known apart.
>
> (Boehn 1932–35: III: 173)

A Japanese decree from 1668 specified:

> Puppet costumes must not be sumptuous. Gold and silver leaf must not be used on anything. But puppet generals only may wear gold and silver hats.
>
> (Shively 1955: 345)

An order of 1643 in the New England colony in Massachusetts Bay provided that:

> The Court, takeing into consideracon the greate, superfluous, & unnecessary expences occaconed by reason of some newe & imodest fashions, as also the ordinary weareing of silver, golde, & silke laces, girdles, hatbands, etc. hath therefore ordered that noe person, either man or woman, shall hereafter make or buy any apparell, either wollen, silke, or lynnen, with any lace on it, silver, golde, silke, or threed, vnder the penalty of forfeiture of such cloathes, etc.
>
> (Shurtleff 1968: I: 126)

The preamble to a Florentine statute of 1433 reads:

> After diligent examination and mature deliberation, the Lords Priors have seen, heard and considered certain regulations issued by the magistrates [ufficiale delle donne] . . . They realize the great desire of these officials to restrain the barbarous and irrepressible bestiality of women, who, not considering the fragility of their nature, but rather with that reprobate and diabolical nature, they force their men, with their honeyed poison, to submit to them. But it is not in accordance with nature for women to be burdened by so many expensive ornaments, and on account of these unbearable expenses, men are avoiding matrimony . . . But women were created to replenish this free city, and to live chastely in matrimony, and not to spend gold and silver on clothing and jewelry. For did not God himself say: 'Increase and multiply and replenish the earth'? The Lord Priors, having diligently considered the regulations recorded below and in order that the city be reformed with good customs, and so that the bestial audacity of these women be restrained, approve and confirm the following regulations . . .
>
> (Bruckner 1971: 181)

Such is sumptuary law.

I propose to avoid tying myself to a definition of sumptuary law. The contention that laws regulating consumption undergo a series of major transformations forms a major part of the argument that will be fleshed out in this work. The other consideration that leads me to abjure definitions is that those offered in the literature are preoccupied with identifying the 'motives' that are taken to underlie the rules enacted. For example, sumptuary law is commonly defined as laws intended to limit or regulate the private expenditure of citizens (Baldwin 1926:9; Miles 1987: 75).[1]

My reservation about teleological definition that gives primacy to the 'motives' of legislation is that it must become ensnared in the difficulty of distinguishing between 'real' and 'justificatory' motives; since such issues are ultimately undecidable it is better to avoid these difficulties. I will, however, be much concerned with the discourses within which sumptuary laws are located and with exploring shifts and variations in these discourses and in tracing their connection with related discourses. Instead I organize my discussion around the terms 'project' and 'governance'; since I make substantial use of these terms it is necessary to elaborate on my usage.

TOWARD A SOCIOLOGY OF GOVERNANCE

I identify my project as being a 'sociology of governance'. I need to insist at the outset that 'governance' is not reducible to 'government'; while governments govern, governance is exercised by a range of institutions, organizations, professions and other forms of social entities that do not necessarily share the constitutionalized attributes of governments. Governance is exercised where a relatively persistent set of often conflicting practices select and construct some social object that is acted on in such a way as to control, restrain, limit and direct the activities of the selected object of governance. Since all social action is action upon other social entities I am concerned to avoid equating governance with all social action; thus while 'control' is an important component of interpersonal relations I do not think it helpful to speak of governance unless one is seeking to focus on some aggregated activity: for example, individual parents 'bring up the kids', but it is pertinent to speak of the 'governance of children' when such practices are sustained and supported not only by other parents, but by doctors, schools and other wider social practices. Accordingly I identify governance with the results of concerted and persistent action of social agents through 'projects' conceived as the practices (and their associated discourses) directed towards the control of other social agents and institutions.

Central to the concepts of 'governance' and 'project' is that they always involve 'attempts' whose characteristic is that while generally more or less concerted they typically produce results such that the project remains, to a greater or less extent, always in need of supplementation, revision, repetition and likely to produce unintended consequences; attempts are thus characterized by a cycle of attempt, followed by partial realization/failure, which in turn initiates fresh or revised attempts. Governance is always an ongoing set of practices that persists until its target or object undergoes some significant shifts to a reconstructed object or is abandoned. It needs to be stressed that objects of governance are always socially constructed and are then activated in and through the specific and hence variable practices of social agents.

One further feature of my usage of the term 'project' requires comment. While the term 'project' tends to import implications of purpose and motive in a way that is particularly apparent with terms like 'policy', I attempt (and it can be no more than that) to restrain the term to refer, not to the goals or motives, but to the persistent sets of discourses and practices of governance.

The 'sociology of governance' has diverse intellectual antecedents. I will do no more than sketch these links. Its most immediate draws on those parts of the work of Michel Foucault in which he explored and expanded the concept of 'government', for example with the neologism 'governmentality' (Foucault 1979), 'techniques of government' (Foucault 1980a) and the 'government of the self' or 'care of the self' (Foucault 1985). One of the reasons why Foucault's work is of such central significance is that in drawing attention to the governance of sexuality he highlighted the patterns discernible in uniquely personalized conduct; in much the same way that Durkheim had done earlier with the phenomenon of suicide, Foucault highlighted in striking and dramatic fashion the presence of the 'social' within the minutiae of 'individual' life. The identification of a historically constructed object of governance such as the obsession with juvenile masturbation that erupted in Victorian England has its own historical specificity (Neumann 1975). Once constructed this object gave rise to a complex interrelationship between child-rearing practices, dormitory arrangements in schools, medical discourses, etc., that operated in some loose combination for a period of time until changing anxieties about juvenile sexuality resulted in the abandonment of masturbation as an object or target of governance and the earlier concerns came to appear as one of those decidedly 'odd' features of the past whose very difference plays such an important part in constructing the modern. My object of inquiry, sumptuary law, is just such an 'odd' historical object of governance that has served to reinforce the separation of past from present. To treat it as an exemplar of the sociology of governance is to explore not just its differences, but also its similarities with current forms of governance of all those arenas of life that at first glance are viewed as personal and private.

While I have been much tempted to write an extended theoretical essay on the links, borrowing and differences of the sociology of governance and Foucault's legacy, I renounced that approach in the hope that my study of sumptuary law contributes more to the development of such an approach than would be achieved in a theoretical essay. I will leave the topic of intellectual antecedents by commenting that I see strong links between my own project and the exciting line of recent work by Graham Burchell, Mitchell Dean, Colin Gordon, Peter Miller, Nikolas Rose and Gary Wickham; whether they see any links with my work I cannot say.[2]

I have also been much tempted by the designation 'sociology of regulation'; indeed the terms 'regulation' and 'governance' are almost interchangeable in my usage. I come down against employing the label 'sociology of regulation' primarily to avoid confusion with other current usages and thus to avoid adding confusion.[3] While avoiding the use of 'regulation' as an identifying label there are many currents of its recent usages that are close to my current concerns, in particular in the focus on the regulation of morals, gender and the private sphere (Newburn 1991; Smart 1992). There are also significant overlaps with the important body of historical scholarship organized around the focus on the 'reform of popular culture' (Burke 1978) and the 'reform of morals' (Bristow 1977). This line of work has tended to focus on the impact of action from above on the traditions and culture of working people. While sumptuary law shares something of this imposition from above it is very much involved either with the self-regulation of the dominant classes or with their action on rising social classes. Hence my treatment embodies an ongoing concern with Gramsci's focus on hegemony as the interaction of cultural interventions in the formations of patterns of cultural and political dominance (Gramsci 1971).

The implications of these remarks on governance and regulation serve to clarify my reservations about the standard identification of sumptuary law with the restraint of extravagance. While such a definition is adequate for many purposes, it has the disadvantage of importing an emphasis upon the justificatory motives invoked by legislators. The equation of sumptuary law with the curtailment of extravagance was a characteristic economic motive associated with the mercantilist views that were influential in the period when sumptuary law was already in decline. Such a definition would encompass a number of marginal cases, such as price fixing regulations and restrictions on the importation of foreign goods. It should be recalled that price regulation was of great importance in most pre-modern societies, manifest in the illusive quest for a 'just price' that taxed medieval theology as much as it did the early political economy. This definitional separation of price regulation and sumptuary regulation requires some justification and certainly this could not be provided if sumptuary law was defined as regulation of expenditure. The exclusion of price regulation says much about the direction of the present project. If the focus of this study was to have been on economic governance or regulation then both price and sumptuary regulation would have to play an important part in the account of the ways in which economic activity became constructed as a suitable object of governance. While I will nevertheless need occasionally to venture into this terrain, my primary focus is upon a different facet of the history of governance. The projects of governance manifest in sumptuary law were directed at a different object. In its simplest form I will argue that sumptuary law was directed at the 'citizen' as the proper subject of governmental action; in contrast price regulation rules involved the governance of specific economic agents. This distinction between citizens and economic agents can never involve a clear and consistent separation. It is necessary to qualify the term citizen; a better formulation might be to say that the target was 'the citizen before citizenship'. My point is that the term 'citizen' tends to refer to those aspects of the participation of people in an already demarcated public sphere. The difficulty is that sumptuary law was active before such delineations were stabilized and secured; a more positive formulation is to suggest that sumptuary law contributed to the delineation of the more of less stable arenas of intervention in the whole texture of social life that was constitutive of the public/private boundaries of modern social life.

The focus on sumptuary governance is thus conceived as providing a paradigmatic case of one major form of regulation without denying its links and connections to other forms of regulation that together created modern government.[4] My treatment of these themes departs in a small, but possibly significant, way from Foucault's treatment of government and governmentality. I am hesitant about the emphasis he places on 'population' coming to be constructed as the general object of government. He argues that before the rise of the new disciplinary powers in the eighteenth and nineteenth centuries, monarchical power had only a weak capacity for individualizing, exhaustive analysis of the social body (Foucault 1980a:151). My point is one which in principle Foucault would probably not have disagreed with; it is that there coexist a multiplicity of targets of regulation and of forms of regulation. These are subject to significant epochal shifts as new configurations are formed from the combination of different regulatory objects and new groupings of regulatory activities. Specifically, I argue that sumptuary regulation was an early form of the project that comes to target as the proper task of government the manifestations of citizenship, understood in terms of the social and moral well-being of an aggregated population, designated by such constructs as 'the commonwealth'.

In order to avoid adopting any teleological view about 'motives' or 'purposes' of sumptuary laws I propose to adopt the following usage: sumptuary laws regulate the conspicuous consumption of 'citizens'; that is to say, sumptuary laws are concerned with the social manifestations of consumption. My sense of 'conspicuous consumption' is wider than that developed in Thorstein Veblen's classic study (Veblen [1899] 1967) that I discuss in detail below. I am not only concerned with class or status emulation, but with all forms of the presentation of the self. I will take the paradigm case of sumptuary law as being the regulation of personal appearance through rules relating to clothing, and social ceremonies associated with the presentation of the self and of economic wealth, in particular baptisms, weddings, funerals and other events in the life-cycle of individuals and kinship groups.

One distinctive feature of this conception of sumptuary law is that it always involves some combination of social, economic and moral regulation. This insistence on the interplay of social, economic and moral regulation will manifest itself in an ongoing concern to tease out and to make explicit the specific forms of combination of these distinct modalities of regulation.

SUMPTUARY PROJECTS

It should be noted that this definitional strategy focuses on the targets or objects of regulation; this helps to avoid introducing any assumptions about the motives of sumptuary regulation. It will be a theme of the analysis that there occur significant shifts in the 'motives', or as I prefer, regulatory projects. By way of a brief outline of these shifts I will distinguish between projects directed to the reproduction of hierarchical social relations based on birth, rank or other status orders, projects regulating the cultural forms of the struggle between feudal or quasi-feudal nobilities and urban mercantile bourgeoisies, and, finally, a shift towards protectionist economic regulation in which the overtly sumptuary aspects become subsumed. This third stage is still present in contemporary luxury taxes, import duties and the like. Yet the sumptuary impulse is never entirely extinguished, despite the disappearance of overt projects directed towards dress; its traces reemerge in myriad modern projects concerned with the regulation of the social and especially in continuing projects of moral regulation.

The overwhelming response of commentators throughout the long life of sumptuary regulation, and this is true whether these views are contemporary or retrospective, has been to view sumptuary laws as doomed to failure. It is insisted that such laws were widely evaded and that little effort was made to enforce them. It is thus not surprising that the overwhelming response of commentators has been dismissive. Thus the *Cambridge Ancient History* opines that 'belief in the value of sumptuary legislation was a delusion which even the most enlightened minds of Rome rarely managed to escape' (Cook 1932: IX: 301). One survey of the history of sumptuary law from the ancient Greeks to the twentieth century has no hesitation in offering the view that:

> throughout history such laws were generally ignored, flagrantly opposed, only slightly enforced, and gradually became obsolete.
> (Phillips and Staley 1961: 674)

So commonplace is this view that it has remained unquestioned. Sumptuary law is regarded as an immature or unsophisticated stage of legal development; it fits readily into Richard Posner's category 'aspirational law', which is characterized by a legal optimism that leads rulers to believe that their desire to achieve some policy goal is sufficient grounds for its enactment (Posner 1990: 8). I will challenge this dismissive view, the most immediate ground being that it seems improbable that a form of social regulation, bearing highly charged economic, political and cultural manifestations and found in virtually all major civilizations and which, furthermore, persisted until, at the very least, the dawn of modernity, should be regarded as a failure such that it is not worth studying, save perhaps for antiquarian interest.

To challenge this overwhelming and pervasive dismissal of the significance of sumptuary law creates the risk that I might fall into the trap of over-compensating and of lapsing into a simple reversal. It is not the intention to argue that sumptuary governance had some intrinsic importance or that it had some, previously unrevealed, profound impact on societies that experienced it. The project is more modest; it is to advance the contention that sumptuary law was significantly associated with the major stages in the rise of modernity. The study of sumptuary law yields significant insight into the characteristics of the changing forms of governance that are associated with the passage from pre-modernity to modernity. It will be further argued that far from disappearing without trace as most commentators have assumed, projects of sumptuary rule left their imprint on modernity. In particular, it will be argued that sumptuary laws have lived on in the ubiquitous quest for moral regulation that found expression in the social purity and prohibition movements of the nineteenth and early twentieth centuries and is today alive and well in the contemporary purity movements and projects of moral regulation.

If I am correct in suggesting that the sumptuary project is still alive, that is a good reason for taking a closer look at this subject. Aside from the question of contemporary relevance there are a number of other important reasons for insisting on the significance of sumptuary law as an object of inquiry.

The argument that I develop is that sumptuary law, while present in many different societies, can best be viewed as existing on the borders of modernity; it can be understood as a first response to modernity. It is this historical location astride an old world and a new world that leads me to focus attention on the way in which sumptuary projects face in two directions at the same time. Sumptuary law was a response to at least three of the most distinctive features of modernity; these I take to be urbanization, the emergence

MODERNITY.

of class as the pervasive form of social relations, and the construction of gender relations that are less and less determined by a natural sexual division of labour. As such, sumptuary law connects 'backwards' to the medieval world by building on the critique of luxury and a general moralization of social relations embodied in the primacy of religious discourses, but it also points 'forward' to a shift of preoccupation with the 'economy', and thus with the role of the state, which involves a radically different way of thinking and understanding in which social relations are constructed and acted upon by the multiple projects of governance. The sumptuary ethic was strongly implicated in some of the most crucial phases of the advance of urbanization and of the transition from mercantile to manufacturing capitalism. With respect to the experiential impact of urbanization, it brought with it the problem of how it is possible to live in close physical proximity with others and sustain relations of mutual dependence with strangers. I will advance and defend a 'recognizability thesis' which views sumptuary law as one significant component in the solution to this potentially traumatic dilemma. The concern to 'recognize' others involved more than just a concern with social hierarchy and status, although this was a significant component of the logic of recognizability that was so important in providing a plausible, even self-evident, rationale for the long-running project of sumptuary regulation.

It is the location of sumptuary law at the borders of modernity that explains the extinction of interest in this phenomenon in high modernity as long as it remained self-confidently preoccupied with growth, expansion and, more generally, with 'progress'. Now that our late twentieth century concerns and anxieties have radically undermined modernity's self-confidence a fresh look at sumptuary law raises the question: how did it come about that whole areas of potential regulatory intervention are at one period heavily colonized and yet at another present every appearance of being completely unregulated? From the vantage point of the late twentieth century it is possible to examine what was involved in the historical shift whereby regulatory activities suddenly abandoned whole fields (or at least appear to have done so) only to engage with and to penetrate some new field of life before moving on to new targets.

Thus sumptuary law will be closely connected with the changing forms of governance and the associated understandings of the nature of governance and governmentality (the activities and the dispositions of government). The different varieties and stages of sumptuary legislation can be studied as corresponding to different stages of state formation and to differences in political statecraft. Such a study may thus reveal evidence concerning the changing principles and premises on which political authority was grounded. In particular this focus will provide the context in which the conceptualization of pre-modern government as 'paternalistic' can be evaluated. In brief, it will be argued that whilst initially attractive the concept of paternalism ends up impeding an adequate understanding of the projects of governance on the boundaries of modernity.

The light thrown by sumptuary law on government and state formation provides a context in which to explore Foucault's interesting suggestion that modern power has taken two rather different forms, 'disciplines' that act on bodies and 'regulation' that acts on 'populations'. He distinguished between 'discipline', 'the anatamo-politics of the human body' and 'regulation' or the 'bio-politics of the population' (Foucault 1978: 149). At first glance sumptuary laws would seem to be an instance of disciplinary power, acting on the detailed choices made by individuals about their appearance or consumption, and thus provide some evidence for a sequential interpretation of social power with the 'failure' of sumptuary law suggesting a shift from discipline to regulation. Yet the discourses within which sumptuary law was embedded were part of a wider concern with economic strategies concerning the aggregate well-being of populations. There is here some encouragement to explore further this relationship between discipline and regulation. A significant shift occurs within the trajectory of sumptuary laws; in the later phase of their existence they changed from a focus on 'personal regulation' to laws focusing on 'protection of public welfare', and the distinctively sumptuary features get lost in a plethora of economic regulation and public health legislation. It seems likely that this change is understandable in terms of Foucault's distinction between discipline and regulation, even though he was insistent that the distinction should not be regarded as sequential.

The exploration of this theme will also be linked to an interest in the processes of state formation; the shift to 'public welfare' focus brings with it new forms of official knowledge, and new and extended governmental capacities. This concern with state formation and governmentalization needs to be connected to the other significant Foucauldian preoccupation with the government of the self and how that is connected with what Mary Douglas argues is the universal project of government, the 'attempts to force one another into good citizenship' (Douglas 1966: 3). This raises the interesting issue of the connection between sumptuary law as a project for the 'government' of consumption, the presentation of self, 'government of the self', and the emerging conceptions of citizenship that pre-date the struggles for representative democracy. Struggles over dress, ornamentation and consumption provide a focus on some of these most general features of the transition to modernity that are located at the most immediate level of the experience of what the currently influential forms of historical scholarship identify with the label 'everyday life'.

This approach invites attention to the question of what impact, if any, sumptuary laws had on everyday life in the towns and cities that were the most characteristic sites of attempts at sumptuary regulation. While the materials on which this study draws do not permit of any very confident generalizations, they do at least serve to place such questions on the agenda as part of an emerging tradition of culturally oriented legal history (Merry 1990; Post 1991). The study of sumptuary law can provide a vehicle for coming to grips with law's capacity to penetrate everyday life; to evaluate the extent, in E.P. Thompson's powerful terms, that the Law may punctuate the limits of behaviour tolerated by the rulers, but does not necessarily 'enter into the cottages, find a mention in the housewife's prayers, decorate the chimney-piece with icons, or inform a view of life' (Thompson 1978: 154).

SUMPTUARY LAW AND MODERNITY

The existence of sumptuary law at the gateway to modernity also invites an inquiry that focuses on the attempt to understand the anxieties and tensions that accompanied the experience of modernity. Sumptuary laws speak to us, usually indirectly, about the impact of plagues, famines and crises of all kinds that were such a significant feature of late medieval and early modern life. These concerns went hand in hand with the ubiquitous preoccupation with a 'world turned upside-down' which might well be treated as the most pervasive social-psychological response to the onset of modernity. I will adopt as a general heuristic strategy in order to explain the dynamics of sumptuary regulation of keeping to the fore the question: with what social tensions or anxieties was the specific sumptuary legislative activity connected? It is not just the perceived experiential anxieties that should be of concern; these provide a starting point, but this methodological strategy requires exploration of the deeper level of the structural tensions, the forms of class, gender and status relations that constitute the bedrock on which sumptuary legislation rested and of which it can best be regarded as a barometer of both popular and governmental anxiety. A further difficulty is that the surface anxieties, what people said they were concerned about, hid one or more layers of 'displaced anxiety', anxieties which were not necessarily spoken and probably not even perceived in consciousness.[5]

Another avenue through which a similar set of themes will be explored is to consider sumptuary laws as a form of symbolic politics. This draws attention to the importance of symbolic struggles that surround the recognition of appropriateness of dress, appearance or demeanour, captured in the rhetorical question 'Who does s/he think s/he is?' It is precisely the capacity to assert and deny social recognition that lies at the heart of all those forms of regulation, including sumptuary laws, that have addressed this relation between being and seeming, with all its capacity for misreading, misrepresentation and the pretence of those whom Bourdieu calls the 'pretentious pretenders' (Bourdieu 1984: 380).

It is the distinctive persistence and longevity of sumptuary that inevitably ensures that the character of its projects change. I will argue that they provide a case study of the 'functional transformation' of legal norms whereby the same legal framework is deployed in changed circumstances and in the service of different projects (Renner 1972). With the rise of modernity, sumptuary laws, rather in the same way as Foucault describes the trajectory of the confession, did not so much die out, but rather spread and changed their form (Foucault 1980a: 63).

Studying the trajectory of sumptuary law has provided a wonderful opportunity to study the construction of gender during the period of the transition to modernity. Dress is central to the construction of gender. It is the clothed body that is one of the key steps that transform males and females into men and women. Sumptuary regulation centrally revolves around the practices that regulate the gendered ordering of appearance; not only do they emerge in a period in which sexual dimorphism in dress becomes more deeply entrenched, but one in which we find a lot of evidence of anxiety about the ordering of gender. Gender relations are central to the concerns over the 'world turned upside-down', and they manifest themselves in a specific anxiety about cross-dressing. Sumptuary laws provide a unique insight into the complex construction of gender in the emergence of modernity. This complexity arises from the variation in the targets of sumptuary ordering; in some contexts women were the prime target of regulation, but at others women seem to have been largely ignored and it was the ostentatious dress of men that attracted the attention of the legislators.

How people dressed and ornamented themselves, and how others responded, and whether or not they sought to regulate that conduct provides an extensive 'text' that supplements the other traces that are left. Not only is the record of dress extensive, but it may often tell us something different from the written text. Dress has that distinctive characteristic of being, at one and the same time, both important and trivial. As such it has the capacity to communicate both in ways that are highly self-conscious, and also at levels at which we should not search for intention, purpose or motive. Dress is a form of consumed material culture and as such involves a complex system of communication. Since so much of the literature about personal appearance and dress is couched in terms of the significant figure of 'fashion' I will attempt to locate fashion both historically and as a semiotic system before examining 'fashion' as a target of regulation.

THE LITERATURE ON SUMPTUARY LAW

Since the literature on sumptuary law is scattered and much of it is far from recent, it may prove helpful to give a brief overview of the English language sources that deal specifically with sumptuary law.

There is no systematic work on the sumptuary laws of antiquity. The only extended treatment of Rome is in the doctoral thesis by Devi Miles (1987) on Roman sumptuary law. On Greece the most extensive treatment of clothing regulation is in an article by Harrianne Mills (1984).

The materials on European sumptuary law are more extensive.

England is best served by the detailed monograph by Frances Baldwin (1926) who provides comprehensive coverage of English sumptuary legislation. Hooper (1915) provides a thorough study of Tudor sumptuary legislation, and also pays attention to proclamations in the period from 1510 to 1604 and is distinctive for his focus on enforcement. A recent, and more sophisticated, study is to be found in the short but rich treatment by N.B. Harte (1976). Written from an economic history perspective, Harte traces the transition from paternalistic sumptuary law to protectionism. On Scotland Frances Shaw (1979) provides the only recent study.

Italy is well covered by a variety of treatments. Diane Hughes (1983), in addition to providing a comprehensive survey of sumptuary legislation in Renaissance Italy, organizes her discussion around many of the questions that have stimulated the present study. Margaret Newett (1907) and Stella Newton (1988) provide studies of Venice, and Ronald Rainey (1985) has written his PhD thesis on sumptuary regulation in Florence.

The fullest treatment of German material is Greenfield's (1918) detailed study of sumptuary regulation in Nürnburg that is organized around the theme of paternalism. Lyndal Roper's (1985 and 1989) work on women in Augsburg provides valuable insight into some aspects of the local sumptuary regime and, for me, epitomizes the richness and texture produced by the best of contemporary history. John Vincent's (1935) study of sumptuary order in Reformation Swiss towns is, like Greenfield's, organized around the motif of paternalism; it is particularly valuable in providing the most extensive treatment of enforcement of sumptuary laws.

France and Spain are both poorly treated by the English language material, possibly because sumptuary law in both countries spanned such a long period it has not been the focus of any sustained attention. The French and Spanish language material is rather dated and there seems to have been little recent interest in the regulation of personal appearance and consumption, which is surprising given the importance of the history of private life in recent French scholarship.

On sumptuary law in the East I have relied heavily on two contrasting studies: Hall (1906, 1908, 1909) and Shively (1964–65); while on China, T'ung-Tsu Ch'ü (1961) proved the most helpful.

A considerable volume of the evidence concerning sumptuary law has come from more a diverse range of historical studies, as will be seen from the bibliography. While I make no claim to be undertaking what most historians would recognize as historical scholarship, I am appreciative of having had this opportunity to get closer to the methods and problems that confront the practising historian.

The second major seam of material which this study has drawn on is the history of costume and fashion. Amongst this extensive genre the most helpful proved to be Bell (1976), Boehn (1932–35), Brenninkmeyer (1963), Davis (1985), Flugel (1950), Hollander (1980), Alison Lurie (1983) and König (1973 – a largely unrecognized work, but probably the most interesting from a social-psychological perspective). Of the more recent and sociologically sophisticated work on the phenomenon of fashion two studies stand out for special mention. Joanne Finkelstein (1991) shares my own interest in the social construction of recognition. The work I found most stimulating was Elizabeth Wilson (1985) which of all the work on fashion is the one most significantly organized around feminist analysis. The genre of 'costume' studies, although extensive, is little concerned with either the social or the legal context but provided some incidental detail of sumptuary rules.

I single out for mention, because it does not fit in any of the above categories, Leigh Schmidt's (1989) study of dress and religion in New England as one of those delightful surprises that lightens the burdens of lengthy, and sometimes lonely, research! Whilst coming out of an entirely different set of concerns, it directly addresses major themes of the present study. The more general intellectual resources of social and historical theory I make no attempt to summarize here; they take their place, and I hope are given their proper recognition, in the course of exposition and debate.

2

A Short History of Sumptuary Law

FROM THE BEGINNING . . .

This chapter provides an intentionally schematic overview of the history of sumptuary law.[1] I offer this because it is a slice of legal and social history that has rarely been told and so will be unfamiliar to many readers. My account follows, with occasional departures, a chronological approach. It seeks to avoid a developmental approach that assumes that history moves in sequential stages on the grounds that this suggests some internal logic or coherence to the phenomenon under investigation. Instead I focus on 'shifts', on changes in national trajectories or in comparison between two or more different sumptuary regimes. The implication is that the identification of such shifts stimulates questions about what was happening and why it happened in the way it did. In selecting illustrations of the major stages and varieties of sumptuary law I have had regard to choosing examples, where possible, from material not otherwise covered in the rest of the book; it is hoped that this makes the coverage more comprehensive and serves to avoid repetition.

In ancient societies people practised differential decoration and ornamentation of the person much of which involved a widespread, but by no means universal, sexual dimorphism in dress, decoration and ornamentation. People also practised a wide variety of alimentary restraints and discriminations, of which ritual abstention, fasting and feasting are well known examples. I have decided to renounce any attempt to grapple with the question of the transition from what may loosely, and however unsatisfactorily, be called customary regimes to ones in which governmentally imposed restrictions on consumption were backed by the mechanisms of a legal order. Accordingly I have restricted my attention to societies with state formations and legal systems. My history accordingly starts with classical Greece and Rome.

THE PRE-HISTORY OF SUMPTUARY LAW: FROM FUNERALS TO WEDDINGS

Classical Greece had an ancient tradition of sumptuary law, but it functioned more as a memory than as an active form of governance.[2] The founding text for Greek sumptuary law, conventionally dated from the early sixth century BC, the Athenian 'laws of Solon', seem to have been a periodically revised compilation rather than a unitary enactment. They provide evidence of the key place of funereal regulation that was interlinked with the control of women. There were restrictions concerned with conspicuous consumption at funerals, the size of funeral processions, and the value of food that could be served. The other dimension was restriction of the role of women at funerals. Women were limited to three mourning shawls and were forbidden to lacerate their cheeks as signs of mourning.

Athenian funereal rules have attracted some interpretive effort (Alexiou 1974; Mills 1984; Toher 1986). Since my concern is primarily with the processes whereby regulatory activity shifts away from funerals towards a more generalized attempt to regulate appearance and dress in particular, I do not have a great deal to offer on the question of why funerals were selected as a significant object of regulation. I am attracted to the view they these rules should be regarded as an aspect of the birth of a new urban order, with the enhanced participation of citizens. The funeral restraints were directed against the old clan-based nobility and were part of a shift from clan to a social dualism of family and state. This process required the undermining of the influence of 'clan cults' of which the display of wealth and influence at funerals was a key ritual. It follows that the focus on controlling the role of women at funerals was not so much a manifestation of projects to control women, but rather stemmed from their central role in clan practices, in particular with prolonged and visible mourning rituals. What is a little less clear is whether or not there was some sense in which funerals were regarded as potential sources of disorder. Alexiou argues that women, by wailing, lacerating their faces and doing so in public, were attracting attention that might amount to a 'social menace, not only indecent, but dangerous' (Alexiou 1974:21). Alexiou suggests the existence of a close connection between the social power of lamentations and the emotional tension needed to sustain the feuds and vendettas characteristic of clan systems.

This interpretation of the link between funerals and clan relations is certainly consistent with the struggles against patrician clan power that dominated medieval Italy, but I have a lingering doubt because it remains unclear what type of disorder was feared. Harrianne Mills adds a further dimension by pointing to the significance of dress regulations in constructing the differentiation of the realms of the sacred and the profane (Mills 1984: 262–63); this suggests that the sumptuary regulation of funerals involved a secularization associated with the rise of civic political power.

In addition to the funerary rules, classical Greece, in a number of cities and islands, had other sumptuary elements. There were rules about ostentation at weddings and restraints on the value of dowries and the price of presents as well as dress rules (for example, a bride was restricted to three robes in her trousseau).

A similar range of funereal restrictions is found at the heart of early Roman sumptuary law, but in its development it exhibits a shift away from funerals and towards alimentary rules regulating the conspicuous consumption of food.[3] Figure 2.1 provides a synoptic view of Roman sumptuary law.

The primary focus in the early period was on funerary rules, again highlighting restriction on the role of women in public mourning rituals, but also exhibiting a more explicit concern with extravagance in funeral expenses, the size of mausoleum, and the size of funeral meals. The formulations used in the Twelve Tables (*c.* 450 BC) are unequivocally concerned with restraining expenditure. In the Tenth Table, Law IV states 'No greater expenses or mourning than is proper shall be permitted in funeral ceremonies.' Law V requires that 'No one shall, hereafter, exceed the limits established by these laws for the celebration of funeral rites.' Law VI requires that the 'funeral pyre shall be constructed from unfinished wood, not from polished wood' (Scott 1973: I: 74).

Subsequently Roman sumptuary laws relinquished concern with funerals, but elaborated the persistent focus upon the regulation of conspicuous display by women and the extravagant consumption of food. The *Lex Oppia* of 215 BC, introduced during the crisis of the Punic wars imposed both expenditure and appearential

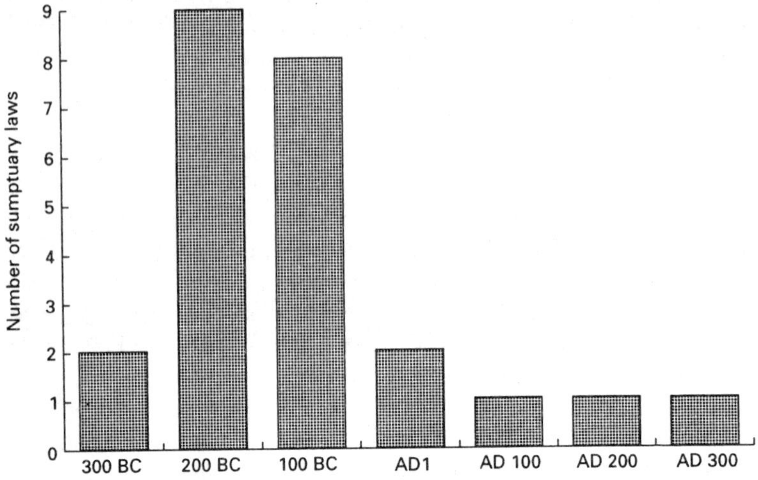

Figure 2.1 Rome: the volume of sumptuary law.

restrictions on woman, limited them to ornaments of half an ounce of gold, forbade the wearing of multicoloured robes, and prohibited them from riding in chariots within the city (Astin 1978).[4] The second strand that came increasingly to the fore concerned alimentary restrictions. For example, the *Lex Orchia* of 215 BC required citizens to dine with their doors open, presumably so that their table could be observed, and restricted the number of guests permitted at entertainments. The *Lex Fannia* of 161 BC prescribed expenditure and frequency for meals and other entertainments, the expenditure being graded by the nature of the festival. The *Lex Didia* of 143 BC extended *Lex Fannia* to all Italy and imposed penalties on guests as well as on hosts (Balsdon 1969).

These dress and alimentary restrictions persisted with reenactment and variation of detail down until the Empire whereupon a distinct shift of focus occurred. It is not that dress and alimentary rules disappeared; for example, both Julius Caesar and Octavius prohibited ordinary citizens from wearing togas with purple edging that was reserved for senators. The significant change was an increasing concern with populationist issues. In 18 BC Augustus embarked on an extensive programme of moral and familial legislative reform. The dress and alimentary rules of the earlier period were reenacted with amendments. The distinctive new concern was with measures to encourage marriage and procreation among the elite by penalizing citizens who did not marry or produce offspring.

The key elements of the Augustan matrimonial legislation was the *Lex Julia de maritandis ordinibus* (18 BC), which was amended and amplified in *Lex Papia Poppaea nuptialis* (AD 9). Male citizens between the age of 25 and 60 were required to be married, as were women between 20 and 50. When a marriage ended through death or divorce both men and women were required to remarry. Exemptions from the obligation to remarry were granted to those who had already produced three children. The sanctions that gave this legislation potential bite were that bachelors or spinsters were denied the entitlement to inherit an estate or legacy under a will unless he or she contracted a marriage within 100 days; a childless married person could only inherit one half of any bequest (Nörr 1981; Corbett 1930: 120).

This legislation was explicitly conceived as a response to a culture of celibacy and other forms of sexual abstinence that had secured a significant hold on the patrician classes (Rousselle 1988). The anxieties generated provided the discursive formation within which Roman social policy was debated. As Moses Finley has expressed it, these anxieties always revolved around the concern to prevent 'the self-destruction of the social élite, caught up on the powerful pressures created by status requirements' (Finley 1985: 139). However, it is worth noting that in addition to these populationist concerns there may well also have been a fiscal motive; where a beneficiary was unmarried or childless the bequest was ceded to the treasury, which may have been significant in a period in which the costs of maintaining the empire were escalating.

While this social engineering legislation was undoubtedly important in its own right, it is not easy to estimate its significance; it remained on the statute book and was subject to detailed revisions over the next three centuries. The legislation does indicate the central role of inheritance as the primary economic institution and thus the means of determining social status. In this respect Rome had become a static society in which its upper classes came to play an increasingly parasitic role. As the economic and military circumstances of the empire deteriorated there were periodic flurries of sumptuary activity, first under Tiberius in the second century AD, and over the next two centuries episodically by Diocletian and Theodosius, who imposed a series of sumptuary laws that were increasingly concerned with the preservation of hierarchy (Norris 1924: I: 101–08). One of the last Roman sumptuary laws, an Edict of Honorius in AD 397, prohibited Roman men from wearing breeches within the precincts of Rome since these were the garments of their enemies, the northern tribes, and were thus seen as barbaric even though they had been adopted by the legionaries fighting in the cold climes of north-western Europe (Boehn 1932: I: 168).

Roman sumptuary law exhibits a shift from funereal to alimentary regulation in its most distinctive and enduring form, designed to restrain extravagance in private hospitality and dining; it proved to be the main link with medieval sumptuary regimes. Although less prominent, perhaps more enduring was the linkage of women's vanity and economic extravagancy that comes to dominate the discourses of luxury.

SUMPTUARY LAWS UNDER FEUDALISM

Sumptuary laws have generally been viewed as attempts to consolidate and reinforce the formalized hierarchy of social relations characteristic of feudal societies. The evidence is contradictory. I will assume for present purposes that the generic term feudalism can be employed to describe both European and the two Asian feudalisms of China and Japan.[5] During the supremacy of European feudalism, while sumptuary laws were periodically enacted, their presence was occasional and episodic. It is only with the decline of feudalism that the emergence of the 'bastard feudalism' that succeeds the monetization of land rents, and the long rise of merchant capitalism, gives rise to what may be regarded as the high period of sumptuary law (Bellamy 1989). It should be noted that this characterization sets up a challenge, which I develop at length in the chapters that follow, to the conventional association of sumptuary law with pre-modern social systems.

In both China and Japan it was only with the subordination of localized militaristic forms of feudalism by centralized and bureaucratized systems of governments associated with formalized social hierarchies that sumptuary law came to the fore. In schematic terms in China it was with the consolidation of the mandarin bureaucracies over local warlordism from the Wei dynasty of AD 220–250 that a strictly defined system of personal status is translated into the legal form of sumptuary codes that were firmly in place by the T'ang period, AD 618–906. While the details underwent bewildering changes, the basic mechanism whereby custom, law, religion and politics operated to provide the meticulous definition of all aspects of the life-styles of the fundamental social categories persisted down to the very brink of the struggles around modernization. In Japan it was under the centralized Tokugawa system between 1600 and 1868 that sumptuary law finds its highest level of development. In both the cases of China and Japan, with the passage of time the key target of sumptuary regulation became the merchant classes whose irresistible rise was eating away at the very possibility of a stable system of social closure required by the bureaucratic regimes.

In China the system of sumptuary laws was an expression of the politico-ideological systematization of norms of personal status (Ch'ü 1961). The *wei payi* system, from its formal articulation during the Wei period, distinguished between *jian min* (good people) who were worthy of consideration and the great majority *liang min* (mean people) who were excluded; this basic conceptualization was to remain intact through all the subsequent dynasties. In its major institutionalization in the T'ang, laws eight primary groups amongst the privileged, stretching from the Emperor's household to the mandarin officials, were identified and made subject to hierarchically defined regulation of life-styles. These regulations were both extensive and intensive. In addition to the extensive coverage of virtually every aspect of life-style, these regulations were distinguished from any others encountered in this study in that they also included rules imposing class exogamy. Some idea of the tyranny of detail is exemplified in two features shared by feudal sumptuary laws in China and in Europe concerning the status attached to falconry. Chinese law specified the species of raptors allowed to each social category. Lower officials and commoners were prohibited from taming 'grey falcons' (probably peregrine falcons), but were allowed to tame 'eagles'; in Europe, England and France both had a similar hierarchy of birds of prey although it was never fully encapsulated in legislation. Similarly furs in both Asia and Europe were also subject to hierarchical ordering. An eleventh century Chinese edict allowed only nobles to wear the fine black sables and ermine, while commoners were permitted only ordinary sable, sheep and mole skins (Wittfogel and Chia-shêng 1949); late medieval English laws employed a similar hierarchical ordering of furs (see Chapter 12).

While the high period of sumptuary law in Japan was in the Tokugawa period between 1600 and 1868 there is evidence of sumptuary regimes under militaristic feudalism.[6] A hierarchical dress code of AD 681 was reputedly modelled on Chinese T'ang law (Hearn 1904). In the main, the sumptuary codes of the feudal period were concerned with regulation within the feudal hierarchy and took little or no interest in merchants and other commoners. Shively identifies the first appearance of concern with frugality in both housing and dress in 1261; he suggests it may reflect a concern with the solvency of vassals (Shively 1964–65). The first comprehensive set of prohibitions affecting the dress and life-style of town dwellers, *chonin,* was introduced in 1649; its contents have a now familiar ring with prohibitions on finer silks and on the use of gold lacquer and gold or silver leaf in interiors or on household articles and saddles. Another comprehensive sumptuary code in 1661 required 'simplicity' in house and pleasure boat construction, and limited conspicuous display at weddings and funerals, and imposed strict limits on the number of dishes whilst entertaining.

Periodic sumptuary legislation followed with marked regularity and was increasingly directed against the *chonin,* a category that became synonymous with the merchant class; this shift was sparked not only by their growing affluence but also by the fact that previously specialized techniques in the production and handling of silk became more widespread and thus opened up wider availability. This provides an illustration of a more general interconnection between technical change and its impact on patterns of consumption. In the twentieth century we have become familiar with the rapidity with which today's innovative and expensive item of conspicuous consumption becomes tomorrow's mass commodity. Study of the shifting relationship between consumption and its regulation needs to attend to the impact of changing production techniques and other factors affecting availability and price. There are two processes here: not only do an expanding range of commodities become available through technical innovation and expansion of trade, but at the same time novelty and distinctiveness in and of themselves come to play an increasingly significant role in opening up trade and commerce. The case of Japan is a useful one from which to insist that this process is not one confined to high modernity, but has been an increasingly significant dynamic from the earliest stages of the development of trade.

This dynamic also helps toward an understanding of the material basis of the conflict between the nobility and the merchants. The increased availability of commodities provided the aristocracies with an ever-wider range of opportunities for self-indulgence and conspicuous consumption. But in so doing it also produced a shift in the balance of economic forces with the dwindling riches of the 'old' classes and the increasing disposable resources of the merchants. Wolfgang Haug's argument that luxury commodities are associated with powerful sensual stimuli can also be applied to the symbolic and erotic significance of sumptuousness in dress in pre-modern societies, and nowhere more so than in Japan (Haug 1986).

When economic change disrupts a 'static' system of social relations emulation becomes an increasingly available strategy by which people lower in the social hierarchy attempt to realize their aspirations towards higher status by modifying their behaviour, their dress and the kinds of goods they purchase. At the same time it becomes even more significant for the economically weakened nobility to resist these changes that express themselves in the frequently voiced anxiety about the difficulty of distinguishing between different categories of persons. In Japan it was the regulation of silk, its varieties and forms that was a primary site at which the struggle between the declining samurai and the rising merchant was fought out. As this tension sharpened it is noticeable that by the eighteenth century sumptuary laws had become more detailed and more frequently sought to inhibit any innovation in consumption. By the end of the century sumptuary discourses become more closely linked to the discourses of governmental economy, frugality and protectionism; sumptuary laws become integrated in the new field of economic government. The Meiji Restoration after 1867 formally abolished sumptuary laws.

In medieval Europe the presence of sumptuary regulation is at first uncertain and irregular. The first traces are found in Charlemagne's extension of the range of governmental action to secure the general conditions of feudal relations. In this context sumptuary features emerge from what was primarily a system of labour regulation. That an edict was necessary specifying that peasants were required to work on the land for six days each week indicates a recognition that feudal relations could not be relied upon to reproduce themselves at the local level. A related anxiety, this time of a security nature, is suggested by the fact that peasants were prohibited from carrying a sword; here, as in Japan, the monopoly of arms was both a practical and a symbolic preoccupation. Symbolism comes to the fore in the provision that peasants were required to walk to church on Sunday carrying a cattle prod; this suggests a concern that peasants should know their place and should be provided with regular reminders of it. It was in this context that the requirement that the clothing of peasants be restricted to a single colour, either black or grey, came about (Bonawitz 1964).

From the early ninth century there is evidence of periodic attempts to link dress to rank, and in the eleventh century to impose restrictions on the colours that were permitted to the peasantry. More regular sumptuary regulation begins to appear by the end of the twelfth century (1157 Genoa, 1188 in France) and becomes more frequent in the thirteenth century (1234 Aragon, 1249 Siena, 1250 Florence, 1256 Castille). There were significant bursts of activity in the final quarter of the century (1276 Bologna, 1277 Padua, 1297 Venice, 1304 Zurich). In the thirteenth century sumptuary enactments came from both church and state; in 1274 Pope Gregory X issued an edict banning 'immoderate ornamentation' throughout Christendom and in 1279 a Papal legate issued regulations on women's apparel in Lombardy. Thereafter sumptuary law became increasing secular, even though there was much reinforcement from the Church of the moral rationale of such restrictions through the critique of luxury (see Chapter 4). By the second half of the fourteenth century sumptuary laws are present in significant numbers over most of Europe (in 1363 England had its first significant sumptuary enactment). By the middle of the fifteenth century Scotland and the German cities and principalities had established sumptuary legislation.

Some patterns are detectable in this early phase of European sumptuary law. They are far from easy to summarize because they are cross-cutting, laid one atop the other across a complex panorama of economic and political regimes. All that I plan to do at this stage is to list (with occasional illustration and comment) some of the more evident shifts that traversed the multiple projects of sumptuary regulation in medieval Europe.

Continuity with ancient societies is evident in the widely imposed restrictions on conspicuous consumption in connection with funerals and weddings and, to a lesser degree, other public celebrations of private rites of passage (births, christenings, betrothals, etc.). The regulation of dress is also present from the beginning, but it becomes increasingly important; it comes to be the typical target of medieval sumptuary law, to such an extent that the term sumptuary law itself, both in its historical usage and my own, becomes almost synonymous with the regulation of dress, ornamentation and personal appearance.

Dress regulation took two distinctive forms, the first being the imposition of expenditure limits (either on whole outfits or on the price per piece of cloth, or on individual items). The second form was to reserve particularly significant types of cloth or style of dress for designated categories; this was done either by granting a privilege to a social category (e.g. only nobles may wear ermine) or by negative prohibition (e.g. no female servant may wear her robes with a train). While the form is not always closely linked to the substance of law a general inference can be drawn from these two types of dress rule: reserved privileges tend to be associated with the internal regulation of a social hierarchy where the concern is to limit or to channel competition that occurs within the dominant classes. The negative prohibition tends to be associated with the imposition of an imagined social order on real or imagined disruptions or challenges from below; typical of this category are rules that relate to merchants, commoners, apprentices, servants and prostitutes.

There was a complex articulation alongside hierarchical considerations in the use of sumptuary dress provisions to regulate gender relations. In its simplest form a sumptuary dress code provides a codification of the dress restrictions for males and for females in each designated social category. This type is epitomized by the summaries or 'breviats' circulated with Elizabethan sumptuary proclamations (see Chapter 12). There were significant shifts as to which sex was targeted for regulation that are explored in Chapter 9. Many ordinances were gender neutral, while others differentially imposed restraints – sometimes it was men who were targeted and at other times it was women; those statutes that target women frequently employed strongly misogynistic attitudes and language. For present purposes, it is sufficient to comment that, on balance, medieval sumptuary law was directed against men more often than it was against women. It was women who came to be the object of sumptuary regulation in the early modern period. However, there is abundant evidence to show that, throughout, enforcement was directed more rigorously against women than it was against men.

SUMPTUARY LAW IN THE EARLY MODERN PERIOD

As European feudalism waned and was replaced by bastard feudalisms in many key areas, and especially in Renaissance Italy, mercantile capital achieved economic power and even political power in some cases. If Europe stood on the brink of modernity then it did so with sumptuary regulation at its most active and extensive. This should be sufficient to dispel the tendency to equate sumptuary projects with the kind of social hierarchy conceived of as typically feudal or pre-modern. Sumptuary laws straddle the often imperceptible but fundamental divide between the pre-modern and the modern. (Table 2.1 and Figure 2.2 provide an overview of the quantity and periodization of sumptuary legislation.)

The economic historian N.G. Harte has been one of the more perceptive recent commentators on sumptuary law. He resolves the periodization of sumptuary law by suggesting that it was an 'identifying characteristic' of the pre-industrial period (Harte 1976: 134). I have no quarrel with this; in virtually all cases the typical dress codes of the late medieval/early modern period had disappeared by the advent of the Industrial Revolution. What Harte's periodization does not grapple with is a more interesting and difficult question about the place of sumptuary law in the early modern period in which commercial capital had come to the fore, a period that spanned the sixteenth to the eighteenth centuries. During this period there was a great volume of sumptuary law and its characteristic was conspicuous consumption in matters of dress and ornamentation. I will add the thesis that dress codes become more, rather than less, preoccupied with the preservation of hierarchy.

My purpose here is to review and illustrate the major trends that manifest themselves in the transition to modernity. I will argue that there was significant continuity; sumptuary regulation that had been born in the heart of feudalism came to expand its range and its volume; it increased rather than decreased with the decline of feudalism. Sumptuary projects become a standard feature of governmental activity in the early modern period and only declined when capitalism had triumphed and the modern state,

Table 2.1 A quantification of sumptuary laws

Location / *Date*	*12th c.*	*13th c.*	*14th c.*	*15th c.*	*16th c.*	*17th c.*	*18th c.*
France	1	4	5	6	13	19	1
England	1	0	5	4	20	1	—
Italian cities (except Florence & Venice)	2	7	16	24	12	17	1
Florence	—	2	13	10	7	21	—
Venice	—	1	8	11	17	28	2
Spain	—	7	7	2	16	4	2
Switzerland			3	0	3	3	2
Germany				3	7	7	2
Scotland				7	12	12	1
North America						9	1

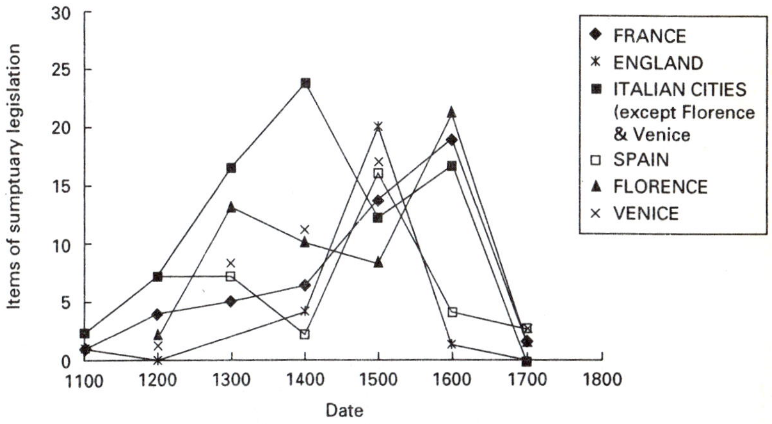

Figure 2.2 European sumptuary law.

but not yet the modern representative state, had come into being. (Figures 2.3 to 2.9 provide an illustration of the volume of sumptuary legislation in Europe.)

With the passage from feudalism to early modernity four major trends affecting sumptuary law are observable. First is the gradual disappearance of funeral and wedding regulations. The second is that dress becomes the central target and dress codes become

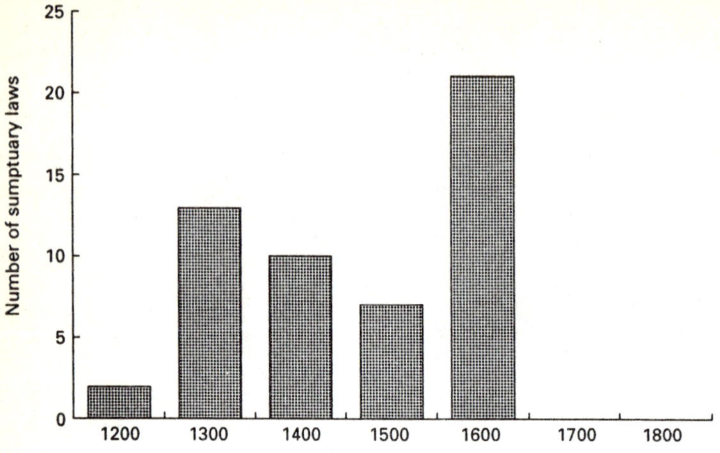

Figure 2.3 Florence: the volume of sumptuary law.

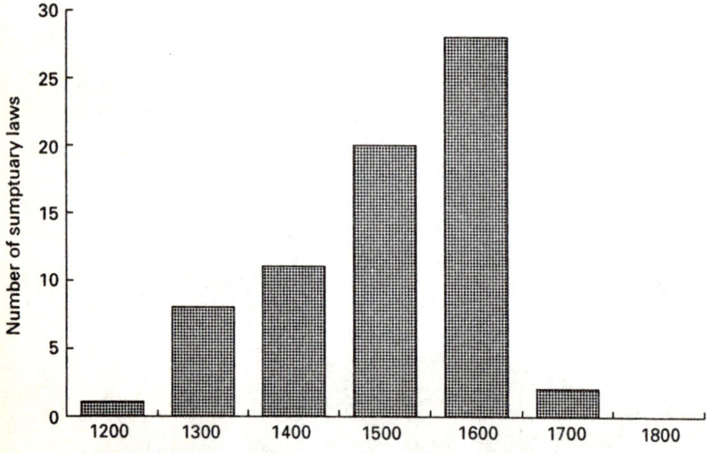

Figure 2.4 Venice: the volume of sumptuary law.

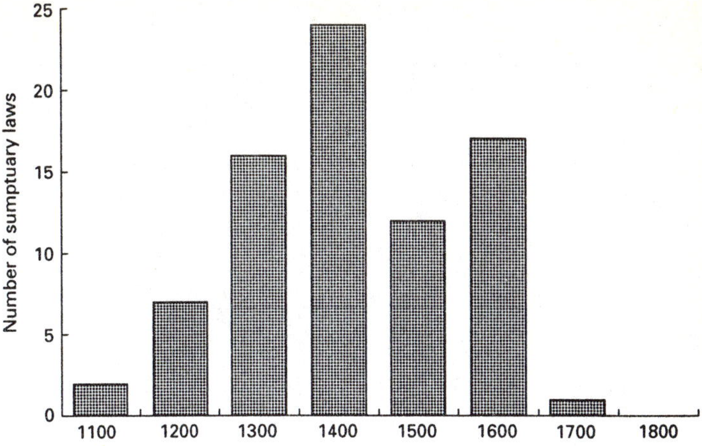

Figure 2.5 Italian cities (excluding Florence and Venice): the volume of sumptuary law.

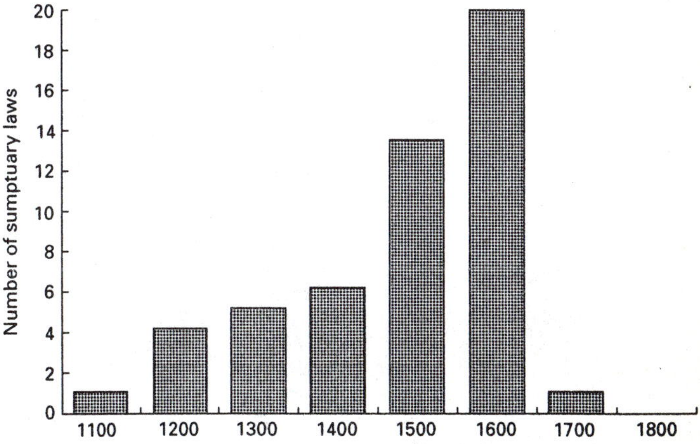

Figure 2.6 France: the volume of sumptuary law.

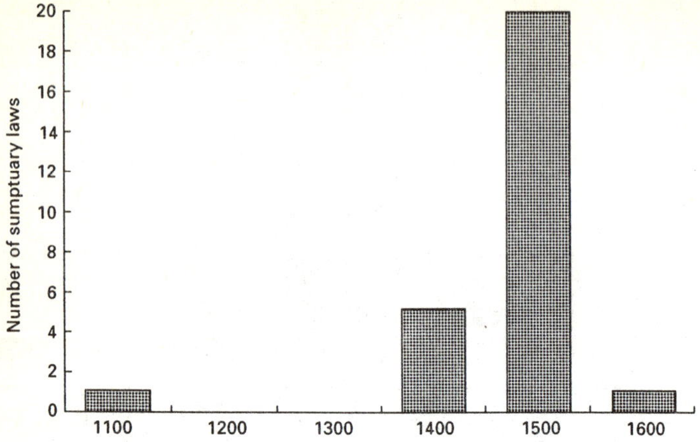

Figure 2.7 England: the volume of sumptuary law.

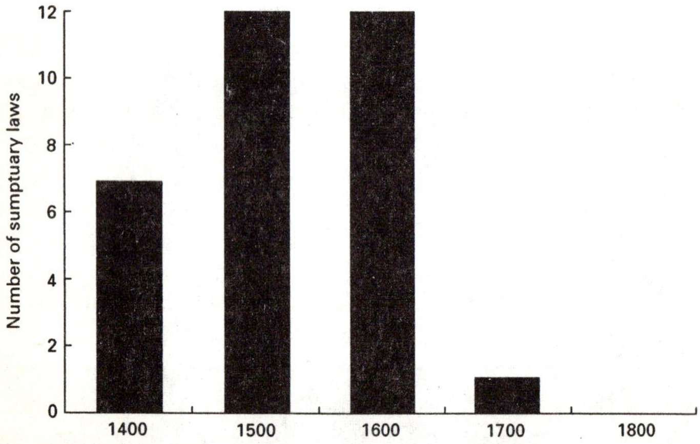

Figure 2.8 Scotland: the volume of sumptuary law.

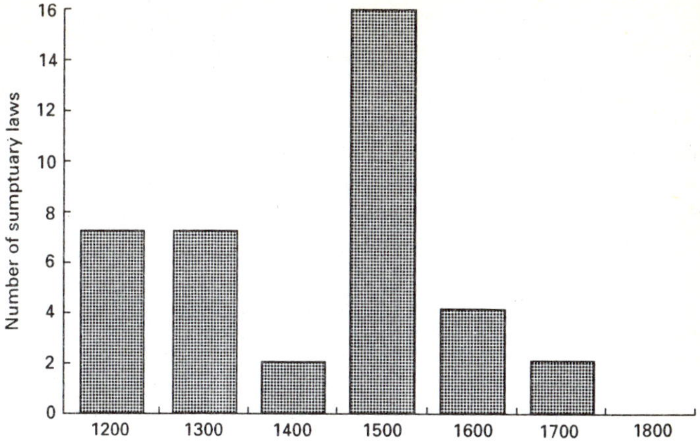

Figure 2.9 Spain: the volume of sumptuary law.

more comprehensive and increasingly codified in form.[7] The third feature is that the legislation becomes more focused upon preservation of the external symbols of class hierarchy. As dress becomes the major regulatory object, attempts at alimentary regulation, whether in the form of general expenditure limits or the reserving of privileged items for the upper classes, decline.[8]

The fourth significant trend involves the shift that takes place against the background of an incipient economic debate, one which flowers again with the rise of classical political economy in the eighteenth century, as to whether expenditure on perishable luxuries, such as food, is economically more beneficial than indulgence in more durable luxuries – clothes, precious metals, jewels.[9] As the restraints on food disappear it becomes harder to sustain the logic that sumptuary laws are motivated by a general concern to restrain extravagance since there is no reason why extravagance on food is less damaging to the nation than extravagance on dress. The fact that by the late Middle Ages dress codes had become the paradigmatic case of sumptuary restriction requires some explanation that goes beyond the critique of extravagance and luxury that had provided the standard and oft repeated legitimation for such sumptuary ordering in previous centuries.

The legitimatory motives that were invoked in the legislative preambles reveal a number of 'shifts' in medieval sumptuary law.

In the early phases sumptuary laws which appealed to the associated phenomena of 'dearth' and 'ruin' gradually gave way before two other loosely connected considerations. The first being that 'extravagance' and 'luxury' became the central discursive features. What is at stake here is a shift away from 'dearth' or 'ruin' concerned with actual or imagined shortage of the means of sustenance, whereas the discourses of extravagance and luxury imply that economic resources are being diverted from more useful or profitable investment. The other strand was the emergence of a conception of a 'national economy'.

The fourth trend in the trajectory of sumptuary law saw a marked turn toward protectionist discourses and preoccupations. This shift was articulated in terms of a sequence of concerns which, while not strictly sequential, go through a number of distinguishable stages. An initial bullionist concern with the outflow of gold and silver was succeeded by considerations about the balance of trade focused on the relationship between imports and exports, and finally became expressed within increasingly protectionist discourses in which the projects became those of advancing some particular domestic trade or industry. An illustrative case of the later approach was the case of Siena where in 1433 citizens were restricted to a single pair of silk sleeves. In 1438 the commune officially sponsored a local silk industry, but it was not until 1460 that sumptuary restrictions on locally produced silk garments were lifted when, as it were, legal ideology caught up with economic exigency (Hughes 1983: 78). A more extensive version of this distinctive admixture and supersession was the official sponsorship of luxury industries in France in the second half of the seventeenth century and the elaboration of protectionism into a national economic policy during the course of which the discourses of luxury waned rapidly in the face of 'national interest' such that imports, especially English ones, become the evil to be combated. I will return to examine the relationship between sumptuary law and economic protectionism in more detail in Chapter 14.

These trends are of course far from universal. The case of Scotland may be cited to illustrate some interesting variations on the trajectory of sumptuary regulation. Sumptuary impositions started a little later than in England – 1424 rather than 1363 – but they lasted significantly longer, with full-blown sumptuary enactments as late as 1691. Scottish sumptuary laws started out with the imposition of what was in essence a two-class hierarchic model that sought to ensure an enduring distinction between the nobility and the urban burghers. These regulations provide rare instances of attempts to prescribe positive dress regulations. The major statute of 1429 required that all men with an income above £20 a year should be well horsed and equipped 'as a gentleman ought to be'; some of these requirements were specific requiring a fur hat, 'doublat habergone' [sleeveless armoured jacket] and the provision of stipulated weaponry (APS II: 18: 8–10[10]).

The discourses within which Scottish laws were located made much more of the invocation of fears of dearth and poverty and this may well have reflected relative economic backwardness. These concerns link up with the fact that Scotland only turned to alimentary regulation after standard dress codes had been attempted. Not until 1551 was a statute passed linking the number of dishes allowed to each social rank (earls not more than 8 dishes, lords 6, barons 4, burghers 3), with hospitality rules stipulating that the number of dishes should be determined by the rank of the chief guest (APS II: 488, *c.* 22).[11] From this point through until 1629 alimentary regulation was the primary form of sumptuary order. In 1581 the quality of provisions that could be supplied to horses was prescribed; they were denied 'hard meat' (oats and hay) in summer (APS III: 225, *c.* 29; APS III: 452, *c.* 40 (1587)). It was not until 1672 that the main focus swung back onto extravagance in dress, and by now this was squarely located within a protectionist discourse. Again, very much at odds with the chronology of the sumptuary regimes elsewhere in Europe, Scotland did not 'discover' the need to regulate funerals, weddings and other ritual occasions for extravagance until the very final phase of its sumptuary initiatives. In 1681 an *Act Restraining the Exorbitant Expense of Marriages, Baptisms and Burials* was passed (APS VIII: 350, *c.*80). It had all the traditional features of this 'early' form of sumptuary enactment, limiting the number of guests on hierarchical principles (Shaw 1979: 92). I attach some significance to the inclusion of a prohibition on the carrying of 'pencels [pennants], banners, and other honours' at burials (J.C. 1891: 297), and suggest that such public events were feared by the English authorities as potential opportunities for the expression of nationalist sentiments and the assertion of the prestige of the clans. This, in turn, supports my reflections about the political role of the archaic restrictions on funerals in Athens that also reappear in thirteenth and fourteenth century Italy as components of struggles against the vestiges of clan power. There are sufficient differences between the patterns of Scottish sumptuary history and those in England and elsewhere in Europe that they would repay the attention of those with an expertise in Scottish history that I do not pretend to possess.

Sumptuary laws were found in virtually every type of political system in medieval and early modern Europe; they were as prevalent in highly centralized nation-states already well on the way to absolutism as they were in the relatively democratic cities and communes. A few broad generalizations are possible. The paradigm cases of protracted state unification, France and Spain, that went on to become highly centralized absolutist states had sumptuary laws by the late twelfth or early thirteenth centuries, and there was a more or less continuous history down until the eighteenth century. The fragmented city-states of Italy and Germany exhibit a mass of sumptuary legislation for much the same period as France and Spain. There was surprisingly little difference between both the temporal span and the general characteristics of the sumptuary law of such divergent cases as England, the great Italian cities like Venice and Florence, and the intensely Protestant Swiss towns. There seems to have been little difference in either the volume or the character of sumptuary regimes in Protestant or Catholic societies.

The city-state of Venice epitomizes the long duration of sumptuary legislation through its rise to mercantile and political power and in its decline. The history of Venetian sumptuary law stretches from the end of the thirteenth century until the end of the eighteenth (Newett 1907; Longworth 1974). Early legislation in 1299 imposed limitations on weddings, feasts and funerals (Newett 1907; Davis 1962: 44; Hale 1973). From 1323 and 1334 regulatory attention shifted to excess in women's dress and to reinforcing ceremonial dress on patrician males (Brucker 1971: 318). From this period the communal treasury records are full of fines for sumptuary violations (Becker 1967: 228). After the plague of 1347–48 the Senate issued sumptuary laws forbidding dark-blue or green raiment to encourage general happiness (Newett 1907: 249). In the fifteenth century a long struggle over dowries and their implications commenced; limits were placed on the size of dowries and wedding costs aimed at discouraging the practice of sending younger daughters into convents (Brucker 1971: 318). In 1472 enforcement officials, *Provveditori sopra le Pompe* [supervisors of luxury], were appointed to enforce the sumptuary ordinances. As the rate of changes in fashion increased legislation became more complex, striving for comprehensive restrictions on the latest fashions. In 1511 the Senate went so far as to order that 'all new fashions are banned' (Okey 1907: 281).

When in 1512, during the political crisis of the League of Cambrai, as Venice's enemies gathered for the attack, the Senate debated dress materials, the size and design of sleeves, fringes and ornaments, belts and headdresses, shoes and slippers, home furnishings and bed-linen (Hughes 1983: 71). In the sixteenth century there was an increasing focus on the hierarchical ordering of appearance and also a more pronounced 'social purity' dimension; it was ordered that men's shirts must cover the entire upper body and be closed at the neck, while women's necklines as usual attracted the legislator's attention (Newton 1988). There was also an expansion of the range of targets with a series of ordinances limiting expenditure on interior decoration; the painting and upholstery of gondolas also attracted attention (Gilbert 1973: 279–80). Sumptuary energy did not slacken in the seventeenth century.[12] Legislative activity persisted into the eighteenth century; the last edict I have record of was from 1781 which continued to complain of the wasteful living of citizens, the destruction of fortunes and the loss of government revenue (Davis 1962: 45).

In Switzerland sumptuary laws spanned nearly 500 years from the very beginning of the fourteenth century until the end of the eighteenth century. John Vincent's study remains the primary source (Vincent 1935); his project was organized around the tradition of costume history, and he used the content of sumptuary prohibition to identify changes in contemporary fashion. What distinguishes his work, and goes way beyond his concern with the empirical history of fashion, is the careful attention he paid to evidence of enforcement in which context I will have cause to return to consider the material he collects. In the meantime some general patterns in Swiss sumptuary law can be identified. In the fourteenth century the focus was, as elsewhere, on the regulation of expenditure on weddings and funerals. Later the same century there is a shift of attention to dress organized around a mix of economic and moral considerations, with typical concern with female décolletage, while requiring that men's coats should be sufficiently long to cover 'his shame' (Vincent 1897: 360). Significantly during the height of the Calvinist ascendancy, although there was vigilant enforcement of sumptuary law, there was no new legislative activity. The mix of moral and economic considerations in the attempt to hold fashion at bay persisted through the sixteenth and seventeenth centuries. Legislation made attendance at church compulsory and prohibited rival activities such as leaving the town during church services. Legislation also prescribed child-rearing patterns: children had to be off the streets after the 'bed bell' (Vincent 1897: 365). A distinctively Swiss extension to the range of sumptuary targets was provided by tight restrictions on sleigh riding; women were banned from riding in sleighs except when accompanied by their fathers or husbands. Sleigh-riding presumably provided opportunities for public display, youthful exuberance and courting (Vincent 1897: 367–68).

It seems evident that there are grounds for stressing the generality of European sumptuary law, a generality that transcends differences in political organization, economic system and dominant religious ideology.

SUMPTUARY LAW IN NORTH AMERICA

North America is a significant case because the sumptuary regimes that were initiated in most, but not all, of the New World colonies were initiated at a time when the sumptuary impulse in Europe, and in particular in England, was showing signs of flagging. Given the close association with England it is significant that England had repealed its last dress legislation around the time the colonists set sail.[13] There was considerable variation between different settlements. The Massachusetts Bay colony has left the fullest record of its sumptuary provisions (Shurtleff 1968), but no such laws existed in Plymouth colony (Demos 1970). From very early days of settlement nearly all colonies had rules concerning non-attendance at Sunday worship, that subsequently acquired the label 'blue laws' and came to have a persisting significance into the twentieth century (Dilloff 1980). The first instance encountered was from Vermont in 1610 where non-attendance could attract the death penalty; more pragmatically in Virginia after 1623 fines for non-attendance could be paid in tobacco (Laband and Heinbuch 1987: 30).

In 1619 the first representative assembly held in Massachusetts approved an enactment 'Against Idleness, Gaming, Drunkenness and Excess in Apparel' (Miller 1928: 94). Much sumptuary energy was directed against the interconnected evils of luxury, fashion and dressing above one's rank (Warwick *et al.* 1965). When in 1638 the Boston court recognized 'the great disorder general through the country in costliness of apparel, and following new fashions' they required the elders to impose sumptuary restrictions, but expressed concern that some of the elders' wives were themselves party to the general disorder of apparel (Flaherty 1972: 185). The hierarchic sumptuary legislation rules did not become concretized until 1651 (Foster 1971: 28). They prohibited particular luxury items such as gold or silver lace, gold or silver buttons, silk hoods or scarves, and 'great boots' to those with an annual income of less than £200.[14] Selectmen were entitled to assess those who dressed above their rank as if they were worth £200 or more and then to tax them accordingly in an interesting example of deploying a fiscal trap against dressing beyond one's means. The boundaries of sumptuary order become very blurred; included alongside sumptuary provisions in Massachusetts in 1639 was a prohibition against the practice of drinking the health of one's companions on the grounds that it is 'a mere useless ceremony'.

The general moral tone is exemplified by a Connecticut law that required that 'no person, Householder or other, shall spend their time idly, or unprofitably' (Flaherty 1972: 180–81); there is no record of what was deemed to constitute 'idleness' but it seems be have borne a meaning close to 'not gainfully employed' or 'vagrant'. By the middle of the eighteenth century the standard dress rules had been repealed or fallen into disuse; but as late as 1750 the Massachusetts General Court prohibited all theatrical entertainment (Weeden 1890: 289). The inclination to control the recreational and cultural consumption of its citizens has never been far below the surface of American life and surfaced powerfully in the twentieth century with Prohibition. These potentialities linger, and are manifest again in the current pornography censorship movement. The nature of the connection between the tradition of sumptuary regulation and the more persistent traditions of moral regulation, social purity and censorship will be discussed in Chapter 11.

ON GAPS AND LINKAGES IN THE SUMPTUARY RECORD

It should be noted that there are some countries for which I have turned up relatively little evidence of the presence of sumptuary laws. It is very likely that this reflects the inadequacy of my coverage and, in particular, the limited availability of works in English. For example, I have only encountered passing references to Portuguese sumptuary law (Hanson 1981; Marques 1971). The most interesting case is that of the Netherlands. Here we have a major player in the growth of mercantile capitalism in Europe and it does seem to be the case that the Dutch had relatively little sumptuary law and what they did have was significantly late. The only two substantial pieces of sumptuary legislation date from the second half of the seventeenth century by which time a comparable country such as England had long ceased to have active sumptuary laws. More significant perhaps is that the sumptuary laws that were passed, in 1655 and 1672 respectively, were instances of 'early' sumptuary law being concerned with expenditure on wedding celebrations and alimentary restrictions against 'unnecessary and sumptuous banquets' (Schama 1987: 182).

The existence of gaps in the record is in part evidence of the limitations of this study, but also indicates that there was considerable variation in the density of sumptuary regulation. To pursue this aspect further would require specialist local and regional knowledge of the social and political locations in which these 'gaps' in the generality of European sumptuary law occur.

Another important source of variation in the sumptuary relates to the complex interconnections between sumptuary and other forms of governmental action. There are numerous instances where a single legislative provision seeks to regulate different types of activity. An English statute in 1388 illustrates this general issue of linkages between different governmental projects. It required rural and urban labourers to desist from 'all playing at Tennis or Football and other Games called Coits, Dice, Casting of the Stone and other such importune Games' on Sundays and Holydays (12 Rich. II, *c.* 6; SR 2: 57[15]), but required them to practise archery. Alongside the quasi-sumptuary dimensions of social order and anti-gambling there was an obvious attempt to direct recreation into a militarily useful direction; I will discuss this and other cases of mixtures of sumptuary and non-sumptuary projects in Chapter 11. To establish linkages between projects is more difficult when they are not part of the same legislative initiatives. For example, the late medieval/early modern period in which sumptuary laws abounded was also a period in which there were important upheavals in the regulation of labour that produced a mass of vagrancy legislation. Another potentially significant linkage between sumptuary law and other projects is with the general field of moral regulation, in particular of prostitution, public health and sanitation regulation. In general it will be argued that an understanding of sumptuary law during its most active period requires attention to the linkages between different regulatory and governmental projects.

The most important linkage that affects the later history of sumptuary law is the connection between restraints on consumption and protectionist economic policies. For example, the question arises as to whether we should regard a French law prohibiting the import of English wool as a sumptuary law or as a very typical instance of economic protectionism. There is, of course, no solution to be found in the realm of definitions. Rather what is involved is a process whereby a series of shifts occur that have the result of disrupting one set of discursive linkages (e.g. that between moralizing luxury and restricting consumption) and establishing another (e.g. that between 'national interest' and restraints on consumption). What is important to note is that the different discursive elements were present from the beginning; what changes is their respective 'weight' and the combinatory repertoires. One way of viewing the general demise of sumptuary law is to see it as a process in which a 'gap', in the form of a discursive separation, occurs between moral regulation and economic regulation. It was at the interface between these traditions that the distinctive phenomenon of sumptuary law existed. As the gap widens, sumptuary law diminishes, if not disappears, while moral and economic regulation march on as central arenas of governmental activity down to the present.

3

Tilting Against the Windmills of Fashion

The faschioun of cloathes now presentlie used not to be cheingit by men or wemen

Act Anent Banquetting and Apparell (Scotland) 1621[1]

THE WINDMILLS OF FASHION

Sumptuary laws were directed at the governance of appearance. They manifested an aspiration to construct an 'order of appearance' that allowed the relevant social facts, in particular about social and economic status, gender and occupation, to be 'read' from the visible signs disclosed by the clothes of the wearer. In the aspiration of the Scottish statute quoted above there is expressed not only a desire to bring fashion under control, but actually to fix it by bringing it to a halt. In England in 1666 Charles II went as far as to announce to his Council a 'resolution of setting a fashion for clothes which he will never alter' (Evelyn 1951: v).[2]

The clothes people wear were (and remain) a significant component of the material, political, economic and aesthetic culture. Clothes are a powerful, if complex, form of communication; but in order to understand the sumptuary impulse it is necessary to consider what is involved in the attempt to 'read' clothing as a system of communication.

What people wear exhibits a fascinating paradox. On the one hand dress is relatively trivial, certainly rarely, if ever, forming part of the 'big questions' of social and political life. Yet on the other hand the importance of clothing is also equally evident. At the individual level people invest significant economic and emotional resources in what they wear; it is as often a site of self-doubt and anxiety as it is of exuberance and self-confidence. And because clothing is so strongly 'visible' it offers us the prospect of both reflective and unreflective readings of the communication that is embedded in it. We all read the appearance of others in every aspect of our lives, but it also invites us to explore beyond our everyday and taken-for-granted reading of ourselves and of others. In this respect an interest in clothing resonates well with contemporary concerns with identity, with communication, with the textual analogy of 'reading' social life.

It is the location of clothes and fashion somewhere between the trivial and the profound that allows us to understand how it has come, at one time or another, to excite so much moral fervour. Even though, at first glance, we are likely to experience the projects that initiated sumptuary law as strange, we can still grasp the powerful urges that produced the preoccupations with appearance. What people wear and how they present themselves can still excite social anxieties and nowhere is this more marked than in inter-generational relations; what young people wear has an entirely predictable capacity to excite the concern, anxieties and fears of their elders. What people wear takes us beyond personal preference or aesthetic judgment; it raises the spectre of morality, invoking notions about what is 'right', 'correct' or 'proper'. I hope to show that attention to what people wear can tell us much about the tensions and anxieties of social time and place.

Much of the literature dealing with clothing as communication has been cast in terms of a discussion about 'fashion' as a distinctive mechanism of change in dress style through imitation. The focus on fashion has given a distinctive inflection to the debates and controversies engendered by sumptuary law. For example, much of the literature about sumptuary law has assumed, explicitly or implicitly, that these projects were concerned with the regulation of fashion. It is important to stress that my concerns are broader in that I do not limit my interest in the social significance of appearance to the specific mechanism of fashion. My interest in approaching sumptuary law as projects of governance directed at the ordering of appearance is not reducible to the question of fashion. Having said this, it is indisputable that fashion plays an important role in the history of sumptuary law, not least because fashion gives access to some of the most self-conscious social involvement with appearance and its ordering. For this reason it is necessary to explore the history of the preoccupation with fashion.

WHAT IS FASHION?

Fashion has a history. The very idea of fashion involves reference to some temporal dimension, a social process that changes over time and distinguishes between 'yesterday's fashions' and 'today's fashion'. While it is not my purpose to chart that history some themes are necessary in order to set the scene. I will use the term fashion in a restricted sense to refer to a process that links the production and consumption of clothes in a context in which both producers and consumers place some conscious valuation on change.[3]

While commonsense responses to the phenomenon of fashion often tend to view it as volatile and unstable, marked by idiosyncratic vagaries and irrational fads, the interests of both historians and sociologists have been stimulated by the fact that despite its superficially erratic features its true significance only emerges when it is perceived that it is a classically 'social' phenomenon. Fashion exhibits long-term trends (or 'trach') that are not amenable to explanation pitched at the level of individual choice (Kroeber and Richardson 1940; Kroeber 1952). These concerns are particularly pertinent for those historians and sociologists who identify their objects of inquiry as being concerned with the 'long-run' (*longue durée*) (Braudel 1972; Freudenberger 1963; Redlich 1963). The present work is concerned to locate sumptuary legislation as a component of governance and of state formation at the juncture between the pre-modern and the modern, even though it goes without saying that there is no moment or location at which the historical finger can be pointed with a triumphal 'There it is'.

Accounts of the origins of fashion offer two rather different stories. The first locates the birth of fashion in the courts of the feudal monarchies which came into being with the rise of Burgundy, whose court at Dijon was to be a dominant influence in the period between 1350 and 1480 after Flanders had been consolidated into the Burgundian kingdom. This led to increased commercial activity and was particularly important to the process of dissemination that is intrinsic to the formation of fashion because the Burgundian court stood on major trade routes (Batterberry 1982).[4] It was at about the same time that Burgundian fashion was beginning to spread to other court societies across Europe that sumptuary laws began to appear with some regularity. Mukerji argues that the early sumptuary legislation was an attempt to reimpose by legislation the medieval codes of dress that were being threatened by the first signs of commercialization inherent in the new spatial reach of fashion (Mukerji 1983: 180). I will argue below that she is wrong in seeing this legislation merely as a 'restoration' of medieval dress codes (Chapter 7).

The reason that some caution is needed about linking the advent of sumptuary legislation with the rise of fashion is that in both England and in the Italian cities of Florence and Venice sumptuary laws were already well established by the early decades of the fourteenth century and predated the eruption of the increasingly self-conscious fashion in the Burgundian court. While the rise of fashion came to provide a distinct focus for the discourses legitimating sumptuary intervention, to stress the link with fashion tends to obscure the more pervasive roots of the sumptuary impulse. This I will trace back to a more persistent concern with social recognizability and the critique of luxury which, as I will argue in more detail in the next chapter, were discourses already firmly in place. For the present it is sufficient to suggest that the rise of a distinctive conception of fashion provided a spur to a sumptuary impulse that was already in place.

The rise of Burgundian fashion was associated with the use of more diverse types of cloth and other materials that became available as a result of the expansion of eastern Mediterranean trade. The Burgundian court is credited with the invention of 'décolleté' style, whose eroticization of the female chest provided an intense site of moralization and regulation down to the present (Brenninkmeyer 1963: 126–29). There emerged a revival of aesthetic concerns, one dimension of which expressed itself in the emergence of tailoring as a field of both economic and creative activity. At the same time sexual dimorphism in dress became fully established, but did so in a form which for much of the next four centuries rendered the male body the primary site for the display of sartorial elegance (Evans 1952). Clothing came to have distinguishable body shapes, sleeves, legs, etc. and head-dresses and hats were elaborated. The major long-term shift was the abandonment of the unisexual long robes that had been dominant since Roman times; in their place there emerged a marked sexual differentiation with long gowns for women, short tight-fitting clothes for men (jacket to waist or hips and tight leg coverings). Agnes Young suggests that long-run trends in basic body shapes exhibit a cyclical character, in women's clothing marked by a circulation of three basic body shapes (Young 1937).[5] Fashion was born as the conscious exploitation of the oscillation between and combination of tightness and looseness and the elaboration of sexual dimorphism (Hollander 1980; Fiero *et al.* 1989).

Although Norbert Elias, perhaps surprisingly, paid little attention to dress as a manifestation of the 'civilizing process' which he identifies with the emergence of 'court society', the link between court and fashion is entirely consistent with his general thematic (Elias 1978, 1982, 1983). Nor did Elias place much significance on the sexualization of court society, something that Sombart saw as emerging from the continual contact between aristocrats without occupation and beautiful women given an elaborated role by the emphasis on self-presentation and self-enhancement dependent on economic resources and the luxury of time and servants for the rituals of grooming. Without detracting from Elias' general thesis about the emergence of self-restraint in court society, it is important to take account of the court as a major site for the eroticization of sexual relations that comes about from the intensification of conspicuous consumption and self-individualization. Struggles over identity and fashion were not exclusively secular; such battles also occurred in the cloisters. Eileen Power suggests that a sideline in the struggles over fashion was one between the male church and nunneries. There was a long history of clerical bewilderment with women and their interest in personal appearance. 'Synods sat, archbishops and bishops shook their heads over golden hairpins and silver belts, jewelled rings, laced shoes, slashed tunics, low-necked dresses, long trains, gay colours, costly materials and furs' (Power 1975: 98).

By the fifteenth century economic and cultural priority had shifted to Italy where sartorial attention focused on the silks and brocades coming from the Eastern Mediterranean and beyond. By the mid-sixteenth century Spanish fashions came to dominate with stiffer cloths, a return to black, and the use of elaborate leatherwork and embroidery. From the mid-seventeenth century leadership in fashion passed to France and the centre of gravity gradually shifted towards the Atlantic, first to Holland and then with England coming to the fore (Brenninkmeyer 1963: 126–29). France's long dominance of the organized fashion industry from the eighteenth century for most of the next two centuries was stimulated by the organized protectionism of French economic policy, associated with state stimulation of a silk industry and, more generally, the luxury industries that were a distinctive feature of French mercantilism, associated with Colbert's policies in the second half of the seventeenth century (Cole 1939; Heckscher 1955). The French developments provide one of the most direct expressions of a more general interdependence of fashion and commerce that operates through the mechanism of cultural diffusion and innovation. Mukerji provides further refinement by harnessing Wallerstein's core–periphery distinction; innovations are generated at the core and are diffused to the periphery through the mechanism of fashion (Mukerji 1983).

There is a broader cultural dynamic that links the emergence of fashion to the contradiction between the secularity of capitalism and the asceticism of Judaeo-Christian culture. Fashion derives its distinctive characteristics from the attempt to emphasize the human body and its beauty in a culture that has tended to despise and denigrate the sensual. Elizabeth Wilson locates the working through of this tension not within court society, but rather from its origins in the early capitalist city, 'the first crucible of this contradiction' where fashion 'links beauty, success, and the city' (Wilson 1985: 9). The cultural dimension had its impact beyond the urban context, clothes seem to acquire an extraordinary aura, the recognition of which is necessary in order to understand the reverential treatment of clothing in the portraits of the period, perhaps most majestically in Rembrandt's treatment of furs. Nor was this accentuation of clothes a matter just for the upper classes; my impression is that in the early modern period many people, including servants and other working people, spent a high percentage of their income on their clothes.

König also emphasizes the urban dynamic of fashion; it was during the thirteenth century, at the precise moment when the urban middle class began its rise to first economic and then political ascendancy, that there occurred a sudden increase in the number of dress regulations (König 1973: 140). Fernand Braudel's account takes a similar tack by treating the rise of fashion as a dimension of a 'uniqueness of the West' thesis. For him:

> the future was to belong to societies fickle enough to care about changing the colours, materials and shapes of costumes, as well as the social order and the map of the world – societies, that is, which were ready to break with the traditions.
>
> (Braudel 1981: 323)[6]

Much, if not all, of the literature on the sociology of fashion bears the stamp of a very specific conception of fashion (Batterberry 1977; Laver 1969a; Roach and Eichler 1965). Since it is one which is becoming increasingly less self-evident it is as well to make explicit what this dominant conception of fashion involved. Fashion has traditionally been viewed as a more or less unitary system (or as a series of rival 'capitals' in which, for example, Paris vies with Rome). The 'fashion system' is conceived of as initiating fashion at the centre; these changes are then communicated radially through fashion magazines and other popular cultural media.[7] A general motivation of imitation is assumed to provide the mechanism of dissemination underlying the completion of the communication process manifest in the multitude of individual decisions about what to buy and what to wear. Quentin Bell captures this sense of fashion in suitably dramatic terms:

> Fashion for those who live within its empire is a force of tremendous and incalculable power. Fierce and at times ruthless in its operation, it governs our behaviour, informs our sexual appetites, colours our erotic imagination . . . and determines our aesthetic valuations.
>
> (Bell 1976: 62)

The feature that preoccupied early sociological approaches to fashion was that, in very much the same way that suicide fascinated Durkheim, it offered a dramatic exemplar of the social reality underlying and determining apparently individual and idiosyncratic choices. From an unreflective standpoint what people wear seems preeminently personal and yet it is simple to demonstrate that 'fashion', involving rules which distinguish between an appropriate from an inappropriate presentation of the self, are formed outside individual consciousness and choice; fashion is thus an exemplar of the 'social' as a force not reducible to the choices and actions of individuals:

> Sartorial custom consists in laws that are imposed without formal sanctions, it is obeyed with wonderful docility and this despite the fact that its laws are unreasonable, arbitrary and not infrequently cruel.
>
> (Bell 1976: 24)

These centrifugal mechanisms increasingly break down during the twentieth century and attention shifts to the mechanism of mass consumption that was an offshoot of the contentious 'mass society' that came to the fore in American social science during the post-Second World War period. However, the theories grounded in the mechanism of imitation still dominate discussion of fashion in the early modern period.

BEYOND IMITATION THEORY

Attempts to understand the dynamics of fashion have been dominated by variants of imitation theory that starts from the presumption that fashion is an essentially hierarchical phenomenon prescribed by some identifiable sartorial authority. Sartorial power is most often conceived as residing with some dominant social group or class whose decisions on what is fashionable are then copied by successive layers of the social hierarchy. Imitation from below induces a pressure on social superiors to display their superiority by further sartorial refinement and innovation in order to distinguish themselves from their inferiors who have adopted their earlier style. Thus a potentially unending cycle of imitation and innovation is set up. Once set in motion the windmill of fashion rolls as if it were self-activating. Fashion is no longer to be conceived as an arena of personal choice; social classes are subject to what Elias aptly termed 'the whip of fashion' (Elias 1983: 65).

The classic formulation of the imitation theory was the product of the distinctive universalizing and evolutionary form of social science that dominated at the close of the nineteenth century and the opening decade of the twentieth century. For Herbert Spencer imitation was conceived as a primary mechanism of his universalization of competition as the driving force of social development (Spencer 1876).[8] Starting from the very beginning the first clothes were the trophies of the hunt or war – skins or other relics of animal and human conquests; these trophies gradually gave way to badges and heraldic symbols. From the beginning dress is never simply functional; it marks distinctions in prowess and rank with the result that:

> the lower-grades have sought to raise themselves into the grades above, by assuming their distinctive marks.
>
> (Spencer 1876 I: 187)

For Spencer this process exemplifies a general evolutionary shift from 'compulsory cooperation' to 'voluntary cooperation', the latter being marked by a tendency to obliterate class-differentiation. He was led to a rather optimistic view of fashion as tending towards equalization and favouring the growth of individuality (1876: 210).

Georg Simmel's version of imitation theory assumed that the species had a dualistic nature in which two forces, those of imitation and differentiation (or individualization), were at work (Simmel 1904: 130). He shared Spencer's evolutionism; imitation characterizes the primitive stage of social development and juvenile personality development. Imitation was further equated with the egalitarian impulse of socialism. He viewed differentiation as characteristically modern, associated with high social development and individual maturity or adulthood[9]. The logic of fashion lies in a passion for self-individualization, an eagerness to distinguish one's self from others, and involves a 'passion for inequality' (Ross 1909: 100). Simmel viewed innovation as emanating from the upper classes and is copied by the lower classes while the upper classes seek out new fashions that, in turn, diffuse downwards. This is the account that has come to be called the 'trickle-down theory' (although Simmel himself never used this phrase).

What is distinctive about these versions of imitation theory is that the competition between social superiors and inferiors is induced by the envy of subordinates. Social superiors are reactive to pressure from below and in so doing given expression to the civilized value of individualism. It was into this somewhat complacent account of the dynamic of fashion that Thorstein Veblen's intervention shifted the focus onto the distinctive patterns of consumption of the ruling class, the 'leisure class', that was his intellectual and political target. Within a now rather dated universalizing anthropology, much informed by Darwinian evolutionism, Veblen constructs a fascinating account of the mechanisms of class differentiation. Capitalism brings with it an expansion of the sphere of consumption and a shift from landed property to monetary wealth. The result is the rise of pecuniary competition and emulation that is manifest in Veblen's enduring concept of 'conspicuous consumption', the mechanics of which he explores in distinguishing between 'vicarious consumption', 'conspicuous leisure' and 'conspicuous waste'. Powerful though his invective is, Veblen's reproach of the leisure class is marked by unquestioned petty bourgeois values that assume the inherent irrationality of conspicuous consumption. As Elias observes this response inhibits Veblen from being able to recognize the social compulsions that necessitate the practices of prestige consumption (Elias 1983: 67). E.P. Thompson takes an important step further by his suggestion that the 'ostentatious display, the powdered wigs and the dress of the great must be seen also – *as they were intended to be seen* – from below, in the auditorium of the theatre of class hegemony and control' (Thompson 1978: 150). It is this step that is crucial in being able to step out of the view-from-above through which all versions of imitation theory operate.

Vicarious consumption involves deriving prestige from the transfer of consumption onto others, epitomized in the medieval period by the competition within the nobility through the display of liveried retainers. 'Vicarious consumption' is of special interest with respect to the story of sumptuary law because of the distinctive, but complex, way in which these laws became gendered, sometimes targeting women and at others being concerned to check male sartorial extravagance. Veblen offers a suggestive account of how women's dress came to be such an important form of conspicuous consumption. He suggests that in pre-modernity vicarious consumption was focused on the class of dependents, liveried retainers and, later, in the bourgeois era on domestic servants. Not only were servants a highly visible form of display, but one which had its own distinctive history. The styles of sartorial elegance of previous periods ossified and the fashionable dress of the upper classes came to be ordained for their servants; thus as wigs were discarded by the upper classes during the eighteenth century they were imposed on their servants. Again towards the end of the nineteenth century, when the wearing of evening dress shifted from the domestic to the public sphere of conspicuous consumption, tails and bow ties were transposed to domestic servants; if the bourgeois man no longer looked like a 'gentleman', then at least his butler could![10]

Veblen suggested that a curious inversion occurred during the course of the nineteenth century; vicarious consumption in the bourgeois household came to be exclusively assigned to wives and daughters. They ceased to be involved in most forms of productive labour, and the forms of labour in which they were engaged, with the important exception of the labour of bearing children, took on the characteristics of consumption rather than production. Such 'occupations' as embroidery, crochet and the other domestic skills were forms of what might be called leisure labour. Wives and daughters increasingly became vehicles of vicarious display; the wealth and prestige of the bourgeois male was displayed in the elegance of his wife and daughters who took on the endlessly demanding idle-work of being 'ladies'.

While Veblen's concerns were firmly located within the nineteenth century similar processes were also at work much earlier among the upper classes in late medieval and early modern society. In both feudal court societies and among the urban bourgeoisie the reconstitution of the sexual division of labour manifested itself in the privatization of the domestic sphere and with it the privatization of women. For present purposes it is sufficient to identify a general process that I will call the feminization of fashion as a process to which some variant of Veblen's vicarious consumption applies. In its turn the feminization of fashion had much older roots in the ubiquitous eroticization of women's bodies and the identification of women's personal worth through appearance, processes that manifest themselves in the way in which the very presence of women is universally judged against prevailing standards of 'beauty' and captured in description of dress, ornamentation or decoration as the very defining characteristics of the existence of women.

While the feminization of fashion was a very long-runing trend, modernity is characterized by a very distinctive change in the male identity. The bourgeois male underwent what has been called 'the great masculine renunciation' that Flugel describes as 'the most remarkable event in the whole history of dress' (Flugel 1950: 110). Men gave up their right to all the brighter, gayer and more varied forms of ornamentation, leaving these entirely to the use of women. It will be necessary from time to time to return to consider the connections between sumptuary law and these shifts in the sartorial role of the sexes although the main period of 'the great renunciation' lies outside the period of this study. For present purposes it is sufficient to note the significant gendered component of the history of conspicuous consumption and that, even in periods when fashion was as much a male as a female phenomenon, there has always existed a significant sexual differentiation. For men fashion has always been public, an expression of political and economic power, while for women fashion always exhibited a more specific dimension of personal worth and self-identity and is manifest in the flowering of narcissism (Turner

1984). Mirrors came to play a significant part in a distinctively gendered preoccupation with personal appearance. While they had been available as rare items of luxury for a long time, it was the invention of silvered mirrors that led to them becoming an essential item for upper-class women by the sixteenth century (Angeloglou 1970; Gunn 1973).[11]

Veblen's category 'conspicuous leisure' manifests itself in abstention from labour and the pursuit of the non-productive consumption of time that may also be associated with ostentatious waste of some economically valuable resource: the pursuit of highly specialized and expensive hobbies, no matter whether they are frivolous or virtuous, all constitute conspicuous leisure. It is epitomized in his discussion of the role of the Victorian 'lady', realized only through time-consuming and intense preoccupation with dress, decorum and demeanour. However, Veblen's treatment is perhaps too strongly overlaid by a moralist preoccupation with 'waste.' This leads him to miss out on the significant role played by ascetic, aesthetic and even scientific pursuits as components of the features of the pursuit of 'distinction' by the upper classes. It may even be suggested that these features achieve growing importance as wider sections of a population become able to participate in simple economic display. This has led to increasing importance being attached to a range of non-essential, but non-profligate activities such as the consumption of and participation in 'high culture', higher learning, charity and 'good works'.[12] In short, the practices of distinction should be regarded as morally neutral; the entirely serious activities of eighteenth century amateur botanists as well as the demanding pursuit of fashion epitomized by figures as Beau Brummel equally exemplify the category 'conspicuous leisure'.

The immediate implication of imitation theories of fashion is that one strategy open to the upper classes is to preserve their symbolic sartorial predominance by seeking to prohibit imitation from below by the imposition of sumptuary laws. However, as will become apparent when examining the history of the style wars between social classes and the part played in them by sumptuary law, the attempt to outlaw imitation and competition from below was a project marked by endemic tensions and contradictions.

Imitation theories of fashion suffer from a number of serious limitations. In the first place imitation theory is readily applicable only when there exists a stable social hierarchy, and when the social as well as sartorial preeminence of the dominant group is accepted by other social classes. This limitation results from the fact that imitation theory imports a rather simple social psychology of class relations; it assumes that inferiors envy superiors and engage in imitative activities to emulate their 'betters' in order to gain recognition and even entry to the privileged group. Thus in the expansionary period of British capitalism did the misnamed 'public schools' acculturate an expanding middle class to the culture, sartorial and otherwise, of the dominant class. But the simple mechanism of imitation is inadequate to understand such a process. A conception of an 'imagined class' makes it possible to grasp that fashion involves more than an imitation of an already existing class, but rather involves the production of just such an imagined class that is not reducible to any simple socio-economic category.[13] The class 'produced' by the English public schools involved a complex mix of elements from a variety of class positions; this 'imagined' class was half bourgeois, half aristocratic.

Imitation theory is typically a view from above. It manifests the self-absorption of a dominant class incapable of imagining any other reason for the behaviour of their 'inferiors' than that they desire to imitate their 'superiors'. The dominant class may be gripped, particularly in periods when it suffers from exhaustion or is already in decline, by an inability to grasp the possibility of aesthetic and self-expressive motives in others.[14] While their economic advantage meant that the dominant class had first access to the new fabrics and materials that were the product of the expansion of trade and the development of the textile industry, this does not justify the view that the aspirations of others for access to these new and exciting resources can adequately be explained by the notions of envy and imitation. There is an interesting story to be told about the process of adaptation and innovation that occurs alongside imitative processes in the history of fashion seen as an active manifestation of class and gender struggles. That such an analysis is possible is suggested by the fascinating innovative processes that have bubbled up from below in the short history of mass consumption and its complex interaction with commercial manipulation by the clothing trades.

As we shall see, imitation theories of fashion become less adequate as soon as class relations are contested and when the expansion of the consumer market creates spaces in which differentiated markets coexist. This is especially evident in the recent past. Since the Second World War the expansion of internal consumer markets has manifested itself in the phenomenon of 'mass fashion' whose dynamic is not reducible to imitation. Its place is taken by an ongoing process of the production and display of a 'collective taste' (Blumer 1969: 282; Horowitz 1975; McCracken 1988). However, in avoiding the simple model of hierarchical imitation theory there has perhaps been a tendency to ignore and to obscure the continuing role of social differentiation and of class relations that has been characteristic of 'mass society' theory. Nor is the situation improved by the Leftist version that deploys a conspiracy theory model that conceives of fashion as the arbitrary product of an alliance of clothing manufacturers, haute couture and fashion magazines. While fashion always involves purposeful interventions designed to change taste any account that ignores the fact that people make decisions on their own account will be incomplete. The history of modern fashion is littered with cases where 'the industry' has failed to induce changes, for example in the length of women's skirts during the 'hemline battle' of 1929–1931 (Weibel 1977: 224). More recently attention has been directed to the phenomenon of 'imitation from above', a process classically exemplified by the basketball fashions of the ghettos of American cities that have dominated the mass fashions of the early 1990s. A distinctive process in which fashion 'trickles up' is by no means new, another classic example being the transition of the ubiquitous blue jeans from being a rural working garment to the height of designer fashion.[15]

Earlier commentators had noted a more generalized 'trickle-up' process. For example, Quentin Bell had noted that the movement of male fashion over the last century has involved the elevation of the leisure fashions of the previous period into the privileged style of the next generation. The Victorian Englishman's weekend wear of blazer and slacks or sports jacket and flannel trousers became the office wear for many in the twentieth century. Bell errs, I believe, in suggesting that this is true only of 'leisure' sports and contends that professionalized sports, such as boxing and soccer, have not had the same impact on fashion. That he could say this confidently in 1976 reveals what he and others have so often pointed to about the rapidity and fluidity of the movement of fashion. One of the most distinctive movements of the 1980s has been the adoption of the uniform of professional sports as the youth fashions that have percolated across the increasingly permeable generational boundaries. It is precisely the uniforms of the great mass spectator sports – baseball, soccer, basketball, cycling, etc. – that provide both the national variation and the globalized trends in youth wear.

Imitation theories are prone to miss the significance of the phenomenon that Quentin Bell calls 'conspicuous outrage', a concept that catches the significant dimension through which fashion is capable of manifesting a defiance or an aggressive non-conformity (Bell 1976: 30). This dimension requires that an adequate account of fashion needs to go beyond conformity and imitation in order to grasp the more active, complex and contradictory reality. For example, low necklines have been a frequent site of outrage, and yet, paradoxically, décolletage has long been a significant component of high sumptuosity. Bell draws attention to the fact that formal female evening wear has frequently favoured a high exposure, in various combinations of chest and back; in contrast day wear has been noticeably more modest. He explains this paradox with ingenuity, suggesting that décolletage harmonizes the display of conspicuous leisure while offering a romanticized view of women (Bell 1976: 142). This coexistence of exposure and respectability is evidence of the capacity of fashion codes to convey ambiguity by allowing a pronounced eroticism to go hand in hand with refined sartorial elegance.

Blumer offers an account that provides an alternative to imitation by focusing on the link between fashion and modernity. Fashion is viewed as 'a collective groping for the proximate future' (Blumer 1969: 281). Thus people 'follow fashion' not to imitate the elite, but simply because it is 'the fashion'. What Blumer comes close to articulating is the idea of the relative autonomy of fashion, in which fashion frees itself from being an expression of an elite culture within a unitary hierarchy and comes to appear to be an independent self-moving process. Here it is important to extrapolate from a reification thesis: just as commodities come to appear independent of their producers and to acquire a value that appears intrinsic, so does fashion come to appear independent of the social status or prestige of those manifesting any particular fashionable artifact or practice. Things are fashionable for no other reason than that they are fashionable. Fashion involves a 'wish to be in fashion, to be abreast of what has good standing, to express new tastes that are emerging in a changing world' (Blumer

1969: 282). Thus fashion is always 'modern'; to be fashionable is to keep abreast of the times. This connection between fashion and modernity was also made by Boehn:

> Dress is the agency through which any new consciousness of the world and one's particular *milieu* is most speedily proclaimed.
> (Boehn 1932: I: 215)

Thus there is a fascinating richness in the contrast between the immediate triviality of fashion and the complex social reality that it can be made to yield up under examination. For Marshall Sahlins 'it is by appearances that civilization turns the basic contradiction of its construction into a miracle of existence: a cohesive society of perfect strangers' (Sahlins 1976: 203). Elizabeth Wilson makes a similar point when she observes that fashion 'is not as senseless as at first appears; it is a statement of the unnaturalness of human social arrangements' (Wilson 1985: 9). Fernand Braudel emphasizes a positive or dynamic dimension:

> Is fashion in fact such a trifling thing? Or is it, as I prefer to think, rather an indication of deeper phenomena – of the energies, possibilities, demands and *joie de vivre* of a given society, economy and civilization?
> (Braudel 1979: 323)

This chapter aspires to grasp both this positive dimension in which clothes and the fashions that mark change and variation reveal also the tensions and ambiguities that are the life-blood of the shifts that make up the social life of fashion. This concern to take personal appearance seriously is greatly facilitated by the considerable advance of cultural sociology in recent years. It is today much easier to pursue as I do here the meaning of dress and fashion, while also being concerned to explore a political economy of the attempt to regulate personal appearance.

BEYOND FASHION: READING CLOTHES

There should be nothing controversial in the claim that clothing operates as a system of communication, that the clothes people wear carry meaning, and thus that it is possible to 'understand' or 'read' clothing. It is, however, less easy to identify just what type of communication is involved. The increased attentiveness to communicative meaning that has been such a significant feature of contemporary scholarship not only requires, but also enables, us to be more precise in posing questions about clothing as communication. Clothing forms a system of 'signs' that people wear that constitute a cultural discourse. Social meanings may be constructed from the elementary contrasts and differentiations that constitute the code or codes that works through the specific combination of the elements which each costume or ensemble brings together, and makes it possible to understand the social meaning of clothing.

If language is the preeminent communicative form it is not surprising that there have been attempts to develop a treatment of dress as a form of language (Lurie 1983; Roach and Eichler 1979; Steele 1985). To draw on the linguistic analogy requires that dress be viewed as exhibiting features such as syntax and grammar. Does dress embody a limited number of simple rules that reveal a potential range of social properties that clothing may be considered as being capable of communicating, such as class or status attributes or gender designations? There is no doubt that specific dress systems contain at least some such rules: for example, much Western clothing has a rule in which opposite buttoning (left over right and right over left) marks a simple gender difference. Such genderized rules are evident in the history of children's fashions; for most of the period under discussion children's appearance was constructed as minaturized replicas of adult dress. Then during the seventeenth century there occurred a distinct feminization of the way in which children were dressed to mark the increasing preoccupation with training for submissiveness (Greven 1977; Muchembled 1985). It was only in the 1920s in a classic example of the 'invention of tradition' that the ubiquitous blue/pink dichotomy was imposed on infants (Paoletti 1987).

The discourses of fashion are replete, like language, with rules that limit and prescribe combinatory features (e.g. top hats go with white ties). Rules of combination revolve around the construction of differentiation through such oppositions as public/private, work/leisure, town/country, day/evening, male/female, adult/adolescent, etc. In some instances dress may 'speak' in much the same way as language. Nowhere is this better illustrated than in Samuel Pepys' description of a sartorial insult delivered in 1666.

Charles II officially sponsored a new style of court dress for the English court, a costume of 'vests' and 'tunics'; the move was designed to assert the independence of the court from French fashions (Evelyn 1951). Pepys reported that the King of France ordered all his footmen to put on vests as 'an ingenious kind of affront' against the English (Pepys 1976: 22/11/1666).

There is a more general sense in which the analogy between fashion and language is helpful. I want to bring out the sense in which dress has the capacity to be eloquent. A particular set of clothes, at the right time and in the right place, 'speaks' with enormous force and immediacy; dress can entirely 'capture' a social position, make a status claim and even secure the moral high-ground.[16] Dress is, of course, more limited in the range of its signification than language, but what has been at stake is not, I suggest, a literal attempt to develop a linguistic model for the communicative properties of clothes, but rather an attempt to mobilize the analogy in order to ground a claim that the communicative dimension of dress and fashion be taken seriously, that dress should not be assumed to be trivial.

Yet to establish the communicative significance of clothing it is not necessary to press the parallel with language in too literal a manner. Indeed there are grounds for resisting this linkage. If we take communication as the starting point then alongside language there exist complex repertoires of non-verbal communication such as visual communication, illustrated by gestures, deportment, processions and demonstrations, advertising, architecture, emblems and many other types (Eco 1979). Clothing is one such form of visual communication. Non-linguistic forms of communication are typically characterized by a limited repertoire of signification; they do not have what can be called the communicative reach of language. Indicatively it is apparent that clothing exhibits a capacity to communicate about such matters as age, social status, gender and national identity, but may also operate within an emotive register being capable of representing mood, playfulness, eroticism, nationalism and a range of sentiments.

With language the speaker or writer is constrained by the structural properties of the language, but is almost completely free in the combinatory power of the language. With clothing it is conventions, rather than structural rules, that limit the potential combinations: that running shoes could be worn with evening dress attests to the absence of any equivalence to rules of grammatical construction. At the same time the range of combinatory elements in dress is more limited and thus the capacity for innovation and complexity is similarly more restricted with the result that dress must be understood as involving a more limited process of signification.

Grant McCracken argues that the capacity of observers to decipher clothing seems to be inherently limited. Dress seems generally to be read as an ensemble, rather than specific readings to be constructed from the connection of its elements, and thus is radically different from the combinatory capacity of language. He found that observers did not seem to be able to 'read' clothing when elements were mixed (e.g. running shoes and evening dress). His respondents became confused unless the images they were shown corresponded to some preconstituted type (e.g. business man vs. hippie). Yet this finding seems to miss the very important sense in which dress does seem to be able to produce meaningful combinations by the use of devices such as side references, borrowings and allusions as when different conventions are linked, for example the deployment of 'peasant' elements in high fashion, or the mix of 'national' conventions, or the deliberate combination of erotic and modest elements. That dress has the capacity to employ such complicated and ambiguous significations is significant, but it is true that clothing as a means of communication does not possess genuine syntagmatic rules governing its combinatory possibility. Dress is perhaps best viewed as a collection of messages rather than a means for their creation (McCracken 1988: 66). It is probably better to abandon the language metaphor as, if not misleading, it is neither necessary nor helpful in order to understand the expressive capacity of the clothes we wear.

To abandon the linguistic metaphor is no great sacrifice since it invites us to follow the trajectory of linguistics itself and to explore dress as a semiotic system. If clothing is approached as having communicative capacity that works through signs that are non-discursive, the visible signs of dress are often closely associated with explicitly discursive features. This combination of the visual and the verbal is particularly evident in the case of high fashion. Roland Barthes' semiotic reading of the 'fashion system' focuses primarily on a reading of fashion journalism that disseminates the aesthetic code of fashion as when 'Yellow is the fashionable colour this season' or 'the youthful accent of this year's fashion' (Barthes 1983).

To make a semiotic turn facilitates engaging with the variety of semiotic elements that coexist in the social construction and understanding of appearances of the clothed body. As Anne Hollander most convincingly demonstrates even in the artistic convention of the nude, the naked body is always significantly clothed (Hollander 1980).[17]

A semiotic approach to clothes needs to grasp that there are different sign systems at work. This is apparent as soon as we contrast uniforms with other forms of clothing. The signs associated with clothing are capable of being organized into codes with general rules that specify the means of interpreting specific signs as with insignia of rank. It is important to stress that signs are rarely capable of carrying much communication without being located within a code. The road sign is one of the simplest forms of signs: while capable of standing alone as with the conventionalized representation of the left or right turn, their full utility is dependent on their location within a code that, for example, contains a generalized distinction, usually conveyed by the framing shape within which the individual sign is located, that distinguishes between an imperative sign and an advisory or warning sign. The code provides rules for the interpretation of the discrete sign.

Uniforms work through codes; they may exhibit a precise (and potentially complex) code that makes possible very precise readings. Military, medical and clerical uniforms make possible the close reading of rank, grade, function, etc. Such codes are capable of extensive expansion when combined with the additional semiotic diversity facilitated by ornamentation and other semiotic devices of which heraldry provides an expanded system both of differentiation, for example by status, and individual recognizability. It was undoubtedly significant that it was the development of medieval enclosed armour that obscured the normal marks of individualization through hair and eye colour, and variation of physiognomy that led to the complex semiotics of heraldry. Medieval symbols were not simply forms of signification or metaphor, but rather were constitutive of that reality (Huizinga 1954). Clothes and the extensive variation made possible by ornamentation suggest the utility of Bourdieu's concept of symbolic capital. It is significant that ornamental detail in dress deploys a symbolism of power-laden practices, the most obvious being the use of military symbolism in buttons, braids, epaulettes and other details or the use of symbols of precious metals, of gold and silver finishes to detailing in buttons, clasps, etc.

Other dress codes that share some of the features of the uniform exist. Mechanisms of 'ritual' designate what come close to being virtually compulsory dress conventions for weddings, funerals and other ritualized social relations and activities; few, for example, violate the ritual requirement to wear black at funerals. The codes of etiquette apply not only to clothing, but also to food and all other items of consumption by specifying what is appropriate to wear or to eat in specified social contexts such that even the most habitual informal dresser succumbs and dons the ubiquitous suit for a job interview. The recognition of the variety of quasi-codified dress regimes leads to the suggestion, to be examined in more detail below, that sumptuary law should be understood as an attempt to put in place precisely such an external and potentially coercive enforcement of dress codes.

However, too much emphasis on the role of codes in semiotic systems needs either to be avoided or, alternatively, to be broadened in order to engage with the emotive and aesthetic dimensions of communication through clothing. Not all social signs are of the same type. If dress has an aesthetic dimension then, like music, it will involve the play of suggestion, emotion, allusion and ambiguity. The 'meaning' of clothing is constructed through communicated images, sentiments and sensibilities. There is no controversy that music and novels are communicative, nor that they communicate in different ways than do road signs and instructional manuals. It is, however, less easy to specify either the nature of this difference and whether aesthetic communication is best treated as a component of semiotic codes. Putting aside the philosophical issues involved as usefully flagging problems that may arise, I will make use of the idea of an aesthetic code. Such codes exhibit ambiguity; in part this ambiguity stems from the complexity of the unconscious symbolism of colour, textures, etc. that involves what Fred Davis aptly describes as an 'awesome, if not overwhelming, ambiguity' (Davis 1985: 17). Jonathan Culler offers one possible route to an understanding of the complexity of aesthetic codes that he suggests involves an 'evasive complexity' through the play upon complexity, paradox and ambiguity (Culler 1976: 100). Aesthetic communication will tend towards transgressive violation or disruption of its own code.

There are two important respects in which dress codes can be understood as evasive. In the first place, dress choices, while they take account of pressures toward conformity, at the same time exhibit self-expression and differentiation. In the simplest case people strive to present themselves as both conforming to the pressure to dress appropriately, while seeking to avoid presenting themselves as identical to others. 'To dress fashionably is both to stand out and to merge with the crowd, to lay claim to the exclusive and to follow the herd' (Wilson 1985: 6). Even where the consumer market is underdeveloped, as was the case in medieval Europe and in the Third World today, individuals can generally be assured that the combinatory choices they make will ensure that they will never be dressed exactly the same as anyone else. Even in formalized dress codes individualization is not absent: soldiers in uniform wear berets at rakish angles and wearers of stylized national costume secure individualization by small variations in figurative detail. The preoccupation that dominates the literature on dress and fashion with the tension between imitation and differentiation can satisfactorily be embraced by thinking of aesthetic codes as being constructed not of stipulative rules, but rather as being constructed in the form of rules that lay down outer limits or boundaries. Such a code might typically take the form 'Clothing item X may be worn in combination with A, B and C, but not with D'. In this context aesthetic codes are simply more complex versions of these limiting codes, but which are always subject to the possibility of innovative transgression.

In attempting to understand dress codes there is another dimension that is less easy to encompass within a semiotic approach. It is now commonplace to decentre the subject and to deny significance of authorial intent. The position of the dresser in connection with fashion invites just such a treatment. Our capacity to undertake a reading of clothes needs to recognize that there frequently exists a radical separation between what people do, and their own understandings and explanations of their conduct. An important key to our understanding of the social significance of clothing will depend on our ability to come to grips with the disjunctive features of personal appearance. In the first place the key issue is that some separation between social meaning and personal intentions seems to be ubiquitous. Accordingly it becomes of the greatest importance to make explicit the implicit meanings that clothes are able to carry and to reconstruct how these work. In some cultural activities, such as the plastic arts, the notion of 'meaning' is self-consciously present and forms a familiar part of their discourses. While 'Fashion' has its own discursive formation, the most generalized being found in the massively consumed genre of 'women's magazines', individuals characteristically refuse to recognize the presence of 'meaning'. It is paradoxical because the presentation of self involves the investment of substantial resources of both time and money, yet individuals maintain at least a public veneer that trivializes precisely these activities. This refusal is nowhere more evident than with respect to the erotic dimensions of the presentation of the self, where denial and repression go hand in hand with the pursuit of an unambiguously sexualized self-presentation. The most likely explanation of this paradox is that the discursive denial of sexualization renders its sartorial pursuit freer and less encumbered by mechanisms of self-restraint. It is this 'refusal' that is intimately connected, in a way I need to specify, with the transgressive role of fashion. Dress allows us to make 'statements' in our presentation of self that would involve much higher risks if they were made in the more explicit medium of spoken language. Visual 'statements' can always be denied or retracted.

There seems to be an essential inexplicitness that surrounds the communicative capacity of clothing. Clothes communicate their messages in a less overt and less conscious manner than does the spoken or written word, but this provides considerable flexibility. Clothes can carry messages that could not be put more explicitly without danger of protest or controversy. On the other hand clothing has obvious limitations as to the range of messages that it can communicate, but dress is not so limited as to be incapable of giving expression to a range of fairly subtle emotional statements. I think that Grant McCracken is wrong when he argues that clothing cannot be used to express irony, scepticism or ambivalence (1988: 67). I suggest it can and does communicate all of these. Irony and scepticism are present in styles that incorporate features of uniforms as in recent fashions organized around army fatigues. Ambivalence is present in the way in which both display and concealment of secondary sexual characteristics figure significantly in the history of women's clothing. In general I suggest that one should assume that visual signs have a greater communicative capacity than suggested by the fairly limited materials with which they work.

Diane Hughes provides a dramatic illustration of the ambiguity, or what she describes as polyvalence, of the semiotic content of the fashion system in her superb social history of the earring. She argues that:

> clothing forms an obvious semiotic system whose polyvalence challenged social organizers to manipulate its codes. The movement of ear-rings from a sign of concupiscence and mark of the outsider to a sign of honour and mark of the entrenched brings to an end the long fifteenth-century struggle between ideals of civic wealth and Franciscan poverty in a victory of aristocratic codification.
>
> (Hughes 1986: 48)

Not only does she draw attention to the fact that fashion codes are always context dependent and thus permit great variability in the signifier–signified relationship. For example, silk plays a central role in the history of sumptuary law, but its role shifts, being sometimes erotic while at other times it manifests conspicuous consumption and, of course, an interplay of the erotic and the exotic. It should not be thought that the erotic and the economic roles are always distinct: the eroticization of wealth plays a significant part in my story. It should be borne in mind that the expansion of fashion is just one feature of a much wider process that involves a growing separation between production and consumption and between work and leisure.

Diane Hughes shows how the earring was imposed upon prostitutes and Jewesses as 'marks of infamy' but came to acquire the status of marks of distinction.[18] The late medieval Italian discourses of sexuality constructed the conspicuous ornamentation of the earring as a sign of sexual immorality; it further produced a degradation discourse linking prostitutes and Jewesses as both 'foreign' and immoral.[19] I want to stress the significance of the discursive linkage that Hughes' case study reveals since I will argue that such discursive linkage or coupling is a distinctive feature of the discourses surrounding sumptuary legislation. The second feature of Hughes' account that I will draw upon is the connection she establishes between the symbolic role of ornamentation and wider social and economic struggles. As I hope to show, the attempt to understand the controversies that have surrounded the ordering of appearance provide one means of assessing the wider dynamics of social struggles.

The emergence of an explicit conception of fashion played a significant part in clothing coming to embody an expression of the emergence of sartorial self-consciousness alongside the more general civilizing process identified by Elias. 'Appropriateness' developed as a concern of securing a linkage between behaviour and 'demeanour', an idea that readily lends itself to a linkage between 'appropriate appearance', 'neatness' and 'respectability', which is contrasted with a self-consciousness of a breach with the past and with the rural 'rusticity' that the rise both of court societies and urban expansion contrasted themselves against. In other words, whilst attributing significance to the phenomenon of fashion, the wider significance of dress and personal appearance should not be reduced to the question of 'fashion' as much of the literature has done (Jaeger 1985: 117).

MISREPRESENTATION, DECEPTION AND DISGUISE

While the clothes people wear provide a rich and complex way in which the social and cultural map may be read, they also create rich possibilities for deceit, dissimulation and subterfuge. To don the appropriate garments can never in itself be 'proof' of the projected message and the associated social position and its entitlements. Virtually anyone, with a little effort, could dress 'like a gentleman or a lady'. To take social appearance at face value is always to take a risk. The problem is not simply that of social fraud and 'gate-crashing', but some of the complexity involved in reading clothes stems from the possibility of playing games with dress, of 'dressing up' and 'dressing down'. Nor is the problem confined to misrepresentation; the separable connection between the body, the self and its appearance allows for a range of other possibilities, from clothes as disguise where the intent is to conceal identity rather than to take on a different one. One can only speculate about the set of motivations that produced the Scottish statute of 1429 prohibiting any woman from coming to church or market with her face covered in such a way that she could not be recognized, 'that sho may nocht be kende' (APS II: 49: 11, 13; quoted in Shaw 1979: 99). The long history of the mask (and to a lesser extent the fan), despite many stylistic variations, has continued to serve as a means of denial, not only of identity, but also of responsibility as epitomized by the use of the mask as licence in traditions such as the masked ball, carnival, fancy dress, etc.[20]

The veil is a case that is significant for its ambiguity: it is a significantly genderized means of disruption of visibility and knowability. On the one hand, the veil operates within a code of modesty and self-denial, but on the other it creates the possibility for deception and evasion. While in many religious discourses it was an expression of female modesty, the veil could also encourage an anonymity regarded as problematic by the city fathers. Thus in Siena officials were empowered to demand of a veiled woman the name of her father or husband (Hughes 1983: 91). The result has been that the veil has both been enforced and refused and more will need to be said about its ambiguity in the context of the regulation of gender relations in Chapter 9 below.

That clothes serve to establish social identities but provide opportunities for misrepresentation has always created a limitation on the possibility of achieving a reliable ordering of appearance. There are two contrasting responses to this inherent limitation. The first is found in attempts to secure a foolproof system of distinguishing marks of which the widespread use of the branding of offenders with undeniable and unerasable marks is the simplest, if most extreme, instance. There is an interesting contrast between the widespread punitive use of branding with marks on the face or the cutting off of ears or noses and more narrowly evidential forms of branding. In the latter case the distinguishing mark was placed on the body but was normally concealed, but when an issue arose such as whether a suspect had committed a previous offence the appropriate inspection could be ordered. In both of these situations the general context is the use of legal power on and over the body of the accused (Muchembled 1985). The long history of 'misrepresentation of office' laws that prohibit wearing of police, military and other uniforms should also be noted.

A very different set of issues was involved in the bizarre proposal of one French nobleman, who very shortly before the French Revolution was concerned about misrepresentation of noble status. He proposed the placing of permanent marks on nobles of the blood. But it was not revealed whether these were to be prominent for all to see or to be placed discreetly for evidential use in case of disputes or other serious causes. The report of this incident by de Tocqueville speaks of a concern 'to ensure their exterior recognition', which seems to suggest the former (1856: 465); one wonders how many French nobles owed their lives to the fact that this scheme was never implemented! In pre-Tokugawa Japan a visual code of tattoo marks revealing the wrongdoer's offence was part of the scheme of penal politics (Hall 1979: Appendix). More generally rules prescribing the wearing of visible distinguishing marks, for example by prostitutes, were supplemented by rules requiring that these marks should not be covered; one English plague proclamation required that those who had been in contact with plague victims should not wear cloaks, the object being to ensure that they did not cover the distinguishing mark that they were required to wear.

The alternative response to the problem of the misrepresentation inherent in clothes is to shift the criteria of social recognition in which clothes may provide prima facie evidence of rank or status, and to employ supplementation by some other special test. The secret password or handshake are simple examples. Of much greater importance are those responses that operate through the imposition of more complex cultural codes or tests: the adoption of a foreign language, such as the adoption of French by the upper classes in Poland and Russia, was such a case. More generally dress codes exist alongside a series of tests or hurdles. Veblen was correct when he insisted that the distinction pursued by the upper classes does not necessarily involve indolence or quiescence; rather it manifests itself in time-consuming and 'demanding' acquisition of 'accomplishments', 'manners', and 'etiquette' that requires the investment of conspicuous non-labour time. He insists, with a nice touch of irony, that 'good-breeding' requires a 'substantial and patent waste of time' (Veblen 1967: 51).

A particularly fruitful way of understanding the dynamic part played by the ordering of appearance in the wider processes of the ordering of social and cultural relations is to make use of Bourdieu's concept of 'distinction' (Bourdieu 1984). This concept has a great advantage over all versions of 'imitation' theory in that it does not assume a simple hierarchy in which all social groups and classes are presumed to have much the same understanding of the vertical ranking. Imitation theory rests on the rather simplistic model of envy; lower positions are presumed to aspire to or at least to be envious of their superiors. In contrast distinction theory makes use of the play between 'to distinguish', that is to distinguish or separate oneself from others, and 'to be distinguished', to fulfil or to display some superiority over others.

The great merit of this approach is that it offers a nuanced account of the mechanisms through which hierarchical class relations are lived. The socially dominant classes work hard to secure the tastes of their own class as 'distinguished', in contrast to the 'vulgar' tastes of the lower orders and the 'pretentious' tastes of intermediate social positions. In addition, Bourdieu's concept makes it possible to focus on the way in which each social group 'distinguishes' itself from others. This mechanism can include self-degradation, for example, the celebration of vulgarity as when drinking and eating are measured by volume rather than by quality. Of particular relevance is the attention that the concept distinction allows to the formation of more positive or self-assertive class identities. This is of importance for the present study because so much of it revolves around the trajectory of the decline of pre-modern nobilities and the rise of the bourgeois classes. Almost without exception, writing on the politics of appearance has viewed the merchant and bourgeois classes as simply imitating the dress styles of the nobility. There was undoubtedly a great deal of passive and obsequious imitation, but there was also a more complex working and playing upon fashion that was part of the process of the emergence of the new economically and culturally dominant class configuration. In brief, 'distinction' can encompass imitation, but can also illuminate innovative practices.

DRESS CODES

If we are to understand the characteristics of dress codes it is important to explore how they are constructed. In the first place they are constructed from a limited number of variables. The existence of these elements makes possible a complex set of relations and distinctions within which people operate as they make choices about their clothing. People come to 'know' about the appropriateness of clothing choices, and this in turn institutes and reinforces a clothing system that can be understood and explained and which involves a semiological system of distinctions, categories and rules of combination. The semiotic content of dress is constructed from the elementary contrasts and differentiations.[21] These contrasts are embodied in the three primary variables around which clothing is constructed: texture, colour and line. One basic pattern is the existence of codes of gender differentiation: female gender is linked to soft fabrics, bright colours and curved line, while masculinity is signed by rough texture, dull colours and angular line. This semiotic order acquires increased fluidity by virtue of its capacity to incorporate reversals within this code as when fashion 'plays' on the existing code by incorporating a discrepant element, for example when female fashion deploys angular 'male' padded shoulders.

Clothes make significant use of signs that operate as indexes in which the connection between sign and that which is signified is substantive. The Rolls-Royce as a sign of wealth is more than symbolic: the high price of the Rolls is an indexical supplement to the communicative capacity. In contrast, colour coding (purple and crimson as signs of nobility) attest to Saussure's insistence on the general rule of the arbitrariness of the connection between sign and that which is signified.[22] The arbitrariness of the true 'sign' is well illustrated in Grant McCracken's study of colour-coding at the Court of Elizabeth I where the symbolic opposition between white and black expressed a political opposition between youth and age (McCracken 1985). One of more extreme deployments of the regulation of colour occurred in Venice after the great plague of 1347–48 when the Senate issued a sumptuary rule forbidding dark-blue or green raiment with the motive of encouraging a return to general happiness (Newett 1907: 249).

One of the most persistent semiotic features of clothing and ornamentation is that it has provided complex and infinitely varied ways of displaying both material and cultural capital. The body is a primary site for the display of economic status; hierarchical statements are made through the wearing of expensive materials. In order to 'read' the dress code of a particular culture one requires some knowledge of the relative values of the different cloths available. For example, both China and Japan have had a complex hierarchy of different grades of silk; similarly Northern Europe has had a strongly hierarchical gradation of furs and often a moralization supplement. For example, in *Piers Plowman* fur is presented as the epitome of depraved luxury and corruption so that when 'Reason' is summoned, he refuses assistance until 'Lady Peacock casts her finery off and locks her furs away in her clothes chest' (Langland 1550). Both silk and furs figure prominently in the history of sumptuary regulation. It should be noted that in the construction of such hierarchies economic value is not the sole consideration. Veblen's distinction between 'conspicuous consumption' and 'conspicuous leisure' draws attention to the fact that some fabrics acquire hierarchic significance not just because of their expense, but because they are delicate and thus unsuitable for work. Thus the continuing sartorial significance of silk is to be accounted for through the combination of its expense and its delicacy. It should be noted, account also needs to be taken of the tactile properties; it is the 'silkiness' of silk alongside its cost and delicacy that accounts for its significant sexualization in many cultures.

The human body has provided a primary site for the display of conspicuous consumption: rings, necklaces, bracelets, earrings and the like provide readily portable means of displaying economic status. Ornaments do more than display wealth; ornamentation also has an aesthetic significance in a double sense. First, the objects of display are themselves aestheticized; rather than wearing bars of gold or uncut stones most cultures add some aesthetic dimension to these objects of consumption. Second, the object aestheticizes the human subject as the locus of display. Nowhere is this more apparent than in the complex coupling of aesthetic and sexual significance associated with the female neck and breast as a site of display, both of precious metals and stones, but also of the body itself, with the valorization of soft and unblemished skin in close proximity to the breasts themselves as primary signifiers of sexuality. This double aesthetic is further evidence of the close link between conspicuous consumption and conspicuous leisure. It is not only in advanced capitalist societies that the aesthetics of display encompass the great majority of the population and are not confined to a privileged or dominant class. In short, dress conceals sexuality at the same time as it displays it.

It should be noted that conspicuous consumption is not confined to the display of economic capital: cultural capital is also a major object to display (Bourdieu and Passeron 1977). Medieval lawyers and doctors were quite frequently the beneficiaries of special relief from the sumptuary provisions by which their economic peers were constrained. It is worth noting that academic dress, more so than that of lawyers, and much more than that of medical doctors, underwent an early ossification to produce the ceremonial cap and gown now reserved for ceremonial occasions (Hargreaves-Mawdsley 1963a). In general it may be observed that the mechanisms that ossify a dress style of a particular period to produce either occupational or status uniforms tend to remove them from the ambit of state regulation. Occupational dress periodically ossified to become the 'liveries' of the guilds. Account needs to be taken of the fertile process, that Hobsbawm has so aptly termed 'the invention of tradition', whereby 'newer' occupations devise costumes within the genre of these older traditions (Hobsbawm and Ranger 1983). Thus the costumes of the English judges and barristers are much more 'modern' than their style suggests (Hargreaves-Mawdsley 1963b). Cultural capital in the form of degrees and honours and the general display of qualifications on visiting cards and curricula vitae plays a significant part in the presentation of modern self.

Dress can thus be approached as a form of communicative action that operates as an extensive semiotic and symbolic system. As Boehn observed 'dress is the agency through which any new consciousness of the world and one's particular *milieu* is most speedily proclaimed' (Boehn 1932: I: 215). It provides a mechanism that links both the self-individualization that operates alongside its capacity to carry quite complex messages about social roles, economic status and political power, while at the same time participating in the reproduction of beliefs and values. I will return to this theme in the discussion of the construction and ordering of gender in Chapter 9 below. More specifically the general thesis can be derived from this consideration of a semiotic approach to dress that sumptuary law operates predominantly through the mechanism of proclaiming an indexical code that seeks to link the regulation of dress to other features of the material and cultural order. Whilst making use of other more purely symbolic devices, sumptuary law may best be read as a social and political project directed towards the reproduction of the dominant forms of class and gender relations. If sumptuary laws are viewed as an attempt to impose a semiotic dress code we can begin to understand the 'failure' of the sumptuary project, not as something to be sneered at and pronounced impossible, but rather as the victim of the inherent instability and trangsressability of clothing as a social device for ordering appearance.

CLOTHES, NATIONAL IDENTITIES AND XENOPHOBIA

That clothes are a vehicle and, in particular, a sign-vehicle (Goffman 1959) is apparent. Less immediately apparent is the connection between clothing and the construction of national identity. A persistent theme of many of the attempts to regulate fashion was the presence of a nationalist theme that was always in danger of spilling over into xenophobia. Sumptuary regulation appealed with significant regularity to a hostility to the 'foreign'. Shakespeare captured this persistent moralization of foreign fashions:

> Report of fashions in proud Italy,
> Whose manners still our tardy apish nation,
> Limps after in base imitation.
> (*Richard II*)

Evidence of the use of sumptuary laws against foreign fashions is to be found throughout Europe. A Florentine decree of 1512 prohibited 'the most shameless dance of the cap and other French dances full of lecherous and sinful gestures' (Gilbert 1973: 279–80). In Moravia licence was allowed to unmarried girls to wear 'city' or even 'foreign' clothes, regarded as more exotic, that were denied to married women (Bogatyre 1971: 56). In 1509 a Venetian proclamation prohibited 'French fashions' and in neighbouring Vicenza men were banned from wearing the 'fashions of our enemies' (Newton 1988: 137). In fifteenth century Nürnburg there was a general prohibition against 'any sort of peculiar cut or innovation, . . . foreign custom or peculiarity' (Greenfield 1918: 118). A Strasbourg ordinance of 1660 moralized those who imitated anything:

> new in clothing from foreign non-German nations, and imitate this regardless of whether it looks good or bad, and through such foolishness let it be seen how little they have the commendable steadfastness for which our old German forefathers had a singular reputation in other things as well as in clothing.
>
> (Vincent 1935: 69–70)

In the early fifteenth century the clothing ordinances of the city of Nürnberg deplored 'newfangledness' (*neuerung, neue Sitten*) and 'foreignness'. At first the Council outlawed each objectionable new innovation; but by the end of the century they made a more comprehensive assault on innovation with a general ban on 'Innovation and Unaccustomed Styles in Apparel, Adornment and Shoes'. Strauss sums up the mood of the city fathers:

> Affluent and confident though the city was, it peered into the future with concern and suspicion.
>
> (Strauss 1966: 114)

John Evelyn epitomized the preoccupation with the link between clothes and national identity when by the mid-seventeenth century the French had resumed their role as the 'natural enemy'. His satirical attack on 'the mode' argued that nations distinguish themselves by their dress and that they advance and conquer others by spreading their 'mode'. This accusation is directed against the French and the English are chided for committing national suicide by voluntarily adopting French fashions. Evelyn went to great lengths to propose a distinctive English style, although it reads more as the adoption of a largely eastern *mélange* of styles; it certainly made no effort to draw on any indigenous national traditions (Evelyn 1951). His plan secured the approval of Charles II but no serious steps to legislate the new fashion into being seem to have been taken.

In an earlier attack in 1577 on 'foreign' styles William Harrison did project some conception of English identity through dress. He derided the current preoccupation with Spanish and French fashions, but looked back to the good old days when 'an Englishman was known abroad by his cloth and contented himself at home with his fine kersey hosen . . . without such cuts and garish colours as are worn in these days and never brought in but by the consent of the French' (Harrison 1968: 148). Similar sentiments were still alive in Wilhelmine Germany up until the threshold of the twentieth century. The critique of luxury persisted, revealing a typically bourgeois anxiety about foreign, and in particular, French fashion (Breckman 1990–91). The attack on foreign fashion in most European countries was to shift imperceptibly, but decisively, towards a more familiar protectionist rhetoric, one which as a matter of principle favours home products over foreign. In this process sumptuary law did not so much die as change its form and it continued life as economic protectionism, a political and economic discourse that is very much alive in the late twentieth century.

However, nationalism and fashion do not always have a simple relation; frequently the assertion of a new national identity goes hand in hand with the adoption of imitative fashion. For example, in the Italian Risorgimento women opted for French fashion and men for English. Disjunctions of this type persist: in the 1960s the mass demonstrations in Japan against US bases were conducted by young people wearing impeccable denims. A much more direct connection between dress and nationalism exists were law is used to suppress dress as an expression of national identity. One element of the English suppression of the Irish was provided by a Tudor statute of 1539 that prohibited the wearing of 'mantles, coat or hood made after the Irish fashion', the dressing of hair in Irish fashion, or the wearing of saffron dyed shirts, smocks or capes; women were specifically prohibited from wearing any item embroidered in the Irish fashion (Walker 1818). Other prohibitions on Irish dress followed that survived until 1610 and included a prohibition on Irishmen wearing moustaches (McClintock 1943: 66–67; Harte 1976: 158). In similar style, when the French occupied Strasbourg in 1681 the inhabitants were required to abandon German costume and to wear French styles. Following the defeat of the Scottish rebellion and Bonnie Prince Charlie's invasion in 1745, the *Act of Dress* banned Highland plaids, trews and kilts (de Marly 1985: 66). The regulation of dress as a means of visible degradation has a long history; we will encounter it in different guise as the imposition of 'marks of infamy' in Chapter 6.

TOWARD A POLITICAL ECONOMY OF FASHION

The embrace of cultural theory does not require the neglect or abandonment of other theoretical approaches. All communicative forms are located within non-discursive relations: their limits are influenced (even if they are not 'determined') by the political and economic context within which they are located. This is as true for material culture as it is for any other social phenomenon, hence it is pertinent to engage with the project of understanding the place of clothing within culture. There is a tendency that is found in both academic and non-academic discussion of fashion to assume either that it is self-contained, governed by some invisible hand that dictates its shifts as skirt lengths rise and fall, and as trousers tighten and widen. Or, alternatively, the assumption is made that shifts in the rules of appearance are mere reflections of operative causes at work elsewhere, whether it be in the boilerhouse of the economy or in the conservatory of the intellect. In order to avoid these extremes that posit either the autonomy or the dependence of fashion, it is necessary to flesh out the idea of dress, as a key instance of consumption, as the intersection of material culture and the regulatory projects of governance.

Harte draws attention to the gap between economic history and the history of costume (Harte 1976: 140). The recognition that in a distinctive way fashion straddles the realms of production, consumption and culture provides an opening that needs to be developed. It must be capable of embracing both a cultural history, attentive to the semiotics of personal appearance, and a political economy of fashion that takes into consideration the role of consumption in economic life and some notion of 'the politics of fashion'. It needs to grapple with the way in which fashion becomes implicated in other forms of political transformation, and in particular with the changing forms of regulatory intervention, of which sumptuary regulation provides the central focus of this work. Before exploring the distinctive regulatory projects of sumptuary law it is necessary to explore the central discursive tradition within which the sumptuary laws were located, namely the discourses of luxury.

4

'As If God Had Not Made Them Fine Enough': Moralizing Luxury

> So proud and lofty do some people go,
> Dressing theirselves like players in a show,
> They patch and paint, and dress with idle stuff,
> As if God had not made them fine enough.

Waterson's 'Christmas is Now Approaching Near' (trad.), *Frost and Fire* (1965)

THE DISCOURSES OF LUXURY

From the first literate societies until high modernity the figure of Luxury has excited moral condemnation and stimulated the regulatory reflex. At the core of the discourses surrounding sumptuary law has been the moralization of luxury. The invocation of luxury is one of the most ancient and most pervasive negative principles around and one through which social criticism has been articulated; this is certainly true in the history of Western society, and probably more widely (Murray 1978).[1] From the Old Testament to Classical Rome, from the medieval divines down to secular Elizabethan England (and beyond), virtually every conceivable ill, whether personal or social, has been at one time or another laid at the door of luxury. Indeed it will be a supplement to my argument to suggest that the discourses of luxury find strong resonances in the preoccupation with inflation as the primary economic evil of the twentieth century.

From the vantage-point of the present we retain a vague sense of 'luxury' as a problematic category. For us it combines some lingering sense of censure with a positive attraction: the designation of consumables, such as hotels and motorcars as 'luxury', is both neutral, designating a segment of the market, and an advertising puff – we may never take one but the attraction of the idea of being pampered and indulged makes the idea of the 'luxury cruise' a potent stimulant. So, while we retain some sense of the more negative construction of luxury, it is by no means simple to retrieve an understanding of exactly what it was that was so wrong with luxury as to make it a focus of moral critique and a target for regulation.

It is important to start with what should perhaps be treated as the material basis of the critique of luxury. It should be borne in mind that few societies outside the developed industrial sphere have freed themselves from the looming shadow of what used to be called 'dearth' and is now called 'famine': the inability to provide for the basic conditions of social reproduction was and remained a widespread social reality. It is in such a context that there exists a tension between the negative activity of 'squandering' economic resources and the persistent significance of the gift relationship as a mechanism for reinforcing social bonds. Luxury was frequently associated with the figure of 'ruin', a persistent discursive strand provided by the fear of 'ruin' in an imagery that brought together economic and moral catastrophe. For example, in England as late as 1661 there were two proclamations imposing a week of fasting because of the 'unreasonableness of the weather, scarcity and famine' (British Library 1851: *c.* 8 (78) and (97)).

The concern with ruin was connected with a range of anxieties, for example that of the older nobility unable to compete with the pressure of conspicuous consumption from the 'nouveaux riches', but also concern with the 'ruin' of the lower orders trapped into competitive consumption that they could ill afford. And then there was a wider preoccupation with moral, or more specifically sexual, ruin, epitomized by the discourses of virginity, prostitution and, yet again, debility. Krafft-Ebing captures these anxieties when he refers to the view that 'the material and moral ruin of the community is steadily brought about by debauchery, adultery and luxury' (Krafft-Ebing 1922: 6). A sense of the medieval term luxury, connotations which have today been lost, is secured not only by being counterposed to frugality, but also to chastity, such that profligacy carried with it sexual and well as economic implications (Tuve 1966: 207–11). Thomas Mun typifies a voice that had been commonplace for at least two centuries that captured the great chain of vice induced by luxury:

> The general leprosie of our piping, potting, feasting, fashion, and the mis-spending of our time in idleness and pleasure . . . hath made us effeminate in our bodies, weak in our knowledge, poor in our treasure, declined in our valour, unfortunate in our enterprises, and condemned by our enemies.
>
> (Mun 1664: 180–81)

But it is easy to see how the moralizing tones can abate and how 'luxury' shifts towards a concern with 'profligacy' that comes to be viewed in more explicitly 'economic' terms as, for example, in the Venetian law of 1360 that explicitly complained that inordinate luxury was detracting from productive investment in shipping and industry (Miskimin 1969: 156).

It is significant that the imagery of present 'indulgence', 'extravagance', or 'profligacy' and their association with an imagined future shortage and hardship remains a persistent feature of the discourses of luxury down to the present. For the purposes of the present study it should be recalled that serious economic shortage was a general condition of existence in pre-modern Europe during the period of both the rise and the decline of sumptuary law.

The discourses of luxury had a life that went far beyond the fear or the memory of dearth and famine. Luxury came to be conceived as both cause and symptom of an evil that was both personal and social. It needs to be stressed that the notion of luxury had no fixed content. There is no stable reference point of need or necessity as its counterpoint; rather the discourses of 'luxury' involved the construction of a system of rhetorical signs, that is of means of setting up a dichotomous discourse which operated through counterposing vices and virtues. What was distinctive about the discourses of luxury was that its counterpoints were never stable.

Luxury has two major discursive counterpoints. In the first place it is socially divisive – it acts like a solvent, loosening and separating the social bonds conceived as necessary to sustain the community.[2] A second, and rather different, expression of the critique of luxury involves the idea that luxury induces weakening or debility, that it undermines or weakens the individual and thus puts the group at risk. This concern with weakening, 'enervating', making soft, etc., involves the interplay of highly charged sets of myths and symbols. National mythology pictures the national ideal, in contrast to the 'other', as simple and hardy; thus Spanish sumptuary law appealed explicitly to a national image of the Spanish as frugal and hardy, in contrast to the luxury that typified the Moorish national enemy (Hume 1896). The past is imagined as a golden age involving a rural, agricultural, hard-working and simple life; thus in one of its dimensions the construction of luxury reveals itself as a critique of modernity or, alternatively, as the expression of anxiety or apprehension of social change. The reference to simplicity invokes the dualism of town and country in a form which treats the urban as problematic and forgets about Marx's description of rural idiocy (Williams 1973; Berman 1982).

The view of luxury as debilitating deploys the powerful genderization associated with the pejorative connotations of the term effeminate. When Plato links luxury and effeminacy he speaks not from great philosophical insight but from the standpoint of common sense or what everyone 'knows' to be true. Plato was joined in this view by, amongst others, St Augustine, Dante, Swift, Montesquieu and Rousseau (Veyne 1990: 248). Luxury is the feminine, and the feminine is not only in itself weak, but – as in the Samson myth – it undermines the masculine principle of self-sufficiency and hardiness. The pervasive mythology of the Garden of Eden provides evidence of a significant early association of luxury, evil and the female: luxury was and remained a feminine personification. For example, the discourse surrounding Roman sumptuary measures relied heavily on images of 'female luxury' and ostentation and betrayed a preoccupation with the dissolution of the male economic mechanism of inheritance of patrimonies (Miles 1987).

These gendered mythologies relate back to national mythology where concern with weakness and debility takes on an explicitly military dimension in which the nation is conceived as being put at peril when its young men are corrupted by luxury.[3] The discursive construction of the sumptuary ethic played powerfully upon both national and gender dimensions of the critique of luxury, establishing links to military concerns (weakness and effeminacy), economic anxiety (luxury versus famine) and national myths ('us' versus 'them'). In addition, the discourses of luxury spoke of a concern with social stasis, of luxury as inappropriate and as the harbinger of a world-turned-upside-down, an imagery that proves to be powerful and evocative of our retrospective view of the bridge from the pre-modern to the modern. It should be noted that the critique of luxury generally took a distinctive biological metaphorical form in which luxury is conceived as invasive, as a disease and infection to combat which requires either surgical or agricultural operations of pruning, weeding, cutting back, etc.

The Christian tradition adds its own distinctive representation. Luxury is conceived as violation of a divinely conceived necessity or natural order, and it is here that 'necessity' is most successfully linked to a sense of hierarchy. The conception of necessity and the natural seems to refer to a view of the world in which God provides all we need, but an imagery in which our needs are presented as simple, powerfully captured in the symbol of bread. The distinctive shift in the religious critique of luxury is from a concern with personal sin to the idea of luxury as a political evil, because it is only then that it becomes 'a suitable case for treatment' through regulation. The two main candidates as the sins that are induced by luxury are the linked but distinguishable sins of pride and envy. A perennial criticism of preoccupation with personal appearance and with fashion is that it is evidence of the sin of pride. Latimer's sermon that 'excessive pride in apparel is odious' (1584: 280) was typical of a torrent of moralization, both religious and secular, that reaches down to the present. An onslaught that reappears over the next two centuries was Phillip Stubbes' attack, in his *Anatomie of the Abuses in England* [1583], upon that greatest abuse 'the sinne of pride and excesse in apparel' that 'induceth man to wickedness and sinne' (1972: n.p.). North (1974: 348) suggests that it is important to distinguish the more traditional attack on pride from the Puritan critique of envy. Envy is not reducible to the more traditional religious critique of pride; pride is self-regarding, while envy is other-regarding. It is envy that in the more modern figure of 'imitation' fuels the pervasive secular concerns with appropriateness in the presentation of self and with the preservation of the natural social order that provides the organizing principle of the sumptuary discourses.

There were theological issues between Protestantism and Catholicism over their treatment of luxury. In its simplest form, while Catholicism condemned luxury as the personal sin of pride, Protestantism was generally more concerned with the consequences that were attributed to this vice, with its immorality and its dissoluteness. This linkage between luxury and immorality became secularized and we find Montesquieu confidently opining that 'public incontinence is the inseparable companion of luxury'

(Montesquieu 1900: 106). Puritanism added a significant inflection to the discourses of luxury. The idea that luxury was wasteful or profligate was pinned down by being contrasted with charity; what was wasted on luxury was not available for charitable works. John Wesley preached against extravagance in dress, such extravagance being condemned because it impedes the charity that is necessary so that believers 'may clothe your poor, naked, shivering fellow-creature!' (Wesley 1984: VII: 20–21).

The earlier Christian concern with the idea of need or necessity continues to find expression in robust secular thinkers like Montesquieu whose view that 'the law ought to give each man only what is necessary for nature' (Montesquieu 1900: 94), was – even in the mid-eighteenth century – giving voice to one of the central tenets that had earlier motivated the sumptuary project. This notion of necessity and simplicity was readily transferable into an anti-capitalist critique, in rather the same way that the Christian opposition to usury had been deployed. Charles Davenant offered just such a traditionalist, anti-capitalist critique of luxury in a form that provides a neat juxtapositioning of social ills:

> Trade, without doubt, is in its nature a pernicious thing; it brings in that wealth which introduces luxury; it gives rise to fraud and avarice, and extinguishes virtue and simplicity of manners; it depraves a people, and makes way for that corruption which never fails to end in slavery, foreign and domestic.
>
> (Davenant 1771: II: 275)

A perennial feature of moralizing discourses is that they make heavy use of 'slippery slope' arguments deriving cataclysmic consequences from unprepossessing vices. Luxury came to be viewed through the metaphor of moral contagion, involving the idea that there is a sequential linkage between vices and sins which accumulatively cause social harms or bring down the wrath of God. Cicero, for example, propounded the sequence that luxury led to avarice, avarice bred audacity, which in turn was the source of all crimes and misdeeds (Cicero 1897). Perhaps the apex of the moralization of luxury was reached in Florence with Savonarola's famed 'bonfires of the vanities' (Alexander 1974; Rainey 1985).[4]

In Tudor England numerous sermons and polemics propounded versions of a 'domino theory' or cascade effect whereby the individual sin of luxury leads to damage to the whole social fabric

(Herrup 1985; Owst 1933). Ben Jonson had his fictional character Touchstone in *Eastward Ho* opine that:

> Of sloth comes pleasure, of pleasure comes riot, of riot comes whoring, of whoring comes spending, of spending comes want, of want comes theft, of theft comes hanging.
>
> (Jonson [1605] 1979: 91)

What is central to the manifold versions of 'moral contagion' discourses is that from an initial attention to some widely diffused vice, 'normal sin', is constructed a slippery slope to personal and national ruin. Some targets persist, such as the moralization of prostitution; others like luxury wane, while others, such as alcohol and tobacco, become new sites of preoccupation and regulatory reflex.

It seems reasonable to suggest for subsequent exploration in the specific context of sumptuary laws that moralizing discourses are unleashed by feelings of social disturbance or anxiety. For example, Sekora suggests that a later revival of the critique of luxury in eighteenth century England was fuelled by a renewed concern about a 'dangerous insubordination' on the part of the lower orders, a concern which had flared on and off over the previous centuries (Sekora 1977: 91). A good illustration of the 'slippery slope' version of the moral contagion critique is the unrestrained polemic against the lower orders from the essayist and active Justice of the Peace, Henry Fielding:

> It [luxury] reaches the very Dregs of the People, who aspiring to a Degree beyond that which belongs to them, and not being able by the Fruits of honest Labour to support the State which they affect, they disdain the Wages to which their Industry would entitle them; and abandoning themselves to Idleness, the more simple and poor spirited betake themselves to Idleness, to a State of Starving and Beggary, while those of more Art and Courage become Thieves, Sharpers and Robbers.
>
> (Fielding [1751] 1988: 77)

Parallels with the discourses of the late twentieth century against 'welfare scroungers' may be noted. As we will see, versions of the critique of luxury attesting to current anxieties remain alive and well in the late twentieth century.

THE NECESSITY OF LUXURY

Confronted with such a massive and persistent moralization of luxury it is of the greatest importance to bring this critique into contact with another reality. Luxury was constitutive of the social formations of pre-modernity. Luxury was not a peripheral phenomenon, a mere excess at the margins; rather it was at the very foundation of the pre-modern social order. As Weber observed, for an aristocratic ruling-class luxury was

> not something 'superfluous' but one of its means of its social self-assertion.
>
> (Weber 1978: II: 1106)

For the nobility within medieval society the maintenance of the splendour of their castles or, as they later came to be called in England, 'stately homes', or the number and the livery of servants and other dependents were not so much expressions of wealth or manifestations of conspicuous consumption, but were necessary confirmations of their social, economic and political position in society. The centrality of luxury in pre-capitalist social formations is deepened by Elias' work on the 'court society' and the 'civilizing process' associated with the rise of a post-feudal nobility (Elias 1978, 1982, 1983). Similar themes are taken up by Le Goff in analysing the distinctive link between courts and emergent urbanism at the end of the twelfth century: he draws attention to the literal connection between lust (*luxuria*) and luxury. The quest to prevail in combat becomes transmuted into a quest for sartorial splendour, and thus links to Elias' focus on the 'civilizing process' (Le Goff 1988b: 184). Rodney Hilton demonstrates that the principal way of life of both lay and ecclesiastic nobility was 'war, luxury and display' for themselves and their retainers. Their expenses reached such prodigious proportions that even at the height of their prosperity they lived on the edge of financial failure; the proximity of 'luxury' and 'ruin' was a condition of the existence of a post-feudal nobility (Hilton 1990).

The life-style of the nobility revolved around what, in a different context, E.P. Thompson described as 'the theatre of the great' (Thompson 1974: 395). During these long-term processes essentially archaic social forms structured around kinship, conviviality, mutuality and, especially, blood feuds gave way before a distinctive 'civility' or refinement of manners. Extravagance in consumption remains central, but its form shifts by imperceptible steps from sumptuous display to a private luxury that produces an elite culture distinguished from popular culture by the emergence of the discriminations designated by the idea of 'taste' (Becker 1989). The patterns of expenditure of the nobility were a necessity and a duty; a duke who did not live like a duke was in some real sense no longer a duke:

> In a society in which every outward manifestation of a person has special significance, expenditure on prestige and display is for the upper classes a necessity which they cannot avoid.
> (Elias 1983: 63)

The display of sumptuosity was an important means through which pre-modern political authority both manifested and reproduced itself (Mertes 1988). Relations of reciprocity within the social hierarchy involved the calculated dispensation of hospitality and 'conviviality' and thus explain why one of the early forms of sumptuary law imposed restrictions on the quality and quantity of food that could be served (Bennett 1992; Heal 1984). The pomp and conspicuousness of the royal presence, the staging of dramatic visitations and appearances was a ubiquitous feature of pre-modern political relations (Anglo 1969). Doug Hay's rightly acclaimed study of the self-display of the power by English law in the ceremonial visitations of the assizes demonstrates that theatricality in display lasts into the eighteenth century (Hay 1975). These ceremonials then undergo a transformation into ceremonials that function as remembrances and as traditions (Hobsbawm and Ranger 1983).

This feature is very closely associated with the idea that there is an 'appropriate' and 'natural' order – one of whose manifestations is expressed in the display of hieratic status. Elias makes the important point that competitive prodigality occurred within a context of coexisting prohibitions and restaints. The duke's palace could not equal the King's in its splendour. What is absent from Elias' account is any consideration of the nature and source of these countervailing restraints.

It is tempting to suggest that sumptuary law might be viewed as providing these restraints on the competitive struggle within the pre-modern nobility. Yet it would be difficult to make out such a case. Elias is undoubtedly correct in the emphasis he places on the paramount role of the architectural presentation of monarchs and nobles through their castles and mansions. It is significant to note that there is no trace in European sumptuary legislation of any restraint on architectural conspicuous consumption. It may be significant to note that just such regulation was central to the sumptuary law of Japan and, in particular, of China. The most immediate contrast between Chinese and European sumptuary legislation was its range and scope. Whilst in Europe dress, and to a lesser extent food, were the primary targets, in China sumptuary law addressed almost every aspect of the style of life, prescribing standards for food, clothing, architecture, furnishings, domestic animals, attendants, boats, carriages, utensils, hats, clothing, houses, carriages, and, after death, coffins, funeral clothes and graves. Architectural regulation was most precise. Not only was the size of houses, in particular the number and size of courtyards, prescribed by rank, but so also were the proportions of archways, doors and other entrances, and many other details of their decoration (for example, the use of tiles with animal motifs), and the style of entrances and gates, including such matters as the use of lances at gates, bird's head door-knockers (Ch'ü 1957, 1961; Marsh 1961). One obvious consequence of architectural sumptuary regulation was that of recognizability; a passerby could tell the status of a house-owner by merely looking at the signs disclosed by the ornamentations on the gate. It also seems likely that another consequence of such regulation was that, while it would not eliminate competitive display, it might provide some channelling as to the fields of expenditure within which competition would occur.

While there was no comparable architectural regulation in Europe, the case that comes nearest to providing some general regulation of expenditure (as distinct from its specific manifestations with regard to dress and food) is the case of the regulation of the number, status and expenditure on liveried retainers. In England there was a persistent pattern of statutory intervention from the mid-fourteenth century (1 Rich. II, *c.* 7; SR 2, 3) and more than twenty statutes and royal proclamations over the next hundred and twenty years until the question of livery disappears from the legislative agenda during the early sixteenth century. Henry VIII in 1514 issued the last proclamation repeating the by then somewhat plaintive demand for the enforcement of the existing statutes of livery (12/10/1514; Hughes and Larkin 1964–69: No. 77).

The regulation of livery and retainers is an interesting case that necessitates a brief detour. It is far from clear whether such regulation should be treated as being 'sumptuary' in character. The regulation of livery clearly has a potentially significant impact on expenditure and one of the major manifestations of the institution was to create identifiable retainers through the use of forms of dress that correspond pretty closely to the modern notion of uniform. On these grounds the regulation of livery would seem to have strong 'sumptuary' characteristics. Yet it is very noticeable that, in the English case at least, there was no discernible contemporary recognition of the connection between livery and regulation directed against excess of apparel. The statutes and proclamations regulating livery and apparel never make cross-reference and appear with a very different periodization. I do not have any satisfactory grasp of the separation between these two regulatory fields; to mark this discomfort and leave the matter open I propose to treat the regulation of livery as being 'quasi-sumptuary' in character.

It is established that patterns of competitive display played a central part in the economic practices and cultural ethos of the pre-modern nobility. What is less clear is what the mechanisms were that served to channel or limit the forms of this competition. Those who have looked at the constitutive role of luxury for the nobility in pre-modern Europe provide us with enough evidence to make a judgment about the character and the form of these mechanisms. I suggest as a provisional hypothesis that the dominant bloc, increasingly the monarch, in association with the royal household and the nobles of the robe (state functionaries), had available mechanisms for influencing the sites and forms of the display of luxury. The classic method was the use by traditional elites of the critique of the 'tasteless', 'brash', 'upstart', 'unsophisticated' rising class or emergent class-fraction. Such mechanisms interpose cultural tests, alongside the measure of economic expenditure, whose acquisition requires the 'expenditure' of much leisure time ('conspicuous leisure' to use Veblen's term) to acquire the 'taste' and 'judgment' not only to gain admission to superior social circles, but also for their economic expenditure to 'count' in the competition of conspicuous consumption.

Perhaps the most coherent countervailing pressure was the ideology of 'chivalry'. For present purposes the most significant aspect of the codes of chivalry was how behaviour and appearance appropriate to status is combined with a celebration of a lifestyle that is ascetic and frugal to the point of austerity (Huizinga 1954). The most immediate implication is that in pre-modern Europe luxury was no mere 'unnecessary' or 'irrational' excess. It was simply a different rationality and a different necessity. In this regard it is worth entering a brief criticism of Veblen's otherwise impressive critique of the historical role of conspicuous consumption for the leisure class. He is guilty of certain 'petty bourgeois' prejudices in that he adopts an unexplored and self-evident distinction between 'work' and 'waste' (Veblen 1967).

The most important consequence that flows from this contextualization of the forms of consumption in pre-capitalist society is that it allows us to understand how the practices of conspicuous consumption could exist side by side with the critique of luxury. The patterns of expenditure and display of the noble classes were not manifestations of luxury, but of necessity. Until this is recognized the existence, alongside the persistent moralizing critiques of luxury, of the conspicuous consumption of the upper classes is at best cynical ideological manipulation and at worst an unsustainable contradiction. Thus Sekora, in his valuable study of the history of the idea of luxury, argues that there existed both a practical tension and a double standard between the immoral lust for false wealth and the natural expression of position, status and self-interest (Sekora 1977: 52).[5]

While there is certainly much more that could be said about the role of luxury in pre-capitalist society the present concern needs to be restricted to the question: what is the connection between the medieval critique of luxury and the existence of sumptuary law? For example, John Sekora suggests that it was the tension between the reality of conspicuous consumption and the moral critique of luxury that lay behind the imperative to embark on energetic sumptuary interventions (Sekora 1977: 53). The logic of such an account is that if the law prescribes the appropriate level of expenditure for each estate or class, then this must contribute to moderating the quest for luxury while, at the same time, permitting visible recognition of rank and status. This suggests the hypothesis that sumptuary law should be regarded as an attempt to mediate the tension or contradiction inherent in post-feudal societies of estates. It will be necessary to return to evaluate this thesis when more evidence has been presented in subsequent chapters about the place of sumptuary law in both pre-modern formations and in the complex transitions created with the rise of capitalist economic formations.

LUXURY AND CAPITALISM

Thus far the discussion of luxury has taken place within a context that has assumed the existence of a more or less coherent system of estates based on the primacy of the extraction of economic surplus from land-holding. What now has to be added to this model is one to take account of the fact that the nature of such post-feudal systems of land-rents necessarily involved a significant expansion of the commodification of economic relations. The phenomenon of luxury and attempts at its regulation, if that is what was at stake with the growth of sumptuary regulation, must now be considered in the light of the development of capitalism.

Werner Sombart's treatment of the connection between luxury and capitalism provides a suitable point of intervention. Sombart is currently undergoing a certain reprise as a forerunner of the contemporary critique of productionism and the reinvigoration of attention to consumption epitomized by Baudrillard's critique of postmodernism and the widespread revitalization of interest in cultural studies and cultural anthropology (Baudrillard 1975; De Certeau 1984; Sahlins 1976; Willams 1980). Sombart argued that it was the imperative of satisfying the greatly expanded demand for luxury, no longer supplied by old localized systems of craft production, that fuelled the imperative of the transition to more extended forms of production for expanding markets, and which led ultimately to the industrial production of the Industrial Revolution of the late eighteenth and early nineteenth centuries. Two features of Sombart's analysis require comment. First it should be noted that his primary target was to challenge all prior analyses of the transition to capitalism, in particular those associated with classical political economy, which following on from Adam Smith, had emphasized the role of thrift in promoting simple accumulation and reproduction of capital. He linked his rejection of a simple accumulation model to a very spirited rejection of Weber's association between Protestantism and capitalism. The second feature of Sombart's account to be noted is that it emphasized the critical role of the growth of 'consumer cities', particularly in Italy, whose rapid expansion was fuelled by the acceleration of luxury or conspicuous consumption. This process was spearheaded by a class of merchants who did not conform to the image of frugal capital accumulators. Rather they enthusiastically engaged in consumption battles with the old nobility who, in such key sites as Venice, were supplanted by this new capitalist nobility. To this emphasis on urbanization and mercantilism Sombart added a psychological dimension by stressing the emergence of new sexual values centred on a 'hedonistic aesthetic conception of woman' (Sombart 1967: 48). For example, he insisted on a feminine imperative underlying the rise in consumption of sugar and of beverages such as cocoa, coffee and tea, and a crucial feminine role in the growth of 'fashion' which was a major factor in the key role of textile industries in the development of first manufacturing and later industrial capitalism. It is by no means clear that this account of capitalist motivation is inconsistent with the negative evaluation of idleness and luxury by early capitalists. Marx provided a delightful description of capitalist indulgence as 'economical' forms of pleasure. The rising merchant capitalists gratified themselves with the 'clear-headed bourgeois intoxication' associated with the rise to prominence of the trinity of powerful stimulants, coffee, tea and tobacco (Haug 1986: 19); in contrast the clergy and aristocracy consumed chocolate and sugar, it perhaps not being insignificant that these emanated from the Catholic colonies in South America.

Another version of the development of capitalism is provided by Jacques Le Goff. He suggests that the urban merchant class has its origins in supplying luxury for the nobility, a market which develops long before regular trade in staple products (Le Goff 1988a). The question of luxury arises as the feudal aristocracy lose all real contact with the land and are transformed into a parasitic 'rentier' class – living off money rents, doomed to idleness, conspicuous consumption and to struggle both *with* and *against* luxury as this class is forced to compete with a new and rising class. In this version sumptuary law is likely to be seen as an attack by the nobility on the aspirant merchant class in order to preserve their traditional precedence.

It is not my intention to venture into the debates on the development of capitalism. My task is very much more modest. The project of trying to understand the rise and fall of sumptuary regulation is confronted by an obvious difficulty. Sumptuary laws flourished under two key configurations: they are to be found in their highest development in both post-feudal estate society dominated by a landed nobility and in the typically capitalistic commercial cities, first of Italy and later of northern Europe. How was it that sumptuary law developed in these apparently antithetical or incompatible environments?

For the present I want to hold on to this paradox. In order to keep these two dimensions actively present I will keep open both strands and will assume a parallel development of the sumptuary impulse in both court society and in the city. But it will do no harm to flag the possibility that an attractive solution to this paradoxical dual development might be that sumptuary law was one of the resultants of the growing interaction and convergence of these two configurations that played such large roles in the development of modern Europe. Elements of this process are evident in such developments as the city government of Venice, which by the mid-fourteenth century had became convinced of the necessity of stemming the advancing tide of luxury and expenditure by creating special magistrates, explicitly named as the supervisors of luxury, *Provveditori sopra le Pompe* (Newett 1907).

Just in case the above discussion has created an impression that the appearance of sumptuary law is nothing more than a defensive response of a declining nobility, whether to restructure intra-class struggle or to hold at bay the competition from a rising merchant class, a few additional comments are necessary. Mercantilism also had its own distinctive critique of luxury which, as I will explore in more detail in Chapter 14, generated its own distinctive advocacy of sumptuary regulation. Mercantilist discourses characteristically compared the national economy to the domestic economy, the state to the family. The motive of economic activity was conceived as being to increase foreign trade and to gain a surplus of wealth and treasure, while at the same time ensuring that the hard-earned surplus was not squandered. In establishing the need for sumptuary restraint, the mercantilists drew heavily on the traditions of the canonists whose critique of luxury grounded the sumptuary regulation. Thus mercantilist calls for sumptuary laws were able to trace a respectable genealogy from the feudal era. The important inflection imparted by mercantilism was, as we will see, to gradually shift the 'enemy' from luxury in general to 'foreign luxuries'.

THE PERSISTENCE OF THE MORALIZATION OF LUXURY

It is important to stress that the critique of luxury should not be tied too closely to pre-modernity and a traditional Catholic treatment of sin. The critique of luxury exhibited remarkable resilience and lasted well into modernity; it is arguable that the condemnation of luxury did not lose both its conventional and its moral force until the late modernity of the twentieth century. Only then does 'luxury' become a positive rather than a negative descriptor. Not only did the hostility to luxury persist, but it also fuelled a lingering desire, and one that might have been more than mere nostalgia, in many for a return to sumptuary regulation.

Persistence may arise from unreflective habit, a deadening conservatism in which 'common sense' is evidently 'bad sense'. There is more to the persistence of the moralization of luxury than can be explained either by conservatism or by theology even though many of its manifestations fit this characterization (Pendarves 1656; Philopoliteios 1685). I want only to give a flavour of this persistence that comes from the pens of people of generally self-consciously advanced views and ones whose intelligence posterity has judged favourably.

Just at the time when the regular routine of sumptuary enactment had dried up in Elizabethan England, Phillip Stubbes was launching one of the most venomous diatribes, and one that was widely invoked over the next three hundred years, against 'pride', of which 'pride of apparel' is the most serious form:

> Pride of apparel, remaining in sight, as an exemplarie of euill, induceth the man to wickedness and sinne.
>
> ([1583] 1972: 22)[6]

Thomas Cranmer forceably linked anxieties about social unrest to the pursuit of luxury and sartorial elegance by the lowest orders:

> The great part of them that be the chief stirrers in these insurrections be ruffians and sturdy idle fellows, which be the causes of their own poverty, commonly resorting to tippling and to alehouses, much drinking and little working, much spending and little getting; and yet they will be clad gorgeously, fare daintiously, and lie softly.
>
> (1846: II: 194)

Arthur Arth identifies the primary cause of poverty as excessive pride in apparel, other causes being identified as 'unmeasurable wasters of meate and drinke' and 'wilful wrangling in law matters' (Arth 1914).

In the seventeenth century Edward Waterhouse, who has been described as England's first sociologist, invoked the discourses of luxury to attribute the decline of families to 'bad marriages', 'prodigality', 'idleness and gambling' and 'pompous housekeeping' (Sharp 1974: 37). In the eighteenth century, long after all sumptuary restraints had been repealed, Jonathan Swift argued that in order to prevent the luxury associated with 'all Excesses in Clothing, Furniture and the like' it is necessary to 'enact and enforce sumptuary Laws against Luxury' (Swift 1951: VI: 95).[7] Defoe, no conservative, but a journalist with an active identification with Whiggish interests, complained that the spirit of luxury and extravagance that 'seems to have seized on the minds of all ranks of men' produced a 'general corruption of manners throughout the kingdom' (Defoe 1738: 93). Sekora goes so far as to argue that throughout the eighteenth century luxury probably was the greatest single issue and the greatest single commonplace (1977: 75). In England John Dennis provided a late voice calling for the revival of sumptuary law for 'the immediate suppression of bare-faced luxury' (Dennis 1711: 86), while the voice of Jean-Jacques Rousseau struck a more modern note in opposing luxury to equality, advocating a luxury duty to prevent increasing inequality of wealth and by insisting that such taxes 'would have the effect of the best sumptuary laws' (Rousseau 1972: 56; Shklar 1978). Into the nineteenth century one still finds respectable historians like Lacroix voicing the criticisms of luxury and fashion as a source of moral contagion 'which has so sorry an influence over public morality, and which opens the gate, so to speak, to all distractions, to all disorder, to all vices' (Lacroix 1931: 1197). He obviously saw nothing unusual in his call 'to repress the license of fashion and to keep watch over costumes from the point of view of morals' (1931: 1198). It should also be remembered that one of the greatest of all historical novels, Thomas Mann's *Buddenbrooks: The Decline of a Family*, first published in 1901, is organized around the critique of luxury in tracing a commercial dynasty through its rise and fall; the final bankruptcy comes through the weakening of self-restraint and austerity as manifest in the furnishings of the Buddenbrook home. The once great family is extinguished when the prodigal son dies of the disease known as 'consumption' with more than a hint that this was not unconnected with a profligacy of consumption. Mann was doing no more than to articulate contemporary German public debates in which luxury remained a central preoccupation. Explicit discussion of the merits of sumptuary law continued, but there was little confidence that the state could control luxury. Rather the German bourgeoisie resorted to generalized moralization in order to discipline its own desires (Breckman 1990–91: 485).

As the sumptuary impulse slackened, features of the moralization of luxury were given new expression and new content. Something of the popular thrust of social moralization, in particular that directed against the moral contagion carried by the lower classes, is taken up by social purity movements (Curtis and Speck 1976). I use this term to designate all forms of populist movements, movements from 'outside' the dominant bloc, if not necessarily from 'below', that focus upon the moralization of some 'normal sin' which is mobilized through a discourse of moral contagion. The classic social purity movements have been those directed against prostitution and alcohol (Bristow 1977). The connection between 'social purity' and the earlier sumptuary projects is the distinctive concern with 'symbolic legislation' in that the concern is much more with the enactment of law than with problems of enforcement (Harrison 1974).[8] Social purity movements mark a shift towards forms of organized political participation; the persistence of the preoccupation with sumptuary regulation never, either during its active or its latent phase, found expression in more than the oft repeated calls for intervention to regulate appearance and consumption.

It is by no means clear what should be made of the long life and proven vitality of the moralization of luxury. One suggestion is that whilst the explicit critique of luxury *per se* has waned, if not entirely disappeared, in the late twentieth century it has survived hidden in the central anxieties and concerns that surround the modern economic 'vice' of inflation. The discourses of inflation provide the organizing trope of what stands out as a distinctively moralizing discourse, one which is scarcely concealed behind the more technocratic concern with balance of payments, public borrowing requirements and the like. The point to be stressed is that while the critique of luxury and fashion strikes us as dated and crudely moralizing, we may be less perceptive of the moralizing core of our contemporary preoccupations and controversies, encapsulated in contemporary preoccupations with the 'fight against inflation'. Luxury and inflation are by no means distant or unconnected concepts. While inflation is in an obvious sense a 'social' or 'collective' ill, it should be noted that the discourses of luxury move fluidly between the personal and the public, between private and national vice. What is significant about the current discourses of inflation is that they have been significantly 'personalized'. The now classical embodiment was in Margaret Thatcher's miniaturization of the nation's inflation to the family's budget, in the course of which transformation inflation was transformed from a 'technical' to a 'moral' issue. Thus 'greedy' workers put the nation in peril; buying on credit is profligate for individuals and ruinous for the economy; and buying 'foreign' harms the national economy. There is another parallel in that it is the failure of the poor to keep a tight hold on the purse-strings which excites moral condemnation, just in the same way as it was the profligate poor of the past who stimulated the regulatory urge. There may also be a connection between the older discourse of luxury and the current discourses of health and exercise in that these counterpose the 'good life' to consumption, whether conspicuous or otherwise; the rewards, however, are no longer spiritual but narcissistic.

THE TRANSFORMATION OF THE DISCOURSES OF LUXURY

Powerful and persistent though the voices of the moralization of luxury were, urbanization and the growth of trade produced, albeit belatedly, a new discourse. It was one that recognized that luxury and fashion have the capacity to breed desires, and that desires rapidly become needs. This shift was for a long while devoid of a public discourse; it made deferential bows to the moralization of luxury as it did to the closely associated critique of usury. The new discourses – if it is not contradictory to speak of them in this way – developed silently. When they did break surface they nevertheless elicited a great panic. Since this work is primarily concerned with sumptuary discourses I am less concerned to treat mercantilist discourse in its historical complexity. For present purposes it is sufficient to treat the riposte in a more emblematic form by drawing attention to the outrage that greeted the dissemination of the writings of Bernard Mandeville. It is significant that this most forceful and coherent alternative to the moralization of luxury does not appear until the beginning of the eighteenth century, a century after England had repealed all of its genuinely sumptuary restraints. His simple thesis that luxury fuelled the fires of economic prosperity was greeted with a wrath that had previously been reserved for heresy.

Mandeville insisted on the link between private vices and public benefits:

> It is the sensual Courtier that sets no Limits to his Luxury; the Fickle Strumpet that invents new fashions every Week. . . . [who] is, right or wrong, the greatest Friend to the Society.
>
> (Mandeville 1957: 355–56)

He sets out to rebut the argument that the pursuit of luxury enervates or saps a nation's energy; in its place he argues that it is luxury that is the engine room of inventiveness and innovation, and thus provides the necessary conditions for national economic prosperity. In advancing his case he played unremittingly on a theme that had long been of the greatest concern to the highest authorities in the land. He emphasized that it was only flourishing trade that could guarantee that the dangerously unstable and increasingly unpredictable poor could be put to work. In passing it should be noted that while Foucault did enormous service in drawing attention to the significance of the discourses of 'population' for the emergence of modern government, there are other candidates that arise earlier and persist longer (Foucault 1978: 25; 1979: 18–19). Perhaps the most significant candidate has been the discourse of unemployment. To comment only on the English case the concern is expressed in the short title of an Elizabethan statute of 1576 as 'setting the poore on worke' (18 Eliz. I: *c.* 3).[9] Mandeville argues that it is only the 'pride' of the wealthy that can set the poor to work.

That Mandeville's views appeared so scandalous at the opening of the eighteenth century is testimony to the intellectual and political hegemony of the discourses of luxury. This is underlined as soon as we note the significant concession that Mandeville makes to the moralization of luxury; recall how he concedes that luxury is a vice and hence the paradox which he works and reworks that it is vice, 'private vice', that yields national prosperity, 'public benefit'.[10] The inference to be drawn from this late and partial critique of the discourses of luxury is that the disappearance of luxury as an appropriate target of governmental intervention cannot be attributed to some change in the intellectual and political climate concerning this central focus that sustained the sumptuary imperative. It was not the decline of the moralization of luxury that 'caused' the decline of sumptuary intervention since the critique of luxury outlasted the sumptuary laws. Two provisional conclusions follow: first, some other account needs to be found for the demise of sumptuary law which does not depend on the erroneous assumption that its roots in the critique of luxury had been undermined; second, it needs to be established that if the critique of luxury persists while sumptuary law declines we should look for some change of target of regulation through which it is expressed.

It is clear that social and economic change did not wait upon the kind of challenge to the discourses of luxury mounted by Mandeville. Much earlier there occurred a more powerful challenge but one that was much less direct, less frontal. The discourses of mercantilism did not confront the moralization of luxury. Rather what happened was that mercantilism took one discursive element, namely 'the economy', emphasized it and elaborated it until it became the predominant element in a new discursive formation that was no longer organized around morals, but around economics. That feature was the concern with a distinctively new sense of the 'national' or 'city' economy.[11] At the core of mercantilism was a concern with the conditions of national prosperity and the heart of the answer that was proposed, which of course only emerged gradually, was in the first instance protectionism. The first stages of the process were projects of unification expressed in such projects as national systems of weights and measures, the dismantling of internal trade barriers and the extension of national legal systems.

This focus on the 'national interest' increasingly comes to be inflected into a mercantilist discourse. Mercantilism embodied much more than the rise of mercantile interests; more significantly I think it was the expression of an expansionary conception of the state in which 'reasons of state' take precedence over all other considerations. Mercantilism thus subordinates all economic activity to the state's interest in power; it seeks to secure the state's power internally against particularistic interests and externally against competitor states. Central to the controversies surrounding political economy before the birth of 'political economy' is that they are confronted with what seems to be an unresolvable dilemma between protectionism and free trade. It is, of course, not surprising in the current epoch of globalization that it is precisely a far from sophisticated version of this same dilemma that occupies the centre of international economic controversies. On the brink of modernity it was clear that the situational advantages of foreign producers and merchants could adversely affect some indigenous economic interest, but attempts to protect that interest resulted not only in a potential diminution of trade, but also in retaliatory action disadvantaging some other domestic interest. It is in this context that fashion as one of the major factors stimulating consumption was so paradoxical. On the one hand the stimulation of demand for some 'new' fashion created the possibility of a radically extended market, which in turn produced not only quantitative expansion, but qualitative change in the technology and organization of production and distribution. At the same time the same fickleness could lead to sudden and irreversible collapse as public interest turned to new garments and different materials. This was especially significant when changes in domestic demand led to the reduction of domestic production in favour of an increase in overseas imports. Not only does such a movement occasion unemployment and other economic ills, but it also comes increasingly to be seen as a matter of governmental concern, with what political economy came to call the balance of trade (Johnson 1932). Early on the problem of trade balance had been largely conceptualized as a problem about bullion, the movement of gold and silver, which was not only a matter of immediate economic concern, but also made direct connection with the more traditional military concerns, the capacity to raise and maintain armies, build and provision ships. One of the decisive steps away from hierarchic sumptuary rules was the growing recognition that as fashion items, such as silk and printed cottons, ceased to be the exclusive wear of a privileged but small class and became items of mass consumption, even though individual enterprises must have been vulnerable to the volatility of fashion, the economic opportunities were considerable. This stage may be characterized as one in which there occurs what Stephen Mennell has aptly described as a 'democratization of luxury' (Mennell 1985).

It was thus without a break with the discourses of luxury that a decisive shift occurred. The emphasis shifted towards an identification of products, ones which had previously been viewed only through the narrow lens of luxury, that came to be regarded as fruitful stimuli of both production and trade. Perhaps the period that was marked by a high level of sumptuary activity should be regarded less as a manifestation of moral prohibitions than as an attempt to deal with the balance of payments problem.[12]

This discursive shift was one in which, under the ideological hegemony of the continuing critique of luxury, a new set of practices and barely audible discourses of mercantilism, the latter comes to subvert the long-established connection between the critique of luxury and the array of sumptuary provisions. These considerations suggest the thesis that while sumptuary law starts out as the embodiment of a traditionally rooted critique of luxury, it becomes an expression of economic protectionism. But once protectionism becomes an explicit motor of state policy it becomes increasingly apparent that the umbilical cord between luxury and national interest has already been severed. To put the same point in different terms, sumptuary law underwent a functional transformation in the course of the rise of state mercantilism; sumptuary law came in as an expression of a pre-modern critique of luxury and goes out as a soon-to-be-discarded vehicle of economic protectionism. Over a long period, and a period in which there were no major turning points, there occurred a 'discursive relocation' in which the issue of dress and of fashion underwent a 'shift' from the discursive field of morality to an economic discourse of trade, protectionism, bullionism, etc.

The process under consideration is one in which a social phenomenon (in the present case sumptuary law) that was at one time integrated into a specific discursive formation (the critique of luxury) becomes detached. The phenomenon then comes to be 'linked up' or associated with some other developing trend, with the result that both the original elements survive rather than one or the other being extinguished. The moralization of luxury persisted well into the nineteenth century, while sumptuary law during the seventeenth century came to be aligned with a new set of discourses (those of protectionism) which themselves survived while the sumptuary discourses themselves disappeared either temporarily (possibly to reemerge elsewhere) or permanently. What is needed is a way of conceptualizing such processes of combination, detachment and recombination. A convenient way to speak of these processes is provided by the metaphor of 'coupling' and 'uncoupling'. This conceptualization, in terms of coupling and uncoupling, draws freely on Habermas' notion of 'uncoupling' (as in the 'uncoupling of system and lifeworld' in Habermas (1986) and (1987)) and more specifically from Gunther Teubner's discussion of 'structural coupling' in the context of autopoietic theory (Teubner 1992).[13] I am attracted to this conceptualization because it facilitates the exploration of shifts in discursive formations where it is rare that one formation simply displaces another; Kuhn may have been correct in arguing that scientific discourses exhibit paradigm shifts, but in social discourses it is processes of recombination, of coupling and uncoupling, that best provide a means of exploring the dynamics of these shifts.

A further illustration of the mechanisms of coupling and uncoupling emerged from the present project: in the late Middle Ages the regulation of games and gambling was closely associated with sumptuary law, associated in the sense that provisions regarding games and gambling were, in England and Scotland at least, found within the statutes regulating excess of apparel. The prohibition of football and card-games was part of the attack on luxury (luxury of time as well as of appearance). Then gradually the regulation of gambling came to the fore. It remained linked with sumptuary regulation, in that it was concerned with non-productive economic activity, but gradually the regulation of gambling became a specific, and significantly, enduring form of the regulation of the pleasures retaining a strongly moralistic content. In the meantime the classical form of appearential ordering through sumptuary enactment waned.

As this inquiry into the grounding of the history of sumptuary law in the critique of luxury developed it became clear that there is always the shadow present of another critique. The critique of luxury has as its supplement what I will call 'the critique of idleness'. This critique is most immediately evident with regard to attempts to impose restraints on popular patterns of feasting and revelry and in the regulation of unlawful games, drinking and gambling. It has an even stronger presence within the discourses of political economy over labour discipline and labour productivity. It erupts with great prominence in the debates over the connection between the work ethic and Protestantism initiated by Max Weber. It plays a crucial part in the discourses of colonialism in grounding the legitimacy of both slave and indentured labour.[14]

The moralization of idleness comes to the fore in respect of the regulation of vagrancy and the growth of the poor laws that connects up at important stages in the story of sumptuary law, in particular in Elizabethan England discussed in Chapter 12. More generally the moralization of luxury intersects at almost every stage with the concerns that have so valuably emerged within the new social history's focus upon the projects of governance directed toward the 'reform of popular culture' (Burke 1978). This impressive and expanding body of work, in quite correctly focusing on 'popular culture', has tended to omit the whole phenomenon of 'labour'/'idleness' as lying outside the sphere of culture. A subsidiary and undeveloped theme in the present work can be read as urging a further expansion of the conception of popular culture.

I have resisted the temptation to make any systematic effort to track the history of the moralization of idleness and the discourses of labour because, not only do they have roots deep in the past, but they are very much alive and active today. Current debates on unemployment and social welfare are traversed by shifting forms of the moralization of idleness. In short, to track the discourses of idleness would be a major project in its own right. For the purposes of the present project I will be content to assert the general supplementation of the discourses of luxury by the moralization of idleness. I will pick up the traces of the discourses on idleness and labour discipline only where they directly impinge on the history of sumptuary law.

The history of the critique of luxury, its persistence and its temporary conjunction with projects of sumptuary regulation must now be brought into proximity with the dynamic of fashion which was the focus of the previous chapter. When these phenomena are viewed together it becomes clear that sumptuary law sits astride a perilous fault-line, an arena rendered unstable by virtue of the opposing pressures. There exists a fundamental contradiction at the heart of every sumptuary project, to which the next chapter addresses itself.

5

The Fundamental Contradiction of Sumptuary Regulation

This chapter is short. It seeks to make clear something that has been implicit in what has gone before, but which should now be stated. A fundamental contradiction lies at the core of the project of sumptuary regulation. I am not the first to have noticed this fact. The most elegant formulation comes from the pen of Montaigne:

> To say that none but princes shall eat turbot, or shall be allowed to wear velvet and gold braid, and to forbid them to the people, what else is this but to give prestige to these things and to increase everyone's desire to enjoy them?
>
> (Montaigne [1572] 1958: 196)

To designate some item of dress or some dish of food as being reserved for others is unlikely to reduce the desire to consume such items on the part of the rest of the population, or at least of those sections of the population within whose economic reach or imagination such items lie.

It should be noted that this formulation of the fundamental contradiction involves some minimal acceptance of a social psychology of imitation. If some economic or cultural asset is restricted to some groups or classes it becomes a potential object of aspiration for others. Such an aspiration is reinforced where that asset is associated with a claim to social superiority. It comes closest to working in these terms when there exists a widespread acceptance of some natural hierarchical social order. The sumptuary regime in some of the early New England colonies was premised on the belief in a natural society of rank that had been imported from Europe with its hierarchy intact, but stripped of its formally designated ranks. The following passage from the Massachusetts magistrates is revealing.

> We declare our utter detestation and dislike that men and women of mean condition, educations, and callings should take upon themselves the garb of gentlemen, by the wearing of gold and silver lace, or buttons, or points at their knees, to walk in great boots; or women of the same rank to wear tiffany [transparent silk or muslin] hoods or scarves, which though allowable to persons of greater estates, or more liberal education, yet we cannot but judge it intolerable in persons of such like condition . . .
>
> (Shurtleff 1986: III: 243)

To concede that some relatively routine items of apparel and ornamentation are legitimate for some and not for others requires a very strong conception of natural social order. Once stripped of the mythology of the nobilities of the robe and the sword, its legitimation and reproduction becomes more difficult to secure. It is interesting that the Puritan sumptuary experiment did not make a more decisive shift towards what might be called a democratic sumptuary regime, as in rationing in time of war, as in Britain during the Second World War, where the legitimation is provided by the priority given to some common good over individual interest. While such democratic conceptions were present in some of the more radical sections of seventeenth century Puritanism, brought to the fore by the exigencies of the English Civil War, it is significant that the Puritan strands that took root on North American soil clung to a more traditional view of the social order.

Gary North, discussing sumptuary law in New England, identifies another and inescapable tension: on the one hand, the godly were enjoined to work diligently and to show themselves through their work, while on the other hand, sumptuary laws sought to perpetuate a static, pre-modern, social hierarchy (North 1974). The Puritan settler was offered no solution to the tension between 'social mobility' and 'fixed status'. It is perhaps too strong to claim that this tension was insoluble. There was a 'solution', one which was employed in both Puritan New England and much earlier in England, that involved the gradual abandonment of hierarchical rank and a substitution of some economic measure, usually in terms of annual income. By 1651 the prohibition on fashion items similar to those listed above (e.g. gold or silver lace, gold or silver buttons, silk hoods or scarves, great boots, etc.) extended to those worth less than £200 per annum. The critical factor with the use of such economic gradations was to determine what percentage of the growing mercantile and professional classes were included within the privileges of fashion (Shammas 1990: 218).[1] However, the resort to such 'modern' criteria for determining sumptuary boundaries itself confirms the fundamental contradiction, for it becomes increasingly difficult to sustain the legitimacy of such arbitrary boundaries and opens the way for struggles from below to lower the threshold of eligibility and from above to raise it, struggles that are characteristic of today's controversies over income tax bands.

In general, any acceptance of imitation theory should be qualified by an insistence that it only holds good until such a point in time when subordinate groups or classes have asserted some alternative scheme of cultural valuation. Thus in radical phases movements of subordinated classes often exhibit a marked repudiation of the cultural values and symbols of the dominant classes.

It follows that the fundamental contradiction is at its sharpest when the social hierarchy is strongly asserted, but is resisted in some measure by those relatively disadvantaged. A society in which there was an extensive internalization of the superiority claims of a dominant class entitling them to privileged consumption would not require sumptuary law. The kicker of sumptuary law is that not only is it beset by a fundamental contradiction but that contradiction sharpens as the position of those claiming privilege becomes less secure in their continued capacity to exercise it. This expresses itself in self-parody when, for example, the illicit status of some item generates its very attraction. There was ongoing reference to sumptuary restraint in novels and plays into the eighteenth century that played on the desire for the illicit. The popular eighteenth century English playwright Colley Cibber had a character express disdain for an item of apparel since 'I do not care for it now it is not prohibited' (quoted Cunnington 1972: 14).

Harte takes this point a step further in suggesting that sumptuary legislation might actually have strengthened the forces for the diffusion of fashion (Harte 1976). For example, perhaps the most famous of all pieces of English sumptuary legislation of 1571 imposed what Shakespeare referred to as a 'statute cap', by providing that every person over the age of six should wear, on

Sundays and holidays, 'a cap of wool . . . made within this realm' (13 Eliz. I: *c*.19; SR 4(1): 555). The imposition of the wool cap seems to have immediately made it unfashionable. On the other hand, the prohibition of an item tended to give it special appeal. Indeed it was the very movements of fashion that provided a spur to the development and growth of the textile industries.

It is from these considerations that the sociological thesis emerges, whose exploration underlines much of what follows, that sumptuary law is rarely, if ever, associated with stable relations of hieratic domination, but is a product of circumstances in which a hieratic social order has come under internal pressure.

The sumptuary project is also beset by a further ramification of the fundamental contradiction. When social rank, status or class comes to be identified with symbolic representations one result is that these 'symbols', rather than the underlying economic or property relations from which they stem, become the target for usurpation from below. It is easy to assert a status claim by donning a purple robe or wearing an ermine cape; with the passage of time the economic capacity to acquire such status items comes within the reach of wider sections of the population. In addition to the economic capacity to acquire symbolic capital, political struggles for access to symbolic goals can often be won more readily than can economic or military concessions. The right of an aspirant group to wear some symbolic item of apparel or to participate in some rituals are important forms of social conflict. The history of sumptuary law reveals a general pattern of a widening of the privileged circles as successive waves of pressure come from below and concessions are granted. The result is that far from clarifying social differences, sumptuary law actually provokes increasing competition and imitation since it is 'cheaper' (economically and politically) for all parties to compete over the symbols than over what those symbols represent. The result is the generation of fierce tensions and rivalries over symbolic distinction. Miles, in his study of Roman sumptuary law, draws attention to competition over two symbolic manifestations of rank, namely the number of gold rings that could be worn and access to prominent seats at the games (Miles 1987).[2] This type of regulation suggests evidence of an anxiety about the dangers of the promiscuous mixing of ranks, but because it instituted strict visibility of rank the regulation itself became a source of significant resentment and thus became a site of struggle.

We can observe a modern day manifestation of the same problem. One consequence of the expansion of the consumer market has been to attach status esteem to 'brand names'. As we saw in Chapter 3 in some cases there is an indexical basis to the priority attached, for example, to Rolls-Royce cars or to Rolex watches. Their status attributes become connected to the fact that they are expensive. But in addition to this 'logic' there are others. The display of branded items with prominent logos requires explanation of the shift, as a result of which clothes manufacturers, who used to include low visibility advertising through labels on the inside of clothes, now have their customers pay an additional premium for the privilege of carrying the manufacturer's logo. The wearer is thereby able to display 'fashion' knowledge, knowing what is in fashion and what is not. In a situation in which a brand becomes 'too popular', the *cognoscenti* 'move on'. Such display may also assert a sense of consumer expertise, knowing and displaying what is 'best', that is of displaying some accumulated cultural capital.[3]

It remains only to comment on the implications that can be drawn from the identification of a fundamental contradiction at the heart of each and every sumptuary project. Many commentators move immediately to pronounce each and every sumptuary project as doomed; it is this response that underlies the general dismissive attitude which is such an overwhelming feature of the literature on sumptuary law. Contradiction and tension is a feature of most if not all fields of social policy: the political and intellectual challenge has always been to find persuasive legitimations both for the object of regulation targeted and the criteria of social differentiation. Controversial though most questions about taxation have been there have been periods of relative stability reflecting a fairly wide consensus about what is to be taxed and how the broad bands are to be drawn. Sumptuary law was not simply a failure; the comparison with tax is suggestive, for while few citizens welcome the opportunity to pay taxes there is a grudging recognition of their necessity. My sense is that we can help achieve an understanding of sumptuary law if we start by conceding that it could well have been conceived by broad sections of the populations of widely different economic and cultural systems as a necessary evil, and like tax to be avoided where the opportunity presented itself, but whose presence was conceded, if always with a grumble.

If sumptuary projects were beset by a fundamental contradiction it seems likely that the purely conservative project of freezing existing social hierarchies is insufficient to explain their persistence. It is necessary to consider next the elements other than hierarchical considerations that fuelled the many sumptuary projects that traversed the transition to modernity.

6

Recognizability: 'The Mingle-Mangle of Apparel'

> Nowhere is suche a confused mingle-mangle of apparell [as in England] and such preposterous excesse thereof, as anyone is permitted to flaunt it out in what apparell he lusteth himself, or can get by with any kind of meanness, so that it is very hard to know who is noble, who is worshipful, who is a gentleman, who is not.
>
> (Phillip Stubbes [1583] 1972: n.p.)

SOCIABILITY AND RECOGNIZABILITY

The quotation above from a Puritan preacher and Elizabethan moralist exemplifies a persistent preoccupation about being able to 'know' or to 'recognize' others. The concern to recognize others is a persistent feature of social life. People have a socially developed capacity to 'read' or interpret 'appearance'; this capacity is inter-personal, as in the capacity to identify the moods and dispositions of familiar persons and to identify others in a crowd. It is with the social interpretation of the identities of 'others' and its connection with attempts to regulate the presentation of identity that this chapter is concerned.

In this focus on 'recognition' I draw attention to its capacity to carry a double sense. On the one hand to 'recognize' is to be able to 'identify' (as in 'I recognized Harold standing at the bus-stop') and on the other to 'recognize' is be 'accorded recognition' (as in 'Jane was awarded a prize in recognition of her contribution'). I will develop the argument that both senses of 'recognize' are involved in the project of the regulation of appearance through sumptuary law. As I came to grasp this double meaning it occurred to me that there is an interesting parallel with Bourdieu's key concept of 'distinction' which also carries a double sense. In the first sense 'distinction' is again about 'identification' ('Marsupials are distinguished from other mammals by the presence of a pouch') and the second sense involves some claim to 'distinction' as superiority (as in 'She achieved distinction as a result of her research on marsupials'). There is then a homology between the concepts of 'recognition' and 'distinction': it is one that I will make use of. Without pursuing this word-play too much further, there are other related terms, such as 'identity', that are capable of bearing a related double sense. The link between these words comes from their place in discourses that traverse the self–other relation. At the outset I want to propose the concept of 'recognizability' as designating a persistent social concern with both aspects of this dualism, with being able to identify others and with processes of claiming and conferring social recognition, advantage or authenticity. In the sense used here recognizability is thus an element in a social terrain of competition and struggle where people seek to secure their identities in the process of identifying with and distinguishing themselves from others. It is in this area, which has come to be designated in another influential strand of social thought as 'the subject', which sumptuary law came to intervene.

The recognizability thesis suggests that sumptuary law revolved around a dual project. On the one hand, it offered a solution to pervasive problems in the process of urbanization of coping in a 'world of strangers' and of living in 'the company of strangers', learning how we are to 'know', to 'identify', to 'recognize' others. Reduced to its simplest the sumptuary imperative was that 'the Ranks of People should be discerned by their Clothes' (Cotton Mather 1694: 71). Or, in the words of a London ordinance of 1351, it was desirable 'that all folks, native and strangers, may have knowledge of what rank others are' (Riley 1968: 267). This problem is solved in the radically anonymous world of the military where insignia of rank allow everyone to know whether to salute or be saluted. On the other hand, the second project of sumptuary law was concerned with efforts to protect and reinforce hierarchical status claims of dominant classes. I will add an important extension to this second strand, namely that the protection of dominant classes by sumptuary laws intensified as the claims to superiority began to lose hegemony and became challenged by new social forces. The discussion of this second limb will be postponed until the next chapter.

RECOGNIZABILITY IN THE COMPANY OF STRANGERS

One significant component of the transformations that mark the complex and uneven transition to modernity stems from the responses to the increasing density of social life that goes hand in hand with the extension of the diversity of social relations. Increased density is manifest in urbanization and diversity in the expansion of commerce, trade and the division of labour. More generally these processes involve both intensive and extensive dimensions (Mann 1985). In the historical period under consideration these changes are highlighted as social and economic life picked up after the deep economic and population crises that occupied much of the fourteenth and fifteenth centuries.

In pre-modern society the person lived within the 'persona' – literally in Latin the mask – a public mask that was both impersonal and objective (Mauss 1979). Personality was objectified in the external marks of status and insignia: under feudalism first the escutcheon and then, with the advent of closed armour, heraldry served to render the occupant recognizable. This form of identity was embedded in sentiments of 'honour' and 'duty' that contributed decisively to the discursive frameworks within which the governance of the self was effected. This framework was more or less rapidly undermined by the advance of urbanization and the rise of monetarization in which bastard-feudalism slowly but inexorably gave way before capitalist economic relations. 'Honour' shifted from being an attribute of inherited rank and became embedded in the personal acquisition of status associated with merit or achievement. Status symbols were no longer exclusive rights buttressed by legal entitlements. The self was no longer pre-defined by birth or 'blood', but had to be constantly reproduced in face-to-face relations.

Much sociological attention has been focused on the process of urbanization and this phase is important in the history of sumptuary law; but before exploring the impact of urbanization the caveat should be entered that processes of intensification of social relations should not be thought of as only occurring in the increased spatial density of the town. These more general processes are illustrated by the transformations that Elias captures in his notion of the 'civilizing processes' that occur with particular intensity in the medieval courts and more generally within the whole field of 'private life' that has become such an important focus of contemporary historical sociology (Elias 1978 and 1982; Ariès and Duby 1987–1991).

The connection between the urban 'world of strangers' and sumptuary law can be explored by examining Lyn Lofland's thesis that the experience of urbanization is marked by a shift in which:

> the preindustrial city is characterized by the dominance of appearential ordering; the modern city, by the dominance of spatial ordering.
>
> (Lofland 1973: x)

This thesis is directed at a broad historical sweep whose target is to draw attention to a major historical transformation that occurs within urban life. The twentieth century city is subject to a spatial ordering that seeks to regulate the public space primarily by means of economic zoning, for example in its simplest form by separating residential, commercial and industrial zones. Zoning illustrates the failures and unintended consequences of governance: the spatial boundaries may become so rigid as to amount to segregation. The most extreme manifestation is found in the downtown cores which either die at night or have a second population that replaces the office workers after dark. There are the two very different 'no-go' areas, the inner city ghettos contrasted with the fortresses, walled, wired and self-selected of age-segregated ghettos of condominium developments across the United States. Lofland's thesis is that this more recent ordering of urban life through spatial regulation replaced the earlier response to the urban experience that was characterized by an ordering of appearance. In the medieval city there was little economic segregation; rich and poor lived and worked cheek by jowl, but were readily recognizable by their occupational dress or by their level of conspicuous consumption. Lofland treats the existence of sumptuary laws as unassailable evidence that pre-industrial urban experience was organized by means of an imposed appearential ordering and, furthermore, that this ordering was hierarchical. Oddly there is no discussion of sumptuary law; it is simply treated as conclusive evidence for the thesis of the transition from appearential to spatial ordering. It will be a major part of my argument to show that the existence of sumptuary regulation discloses something significantly more complex than a transition from appearential to spatial ordering.

Sumptuary law provides evidence of two distinguishable, and significantly different, attempts at the ordering of social appearance. On the one hand, it manifests a concern with an effort to secure and stabilize the ordinary mechanisms of recognition in a world characterized by increasing social density. On the other hand, it can be understood as a response to a challenge to the old order from below, in particular by the distinct strategies of the urban merchant classes who increasingly came to assert their own marks of distinction. These two features can be distinguished analytically, but in practice they often interpenetrate. Looked at separately they help us to understand how it was that the necessity of an appearential ordering seemed to form such a strong component of the common sense of the pre-modern world without necessarily being associated with any sustained efforts at enforcement. In this respect we can regard the existence of sumptuary law as declaratory, that is as evidencing a desire for some stability to be secured by ensuring recognizability in a world which made it more difficult to recognize and to give recognition to others.

Urbanization brought with it a troubling set of shifts in the distinction between the public and the private. For example, Richard Sennett draws attention to the paradox that in an urban environment hierarchic dress rules became increasingly unenforceable as, in a world of strangers, we know less and less what some stranger is 'entitled' to wear. Yet despite these obvious difficulties, there remained a widespread desire for an appearential ordering (Sennett 1974: 66). In similar vein Turkel draws attention to the connection between urbanization and the rise of impersonalization and anonymity, whilst the desire to 'know' and 'recognize' others intensified, so at the same time did the capacity of clothing to induce some feigned appearance, to dissimulate, increase (Turkel 1992). In a world of strangers the capacity of appearance to mislead and to misrepresent (so important in constituting the nuances of fashion) through the use of costumes, uniforms, wigs, make-up, etc. increases apace. In particular as 'fashion' comes to the fore as a distinctive form of aesthetic governance, fashion itself is constructed out of this capacity to both represent and misrepresent. Similarly, social transgressions and crimes increasingly come to involve deceit and disguise, one manifestation being that offenders adopt a dress or appearential style appropriate to their target victims (Weisser 1979).

Clothing provides mechanisms for securing both impersonality and individualization in the same way that fashion involves both conformity and individuation. Impersonality and, in more extreme form, disguise provides the freedom of anonymity. The veil provides an interesting example and will be explored more fully later in this chapter. While, on the one hand, the veil is a mark of female piety and a sign of patriarchal deference, it is, at the same time, a means of snatching autonomy and anonymity, and is thus capable of becoming a sign of licence and by this route exhibits a capacity for eroticization.

A concern that the social environment be recognizable is a fairly general feature of sociality. The difficulty people encounter in making sense of the circumstances in which they find themselves revolves around the blurring and confusion between what presents itself as natural and the socially constructed. Thus dimensions of sex and age appear natural and carry heavy social signification; social rank or status never becomes finally secured in such a naturalization. However well inscribed deference may be it is always vulnerable to the democratic prod of the fallibility of the occupants of even the most elevated position. Whether statuses are naturalized or not, they are always part of a system of social recognition. There is evidence of this as a very ordinary desire for recognizability and recognition in the interesting trend in the world of strangers of the later Middle Ages towards the formation of large numbers of horizontal social organizations. A wide range of organizations, confraternities, guilds, regiments, orders of lay knights and others were created, all identifying themselves by symbols of recognition, 'cognizances' (crosses, ribbons, etc.). In addition to the economic associations typified by the guilds there were contractual associations founded on vows and oaths, not all of which were economic in motivation, and which linger in such practices as freemasonry (Braunstein 1988: 577).

THE ABSENCE OF OCCUPATIONAL SUMPTUARY REGULATION

There is one particular difficulty with my argument that needs to be addressed. There undoubtedly existed a connection between a widespread desire for stable representation of social identities through appearance and the expansion of sumptuary regulation.

The problem stems from the almost complete absence of rules governing occupational dress within the great mass of sumptuary legislation. Aside from the special case of prostitution, about which more later, sumptuary laws rarely, if ever, laid down rules about occupational dress.[1] For the great majority of the population occupation was a central aspect of their identity; this was true well back into feudal society once any significant division of labour had emerged. If sumptuary laws were concerned with social recognizability, why was it that there was so little evidence of the formal regulation of occupational attire? It is necessary to offer some account of this absence.

There did exist a number of instances of the regulation of occupational dress that exhibited certain sumptuary features. Some evidence of occupational sumptuary laws comes in an article by Chevalier (Chevalier 1947). He locates his account in an economic context in which in the late Middle Ages through much of Europe artisans were becoming increasingly dependent upon and thus subordinated to the merchant class. The latter took advantage by imposing regulation on the dress of artisans. He gives the example of the corporation of the town of Halberstadt which decreed that journeymen must only appear out of doors wearing doublet, cap and cloak. He goes on to suggest that there were widespread rules requiring that artisans and craftsmen be recognizable by carrying some mark of their trades. For example, coopers and smiths carried hammer and axe, carpenters carried rules, bakers wore white aprons and linen bags over their shoulders, etc. Unfortunately few source references are provided and it is difficult to evaluate his analysis. It is by no means clear that the trend of occupational dress referred to emanated from sumptuary regulation. Since other evidence is not forthcoming to support his claims, I am inclined to think that Chevalier is discussing the emergence of trade practices that led to the self-governance of occupational dress. Two related but distinguishable practices developed. The first was the adoption of ceremonial dress by guilds and liveried companies: such practices were quasi-heraldic and were significant with respect to pageants, processions and other ceremonial occasions.[2] The implication to be drawn is that ceremonial costumes were not designed to produce an everyday system of social recognizability, except possibly in terms of the elaborate internal hierarchies that had much in common with the highly complex stratifications practised by the landed nobility.

The second form of occupational dress was the voluntary adoption of distinguishing occupational costume as an immediate form of recognizability that became the first form of advertising. The main stages in the development of occupational dress can be roughly sketched. In the first place there occurred some general process of functional differentiation. Certain features of work dress can be connected with functional characteristics – for example, cobblers and blacksmiths wore leather aprons; masons wore white aprons, etc.[3] Gradually the symbols of recognizability became concentrated on some distinctive external garment and, in particular, on an item of headwear. Those who plied their trade in public, at markets, in shops and stalls, and in the streets had reason to assume easy marks of recognition. In England butchers adopted straw hats and blue aprons with horizontal white stripes while carpenters wore square paper caps.[4] These visible signs were supplemented by a cacophony of distinctive calls, cries and chants.

Work clothes also came to exhibit a certain degree of functional symbolism. For example, in England from medieval times the rural labour market was organized through 'fairs' or 'statty fairs' (statute fairs).[5] At these employment fairs people seeking employment would display their occupation by braids tied to their hats (waggoner with whip cord, cowman with cow-hair, shepherds with wool, and gardeners with flowers) or by the carrying of some characteristic work implement of which the shepherd's crook is perhaps the best known. Women seeking employment as domestic servants differentiated themselves through a colour-coding of their aprons: cooks with coloured aprons, nursery maids with white, and chamber maids with lawn aprons (Cunnington and Lucas 1967: 377).

The use of formalized symbolism was a parallel development such as the use of 'cognizances', symbols of guilds or livery companies emblazoned on sleeves and shoulders. More generally the emergence of ceremonial dress and uniforms involved the ossification of distinctive apparel itself disconnected from occupational attire, as with the liveries granted to guilds and liveried companies. Another development was the emergence of uniforms for a wide range of occupations – post, railways, police, nurses and many others (Joseph and Alex 1972).[6] A persistent and expanding consideration was the role of occupational dress in trade advertisement.

Livery might be regarded as a quasi-occupational form of dress, but in either of its two different forms it would probably be wrong to regard it in this light. In its first form as a uniform of household retainers to the nobility it was distinctly feudal in form; it evidenced a personal relationship to a lord and focused on the affirmation of recognition and distinction of the lord rather than the wearer. In its second form, livery referred to the ceremonial costumes granted to occupational guilds, as in the English case of liveried companies. I have come across no evidence that there was any connection between functional working clothes and these ceremonial liveries.

As already noted, there is little evidence of any general attempt as part of wider sumptuary projects to regulate work clothing. The few examples that I have come across are 'exceptions that prove the rule' cases, usually stemming from situational circumstances. In fourteenth century England the crown sometimes resorted to the impressment of labour for major construction projects. The Sheriff of York supplied those impressed with red caps and liveries; it seems reasonable to infer that this was a means of hampering attempts at desertion. In 1582 the Common Council of London ordered apprentices to wear 'no apparel but what he receives from his Master'; another decree in 1611 ruled that no apprentice should wear a hat costing more than 5s., no 'Spanish shoes', no 'tuft or lock' in the hair that had to be 'cut short in a decent comely manner'; these rules seem to involve a sumptuary rather than an occupational regulation (Cunnington and Lucas 1967: 380). There is some evidence of compulsory badges. For example, the Lord Mayor of London required drovers bringing stock to market at Smithfield to wear a leather armband with a number on it. The concern seems to have been with providing a means of reporting cruelty to cattle (Cunnington and Lucas 1967: 377).

The absence of occupational sumptuary law is at first glance surprising in that, aside from age and sex, occupation is certainly one of the most available indicators of social position. It is possible that the absence of occupational dress laws is easily explained on the grounds they were not necessary since there was already in place a voluntary system of occupational identification: butchers, bakers and candlestick makers were recognizable and were so because occupational dress was both good business practice and fitted in well with the kind of associationalism, typified by the guilds, that was one of the characteristic responses to a world of strangers. It is certainly evident that, from at least Chaucer onwards, people and their occupations were closely linked in both appearance and association.

It remains unclear whether this absence of any generalized regulation of occupational dress is consistent with my contention that there existed a strong desire amongst a wide cross-section for an appearential ordering. A desire to distinguish by rank or degree was widespread in early modern society. The most telling evidence is the ubiquity of hierarchic forms of social organization. The organizational expressions of civil society, whether urban or rural, secular or religious, all exhibited strongly hierarchical forms. The handicraft guilds and the quasi-religious confraternities were, in both their structure and the costumes used in public ceremonial, unambiguously hieratic.

My answer to the question as to why there were so few occupational sumptuary laws is in the first place that they were not necessary; an adequate system of occupational recognizability was generated by other means and did not require legislative intervention. Later, in Chapter 14, I will argue that the same logic is at work in the reappearance of extensive occupational uniforms in the second half of the twentieth century. These considerations permit the theoretical generalization that the work of governance gets done (but never completed) through different practices: nothing in principle determines whether state practices, occupational interests or market forces provide the vehicle for the regulation of social visibility. In brief, things get done. The task is to unravel the interaction between these practices and their associated discourses that inscribes governance on social relations.

The absence of regimes of occupational sumptuary law underlines the central dynamic of the discourses of luxury discussed in Chapter 4. However committed people were to conspicuous consumption they do not seem to have made their occupational wear the main occasion for the display of luxury.[7] In general, occupational dress did not activate the critique of luxury that provided the principle stimulant for sumptuary intervention.

The literary record so heavily over-represents the privileged classes that we cannot be entirely confident about the attitudes of the labouring classes. However, there does seem to be some grounds for suggesting that most people accepted an appearential order as not only natural, but desirable. Such a sentiment is, for example, engagingly captured in the autobiography of an eighteenth century Anglican rector in America who came from a poor farming background.

> A periwig, in those days, was a distinguishing badge of gentle folk – and when I saw a man riding the road, near our house, with a wig on, it would so alarm my fears, and give me such a disagreeable feeling, that, I dare say, I would run off, as for my life. Such ideas of the difference between 'gentle' and 'simple', were, I believe, universal among all of my rank and age.
>
> (Jarrett 1952: 361)

The lower orders, as Gerald Strauss demonstrates, invoked the traditional hierarchy in protectionist moves to prevent competition from above. A Nürnberg writ from the mid-sixteenth century insisted that 'nobles are forbidden for the sake of their nobility to engage in burgherly enterprises and lowly trades' (Strauss 1986: 11).

These few instances do not substantiate the claim of widespread acceptance of hierarchic dress codes, but they do provide something of a peg on which to hang the contention that evidence about the connection between sumptuary law and the reproduction of hierarchic rank is not in itself evidence that it was always imposed from above. In turning now to consider the connection between sumptuary law and the reproduction of social hierarchy the possible existence of a hegemonic preoccupation with rank and status should be borne in mind. This idea will later come into play in Chapter 8 where it will be necessary to try to understand why urban sumptuary codes, implemented by unambiguously bourgeois classes, both in the city states and at the national level in the early modern period, were similarly concerned to provide external appearential evidence of a hierarchic social order, whether real or imaginary.

RECOGNIZABILITY AND HIERARCHY

The most visible feature of the sumptuary laws was that they protected and reinforced the hierarchical status relations that dominated late medieval and early modern life. Sumptuary laws were representations and re-presentations of the social hierarchy and they served not only to identify individuals to one another but also to regulate the visible expression of that hierarchy by regulating access to items of dress or ornamentation that carried the symbolic expression of that hierarchy. The most general form of such regulation was to reserve for the upper ranks some privileged items of social visibility. Generally the regulated items singled out in sumptuary laws were expensive indexical symbols of hierarchy.

Sumptuary legislation classically takes the form of negative prohibitions: it forbids certain categories of persons to wear stipulated cloths, garments or ornamentation. This negative form becomes apparent when an exception appears. The earliest Scottish sumptuary statute of 1429 is the only one encountered that lays down a positive duty. It required that all men with an income over £20 p.a. should be well horsed and equipped 'as a gentleman ought to be', and yeomen with £20 in goods should be well turned out and own a bow, buckler and knife (APS II: 18: 11–12). This provision is worth recording to emphasize the overwhelmingly negative form of sumptuary legislation.

The project of imposing hierarchical access to sumptuous and prestigious wear is exemplified in an early Elizabethan proclamation, 'Proclamation Against Excess in Apparel', which announced the intention to enforce the extant sumptuary legislation[8] and circulated as a schedule that was repeated many times over during the next forty years. A synopsis or tabular summary of the rules is in the following terms:

None shall wear in his apparel any:

cloth of gold, silver, or tinsel; satin, silk, or cloth mixed with gold or silver, nor any sables; except earls and all of superior degrees, and viscounts and barons in their doublets and sleeveless coats;

woollen cloth made out of the realm; velvet, crimson, scarlet, or blue; furs, black genets, lucerns; except dukes, marquises, earls or their children, barons, and knights of the order;

velvet in gowns, coats, or outermost garments; furs of leopards; embroidery, pricking or printing with gold, silver, or silk; except baron's sons, knights, or men that may dispend £200 by year;

taffeta, satin, damask, or silk camlet in his outermost garments; velvet, otherwise than in jackets, doublets, etc., fur whereof the kind groweth not within the Queen's dominions, except grey genets, budge; except a man may dispend £100 by year.[9]

In the late thirteenth century the following section from a sumptuary edict from Castille reveals the same detailed attention to hierarchic regulation:

> XIV. No grandee, knight, or any other man whomsoever may have more than four suits of clothing each year; and those may not bear ermine, drawnwork, silk, gold or silver thread, elaborate needlework, gold embroidery, pelts, trimmings, or any real or elaborate material whatever except fur and cloth; one suit of clothing may not be covered with another; no one except the King may wear a scarlet rain cloak; no one may have more than two mantles per year and a rain cloak should last for two years; no one may wear sendal [rich silk] or silk except the King or a noble knight (except as lining in clothing); no one may wear marten furs except the King, a noble, a grandee, or a bridegroom if he is the son of a grandee; no one may wear silver, crystal, buttons, long chains, ermine, or otter on their cloaks or robes except around the edges of their mantle; and no grandee may wear travelling costume in court.
>
> (Anon 1963: 99)

These two provisions, distant in both time and place, illustrate the preoccupation of much sumptuary legislation with detailed specification of hierarchical entitlements. The close attention to detail is further reinforced when small changes were made in successive provisions. It would be tedious to provide much detailed evidence on this point. The most accessible evidence comes from the Elizabethan proclamations over the period 1559 to 1597, during which time there were nineteen proclamations dealing with excess of apparel. Their common form was a repetition of the tabular presentation followed by some 'necessary additions' (Fig. 6.1). These additions sometimes sought to regulate new fashions, and at other times to add items that had previously escaped mention. Around 1565 new innovations in men's hose elicited additional rules about both the quantity and quality of material used, while in 1575 a certain desperation is evident in the proclamation that, in the course of detailing additional restrictions, prohibited anyone from 'devising any new forms of apparel' (Dyson 1618: No. 168).

A general characteristic of the discursive construction of sumptuary legislation, usually appearing in the preamble, was the direct linkage of social recognizability and hierarchical order. In 1530 the Augsburg Diet drew up fresh clothing regulations 'to ensure that each class should be clearly recognized apart' (Boehn 1932–35: II: 193–194). The 1533 English statute, 'Act for Reformation of Excess in Apparel', brilliantly captures the sense in which recognition and social hierarchy go hand in hand when it complains of 'the subversion of good and politic order in knowledge and distinction of people according to their estates, pre-eminences, dignities and degrees'.[10] In similar vein a proclamation of 1566, 'Enforcing Statutes of Apparel', speaks of 'the disorder and confusion of the degrees of all estates . . . and finally to the subversion of all good order'.[11] As a final example a Nürnburg law of 1657 commenced:

> It is unfortunately an established fact that both men and women-folk have, in utterly irresponsible manner, driven extravagance in dress and new styles to such shameful and wanton extremes that the different classes are barely to be known apart.
>
> (Boehn 1932–35: III: 173)

Note how 'extravagance' and 'recognizability' get juxtaposed in these legislative discourses.

While sumptuary regulation exhibited a preoccupation with the detailed construction of an appearential hierarchy there were certain primary targets – items of apparel, materials or valuables – that recured. It is thus appropriate to consider the major regulatory targets or objects of regulation. Joanne Finkelstein suggests that frequently the items selected for regulation were themselves central to the organization of the economy. She does not pursue this interesting point very far, but does suggest that very widespread prohibitions or restrictions on gold can be understood as attempts to preserve the social order by 'guarding against the accumulation of too much wealth by those who might challenge the status quo' (1991: 138). We can get closer to the sumptuary project by grasping the way in which Finkelstein here ends up completely misunderstanding the nature of sumptuary law. I have not come across a single sumptuary regulation that prohibited ownership of gold or silver, or other economically significant resources; what sumptuary law prohibits is the display of that wealth, not the wealth itself. It is for this reason that it has to be insisted that sumptuary law is concerned with the symbolic representation and

MEN'S APPAREL

NONE SHALL WEAR

NONE SHALL WEAR	Except
Cloth of gold, Silver tissue, Silk of purple colour	Earls and above that rank, and Knights of the Garter in their purple mantles.
Cloth of gold or silver, tinselled satin, silk or cloth mixed or embroidered with gold or silver. Foreign woollen cloth	Barons and above that rank. Knights of Garter, and Privy Councillors.
Any lace of gold or silver, mixed with gold and silver, or with gold or silver and silk. Spurs, swords, rapiers, daggers, buckles or studs of girdles, etc. — Gilt or damasked with gold or silver silvered	Barons' sons and all above that rank. Gentlemen attending upon the Queen in house or chamber. Those who have been employed in embassies. Those with net income of 500 marks per year for life. Knights (as regards daggers, spurs, etc.); Captains.
Velvet in — Gowns, Cloaks, Coats and upper garments; Embroidered with silk; Netherstocks of silk	Knights and all above that rank; their heirs apparent; those with net income of £200, and all excepted in preceding article.
Velvet in — Jerkins, Hose, Doublets; Satin, Damask, Taffeta, Grograin in — Gowns, Cloaks, Coats, etc.	Knights' eldest sons, and all above that rank. Those with net income of £100. Those excepted above.
Velvet, Gilding, Silvering, etc., Studs, Buckles, or other garniture, gilt, silvered, etc. in — Saddles, Bridles, Stirrups, and all furniture of horse	Barons' sons and all above that rank; Knights; Men with incomes of 500 marks etc. as above.

Figure 6.1 Sumptuary Proclamation 10 Eliz. I, 1575–76: 'A brief content of certain clauses of the statutes of King Henry VIII (24 Hen. VIII, *c.* 13, 1533) and Queen Mary (1 & 2 Philip & Mary, *c.* 2, 1555), with some moderation thereof, and other provisions to be observed according to Her Majesty's Proclamation.'

WOMEN'S APPAREL

NONE SHALL WEAR

None shall wear		Except
Cloth of gold or silver tissued, Purple silk	Except	Countesses and all above that rank.
(Viscountesses may wear cloth of gold or silver tissued only in their kirtles)		
Silk or cloth, mixed or embroidered with pearl, gold or silver	Except	Baronesses and all above that rank.
Cloth of gold and silver only in linings of garments, etc.	Except	Wives of Barons eldest sons and all above that rank. Barons daughters.
Cloth of silver in kirtles only.	Except	Knights wives and all above that rank.
Embroideries of gold or silver. Lace of gold or silver or mixed with gold, silver or silk. Headdresses trimmed with pearl.	Except	Wives of Barons eldest sons and all above that rank. Barons daughters. Wives of Knights of Garter or of Privy Councillors. Maids of honor, Ladies, etc. of Privy Chamber. Those with income of 500 marks a year
Velvet in upper garments. Embroidery with silk. Netherstocks of silk.	Except	Knights wives and all above that rank, and those expected above. Those with incomes of £200.
Velvet in {Kirtles, Petticoats}; Satin {Gowns, Cloaks and other outer garments}	Except	Wives of knights eldest sons, and all above that rank. Gentlewomen attendant upon countlesses, viscountesses, etc Those with incomes of £100.
Satin in Kirtles, Damask, Tufted taffeta in Gowns, Plain Grograin	Except	Gentlemens wives, bearing arms, and all above that rank, etc.

consumption of wealth rather than with wealth itself.

The regulation of symbolic vehicles of social hierarchy can be investigated by attending to the 'objects of regulation'. Gold and silver have a special place in economic history as providing, at one and the same time, the means of displaying wealth and the means of economic calculation and exchange; the gold coin is both wealth and its symbolic representation. One of the manifestations of the fundamental contradiction of sumptuary law is that, while the economic ethic of early modernity encouraged the accumulation of wealth through trade and commerce, the sumptuary regimes restricted or prohibited either the direct or indirect display of the wealth so accumulated.

A very special target of the sumptuary legislator over many centuries and in many countries concerned the combination of precious metals with textiles to produce sumptuous materials, in particular cloth of gold and cloth of silver. For example, Japanese sumptuary law restricted the use of gold lacquer and gold-leaf in household interiors and on saddles. The preoccupation with either restricting or prohibiting these materials rehearsed the usual mix of concerns about luxury and hierarchical recognition. In addition there was an economic concern about the 'loss' of gold and silver involved. Bullionism, the concern to protect the accumulation of gold and silver and to avoid its dispersal, was one of the first stages in the development of mercantilism as a coherent economic programme of governmental concern. As the health of the late twentieth century nations is measured by one or more privileged indices, whether inflation or interest rate, GNP, etc., in the medieval and early modern world the stock of bullion was the measure of national economic and military strength. We encounter here a connection that will become more important, namely that where there is a connection between a sumptuary motive and a mercantilist motive state regulation shifts readily from one regulatory discourse to the other.

Attention has already been drawn to the part played by conspicuous consumption in the life-style of the post-feudal nobility. While the European pattern of consumption by the nobility is rarely a direct form of the gift or potlatch system, where inequality of accumulated wealth is 'exchanged' for status recognition in its distribution, the conspicuous consumption of the nobility had distributional dimensions. Recall that the polemic from Stubbes at the head of this chapter complained not only of flaunting display but of 'meanness'. The ranks of the hierarchy needed to be able to maintain a particular level of consumption, and the associated distributional features were a component of the legitimation of hierarchy. An Elizabethan proclamation of 1597 reveals a very interesting combination of 'motives' or grounds of legitimation in its exhortatory preamble which links the 'immeasurable' expense of superfluous apparel, particularly of wives and children, to the decline of hospitality that in turn leads to a confusion of ranks (39 Eliz. 6/7/1597; Dyson 1618: No. 343).

During the seventeenth century concern about the decline of hospitality by the English nobility was linked to an emerging anxiety that they were not devoting sufficient attention to the visible representation of hierarchy throughout the kingdom because they were spending more and more time in London. Several proclamations sought to remove the nobility back to their estates and in doing so revealed an interesting set of motives. Only one of these relates to the current interest in keeping alive the hierarchical order through its active display in the countryside. This concern is mixed with a military concern in periods of anxiety about invasion or about civil unrest. The nobility were expected to provide military mobilization and leadership. On the other hand edicts against the minor nobility and upper gentry who were busily establishing an expanded version of a 'court society' in London, promoting a 'season' for conspicuous consumption associated with the 'coming out' of marriageable daughters that was to survive into the twentieth century, were part of that older tradition of the moralization of luxury.

The attempt to reserve the most significant symbolic expressions of social status such as gold, silver and jewels for the exclusive use of the designated hierarchic group was not only about the denial of these status attributes to the rising bourgeoisie, but was a means of reproducing the recognizability of the hierarchic order. This concern with recognizability can be examined in more detail by attending to some of the other most frequently indicted objects of regulation. Throughout the whole span of European sumptuary law the most frequently regulated items were furs and silks.

Fur, silk and social hierarchy

Furs have provided a persistent expressive mechanism for the visible display of social hierarchy and thus have been a persistent target of regulation. But why furs? In the first place there are deep roots to the ornamental role of trophies: the horns, head or fur of the victim of the chase attest to the prowess of the male hunter and thus become sources of status. Manifestation of the link between trophies and hunting have remained remarkably enduring features of masculinity: taxidermy still flourishes, antlers are still attached to walls and fish that did not get away still achieve a gruesome immortality. We can add an interesting note to Veblen's thesis concerning the rise of vicarious consumption whereby men transfer their consumption of trophies onto women. Throughout the Middle Ages and the pre-modern world furs were of enormous importance; they provided warmth and comfort and, at the same time, displayed the status of their wearers. Their potential as both material and symbolic capital was enhanced by their durability. Medieval wills are replete with the disposition of large numbers of both fur robes and complete furs. Any examination of the history of portraiture will reveal the enormous significance of the fur as the preferred drapery through which to display the social and economic pride of the subject (Hollander 1980). Pictorially furs dominated the self-presentation of the medieval upper classes.[12]

Rather suddenly during the eighteenth century Western European men stopped wearing furs and in an act of symbolic renunciation made the fur coat an exclusively gendered garment. In Europe the fur coat for much of the nineteenth and twentieth centuries became one of the most immediately recognizable signs of vicarious display of wealth on the backs and shoulders of the wives and mistresses of the wealthy and powerful. In this role fur signifies the transfer of trophy from male to female and, in turn, provides an opening to understand the eroticization of fur. Interestingly, males retained for themselves access to the wearing of reversed furs in the form of sheepskins, flying-jackets and more generally of leather garments. The latter then secured some gender-neutral status attributes with their absorption into mass fashion.[13]

The other significant attribute of fur was that it exhibited its own hierarchy of sumptuous prestige. Ermine and sable were consistently reserved for the highest social rank. For much of the middle ages squirrel furs, in particular the flecked variety from northern regions that resembled ermine, had high status. It is interesting to note that some changes of rank occurred: fox fur, for example, rose in esteem while squirrel fell in the more recent period, but it does not seem that these changes were reflections of scarcity. In general the prestige of furs seems to have been strongly linked with their indexical economic value; the rarer and more expensive the fur, the greater its social prestige. The more significant point is to stress the consistent sumptuary importance attached to furs; only the very recent rise of environmental concerns seems to have, probably finally, undermined the fur as a means of displaying wealth and social standing.[14]

The possibility of detailed hierarchical status display, and thus correspondingly the opportunity for its regulation, was progressively expanded by the increased variety of cloths that were one of the earliest consequences of the advance of medieval trade. The opening up of trade routes to the East brought silk to the fore. There is an interesting set of parallels between silk and furs. First it has indexical significance; it was its scarcity and cost that first gave silk its sartorial importance. For most of the medieval and early modern period silk was the preferred vehicle of sumptuous display for both men and women. Silk, like fur, was later subject to male renunciation and the genderization of silk as a vehicle for the vicarious display of women became linked to the eroticization of silk. Silk offers one significant distinction from fur in that it dramatically manifests the disassociation of sartorial display from work through Veblen's conspicuous leisure. Its delicacy displayed the conspicuous leisure of its wearer.

In the main the signifiers of social status and the targets of sumptuary regulation were themselves indices of the wealth and status they communicated. The history of sumptuary law also involves evidence of pure symbolism. The attempt to impose a colour-coded status hierarchy emerges now and again although it is mainly associated with pre-modern social forms. The best known case of colour regulation was the effort made by Roman emperors to reserve the colour purple. In 46 BC Julius Caesar introduced *Lex Iulia sumptuaria* which, in addition to detailed regulation of women's dress, imposed restrictions on the use of purple robes (Mommsen 1862–66: IV: 522). In 36 BC Octavian prohibited the practice of ordinary citizens wearing the purple robe, which was again reserved for senatorial rank. As late as AD 382 the *Lex Vestiaria* reserved purple robes for the Emperor, while senators and other officials were allowed white mantles with purple borders (Boehn 1932–35: I: 174). With fine attention to detail Chinese emperors reserved only certain specified shades of purple for use by the imperial household (Kracke 1975: 255) and went further in reserving specific symbolic representations of the number, colour and configuration of the dragons on the ceremonial 'dragon robes' (Cammann 1952: 52–57).

The attempt to monopolize purple was also present in English sumptuary legislation. It first appeared in 1463 when it was enacted that 'no person under the estate of a lord [may] wear any manner of cloth or silk being of the colour of purple' (3 Edw. IV: *c.* 5; SR 2: 399–402). The same restriction was embedded in what was probably the most important and certainly the most detailed English sumptuary statute: the 'Act for the Reformation of Excess in Apparel' of 1533 reserved purple silk, in clothes or on horses for members of the royal family.[15] It further restricted crimson, scarlet or blue velvets to the upper nobility (duke, marquis or earl).[16] These colour restrictions were applied not only to clothes, but also to carriages and horse furniture. This regulation of means of transport is a significant feature of sumptuary legislation and is strong evidence that control of conspicuous consumption was the most persistent motive since no form of self-display was more visible than the use of ornate carriages and sumptuously decked horses; there was quite literally no more visible form of conspicuous consumption.

Next to the colour purple, scarlet was the most popular target of sumptuary regulation. Scarlet was persistently reserved for royal families in both France and Spain in the late Middle Ages. Occasionally one detects a widening of a privileged group: after a long period when scarlet had been a prerogative of the French royal family a law of 1328 extended the privilege to princes and knights; but by the fifteenth century scarlet was again limited to the king.

The semiotic properties of clothing and ornamentation allow for the construction of more or less complicated 'visible codes' of legibility.[17] Many of the most pervasive codes are inscribed within custom, such as the ubiquitous wearing of engagement and wedding rings in most European cultures. In the course of the history of sumptuary regulation there were cases in which these codes were given legal form. In traditional China certain colours were reserved for the garments of different classes and different ranks of officials. What is interesting is that this 'colour coding of class' underwent significant changes over time. Ch'ü records this fact but offers no explanation of why particular colours rose and fell as designators of status (Ch'ü 1961). It would be fascinating to trace how it came about that blue was at one time reserved for high officials then 'sank' to become the legislatively approved colour for commoners. An interesting additional touch is the existence of positive injunction that mothers and wives of officials are ordered to dress in accordance with the rank of their husbands or sons. It seems likely that what was involved here was the predominance of a male occupational hierarchy in which the recognizability of women was provided for by the patriarchal assignment of status.

The obverse of reserving symbolic colours for privileged categories and denying it to others was occasional efforts to impose drab colours on subordinates. For example, a Scottish statute of 1457 laid down that labourers, husbandmen and their wives were permitted to wear specific colours (light blue, green and red) on holidays only; on working days they were restricted to white or grey (hence 'commoner's grey') (APS II: 49, *c.* 13).

DISTINGUISHING MARKS

Probably the most obvious expression of a concern with recognizability is where the attempt is made to impose distinguishing marks on particular categories of persons. The most widespread use of distinguishing marks was to impose visibility upon prostitutes. Virtually every sumptuary regime has, at one time or another, sought to impose 'marks of infamy' on prostitutes. They have been required to wear coloured patches (yellow for some reason being the most widely employed), special hats, special shoes, to wear bells and other means to provide visible and audible evidence of the preoccupation with distinguishing between 'good girls' and 'bad girls'. Since the control of prostitutes is so centrally a matter of the regulation of gender, I postpone further discussion of prostitution until Chapter 9.

More generally, social visibility or recognizability has been of particular significance for women: whereas men derive their recognition from their public roles, women have taken their social position not as themselves, but through patriarchal precedents derived from their fathers or husbands.

There was an interesting piece of legislation from Bologna in

1474. To the best of my knowledge it is unique in European sumptuary legislation in that it provided a visible code of social status specifically for women. Gold gowns were reserved for the wives and daughters of knights; sleeves of gold for those of notaries and bankers; crimson dresses for the wives and daughters of artisans of the senior guilds; only crimson sleeves for women attached to men in humbler trades (Hughes 1983). Some sumptuary ordinances allowed greater licence to the young and unmarried. Marriage itself marked a passage from one sumptuary status to another; for example, in Genoa after 1499 sumptuary restrictions were imposed three years after marriage, presumably drawing a distinction between brides and matrons. A quasi-sumptuary provision for women in the Moravian community in eighteenth century Philadelphia used the ribbons with which their caps were tied as a detailed colour-coding separating women into distinct 'choirs' (married – blue; widows – white; unmarried – pink; girls from 12–16 – red) (Ritter 1857: 85, 145).

The attempt to prescribe visibility finds its most dramatic expression in the use of the branding of the flesh with an authoritative and irreversible imprint of its crimes. Branding allows considerable potential for the symbolization of wrongs. The Japanese harnessed the techniques of tattooing to provide a highly legible code in which the nature of the offence could be read from the body or facial tattoo (Richie 1973). John Hall's study of Tokugawa legislation ends with some extraordinary prints that in possibly unintended juxtapositioning of tattoo marks and physical punishments reveal the fertility of the human imagination for imposing its mark upon the body (Hall 1909).

Through most of medieval and early modern Europe the branding iron exhibited a limited flexibility by the imprint of signifying letters into the burnt flesh of those judged to merit such designation. In England branding was mainly directed against 'vagabonds', a class always contrasted with 'the poor' in a categorization that persists into modernity as the 'deserving poor'. Branding first appears in English legislation in the late fourteenth century in an attempt to control the movement of labour that had become a serious concern of the landed classes. A statute of 1361 required that fugitives, those leaving employers without leave, be branded with 'F' on the forehead for 'falsity'.[18] A statute of 1547 provided that sturdy beggars should be branded with 'V' for vagabond on the chest and an 'S' for a second offence (Aydelotte 1967).[19] An

Act of 1604 required that 'incorrigible rogues' be 'branded in the left shoulder with a hot burning iron' with an 'R' (Beier 1985).[20]

Branding was not simply a coercive means of imposing recognizability; it was also about an old and pervasive conception of the legibility of character. It was widely held that the nature and character of individuals could be read from physical characteristics, and in particular from physiognomy (Finkelstein 1991: 17–40; Porter 1985). Once the character was revealed, despite Christian notions of redemption, it was regarded as immutable. It was thus a short step to the view that branding provided a ready means of conveying this information to others confronted by the intractable problem that the rootless vagabonds seemed to pose.[21] As with sumptuary offences, there is a decided lack of records of the imposition of these punishments; obviously the summary nature of these offences reduces the likelihood of records. It seems reasonable to think that in a system which was primarily concerned to compel beggars and vagabonds to return to their place of origin or to keep moving, the fear of branding was a valuable threat in the armoury of authority.

The threat of branding and periodic intense campaigns of whipping beggars, such as the one that reached a frenzy in England between 1569 and 1572, associated with anxiety about the possible connections between itinerant beggars and the spread of religious revolts, and again after 1591 with the moral panic after the Armada about foreign agents and disguises, were the coercive responses to a perceived crisis of social order. These responses coexisted with less punitive forms of imposing distinguishing marks made familiar to modern sensibilities by Nathaniel Hawthorne's famous 'scarlet letter' (Hawthorne 1981).[22] Such external markings have deep roots in the practices of popular justice in which many forms of manipulating shame and exposure were well known in medieval Europe: for example, in the English village practice of the 'skimmington' mock-procession was used to bring ridicule on either husbands or wives for infidelity or ill-treatment.[23] The local archdeacon's courts used the penalty of making moral offenders stand in a white sheet during the church service. In colonial America a system of external letters was attached to the clothing of offenders, or the wrongdoer was required to wear a rope or halter around the neck (Miller 1966: 258).

There was a more governmental response to the expanding crisis in Europe of the unemployed. 'Licences' to beg and the requirement of 'passports' had been used intermittently since the fourteenth century, and such techniques became increasingly important in the course of the sixteenth century (Beier 1985). 'Badging' of licensed beggars was probably adopted directly from the 'distinguishing marks' imposed on European Jewry.[24] The imposition of a cloth 'V' was adopted in York in 1516 and by London's Court of Aldermen in the same year, and was extended to the whole country in 1563. In these and other cities licensing was seen as the solution; it preserved some lineage of charity while serving the more pressing need of controlling the pressure of numbers that was particularly severe in the major cities. Beggars were required to wear 'some notable badge or token' on their breast or back. Alongside the overt evidential role, badging functioned also as a degradation ceremony (Richards 1990).[25]

A WORLD TURNED UPSIDE DOWN

One of the things that confirms some experiential reality of a temporal boundary between the pre-modern and the modern is the pervasive disturbed and anxious words in which the past speaks to us. And this remains true even if we find it difficult to identify a chronological moment or period in which to locate that transition. There are two figurative forms that reappear as people try to grapple and come to terms with social change. One is the notion of 'the world we have lost'. Peter Laslett deploys this figure to great effect to capture the profundity of the changes experienced in inter-personal and familial relations in the transition to modernity (Laslett 1965). This figure embraces a mood of regret about the passing of a life that was known and familiar and which was valorized through its simplicity. Such invocations are alive and well today, and are most intrusively harnessed by a retreat into nostalgia in advertising, as, for example, when heavy dray-horses pull carts loaded with beer in wooden casks through rural landscapes in order to sell today's chemical preparations in cans to the residents of concrete jungles. The boundary between nostalgia and an affirmation of the past is fragile, but its significance is not reduced by that instability.[26] An element of the sumptuary project was to provide symbolic affirmation of a sense of social recognizability; and furthermore this sense of the knowability and familiarity was shared, albeit differentially, by subordinate social groups.

The concern to capture and to encapsulate symbolically the familiarity of the past can be contrasted with a response at the other end of the continuum of responses to modernization. Just as the first sense is captured by the notion of 'a world we have lost', so this other response is captured in the imagery of a 'world turned upside-down'.[27] The 'upside-down' imagery has exhibited remarkable persistence as an expression of a deep anxiety and pessimistic projection in the face of social change. This imagery is alive and well today. The role of extrapolation through the device of 'slippery slope' arguments has played a large part in both the intellectual and emotional construction of conservative responses to social change. E.S. Turner captures this with great humorous effect in tracing the predictions of doom and disaster that were unleashed during debates over social reforms such as the removal of the impediment to marriage to a deceased wife's sister (Turner 1950). Humour aside, such constructions have played a powerful role not only in popular political debates but in the courts where appeal to the dangers of the 'slippery slope' has been a significant line of defence against both social and legal change.

The enormous effort that was involved in the multitude of sumptuary projects, evident even if only a simple quantitative account is taken of the volume of sumptuary enactments, needs to be stressed. These projects were not passing whims of the rulers. Their increase during periods of military, economic and social crisis suggests that, despite the way in which the sumptuary dimension of European history has been forgotten, sumptuary regulation was at many important historical turning points a major political question. For example, the Diet of Worms in 1521, one of the critical turning points in the political realignments of Reformation Europe, took the time to articulate the urgent need for sumptuary legislation in order to maintain the visibility of social status as manifest in attire (Greenfield 1918: 128).

Dress has long excited fear of the demise of the world that is known. The preoccupation expressed in much of the hierarchical sumptuary law was that a society without discernible ranks and thus devoid of recognizability lacked a necessary precondition of normal social life. The decline or demise of the known freezes responses and induces fear because no other ways of relating to others can be envisaged. Hovering around the margins of sumptuary discourses is the fear of social collapse if the natural and necessary social order is not preserved. As the earlier exploration of fashion revealed, it is the quest to achieve both individuality and conformity that provides the motive force for change in self-presentation. It is the ambiguity at the heart of dress as a semiotic system that results in clothing being interpreted in extreme forms. Shifts in the exposure of flesh or accentuation of physical features frequently gave rise to images of a world turned upside-down. Aside from the polemical assaults on luxury and its connection with fashion, discussed in Chapter 3, the preambles to sumptuary statutes reveal an interesting mix of social ills that are to be corrected by legislative action. For example, the Preamble to an English statute of 1463 complained that:

> the commons of the said realm, as well Men as Women, have worn and daily do wear excessive and inordinate array (and Apparel) to the great Displeasure of God, and impoverishing of this realm of England and to the enriching of other strange Realms and Countries to the final Destruction of Husbandry of this said Realm.
>
> (3 Edw. IV: *c.* 5; SR 2: 399–402)

The complaint of displeasing the deity was a standard moral trope, national impoverishment is part of an already familiar economic discourse, but the 'destruction of husbandry' was a classically catastrophic and radically improbable outcome of indulgence in conspicuous consumption. It is doubtful that anyone believed that the English peasants were about to lay down their hoes and desert the cultivation of the soil. But if the catastrophic scenario was not persuasive, why was it there?

The answer I suggest is that the variations in the justifications and legitimations offered for enacting sumptuary controls are capable of speaking to us about the anxieties and preoccupations current at the time of their conception. Further, but beyond my present concern, it should be noted that while circumstances change, certain of these ideological responses become routinized long after the circumstances to which they relate have passed. My suggestion is that the prediction of the 'destruction of husbandry' reveals not only a general anxiety about a continuing shortage of agricultural labour, but relates specifically to a period of considerable upward pressure on agricultural wages. Then it begins to make sense; if rural wages are rising and this leads to an expansion of commodification, then the image of the agricultural labourer decked in finery and refusing to work at least 'makes sense', albeit not very good sense.

Thus while the most general social anxiety invoked in the discourses of the sumptuary ethic was a response to the changing configuration of class and status relations, there were always more specific combinations of concerns and anxieties disclosed. The most persistent of these surrounded gender and sex. At this stage it is sufficient to note that there is a marked variation in both the extent to which and the direction in which gender issues are incorporated in sumptuary discourses. During some periods males were the main target while at other times it was women who were targeted. Also present, although less frequently than the question of gender, were anxieties about the age structure. Here, interestingly, it was always young men who were the target; the clothing of young males of the dominant classes was constructed as evidence of insubordination. Even more persistent was the preoccupation with apprentices: my sense is that the label 'apprentice' signified more than the indentured, but expressed a wider anxiety about one of the most distinctive features of the urbanization process, the influx of large numbers of unattached young men no longer firmly bound to kinship and familial relations who dramatically signified the demise of the old order.

The other side of this upheaval, the emergence of uprooted females in the urban environment, was expressed in the linked concerns that were most visibly expressed in the persistent preoccupation with the regulation of prostitutes, and less visibly, but I suggest similarly manifesting the response to rapidly changing urban demography, with the attempts embedded in sumptuary law to regulate servants. The 'servant problem' was overwhelmingly about the regulation of young women whose presence in the urban environment revealed a weakening of their linkage to the patriarchal order. In Chapter 9 I will try to make sense of the historical specificity and variation of these shifts in relation to gender and age.

There is a methodological implication to be extracted from these considerations. The history of sumptuary regulation is to read by attending to the specific discursive combination revealed in the preambles and the texts of the myriad edicts, statutes, ordinances and proclamations that made up the raw material of the sumptuary projects that span the transition from pre-modernity to modernity. These texts provide an access through which to address the way in which the different strands of discourse are invoked and mobilized. It is the combination or 'coupling' of these themes that make it possible to understand the social anxieties that are reflected in the great mass of regulatory interventions.

The general thesis that emerges is that the transition to urbanization and modernity was marked by a 'crisis of recognizability' that manifested a concern with the passing of the forms of social relations inherent in the various forms of European feudalism as these underwent the protracted birth of capitalist social relations. Herein lies the general historical location of the phenomenon of sumptuary law. The attempt to regulate appearance as evidence of a concern on the part of the dominant classes is reinforced by the changed material circumstance of the slow but ineluctable expansion of the consumption of commodities, in which the production of ever greater variety of cloths played such a significant role. As fashion expanded it became more accessible to wider sections of the population and, correspondingly, the possibilities of competitive conspicuous consumption were augmented. Thus anxieties and complaints about the difficulty of reading rank from appearance had a materiality. In other words, the energy invested in projects of sumptuary regulation cannot be understood simply in their own discursive forms but one must attend to the ideological and symbolic dimensions and, in particular, to the materiality of the circumstances that unleashed these preoccupations. The concern manifested by legislators throughout Europe was with a construction of social disorder, with a 'world turned upside-down'. From the perspective of the legislators the problem was that changing social appearance, captured in the preoccupation with 'fashion', bred disorder. 'Laws on the disorder of clothes and the disruptiveness of fashion seem to have reflected a growing, if less easily expressible, sense of social disorder' (Hughes 1983: 90). Or, as Simmel expressed it, their concern was with a society in which differentiation had got out of hand (Simmel 1904: 135).

COUNTERFEITING APPEARANCE

A problem endemic in any attempt to stabilize the social order through appearential ordering stems from the fact that clothing can only secure the external manifestations of rank and status attributes. Appearance is eloquent and – quite literally – powerful; there is an important truth in the clichés about 'first appearances'. Thus visible self-presentation creates endless possibilities for the perpetration of fraud and misrepresentation. It is for this reason that the discourses of clothing and fashion exhibit an ongoing concern with the counterfeiting of status claims. While external appearance can be read for signs of deeper attributes, to 'dress like a gentleman' or to 'look like a lady' can never provide any stable guarantee of those status claims. This inescapable unreliability of appearential ordering was probably the single most important cause of the abandonment of the projects of sumptuary regulation. The absence of guarantees of appearential status is the practical consequence of the semiotic ambiguity that lies at the heart of fashion that was explored in Chapter 3.

One measure of the significance of recognizability is the use of 'disguise' in early and medieval literature in which kings, princesses, etc., avoided recognition by the wearing of a cloak or simple clothing (tales of the Caliph Al-Rashid, Shakespeare's plays, etc.). For example, in *The Odyssey* Athene helps Odysseus against his enemies: 'I shall make you unrecognizable to all mortals' (Homer 1974: 184). She turns him into an old man and 'she threw other clothing about him'. Odysseus was not recognized by his servants or his wife.

Laws, sumptuary and others, intervened, albeit rather unsystematically, against disguise and misrepresentation. A very explicit visible fraud also appeared towards the end of the fifteenth century when 'able-bodied beggars' sought to evade the increasingly rigorous vagrancy legislation by counterfeiting their appearance. Two favoured personae were those of the pilgrim and the discharged soldier or sailor. The legislation responded by requiring evidence of status – authorization for pilgrimage from parish priest or discharge papers from naval or military authorities.[28] Here, of course, is what became the characteristic means of establishing identity that was to last until the advent of the computer that dispensed with the need for a police who checked that 'our papers are in order'.

Tudor vagrancy statutes specifically prohibited vagabonds disguising themselves as Egyptians (gypsies) or wandering in company with them.[29] The interpretation of this provision that seems to fit is that vagabonds were using the claim that they were gypsies to legitimate an itinerant life. Another English statute in 1540 contained explicit provision against disguises, penalizing anyone with 'his face hid or covered with hood or visor or with his face painted or himself otherwise disguised, with the intent that he would not be known'.[30]

A Venetian provision of 1339 directed at nocturnal disorder forbade any person to walk about the city disguised so as 'not to be recognizable'. A further measure in 1443 provided for a heavy fine for men wearing women's dress. In 1443 a new target came into prominence – head covering and veiling. One address to the Venetian Senate referred to:

> an abominable fashion [that] has been introduced among our ladies . . . who go about with the head and face covered, contrary to the ancient and good custom; under which dishonest mode various dishonest acts have been and every day are committed, against the honour of God and of our dominion.
>
> (Newett 1907: 268)

It would be interesting to know what 'dishonest acts' the speaker had in mind; it is probably reasonable to infer that the anxiety was that women might be enjoying the freedom to move incognito around the city.

As we have seen, veils were a considerable source of anxiety; while on the one hand the symbols of piety, or at least of church attendance, they also served as a very effective device of both allure and invisibility as did masks and fans. Venetian ladies were masked when they visited the coffee-houses that were forbidden to persons of rank (Braudel 1982: 489). Barthes makes the point that veiling secures both transparency and invisibility (Barthes 1983: 128).[31] Clothing and associated display operate as a mechanism for claiming an identity within a public arena. They provide the means for securing the double sense of recognizability; yet it is always ('always already' in Althusser's sense) fallible and vulnerable and thus can never be free of anxiety. Maybe it was because of this ambivalence that veils, while much talked about, were rarely the explicit targets of regulation.[32]

Personation offences have existed in most jurisdictions and are alive and well today. The most widespread are offences of misrepresentation of office that prohibit the wearing of police, military and other specified uniforms. Such laws do not come within the field of sumptuary law since they are typically invoked only in connection with the commission of some other offence. This form of the regulation of appearance does not further impinge on the investigation of sumptuary law.

The unreliability of external appearance is compounded by two key processes. In the transition from social relations dominated by face-to-face relations to those in which the major experience is that of living in a world of strangers, encounters with 'strangers' cannot be guaranteed. We can no longer 'know' who we encounter, but neither can we 'read' their self-presentation with reliability. It should be recalled that versions of physiognomy were widely popular in late medieval and early modern society; such ideas heightened the tension between 'character' and 'appearance' (Porter 1985). This difficulty was compounded by the expansion of consumption that brought the means of appearential misrepresentation within the means of ever larger populations. The central process was the one that brought the means of conspicuous consumption within the reach of the rising bourgeois classes. It is one of the paradoxes of the history of sumptuary law that while it was much concerned to secure a stable connection between appearance and entitlement, the social conditions in which it did so were everyday making the achievement of its goals ever more unrealizable. This insight provides a more adequate understanding of the 'failure' of sumptuary law; it was not doomed to failure, but rather it was an attempt to grapple with a set of social and economic changes that would sooner or later swamp the ideas that social recognizability could be secured and stabilized through law.

Although the concern with recognizing others persists, the legibility of appearance by the eye is displaced by two very different processes. On the one hand there are the mechanisms of 'distinction' which employ more complex cultural barriers, for example, of accent or use of a foreign language. Such rites of passage in securing recognition are more expensive and time-consuming than acquiring the appropriate external appearance. On the other hand there is the powerful democracy of the credit card; if people have the means (or even if they don't) most social doors are opened. But for those who interpret this as the final victory of democracy it needs to be stressed that just as soon as the credit card opens all doors, the doors that it opens become socially less significant. Today the mechanisms of distinction operate, not through a set of difficult to acquire criteria that are tightly controlled by some dominant group; rather there has occurred what may be described as a segmentation of distinction. A plurality of different elites generate and police their own favoured codes of distinction. Social pluralism, within important economic and cultural constraints, offers choices that are not constrained by a pre-existing hierarchy. The field of conspicuous consumption has almost entirely been surrendered to transient figures from the world of popular entertainment and sports, who provide the vicarious consumption for the great mass of the population. Perhaps the post-modern condition marks the final end of distinction under the full blaze of the spotlight that now never leaves their universally distinguishable and recognizable images.

ON THE BORDERS OF MODERNITY

A distinctive feature of the history of sumptuary regulation is that it spans the transition from pre-modernity to modernity. It was an active component of the classical civilizations of Greece and Rome and was a characteristic feature of the structured hierarchies of both Europe and of China and Japan. This has led to most accounts of sumptuary regulation associating sumptuary law with pre-modernity and viewing its demise as providing evidence of the profound changes in the nature of government associated with modernization. Yet an account that is restricted to linking sumptuary regulation with pre-modernity is radically inadequate if for no other reason than that the sumptuary ethic was strongly implicated in some of the most crucial phases of the advance of urbanization and of the transition from mercantile to manufacturing capitalism. The most extensive and intensive phase of sumptuary law was to be found not only in the great Italian mercantile cities of Venice and Florence, but in the German, Dutch and English cities as they became the key sites of the next phase of capitalist development. It is possible that this conjunction was an example of uneven development; sumptuary rule was going through its death throes during precisely the same period that the distinctively modern forms of economic and social relations rose to predominance in the towns and cities of north-western Europe. The key question is whether sumptuary law was or was not closely or significantly associated with any part of those changes that were distinctively new, for if it was it will be necessary to conclude that it was not merely some residue.

The first phase of sumptuary law provided an important instance of efforts to reinforce and to legitimize the hierarchical social order of both Eastern and Western feudalisms. However, sumptuary law had a second life, one which seemed to offer a solution to one of the most difficult transitions of the modernizing process. Urbanization brought with it the problem of how it is possible to live in close physical proximity and to sustain relations of mutual dependence with strangers. Sumptuary laws attempted to provide one possible solution to this potentially traumatic dilemma. It responded to a deep-rooted concern that the participants in casual and fleeting social contact could be mutually recognizable.

One significant implication of the recognizability thesis is that sumptuary law which had previously only served the function of reproducing the social hierarchy had undergone the kind of change that Karl Renner described as a 'functional transformation' in that, with little or no change in either content or form, it had come to play a different social function (Renner 1972: 87–90). What is significant about Renner's thesis is that it draws attention to the way in which, without any change to the content of the legal rule, by virtue of changes in the other elements with which it is associated it can achieve quite different effects. Once sumptuary law ceased to be exclusively concerned with the maintenance of hierarchical relations, it became reactivated as a means of holding-out the prospect of stabilizing recognizability in the new urban world of strangers. However, while addressing an issue posed by modernity, sumptuary law never fully put aside its original association with the hierarchical principles of pre-modernity. In so doing sumptuary law sought a stabilization of appearance that was ever less realizable as the externalities of hierarchy became subject to major change and were more openly challenged. The result was that as a significant force of social regulation sumptuary law barely survived into modernity. Yet much of the reason for its flickering reappearances stems from a certain interest, always in danger of lapsing into nostalgia, in a world of recognizability.

7

Style Wars: Fashion and the Class Struggle before Classes[1]

INTRODUCTION: STYLE WARS AND CLASS STRUGGLE

The most active period of sumptuary regulation occurred between the demise of feudalism and the rise of manufacturing capitalism. That period is traversed by complex cultural, economic and political struggles. The sumptuary laws were a part of those struggles. But precisely what part they played is important and potentially controversial. Before addressing this broad question some comments are needed about the way in which notions of 'struggle' and 'class struggle' will be employed. The period under consideration is marked by competitive struggles between social interests that at the very end of the period under consideration manifest themselves as social classes. By this I mean a notion of class that involves some self-consciousness of and identification with a relatively stable configuration of economic, political and cultural interests. In order to make use of the metaphor of classes and class struggle it is necessary to insist that much of the period under consideration is characterized by what E.P. Thompson has called 'class struggle before classes' (Thompson 1978). My usage involves an intentionally broad conception of classes. It is one that makes no assumptions that 'classes' have any necessary or preconstituted unity. There are important respects in which it might be desirable to avoid the term 'class' altogether, but no other term captures the sense of emergent recognition of collective interests and separation from other social aggregates.

Class struggles, in the full sense, realize themselves in the political and economic arenas in outcomes involving reciprocal advantage and disadvantage. It is a distinctive feature of 'class struggle before classes' that, while in some ultimate sense its outcome and rewards bear fruit in political and economic terms, these are not necessarily the terms in which the struggles are fought out. Struggles waged in the name, for example, of religion are not mere ciphers of some root essence of class interests. It is therefore of the greatest importance to insist that struggles over and around symbolic capital are not themselves symbolic; that is, they are not displaced activities in which what is struggled over is more or less clearly understood by the participants to be about a more important or deeper conflict that exists, but which is not spoken of or acknowledged.

It is with these considerations in mind that I want to insist that struggles over appearance and its regulation were important. Style wars are class wars; they are made up of battles over dress, fashion and appearance. A striking feature of the great bulk of sumptuary law is that it was directed at conceptions and images of the social order. It was concerned with attempts to protect hierarchical conceptions of social relations, to resist some of the most directly visible manifestations of rising social groups either challenging or undermining the incumbents of advantaged social positions. Sumptuary laws revolved around resistance to those innovations and changes that were judged to be inconsistent with the prevalent vision of the social order. This chapter is concerned to make sense of these controversies and the regulatory interventions to which they gave rise.

The case to be developed is that sumptuary law was present during the long and uneven transition between the pre-modern and the modern world. Whether sumptuary law played any active part, either positively or negatively, in that process can only be assessed in the course of the investigation.

Some explanation is necessary of the way in which the idea of the pre-modern/modern transition is being used. The critique of the Enlightenment emanating from post-structuralist and post-modernist intellectual positions has put the very idea of modernity under a shadow. A critique of 'Modernity' (contrasted with 'modernity'), that is of a preconstituted, coherent and totalizing project, is well-founded. But the risk of sweeping aside any notion of a transition from the pre-modern to the modern is that it obliterates the profoundly important sense in which distinctively new forms of governance were directed towards 'social change', towards improvement, reform, betterment and a host of other conceptions of change. Without such conceptions it would be impossible to begin to think how it came about that new objects of governance, whether it be 'godly government', 'the population' or 'the national economy', came to be constructed and acted upon.

The issue to be decided is whether sumptuary law was a late defensive measure by the remnants of feudalism or whether it was in any way associated with the early moves towards the new projects of governance for which the term 'modernity' still serves as a useful shorthand. With a considerable number of hesitations and reservations I will be arguing that sumptuary law has an important connection with the processes of modernization. This case will be developed through the following stages. I will first examine the place of restrictions on consumption in pre-modern societies and consider their affinity to sumptuary rules. I will then criticize the most prevalent account of sumptuarism that treats it as a conservative project of declining feudalism to hold back the advance of the rising mercantile bourgeoisie. This prepares the way for an examination of the ways in which the sumptuary laws of Europe were used in the protracted engagement between the landed nobility (and the urban patrician classes) and the emergent mercantile and bourgeois classes which exhibited both intra-class and inter-class dimensions and which spanned the period from 1400 to 1800.

Restrictions on consumption before commodities

Where did the restrictions on consumption that were discursively linked with social rank or status come from? Only a few comments on this wide question need to be made for the purposes of the present inquiry. It seems sensible to set aside those rules that reinforce the distinction between the sacred and the profane as not primarily involving status. The most general point of philosophical anthropology to be made is to suggest that sumptuary restrictions only follow on from the appearance of some fragility in or challenge to some existing pattern of social differentiation. Simple economic differentiation involves some system of positive duties of a public character. Its most general form is the gift relationship and in its more specific form is to be found in the Roman patrician's obligation to lay on games, the feudal lord's duty to lay on feasts or in the expectation laid on the Venetian nobility to erect a new piazza or some other public building.[2] In the first instance the obligation to confer public benefits is not associated with the imposition of prohibitions on others. Associated with the duties attached to their social role, the privileged acquire or appropriate privileged forms of activity or consumption. Such privileges come to be the symbolic representation of a privilege asserted and a privilege recognized or conceded by others. The critical stage of development occurs when the privileged begin to impose negative restrictions on social subordinates, for example when they are denied access to the privileging practices.

A wide variety of restrictions on the use and disposal of artefacts are known to both anthropology and pre-modern history. The use and handling of sacred or ritual objects was often restricted to specified categories of persons. The manner in which things are to be disposed of may be prescribed, for example when things may pass as gifts, but are excluded from barter or other forms of trade. Certain types of objects can be reserved for identified categories of persons. Two different types of such restrictions are illustrated among the Lozi of Zimbabwe where fly-whisks made from the eland are 'kingly things' whose use and possession is restricted to royal persons;[3] in contrast the royal monopoly in elephant tusks is a restriction upon 'economic' dealings in these items (Gluckman 1983). Although these are not Gluckman's terms we can distinguish between a royal privilege and a royal monopoly.

Mary Douglas offers a functional analysis of such exclusionary norms and customs. She distinguishes between two main functions: the first is to provide conditions for entry into high-status positions, and the second is to reduce or even eliminate competition in the interest of a fixed pattern of status (Douglas 1967). The problem with functionalist accounts is that they tend to assume as settled that which is most problematic. Status restrictions on consumption 'work' when the social relations to which they relate are widely accepted or internalized by those who would otherwise regard themselves as disadvantaged. Only where a hierarchical status system is stable, that is its normative presuppositions are widely internalized and there is little or no resistance, do hierarchic rules concerning consumption contribute to the continuing reproduction of these hierarchic relations. The most that we can say is that hierarchic consumption rules may provide a mechanism of ideological reinforcement; if some high status category has exclusive entitlement to consume or use some resource then this confirms and underlines their social superiority.

The more difficult problem is, given the ubiquitous nature of these hierarchic consumption norms, how and why do some of them find their way into a specifically legal form, as sumptuary laws? Is this simply a natural extension of the fact of hierarchical social ordering? Or, alternatively, is hierarchic sumptuary law evidence of the failure or breakdown of non-legal hierarchical social ordering? There are two general claims to be advanced. First, sumptuary laws played no significant part during the formative period of hierarchic social order. Second, sumptuary laws do not figure significantly until hierarchical social orders come under serious pressure.

My contention that sumptuary laws were not present in the formative period of hierarchic social order requires some comment. In a literal sense it is simply not true; there were sumptuary rules in a number of the ancient civilizations. What is significant is that they were not only few in number, but were decidedly random. For example, in Egypt there were restrictive rules about the wearing of sandals, but there seems to have been no other appearential regulation. It seems reasonable to conclude that the reproduction of the specific social hierarchies were not dependent to any significant degree upon sumptuary ordering.

More important for my case is that in the high period of European feudalism, while there was some sumptuary law, it was infrequent and patchy. On the contrary, sumptuary laws only become apparent as the feudal order waned. It is only in late feudalism or bastard feudalism that sumptuary laws became frequent and widespread. Thus in England the first major pieces of sumptuary legislation appeared in the mid-fourteenth century and only became a regular feature of legislative activity in the later fifteenth and early sixteenth century.[4] In Russia it was not until the later stage of Russian feudalism that sumptuary laws began to make their appearance in the eighteenth century and then it was very much conceived as a component of a Westernizing project. The picture is very similar in Japan: it was not until after classical Japanese feudalism had fallen at the end of the sixteenth century that sumptuary law became significant. The high period of sumptuary law in Japan was in the Tokugawa period with a large body of legislation between 1649 and 1793.[5] While in feudal Japan there had been episodic sumptuary interventions, during the bureaucratized feudalism of the Tokugawa period the defining characteristic of the mass of sumptuary regulation was what Hearn aptly called its 'ferocity of detail' (Hearn 1904: 187).

My second thesis, that sumptuary law did not come into its own until fixed status hierarchies were challenged from below, follows from the foregoing claim that sumptuary law should be regarded as a late-feudal or even post-feudal phenomenon. In its simplest form it was the merchant classes that induced the rise of sumptuary regulation. It is only with the rise of mercantile capitalism that sumptuary laws became a regular feature of the governance of social order. The most obvious inference to be drawn is that sumptuary law was an expression of a conservative defence of a hierarchical social order whose mode of existence came to be threatened by the rise of new economic and social forces. Furthermore it was an attempt to mount a defence of the old order that, quite simply, came too late. Sumptuary law was a case of the proverbial attempt to shut the stable gate after the horse had bolted.

There is undoubtedly a substantial kernel of truth in this interpretation. I will explore some of its more important dimensions below. Before doing so I want to introduce an important qualification. This alternative thesis is that the conservative defence of hierarchy thesis is not sufficient to explain the more significant fact that sumptuary laws survived the demise of the old nobility.

The conservation of stable status systems?

The most frequently encountered view of sumptuary law is that it was one of the mechanisms by which the rigidly stratified social societies of pre-modernity protected their hierarchical structure from the vicissitudes of change. Daniel Miller provides a neat formulation of this widely held view:

> In a period of strong social stratification, objects tend to reflect given social hierarchies. At such a time, sumptuary laws may be passed which forbid the use of particular goods to those who are deemed to be below a certain station in life.
>
> (Miller 1987: 135)

In the language of a related theoretical tradition, sumptuary laws freeze and reproduce 'social distance'. Max Weber, for example, applied the term 'social closure' to any practice that aimed at the monopolization of social rewards by a group of eligibles against those outside the group. The grounds of such exclusionary practices have been varied: age, sex, ethnicity, religion, language, nationality and colour being the most frequent.

T.H. Marshall, in his classic paper on citizenship and social class, provides the following formulation of the mechanics of social closure:

> When a section of society is threatened by invasion from below . . . they protect themselves by constructing barriers out of those attributes and symbols of social difference which are the most difficult to acquire. Conspicuous expenditure can be copied by those who get rich quick, but correct manners, the right accent, the 'old school tie' are esoteric mysteries and jealously guarded monopolies.
>
> (Marshall 1963: 195–96)

What is suggestive in Marshall's formulation is the idea that attempts to regulate conspicuous consumption are fundamentally undermined once those below acquire the means to engage in direct competition with those seeking to shore up social barriers. Ferdinand Tönnies captured the link between closure and fashion: 'Fashion is the incessantly rebuilt barrier by which high society takes pains to shut itself off from the middle stratum in society' (Tönnies 1961: 121). This leads to the thesis that sumptuary laws become displaced from direct consumption into fields of what may be called 'symbolic distinction', forms of cultural capital whose acquisition requires the expenditure of conspicuous 'leisure' that often turns out to be 'work'. In this process a shift of great importance occurs. Social distance comes increasingly to feature 'tests' that are powerful precisely because they are not formalized (for example, the test of using the 'proper' accent is by its nature informal and thus remains invisible to those against whom it is deployed). Once the criteria of social rank shift from economic to cultural tests, then such tests can no longer be inscribed in legislative form. Class competition decreasingly took a form that relied, to any significant degree, upon appearential ordering and thus in which sumptuary legislation played any major part. In other words, sumptuary law did not so much fail as change its form – it moved from the arena of public legislation to that of private governance.

While Foucault would not generally be considered as being concerned with social closure, his account of the rise of normalization describes a related process. He draws attention to the way in which distinctive signs expressing status, privilege and affiliation (for example, noble versus commoner, amateur versus professional) tend to be replaced, or at least supplemented, by a whole ladder of normalization, the rungs of which serve to classify, hierarchize and distribute social rank. In his account of the interconnection between urbanization and the growth of his expanded conception of policing, Foucault provides an interesting formulation. The aims of early policing were twofold: they provided the city with adornment and splendour, and they fostered working and trading relations. In this conception policing is conceived as a form of rational intervention wielding political power over citizens by controlling all forms of 'communication' (work, production, exchange and accommodation):

> In short, life is the object of the police: the indispensable, the useful, and the superfluous.
>
> (Foucault 1981: 250)

While Foucault almost certainly did not have sumptuary law in mind, it is clear that the idea of the policing of 'the superfluous' captures to perfection the interventionist role of the early modern city fathers in appointing, as they did in Italian cities of the Renaissance, special magistrates and paying informers to pursue the display of the superfluous finery by the citizenry.[6]

Chandra Mukerji argues a closely related position when she suggests that European sumptuary law emerged, first in Italy and then in England, at the precise time when Burgundian fashion was beginning to spread and to create the first true 'fashion'. Thus early sumptuary legislation was an attempt to 'reimpose by legislation the medieval codes of dress that were being threatened by the first signs of modern fashion' (Mukerji 1983: 180). My resistance to Mukerji's account is that the content of early sumptuary legislation cannot be understood as an attempt to reimpose prior dress codes. On the contrary, they were attempts to produce some stabilization in the use of the cloths, materials and ornamentation techniques that were the material manifestations of the 'invention' of fashion. The ancient and medieval sumptuary rules were unstructured and episodic. The 'modern' systematic sumptuary laws that first emerged in the late thirteenth century were, as I have tried to show, a response to the emerging crisis of the old order. True they were motivated by a concern to preserve the appearential cultural capital of the nobility, but their most general characteristic was to monopolize the fashions that were coming into existence rather than to reimpose a previous dress code.

These considerations lead to the conclusion that there was more to sumptuary law than the attempt to impose a legislative freeze on an existing social hierarchy. Instead sumptuary law should be understood as a manifestation of the crisis of the old order, an attempt to sustain social advantages that were already being threatened. König connects this theme of class relations to fashion as the motive for legislative intervention:

> The strict class order of society thus knew only differentiation, but not imitation; at the earliest imitation occurred only when the existing social order began to disintegrate. We therefore cannot claim that the principal origin of fashion should be traced to the class structure in that the lower estates imitated the upper ones, thus forcing them to change their style of dress continuously. Imitation started only when the class order began to break up.
>
> (König 1973: 99)

It is to a more detailed examination of the processes involved in this rearguard action that I now turn.

THE NOBILITY RESISTS THE ADVANCING MERCHANTS

The most general indicator of the emergence of any sustained attempt at sumptuary regulation was the appearance of an expanding class of merchants, a process that went hand in hand with monetarization and commodification. As money, rather than the ownership or control of land, becomes the indicator of wealth, the nobilities come to conceive of the merchants as a potential threat to the supremacy of the landed interest. Sumptuary laws came into play when social distance was beginning to 'close' as when an emergent class closed in on a declining class (Gies 1978: 18–22). Rodney Hilton, in discussing the decline of the English landed nobility, focuses on a general pattern of apparent upward mobility during the fifteenth century:

> The chief manifestation of this mobility was that the old landed aristocracy . . . was being penetrated from below by merchants and other rich commoners. This was why it was necessary to sharpen the definition of social boundaries as was done in sumptuary legislation.
>
> (Hilton 1990: 173)

Care should be taken over the 'penetration from below' thesis in the light of the work of Lawrence Stone that, albeit for a slightly later period than that discussed by Hilton, throws doubt on the idea that the English landed aristocracy survived by cynically incorporating mercantile wealth and genes into its ranks (Stone 1967; L. and J. Stone 1984). For present purposes it is sufficient to insist on two related features: first, a relative decline of the landed aristocracy *vis-à-vis* the other social classes and, second, a general demographic mobility of the whole of the lower classes. These processes gave rise to a widespread social preoccupation on the part of the upper classes with an anxiety that the social order was in danger.

We can leave the specific dynamics of these class relations open. It is sufficient to note that their general form involved a declining rentier aristocracy conceiving of itself as threatened by an urban mercantile bourgeoisie. The struggle surrounding the appearential ordering was, quite literally, fuelled by the expansion in the availability of ever more varied and sumptuous cloths, jewels and the wherewithal to fight the battle for distinction. This was brought within reach by the spread and extension of trade by merchants who flourished as a direct result of the conspicuous consumption of the nobility. It is significant that it was precisely this recently created luxury market that became economically significant.[7] This dynamic is illustrated in Toulouse where the rise of the new urban mercantile elite produced a defensive sumptuary response from the nobility in 1550 when the 'parlement' forbade non-nobles from wearing silk (Schneider 1989: 26–27).

In the light of these features of the relationship between the landed nobility and the urban merchant classes the sumptuary legislation that spanned the late medieval and the early modern period can best be understood as a 'weak' attempt to sustain a previous social advantage. In this view sumptuary law is seen as a 'weak' response of a declining class in that, however fervently and passionately change is resisted, it was already too late in that the social forces that were the bearers of social change (e.g. trade, commerce, money, commodities, etc.) were already in existence. Marilyn Horn captures the fate of a declining nobility:

> When a ruling class finds itself unable to maintain its position of fashion supremacy through the control of wealth, it often restricts the consumption of the lesser citizen through the enactment of sumptuary laws.
>
> (Horn 1968: 206)

An impressive application of this model is provided in Donald Shively's account of Japanese sumptuary law. His is a sophisticated account that manages to avoid the arrogance of modernism that treats the projects of sumptuary regulation with disdain (Shively 1964–65). The most active period of sumptuary regulation was during the Tokugawa period, from 1600–1868.[8] The order of social classes was written into the system as being essential to the structure of the regime, but what distinguished the legislation of this period from, for example, the classical Chinese hierarchic model, was that the law betrayed, both directly and indirectly, a consciousness that the real target was the increasing economic power of the urban merchants.

Japanese sumptuary law reflects back the class struggle between the samurai and the merchants. While the merchants were advancing their economic position, the samurai were dependent upon fixed incomes and were relatively disadvantaged during this extended period of commodification and monetarization (Reischauer and Fairbank 1958). This manifests itself clearly in the regulation of the closely linked fields of prostitution and the theatre. It was in the 'districts of pleasure' more than in any other arena of social life where money, and not status, was paramount.

Shively places heavy emphasis on the primacy of samurai resentment of arrogant merchants. Since this sentiment could have an adverse effect on the morale of the samurai class, and since they were in an important sense the base for the Tokugawa order, the government had a strong interest in prescribing a proper correspondence between status and consumption. The first comprehensive set of prohibitions affecting *chonin* (merchants and town dwellers) in 1649 prohibited the finer grades of silk, the use of gold lacquer and gold or silver leaf in house interiors or on household articles and saddles.

Japanese sumptuary law included distinctive spatial dimensions. There was detailed regulation of the geographical distribution of the different social classes within the castle-towns, with the higher classes on more elevated land. Thus social distance was minutely reproduced in both spatial distance and in the social visibility of rank. Another distinctive feature of Japanese law was its preoccupation with the regulation of the theatre. From the beginning of the seventeenth century strenuous efforts were made to regulate the popular *kabuki* theatre. Shively suggests that this revealed a fear that if merchants were able to give cultural expression to their growing wealth, manifest in the extraordinary sumptuousness of costumes and sets, this 'would excite the envy of the theoretically superior samurai' (Shively 1955: 344):[9]

> It is generally under circumstances of this type, when changing economic conditions are affecting the relationships in a carefully ordered society, that the government will attempt to maintain the distinctions between classes by issuing sumptuary laws.
>
> (Shively 1964–65: 124)

A distinctive feature of Japanese sumptuary legislation that was largely absent from European sumptuary law was the attention paid to restrictions placed upon the direct producers. As the producers of the wealth, especially rice, on which the system depended for both consumption and as the medium of exchange, the peasantry were ordered to lead a life of severe limitation. For example, in order to conserve rice they were forbidden to make or drink sake and they were forbidden to ride horses or oxen which were to be reserved for cultivation. They were legally enjoined to show respect for their superiors. Efforts were also made to immunize farmers from outside influence; for example, merchants were forbidden to enter villages, many articles were banned from sale to villagers, they were forbidden books to discourage education, and were prohibited from owning weapons.

Other cases in which sumptuary law was used expressly against the merchant classes to inhibit their capacity to compete with an established dominant hierarchy occurred. The early Scottish sumptuary act of 1457 seemed to select merchants as its particular target; they were banned from wearing marten furs, silk or scarlet cloth, and their wives were restricted to short kerchiefs for their headdresses (APS II: 49: *c.* 11, 13). Three centuries later in Turkey at the end of the eighteenth century a renewed attempt was made by Selim III to use dress regulations to mark social estates; for example, merchants were forbidden to wear furs, these being reserved for state functionaries (Karpat 1973: 86).

A rather different picture with regard to the treatment of merchants emerges in the English sumptuary legislation. The first major statute of apparel in 1363 was in many respects the most systematic. The 'Statute Concerning Diet and Apparel' (37 Edw. III: *cc.* 8–14; SR 1: 380–81) devoted a chapter to each of seven social groups. Merchants were dealt with alongside the other urban categories citizens and handicraftsmen through the strategy of fixing their social status, and thus their clothing, by the imposition of a linkage between their wealth and the annual rents of the minor landed gentry (esquires and gentlemen). Urban dwellers possessing goods to the value of £1000 were treated the same as gentry with annual rents of £200, and merchants worth £500 were placed on the same sumptuary level as gentry worth £100 a year.

Some commentators have interpreted this provision as seriously discriminating against townspeople by noting the 5:1 monetary ratio (Harte 1976: 134–35; Miller 1928: 89–90). This is unwarranted because the figures compare different values (capital versus annual rents). It seems likely that these figures represent fairly similar disposable incomes. What needs to be noted is that at this very early stage in the development of the English merchant class their sumptuary entitlements were pegged at the level of the lower gentry, that is the merchants were slotted into the rural hierarchy.

The subsequent legislation departs from this model. Specific criteria that relate to the different sources of income of the gentry and merchants disappear from the subsequent acts of apparel. Exactly a century after the 1363 statute came the second apparel statute. While providing more detailed differentiation within the landed nobility it treated urban wealth fairly even-handedly by imposing the same restrictions on all those in possession of an annual income of £40 (3 Edw. IV: *c.* 5; SR 2: 399–402). In addition specific provision was made for urban officials (mayors, sheriffs, aldermen) who were given the same privileges as specified grades of knights and the lower gentry. As sumptuary enactments came more regularly over the next century, with major sumptuary enactments in 1483, 1510, 1514, 1515, 1533 and 1553, attention to the regulation of the rapidly expanding merchant class disappeared below the visible surface of the legislation.[10] These statutes became increasingly dominated by the attempt to inscribe precise differentiations between the upper nobility as new ranks and subdivisions were created. This suggests that the preoccupation was to restrict intra-class competition within the nobility, and this will be discussed in the next section. The second feature is that the imprecise categories of 'esquire' and 'gentleman' became courtesy titles and sumptuary gradations increasingly were imposed on the basis of annual income from lands rather than by rank or title. While the values specified varied somewhat, there was a fairly standard gradation between rent values of £100, £40 and £20. The statutory provisions make no reference to how urban categories, many of whom would not be classifiable under these categories, were to be treated.

Two alternative interpretations suggest themselves. By making no express provision for urban criteria merchants were dropped below the level of the gentry and were thereby reduced to the level of rural yeoman farmers and urban artisans who were denied most sumptuary refinements. This seems unlikely since it is probable that the attempt to impose such a sharp degradation ceremony upon the merchant classes would have elicited complaints and resistance such as to leave its trace in the historical record, and there is no such evidence. This view is supported by the fact that just one in this series of statutes, that of 1515 (7 Hen. VIII: *c.* 6; SR 3: 179–82), does return briefly to stipulating an equation of land rents and possessions (an annual rent of £10 is equated to possession of goods valued at £100). The second interpretation is that the thrust of English sumptuary legislation became increasingly concerned with the intra-class relations within the landed nobles and gentry and for this reason became less and less concerned with inter-class regulation of the rising merchant bourgeoisie. The gradual disappearance of any specific reference to merchant categories, the continued protection of the interests of urban officials, and the increasingly narrow subdivisions within the ranks of the nobility all support this view.[11] The interpretation advanced above is somewhat disrupted by the complaints and diatribes that urged renewed sumptuary legislation and more rigorous enforcement and, as we have seen, complained about the difficulty of recognizing social rank. These discourses have the social disorder of the urban street as their most frequent point of reference. This does not undermine the importance of intra-class regulation, but is simply evidence that all projects of governance are multivocal in stitching together different discursive elements.

Conclusive interpretation is significantly handicapped by the lack of information about the patterns of enforcement of English sumptuary legislation, a topic that will be explored in more detail in Chapter 13. There was certainly no sustained targeting of the pretensions of the merchants, who experienced an expansion in their numbers and their individual and collective wealth during the sixteenth century which was the most fertile period of sumptuary legislative activity. Had the mercantile bourgeoisie been the primary target it seems reasonable to infer that any such targeting would be discernible. If sumptuary law was less concerned with holding back the merchants than the orthodox account suggests, then it is necessary to examine more closely the role of sumptuary law in the regulation of intra-class relations.

THE NOBILITY REGULATES ITSELF? SUMPTUARY LAW AND INTRA-CLASS RELATIONS

The evidence to support the conventional thesis that sumptuary laws were a device promoted by the declining nobility to ward off the competitive encroachments of a rising merchant bourgeoisie is at best ambiguous. Is the evidence any better to support the thesis that sumptuary laws were a form of intra-class regulation, by which the nobility sought to reduce competition within its own ranks? It would be unwise to pursue a simple reversal of the conventional thesis that the nobles used sumptuary legislation to restrain competition from the merchants. It seems intuitively more attractive to explore the view that sumptuary law exhibited both inter-class and intra-class dimensions. Within hierarchical orders, in particular in the case of European feudalism, the intra-class dimension took the form of 'rivalry' that exists within and between the upper fractions of the feudal order.

The inter-class dimension involves 'competition' between the rising mercantile bourgeoisie and the feudal nobility and gentry. The feudal nobility underwent a major transformation of their economic circumstances. They more or less rapidly became a rentier class and became separated from any immediate involvement in productive activity and thus shifted their mode of existence to one orientated towards a changed preoccupation with consumption for its own sake. It is precisely under these conditions that fashion itself became a 'way of life'. This fundamental shift occurred at much the same time as the merchant class was expanding during the commercial revolution of the late Middle Ages. For the nobility there existed a concern to distinguish themselves from the lower classes and to pursue the internal 'rivalry' within the upper classes. Indeed it is likely that the internal rivalry was more important than the inter-class competition. The nobility exhausted themselves on conspicuous consumption whilst the new forces of the bourgeoisie had meanwhile occupied one economic position after another.

Bourdieu provides an important opening:

> The field of cultural production is the area par excellence of clashes between the dominant fraction of the dominant class . . . and the dominated fractions who are totally involved in this struggle.
>
> (Bourdieu 1980: 285)

Bourdieu's own focus is on the realms of 'high culture', but it seems entirely plausible to apply this idea of an ongoing struggle within the dominant class over all forms of cultural practices, including the fields of dress and fashion. The very indirectness and ambiguity of the language of fashion made it possible for subordinate fractions to challenge the dominant in ways that did not have to be fully confrontational. There is always a contest between those who have 'made it' and 'aspirants' who aspire to 'make their name'. One of the classical forms of this confrontation, whether in high culture or in fashion, was that between 'classicism' or 'traditionalism' and 'innovation'. All of this seems to have very considerable potential for an understanding of the dynamic of the struggles over appearance and its regulation. There is an important temporal dimension to the struggles in the cultural field. Struggles over appearance and fashion can fruitfully be grasped as attempts to stamp an identity on the present, to be 'in fashion'.

Irving Goffman took a different cut into these issues. If class is manifest in a specific system of class symbols that always encounter the problem of misrepresentation or misappropriation, this generates the necessity for 'restrictive devices', that is for the cultivation of restrictions exemplified in the acquisition of 'taste' acquired through long immersion in non-remunerative pursuits such as the acquisition of a foreign language. This mechanism is the process that Veblen called vicarious leisure. The existence of such restrictive mechanisms provoked routine methods of subversion. For example, the English 'public schools' inculcated the attributes of the aristocracy into the middle class. Status attributes that were once unchallenged become exhausted or find themselves in competition with new sources of status as part of a long process in which 'blood' comes to be replaced by the fascinating term 'breeding', that while carrying connotations of genetic inheritance is strictly a cultural acquisition whose dependence on wealth is real but repressed.

Goffman describes the exhaustion of distinction in the following terms:

> It is therefore common for a whole class of persons to find themselves with symbols and expectations which their economic and social position can no longer support.
>
> (Goffman 1951: 303)

A declining class is forced to rely more and more upon symbols that do not involve current outlay; but this in turn operates to lower the value of these symbols in the eyes of others. It follows from this that class symbols are not static, but are subject to processes of circulation, both upward and downward. Important agents in these circulatory activities are those that Goffman calls 'curator groups', such as domestic servants, tailors, interior decorators and others who function to preserve and perpetuate a set of class symbols in which they are expert, but are not themselves entitled to use. The twentieth century has witnessed a paradoxical 'democratization' of class cultural capital; under the label 'the rich and famous', an elite drawn mainly from the entertainment industries secure self-promotion by exposing its life-style to a mass audience while to other elites such people lack any credible distinction.

Almost all of the discussion of the symbolic dimension of class relations is premissed on the existence of a single hierarchy. Such a view has a decreasing applicability to the pluralization of hierarchies characteristic of the twentieth century. This matter need not detain us long since my concerns are with an earlier period; it is, however, worth commenting that Bourdieu's concept of 'distinction' has a utility that goes beyond his own application. The concept 'distinction' helps to make sense of the competitions between the different sections of the privileged to secure their advantage. It was Max Weber who suggested that in 'patrician cities' such as Venice the form of political domination often involved:

> the simultaneous preservation of very strict mutual control of the noble families over each other.
>
> (Weber 1978: II: 1271)

There does seems to be evidence that the Council of Ten were much preoccupied with the supervision of the nobility itself (Pullan 1973). The most persistent strand of sumptuary law was in significant measure concerned with the self-regulation of the patrician class. This is a case in which the boundary between a dress code and a uniform is difficult to determine (Lane 1973). The *veste patrizia* consisted of cumbersome ornate robes and incorporated a complex colour code demarcating different ranks and governmental roles. The *veste* started out as the everyday wear of the patrician class, but it became increasingly unpopular and unfashionable. The dress code was repeated more strenuously as time went by, and more draconian punishments were stipulated, at one point rising to the threat of five years' imprisonment (Andrieux 1972; Rowdon 1970: 20).

Self-regulation poses special problems with regard to enforcement. All commentators emphasize that the enforcement of the *veste patrizia* was lax. But since the patrician class had a large measure of control over the content of the dress code in force, why would they increase the severity of the sanction and then not bother to enforce it? It is far from clear that even any symbolic benefit could accrue. Any further pursuit of a more satisfactory answer would need a much closer engagement with the history and social structure of Venice than I can offer. The long-run solution was that the *veste patrizia* becomes fully a uniform to be worn only on ceremonial occasions. The generality of Venetian sumptuary law was significantly egalitarian; almost the only trace of class differentiation is to be found in the penalties prescribed. Gentlemen were often subject to heavier fines than plebeians, although the latter were subjected to summary justice (Newett

1907: 249). I have no evidence as to whether this resulted in differential class enforcement.

In Nürnberg the early sumptuary legislation was directed primarily at the established merchant classes. During the course of the fifteenth century it was extended to the lesser trades and, eventually, to artisans and apprentices. Fines specified for patrician offenders were routinely heavy, but such provisions need to be read in the context of enforcement practices that pervasively seem to have favoured the patrician classes (Strauss 1966).[12] By the late seventeenth century dress ordinances in Nürnberg had become more class specific. Extravagance was still the target, but now there were different standards for different social ranks (Greenfield 1918).

In the non-urban and economically underdeveloped Sicily of the sixteenth century the political representatives of the nobility seem to have realized that competitive consumption was harming their mutual interests by depleting their limited resources. Accordingly it was their representatives in Parliament who petitioned the monarchical government for sumptuary regulation. The result was a general sumptuary ordinance which banned the use of gold and silver in clothing, prohibited silk in liveries, restricted the number of carriages, and imposed a limit of two grooms and three pages per noble. There is some suggestion that one concern was to ensure sufficient labour for agricultural purposes (Smith 1968). It is interesting to note that these measures sparked a demonstration from tradesmen and artisans complaining that these sumptuary restrictions were causing unemployment. This example raises an interesting issue, namely the possibility that the representatives of a class play a strategic role that conflicts with the immediate interests of the class; it is likely that many Sicilian nobles resented and resisted restrictions placed upon their conspicuous consumption. I am reminded of Marx's discussion of factory legislation in which the interests of capital 'in general' conflict with the immediate interests of individual capitalists.

Rather than attempting to restrict competition within the nobility, the practices of the French court, especially during the reign of Louis XIV, are frequently referred to as being designed to foster competition among the court nobility. Many accounts suggest that royal policy encouraged conspicuous consumption in order to dissipate wealth that might otherwise have been used to challenge royal power. The conventional account claims that the French nobility deployed all their assets and worked their way ever deeper into debt. These accounts seem to have an apocryphal flavour and I am hesitant to place much reliance upon them.

There is, on balance, insufficient evidence to conclude with much confidence that sumptuary legislation was widely used as a means of imposing self-regulation upon a dominant class. That it was used in this way is not in doubt, but it is far from clear whether there was any general pattern. What is significant is that both the general theses examined thus far, namely that sumptuary law was used to head off competition from below and that it was concerned to regulate the internal relations of the dominant bloc, find some supporting evidence, but insufficient to attribute any strong claim concerning their generality. A third possibility that will now be explored is that sumptuary regulation was an early expression of bourgeois power involving a general conception of the desirability of appearential ordering and a desire to impose limitations on the cultural and political pretensions of the nobility.

THE BOURGEOISIE STRIKES BACK

A decisive component of the urban experience was the emergence of an internal class differentiation whose first expression involved the emergence of patrician families distinguished by both wealth and a socially appropriate style of life, revolving around hospitality and conspicuous consumption (Weber 1978: II: 1239–40). This suggests the possibility of a dual motive for sumptuary regulation: first, on the part of patricians to preserve their distinctive life-style and, second, for non-patrician regimes often preoccupied with securing solidarity against external political authorities, to make use of sumptuary laws as constraints on the privileged patricians in the interests of urban unity.

In attempting to understand the part played by sumptuary law in the class and other struggles that traversed the beginnings of modernity it is desirable to avoid a static model in which sumptuary law is conceived of as simply playing the role of reproducing pre-modern patterns of social relations (Blanshei 1976; Pirenne 1956). It is important to go beyond the simple imitation model that assumes that subordinate classes and strata inevitably imitate their 'betters'. What is needed to supplement this account is the development of the idea of transformative emulation. Such a conception may provide a means of encompassing a more dynamic view of competitive processes to include a transcendent emulation that changes or modifies the criteria, whether economic or cultural, of social status. The important idea is that a rising social class distinguishes its own aspirations from the embedded values of an old order and comes, haltingly at first, to find the means of articulating the values, symbols and practices of a new way of life. There emerged a distinctively bourgeois pattern of consumption, in which the merchant class did not merely imitate the nobility, but came to adopt new patterns of cultural consumption along with the espousal of the more extensively studied new valuations of work and economic activity. For Bourdieu:

> struggles for recognition are a fundamental dimension of social life and what is at stake in them is the accumulation of a particular form of capital, honour in the sense of reputation and prestige, and that there is, therefore, a specific logic behind the accumulation of symbolic capital, as capital founded on cognition [connaissance] and recognition [reconnaissance].
>
> (Bourdieu 1990: 22)

In the first place it is clear that the early modern merchants and burghers were not opposed to the project of imposing an appearential order. As Lofland comments, the burgher classes were not ideologically opposed to the visible display of status distinctions (1973: 57). Greenfield goes further: he notes that by the end of the fourteenth century the representatives of the craft guilds had secured representation in the city government in Nürnberg and now sat alongside the patricians, and even became burgomasters. The significant result was that:

> any sumptuary law which bound the rising commercial class – covetous of high station, and as sumptuous in display as the gentry – were of the merchants' own making.
>
> (Greenfield 1918: 25)

A century later, in the compendious 'Wedding Manual' of 1485, the Preamble was at pains to stress that the regulations were to be applied to all, not just the well-to-do, and were to be observed without distinction. It was not until the early sixteenth century that anxiety came to be expressed about the obliteration of social distinctions, with the result that the sumptuary laws paid increasing attention to maintaining the lines of class stratification and the regulations imposed discrimination along the lines of social rank (Greenfield 1918: 51).

An interesting illustration of a bourgeois commitment to some version of the sumptuary project is provided by the case of colonial America. In the New England colonies a wide-ranging sumptuary regulation was instituted similar to that which had only been recently abandoned or repealed in England not long before the colonists had embarked for the New World. Yet what was erected in Massachusetts Bay and in Connecticut was not a pale imitation of a European model.[13] The sumptuary regime in the American colonies provides confirmation that, radical though the religious breach often was with England, the colonists brought with them highly conventional views about the social structure. Puritan theology, as codified in the 'Larger Catechism of the Westminster Confession of Faith', involved a hierarchical interpretation of the Fifth Commandment, 'Honour thy Father and thy Mother':

> By father and mother . . . are meant not only natural parents, but all superiors in age and gifts; as especially such as, by God's ordinance, are over us in place of authority, whether in family, church, or commonwealth.
>
> (1647: S. 124)

These attitudes were reflected in the prevailing views on social appearance. The magistrates and deputies of Massachusetts in 1651 prohibited the appearential signifiers of the status of gentlemen to 'men and women of mean condition, educations, and callings' (Shurtleff 1968: III: 243).

The sumptuary laws in New England led to an inescapable tension. On the one hand, the godly were enjoined to work diligently and to show themselves through their work, while on the other hand, sumptuary law sought to perpetuate a static, premodern, social hierarchy (North 1974). What North fails to see is that there was an attempt to address this tension within sumptuary law. In both New England and much earlier in Europe, there was a progressive move away from the definition of social position by blood towards the 'new' economic criterion of 'income'. By 1651 Massachusetts Bay was prohibiting gold or silver lace, gold or silver buttons, silk hoods, etc. to all those whose annual income was less than £200 (Shammas 1990: 218). The interesting question would be to determine what sections of the middle class were thereby included and which excluded; around that boundary tensions might be visible and resistance generated. In addition, exemptions were granted to those below this economic position who were holders of public office or with education or employment 'above the ordinary degree'. This suggests that many of the respectable and governing persons had a lower income than that specified. In England in an earlier period income gradations had, as we have seen above, been used to impose sumptuary boundaries based on annual rents or the cash value of possessions.

Joan Kent's fascinating study of the attitudes of Elizabethan Parliamentarians toward personal regulation throws light on the paradoxes of the projects of sumptuary regulation (Kent 1973). There was a widespread preparedness to regulate the lower orders, but there was much more outspoken opposition to attempts to impose regulation on the upper classes. One key disagreement revolved around where the appropriate boundaries or cut-offs should be. What was going on, I suggest, was a complex juggling for relative class advantage; in the name of the protection of the social hierarchy each class fraction sought to protect its own relative advantages and to prevent encroachment from its competitors. It is, however, significant that there is no reference in Kent's account of any talk of the need for self-restraint on the part of the upper classes.

Thus far it looks pretty much as if the broad picture is one in which, when bourgeois classes secured or participated in political power, they were happy to take over, largely unchanged, the presuppositions and practices surrounding sumptuary regulation. There is even some evidence that the commercial classes had a special affinity for sumptuary interventions. Italy provides an interesting case study since there was a considerable alternation of political power between patrician and burgher classes (Pullan 1973; Blanshei 1976).

Florence more than any other Italian city exemplifies a sequence of sharp struggles between a merchant class and an older nobility. During the brief rule of the artisanal guilds in Florence in the 1290s and again briefly after the Ciompi revolt in 1378, there was a bout of restrictive legislation against the patrician classes; they were required to take oaths of obedience to the commune and to pay heavy bonds to guarantee good behaviour (Schevill 1936: Trexler 1984). From the late thirteenth century during periods when the commune was dominated by the guilds, in particular by the merchant guilds (*arti maggiori*), legislation, both fiscal and sumptuary, was directed against the upper classes or magnates who were conceived of as 'unruly', a term suggesting both a threat to the existing order, as well as notions of disorderly and profligate conduct. Taxes were accordingly imposed on property rather than income and various restrictions were imposed on consumption. For example, in 1281 the commune enacted restrictions on the size of funeral candles and palls. These provisions seemed also to have a fiscal motive. Exemptions from these funerary restrictions later began to be sold by the commune and during the first eight years of this practice, over 233 exemptions were purchased, probably mainly by notables since funerals were very much a matter of displaying status (Strocchia 1989: 135–37).

Diane Hughes suggests that much of Florence's regulation of dress should be understood as a curb on aristocratic display, but which at the same time established appearential restraint as a 'symbol of republican virtue' (Hughes 1983: 74). A statute of 1356 launched a fierce attack on the 'arrogance' of the Florentine patricians, the *magnati*. Under another ordinance patricians were excluded from holding public office. Family heads were required to post bonds as security for good behaviour of family members; heavy penalties were imposed upon any *magnati* adjudged to have injured or insulted a commoner. Limits were imposed on the number of wedding guests. Rainey suggests that this should be regarded as a 'public order' measure since weddings often degenerated into unruly displays of the rivalries between the great Florentine families. Rainey further argues that the sumptuary dress regulations themselves were not aimed at the patrician class since they were all knights and thereby exempt from most of the regulations concerning dress, weddings and other ceremonies. He regards the early Florentine sumptuary legislation as being designed to keep wealthy commoners, *popolani*, from behaving like magnates (Rainey 1985: 141–42).

A similarly protracted struggle occurred in Siena between *popolani* and *magnati*; both had periods in power during which they imposed sumptuary laws. A similar concern with repressing the display of wealth by the patrician class probably underlaid the infrequent sumptuary interventions. Between 1277 and 1355 a period of self-conscious merchant power was embodied in the 'Council of Nine' that excluded any representation from the nobility. Merchant power expressed itself in some major sumptuary legislation which was increasingly directed against the aristocracy by specifically prohibiting materials dear to the patricians (Hughes 1983: 73).

In the Netherlands at a later period the most significant developments were the Amsterdam ordinance of 1655 restricting marriage feasts, and that in 1672 against 'unnecessary and sumptuous banquets'. These elaborate and extended feasts were often highly sensitive; while they were often a major component of social solidarity they easily spilled over, particularly in times of crisis, into occasions for class envy and social disorder. It was under these circumstances that the Regents of Dutch towns occasionally invoked sumptuary restrictions on the duration and size of banquets (Schama 1987: 182).

It seems safe to conclude that where bourgeois interests held legislative power they used this power to impose sumptuary restrictions or fiscal burdens on the patrician classes, but this needs to be understood in a context in which there was a widely shared ideological consensus about the desirability of sumptuary regulation that cut across class and religious boundaries. In contrast, despotic and aristocratic governments were less inclined to engage in sumptuary activity. Milan, after a brief period of democratic rule in the thirteenth century, was ruled thereafter as a dukedom, when there was far less sumptuary regulation than in its more democratic neighbours and competitors; one sumptuary law was introduced in 1396 and was reissued virtually untouched in 1480. On the other hand the periods of Medici rule in Florence did not seem to reduce significantly the flow of sumptuary regulation. It is evident that the association between sumptuary laws and economic class interest is complex. I will return to this issue in the next chapter when considering whether there was a distinctive form of urban sumptuary law.

Jacques Heers and Ronald Weissman add an important dimension to the discussion of the political tendency of sumptuary regulation. They insist that the social forces at struggle cannot be reduced to modern 'economic classes' and suggest that kinship lineages of 'family clans' were important social forces in medieval and early modern society (Heers 1977; Weissman 1982 and 1989). Heers advances the interesting hypothesis that sumptuary laws were significantly directed against the forms of display that both constituted and displayed the power of family clans, exemplified by ostentatious weddings and funerals. Such displays were a potential source of disorder since they could ignite clan vendettas into public disorder and even civil war. He argues that sumptuary restraints on what he calls the 'luxury of assembly' are to be found more frequently in urban legislation than in royal ordinances since family clans posed more of a threat to the municipal authorities than to royal power (Heers 1977: 76–77). His findings are broadly consistent with the case argued here, although one proviso is necessary. Heers tends to assume that all municipal authorities were hostile to the power of family clans and in so doing he fails to take account of the fact that an important component of the dynamics of power in city politics was that in many cities patrician interests as systems of family clans secured political power, as the most famous case of the Medici in Florence shows.

A more detailed study of the correlation between laws against the luxury of assembly and the local balance of political power would be necessary to confirm his thesis. As I have shown above, the Italian evidence is ambiguous and there do not seem to have been major differences between the content of the sumptuary laws between 'democratic' municipalities and those under the sway of patrician family clans. It is, of course, important to bear in mind that the pervasiveness of clan-like forms of organization existed among the more 'democratic' burgher classes so that the immediate social forces in contention were family clans from and representing different strata.

I have been careful to avoid the suggestion that sumptuary laws were an actively modernizing phenomenon. Marc Raeff's work on the somewhat broader field of administrative and police regulations in early modern Germany does make just such a claim. He identifies the fully conscious aim on the part of the senior burghers to discipline society as a truly innovative project[14]. Their ordinances aimed to adapt the population to the performance and attainment of the economic and productive goals set by the state. This discipline aimed to instil a new set of attitudes, ones that broke with the pre-modern pattern of lives that strove to survive dearth and in periods of relative surplus to engage in unrestrained consumption (Raeff 1983: 87–88). He interprets the enormous legislative energy directed towards restraining feasting, drinking, gaming and other indulgences as attempts to promote the work ethic, but also as projects of the Protestant Reformation directed towards the suppression of pagan and idolatrous festivities forming part of the struggle against Catholicism.[15] It is possible that Raeff goes a little too far in treating sumptuary law as a harbinger of modernity; I will offer an assessment of his thesis in the context of the link between sumptuary law and urban government in the next chapter. For the time being it is sufficient to note that he does, however, provide perhaps the most important reason for rejecting the conventional equation of sumptuary law with pre-modernity, namely that it was alive and active at the same time as other unambiguously modernizing projects.

Gerald Strauss argues that in Nürnberg the patricians were often the target of sumptuary legislation even where this was couched in universal terms since the prohibitions involved were much more likely to affect the well-to-do than the 'middling sort', for example bans on attending out-of-town weddings, limits on the cash value of presents, and a ban on imported pastries for weddings (Strauss 1966). In similar vein Lyndal Roper shows that during the sixteenth century Augsburg's sumptuary laws revealed a pattern of increasing class stratification. For example, an enactment in 1575 imposed a class differential on the permitted expenditure on wedding rings: 150 gulden for patricians, 75 for merchants, and only 3 for ordinary members of the commune (Roper 1985b: 80). I leave over until the next chapter the interesting suggestion made by Diane Hughes that there was a distinctive form of 'urban sumptuary law'.

It is a conventional response from the vantage point of the late twentieth century to view the sumptuary impulse as a species of 'puritanism', carrying with it connotations of restrictive intervention in the field of personal choice. This imagery is reinforced because most of the obvious cases of quasi-sumptuary rule during the present century, such as Prohibition in the United States, have had precisely such an intrusive moralizing character. It is important to consider briefly the evidence concerning the connection between the Reformation and sumptuary law. Did the Reformation lead to any intensification or change of focus in European sumptuary law during the sixteenth century? Greenfield, in his study of Nürnberg, comes to the conclusion that there was no discernible shift in the character of the sumptuary laws that can be attributed to the local Reformation of 1526 which would substantiate the view that associated the Reformation with a tightening of regulation in general, and of personal regulation in particular (Greenfield 1918: 87). A very similar conclusion is arrived at by John Vincent, that in the heartland of the Swiss Reformation there was no discernible change or intensification of sumptuary intervention (Vincent 1935). Even during the height of Calvin's power in Geneva there was no new sumptuary legislation, although there may have been some increase in the rate of enforcement of the existing ordinances; there were around 800 arrests, that resulted in 76 banishments and 58 death sentences for sumptuary and moral offences (Van Paasen 1960: 233).

What seems clear is that the protracted rise of bourgeois economic and political power involved a considerable degree of sumptuary continuity. It is this fact that underlines the theme which runs through this book of locating sumptuary law as a phenomenon on the boundaries of modernity. Yet with the consolidation of bourgeois power during the course of the eighteenth and nineteenth centuries sumptuary law in its most general form, the regulation of personal appearance and consumption, disappeared. Symbolically it was the General Assembly thrown up by the French Revolution that explicitly abolished all laws relating to distinctions in dress (Barber and Loebel 1953: 325). Elsewhere they merely fell into disuse or were repealed without fanfare. In summary, sumptuary law was a phenomenon of the early bourgeois period, but not of mature capitalism.

FASHION AS CLASS STRUGGLE

The cultural studies movement secured a certain intellectual notoriety by its insistence that cultural phenomena that had long been regarded as either peripheral or derivate (or both) by those who had focused their attention on the 'serious' business of class struggle were indeed important. It is within this tradition that a certain mischievous pleasure can be derived by insisting that something so frivolous, trivial and peripheral as fashion can be talked of in the same breath as class struggle. There is a deeply serious core to the project of exploring the connection between fashion and class struggle. While I employ the language of class, as I indicated at the outset, I am mindful of the limitations of 'class' conceptualizations and thus include discussion of the non-class social forces which are especially important in the period under consideration. The rise of fashion was, as we have seen, a central feature of the way of life of the dominant classes of the pre-modern era. No longer feudal, the landed nobility extracted monetary rents and dues and were thus able to participate in a developing consumer market. The increasingly tenuous claims to privilege by virtue of birth found expression in the preoccupation with the display of conspicuous consumption as a central feature of the identity of this declining social force.[16]

Rising classes have to find new ways of asserting their claims, first to recognition and later to superiority, but at the early stages of these processes they rely on competitive emulation through the social display of style, fashion and elegance. One result is that fashion became a vehicle for the rising class. As the mercantile bourgeoisie moved from cringing dependence on the nobility to increasingly assertive forms of life there was born a new principle of social organization in which 'money' displaced 'blood'. What makes fashion 'serious' is that the linked processes of urbanization and commercialization (or commodification) transformed the relationship between the public and the private. The reallocation of interior space and new possibilities of interior design has received much attention in recent years as a range of intellectual concerns and traditions have converged on the history of 'private life' as a focus for scholarly attention (Veyne 1987; Braudel 1989; Ariès and Duby 1987–91). Paralleling the new intimate interiors was a dawning world of busy streets and strangers in which the display of fashion took place.[17]

Fashion then was a highly visible feature of the identity and self-expression of the social forces that were shaping the modern world:

> Fashion, indeed, is born only in social struggle, and it is typical of new and struggling societies and times of violent social change which give birth to new social orders that styles change with equal violence.
>
> (Binder 1958: 333)

As Quentin Bell points out, the major contenders in such historic struggles as the English Civil War and French Revolution had distinctive and memorable sartorial differences, as did the combatants in many other important episodes of social conflict (Bell 1976: Ch. 6). The revolutionary process generally received sartorial expression. This serves to underline my concern not to give too general an endorsement to the phenomenon of imitation. The more self-conscious a social force became the less likely it was to engage in purely imitative behaviour. The means of sartorial expression are never limitless, so that attention to the dynamics of the class struggle in the field of fashion would need to attend to the differential use of the available materials and other resources. In general the existence of explicit class consciousness weakens the purely imitative dynamic, but rather expresses itself in the quest for a distinctive separation from the old ruling class. The literature of the history of costume has without exception worked within the assumptions of either imitation theory or of the existence of some natural social order of ranks and grades. A history of costume written from the standpoint of a theory of distinction as competitive class conflict would be likely to produce very different results. It would need to watch for key moments at which an increasingly self-expressive bourgeoisie asserted their own characteristic styles. There was a long-running shift in the geographical location of leadership in fashion to the more bourgeois countries of Northern Europe. In this way certain distinctive bourgeois fashion values were imposed on the aristocracy.

What took place was both a cultural and an economic appropriation. The merchant bourgeoisie indulged the nobility's love of luxury and fashion and in so doing they appropriated, through the mechanisms of debt and interest, the dwindling power of the aristocracy (Haug 1986). There is a place here to apply Gramsci's concept of hegemony to the control of appearance as a manifestation of class struggle. This facilitates coming to grips with the role of transformative emulation whereby a simple 'emulation of one's betters' becomes transformed into a transcendent emulation where the criteria of social worth become transformed, such as when a rising social class comes to reject the embedded values of an old order. As I have suggested, the merchant class did not merely ape their 'betters' but adopted new patterns of cultural consumption that are conveyed to us in the distinctive appearance of the solid and sober burghers decked in fine furs that are familiar in the portraits by Van Eyck, Holbein and Rembrandt.

In asserting their own worth the merchant classes did not hesitate to regulate the artisans. In a number of cities the merchants imposed fixed regulation on the dress of the trades, for example the corporation of the town of Halberstadt decreed that journeymen must only appear out of doors wearing doublet, cap and cloak (Chevalier 1947). Apprentices were a favourite target of regulation, but I suspect that this was more a matter of generational than class relations. However, there is much less consistent evidence of attempts by the merchant classes to impose sumptuary restraint on the working trades and labouring classes; it will be necessary to explore this aspect of inter-class relations in the next chapter which focuses on urban sumptuary law.

The history of sumptuary law during the bourgeois epoch exhibits what might be called a 'democratization' of the sumptuary imperative. Attempts to reproduce a hierarchical social order were gradually abandoned. In many cases no new sumptuary projects were generated, but in a number a more universal sumptuary standard was imposed, in which the whole population was subjected to the same limits. The Scottish case illustrates this process well. The first sumptuary legislation in 1429 divided society into three broad classes and set a standard of dress for each: lords and knights with income over 200 marks, gentlemen and burgesses, and the third group of yeomen and commoners (APS II: 18: 8–10). There were minor adjustments to these categories until in 1672 the classifications were reduced to two broad groups, a 'privileged' group of nobility and wealthy gentry, and then the rest of the population (APS III: 71–72: *c.* 21). This bipolar stratification was largely removed just one year later in an Act of 1673 (APS III: 212: *c.* 3). This Act rescinded that part of the Act of 1672 that had forbidden all but the privileged group from wearing silk fabrics and trimmings, beaver hats and lace; anyone could now wear these. The result was to deprive the privileged classes of most of their legal sumptuary advantages. The lifting of the restrictions was explained in terms of the employment provided to the poor by the manufacture of these items. All differential restrictions were finally removed in 1681 (APS VIII: 348–49, *c.* 78). Thereafter the legislation was directed at the whole population. The disappearance of status distinctions came about because of the emergence of a distinct shift in the rationale for sumptuary intervention to a more conscious concern with economic development and protectionism, a process to be examined in more detail in Chapter 14.

Dress, appearance and fashion and the projects that sought to regulate them cannot be adequately understood in terms of the various forms of imitation theory. Rather, both fashion itself and its regulation need to be understood as the product of specific forms of class and other formations of hierarchical relations under pressure of change, competition and conflict. The high period of sumptuary regulation in Europe that spanned the period between the late Middle Ages and the early modern period, say from 1300 to 1600, was both an expression of and a vehicle for these shifting social relations. The economic and political weakening of the nobilities, whether feudal or patrician, found them in circumstances in which they were less and less able to guarantee the defence of their sartorial distinction against the rising merchant class. The demand for the regulation of consumption thus typically invoked the dual motives, on the one hand the fear of their own economic 'ruin', and on the other the anxiety over preserving their distinctive 'recognizability' from subordinate classes that was explored in the previous chapter.

Sumptuary law gave voice to social problems that could not be fully solved through legislative control over their outward signs or expressions. Hughes explains the context of Italian sumptuary law in a way that has a wider applicability:

> In Renaissance Italy, a society that dreamed of order while facing the daily consequences of class fluidity, they had to be controlled by legislation.
>
> (Hughes 1983: 99)

Hughes' formulation requires some reworking because it carries the implication that sumptuary law actually 'controlled' the underlining sources of tension. This it almost certainly did not do. Rather, sumptuary law provided a discursive field that allowed expression of these tensions and in an important sense was successful in creating projects of governance, along with the appropriate legitimations, that together with other political and religious discourses addressed these deep-seated, multi-dimensional problems of the shifting class relations on the borders of modernity.

8

Governing the City: Regulation, State Formation and the Coming of Modernity

URBANISM AND SUMPTUARY REGULATION

The city and the experience of urban existence are important components of shifts which mark a profound change in the forms of social life. Bearing in mind my earlier concern to avoid any suggestion of a totalizing notion of 'Modernity', it is nevertheless important to insist that the term 'modernity' is a useful shorthand for designating what was novel and distinctive about the city. Yet it does not follow that the city is quintessentially modern. Rather it can be said that some of the most distinctive developments in the forms of social life occurred in an urban environment. And it is possible to push this a stage further by saying that these developments probably could only have occurred within cities. The classic formulation of the connection between modernity and urbanization was voiced by Ernst Troeltsch who viewed the emergence of large numbers of towns from the twelfth century onwards 'as a preparation and foundation for the modern world' (Troeltsch 1931: I: 255).

In the previous chapter it was argued that sumptuary law should not be regarded as a late manifestation of the death throes of feudalism. I have suggested that sumptuary law can usefully be regarded as a phenomenon inhabiting the threshold of modernity, without itself being a component of that configuration of forms of social life. Such a view has an obvious attraction in suggesting that there was some affinity between the urban experience and sumptuary regulation, but in such a way that does not necessarily imply any causality in that connection. It was cities, widely different cities, with which sumptuary law was most closely associated. This chapter explores the link between urbanism and sumptuary law.

One way or another the previous chapter on class and sumptuary law had a good deal to say about cities, particularly with respect to the dimension of 'class conflict' between patrician and burgher interests. I will take it as read that Weber was correct in identifying the trend toward hierarchical class and status divisions as one of the distinctive characteristics of the process of urbanization. It was Weber who first advanced the thesis that cities were more importantly centres of consumption rather than of production, a thesis that has been elaborated upon and developed in the more recent sociology of consumption. This process is brought vividly to light in the case of London. The relocation, both permanent and seasonal, of the provincial gentry to London was a source of anxiety throughout the Tudor and Stuart period. The concern was that the mechanisms of rural governance could not operate if the 'master' and the 'mistress' were away for much of the year. Elizabeth wanted them at their bases as invasion fears mounted and James I issued proclamations trying to move them back to their country seats (Fisher 1948). As London became a site (in a very literal spatial sense with its parks and squares) of conspicuous consumption so it also became a location for the distinctive luxury and service forms of production.

However, it is with another of Weber's general characterizations of the urban experience that this chapter will be mainly concerned. The city exhibited an alternative tendency towards solidarity and cohesion that united diverse populations as having distinctive urban interests. In the first place the towns were counterposed to feudal interests, but more importantly cities were constituted from the constellation of cooperative and competitive relations between autonomous social groups, of which the guilds provided the paradigm case. Weber gave sharp focus to this relationship in his formulation that cities did not originate in guilds, but rather that guilds originated in cities (Weber 1978: II: 1239–40). The guilds were significant in that they both required alliances between economically independent groups while, at the same time, they focused and objectified competition. It was thus the dual poles of competition and cooperation that laid down much of the distinctive character of the urban experience. The nature of the socio-economic relations involved is captured by the idea of guilds as 'sworn confraternities' with a capacity for both self-regulation and for collaborative legislative activity (Weber 1978: II: 1243).[1] Something of the flavour of the contractual basis of citizenship is captured in the oath from the city of Beauvais in Picardy: 'All men within the walls of the city and in the suburb shall swear the commune; each shall aid the other in the manner he thinks right; if any man who has sworn the commune suffers a violation of rights, and a claim comes before the peers of the commune, they shall do justice against the person or the property of the offender' (quoted Berman 1983: 295).

In the long-run, that is in the transition to industrial capitalism, it was the incipient competition that exploded as the class struggle between labour and capital became the dominant socio-economic relation. In the process, the cities learnt for themselves new forms of social and political relations. Particularly important for present purposes is the distinctive form of government to which the cities gave rise and of which sumptuary laws were a significant manifestation. But since sumptuary laws had long predated the distinctive forms of governance of the early modern city it becomes necessary to pose the question: was there a distinctive form of 'urban sumptuary law'? This question will be addressed in the next section.

The urban experience was one of considerable anxiety and danger alongside the obvious advantages and attractions. Of the dangers one only has to recall the endurance of fire and plague which were something within the direct experience of almost every urban dweller well into the nineteenth century. Urban life was beset by social disorder or the perception of social disorder. We have already encountered the anxieties generated by the difficulties attendant upon the concern with recognizing others in the jostle of the urban streets or in their night-time gloom. With urbanization came an intensification of the public/private divide, while its boundaries underwent radical and perplexing shifts. While drawing attention to the risks that were characteristic of the urban experience it is important to keep firmly in mind that towns and cities acted as magnets, not least because they offered a positive expectation of choice and self-determination that was absent in rural society (Cox 1965).

Elizabeth Wilson gets it just right when she refers to prostitution as the metaphor for urban disorder (Wilson 1992: 91). The encounters on the streets were uncontrolled; there is a sense of both promiscuity and alienation in the daily contacts of urban life that bred an anxiety, one that is still present in the late twentieth century but was potent in the late Middle Ages, about the mixing across social rank and across occupation of young men and women that manifests itself in concerns of social breakdown, of immorality, of contagion, of risk and of excitement (Corbin 1990; Berman 1983). I will return to some of these themes in taking a closer look at prostitution as the signifier of both men's voyeuristic mastery of the streets and, at the same time, the freedom of and familiarity with the streets exhibited by prostitutes that gave them a partial autonomy rarely gained in the increasingly closed domestic world that women came to inhabit. The streets became and remained sexually charged public spaces that elicited strong and continuing regulatory impulses. The compelling sense that 'something must be done', the concern with urban disorder, was one of the more important well-springs of the sumptuary impulse.

Along with this general characterization of the urban context of late medieval society the present study needs to take note of some other features, but without any pretence at providing a general sociology of the city. Particularly important for a study of the regulation of consumption is Sombart's attempt to grasp the distinctiveness of the urban experience by emphasizing the rise of 'consumer cities', particularly in Italy, whose rapid expansion was initiated by the rise of conspicuous consumption, spearheaded by a class of merchant 'nouveaux riches'. This class was epitomized by the diary-keeping merchant of Prato (1335–1410) who inscribed the covers of his ledgers with the words 'In the name of God and of profit' (Origo 1957: 5; Brooke 1971: 244). Since it is already clear that sumptuary rules bore a strongly gendered content it is also worth noting that Sombart added a psychological dimension to his account of the rise of capitalism in identifying the emergence of new sexual values organized around what he called a 'hedonistic aesthetic conception of woman' (1967: 46). It will be necessary to return to this issue in examining sumptuary law and gender in Chapter 9. For present purposes it is sufficient to note the link between sex and conspicuous consumption.

URBAN SUMPTUARY LAW?

How do we explain the prevalence of sumptuary law in the great cities that were the harbingers of modern capitalism? The orthodox contention that sumptuary laws were a feudal relic cannot account for the mounting volume of sumptuary law in so many of the cities that sprang up in post-feudal Europe. One obvious and attractive possibility is to distinguish different varieties of sumptuary law and to propose the existence of a distinctively urban sumptuary law.

This strategy has been followed by Diane Hughes who explicitly links the expansion of sumptuary law with those cities of northern Italy that were forced to admit the popular classes of merchants and guild artisans into government. In the course of developing this theme she introduces the idea that a distinction is needed between 'urban sumptuary law' and 'aristocratic sumptuary law'. Urban sumptuary law takes one of two possible forms; it is either universalistic (imposes the same restraint on all, e.g. 'No person shall wear rings of more than 2 oz. of gold') or, alternatively, it is employed by the contending classes of patricians and merchants in fighting out their conflicts of interest. Aristocratic sumptuary law on the other hand, associated with the great monarchical states, was directed at the regulation of dress and other forms of consumption according to social hierarchy (Hughes 1983: 73).

This distinction between 'urban' and 'aristocratic' sumptuary law certainly works well for Hughes' study of sumptuary law in Renaissance Italy. My concern is whether this (or some similar) general distinction can be usefully employed in the more extensive study of the sumptuary tradition with which this book engages. I proceed with some caution to criticize Hughes' distinction because I had for some time worked with a very similar classification as my own working model. It was only when I tried to work through the implications of her proposal that I became less comfortable with it. There is no doubt that this model is intuitively attractive. There is also no doubt either that it covers some cases; the best fit is between Hughes' 'aristocratic' category and the absolute monarchies of, for example, early modern France and Spain. My reservation is that the distinction does not succeed in capturing sufficient of the historical record. Even making allowance for the general caveat that no conceptual or theoretical model can be expected to produce a neat fit with reality, the gap is just too great. The main problem is that the hierarchical sumptuary ordering that Hughes associates with the 'aristocratic' category is just far too persistent. Too many thoroughly respectable non-aristocratic societies persisted with hierarchic dress codes – recall, for example, the lines of sumptuary division drawn in Puritan New England, discussed in the previous chapter. Conversely, there were far too few cities that practised the universal sumptuary legislation that imposed uniform restrictions across the classes. Even more problematic is the fact that the hierarchic form of sumptuary law most frequently succeeds (rather than precedes) the more universalistic forms of sumptuary rules. Conversely it is in societies that correspond most closely to a hierarchic model of fixed social ranks that are more likely to have universalistic sumptuary rules. The detailed evidence concerning the history of sumptuary laws in European urban life examined in this chapter suggests that the distinction between 'urban' and 'aristocratic' sumptuary law cannot be sustained.

Another classificatory approach is used by a diverse set of authors who propose the view that there were a limited number of 'motives' that prompted sumptuary legislation. The different types of sumptuary law are viewed as deriving from the different motives (or combination of motives) which the specific instances manifested. This perspective typically identifies a set of motives that includes some or all of the following: hierarchical (preservation of class distinctions), moral (curbing luxury), public order, economic (domestic trade protection) or populationist (facilitating early marriage) motives that are mixed in various combinations. In the more sophisticated versions some combinations are identified as being more likely to occur than others – elective affinity – while other combinations are unlikely or unstable. For most purposes this approach is a serviceable means of classifying the various forms of sumptuary law.

However, the concept of motive has serious shortcomings in that it tends to conflate its most immediate sense, the subjective intentions of those sponsoring or instituting sumptuary laws, with a more functional concern with the social results or consequences that are produced. In some instances the two dimensions will converge and analysis in terms of motives raises no difficulties. It is when subjective intention and social function diverge that talk of motives becomes either unhelpful or positively misleading. The most obvious case is where what is taken as motive is nothing more than a legitimatory discourse, for example the legitimation appealed to when restraints were imposed on women's dress was the necessity of restraining the natural vanity of women. Nor do I think it a sound procedure to seek to go behind the shroud of such legitimatory discourses to search for a 'real' motive. Not only does this tend to produce a conspiracy theory approach, but such a procedure allows no practices of verification or falsification (except in those rare cases where some secret memorandum may have set down the 'real' motives). The other problem with motives is that there is a tendency to assume that motives themselves are coherent and thus capable of making sense of the associated practices.

There is an alternative approach that much of the remainder of the book will be concerned to explore. The key concept is that of governance. Governance can be contrasted with motives because governance focuses attention on the results or effects of social action while remaining agnostic as to origins and causes. This agnosticism does not mean the abolition of the inquiry into causes underlying mechanisms of governance.[2] For example, the project of the Calvinist 'holy government' of family and city discussed in more detail in the next chapter exhibits close links between motives, discourses and practices. But the concept of governance comes into its own when no such unity is present. First it insists that governance is not only the work of 'governments', but that it arises from the mundane activities of people grappling with the exigencies of life. Such practices have no necessary coherence, participants do not necessarily have any clear view of the results at which they aim or if they do the outcome will, more often than not, fail to secure their imagined goal. The use of the concept 'governance' does bring with it another important assumption that needs to made explicit. It is that our species seems to exhibit what might be called a 'will to governance'. This, I think, is apparent in the extraordinary energies expended on the governance of the self.[3] Underlying such activity is a pervasive concern to control (and control here should not be equated with dominance) selected aspects of one's circumstances. Of critical importance is the process which forms the objects of governance, which situational aspects are selected as objects of knowledge to which there corresponds some appropriate set of practices. This knowledge and the associated practices are described as 'projects', which is my preferred alternative to 'motives'. Projects do not entirely drop all elements of intentionality; what people think they are doing is not unimportant, but must be put in the context of what they know and what they do.[4] Projects are repeatable practices of control of a selected 'target' or 'object' which may or may not be associated with some conception of motives or purposes. Central to projects of governance are the processes for the collection and handling of knowledge, the formation of policies, the selection of tactics and techniques and the regularized practices that result. These distinct phases are most apparent in bureaucracies and professionalized agencies, but are identifiable in even the most informal and unselfconscious forms of governance. Such a conception of governance traverses the traditional distinction between public and private, state and civil society. Governance is not something restricted to the public sphere; rather it is the very stuff of the social.

The sociology of governance builds on two of Foucault's terms, 'governmentality' and 'government of the self'. Governmentality focuses on the forms of mentality, the knowledges, procedures of administration and ways of constructing social objects capable of being governed, the techniques and tactics deployed. Of special importance is the way in which 'the population' and 'the economy' came to be constructed as objects of governance. The formation of objects of governance is not just a matter of 'goals' or 'motives', but rather focuses on the way in which specific social practices and social relations come to be selected as 'proper' targets of governance.[5] The direction or thrust of governance is rarely, if ever, the expression of a unitary will; the projects of governance are typically the resultant of a set of practices, tactics and techniques. In other words, while retaining some of the concerns captured by the concept 'motives', this approach goes beyond the subjective intentions of agents to ask what are the conditions of possibility for some particular motive to be adopted and pursued.

The radical implications of Foucault's thought are captured by his oxymoron 'the government of the self'. The significance of this idea starts from the way it undermines the commonsense equation of 'government' with external control or top-down imposition and as a one-way process in which those that govern do so to those who are governed. The concept of self-governance draws attention to the truth that an enormous amount of governing of the self gets done without any reference to external social agents or to sanctions. Perhaps the most fascinating issues revolve around the interactions between the 'governance of the self' and the 'governance of others'.

The concept of governance focuses on the content of the processes of governing; it unashamedly brings to the fore the 'how' of governing, what gets done, by whom, what means are employed, and with what consequences. In coming close to a technical interest in the mechanics of governance the approach needs to be very insistent upon the 'limits of governance'. It would go only slightly too far to say that governance always fails; perhaps it would be better to post as a warning notice that never as much governing gets done as is intended nor does the governing that does get done very frequently produce anything closely resembling the intentions of the participants. Governance is always incomplete and always subject to avoidance, evasion and resistance.

Applying this conception of governance to the topic of sumptuary law it is possible to identify a number of persistent 'sumptuary projects'. A 'project' is not reducible to a 'motive' in that it makes no necessary reference to the intentions of participants. In practice this facilitates the focus of attention on two key features: first, what gets done and the techniques employed; second, what discourse(s) are associated with these practices. One additional implication needs to be added. The movement between practices/techniques and discourses creates the possibility of a form of analysis that goes behind both elements to discover connections not immediately visible on the surface of the practices or the discourses. For example, in Chapter 6 a demonstration was offered of the connection between hierarchic dress codes and a more pervasive quest for recognizability. In Chapter 9 I explore the way in which the regulation of the dress of prostitutes can be understood as a component of the governance of 'normal' heterosexuality. And as a final example, in Chapter 13 I show how sumptuary laws were linked to the governance of labour mobility and the moral regulation of the poor.

I distinguish between moral regulation, economic protectionism, populationism and the reproduction of social hierarchy. First, projects of moral governance embrace a range of preoccupations that connect up the moralization of luxury to misogynist anxieties about gender relations. Moral projects are for most if not the whole of the period under study brought under the general umbrella of preoccupations about degeneracy and impending ruin. Second, there are economic projects organized around the construction of a distinct concept of a 'national economy' conceived of as existing in competition with other national economies through the medium of trade. Third, and worth separating from the economic although closely connected, are populationist projects concerned with a similarly 'national' preoccupation about marriage, fertility and health. Fourth are projects organized around the reproduction of social hierarchy; to focus attention on the importance I have attached to 'distinction', these projects may be called 'diacritic' in the sense of being concerned to distinguish different social categories. Finally, a potential candidate for independent status, but potentially subsumable within the other heads, is conservatism – projects organized around the preservation of the known which may be associated with a fear of the new. It should be stressed that these categories are neither closed nor watertight.

I am not much concerned about the classification of sumptuary projects. Rather I am anxious to explore the contention that what is interesting and should command our attention are the combinations in which these projects manifest themselves. Pure projects of sumptuary governance rarely, if ever, appear. So rather than look for a one-dimensional shift, as in Hughes' idea of a shift from aristocratic to urban sumptuary law, a focus on the historical patterns produced by shifting combinations of sumptuary projects is likely to be a more rewarding approach than that offered by traditional evolutionary typologies.

In order to carry out the type of analysis being suggested it is necessary to introduce a few additional basic concepts. In the first place it is necessary to be able to identify the 'targets' of governance, the 'objects' of regulation (always 'social' entities). The 'agents' of regulation refer to the categories of persons carrying out the regulatory practices; the 'form' and the 'sanctions' identify the tactics, techniques and resources put into motion. These elements combine together to make up what I will call 'projects of governance'. Applied to sumptuary law it is possible to identify a small number of general sumptuary projects that are concerned with expenditure, appearance, gender, luxury and trade. What constitute the distinctive features of particular historical forms of sumptuary regulation are the combination of these elements. It is for these reasons that I resist the idea of positing a developmental typology of 'stages' of sumptuary law.

FROM APPEARENTIAL TO SPATIAL ORDERING?

In Chapter 6 Lofland's thesis that urban history is marked by a shift from an appearential order to a spatial order was introduced.

It now requires further attention in order to extend my contention that the urban experience has always involved an interaction between appearential and spatial ordering rather than a transition from one to the other.[6] The regulatory practices that developed within the medieval city were from an early stage concerned with spatial ordering. This is true of both sumptuary and other forms of regulation. There was widespread spatial regulation of economic activity through the positive designation of market locations or, negatively, the prohibition of specific economic activities from designated locations.[7] What is required is a broad conception of 'space' that makes it possible to grasp the continuum between 'social space' and 'physical space'.

As we have seen, the orthodox account views sumptuary law as involving the project of the production and reproduction of social closure. It may be worth thinking of social closure and enclosure as being more closely connected with a more modern project, namely the first stages of citizenship associated with the 'communal citizenship' of the medieval city understood as a two-fold process. On the one hand, the circle of participation widens; the lower orders become 'enclosed' within the space 'social body' (a metaphor approaching literalness within the physical space of the city walls or boundaries). On the other hand, mechanisms of social closure change their form, from 'blood' and birth, via symbols (shields, livery, uniforms, etc.) to more exclusively economic participation via guilds and other formal and informal mechanisms. As Maffesoli (1991) argues, groups constitute themselves through the 'formism' of the symbolism that attaches itself to a sign (a garment, a habit, a taste, etc.). The implication of this is that sumptuary law operates on and is implicated in both the mechanisms of 'enclosure' and 'closure'.

Shively identifies the distinctive feature of Japanese sumptuary legislation as being its concern with the combination of distance-space-decoration. Thus, for example, there was close regulation of the geographical distribution of the different social classes within the castle-town, with the higher classes on more elevated land. Thus social distance was minutely reproduced in spatial distance and in visibility of rank (Shively 1964; McClain 1982). Similarly in China the spatial characteristics of houses, their length and the number of courtyards was linked to rank; so also were the proportions of archways, doors and other entrances, and many other details of their decoration, such that the rank of the occupants could be immediately read from the location of the residence and its spatial organization (Ch'ü 1961).

Perhaps the most obvious example of the interconnection between appearential and spatial regulation occurs in one of the most prolific fields of sumptuary activity, namely the regulation of prostitution. Throughout most of early and pre-modern Europe prostitution excited the regulatory impulse. I will have more to say about the governance of prostitution as a form of gender regulation in Chapter 9. For present purposes it is sufficient to note that in addition to the great volume of edicts aimed at controlling the appearance of prostitutes, they were subject to extensive temporal and spatial regulation. Typical were attempts to keep brothels outside the city walls or, at least, confined to specific locations. It was also common for attempts to be made to keep prostitutes away from the most respectable and sanctified venues. The squares and piazzas were frequently sites of restrictions as were the precincts of churches. More problematic was the dual characteristic of festivals and processions; on the one hand, they had close connection with the church, but on the other they involved occasions for release and for deviant pleasures. The pressures to both recognize and repudiate the role of prostitution shows through in some of the tensions in the regulation and the suspension of regulation that such occasions elicited.

In general, sumptuary regulation involved the manipulation of social space, time and appearance. With regard to the second of these, Trexler points to a significant temporal dimension in social regulation: through a mix of religious and secular regulation, including sumptuary regulation, a 'shaped time' is generated in that specific types of permitted or prohibited behaviour comes to be associated with specific times (Trexler 1980: 75). For example, sumptuary laws were frequently suspended during designated festivals and celebrations or during certain ceremonial visits, as when Pope Pious II visited Florence in 1459. The most pervasive temporal preoccupations in early modern cities concerned the increasingly difficult task of securing Sunday observance. Not only was it a matter of policing church attendance, but also of prohibiting both economic activity and recreational practices. In England there was an additional dimension to the regulation of time. Legislation set up an interesting association between the use of Sundays, prohibition of undesirable recreations, and the provision for the exigencies of national defence. A long series of statutes and proclamations, stretching between 1388 and 1608, prohibited the playing of many popular sports, recreations and pastimes on Sundays, which will be discussed in more detail in Chapter 11.

What now needs to be considered is whether there occurred an intensification of urban governance. An intensification might involve some combination of an extension and an intensification of governance. Extending governance involved activities that previously had not been controlled coming to be regulated. Sumptuary law may well have been just one of an expanded range of such activities. The intensification of governance involved the forms of regulation practised becoming more severe or more thorough and efficient. The severity of regulation, in contrast to its volume, is more difficult to judge. Mere harshness of sanctions might be an indicator but would not necessarily get to grips with its intrusiveness, how much difference it made to everyday life. Nor is it a matter of the efficiency of the regulatory capacity of the authorities, for it is rarely technical questions alone that determine the degree or intensity of regulation.

My view, and it can be no more than impressionistic, is that sumptuary laws failed to penetrate significantly into the everyday world. It is always difficult to prove a negative, but my perusal of a cross-section of diaries from the periods of high sumptuary activity suggests that few experienced any immediate anxiety about such rules. The diaries generally attest to the everyday importance of clothes; many describe garments that would in all probability have been proscribed by the sumptuary law of the day. This impression is supported by the dearth of evidence of prosecution for sumptuary offences from most of the jurisdictions involved. I will scrutinize the available evidence in more detail in Chapter 13 below; for the present I only want to lodge the contention that absence of evidence of systematic enforcement does not of itself establish that sumptuary law was ineffectual or unimportant.

Sumptuary law was one element of a process in which the regulatory reach was being expanded, more aspects of social life were becoming the objects of disciplinary or regulatory activity. But there was little sense that the regulatory screw was being tightened. What needs to be engaged with is why a significant expansion in governance occurred. Because much of this expansion, like many other significant changes, occurred in the cities of Europe it seems likely that it was connected with some of the distinctive social changes that came about with urbanization. This feature could well have been the increased density of urban life, the shifting boundary between public and private or the commodification of economic relations (phenomena that are themselves internally connected).

For present purposes it is sufficient to note that sumptuary activity occurs at much the same time as the urban authorities were busily engaging in a wide range of other regulatory activity. Very much to the fore was the governance of public health. Typical were the attempts to regulate what kind of garbage could be disposed of in the streets, public thoroughfares and water systems, and what animals could be kept where. The question of pigs provided a rich and fertile convergence as a link between garbage and the place of animals in urban space. The ambiguous location of pigs in the history of urban regulation was further compounded by the fact that they had come to play the dramatic role of defendants in criminal trials where they were accused, tried, tortured and convicted for a wide range of offences; the most common offence committed by pigs was assault or causing the death of a child (Evans 1906). The fact of pigs eating garbage in the streets was presumably the circumstance for the alleged attacks on children with whom they must have shared the same urban space. Conviction led them to 'execution' at the hands of the hangman rather than of the butcher; and as a significant semiotic testimony to the animal's criminal capacity they would be dressed in human clothes before being dispatched.

A note of caution should be entered against a widespread tendency to attach a developmental significance to this expansion of regulation. It does not follow that a quantitative expansion of regulatory intervention means that this activity becomes more coherent and systemic. Marc Raeff in his important study of the German city ordinances *(Landes-* and *Polizei-ordnungen)* was more prepared than I think his material justified to conclude that the new 'codified' ordinances involved a conscious effort to bring about 'coherence, regularity, and continuity' which characterized the cities whose politics he captured in his title as 'well-ordered police state' (Raeff 1983: 2t). He argues that:

> an essential aim of these ordinances in the area of social life was to undermine, constrict, and eventually to eliminate what may be called traditional (premodern) patterns of social behavior.
> (Raeff 1983: 85)

He viewed this distinctively urban legislation as part of a process that 'helped to turn legislation into a tool for bringing about dynamic modernization as an end in itself' (1983: 171). He went on to link this activity, first with the Enlightenment and then with the modern welfare state:

> The goals and practices of the well-ordered police state not only foreshadowed but endeavored to implement the notions usually associated with the Enlightenment.
>
> (1983: 252)

> The modern welfare state presents us with an updated version of the basic conceptions of the well-ordered police state.
>
> (1983: 254)

In contrast to this far-sighted vision, it seems more likely that the ordinances were only 'codified' in the sense that they brought together many discrete regulatory initiatives. In other words, it is risky to assume that anything more than administrative convenience is involved in the production of these ordinances. The ordinances read, I suggest, much like modern city ordinances and by-laws that do not aspire to coherence, but merely convenience, in that they bring together sets of rules and regulations on related topics.[8] My caution stems from a reluctance to read into the past the necessary seeds of the present. It is generally unsound to attribute long-range and large-scale projections to people grappling with the immediate pressures of the daily government in difficult and confusing times.[9]

This more contextual evaluation of the expansion of governance is captured by Jeff Minson. The 'police' forms of intervention should be understood as conservative and not as harbingers of modernity; neither should the medieval police be regarded as harbingers of the welfare state. What is significant is that interventions such as sumptuary law, the reform of manners and the 'medical police' bear on the specificity of personal life and thereby personal and domestic life became matters of political and economic moment. The regulation of personal life was the product of a transformation of policing associated with the rise of liberal forms of government embracing both political and non-political modes of regulation (Minson 1985: 106).

What remains indisputable from the evidence of Raeff, and of others, is that extensive and self-conscious regulatory projects were an important feature of the governance of the early modern cities of Europe. Further, it is also clear that sumptuary ordinances were associated with a wide range of other regulatory initiatives. Distinctively sumptuary projects became increasingly closely entwined with public health matters, moral regulation, the control of the labour market and of vagrancy and, perhaps most important of all, with the burgeoning field of economic policy. This makes it possible to sketch the thesis that as these arenas of modern governmental activity became more clearly elaborated and distinguished one from the other, the purely sumptuary dimension did not so much die away, but rather became dispersed within a range of more or less self-contained fields of both public and private regulation. This thesis is explored in more detail in Chapter 14.

It is with the rise of the city that there occurs what Le Goff, Foucault and others have seen as an intensification of governance. The prevalence of sumptuary laws in significant periods of the expansion of European cities is an early manifestation of this regulatory impulse. This process may be viewed through a Durkheimian perspective as one in which increasing social differentiation no longer makes it possible for people to know and to agree upon precisely how they must eat or dress in every situation, or the gestures they must perform. As Durkheim made clear 'moral and legal prescriptions lose clarity and preciseness, they no longer regulate any save the most general forms of behaviour, and these only in a very general way, stating what should be done, not how it should be done' (quoted in Lukes and Scull 1983: 55). Sumptuary law came to the fore in the pre-modern and early modern city as a mechanism that partially closed the gap between the pre-modern and the modern. These shifts towards a specificity of regulation were not merely urban phenomena, but were to be found more widely during this period. As Jeff Minson points out:

> sumptuary law, reform of manners, medical police all bear on the minutiae of personal life. Personal and domestic hygiene become matters of political and economic moment.
>
> (Minson 1985: 106)

Jacques Le Goff, for example, draws attention to the way in which the late medieval church came to require an ever closer interrogation by priests about the sexual practices of their flock, about the style, time and frequency of intercourse (Le Goff 1988b). There is a certain similarity here between the Church's intervention in everyday life and sumptuary regulation that might be said to be a form of legal regulation focusing on the visible face of everyday life. These considerations seem to suggest that the presence of sumptuary laws in the cities can be seen as facing both ways, as both a manifestation of the rise of modernity and as a form of resistance thereto.

GOVERNMENTALITY AND STATE FORMATION

Thus far the consideration of the place of sumptuary law in the emergent cities of Europe has focused on changes in the nature of governmental activity. I will now consider whether it is possible to identify more closely the connection between sumptuary law and the forms of government characteristic of urban Europe. In his paper on 'governmentality' Foucault drew a distinction between two forms of government. The first, 'the state of justice' of the Middle Ages, he characterized as a 'society of laws'. The second, the 'administrative state' of the fifteenth and sixteenth centuries, corresponded to a 'society of regulation' (1979: 21). These forms precede the distinctively modern form of government through 'surveillance'. Foucault's typology suggests the question: should we regard the prevalence of urban sumptuary law as confirmation of increasing importance of regulation in the 'administrative state'?

In the first place this connection between regulation and administration fits with another distinctive Foucauldian theme, namely that of his expanded conception of 'policing' which revolves around the thesis that the 'police's true object is man' (1981: 248). Policing thus conceived has a dual aim: on the one hand to provide the city with adornment, form and splendour and, on the other, to stimulate productive working and trading relations in order to expand the well-being and prosperity of the city. This Foucauldian conception of policing resonates with what might be called the economic side of sumptuary regulation, with its concern that resources should not be wasted, that people should apply both their capital and their labour purposefully for their individual benefit and for that of the community. However, the rationalism at the heart of Foucault's conception does not mesh readily with the moralizing dimension of most, if not all, sumptuary projects.

It is instructive to compare Foucault's account of early modern regulation with that offered by Gerhard Oestreich of 'social discipline' in early modern Europe (Oestreich 1982). Central to Oestreich's account is the identification of discipline as having two dimensions, that of individual self-discipline (the conquering of passion and emotion) and social discipline. In the process of state formation it is discipline that is more important than sovereignty; the central concern is to intensify, revitalize and discipline public life. Here we encounter Foucault's 'expanded' conception of police in a new guise. 'Police' for Oestreich encompasses the whole of 'civil organization' and 'the regulation, discipline, and control of a community' (1982: 156).

This conception of police develops in urban Europe from the late medieval period. It is a response to increased demand for labour, the drift from country to towns and increased social density, all of which generated pressures towards 'new modes of life' that were characterized by greater variation in life-style which, in turn, generated a perceived need for more discipline. These strategies are manifested in an enormous regulatory productivity that was exemplified in the police ordinance for the city of Strasbourg from 1628. What is significant to note is how its regulatory range covers both the public and the private spheres, the criminal and the civil. It included moral regulations (Sunday observance, sorcery, blasphemy, cursing), many public health rules, child rearing practices, control of servants, and relations between innkeepers and guests. It contained extensive sumptuary regulations (dress, funerals, festivities, weddings, drinking, etc.); begging, almsgiving and vagrancy; the status of Jews; and economic regulation (weights and measures, usury and monopolies) (Oestreich 1982: 158).

Looked at from the standpoint of state formation such mechanisms of urban governance attest to the considerable space that existed for forms of authority below the level of the central state, from the governments of communes, to the councils of the guilds to patriarchal familial power. These forms of governance only gradually became 'overlaid' by the institutions, regulations and practices of governments as such. At the same time there were significant continuities with pre-modern social relations, exemplified in the persisting importance of pre-modern forms of communal activity. Festivals, processions and carnivals were central features of the public participation of the inhabitants of urban communities. Similarly, fairs and markets were not only the major form of exchange relations, but also of communal experience; they were also closely linked to libidinal pursuits and to 'excitement' (O'Malley 1992). The disciplinary response, manifested particularly in the governance of the self, the preoccupation with decency, diligence, gravity, modesty, orderliness, prudence, reason, self-control, sobriety and thrift, was epitomized by the concern to effect the 'triumph of lent over carnival' (Burke 1978). The guilds sustained a governmental role, to some extent independent of whether they held formal political power; they continued to engage in local legislation until, in the case of most German cities well into the eighteenth century, their judicial and legislative powers were stripped by Imperial decree (Wegert 1981).

Down to the present, consumption has expanded its association with pleasure and self-realization. One significant consequence is that in the course of the extension of commodification, discipline, – apparently so essential for production oriented to the market – is always at risk of being undermined by the hedonistic culture of consumption, the society of the spectacle, that systematically eats away at the culture of work and production. This provides one way of understanding the tensions between modernization and continuity that surrounded urban governance. This tension was strongly reflected in the discourses surrounding sumptuary law; it both sought to preserve traditions by valorizing the old ways and traditional values and, at the same time, strove to inculcate a new economic rationality of thrift, investment and self-sufficiency.

While urban life rendered social relations more transparent, even though impersonal, it was accompanied by the dramatic privatization that sketched out the new monochrome configuration of public and private zones within urban space. It has been the retrospective appreciation of the significance of Norbert Elias' previously neglected work that has made the study of everyday life into the serious, more rigorous and rapidly expanding enterprise that it is today. For the period traversed by this study this new seriousness attached to the history of the private is exemplified by the monumental studies brought together by Philippe Ariès and Georges Duby (1987-1991). The discovery of silent, and thus private, reading is only one startling revelation of the transformation of everyday life toward the end of the Middle Ages. This intense privatization of life brought with it not only an ever more sharply defined separation between public sumptuousness and private luxury that had profound impact on the controversies over conspicuous consumption, but also a more rigorous interrogation of the proper scope of governance.

From different standpoints, religious and secular, economic and moral, those who governed seemed always to be faced with a sense of the 'disorder' that must have seemed endemic to urban existence. This sentiment seems easy to understand from the vantage point of the late twentieth century when, after seeming to have learned to live with urban and then suburban life, we are now going through a period of dramatically increased insecurity about the very possibility of urban life. For those charged with governing late medieval cities the sense of disorder was manifest not only in the subject of this study, the disorder of social appearances, but in the dislocations threatened by the ubiquitous figures of 'masterless men', the transients, vagrants and beggars whose arrival in the cities was evidence of the break-up of the old order and appeared such a threat to the new. These anxieties and preoccupations link with the focus on the regulation of appearance since both strands provided a powerful stimulus to the practices and ideologies of moral regulation.

These concerns and preoccupations with urban life are strongly reflected in the religious controversies that traverse our period. The contest in England between Anglicanism and Puritanism overran the printing presses of the late sixteenth and early seventeenth centuries. The Anglicans invoked an image of a good old England of paternal lords and sturdy yeomen who lived in harmony. The Puritans were preoccupied with the contemporary fact of 'disorder'. Their prescription required the fostering of discipline (in its double sense of public governance and self-discipline) and congregationalism (the rejection of the universalism of the 'parish' for the community of believers). This combination gave rise to congregational discipline, founded on mutual surveillance, that Walzer describes as 'a close system of collective watchfulness' (Walzer 1965: 221). This has important bearings on the attempt to understand sumptuary regimes since they rested upon a mix of a strong sense of governance as having a duty to ensure what is proper and appropriate and, at the same time, a strong sense that one's neighbour's business is one's own.

Nowhere was the combination stronger than in the sumptuary discourses of the New England colonies. On 3 September 1634 the Court of the Massachusetts Bay provided the following open-ended licence for one person to initiate trouble for another:

> Moreover, it is agreed, if any man shall judge the wearing of any of the aforenamed particular [fashion items], new fashions, or long hair, or anything of the like nature, to be uncomely, or prejudicial to the common good, and the party offending reform not the same upon notice given him.
>
> (Shurtleff 1968: 89)

It is important to underline that the agendas of appearential legislation were never far removed from the more general attempts at legislative moralization directed against such activities as dancing, bear-baiting, swearing and Sunday sports. Back in England ale-houses were a particular target for regulation just at the time when dress rules disappeared from the statute book. The links between sumptuary regulation and moral regulation will be taken up again in Chapter 11.

There is widespread agreement from different theoretical and political perspectives that the city as a political, economic and social form was a decisive condition for the emergence of industrial capitalism and representative democracy. Gianfranco Poggi, for example, suggests that the distinctive form of the 'Standestatt' represented an important stage in the formation of the modern state. The 'estates' that took on political organization still had their roots in feudal arrangements. The towns gave rise to a collective capacity formed as centres of solidaristic action by otherwise powerless individuals (Poggi 1978: 37). An important feature of this process was the securing of 'free' legal status for individuals as citizens and the corporate status of the guilds that became the primary form of self-organization of economically decisive sections of the population. Urban guilds and corporations were like nurseries in which self-respect and dignity emerged, along with feelings of fellowship and mutual respect, and thus effected a radical break from the dependencies of the lord-vassal relations of feudalism (Gurevich 1985).

Not only was self-organization important, but so also were the mechanisms that brought together the different 'estates' or strata of self-organized citizens. The distinctive political expression was the emergence of the late medieval assemblies or 'parlements' that Poggi sees as the key institutional expression of this stage of development. For present purposes the most important consequence was the emergence of a distinct process of 'legislation', that Poggi describes as a 'momentous innovation' (1978: 55). Legislation came to be conceived of as a process of self-conscious deliberation in contrast to a conception of legislation as an edict, as expression of royal will or command. In a significant respect these processes can be regarded as the birth of 'politics' that led to an expanding range and diversity of regulatory activity. Most cities undertook a considerable expansion of what is perhaps best regarded as distinctively 'urban legislation'. Much of it was directly 'economic' guaranteeing market conditions and practices, weights and measures, price and quality controls. Another important arena was that of sanitary regulation dealing with the keeping of animals, disposal of refuge, preservation of water supply and the upkeep of highways. Such urban regulation also included aspects of the regulation of private life (dowries, marriages, servants, apparel) and matters relating to the expansion of 'civic public life' exhibiting elements of town planning with regard to the construction of churches, town halls and public spaces (Black 1984).

There are a number of things that need to be noted about this expansion of governance. In the first place it frequently occurs with little or no attention to the possibility of enforcement. There remains a persisting sense in which legislation was conceived as a form of public exhortation. This feature will assume potential significance when I come to consider the enforcement of sumptuary law. The absence of sustained enforcement is typically regarded as evidence that this variety of regulation was not 'for real' and was doomed to failure. It may be that this conventional view is not simply a misunderstanding of sumptuary law, but is more generally a misapprehension of the early forms of regulatory legislation. Poggi offers the instructive example of the activity of the Parlement of Franche-Comté that in the opening decades of the sixteenth century embarked upon a broad range of regulation that included amongst its targets: general security, crime, heresy, access to pasturage and vineyards, the targets and seasons for hunting, control of craft skills and product standards, weights and measures, the maintenance of roads and waterways, control over the export of salt, iron, wine and wheat, and the fixing of prices of meals at inns. The simple but fundamental point to be made is that sumptuary law was one amongst an extraordinary expansion of projects of governance.

A significant dimension of legislative activities in late medieval cities was the extent to which they contributed to the processes of state formation. Some care is needed because there may be a temptation to suggest that this dramatic expansion of urban legislative activity must have contributed to these processes. In the context of his study of the temperance movement in England, Brian Harrison (1971) makes the important point that not all legislative activity contributes to state formation. He contrasts the temperance movement with the kind of social reform movements that MacDonagh (1961) studied, such as the safety of emigrant passengers at sea. The temperance movement induced none of the collection of 'scientific' data or appointrnent of inspectors or other regulatory agents that were so important. It is even more important in the context of the late medieval city to be cautious about concluding that projects of sumptuary regulation can be understood as processes of state formation. My strong inclination is to think that the considerable output of sumptuary legislation had little or nothing to contribute. Perhaps the significance of the 'invention' of legislation in the early modern city, of which the sumptuary form was one widespread expression, should be viewed as providing some of the preconditions of subsequent state formation. However, these reflections do point to the importance of keeping in view the other regulatory projects that appeared during periods of active sumptuary interventions.

PATERNALISM, URBAN GOVERNMENT AND THE REFORMATION

A frequently encountered explanation of the prevalence of sumptuary laws in the late medieval and early modern city was that it manifested a predisposition towards a paternalistic mode of government. Some commentators, but by no means all, offer the extension that urban paternalism was associated with the coming of the Reformation in the first half of the sixteenth century. Kent Greenfield, in one of the most thorough studies of urban sumptuary law, argued that medieval sumptuary regulation was neither 'police regulation' nor 'economic regulation', but rather stemmed from a 'paternal' conception of government that manifested itself in an 'impulse to care for intimate processes of the citizen's life' (Greenfield 1918: 133). His concept of paternalism was one that viewed the state as assuming responsibility for economic thrift and the moral standard of family life, a concern that went hand in hand with the minute regulation of such matters as prices, wage rates and the like. Greenfield's account of the government of Nurnberg identifies a persistent paternalism that, significantly, reached across the most important political and intellectual upheaval, namely the coming of the Reformation. Thus as detailed in the previous chapter, he rejects the existence of any causal connection between the advent of the Reformation and sumptuary laws.

Gerald Strauss, who like Greenfield has focused his work on Nurnberg, likens paternalism rather literally to the voice of 'an offended, sometimes outraged parent correcting his prodigal offspring' (Strauss 1966: 112). His description of paternal governmentality is striking: 'Affluent and confident though the city was, it peered into the future with concern and suspicion' (1966: 114). Yet this formulation, and maybe the concept 'paternalism' itself, only engages with the backward-looking gaze of city government. The city fathers are presented as only wanting to preserve a society functioning through the operation of a mutually beneficial system of cooperation and interdeyendence. Strauss, like Greenfield and others, contends that the Reformation made no appreciable difference to the city's sumptuary legislation. Indeed, if anything, there was a certain relaxation associated with advancing prosperity, as a result of which finer cloths and heavier gold chains were allowed (Strauss 1966: 113).

Other strands of historical scholarship, significantly those less directly concerned with sumptuary law, do attribute greater significance to the Reformation as ushering in new and distinctive forms of governance. In particular, attention is focused on the role of the Reformation in the field of moral regulation. Merry Weisner (1988) argues that urban paternalism in Germany became increasingly concerned with morality. This resulted in both an extension of regulation into the household, but also an exclusion of certain groups from 'the public good'. These trends manifested themselves in increasingly interventionist regulation of domestic servants and of prostitution. By the end of the sixteenth century, control over servants reached its strictest and this coincided with the intensification of sumptuary clothing laws. This regulation was much concerned with the maintenance of the visible distinctions between master/mistress and servant relations. From the end of the fifteenth century there were attempts to hide the visibility of prostitution. Prostitutes were forbidden, for example, to sit outside the brothel and from occupying the front pews at church. During the first half of the sixteenth century throughout Germany city ordinances closed the brothels. The ideology of concern with the 'good of the community' came to demand a wider scope and increasingly embraced an expanding concern for decorum, order and morality.

Lorna Abray shows how in Strasbourg, Protestant city authorities expanded their jurisdiction, for example by the abolition of the consistory courts. One important dynamic was the struggle for jurisdiction over moral regulation. In 1529 a lay Marriage Court was established with jurisdiction over marriage, divorce and many sexual offences. By 1548 a more permanent lay jurisdiction was secured with the establishment of the Morals Board with jurisdiction over blasphemy, cursing, gambling, drunkenness and sexual offences (Abray 1985). The struggle revolved around the conflict between lay and clerical forces; there is little evidence of any significant change in the social objects against which that jurisdiction was wielded or of any significant new legislative activity. Evidence from Nordlingen into the late seventeenth century suggests the existence of a wide and intrusive moral regulation. An ordinance of 1672 forbade daughters of artisans and labourers to squander their dowry on provocative clothing. The control of weddings through limits on the number of guests and number of courses at wedding feasts persisted until mid-century. A wide range of popular activities and recreations were forbidden in moves that were typical of projects to reform popular morals: nude swimming, night revelry, 'tobacco-drinking' and the throwing of snowballs were all forbidden (Friedrichs 1979).

Lyndal Roper's impressive studies of Augsburg argue that the closure of the town brothel in 1532 was part of a wider programme of moral regulation which was ushered in by the Reformation (Roper 1985a). Although he has little to say about sumptuary law, mention should also be made of Hsia's study of social discipline during the three main variant (Lutheran, Calvinist and Catholic) Reformations that traversed Germany and central Europe (Hsia 1989). His position is consistent with those accounts that view the Reformation as involving an intensification of regulation characterized by a more systematic intervention of the 'moral police'.

These studies all, directly or indirectly, raise two important questions. The first is whether there was a connection between the advent of the Reformation and the expansion of paternalistic moral regulation. The second question is whether there was any link between the Reformation and sumptuary laws. The implication of these two questions is that if there is some demonstrable connection between the Reformation and moral regulation, but not between the Reformation and sumptuary laws, then this suggests that sumptuary law should not be regarded as, in any significant respect, an expression either of the Reformation or of moral regulation.

There seems to be widespread agreement that there was some generalized connection between the Reformation as it impacted on conceptions and practices of government and a preoccupation with moral regulation. This did not always mean that this predisposition yielded significant practical results. For example, in Elizabethan England Puritan parliamentarians urged increased moral legislation, but without much success (Kent 1973). During the Cromwellian period there was similarly much advocacy of moral regulation, but there was little legislative or administrative productivity. There was a series of attempts to renew sumptuary legislation, all of which foundered. While Puritan influence did lead to efforts to control a variety of aspects of personal behaviour, such as swearing, alehouses, gambling, Sabbath-observance and holiday jollifying, this was very much a continuation of a line of legislation from the Tudor period (Harte 1976: 151).

There is a surprising consensus from a range of studies that while the Reformation either sustained or accelerated moral regulation there is no evidence that points to extensive sumptuary initiatives during or immediately after the Reformation. While there are lines of connection between sumptuary law and matters of moral regulation, we need to recognize that what seems to have been clear to the burghers of the Reformation was that sumptuary law was a distinctively secular matter. The only claims that run counter are from sources that rely on a very impressionistic association between Puritanism and moral regulation on the one hand, and between moral regulation and sumptuary law on the other. The Reformation wrought profound changes with respect to who held power and the forms of constitutional relations between church and state, but there was a remarkable degree of continuity with respect to the objects of governance (Ozment 1975; Davis 1975). Thus the regulatory activities of the city governments of Northern Europe after the Reformation reveal a significant continuity with their predecessors. Sumptuary regulation persisted, but at a somewhat reduced frequency and intensity. This suggests that, at least for present purposes, any discussion that places a significant reliance on the identification of urban government as 'paternalist' tends to emphasize only its conservative face, significant though this was, at the expense of the stuttering and unplanned steps into the future that also marked the practices of city government. One question which the available material has not made it possible to explore is the relationship between sumptuary regulation and the forms of Catholic Reformation. The characteristic concern of Tridentine politics with the reform of popular culture would suggest that sumptuary law would continue as before or even expand (Greyerz 1984). Unfortunately my own data is at its sketchiest for those regions most affected, but there certainly appears to be continuity rather than disruption of the sumptuary record.

With these considerations in mind it seems more fruitful to rely on the conception of discipline rather than paternalism as an organizing theme. This discussion suggests the need to highlight a feature implicit in Foucault's concept. It will be recalled that one of his most significant contentions is that 'power' is never entirely negative, but must be understood as having a positive dimension.[10] Similarly it is necessary to free 'discipline' from exclusively negative attributes. Programmatically Foucault was committed to such a treatment, though it is significant that given the preponderant emphasis he placed on the connection between discipline and surveillance, especially apparent in his studies of asylums and prisons, in practice he reproduced a negative conception of discipline. In contrast my exploration of the trajectory of urban government points to a conception of discipline as a set of practices traversed by both positive dimensions, in the concern for predictability and efficiency, and negative dimensions, concerned with the preservation of the old ways and with imposing moralistic restrictions.

One of the major features of the shifting conception of discipline was a profound change in the role of government with respect to economic protectionism. The emergence of distinct urban economies was marked by a wide range of protectionism, both internal and external. Examples of this activity were restrictions on the number of apprentices, on the admission of new masters, prohibition of 'putting-out', and restrictions on forestalling and other manipulations of the market. Concern with 'the economy' was, however, not something confined to the cities, but was just as evident in the centralized states. For reasons of ease of exposition I will deal with the vital question of the relationship between economic governance and sumptuary law as a separate topic in Chapter 14. For present purposes it is sufficient to introduce an argument that will become increasingly important. It is that sumptuary law is gradually and unintentionally submerged by economic projects. In the first instance cities had an abiding fiscal motive in the light of which it came to make good 'economic' sense to refrain from prohibiting certain styles of dress or ornamentation, but instead to impose a tax or to grant exemptions against contributions to the city's coffers. By extension it became increasingly frequent for what started out as sumptuary restraints to become import restrictions. It was not a big step then to promote domestic industries on import substitution grounds. It was through such mechallisms, that may provisionally be identified as protectionist, that the 'government of the economy' became transformed (Rose and Miller 1990). Sumptuary laws underwent a metamorphosis and remerged protectionism. Having introduced this theme that will be pursued and elaborated on in subsequent chapters, I conclude the present chapter with some synoptic views of the link between city government and sumptuary law in three case studies.

SOME COMPARISONS: FLORENCE, NÜRNBERG AND LONDON

Trajectories of Florentine sumptuary legislation

For longer periods than any other Italian city, Florence was politically dominated by the guilds, in particular by the merchant guilds *(arti maggiori)*. During such periods much of the legislation was directed against the 'unruly' upper classes or magnates, for example by the imposition of taxes on property rather than on income. Sumptuary laws commenced in 1281 and from the very beginning the commune adopted the very distinctive strategy of issuing licences allowing the wearing of otherwise forbidden apparel. A payment of 50 lire secured entitlement to wear prohibited head ornaments, gold-silver decorations on cloaks, and pearls. This fiscal tactic tied sumptuarv rules closely to the *gabelle* tax that already existed on salt, wine and dowries (Rainey 1985). Florence was unique in this early linking of sumptuary restrictions with fiscal and administrative motives (Kantorowitz and Denholm-Young 1970: 358).

The first major revision and consolidation of sumptuary legislation took place in 1322 with the 'Statute of the Captain of the People'. Its preamble identified its aim as being 'to eliminate the ostentation that has led to lascivious and thoughtless expense'. Interestingly both men and women were forbidden ornaments bearing the likenesses of trees, flowers, animals and birds. This rule probably combines a restriction on the expense of embroidery, a frequent target of sumptuary rules, along with a more religious regulation of the representation of images. More significantly this law imposed a numerical limit on the number of garments owned and also a value limit on clothes and ornaments for both men and women; such rules obviously implied the possibility of the inspection of private homes (Rainey 1985: 95). By the end of the thirteenth century women had been ordered to register all dresses over a certain value. From the 1330s enforcement of sumptuary legislation had been placed in the hands of an *ufficiale delle donne*; it was specified that this post sllould be held by a foreigner, a 'true Guelf', along with four assistants, who had power to impose penalties without recourse to appeal. Rainey reports that in 1427 an attempt was made to create a permanent sumptuary magistracy, but this failed because tlle unpopularity of the job resulted in no applicants being forthcoming![11]

It is known that from 1343 the city government, the *Signoria,* had sent out inspectors to examine domestic clothes chests. Items in breach of the provisions of the sumptuary code might continue to be worn as long as they were taxed and marked with a special lead seal bearing the Florentine lily on one side and a cross on the other. Women had to line up to have such items listed in a register (de Marly 1985:19). While some of the legislation itself was directed against both sexes, the overwhelming thrust of sumptuary discourses and enforcement was against women, though it should be noted that young men were also a significant target.

A renewed sumptuary initiative was launched in 1356 with the enactment of an extended *pragmati,* arranged in 43 chapters. Their content was directed mainly against women's apparel, in particular against luxury clothes and extravagant ornamentation. The wives of knights were exempted from most, but not all provisions. Regulation was extended to the clothing of children and of servants. The restrictions on the number of wedding guests was evidently a 'public order' measure since it was complained that weddings got out of hand, presumably as a result of rivalries between the great Florentine families.

The threat of invasion in the winter of 1358-59 led to the enactment of forced loans, the imposition of a wealth tax, and further restrictions on dress, weddings and baptisms. From 1363 for an annual *gabelle* tax of 100 florins permission was obtained to wear pearls, precious stones and mother-of-pearl. Something of the general style of Florentine sumptuary law can be gleaned from the extensive sumptuary ordinance of 1373 whose preamble ran:

> Considering the Commune's need for revenue to pay current expenses [it is enacted that]: First, all women and girls, whether married or not, whether betrothed or not, of whatever age, rank and condition . . . who wear – or who wear in future – any gold, silver, pearls, precious stones, bells, ribbons of gold or silver, or cloth of silk brocade on their bodies or heads . . . for the ornamentation of their bodies . . . will be required to pay each year . . . the sum of 50 florins . . . to the treasurer of the gabelle on contracts.
>
> (Brucker 1971: 180)

The sumptuary tax in the form of the *gabelle* was, with occasional interruptions, to remain a central feature of Florentine sumptuary regulation for the next three centuries. It manifests the fiscal dilemma - the tax is justified in the name of sumptuary restraint, but the government relies upon its yield. In 1377 another lengthy pragmatica directed specific focus 'to eliminate the excesses of women and youths' (Rainey 1985: 200). Interestingly it largely removed all purchase of exemptions by means of the *gabelle* taxes.

In June 1363 restrictions had been imposed on funerals during a plague outbreak: severe restrictions were imposed on funeral processions and on the price of coffins, revealing an interesting cross-over between sumptuary and public health projects (Barr 1989: 108). In a further onslaught on weddings, in 1370 caterers were required to report all wedding feasts, the number of guests and the dishes consumed to the notary of the Guild of Spice Merchants (incongruously between 1385 and 1389 these descriptions were entered in the Book of the Dead that listed all burials). This provision suggests a conceptual linkage in which the 'sumptuary imagination' viewed both weddings and funerals as public events of conspicuous consumption (Herlihy 1980: 139–40).

The Ciompi revolt of 1378 brought the artisans from the middle and lower guilds to political power for a brief period until 1382, briefly replacing the patrician oligarchy, drawn from the upper strata of long-established merchants (Brucker 1977). No new sumptuary legislation was attempted until the patricians returned to power, and their first measure in 1384 was simply a reworking of the 1377 rules. The *gabelle* system was revived and further extended and from 1384 the commune started to sell exemptions from funeral regulations. Funerals and weddings had considerable importance for the patrician classes in establishing and maintaining status, but it is not clear whether the commune was milking the nobility or granting privileges to anyone who could afford them (Strocchia 1989: 135–37). I have not been able to establish any pattern in, let alone explanation of, the movement backwards and forwards between licensing and prohibition, nor does it appear to be a topic that has attracted the attention of specialists in Florentine history.

Richard Trexler suggests the existence of a general connection between the perception of crisis and the resort to renewed sumptuary endeavours. When crises occurred, whether military threat, earthquakes, winds, droughts or plague, the city's first response was to marshal its traditional expressive public rituals of prayer and procession. Crises were often explained in terms of discourses of moral degeneration; one oft repeated target was the theme of degeneration through either moral laxity (in particular homosexuality) or the sumptuousness of dress (Trexler 1980: 350). For example, a serious flood in 1333 was attributed to the combined evils of avarice, usury, women's dress, drunkenness and gluttony, and resulted in another sumptuary enactment. Fear of pending calamities was attributed to women's dress and produced legislation in 1449 (1980: 380).

In the aftermath of the protracted economic and military crisis, war with Genoa, plague and unemployment between 1411 and 1414 came the 'great Code' of 1415 that, for a while, instituted a complete ban on the use of pearls and precious stones (Kantorowitz and Denholm-Young 1970: 358). By the 1430s the decline of republican Florence had set in. During the crisis years of that decade there was an upsurge in regulation of the extravagance of women, and against male moral offences, particularly homosexuality (Brucker 1971:179). Sumptuary ordinances were increasingly linked to misogynistic denunciations of women. During a debate in 1433 in the *Signorin* women were rebuked for their 'reprobate and diabolical nature' by means of which they forced their husbands to indulge them in luxury. As we shall see this trope is a common element in the important politics that surrounds what I will call the political economy of marriage; I leave aside discussion until a later chapter, but it should be noted that much of the information on this topic comes from Florence. In general terms, what motivated the city fathers was the populationist concern with the age of marriage, which was regarded as the key determinant of the size of families. The allegation was that female luxury led men, on account of the 'unbearable expense', to postpone marriage (Brucker 1971: 181).

The coming of the autocratic rule of the nobles associated with the Medici accession in 1434 and the demise of civic Florence exhibited significant continuity in sumptuary matters. The Medici carried on the struggle that at one time or another has been waged in every jurisdiction against decolletage. These battles have always oscillated from a complete prohibition of any exposure of women's throats or necks. Ten years later, in 1444, there was a relaxation and women were allowed a precisely stipulated 3 cm below the collarbone and twice that at the back (Hughes 1983: 83). While in many jurisdictions sumptuary regulation of weddings and funerals disappeared and sumptuary law was narrowly associated with dress codes, Florence kept all these major forms of law active. In 1473, the year of the consolidation of power by Lorenzo de Medici, severe restrictions were placed on funeral expenses and there was a renewed onslaught on alimentary consumption with a law that Trexler describes as being 'without parallel', prescribing the food that could be served, the plates on which it was served, and the expense that could be incurred (Trexler 1980: 409).

Each stage of Florentine sumptuary law seems to have been characterized by distinct and shifting projects. In the fourteenth century restraints on the magnati were balanced with attempts to inhibit the *popolnni* from imitating the 1nn,~rnnti. In the late fourteenth and early fifteenth centuries sumptuary law became largely a fiscal device. Later in the fifteenth century populationist projects come to the fore. With the reestablishment of the Florentine republic in 1527, after generations of Medici rule, one of the first acts of the commune was to introduce a new sumptuary law (Hughes 1983: 75). The Medici restoration of 1531 in turn resulted in a steady stream of sumptuary enactments. Twenty-one sumptuary statutes were passed during the seventeenth century until the sumptuary ethic expired towards the end of the century (Burke 1987: 144). The sumptuary discourses became harsher, focusing on combating 'permissiveness', with more extensive attempts to prohibit rather than to restrain female fashion. Regulations were increasingly directed at both women and men, and became particularly focused on young men, suggesting some renewed generational tension. This last phase of Florentine sumptuary law was directed at the moral reform of young men who were perceived as precipitating the collapse of the burgher values that had been central to the republican tradition of Florence.[12]

Nürnberg

Kent Greenfield's study of the sumptuary legislation of Nürnberg has stood the test of time well (Greenfield 1918). It remains the most sophisticated monograph on sumptuary law; only Diane Hughes' smaller scale project on Florence surpasses it in intellectual flair and originality (Hughes 1983). 1 will rely heavily on Greenfield's material, with some additions culled from Gerald Strauss (1966). I will, however, be using Greenfield's material against his own interpretation. He argues that the early sumptuary laws in Nürnberg were directed at the protection of morals, while the later rules were increasingly concerned with the maintenance of class differentials. This thesis contrasts with my analysis of sumptuary law in Florence. There is agreement around the thesis that, despite conventional wisdom, sumptuary law is not subsumed by the preservation of hierarchy, but rather that this only becomes predominant at a later stage. My argument with Greenfield is over his claim that sumptuary law had its roots in moral regulation; this like the hierarchy argument is one-dimensional.

Sumptuary law is in evidence in Nürnberg from the late thirteenth century.[13] The early sumptuary law in medieval Nürnberg in the thirteenth and fourteenth centuries was typical of that in other countries during the same period. Its central focus was on the regulation of the public celebration of private ceremonies, in particular weddings and funerals, and to a lesser extent on christenings and baptisms. Later there seems to have been a distinct shift of focus: funerals attracted less attention, while weddings became the primary target of sumptuary laws in medieval Nürnberg.

The marriage laws of Nürnberg in the thirteenth and fourteenth centuries lacked coherent structure and were a series of haphazard cumulative prohibitions. Their flavour can be gleaned from the following examples. A maximum of 12 wedding guests, six of each sex, were permitted; the bride and the groom could only be accompanied by two (and later four) friends. Out-of-town fiddlers or other musicians were prohibited.[14] Wedding presents were prohibited at one point in time, but more generally were limited by value or by number. The wedding feast was greatly restricted by an edict that no food was to be served save to the spouses' parents and out-of-town guests. Later a rather strange rule stipulated that a maximum of six maidens could be invited to the wedding party, but could only be served with fruit and wine. Anyone who intended to host a wedding in their house was required to visit the town-hall, read the regulations and make a promise to the burgomaster to obey them.

The great bulk of early sumptuary regulation sought to place restrictions on these very traditional familial occasions for celebration, indulgence and conspicuous consumption. Weddings, funerals and the like had long been public events, providing evidence as rites of passage of changes in social status. Marc Raeff suggests that this early form of sumptuary regulation pursued a compartmentalization of social life, establishing a distinctive separation between public and private (Raeff 1983: 78–79). I think that Raeff is wrong here. My sense is that these forms of sumptuary law established a distinctive fusion of the public and private; it is only later when a dichotomous conception of the public/private distinction becomes established that the modernist dichotomous thought becomes possible which defines anything that is not subject to regulation as therefore being private.

The more general question is: how are we to understand this distinctively medieval practice of regulating weddings? Greenfield is, I suggest, wrong in thinking that this species of rules was concerned with moral regulation. A more persuasive explanation is that the primary concern was with the reform of popular culture and the regulation of labour discipline supplemented by a moral gloss. The primary concern seems to have been with the economic burden of unrestrained festivities, particularly where com munities were gripped by competitive rivalries; this is supplemented with a concern that prolonged celebrations disrupted normal work activity. What is interesting about this economic conception is the emphasis on the zero-sum view that consumption necessarily depleted a family's resources and thus ignored the role of hospitality and reciprocity as having their own economic rationality. I had anticipated when I first started exploring this phase of sumptuary activity that the paternalistic concern was likely to have been a concern about families getting into debt to finance revelries. This would have tied into the almost universal medieval preoccupation with usury. It is, I believe, of considerable significance that I have found not a single trace of any discursive linkage of sumptuary restrictions with debt or usury either in Nürnberg or from anywhere else. Rather the discourses focused on the much more ancient anxiety about 'ruin'; it was the consumption of the economic reserves, of grain, seed and livestock, that could spell disaster during adverse climatic conditions.

The moral gloss that supplemented and served to legitimate these economic worries was the sense that extravagant feasting undermined the necessary regularity of work discipline. Here I think more needs to be made of the detail that Greenfield refers to but does not explore. The early wedding restrictions seem to have been emanations from urhan Nürnberg that were directed primarily against the peasantry of the hinterland. Assuming that Weber was correct in his observation that cities were centres of consumption rather than of production, it is possible that peasant self-indulgence was conceived of as disrupting supplies to the city. This concern takes on more substance in the light of the crisis caused by the widespread labour shortage that resulted from the succession of famines and plagues in the early fourteenth century.

A more general consideration is that peasant consumption of their fragile surpluses on weddings and other festivities was characteristic of pre-capitalist agriculture. There were only limited possibilities for capital accumulation; periodic communal consumption of the surplus had long and tenuous roots. This leads me to my suggestion that projects for the reform of popular culture were a significant element of these restrictions on feasting. It is precisely that these practices were so deeply traditional, so at variance with the formative bourgeois consciousness that was developing in the towns. More generally the sumptuary laws directed against weddings, funerals and other festivities should be seen as a manifestation of projects of the reform of popular culture (Burke 1978). The authorities employed sumptuary law as a way of disciplining patterns of consumption which were seen as being both irrational and disorderly; the situational rationality of the sociability of the peasantry conflicted with the emergent bourgeois rationality. It was this widening cultural gap that was articulated through the sumptuary discourses which were taken up and extended by the new urban rulers.

The advance of the self-discipline that Elias locates within courtly society was paralleled by forms of self-restraint through which urban experience differentiated itself from the surrounding rural society. This ideological differentiation is rendered support from theology by a growing condemnation of peasant culture as pagan, a critique that becomes sharper and more insistent with the coming of the Reformation (Greyerz 1984). And here, perhaps, we can reintroduce Greenfield's perception of the moral roots of the restrictions of feasting, because such occasions were associated with relaxation of the work-a-day social and sexual norms, an anxiety of transgression that becomes inflated in bourgeois consciousness.[15]

Whatever configuration of these explanatory elements we might settle on if studies of the same detail as Greenfield's were available to provide comparisons with the sumptuary histories of other early urban communities, we can underline the contrast with the case of Florence where the funereal and wedding restrictions were more an inter-class matter between the already thoroughly urban patricians and merchants. The form of early sumptuary legislation had an explicitly universalistic formulation and this need not undermine my argument that it had an anti-peasant ideological content. During the course of the fifteenth century the Nürnberg edicts became more obviously focused on the internal relations of the city. Restrictions were specifically directed at artisans and apprentices, presumably because they were more numerous and were gradually increasing their purchasing power. Nevertheless the fines stipulated for patrician offenders were differentially heavy and there was explicit reference to the importance of setting a good example.

Nürnberg's sumptuary laws remind us of the important connection between age and status on the borders of modernity. While differential treatment of women by familial status was widespread, Nürnberg is interesting in imposing specific age differentiations on men. No man over 50 was to wear red buckram, while no man under 32 was allowed to trim his cloak with beaver fur. There was also evidence of concern with male decency: male jackets had to reach at least two inches below the crutch. The motive for the ban on men parting their hair is less clear; it may well have been an attempt to resist 'foreign' fashion. The clothing ordinances came to deplore 'new-fangledness' (*neue Sitten*) and 'foreignness'. At first the council outlawed each objectionable new innovation as it appeared on the streets. By the end of the fifteenth century they moved to a more comprehensive assault on innovation with a general ban on 'Innovation and Unaccustomed Styles in Apparel, Adornment and Shoes' (Strauss 1966: 113; Greenfield 1918: 109).

As we have already seen, early Florentine laws were gender-neutral in formulation but fairly rapidly changed to target women. Assuming that Greenfield's translations can be relied upon, the women of Nürnberg do not seem to have been discriminated against in sumptuary matters.[16] An enactment of 1657 complained:

> It is unfortunately an established fact that both men and women-folk have, in utterly irresponsible manner, driven extravagance in dress and new styles to such shameful and wanton extremes that the different classes are barely to be known apart.
>
> (Boehn 1932-35: III: 173)

Unfortunately Greenfield did not have available sources through which to explore the enforcement of sumptuary law and the more specific issue of gender discrimination in enforcement practices. It will be necessary to interrogate the gendered nature of sumptuary law in more detail in the next chapter.

Towards the end of the seventeenth century Greenfield detected mounting evidence of a new concern with the maintenance of social class distinctions in dress (1918: 126). One ordinance was entitled 'Ordinance and prohibition of August 8, 1568 regarding vain display, and what is permissible and proper in clothing and other things for each man according to his rank' (1918: 130). It is again worthwhile emphasizing this late arrival of the hierarchic motive that does so much to undermine the standard interpretation of sumptuary law. Four ranks were recognized: old noble families, respectable merchants, and traders, while the fourth class was a miscellany of other occupations. This fourth class also included all those who had been in Nürnberg for only a few years, thus providing evidence of the strong associational ethic. The regulation was accordingly divided into four parts and reveals enormous attention to detail, down to the length of the ribbons used to decorate the horses drawing bridal coaches. Evidence of concern with public recognizability and with the conspicuousness of display is suggested by the prominence of regulations concerning travelling equipage (e.g. material of saddle cloths, pompoms on heads of coach-horses, etc.).

London

England presents a contrast to both Florence and Nürnberg. The overwhelming volume of sumptuary law emanated from the central state in the form of national legislation. There were only occasional examples of local sumptuary initiatives in England. For example, in 1344 the 'Little Red Book' of the by-laws of the Corporation of Bristol laid down expenditure limits on furs for different categories of citizens (Bickeley 19()0). The City of Coventry issued sumptuary regulations of its own prohibiting 'common folk' from wearing fox or lamb fur, and silk or satin in their doublets (de Marly 1985: 34)

London, however, presents a somewhat different case since it was such an overwhelming presence of both economic and political power, and was also a site of so much conspicuous consumption. The result was that the powerful merchants who ran the City of London became embroiled in sumptuary matters. Periodically the city fathers issued their own sumptuary ordinances. Sometimes they were clearly acting as a conveyor belt transmitting royal proclamations to the citizens. At other times they seem to have acted on their own initiative in devising local sumptuary rules. In England there was little or no national attempt to regulate prostitution; it seems to have been regárded as a London problem only. So decrees were issued in the fourteenth and fifteenth centuries prohibiting 'women of evil life' from wearing fur hoods (except lamb's wool or rabbit) (Wadmore 1902). Then in 1559 the P'rivy Council proposed to the City Corporation the appointment of two 'watchers' per parish; while prostitutes were a particular target the aim seems to have been to gather reports on general compliance with dress regulations (Hooper 1915: 441).

A proclamation of 1562 'Enforcing Statutes of Apparel' required the Lord Mayor to appoint four 'substantial and well-meaning men' in every ward who were to be allowed to retain a moiety of the proceeds of forfeiture of illicit garments. The Mayor was instructed to organize searches of the premises of all tailors and hosiers every eight days (4 Eliz. 1, Procl. 6/5/1562; Dyson 1618: No. 45). Attempts were made to impose bond payments on tailors and hosiers to ensure that they only made permitted garments, but resistance was encountered; for example, in Blackfriars ward warrants had to be issued before the tailors and hosiers would appear before the aldermen.

There is also evidence that many of the guilds engaged in their own regulatory activity. The Merchant Taylors, for example, issued regulations enjoining modesty in dress and actually committed members to jail for excess apparel (Clode 1875: 205;1888: I: 351). As the guild's ceremonial activities, always an important feature of guild life, became increasingly integrated with the City of London their dress regulations tended to become ossified, concerned exclusively with the ceremonial wear of their officials.

There was clearly considerable variation in the degree and form of involvement of European cities in the production and enforcement of sumptuary law. France was, as might well have been predicted, mid-way between the centralized model of England and the dispersed and semi-autonomous pattern of the Italian and German cities. There was a steady stream of legislation, mainly on dress matters, from the end of the thirteenth century. French sumptuary law outlasted English legislative endeavours because, as we will see, two factors aided its retention. In the first place the French court remained politically important for much longer than the English, and secondly the French state proved very adept at harnessing sumptuary mechanisms to the goals of economic protectionism. In brief, French sumptuary laws lasted until the eve of the Revolution. Alongside the central dress restrictions there was a mass of particularistic ordinances from many, if not all, of the more important cities.

The lesson to be derived from the involvement of the cities of Europe in the history of sumptuary law underlines my resistance to the view that sumptuary law is to be understood as a defensive or conservative device of a fast declining post-feudal aristocracy. In the towns and cities of Europe sumptuary law was a part of the context in which the developments that shaped the configurations of modernity were in progress. It is of particular significance that the imposition of laws specifically directed at the reproduction of hierarchical class relations came late rather than early in most European cities.

9

Gender Wars: Sex, Power and Resistance

DRESS AND THE REPRODUCTION OF GENDER

The most persistent form of sumptuary law was directed at the regulation of dress. Since dress is one of the central mechanisms through which gender is reproduced, it follows that a central feature of any inquiry into sumptuary law must be to explore the part that it played in the gender wars. Sumptuary law exhibited considerable variability in its presentation of gender; sometimes it was gender-neutral (e.g. 'no person, man or woman, may wear . . .'), at other times it was explicit in directing its restrictions against a particular sex (e.g. 'no woman may wear . . .'), while on occasions women were specifically exempted from the sumptuary rules.[1] It is significant that the target sex changed over time. Sometimes men and at other times women were the explicit target. On the surface no pattern is immediately discernible. This chapter will be concerned to explore whether or not it is possible to make sense of this variability and to do so in the context of the historical dynamic of gender relations.

It is important to note at the outset that the information available, limited though it is, concerning the enforcement of sumptuary laws points unambiguously at the fact that, in so far as sumptuary laws were enforced, they were enforced overwhelmingly against women. This preliminary view does not yet provide an answer to the question of the extent to which this enforcement against women is independent of the targeting of the legislation itself. It will be necessary to investigate whether it made any difference if the rules themselves were directed against men, women or both sexes.

As I argued in Chapter 3 clothes play a significant part in the construction of gender relations. Dress provides one significant discursive apparatus through which gender relations have been lived, experienced and thought about. Clothes facilitate the expression of ideas about hierarchy, equality, community, purity, sexuality, sin, pride, shame, and most important of all they articulate the displaced anxieties about the contemporary state of gender relations. I use the term 'displaced anxiety' to make the point that the anxieties involved were not necessarily or 'really' about dress itself, but that this provided a way of thinking and articulating a more pervasive set of preoccupations about sex, gender, family, authority and much more (Newburn 1992: 171).

Marshall Sahlins provides an approach to grappling with the way in which clothes provide a mechanism through which gender may be thought and spoken (Sahlins 1976: 177–204). Given the centrality of the dichotomous conceptualization of gender – male/female, masculine/feminine – he suggests that there are a limited number of simple or basic rules that reveal this general dichotomous structure of thought about gender. This dichotomy is inscribed in a multitude of ways, and as testimony to them all I will cite the ubiquity of the rule that buttons are on opposite sides for males and females; blouses are separated from shirts by this simple opposition, but the 'odd' feel of a garment that buttons the 'wrong' way is one that everybody knows.[2] Sahlins suggests an analysis of the gender dichotomy in terms of three elementary values, texture, line and colour, that serve to distinguish male and female in terms of binary sets (e.g. rough/smooth, straight/curved, sombre/bright). These 'natural' associations are amplified through the repetition of these binary distinctions in a way that contributes to the reproduction of the gendered dichotomy.[3] Clothes teach people much about what it means to be a woman or a man within each culture.

An alternative route by which to address these issues is to employ a Freudian approach focusing on the existence of differential 'erotogenic zones' and of women's clothing as revolving around permissible forms of what Valerie Steele calls 'passive exhibitionism' (Steele 1985: 25). The sexual symbolism of clothes finds expression in Freud's stress on the 'libido for looking'. Clothes allow both an active and a passive expression of the libido for looking and for touching, and the extension of their normal forms into voyeurism, exhibitionism and fetishism. On this account men repress their exhibitionism, but have more developed active voyeurism, while women manifest a more passive form, expressed in 'the desire to be looked at' (Freud 1953–75: 14; 126–130). This voyeurism/exhibitionism dimension in turn connects with my stress in Chapter 3 on the potentiality for 'deliberate' ambiguity in the semiotics of clothing that allows the simultaneous expression of sexuality and its denial.

It is also important to keep in mind the instability of gender identities. Dress involves both play and transgression that work through major and minor disruptions of the taken-for-grantedness of gendered dichotomies. For example, Susan Shapiro (1973) notes the power of fashion to muddle, to change or to adulterate sexual identity. If dress both expresses and transgresses gender then this suggests the potential significance of those practices that serve to stabilize gendered identities: customs, etiquette, norms and rules operate to reproduce gendered identities (Brundage 1987). This in turn suggests the interesting hypothesis that this chapter explores, namely that sumptuary laws served, in part at least, as a project to stabilize sex/gender identities. There is an additional historical dimension that generates the need to explain why the shift occurred in which increased significance came to be attached to women's dress. Not only did it become more ornamental than men's, but it became a widely familiar focus for displaced anxieties. This suggests the importance of inquiring into what bearing, if any, this feminization of fashion had on the trajectory of sumptuary law. Is it the case that as fashion became feminized sumptuary law increasingly targeted women? These issues about the connection between dress, gender and sumptuary law are the subject matter of this chapter.

GENDER, DRESS AND FASHION

Dress demarcates and secures gender. Clothing is one of the basic mechanisms that provides for the legibility of sex and gender. If clothes convey and represent gender it follows that projects concerned with the regulation of dress must, whether intentionally or not, have an impact on the regulation of gender. It should be borne in mind that clothing works both ways; it is both a means of reading others and a means of displaying the identity of the wearer. It is necessary to move backwards and forwards asking 'What identity is being displayed?' and 'How is this clothing being read by observers?' Fashion provides a means by and through which the shifting discourses of gender may be read.

Although all clothing systems have exhibited some gender differentiation it was not until toward the end of the thirteenth century that there occurred a sharp sexual differentiation in clothing. Before that time the clothing of both men and women involved wrapping the body in one or more layers of single pieces of fabric cut in some variant of the rectangle. These robes varied in length as an indicator of social status, with shorter garments being used by those engaged in manual labour. There was undoubtedly gender differentiation in the way in which robes were worn and in their ornamentation. The significant development in Europe from the late thirteenth century was the emergence of a stable, yet infinitely variable, dichotomy that is recognizably linked to a generic distinction between trousers and skirts.

The other significant gendered variable in fashion was the shift in the degree of elaboration of men's and women's dress. In some periods fashion seemed to impinge on men's dress and it underwent more or less rapid shifts with respect to some combination of the materials used, the cut or line of garments, the range and form of ornamentation, or the colour or texture thereof. At other periods men's dress remained more or less static whilst women's dress underwent sharp change or elaboration. It is only around the time of the Industrial Revolution that the pattern became established, which has remained more or less intact to the present, whereby women's dress exhibited greater variation and more frequent changes, becoming the very object of fashion itself, while men's dress was more stable and less subject to the injunctions of fashion.[4]

The connection between gender and fashion has its own history. My sense is that the explanation of the shifts of focus between men and women as the bearers of contemporary fashion and their periodization is far from settled. I content myself with drawing attention to some links with a number of themes already developed in this study: gender dichotomy in dress has been centrally concerned with 'recognizability'; it manifests itself as a concern to establish some natural and stable connection between sex, gender and social role. Significantly in the period under consideration there were always a number of significant female statuses. Since the position of women was defined by reference to their relations with men as heads of families, the statuses of daughter, bride, mother, matron and widow were each significant and generally found expression in codes of dress and rules of fashion.

Since dress discloses gender it also expresses, directly or

indirectly, the sexual politics of the age. Since sexual politics rarely manifests itself directly it is typically a field dominated by displaced anxieties. With respect to sex/gender the general form of these anxieties is concern with departures from some (presumed) 'natural' structure of sex/gender relations. One of the most typical social anxieties occurs in the face of social change that appears to undermine the known and taken-for-granted gender order. There is no surprise in discovering that men across late medieval and early modern Europe expressed many of their social anxieties in complaints about women in general and their dress in particular, and exhibited an inclination to generate moral panic around disruptions to commonsense conceptions of a natural order of gender relations. It is evident that the sumptuary tradition both reflects and manifests these concerns.

The social anxieties were standardly articulated in terms of the dress and social demeanour of women; they spoke of a complex of only very loosely connected themes. A fluctuating but persistent theme expressed a moral preoccupation with female modesty that mingled with a concern about the controllability of women. By far the most persistent discursive theme fixated on the vanity of women; this resonated with an implicit appeal to male economic interests in that wives and daughters were construed as both extravagant and irresponsible and thus a threat to family prosperity. There was a complex web of connections in the discursive construction of the sumptuary critique that links gender problematics to a variety of dangers, military (weakness and effeminacy), economic (luxury/dearth) and social (nationalism/foreignness, world-turned-upside-down).

The diatribes against women's vanity and their preoccupation with fashion was part of the longstanding misogynous discourses that stretched back into early Christianity and beyond. It is the very persistence of these themes that requires a certain caution before concluding that sumptuary laws were significantly directed toward the regulation of women. Since sumptuary laws were so closely tied to the regulation of dress, and that dress was and is such a central component of gender identity, it is important to pose the question: to what extent should we regard the protection of gender boundaries as providing a consistent thematic in the history of sumptuary legislation? Beyond this lies the question: to what extent can it be demonstrated that the protection of some specific conception of the gender order plays some part as a contributory project underlying the sumptuary impulse? In brief, was the attempt to regulate dress an attempt to police women?

In order to address these questions it is necessary to consider the gender dimorphism of dress and its connection with the social institution of fashion. The important question is: what bearing does it have for the understanding of sumptuary law that during its active period women came increasingly to be judged by and thus preoccupied with their appearance, such that fashion and femininity become inextricably linked. One articulate woman of Bologna, Nicolosa Sanuit, urging Cardinal Bessarion to remove sumptuary restrictions, captured the core issue with great precision. She argued that women deserved freedom of choice in clothes because it was to clothes that they had been reduced: 'Ornament and apparel, because they are our insignia of worth, we cannot suffer to be taken from us' (quoted Hughes 1983: 87). Thus 'social visibility' and 'recognizability' are of particular significance for women. Whereas men derive their recognition from their public roles, women being excluded from such roles take their social positions either derivatively from their fathers/husbands or by means of the primary form of their social presence, that is their visibility, their capacity to be seen, the object of the gaze, as an entity to be looked at.

It is considerations of this type that lead Harrianne Mills to address another facet of the dichotomization of gendered appearance. While men's dress expresses a 'hierarchical principle' of class or status manifesting self-aggrandisement, women's dress is an expression of a 'seduction principle', of sex-consciousness. This view, although it is cast within an essentialist view of sex difference, nevertheless has interesting implications for our understanding of sumptuary law. For men it is a matter of economic or class regulation and for women sumptuary law manifests considerations of moral regulation and respectability (Mills 1984: 255–56). In a similar vein Diane Hughes suggests that sumptuary laws were imposed 'to control women's appetites and men's social ambitions' (Hughes 1976: 49).

In this connection it is important to stress that the visibility of women is not only a matter of personal self-presentation, but that status or class are woven into gender and also rendered visible. For example, in a law from Bologna in 1474 a visible code of social status in women's dress was provided: gold dresses for the wives and daughters of knights; sleeves of gold for those of notaries and bankers; crimson dresses for major artisans and, finally, women linked to the lower trades were permitted only crimson sleeves (Hughes 1983: 98). Class and personal presentation frequently became closely associated. I have noticed that the girdle was one of the most frequent targets of sumptuary attention and probably deserves an essay in its own right. The girdle itself tended to be a site of what might be called condensed conspicuous consumption by virtue of its elaborate and costly ornamentation; in addition a purse often hung from the bejewelled girdle that was worn on the outside, its positioning between waist and hips varying with the flux of fashion, with the ostensible justification of carrying money for alms also providing a way in which women were able to display wealth (Fiero 1989: 52).

THE BODY AS A SITE OF REGULATION

There is a fundamental but somehow imperceptible shift from the situation in which the focus rests on the objects of conspicuous consumption to one in which it is the body itself, and paramountly woman's body, that becomes the object of moralization and of regulatory attention. The sites of condensed conspicuous consumption shift with time to different parts of the female anatomy. Wealth, in the form of precious stones or metal, is displayed against the eroticized backdrop of the woman's body (Turner 1984). Some sites of display, particularly the face, neck, ears and chest, have secured an almost universal significance. What has been insufficiently discussed is the complex investments, discourses and struggles that have been waged around these sites over time. Diane Hughes' brilliant study of the social and sexual history of the earring in northern Italy illustrates these dimensions. She tells of the passage of the earring from being the mark of the outsider, the North-African jewess, via the sexual display of prostitutes, to the achievement of a preeminent site for the display of male wealth and eroticized invitation to focus the gaze upon the wearer's face, a fixation of the gaze that has persisted down to the present:

> The movement of ear-rings from a sign of concupiscence and mark of the outsider to a sign of honour and mark of the entrenched brings to an end the long fifteenth-century struggle

> between ideals of civic wealth and Franciscan poverty in a victory of aristocratic codification.
>
> (Hughes 1986: 48)

The rise of Christianity to hegemony had major ramifications for daily life, particularly with respect to the body. The key ambivalence with regard to the body stems from the notion that God's incarnation in the body of man was also his humiliation. Thus 'original sin' was at first a sin of intellectual pride manifest in the quest for knowledge viewed in opposition to faith. Medieval Christianity transformed this intellectual sin into a sexual sin, a sin that revolved around and was encapsulated in the body of woman. There is a connection here between the Church's intervention in and moralization of everyday life and the sumptuary regulation viewed as a concern with the visible face of everyday life.

The most important site of these struggles over conspicuous consumption, vicarious display and women's bodies has been fought for centuries over décolletage, the permitted exposure of the flesh between neck and breasts. It is not only the flesh that is significant but its use as the primary site of exhibition, an eroticized version of the jeweller's green baize on which expensive jewellery is laid out. What needs to be stressed is the complex interconnection between flesh and cloth, between the naked and the clothed and their interplay, as with diaphanous materials that expose rather than conceal. The contested flesh expands and retreats; in Puritan New England 'naked arms' were penalized (Miller 1966: 113).

John Flugel provides a Freudian analysis of the significance of décolletage: 'Women thereby introduced the principle of the deliberate mutual reinforcement of the attractions exercised by clothes and nakedness' (Flugel 1950: 106). He accounts for this dialectic of concealment/exposure in the more diffuse sexual libido in women than in men; in women the whole body is sexualized, while in men it is genitally focused. It may not be necessary to be committed to the explicit Freudianism of Flugel's account to appreciate the importance of the attention it draws to the coexistence of the tendencies that make women both more modest and more exhibitionist, in that both their shame and their attractiveness relate to the whole body. This greater diffusion of female sexuality ensures the persistent ambiguity that marks women's existence between sexual exhibitionism and modesty.

The more significant problem with this type of account is that it assumes some version of a feminine essentialism in which women as a generic category express in their appearance and behaviour some innate characteristics. At the opposite extreme are those accounts, today most typically found in radical feminism, in which women are constructed as passive victims of an all-powerful male compulsion. In this version it is men who eroticize the female body and thus require women, at pain of exclusion from security and other benefits, to participate in their own eroticization. What neither of these polarities can grapple with is the coexistence of display and concealment, perhaps the best exemplification of which is the way in which female modesty is never simply denial or purity, but is itself a complex form of eroticization. It is this which lies at the heart of the tension between the celebration and denial of female sexuality, and which manifests itself in the multiple patriarchal regulation of women and their bodies. As Elizabeth Wilson expresses it:

> The fashion project [is] at one level an attempt to emphasize the human body and its beauty in a culture that has tended to despise and denigrate the sensual.
>
> (Wilson 1985: 9)

The regulation of women's neckline has long been one of the key sites of sumptuary intervention.[5] The length of skirts is the other obvious example of the exposure of the female body as a site of struggle. Sumptuary laws exhibited a preoccupation, in the name of modesty and morality, with female necklines and, to a lesser extent, with exposed backs. There were many attempts to specify a permitted exposure by a stipulation of the distance of cut below either the base of the neck or the collarbone. For example, a Milanese sumptuary law of 1498 outlawed women's dresses with necklines lower than one finger (placed sideways, it was specified) below the collarbone. In Florence in 1464 there was a relaxation on décolletage; women were allowed an exposure of 3 cm below the collarbone and twice that at the back (Hughes 1983: 83). During the fifteenth century the laws of Nürnberg were more severe, allowing necklines only one finger's breadth below the throat (Greenfield 1918: 109). In the Papal City of Perugia a law of 1342 reflected the ecclesiastical preoccupation with modesty in women by prohibiting décolletage below the collarbone. In Bern in 1681 of the 133 women prosecuted for sumptuary violations 65 per cent of these concerned low necklines (Vincent 1935: 183).

The tension between exposure and concealment in women's dress is manifest in that, alongside the preoccupation with the depth of the neckline, there was also anxiety over another form of concealment. The veil has led an ambivalent existence. On the one hand it exhibits piety and modesty, but on the other hand veils signify allure by facilitating concealment of identity. In Italy there were tensions between clerical and secular sumptuary activity over the wearing of veils. While the Church favoured head covering as symbolizing religious piety and exemplifying sexual modesty, the secular authorities were concerned that veils could also encourage conspicuous consumption through the use of extravagant materials and jewelling. In addition veils allowed women a problematic anonymity. In Siena officials were empowered to demand of a veiled woman the name of her father or husband (Hughes 1983: 79). What was at stake was the degree of freedom veils allowed for assignations that breached patriarchal control and exhibited some degree of personal and sexual licence. This is borne out by the fact that prostitutes were frequently forbidden to wear veils; Richards cites such prohibitions from Avignon, Arles and Nîmes (Richards 1990: 11).

Alongside the general link between the female body and economic wealth other forms of status differentiation impacted on women. For example, it was typically the case that greater licence was allowed to unmarried women; marriage itself marked a passage from one sumptuary status to another. For example, a Bern ordinance in 1637 allowed unmarried girls a range of ornamentation of costume and head-dress not permitted to married women (Vincent 1935: 62). But in the opposite direction Siena had a sumptuary law in which the maximum length of women's skirts was prescribed; unmarried women were forbidden the long trains that were the prerogative of matrons (Waley 1991: 159).

WOMEN AND VICARIOUS CONSUMPTION

Perhaps the most influential account of the progressive elevation in significance of female dress takes off from Thorstein Veblen's concept of 'vicarious consumption'. He identified a general tendency for conspicuous consumption to involve a transfer of consumption onto others, for example from masters onto servants and retainers, or from husbands onto wives and daughters (Veblen 1899: 49). Veblen did suggest a distinct periodization in which vicarious consumption of leisure is first practised by a class of dependents of whom liveried retainers are the prime example, one epitomized by the elegant simplicity of the seventeenth century French aristocrat making his entrance at court surrounded by servants in gold embroidered costumes (Flandrin 1989: 265). Veblen suggested that it was only later, with the shrinkage of the servant class, that the key role in vicarious consumption, and for that matter with respect to conspicuous leisure, devolved upon the wife alone (1899: 81).[6] König, for example, explains the sexual dimorphism of modern fashion in terms of a Veblenesque 'vicarious consumption' thesis: men confer the task of sartorial rivalry upon their wives while they pursue their careers (1973: 156). When women become explicitly associated with display and consumption another relationship to consumption emerges. Women, possibly as a means of underlining dependence, come to be expected to exercise certain constraints on consumption; familiar examples have been expectations that women abstain from popular male activities such as drinking alcohol and smoking tobacco.[7] These restraints were part of a concern to distinguish between respectable women and others (which I have more to say about later in the chapter). There is also a sense in which these norms are part of a pervasive pattern that sustains gender as dichotomous, in which masculinity and femininity are conceived as opposites, one dimension of which is the opposition between male licence and female restraint.

Another paradoxical dimension of vicarious consumption is that it is demanding of time, energy and commitment; to be 'a lady' involves 'hard work'.[8] The most significant long-term process at work was the transformation of women's relationship to 'work', the privatization of domestic work and the exclusion from 'public' work being the fundamental process. One key expression of conspicuous consumption becomes the male capacity to support the vicarious consumption of wife and family; the 'housewife' was the special invention of this process. Men abandon leisure to realize themselves in work in the public sphere in such a way as to highlight the conspicuous leisure of their non-productive wives. In short, the wife models and displays the fashions that testify to and render legible the social position that men acquire through engagement in public life. This suggests that while Engels and others were correct in drawing attention to the significance of the separation of women from economically productive labour, more fundamental was the elevation of women's role in the arena of consumption. Not only was there the continuing responsibility for domestic consumption, but for the upper classes initially and, more recently, the middle classes and the upper strata of the working class, women increasingly became media for the display and consumption of status-conferring income.

By a variety of routes 'consumption' has become in recent years an increasingly significant focus of inquiry. In part this move was a necessary reaction to compensate for the Marxist preoccupation with production (Baudrillard 1975; Braudel 1982), but it has also been embedded in the emergence of the history of 'everyday life' (Lefebvre 1971; Ariès and Duby 1987–91). It has spawned a general sociology of consumption (Sahlins 1976; De Certeau 1984; McCracken 1988; Mukerji 1983). The reflex in history of the shift to consumption has been gradually to push back the 'origins' of the phenomenon under scrutiny. The 'consumer revolution' that started life as an adjunct of the sociologies of mid-twentieth century 'mass society' has found itself being relocated earlier. Recently there has been a marked trend to push back beyond the nineteenth century and to focus attention on a 'consumer revolution' during the eighteenth century (Campbell 1987; McKendrick 1982; Lemire 1990–91, 1991) and yet further back into pre-industrial societies (Weatherill 1988; Shammas 1990). Without developing the theme I want to suggest that, rather than seeking to locate the origins of a unitary 'consumer revolution', it is perhaps more fruitful to think in terms of a series of protracted and overlapping consumer revolutions each of which has associated with it distinctive patterns of consumption. Each of these phases is likely to have been associated with stages in the social history of fashion in which different items of consumption, in particular different forms of cloth, came to the fore. Alongside the history of cotton, which has a special place in economic history, it would be necessary to attend to such things as furs (Veale 1966; Ewing 1981), silk (Feltwell 1990; Warner 1921) and other commodities such as cloth of gold that have played significant roles in the history of fashion.

Within such a general social history of 'fashion as consumption' it is important to stress the ongoing links between general consumption and the specific mechanisms of what Stuart Hall has called 'eroticized consumption' in which the 'pleasurable and pleasured feminine' is both subject and object (Hall 1980: 25). With respect to the history of sumptuary regulation it has been the dress and appearance of women that have been the key interpellated subjects.[9] Fashion has been one of the primary mechanisms that has, in a literal way, 'hailed' women, generating both personal identity and social recognizability.

One significant implication of emphasizing the role of consumption and its link to fashion is that it allows us to make better sense of the role of women in the transition to modernity, a process that reaches its apogee with the late-Victorian phenomenon of 'the housewife' as radically, but burdensomely, separated from production and from labour and confined to the sphere of consumption. The connection that needs to be explored is that between gender and urbanization.

These developments brought to the forefront projects of the 'governance of the family'. Ronnie Hsia argues that there were significant parallels between the Protestant Reformation and the Catholic Reformation, a concept he persuasively argues is to be preferred to the conventional term Counter-Reformation (Hsia 1989). But perhaps we need to hesitate before espousing his notion of the 'moral police' because this implies a degree of coherence and integration in the governance of the family. Rather it is important to stress the multiplicity of projects of governance that seized on the family as their regulatory object. The Reformation was characterized by projects pursued by both secular and clerical authorities. This, I suggest, illustrates an important feature of governance, namely that it is rarely a unitary set of practices, but rather is likely to involve conflicting projects that are just as likely to cancel each other out.

Lyndal Roper's wonderful study of the 'holy household' of Reformation Augsburg suggests some themes that are of wider applicability (Roper 1989). Roper argues that the central vision of the urban Reformation was of women's incorporation in the artisanal household with a division of labour between husbands and wives, under the leadership of their husbands, as both a productive and domestic unit. The key vehicle that institutionalized this vision was the craft guilds; significantly they frequently restricted membership to married men, excluding both women and unmarried men, on the presumption that the basic economic unit was the household workshop. The guilds conceived of themselves as enshrining in their ordinances an 'ideal' hierarchical and distinctively male order (Swanson 1988). Such a model valorized a womanhood of robust, competent and hard-working partners. The centrality of this conception of the self-sufficient household workshop is attested to by the rule that any man unable to support his wife and family and becoming dependent on poor-relief was, under Augsburg's poor law ordinances of 1522, required to wear the civic symbol as a visible badge of his fecklessness (Roper 1989: 54).

My suggestion is that this model of the domestic economy, with its complex articulation of inequality and partnership, was never widespread, but it remained an ideologically powerful imagery of contractualist views of marital cooperation and the sexual division of labour.[10] The significance of the success of the guild system in producing a class of small manufacturers and merchants was that it left wives stranded as production and business expanded to move outside the household. These circumstances provide the material conditions for women as the bearers of vicarious consumption.

These economic changes affecting the emerging bourgeoisie had already, by a different route, impacted on the landed classes. What was distinctive about the post-feudal nobility was the transformation of its economic base. They had become a rentier class, dependent on the collection of money rents, tithes and taxes and thus separated from any immediate involvement in productive activity. There was thus a profound shift in their mode of existence that became increasingly oriented towards consumption. The result was that the two great opposed classes, the landed nobility and the urban bourgeoisie, underwent different lines of economic development, but ones that led to a shared transformation in the material position of women that linked them to the realm of consumption and to the social role of being agents of vicarious consumption. The epochal competition between the landed and bourgeois interests was, in part, symbolically fought out through the medium of fashion that was practised, usually with enthusiasm, by women.

It is not surprising that there existed a shared ideological climate in which men of both the nobility and the bourgeoisie alike assented to the desirability of the regulation of appearance whilst seeking to avoid its application. We know very little about what the women of either class thought about these matters. This strange conjunction in the circumstances of the major social forces contributes, I suggest, to unlocking much of the mystery surrounding sumptuary law, since it helps us to understand why sumptuary laws were such a typical feature of social life on the margins of modernity while evasion and lack of enforcement seem to have been their fate.

THE AESTHETIC EROTICIZATION OF WOMEN

In the previous chapter I noted that with the rise of capitalism there emerged a set of new sexual values organized around what Sombart had called a 'hedonistic aesthetic conception of woman' (1967: 46). What this involved was a rather specific eroticization of women. It was a sexualization of the clothed and ornamented body of women. Since we still live in an era in which this form of eroticization is dominant it is important to note its characteristics. At its core is the valorization of the commitment first and foremost of both time and labour to personal grooming, typically illustrated in the importance of hair and its brushing, curling or substitution by wigs, and of care of the skin, its texture and its colour. It should be noted that the focus of attention in grooming shifts over time with respect to such practices as bathing and perfuming of the body (Corbin 1986). Time and commitment are also important both in the acquisition of skills (for example, in the application of make-up) and taste, the understanding of colour, texture and other factors that produce a sense of fashion. The end result of this 'labour of ornamentation', as a form of vicarious leisure, is to produce women as having what Colin Mercer calls the quality of 'to-be-looked-at-ness' (Mercer 1983). In this respect voyeurism and fetishism are not so much deviations as natural extensions of 'the gaze' that exists in symbiotic relation with the decorated and ornamented body. I am struck here by Anne Hollander's powerful demonstration that throughout the history of the nude in art the naked female body is always powerfully ornamented by the surrounding drapes (Hollander 1980: xiii).

It is not surprising that these grooming skills first become developed around court society. Only here are there the resources of time, materials and wealth for the elaboration of fashion as a primary component of life for some women and the trades that grow up to service these needs. At core fashion and the ornamental reification of women involves the contact between male aristocrats without productive occupation and beautiful women with their beauty as an occupation (Brennickmeyer 1963: 125). The long-running trend towards the heightened ornamentation of women is disrupted by periodic cultural reactions that give rise to the sexualization of the 'natural' and the 'unspoilt', but these shifts in favour of naturalism produce in practice ever more sophisticated appearential techniques, such as when make-up is used to deny contrivance by simulating a natural look.

The corollary of the ornamentation of women was the remarkable sartorial turn that men underwent – what has been aptly described as the 'great renunciation'. Flugel describes the process in the following terms:

> If . . . women gained a great victory in the adoption of the principle of erotic exposure, men may be said to have suffered a great defeat in the sudden reduction of male sartorial decorativeness which took place at the end of the eighteenth century . . . [M]en gave up their right to all the brighter, gayer, more elaborate, and more varied forms of ornamentation, leaving them entirely to the use of women.
>
> (Flugel 1950: 110–11)

Thereafter, men became merely useful. The origins of this shift lie in the repudiation of the privileges of the old order that the French Revolution, in particular, demolished. The new social order for men involved greater uniformity and simplicity with the shift from the private sphere of the social to the workplace as the primary arena of male activity, one marked by strictly utilitarian criteria. Thereafter men, first of the bourgeoisie but spreading rapidly to all classes, demonstrated by means of the sombreness and severity of cut, the correct creases and fresh starched linen their practical relationship with the economic world:

> This masculine escape from the task of displaying the higher sumptuousity naturally mitigated to a great extent the necessity for emulation, or rather it made the process vicarious instead of being direct. . . . Men might escape the demands of conspicuous consumption, but women could not.
>
> (Bell 1976: 141)

König, following a similar line to Flugel, argues that male austerity in dress attests to the bourgeois opposition against the ostentation of the old order. He argues that this explains why it was that England, 'the birthplace of rampant puritanism', secured and retained leadership in men's fashions. In contrast, it has been France, largely unaffected by the Reformation, that still leads in women's fashions (König 1973: 156).

While there is much to commend these accounts of the male renunciation there is one consideration that tells against them and suggests a much earlier adoption of male severity in dress. As fashion followed political or military power it was significant that during the period of Spanish supremacy in the sixteenth century there was a marked shift towards male sartorial austerity with severe black styles predominating. A similar feature, probably also under Spanish influence, was the dark and heavy styles favoured by the Dutch merchants. These fashions were not, I suggest, expressions of the capitalist work ethic, but rather of the 'gravitas' of paternalism.

For present purposes it is significant to note that women have come increasingly to be associated with vicarious consumption and ornamentation. The attribute of ornament is readily transferable to the person; thus women themselves came to be conceived as ornaments. This defines a significant element of their 'work', the long investment of time and energy devoted to personal appearance. This construction of woman as ornament involves a profoundly paradoxical dimension. On the one hand there is a cultural valorization of beauty that exists, hand in hand, with a reduction and reification in which the person becomes simply an ornament. Howard Bloch neatly captures this specific form of reification:

> If man's desire for ornament . . . is analogous to man's desire for woman, it is because woman is conceived as ornament.
> (Bloch 1989: 12)

Once reified in this way the link between ornamentation and contrivance comes to the fore. It is this which leads women to be automatically associated with both the role of decorative supplement and also with artifice, deception and subterfuge in patriarchal discourses. There is also an association of the contrivance of ornamentation with a sense of the insubstantial or superficial, a logic that leads immediately to a standard trope of sumptuary discourses, to the denunciation of dress, fashion and ornamentation as the 'vanity of women'.

What is important in this analysis is that it is concerned to identify the material roots of the constructions of gender and to avoid attributing them to some all-pervasive misogyny presumed to haunt the male soul.[11] Thus we are better able to understand how it was that the discourses surrounding sumptuary legislation came to be constructed in a way that tends to focus upon the appearance of women as the proper target of regulation.

The feminization of fashion and the role of vicarious display are processes that attest to the economic and familial power of men. It should not be thought that women are the mere victims of male power. In the first place women 'collaborated' for too long and with too much enthusiasm for it to be plausible to regard fashion as a form of female victimization. As the elegant testimony of Nicolosa Sanuit, quoted above, testifies, clothes as 'our insignia of worth' have provided women with significant arenas, not only of self-expression, but also, as I hope to demonstrate below, of resistance. One line of analysis is to explore the dynamics of gender wars in the economic sphere. As Merry Weisner argues, in the Middle Ages women were under attack in respect of their grip on skilled occupations such as brewing; there was an increase in restrictive regulation as women were denied participation in the guild system and were more generally expelled from the public sphere (Weisner 1986). Others have argued about whether the general economic and political position of women improved or declined (Herlihy 1976; Duby 1983). I will pursue some of these issues in my discussion of the political economy of marriage in Chapter 10.

Important though such material factors are for the history of gender relations, their dynamics are primarily inscribed in deeply embedded mentalities, practices and discourses that have their own logics which are not reducible to economic or other material sources. The immediate implication is that fashion cannot be reduced to a male conspiracy that ensnares women in a trivial preoccupation with personal appearance. Given the denial of access to other forms of self-expression, clothing, ornamentation and grooming have provided generations of women with the means of identity, self-presentation and access to valued social status. The history of sumptuary laws is in part a history of gender wars over access to and the forms of utilization of the resources of self-presentation.

Cross-dressing, danger and recognizability

A strand that keeps reappearing in the record is the interaction of sumptuary law with anxieties and fears generated by cross-dressing or 'gender-bending'. The literary and political critique of 'transvestism' and 'cross-dressing' has a history that stretches back to the Bible and beyond (Dekker and Pol 1988; Evans and Thornton 1989). Biblical authority comes from Deuteronomy: 'The woman shall not wear that which pertaineth unto a man, neither shall a man put on a woman's garment; for all that do so are abomination unto the Lord thy God' (*Deuteronomy* 22: 5). The critique, whether moralizing or satirical, exhibits a remarkably consistent content with a preoccupation with 'effeminate' men and 'masculine' women. Perhaps the most revealing motif is the recurrent fear of a degenerate, topsy-turvy world that must inevitably follow from cross-dressing and which brings in its train serious social perils. The most frequently invoked images are of military weakness, but there are also strands of the critique of luxury with the fear that transvestism leads to dearth and famine at the societal level and, more locally, to the decline of noble or worthy families. In general the critique is rooted in an organic conception of society morbidly preoccupied with decline and degeneracy.

Since gender is a cultural construct and thus liable to instability, it follows that it must constantly be reinforced to preserve a stable and dichotomous conception of male/female, masculinity/femininity. Appearance is central to the visibility and recognizability of gender. It is fear of gender instability that renders fashion important, but this importance is also linked to the playful and transgressive capacities of fashion. It is significant that important traditions of popular culture and entertainment contain transgressive moments that have passed down to us as trans-sexual roles in Christmas pantomimes and as drag comedians (Clark 1980: Ladurie 1981). The use of cross-dressing as a form of disguise or misrepresentation has periodically been associated with popular radicalism; in Britain cross-dressing manifested itself in the 'Porteus riots' in Edinburgh 1736, 'Lady Skimmington' leading invasions against the royal enclosure of forests in 1812, 'General Ludd's wives' in Luddite actions, and 'Rebecca' leading Welsh resistance to turnpike tolls (Ackroyd 1979).

The authorities, whether civil or clerical, have always been concerned to hold the line of dichotomized gender and have promulgated the fear that any tampering with it could only be at the price of political, economic, social and sexual chaos (Shapiro 1987: 126). But despite this moralization fashion has long employed transgressive elements. This has, until recently, largely been a one-way traffic; female fashion has 'borrowed' themes from male dress to produce very varied effects and responses that stretch from the protracted battles over women wearing trousers to the 'sophisticated' styles of female singers and dancers in male evening dress that were so important in the inter-war period (Garber 1992).

Cross-dressing is a dimension of recognizability that is generated by the capacity of clothing to facilitate misrepresentation (Horn 1968: 206). Marilyn Horn then links this to the existence of laws prohibiting cross-dressing and suggests that these laws were directed more against male cross-dressing than female cross-dressers. Unfortunately she does not provide details of the evidence that she relies upon to reach this conclusion. Presumably the main factor here is a homophobic response that views the wearing of female attire as 'effeminate'. My sense is that while the fear of homosexuality is a significant element in the attempt to prohibit cross-dressing, it is more generally women who have been the targets of such regulation because they are seen as attempting to usurp male opportunity and advantage as epitomized in the varied history of women sailors and soldiers (Rose 1984; Dekker and Pol 1988; Garber 1992).

The empirical evidence is inconclusive. I suspect that acts of repression against cross-dressing will have been carried out under catch-all public order provisions. There have been very few explicit criminalizations of cross-dressing. What survives are a few episodic details. For example, in Venice a measure in 1443 provided heavy fines for men wearing a woman's dress (Newett 1906: 269). In fifteenth century France Louis XI imposed punishments on prostitutes for wearing men's clothes on the streets of Paris. In 1471 records report the sale of a confiscated man's black-belted robe and a hat from one Jehanne la Thibaude who was then imprisoned (Lacroix 1931: 823). In Strasbourg an ordinance of 1660 bemoaned that 'men ornament their hair like women, weave silk ribbons, ringlets, and other things in their wigs, and add other female fancies' (Vincent 1935: 69–70). It is also worth noting that some popular ritual punishments, associated with the tradition of 'charivaris', dressed offenders (scolding wives and beating husbands) in the clothes of the opposite sex, sat them backwards on a horse and paraded them around town (Davis 1971; Fabre 1989: 559; Ingram 1984).

The persistence of the moralization of fashion

As we have already seen, moralization was rarely far below the surface in the sumptuary regulation of women's dress. This moralization involved complex responses to erotic aestheticism and the periodic fixations upon the exposure of flesh and the accentuation of secondary sexual characteristics. These preoccupations have exhibited remarkable resilience and are rarely absent from the projects of moral regulation or from the succession of purity movements that have erupted time and again since the distinctive emergence of populist movements during the seventeenth century (Bristow 1977; Harrison 1974; Downs 1989; Newburn 1992). Anachronistic though it now seems it is worthwhile to remind ourselves that an Italian earthquake near Naples in July 1930 was greeted by a Catholic bishop insisting that it was 'a scourge brandished by the merciful hand of the Almighty' because of the 'present scandalous female fashions' (Flugel 1950: 58). The dress reform movement that swept Europe and America in the late nineteenth century exhibited a fascinating mix of feminism and moral conservatism (Newton 1974; Roach 1979); in the United States legislation against corsets was broached in a number of states, although never passed, but such moves succeeded in Russia and in Romania, both in 1899, and also in Bulgaria where girls were not admitted to schools wearing corsets (Kunzle 1982). After the arrival of shorter skirts in the mid-1920s in the USA several state bills were introduced: Utah proscribed 'skirts higher than 3 inches above the ankle'; in Ohio 'any female over 14 years of age was to be prohibited from wearing a skirt which does not reach the part of the foot known as the instep' (Laver 1969a). It was the changes effected by the 1914–18 War and the emergence of sporting activities for women, in particular the bicycle, that liberated women from the role so well captured in Helene Robert's evocative phrase 'exquisite slaves' (Roberts 1977). The predilection for attempts to legislate morality, 'morals by statute', did not entirely disappear; it was a characteristic response of the American residues of the sturdy Puritan tradition and is still capable of resurfacing, whether in Prohibition or in anti-pornography ordinances.

An intellectual tendency to the moralization of fashion also exhibits a remarkable tenacity; Lacroix, the nineteenth century French historian, exemplifies this tradition:

> The mode [fashion] is ordinarily but a form and an expression of luxury, which has so sorry an influence over public morality, and which opens the gate, so to speak, to all distractions, to all disorder, to all vices. The love of luxury leads to debauchery and counsels Prostitution; it is the attraction and the bait of the evil passions.
>
> (Lacroix 1931: 1197)

While today such moralization sounds anachronistic, it does underline the long lineage of such discourses. I abstain from discussing whether the rapid transformations in gender relations in the late twentieth century will elicit a renewed remoralization of women's bodies or whether such discourses will finally have run their course.

THE SHIFTING TARGETS OF SUMPTUARY LAW

While it is true that the appearance of women was an important target of sumptuary laws, it is of the utmost importance to recognize that their gender content shows considerable variation. While in many instances sumptuary laws were directed against women, in other cases men were their primary targets while in yet others these laws exhibited an almost self-conscious gender-neutrality in their formulation. This section will explore and attempt to make sense of these shifting targets of sumptuary regulation.

There is no simple chronology to the gender fluctuations in sumptuary law and there is also considerable national variation. As a highly provisional thesis it can be suggested that in medieval sumptuary laws men were the primary target while with the rise of an urban mercantile class the focus of sumptuary law shifted to women's dress. An explanation that fits neatly with this thesis is that sumptuary law simply 'followed' fashion; when male fashion predominated it was the object of sumptuary law and with the rise of female fashion so the target of sumptuary law changed. This contains some partial truth; in high medieval court societies male display and sumptuousity was a symbolic representation and articulation of political relations; not only was women's dress less ostentatious, but women themselves were less publicly visible as the household became transformed from a public into a private arena within which women became increasingly privatized. For example, Thrupp's analysis of inventories and wills establishes that at least until the beginning of the sixteenth century women had fewer and less luxurious clothes than men (Thrupp 1948: 148–49). Unfortunately for the utility of the simple thesis, women were already the objects of sumptuary regulation, both before and after any decline in masculine conspicuous consumption. A second aspect of the simple thesis is a 'class thesis' version in which women's fashion only became an important target of sumptuary law when urbanization brought the rise of a merchant bourgeoisie able and willing to compete with the old nobility. The wealthy burghers strove to exhibit their wealth by having their wives wear clothes that emphasized the leisure to which their wealth had assigned them.[12] What counts against this class competition model is that there is no evidence which points towards a concentration or culmination of attack on the vicarious display of the urban merchants. For example, in the case of England the period of sharpening tension between old and new wealth in the mid-sixteenth century was precisely the period during which women became exempted from sumptuary restrictions.[13] That the pattern in England was not untypical is demonstrated by a fairly similar one in France. Francis I issued a decree in 1543 prohibiting gentlemen from using gold and silver brocade; this law was reenacted several times (Boehn 1932–35: II: 133). In general women seem to have been largely exempted from French dress restrictions (Quicherat 1875: 333). An interesting stage in English sumptuary history is an apparent shift that occured in 1574 with a sudden reversal in which sumptuary restrictions seem to have been reimposed on women; this episode will be explored in some detail in Chapter 12.[14]

The real deficiency in the class thesis is its one-dimensional character. There is no doubt that class was an important dynamic, but it existed alongside at least two other independent mechanisms. The pursuit of fashion and conspicuous consumption by women (certainly among the upper classes, but probably extending much further) in the prevailing transactional marriage market was regarded as proper, legitimate and even necessary. What I will call 'the political economy of marriage' involved mechanisms not reducible to inter-class competition, but involved shifting gender roles within changing kinship patterns and requires separate consideration (see Chapter 10). The other major factor was the role of theological discourses and the political struggles between church and secular authorities in which fluctuating tides of misogynous sentiment were mobilized. This provides, I suggest, the bedrock in which the moralization and control of women was the persistent manifestation, but whose content varied significantly as the struggles washed back and forth. My sense is that what deserves more attention is not so much an increasing regulation of women, but rather the rise of distinctively public forms of regulation that are exemplified by sumptuary laws.

This involves the need to distinguish between familial forms by reference to the forms of discipline they deploy. In extended patrilineal systems the control of women remained internal, exemplified in classical Rome, where the *pater familias* was given jurisdiction over the wrongs committed by the women of his household. The rise of more nucleated family forms seems to have been associated with the rise of more public forms of control. It is important not to imply a one-way process; rather it is better to think in terms of shifting sites of the private and the public (Castan 1989).[15] For example, in a debate on proposed sumptuary legislation in 1621 one MP in the Commons gave as the justification for statutory regulation of women's clothes that 'laws may rule them though their husband's cannot' (quoted by Harte 1976: 149). This suggests evidence of anxiety; women are viewed as becoming uncontrollable and thus in need of external intervention. What men are unable to do on their own, aggregated patriarchal power might secure.

It may be that the more symbolic dimensions of these regulatory discourses should be given greater significance. It is not a matter of whether women were controlled by either private or public powers, but rather that sumptuary laws, along with sermons from pulpits and moralizing tracts, provided a pervasive ideological legitimation for the general deprecation of women. Such a view is entirely consistent with the otherwise paradoxically strong legislative urge accompanied by low enforcement patterns.

It is well to make clear that men were not entirely exempt from moral regulation of their clothing. In Nürnberg male decency was to be ensured by the rule that their coats and capes had to be at least two finger breadths below the crutch (Strauss 1966: 112). The flies on male breeches also attracted regulatory attention. It was insisted that they must not be 'stuffed or artificially enlarged'; to wear the fly uncovered was 'not only against God, but contrary to decency and manly breeding' (Greenfield 1918: 116). In England the major sumptuary law of 1463 laid down that only nobles 'shall wear . . . any gown, jacket, or coat, unless it be of such length that the same, he being upright, may cover his privy members and buttocks' (3 Edw. IV: *c.* 5; SR 2: 399–402).[16] In Siena men were required to wear their hair short 'so that at least part of their neck is visible' (Waley 1991: 158). In Venice in 1509 men were not supposed to wear a beard of more than 12 days' growth (Newton 1988).

Despite these occasional attentions to features of male attire it remains to pose the general question of why it was that women's dress formed the main target of sumptuary regulation. What was it about women's dress that men (and in particular those who governed) found threatening? With reference to Florence, Rainey suggests that the primary anxiety revolved around the political economy of marriage or the population problem, the basic model being that female extravagance led to dowry inflation, which in turn resulted in a postponement of marriage and a consequential decline in the birth-rate.

There was undoubtedly another important factor involved in the shift towards the imposition of the primary sumptuary burden on women, namely that they got caught up in the major struggles between religious and secular authority which were the central political and intellectual focus of the high Middle Ages. The Gregorian reforms that resulted from the rupture of a fused church-state in 1075 were struggles over the terms and boundaries of that separation (Berman 1983). One important manifestation of those arguments was over the respective jurisdictions of ecclesiastical and secular courts, a struggle that reemerged as a central component of the Reformation, and was not finally resolved in some jurisdictions until the eighteenth and even the nineteenth centuries. The reason that these big currents sweeping European history connect up with the more prosaic issue of the regulation of women's dress is that one of the most vexed issues in the church-state settlement was jurisdiction over women, or rather what has so often been regarded as the same thing, over moral offences, marriage and family law.

I am sure that there is much more to be told by those grounded in ecclesiastical history about the rule of ecclesiastical jurisdiction in the construction of the sumptuary tradition than I am able to tell here. There are two aspects on which I want to comment. The first is that rather in the same way that the nineteenth century provided extended opportunities for the discourses of sexuality, the theological controversies from the twelfth century onwards set up an agenda that for the next few centuries created endless opportunities for men to talk about women. I consider the misogynistic aspects of these controversies in the next chapter; here I only want to clarify the link between women and the controversies between secular and sacred authority. There was consensus over the inferiority of women, the necessity of their subordination to their fathers and husbands (Kelso 1956; Schroeder 1990), but there occurred a distinctive bifurcation in the discourses about women. The Church continued to assert the identity of questions about women with morality; in this tradition the sin of luxury is a sin allied to pride and envy. The distinctively secular discourses, also organized around the concept of luxury, came to be constructed rather differently as the economic wrong of extravagance.

The discourses of sumptuary law for most of their active period blend together these two distinctive discursive traditions and only very gradually, as will be examined in more detail in Chapter 14, do these discourses separate and the secular economic discourse comes to dominate just as sumptuary law passes into the general realm of economic regulation. This new discourse on luxury was probably associated with a shift to what might be called the privatization of luxury. In the process the public display of sumptuousness was displaced by the private consumption of luxury and the elevation of taste (Chartier 1989: 164). The significance of the medieval bifurcated discourses on women and luxury is that they reinforced each other; theology and 'common sense' both pointed to women as a source of spiritual, sexual and economic danger.

The second way in which church-state relations impinged on women is that there was often close cooperation between the church and secular authorities in promoting sumptuary law. In Italy, in particular, there is evidence that the targeting of women points to the presence of the ecclesiastical hand behind sumptuary law during the late Middle Ages. The morality of women was a central preoccupation and dress and ornamentation was the readily visible sign of immorality; the immoral character could be read from the immodest clothing. The general complaint, found in the preambles to sumptuary statutes in many Italian cities during the fourteenth and fifteenth centuries, was that women were 'the ruin of men' (Hughes 1983: 88). My suggestion is that this exemplifies the dualism of the discourses on women and luxury: on the one hand it embodies a moral critique rooted in the misogyny that derived from the central role of the myth of the Garden of Eden in the theology of the Church and, on the other hand, it involves the economic critique in which female 'vanities' and extravagances were constructed not only as burdens on men as husbands, but, more importantly, as threatening the family estate or patrimony.

Hughes argues that sumptuary restrictions and prosecutions were directed significantly against married women and that greater licence was allowed to unmarried women. Since Italian wives retained legal title to their dowries it was in the interests of husbands, who relied on the dowry as loan capital for their businesses, to prevent their wives 'wasting' the dowry on conspicuous consumption. Hughes provides the data given in Table 9.1 and Figure. 9.1 of the historical trajectory of Italian sumptuary legislation. Hughes' evidence indicates the decline of sumptuary restraint on funerals and weddings and a clear increase in the focus on the regulation of women's dress.

Hughes' analysis is confirmed by Rainey's study. Early sumptuary legislation was gender-neutral, but with the important pragmatic of 1356 women become the central target of Florentine sumptuary legislation (Rainey 1985: 141–42). Cases against men were rare; prosecutions of males related mainly to embellishments on hats and cloaks and on 'ruffles'. Thirty pieces of legislation on women's dress and ornaments were passed during the Quattrocento. Rainey notes an interesting shift in the late fifteenth century when regulation was increasingly directed at young men. Unfortunately Rainey does not explore this development further, but it seems to suggest some increasing inter-generational tension as an additional feature of the gender politics of sumptuary regulation. Such shifts do not undermine the general conclusion that there is a characteristic linkage between sumptuary law and the regulation of women, but draw attention to the fact that this connection is never simple and is subject to significant variation. Since traditional patriarchy was a system of gerontocracy patriarchal power was not only directed at all women, but also against young men (Turner 1984: 152–53).[17]

Table 9.1 Variation in types of sumptuary offences in Italy over time in Bologna, Siena and Venice between the thirteenth and sixteenth centuries

Date (Century)	*F*	*W*	*CW*	*CM*
Bologna				
13th	15	15	6	1
14th	0	1	19	0
15th	2	2	34	0
Siena				
13th	0	1	0	0
14th	17	15	15	2
15th	7	1	33	0
Venice				
13th	15	15	6	1
14th	0	1	19	0
15th	2	2	34	0

F = Funeral
W = Weddings
CW = clothing (women)
CM = clothing (men)

Source: Hughes (1983: 85).

GOOD GIRLS/BAD GIRLS

An important component of the way in which sumptuary laws were implicated in the regulation of women has been the prominent and persistent legislative strategy of constructing and policing a distinction between 'good girls' and 'bad girls', between the respectable and the dissolute, the virtuous and the vicious. These antimonies were central to the whole medieval Christian construction of women that spoke in the same breath of the natural modesty and sexual passivity of women while identifying women as sexually dangerous, subjecting men to the temptations of the flesh (Brundage 1987). Then as now, the mirror held up to women was the peril of departing from virtue conjured by the image of the whore. As Lyndal Roper argues, the whore was a moral rather than an occupational category; she stood for the lust of all women

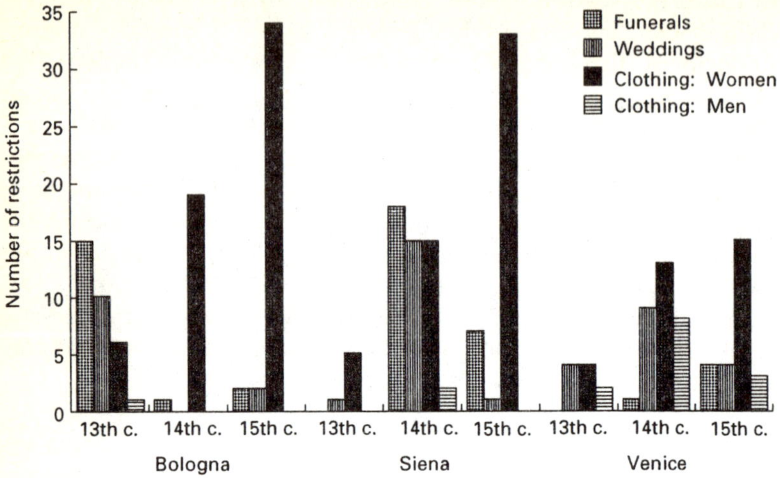

Source: Hughes 1983:85

Figure 9.1 Changing pattern of sumptuary regulation.

grounded in the belief that women's lusts were to be feared as unbridled and demonic (Roper 1985a: 21).

This focus on the sexual danger posed by women finds its expression in the use made in sumptuary regulation of two apparently contradictory tactics. The first played on the distinction between the respectable and the whore by denying fashionable or luxurious dress to prostitutes in order to decrease the attraction of prostitution as a way of life and the attraction of prostitutes to men, while 'rewarding' the virtuous by granting them access to fashionable attire. The second tactic was diametrically opposed to the first; it was to allow fashion and luxury to prostitutes in the hope that respectable women would be discouraged from emulating their sinful sisters in order to protect and confirm their own respectability.

The first strategy was concerned to minimize what a London proclamation from 1538 described with perfect clarity as 'the evil example of the gorgeous apparel of the common women of the stews [brothels] to the great temptation of young maidens, wives and apprentices' (Karras 1989: 421). The authorities sought to impose degrading restrictions on prostitutes. These took two forms:

in the first prostitutes were simply forbidden to wear currently fashionable garments, while the second imposed 'marks of infamy' upon them (this second tactic I discuss in the next section). The imposition of sumptuary restrictions on women who fell outside the constructed limits of respectability involved diverse restrictions. In Seville in the fourteenth century concubines were prohibited from wearing long trains, furs or other ornaments, these being expressly reserved for honourable women (Perry 1990: 48). In 1537 Charles V of Spain passed prohibitions banning 'public women' from wearing silk (Anderson 1979: 204).

In England a City of London Proclamation, 'As to the Dress of Common Women Within the City', epitomizes the attempt to construct the dichotomy between good girls and bad girls:

> Whereas the common lewd who dwell in the city of London . . . have now of late assumed the fashion of being clad and attired in the manner and dress of good and noble dames and damsels of the realm in unreasonable manner, it is Ordered by the Mayor, Aldermen and Commons that no such lewd woman shall be so daring as to be attired either by day or night in any kind of vesture trimmed with fur such as miniver [white squirrel], grey work [badger], squirrel . . . or any other manner of noble budge [lamb's-wool] or lined with sendal [rich diaphanous silk], bokerames [buckram], samytes [another rich silk] or any other noble lining nor yet to be clothed either in coat, surcoat or hood relieved with fur or lining, on pain of forfeiting the said vestments; But shall go openly with a hood of ray [striped] cloth, single [unlined]; and with vestments neither trimmed with fur nor yet with lining, and without any manner of relief, that all folks native and strangers may have knowledge of what kind they are.
>
> (Burford 1973: 93)

What is fascinating about this passage is that, while it has the form of a typical hierarchic appearential order, it combines negative restrictions with the imposition of distinguishing marks.

An ordinance of 1360 issued by the Provost of Paris forbade prostitutes from wearing embroidery or other ornamentation on their hoods. A statute in 1426 forbade prostitutes a range of ornamentations 'which are the ornaments of women of honour'. Another ordinance in 1415 was devoted exclusively to prostitution;

prostitutes were forbidden to wear gold or silver on their hoods or robes, golden or gilded girdles, habits lined with grey squirrel or vair or other 'respectable' furs, and silver shoe buckles (Lacroix 1931: 816–18). Many of the prohibitions were clearly directed at securing recognizability by avoiding any risk that prostitutes might be mistaken for respectable women. In a number of German cities prostitutes were forbidden to leave their hair uncovered as this was a sign of an unmarried girl. If two prostitutes were out together they were required to walk side-by-side and not one behind the other to avoid them being mistaken for a mistress accompanied by her maid servant.

A distinctive feature of the record of the regulation of prostitution in England was that it emanated from municipal rather than from state legislation. The London dress ordinance of 1351, quoted above, contained a fascinating exemption to the dress restrictions: they did not apply if the prostitute was of noble birth (Burford 1976: 73).[18] A fifteenth century regulation for the Southwark stews prohibited prostitutes from wearing aprons (Karras 1989: 399).[19] Karras offers the explanation that aprons were worn by bishops and that for prostitutes to wear such a garment might be treated as mocking the Bishop of Winchester in whose diocese the Southwark stews were located.

Prostitutes were also subjected to much spatial regulation (Harsin 1985; Karras 1989). In medieval France many towns confined them outside the town walls, while Toulouse banned them from the centre of town; there was widespread exclusion of prostitutes from taverns, and restrictions on soliciting, particularly when this involved chanting, were common (Otis 1985). They were forbidden to sit outside the brothel (Frankfurt 1472 and 1478), excluded from the front pews in church in Strasbourg, and they were banned from attending public dances in Nürnburg (Weisner 1988); prohibitions against solicitation near churches and on Sundays and holy days were widespread (Salusbury 1939).

The second general tactic was directed towards shaming respectable women. The right to wear luxurious fashions was conferred on prostitutes in the hope that motives of modesty and shame would restrain 'respectable' women from wearing (and possibly even desiring) these ostentatious and expensive items. In 1564 Philip II of Spain deliberately tried the new tactic of 'shaming' by allowing only prostitutes to wear prohibited finery. Later Philip IV, in a sumptuary decree in 1639, also employed the shaming tactic; only prostitutes were allowed to wear the then fashionable *guarda infante* (metal hooped skirt whose metal plate banged against a similar plate attached to the heel of the wearer's shoes to make a very distinctive noise of passage). Montaigne collected the following examples of the use of the shaming tactic in France. Only public whores were allowed to wear gold ornaments and embroidered dresses; for males only pimps were allowed gold rings (Montaigne 1958: 197). Not only did French laws deny prostitutes some of the vestimentary adornments allowed to respectable women, in particular the 'coif' or veil; in Arles respectable women were encouraged to rip off a veil if a prostitute was found wearing one. Conversely to remove a woman's head-dress was equivalent to accusing her of prostitution or debauchery (Rossiaud 1988: 57).

In Siena only prostitutes were allowed to wear items such as platform soles, cloth of gold, veils, etc. that were prohibited to respectable women (Hughes 1983: 92). A Florentine pragmatic of 1337 explicitly allowed prostitutes to wear garments of any kind; not only was this an attempt to discourage excess in dress by respectable women but there was also an explicit tolerance of prostitution in a period when men were marrying later and prostitution was regarded as a preferred alternative to the homosexuality which excited considerable civic anxiety (Trexler 1980: 350). In Scotland an Act of 1567 stipulated that it was unlawful for any woman, except for prostitutes, to attire themselves above their station; 'it be lauchfull to na wemen to weir abone their estair except howris [whores]' (APS III: 40: *c.* 41). Harte comments that this was 'perhaps the shortest and most direct of all laws controlling dress' (Harte 1976: 148).

Lyndal Roper's analysis, derived from her study of Augsburg, undoubtedly has a wider pertinence. She argues that the finery of prostitutes was a mockery of patrician or noble dress, favouring much jewellery, dramatic feathered hats and the like. She suggests that clothes had a very deep imaginative significance for the prostitutes themselves; extravagant dress was a way of displaying a wealth beyond the normal expectations of the social class from which they were drawn and was a distinct improvement on the drab dress allowed to servant women of their own class (Roper 1985a: 20).

MARKS OF INFAMY AND THE REGULATION OF PROSTITUTION

In Chapter 6 the use of distinguishing marks branded on the bodies of its victims or sewn onto their clothing was discussed. This use of distinguishing marks achieved its most varied and widespread manifestation in the imposition of 'marks of infamy' on prostitutes. The logic of these practices was another species of the 'shaming' strategy in the service of the wider project of securing social recognizability. The tactic was a public degradation ceremony requiring the wearing of some mark that proclaims the bearer's status to one and all. But there was a second feature that underpinned the logic of distinguishing marks. To mark the prostitute drew a clear and unambiguous line between 'good girls' and 'bad girls'. As recently as the Wolfenden Report (1957) one of the major reasons for criminalizing the act of solicitation was not a concern with prostitution itself, but what was seen as a need to avoid the embarrassment to 'good girls' in areas used by prostitutes of being propositioned by men unable to distinguish prostitutes from respectable women. Dostoevsky, in *Crime and Punishment,* had the garrulous Marmelador in the tavern refer to his daughter having a yellow ticket or yellow passport. Later he complains 'my daughter Sofya Semyonovna has been forced to take a yellow ticket; owing to that she is unable to go on living with us. For our landlady would not hear of it' (Dostoevsky 1973: 16).

The imposition of marks of infamy upon prostitutes has a long history. In classical Greece distinctive brightly coloured wear was required for *hetairai* (Mills 1984: 264). In the Middle Ages the wide dissemination of the imposition of distinguishing marks flowed from the 4th Lateran Council in 1215, a requirement repeated at nine subsequent Church Councils until 1370. The general form employed was to require a red cord (*aiguillette*).[20] The alternative form was a yellow felt circle, the *rouelle,* that originated in France; its colour was changed to red and white by John II of France in 1363 probably as a fiscal measure to levy what amounted to a tax on prostitution (Richards 1990: 108–10).

The distinguishing marks imposed were to vary widely across Europe: a yellow scarf in Vienna; in Leipzig a yellow cloak trimmed with blue; a red cap in Bern and Zurich; in Bergano a yellow cloak; a striped tunic in Marseilles; in Bristol a striped hood; in Strasbourg a black-and-white sugarloaf hat; in Nîmes an alternate colour sleeve; while Florence imposed gloves and a bell attached to the hat (Otis 1985; Richards 1990: 11). In Venice yellow scarves were required; in Milan a cloak of common fustian was ordered (changed to white in a 1412 law and then to black in 1498) (Hughes 1983: 92). Avignon and Dijon required a white badge four fingers wide on the arm; Toulouse a white cap and ribbon (Geremek 1987).

In France ordinances requiring prostitutes to wear visible signs were widespread and oft repeated, for example in 1441 and 1458 in Avignon, 1468 and 1475 in Lyons (Otis 1985; Rossiaud 1988). The strangest rule is one reported by Leah Otis from Castres in 1375 that required prostitutes to wear a man's hat and a scarlet belt; given the general anxiety generated by cross-dressing I cannot offer a speculation as to the logic behind this rule.

Significantly it was the same 4th Lateran Council of 1215 that had generalized distinguishing marks for prostitutes whose Canon 68 required that Jews at all times be distinguished from Christians by their dress (Rubens 1967; Finkelstein 1972; Heer 1962).[21]

Prostitutes in Augsburg were required to wear a distinguishing mark of a broad green stripe on their veils; they were forbidden to wear wreaths which were the distinguishing mark for unmarried women, or to wear any silk or rosaries. In other German towns distinguishing marks varied, for example a yellow stripe or red beret were imposed in some cities (Roper 1985a). In many German cities during the fifteenth century the requirement of yellow bands and veils was common and was also imposed on women discovered 'living-in-sin' (Weisner 1988).

In fourteenth century Seville prostitutes had to wear yellow head coverings, but Mary Perry found evidence that many 'honorable' women wore yellow head-dresses (Perry 1978: 204). She suggests that this might be explained by a general lack of enforcement or, alternatively, that it was a show of 'daring' by the respectable. She suggests that distinguishing marks carry the significant implication that both secular and ecclesiastical authorities tolerated prostitution as long as prostitutes distinguished themselves and that this served to confirm and reproduce the grand dichotomization into good and evil women (Perry 1990: 49).

Despite the attempt to impose a visible ordering of respectability there is an inherent ambiguity in distinguishing marks; while setting prostitutes apart, they signified a certain acceptance of prostitution, since it enabled men to recognize unattached women, with whom there was no sin in the consummation of lust. This is but an early instance of the dilemma of all regulationist approaches to prostitution in that they lay themselves open to the charge that in seeking to regulate prostitution they thereby condone it, or, as in the important current instance, to propose needle exchange programmes is met with the charge of encouraging drug use. Over much of Southern France there was a special jurisdiction responsible for the regulation of prostitutes. In Lyons through to Artois each town had a *roi des ribauds* (king of the ribalds) who was often the local executioner who 'reigned over the rabble, he supervised prostitution and disciplined women of doubtful morals, and he exercised control over lepers' (Rossiaud 1988: 58). Prostitution was a fertile arena for spawning regulatory activity, but activity that was significantly varied in its intensity.

In modern times the imposition of distinguishing marks has been employed in political struggles. An attempt in Spain during the eighteenth century to abolish the sombrero resulted in a rebellion that led to the dismissal of the prime minister. During the Ottoman Empire sumptuary rules were used to impose subjection on Greeks and Armenians: Turkish officers were required to cut the skirts of Greek and Armenian women to a prescribed length; Greek subjects were required to wear dark caps as a sign of servitude, Armenians had to wear balloon-shaped head-dresses and Jews brimless caps; Turks themselves were required to wear the red fez as mark of respect to the Sultan. It is reported that 'resistance closely approximating to civil war was the result' (Hurlock 1965: 301).

RESISTANCE: DECLARED AND UNDECLARED GENDER WARS

If women got the worst of sumptuary laws and of the generalized misogynistic discourses within which they were located, they were rarely passive in their response. Leigh Schmidt suggests that women's resistance to both formal and informal dress codes constituted a challenge to male authority. Contestation over dress embodied 'both a male expression of hegemony and a female struggle for autonomous self-expression' (Schmidt 1989: 44). It is this endemic, everyday reality of control and resistance that I am calling 'gender wars'. A central feature of these wars is that they are both declared and undeclared. Resistance is complex: it always involves 'making the best of' the given situation and, at the same time, subverting that given in order to turn it to advantage. The epitome of such resistance is, for example, glimpsed in Paul Vielle's study of Iranian women. The restrictions and isolation that characterize much of the life experience of Iranian women is transformed, if only partially, into an arena of self-sufficiency, stoicism, strategic planning and even power (Vielle 1978). It is important to recognize the diversity and ubiquity of resistance, but at the same time there is a risk in romanticizing resistance; I have in mind a certain phase of radical criminology that celebrated every anti-social act of youthful rebellion as resistance to capitalism (Taylor et al. 1972). It should be borne in mind that there is always a likelihood that resistance is as much a form of accommodation to power as it is a challenge to it. For example, when workers take longer breaks than those agreed, while it may be pleasing to grab a few minutes of the boss's time, it nevertheless concedes control of the rest of the time to the employer. What is ultimately important about resistance is that it impedes the internalization of the act of power as an act of the self. There is a world of difference in doing something because it is 'natural', 'normal', 'right and proper', and doing it because one has to, not because one wants to. Grudging, silent, acquiescent conformity is always a potential site from which opposition can spring; at the outer limits even apathy is registrable as resistance that can provide a springboard for opposition (Corrigan 1988).

With regard to dress, women have long turned the burden of conspicuous consumption to their advantage by taking a close interest in clothing and their personal appearance. In an important material sense it secures for women a claim on both capital and income, and beyond this it provides a socially important form of cultural capital. At the same time involvement with dress and appearance secures important components of personal identity, self-expression and social self-confidence. With regard to dress the idea of 'resistance' is complex and needs to be understood in terms of the general tension between modesty and display. Perhaps the most perennial forms of resistance are those that push at the boundaries of conformity by deploying complex combinations of conformity and transgression.

Sumptuary laws created ideal conditions for resistance. They distinctively formed an area of law which, in principle at least, impacted most significantly on the upper classes. In general we know rather more about lower class resistance (Hall and Jefferson 1976; Scott 1985). For example, it is easy to recognize the resistance exhibited in the form of parodies or mock ceremonial, as when 'mock' trials served as a vent against the oppressive ritual of the law courts (Darnton 1985; Thompson 1991). Until quite recently, with the developing interest in the crimes of the powerful and the vicissitudes of the regulation of finance capital, less was known about the forms of resistance of the upper classes.

The most striking feature is the way in which women's resistance played upon the formalistic qualities of law and thereby forced a spiralling complexity and superfluity of detail upon sumptuary codes. When Cardinal Latino, papal legate to Lombardy and Romagna, ordered women to wear veils this generated an enjoyable form of resistance when women took to wearing highly sumptuous veils made of materials such as gold and silver thread that were prohibited in other garments (Sedgwick 1933). In Florence when a sumptuary law prescribed how low a neckline might be, evasion was charmingly simply – a low neckline combined with some diaphanous materials covering breasts and shoulders. When Florentine women were accused of wearing prohibited hat-bands they resorted to the expedient of unstitching the band and claiming that it was an unregulated 'garland'. One of my favourite legalistic evasions was when a Florentine woman, who was charged with violation of rules regarding the number of buttons that could be worn on the sleeves of a garment, insisted in her defence that the notions complained of were not 'buttons', but rather were *coppelle* since there were no buttonholes (Rainey 1985: 210; Hughes 1983: 69–70). In 1433 the Venetian Senate forbade women from wearing dresses made with cloth of gold or silver; the women responded by adopting a fashion in which sleeve linings were made from the prohibited material worn with the sleeves slashed to reveal the splendid lining. The Senate responded by closing this loophole, forbidding cloth of gold in both gowns and linings (Hughes 1983: 70). Interesting official evidence of avoidance and resistance comes from Scotland. The preamble of a Privy Council proclamation of 1684 complains:

> Yet several women even in our capital city of Edinburgh and elsewhere throughout this kingdom have presumed to go abroad with clothes made of the said prohibited stuffs upon pretext

that they are only nightgowns, undresses [informal wear] or mantois [cloaks].

(Burton 1877: VIII: 496–97)

There is also evidence of more conventional forms of political resistance. In Rome in 215 BC the sumptuary law, *Lex Oppia*, was introduced as emergency legislation during the Punic Wars; it placed general restrictions on women's dress and extravagance. Once the military crisis was over there was pressure to repeal the law. Livy reports that in 195 BC when repeal was debated in the Senate it was opposed by Cato, one of the consuls. He protested that women 'whom neither counsel, nor shame, nor their husbands' orders could keep at home, blockaded every street in the city and every entrance to the Forum' (quoted Lefkowitz and Fant 1982: 177). The demonstrations continued the next day; after an initial veto of the repeal by the tribunes, the demonstration continued until they withdrew their veto and the repeal was finally passed. However, such concerted action by women against the Oppian law is the only example of anything approaching concerted political opposition to sumptuary laws that I have discovered. It must wait until the discussion of the enforcement of and reaction to sumptuary law in Chapter 13 before considering the implications of this lack of active resistance; in the meantime I sketch an overview of the gendered dimensions in the enforcement of sumptuary law.

ENFORCEMENT AND GENDER

During the long history of sumptuary regulation its targets have varied. As established above, it was sometimes gender-neutral while at other times it was directed against the conspicuous consumption of men. Yet there were major periods in which it was directed mainly against women. In broad terms this fluctuation can be summarized in the following overview. In the classical civilizations of the Mediterranean, sumptuary restrictions, especially those concerning funerals, were directed primarily against women. Yet the other major target of sumptuary restriction during this period, alimentary restrictions, should undoubtedly be regarded as impacting on men since they were the major participants in the feasts that were the predominant form of conspicuous consumption.

During the Middle Ages sumptuary laws were directed mainly against men although, as we have seen, there is some evidence of periodic attacks on women. However, from the early modern period sumptuary laws became more and more consistently targeted against women. In so far as men were prosecuted it was the new category of young male apprentices whose conspicuous consumption activated their male masters and political superiors; but for every apprentice charged there seems to have been an equal or larger number of female servants who bore whatever wrath the sumptuary impulse was able to summon.

In addition to the content of the legislation itself we have sufficient evidence, even though it is disappointingly limited, to show that in all periods it was women who bore the brunt of whatever enforcement there was. Much of the evidence available is so limited that the pattern of enforcement is little better than anecdotal. To take the case of Italy about which our general knowledge of its sumptuary regimes is the most extensive, in every case of prosecution of which I have details, the target was female. Where the named defendant was a man, in every case he was being prosecuted because of violations committed by a wife, daughter or female servant. Because of the extensive character of the archival sources for many Italian cities further research by specialists in Italian social and legal history could undoubtedly add much to our understanding of the gender dimensions of the enforcement process.

I confine further comments to the valuable but limited cases in which we do have evidence of the gender patterns of the enforcement of sumptuary law. Of the greatest value is John Vincent's study of sumptuary law in the Swiss cities of Basel, Bern and Zurich (Vincent 1935). For the period in which his work was published his attention to gender issues is particularly valuable. His study is also unique for the remarkably thorough attention he devotes to questions of enforcement and his refusal to adopt the consensus view of the unenforceability of sumptuary law. He was fortunate in that the Swiss records seem to have been remarkably complete.

The language of the sumptuary ordinances of the cities of Basel, Bern and Zurich exhibit an anxious concern to be systematically gender-neutral in their formulation. The Zurich Ordinance of 1650 is typical in this respect:

Table 9.2 Cases before the Basel Reformations-Kammer 1681–1794

Date	*Women's dress*	*Men's dress*	*Sunday observance*	*Dancing*	*Total*	*Dismissed*
1681	134	7	93	30	287	76
1682	45	3	97	6	156	—
1692	16	6	37	40	99	—
1700	13	1	13	33	60	—
1705	44	0	52	1	102	—
1709	62	0	53	1	118	—
1715	8	0	68	10	90	56
1718	0	0	0	10	10	10
1720	0	0	—	—	—	32
1727	210	9	3	0	283	93
1733	98	5	64	45	209	106
1737	51	8	41	39	152	122
1745	30	9	26	—	82	37
1751	2	0	23	10	40	6
1755	6	0	3	2	16	11
1762	12	2	3	3	23	10
1766	31	0	13	9	67	27
1770	34	12	2	2	62	23
1794	3	0	108	108	126	2

Source: Derived from figures in Vincent 1935.

> We command with great earnestness and under heavy penalty that every person in city or country, whether cleric or layman, high class or low, woman or man, young or old, burger or peasant, attend to and use the clothing befitting his class both at home and abroad.
>
> (Vincent 1935: 143)

Yet the evidence that Vincent collected reveals that it was women who were the primary recipients of the enforcement energies of the courts. The figures in Table 9.2 reveal that those who were prosecuted for dress offences were overwhelming women; in Basel between 1681 and 1794 only 62 men were brought before the court while 799 women appeared. In no single year were more men than women prosecuted. Unfortunately Vincent provided no breakdown by sex of those charged with the Sunday observance or dancing offences. For Zurich, he provides yearly figures for most years between 1709 and 1797; while only 314 men were prosecuted, 1014 women came before the court for dress offences. In most years more women than men were prosecuted; but in some years, generally those with low prosecution rates, more men were charged, with the unexplained exception of 1719 when eight women appeared while 52 men were prosecuted.

The only other site of sumptuary activity for which anything approaching statistics are available is from the New England colonies. In Essex County (Massachusetts) there was a flurry of prosecutions in 1653; the court record reveals a pattern similar to the more detailed figures from Switzerland. A total of 14 women were successfully prosecuted as compared to only three men; of those against whom charges were dismissed there were three men but only one woman (Essex County 1911).

Limited though the evidence is, there is little doubt that it confirms the impressionistic account of many commentators that even where the substantive content of the sumptuary legislation was gender-neutral the laws were preponderantly enforced against women. It is unlikely that men were more assiduous in observing the restraints imposed on conspicuous consumption, while women more consistently flouted them and found themselves before the courts. Much more likely is the interpretation that holds for law enforcement in general, that officials charged with enforcement and courts are and remain reluctant to take action against and to convict those like themselves and, conversely, are more likely to act against those whose social rank is below their own. It would indeed be fascinating to know the class breakdown of the Swiss cases studied by Vincent in order to examine whether upper-class women were less likely to be prosecuted than their lower-class sisters.

Sketchy though the evidence is, it is undoubtedly the case that sumptuary laws were a component of the wider processes in which women were the targets of regulation and control. Women excited the regulatory energy of men in such a diverse range of societies over a long historical period. Alongside the specific preoccupation with the regulation of dress and appearance, the tendency to apply that regulation against women was overdetermined by a generalized moralization of women that is most evident in the regulation of prostitution. It remains to ask the obvious question of what it was about women that attracted male regulatory zeal. This question needs to be posed in the context of the pervasive misogynous views that dominated the active period of sumptuary initiatives; this forms the subject matter of the next chapter.

10

Misogyny and the Political Economy of Marriage: 'The Detestable Wickedness of Women'[1]

MISOGYNY AND THE SUMPTUARY ETHIC

An inescapable feature of the sumptuary discourses is that frequently, although not universally, they deployed an all too apparent misogyny. The most common manifestation was a presumed link between the critique of luxury and the vanity of women. This chapter may perhaps be regarded as something of a digression. I confess that in finding myself in the unfamiliar territory of pre-modern social history I was disconcerted by the misogyny exhibited by the men who debated in the public arena and made the laws. One response might have been to adopt the entirely plausible view that misogyny was a well-known ideological component of patriarchal forms of power and to pass on to other matters. However, I kept finding myself asking questions about why it was that misogyny was so widespread and unquestioned. In a simple minded way I was struck by the paradox of the coexistence of these vitriolic discourses and the evident powerlessness of women. As I started to track this issue it receded further and further into the early cultures that had formed modern civilizations. The question of the roots of misogyny simply became 'too big' and I came to accept the limit that the best I could do was to try to trace the connection between misogynous discourses and the sumptuary impulse.

One significant site of contestation in which the relations between men and women has been centrally focused is the institution of marriage. In exploring some facets of the history of marriage I introduce what I hope may prove to be a more widely usable concept, the political economy of marriage. This concept is directed towards making explicit the material interests involved in the social institution of marriage, of which the most important are economic interests, the interests in the control over sexuality and biological reproduction. The concept seeks to set up a heuristic distinction between these material interests and the ideological forms, in particular misogyny, through which these interests are thought and argued over.

As soon as this conceptual framework is explored it becomes apparent that any view which sees marriage exclusively as a site of contestation that counterposes women and men is inadequate. In the medieval and early modern period marriage was predominantly an economic, political and social relationship between kinship groups. It is necessary to look wider than the relations between husbands and wives. In the first place the central interests among the propertied classes were dynastic propertied interests and marriage figured as a central mechanism, particularly in view of the limitations on testamentary dispositions. Beyond these economic interests we need to bring into play the different interests associated with the social roles of kinship groups. Given the importance of dowries in the making of marriages, the interests of fathers were far from homogeneous; they varied both over time, depending on whether the father was currently concerned with the marriage of a daughter or son, and between different men, depending on the sex of their children.

The persistence of misogynous attitudes in European history is confirmed, but not necessarily explained, by the central part it plays in the roots of Christianity in early forms of patriarchal kinship systems. The Old Testament strikingly displays the connection between misogyny and the critique of luxury and female ornamentation:

> Moreover the Lord saith, Because the daughters of Zion are haughty, and walk with stretched forth necks and wanton eyes, walking and mincing as they go, and making a tinkling with their feet: Therefore the Lord will smite with a scab the crown off the head of the daughters of Zion, and the Lord will discover their secret parts. In that day the Lord will take away the bravery of their tinkling ornaments about their feet, and their cauls, and their round tires like the moon, the chains, and the bracelets, and the mufflers, the bonnets, and the ornaments

> of the legs, and the headbands, and the tablets, and the earrings, the rings, and nose jewels, the changeable suits of apparel, and the mantles, and the wimples, and the crisping pins, the glasses, and the fine liner, and the hoods, and the veils. And it shall come to pass, that instead of sweet smell there shall be stink; and instead of a girdle a rent; and instead of well set hair baldness; and instead of a stomacher a girding of sackcloth; and burning instead of beauty.
>
> (Isaiah 3: 16–24)

These concerns were not only reproduced in the New Testament, but were to be repeatedly reproduced from pulpit and in text.

> Women should adorn themselves modestly and sensibly in seemly apparel, not with braided hair or gold or pearls or costly attire but by good deeds as befits women who profess religion. Let a woman learn in silence with all submissiveness. I permit no woman to teach or to have authority over men; she is to keep silent.
>
> (Timothy II 2: 9–15)

These themes were developed and elaborated within Christian doctrine. Tertullian writing around AD 202, like many others, drew heavily from Genesis to link all women with Eve's disobedience. The central requirement imposed on women was that of modesty which was required as repentance for Eve's sin, the first sin, the cause of human perdition. Women were 'the devil's gateway' on whose account Christ had to die (Tertullian 1982: 14–25).

Recent feminist histories have confirmed the ubiquitous presence of the discourses of misogyny throughout European history (Fiero 1989; Pagels 1988; Rogers 1966; Rose 1986; Wilson and Makowski 1990). These misogynous discourses were structured around the claim, one that stretches from Aristotle to Aquinas, that women were inferior since biologically they were defective males, and were linked to the view that the male contributed more on conception than the female (Rousselle 1988). The notion of male superiority was extended to intelligence and hence to a rational/irrational or reason/passion dichotomy (Turner 1984: 37); from this was derived the presumed fickleness and weak-mindedness of women (Fiero 1989).

The intellectual apparatus of medieval misogyny started from the 'derivative' nature of the female, drawn from Adam's rib, which was in turn linked to both the inferiority and the perversity of the female. The great misogynistic early Christian writers were obsessed with the moral implications of female ornamentation and were preoccupied with veils, jewels, make-up and the like, and thus made the connection with both the theological and secular critiques of luxury. The pervasive Christian ambivalence towards the body and sexuality is carried over into an association with dress and ornamentation in the denunciation of the pride and shamelessness of women. The vilification of women, subordinated and relatively powerless though they were, did not inhibit them from being held responsible for all the sins of the world, not only their own but those of men as well. This logic is exemplified in the sermons on sin of the Castillian, Alfonso de Toledo; the range and scope of the present ills he laid at the feet of women is breathtaking (Toledo [1438] 1959). However, it is important to recognize that the discourses of misogyny were by no means as linear as this summary suggests and that they were riven with paradoxes (Bloch 1989). Perhaps the most important of these is that misogyny was at one and the same time a recognition of the senses and a desire to escape the senses, and in particular the body, and with a quest for totality or wholeness. This provides the beginnings of a link to the persistent espousal of virginity and of sexual abstinence that allows us to see the misogynous content in the courtly love tradition that lurks behind its valorization of the feminine (Kahn Blumstein 1977; Power 1975: 30–32).

The 'original sin', the responsibility for which was firmly located with Eve, was at first one of intellectual pride, a quest for knowledge counterposed to faith, but medieval Christianity transformed this original sin into a sexual sin. This sin was both a manifestation of and a legitimation of misogyny, one that was encapsulated in the body of woman (Pagels 1988). Alongside this pervasive theological and secular reproduction of misogynous discourses, I sense a point in time when there occurred an intensification of misogynous rhetoric which, in the English case, can be dated from around the second quarter of the sixteenth century. At this historical juncture the misogynous content seems, not just to be taken for granted, but reaches an almost hysterical pitch and intensity. For example, the sermons of Elizabethan England were full of a combination of critiques of luxury, condemnations of the fickleness of fashion, the dangers to national prosperity, dire warnings of the threat to social stability, and misogynous attacks on women as shallow and extravagant (Anon 1908). The 'Homily on Marriage' had to be read out in church every Sunday in Elizabethan England:

> The woman is a weak creature not endued with like strength and constancy of mind; therefore, they be the sooner disquieted, and they be the more prone to all weak affections and dispositions of the mind, more than men be; and lighter they be, and more vain in their fantasies and opinions. . . . Ye wives be in subjection to obey your husbands . . . for the husband is the head of the woman, as Christ is the head of the Church.
>
> (Quoted Stone 1977: 198)

Stern Protestant injunctions about the duty of the wife were provided by Whately:

> If ever thou purpose to be a good wife, and to live comfortably, set down this with thyself: mine husband is my superior, my better; he hath authority and rule over me; nature hath given it to him . . . God hath given it to him.
>
> (Whately 1617: 36)

In similar vein Robert Cleaver's widely cited, and probably widely read, *A Godly Form of Household Government*, a moralizing text from 1612, identified sumptuary restraint as a wife's third duty to her husband, after reverence and obedience, within a wholly misogynistic viewpoint. He was particularly preoccupied by hairstyle, especially with braided hair. He referred to 'the horrible abuse and excessive pride that many women are guilty of' in this respect (Cleaver 1612: 242).

It was through the Protestant connection that the link between misogyny and sumptuary law found its way into the New England colonies. Many American communities, drawing on biblical authority, articulated strongly misogynistic discourses linking modesty, meekness, submissiveness and obedience as the means of chastening the sensuality of women. Schmidt identifies a flourishing trade in misogynist tracts with such dramatic titles as *A Just and Seasonable Reprehension of Naked Breasts and Shoulders* [1678] and *Hoop Petticoats Arraigned and Condemned* [1722] (Schmidt 1989: 34).

It would be easy to fill many more pages with this evidence of misogynous disquisitions. If the important phases of the history of sumptuary law occurred on the borders of modernity, and these were systematically associated with misogynous discourses, then it is important to attend to transformations in the forms of the family and the governance of the family. If we narrow the focus of attention to England we can make use of Lawrence Stone's sophisticated model of the historical shifts in family form. Stone distinguishes between the 'open lineage family' that spans the period from antiquity through to the sixteenth century, and the 'restricted patriarchal nuclear family' that he dates rather precisely as rising around 1530 and surrendering its dominance to the distinctively modern 'closed domesticated nuclear family' around 1640, before expiring by the beginning of the eighteenth century (Stone 1977: 7–9).

The attraction of Stone's periodization is that it offers the suggestive thesis that the intensification of misogyny in the sixteenth century may have been linked to the rise of the 'restricted patriarchal nuclear family'. This new family form involved a reinforcement of patriarchy, of the authority of husband and father, and at the same time removed both wives and children from the potential personal and political supports that were present in the previous kinship familial form. My suggestion is that such a shift was reinforced by a simultaneous reinforcement of misogyny, one which explicitly stressed wifely subordination and obedience. By extension this seems to be linked to an intensification in the attempts to institute sumptuary regulation. It might even provide an opening by which to explain the sudden removal of the previous exemption of women from English sumptuary regulation identified in the previous chapter. Much more would be needed to be done by specialists in this period before this analysis could be advanced with more confidence than I am able to offer. For the time being I make no stronger claim than that my account is consistent with Stone's justly influential periodization of the history of the English family.

PATRIARCHY AND MISOGYNY

If misogyny was a prevalent and persistent ideological manifestation in late medieval and early modern society it is possible that it was an expression of the patriarchal forms of social relations. I follow Bryan Turner in identifying patriarchy as involving 'the systematic social closure of women from the public sphere by legal, political and economic arrangements that operate in favour of men.... Patriarchy is an objective social structure which is maintained and constituted by a complex system of legal regulations, political organization and economic arrangements' (Turner 1984: 154). Since the introduction of the concept of patriarchy by Kate Millett (1970) it has been used in a variety of very different ways, but increasingly has become synonymous with any form of social relations exhibiting the subordination of women. To be useful the concept needs to be employed to designate more specific forms of relationships for, as McDonough and Harrison (1978: 12) insist, patriarchy takes specific forms under different relations of production and it is important to avoid any trans-historical conception of patriarchy as the generalized rule of men.

For present purposes the primary focus will be on the pre-modern period. 'Patriarchy' will be employed to designate a system of property relations in which inheritance was organized through kinship systems passing through the male line, most typically that of primogeniture. These property relations were in turn supported by political relations in which all levels located power in the hands of the senior male within the relevant kinship category. Of particular importance is that the state was conceived through the metaphor of the family in which lines of authority and corresponding duties of obedience embodied the 'natural' supremacy of the 'head of the family'. Political authority is identified with the rule of the father over the family; as the father is owed absolute obedience, so to was the king since both family and monarchy were assumed to be 'natural' institutions (Schochet 1974). These ideas were encapsulated in Sir William Dugdale's jurisprudential thesis that government was, from the beginning, in the hands of the Father of the Household (Dugdale 1666: 12). Patriarchy was closely connected with gerontocracy in which patriarchal power was not only directed against all women, but also at a large proportion of men, all other than first-born sons.

It is important to bear in mind that during the period under discussion, while companionship, love and sexual desire could help bind a marriage, these were secondary considerations:

> As an institution marriage created an alliance between families and kin groups, building social, economic and political ties of

> crucial importance to large numbers of persons. Finally marriage acted as the most important vehicle for the transfer of property.
>
> (Stone 1990: 6)

In late medieval Europe there were two distinct economic expressions of patriarchy. In the first place post-feudal landed estates were now dependent on money rents, but were still organized as familial dynasties preoccupied with the preservation and expansion of the patrimony. Protecting the patrimony involved a concern with the making of marriages as alliances. The other form of patriarchy was the one so aptly labelled the 'holy household' by Lyndal Roper (1989). It was characterized by the economic relations of the urban guilds in which economic production was located within a household constituted by specific economic roles for husband, wife, journeymen, apprentices and servants.

The central core of these familial discourses revolved around the 'government of the household'. Increasingly this was conceived as embodying the local unity of the sovereign state in a context that Lawrence Stone characterizes in terms of an 'authoritarian family' and an 'authoritarian nation state' which were presented as solutions to an 'intolerable sense of anxiety, and a deep yearning for order' (Stone 1977: 217). An important implication of this conceptualization is that the advent of capitalism undermined the patriarchal household on which patriarchy was founded; it follows that patriarchalism increasingly became an ideological manifestation disconnected from the primary forms of economic relations.

It is now necessary to inquire whether there is some necessary connection between patriarchy and misogyny. In late medieval patriarchy, especially in the urban household form, the most coherent ideological expression was, I suggest, not misogyny, but rather was organized around the general construct of 'separate spheres' in which a presumed 'natural' division of labour identified specific roles for males and females alongside the central role of the quintessentially patriarchal 'head of family'. This headship in the family increasingly dispensed with gerontocracy as the economically active male came to occupy this role. This natural division of labour found its ideological expression in an elaborated set of dichotomies organized around the public/private. One of its more important manifestations was the dichotomy between reason and desire; the counterposing of female passion and male reason undoubtedly provided one of the cultural props of patriarchy. A second dichotomy, that between production and consumption, returns us to the domain of sumptuary regulation and helps to explain the conjunction between patriarchy and the projects of sumptuary restraint.

The association between women and vicarious consumption generated the standard trope of the sumptuary ethic that linked the consumption by women to luxury and extravagance, a trope epitomized in the preamble to the edict of the Venetian Senate in 1504 that declared against fashion on the grounds that:

> among all the superfluous and useless expenditure for the purpose of ostentation made by the women of this our city, the most injurious to the substance of the gentlemen and citizens is the constant change made by women in the form of their clothes. . . . It is convenient that what the aforesaid women have once desired, with the same they should be obliged to be content. . . . For the future no new style may be adopted in the garments of the women.
>
> (Quoted in Newett 1907: 247–48)

Thus not only are women expensive, but this is articulated with the quasi-misogynous view that women are light, fanciful and irresponsible. That nevertheless falls far short of the vilification and the attribution of blame upon women for social ills that characterized misogynistic discourses.

If the ideology of separate spheres was the natural and coherent expression of late medieval patriarchal rule that provided a hegemonic legitimation of male dominance and female subordination, then it remains to ask why it was that misogynous discourses were so prevalent. There is a plausible argument that supports two related if antithetical views, one which sees women experiencing a significant historical defeat toward the close of the medieval period and the other that sees them as mounting an assault on the bastions of male power. The first position argues that there occurred a real decline in the circumstances of women which resulted in the delivery of an ideological *coup de grâce* with the emergence of strongly misogynistic discourses reviving the doctrines of the early Christian fathers, with St Jerome playing the role of the patron saint of a misogyny in which 'woman is the gate of the devil, the path of wickedness, the sting of the serpent, in a word, a perilous object' (quoted in Heer 1962: 110). More specific attempts to locate the content of this historic defeat of women come from Merry Weisner (1986) and Judith Bennett (1991) who argue that in the late Middle Ages women came under attack with respect to their grip on skilled occupations; both cite brewing as their major instance. This expulsion of women from the public sphere was not without resistance and this sharpening of the gender war was accompanied by an upsurge in misogynistic attacks.

The other side of the coin suggests that women were beginning to escape from the fatalistic subordination that had persisted since antiquity. As they came to assert themselves they were rebuffed by an upsurge in misogyny from men determined to maintain their long accustomed advantages. According to this view women achieved a greater social visibility and freedom during the later Middle Ages; but this fuelled the wrath of medieval preachers who denounced women's sexuality, lack of modesty and their breach of sumptuary restrictions on apparel. This expansion of misogynistic discourses coincided with a shift from the purely religious domain to the secular (Fiero et al. 1989; Kelso 1959). Rogers (1966) extends this line of argument into the social-psychological realm by arguing that these early feminist stirrings resulted in the appearance of male anxieties about their capacity to maintain and reproduce patriarchy. These anxieties produced what might be described as a misogynistic 'backlash' drawing heavily on the Christian denigration of sex and a sexual guilt in Oedipal form which expressed itself in a preoccupation with the presumed insubordination of women. Certainly this view fits neatly with the characteristic manifestations of the sumptuary discourses. However, neither of these positions, the 'historic defeat' or 'the backlash' against signs of autonomy, seems as yet to have sufficient evidence to ground the interpretations that are derived from them. This still leaves the nagging question of explaining the one persistent element, namely that there was a marked upsurge in the misogynous vilification of women. I offer the suggestion that attention should be paid to the considerable autonomy of theological thought and religious organization. The polarization of the Christian tradition and the ferocity of the struggles it engendered during the Reformation found one of its expressions in an intensification of the endemic misogyny that Christianity had inherited from its historical roots in the authoritarian tribalism from which it emerged.

This leads to the suggestion that the Protestant and Catholic Reformations tried to outbid each other in the sectarianism characteristic of major ideological contestations, and misogyny was one of the components of this religious sectarianism.

Before leaving this attempt to account for the misogynous context of the sumptuary phenomenon there was one further set of views, again coming in antithetical form, which is worth reviewing. Significantly these views ask the forward-looking question about whether there is a link between misogyny and the rise of capitalism. One side suggests that misogyny had a distinctive bourgeois lineage; its emphasis on the perfidy of women was the obverse of the emergent and essentially masculine work ethic (Power 1975: 30–32). The weakness of this view is that its reading of the Reformation as narrowly authoritarian entirely ignores the fact that the upsurge of misogyny occurs across Christianity's sectarian divide. On the other side the emergent bourgeoisie is viewed more charitably; alongside the predominance of misogynous discourses there arises a distinct and novel concern with women's rights within the merchant classes (Wright 1953). Again I do not have the means to engage in an adequate assessment of this view. I leave the matter of misogyny with the feeling of puzzlement with which I originally approached it. Whether we judge the position of women to be in forward or reverse gear, whether the key sources of misogyny reside with the new or the old classes, the general subordination of women seems during the period under consideration to be so secure with only the most fleeting expression of alternative possibilities, for example in the writings of Christine de Pisan (1985). Yet it was unquestionably the case that misogynous discourses were rampant and showed a bitter tenacity.

With variations in its intensity and vituperativeness, the strident voice of misogyny reappears time and time again down to the present. Since most of this is outside my main period of study I offer just one instance. Whilst reading in the sociology of fashion I was brought up with a start on encountering the passage that follows from Georg Simmel who, although less widely read today, is still regarded as one of the key figures in the history of the social sciences:

> It is one of the pleasures of the judge of human nature, although somewhat cruel withal, to feel the anxiousness with which woman clings to the commonplace contents and forms of social

> intercourse. The impossibility of enticing her beyond the most banal and trite forms of expression, which often drives one to despair. . .
>
> (Simmel 1904: 146–47)

POPULATIONISM

Given the persistence of the misogynous discourses it is little surprise that sumptuary laws were cast in their mould. Yet the burden of my argument has been that sumptuary laws gave voice to social anxieties, which in turn reverberated from social and economic problems that could not be fully solved through legislative control over their outward signs. If sumptuary laws addressed the superficialities and visible surface of social problems and the anxieties they engendered, what was their substance? I have argued that the impulse of sumptuary regulation revolved around issues of both class and gender. These issues came together in complex interconnection and were involved in the expansion of governmental reach that in turn provided a major impulse toward the processes of state formation. These projects reached their fullest development in the seventeenth and eighteenth centuries with the emergence of organized intervention directed towards influencing both the size and the condition of the population. These interventions have been explored through Rosen's term 'medical police' (Rosen 1974), Marc Raeff's 'well-ordered police state' (Raeff 1983) and Foucault's widely influential exploration of the expanded conception of 'police' (Foucault 1980b). Another side of these projects can be grouped under the label of populationism, where they involved any use of mechanisms of public policy and data collection (e.g. political arithmetic, censuses and fertility rates) directed towards the governance of the size and quality of the population from the standpoint of military, fiscal or other economic considerations. While it is undoubtedly correct that the eighteenth century marked a new level of intensity of preoccupation with populationism, populationist politics have a much longer lineage. Heckscher, for example, insists that the whole period of mercantilism was associated throughout Europe with a 'fanatical desire to increase population' (Heckscher 1955: 158). Populationism exhibits significant links with the general theme of the political economy of marriage and thus with the gender wars brought to the surface in sumptuary regulation. I will select two key periods to explore this link between populationism, the political economy of marriage and sumptuary law.

The two most significant cases are those of Imperial Rome and Renaissance Florence. The Augustan matrimonial legislation of 18 BC, *Lex Julia de maritandis ordinibus,* and the subsequent *Lex Papia Poppaea nuptialis* (AD 9) were unambiguously populationist. The earlier laws relied on negative prohibition, but later shifted to employing positive inducements to encourage marriage and procreation. The legislation was constructed from a variety of discursive elements, moral regulation starting from concern about adultery, populationist concerns about the birth rate and a symbolic politics that appealed to the class interest of the elite with fears of the populous underclasses and the 'new' Romans and, perhaps most importantly, shifts in property relations and the role of inheritance. Men between 25 and 60 were required to be married, as were women between 20 and 50. After the termination of a marriage through death or divorce both men and women were required to remarry. The restrictions on the testamentary capacity of bachelors or spinsters and on the childless married were quite explicitly directed towards resisting what was perceived as the disastrous decline in the fertility of the Roman ruling class, the quasi-aristocracy of senatorial rank (Norr 1981). More broadly it was directed against the very distinctive ethic of celibacy that had been embraced by significant numbers of ruling class men (Rousselle 1988).[2]

Medieval Florentine politics, as indeed that in other Italian cities, was much concerned with populationist issues. The concern with population was induced by military-political considerations in the face of the intensifying competition between the city-states and also in response to the devastation wrought by the series of plagues that decimated the population. The Florentine legislation time and time again appealed to a logic that linked women's extravagance, male poverty, the dispersal of patrimonial estates, and a male reluctance to marry, or at least to marry early enough to secure a rising fertility rate. The crucial material factor for populationist policies was the institution of dowry payments. It was the dowry that formed the key instance that I discuss as exemplifying the political economy of marriage and the part played therein by the sumptuary laws.

THE POLITICAL ECONOMY OF MARRIAGE

Renaissance Italian society was one characterized by ideologies of rank and of patriarchy; significantly money became the most powerful determinate of both personal status and of inheritance. Central to the making of marriages and the constitution of kinship relationships was the payment of dowries by the bride's family.[3] Any factors that led to an increase in the size of dowries and the associated wedding gifts made it more difficult for fathers to secure marriages for their daughters. The complexity of the political economy of marriage is illustrated by the fact that bigger dowries, perhaps paradoxically, weakened the position of husbands in the household as they became increasingly dependent upon the capital brought in by their wives. These processes became visible from the thirteenth century. In these circumstances men, as individuals and as legislators, ranted against female folly and extravagance. Yet they were locked into the paradox that they were implicated in this folly in that they lived off the dowries and paid for the forbidden dresses whose splendour confirmed their own status.

During a debate on a proposed sumptuary enactment in Florence in 1433, a leading magistrate referred to 'the barbarous and irresponsible bestiality of women. . . . [who] force their husbands with honeyed poison to submit to them' (quoted in Brucker 1971: 180–81). In rather similar terms a Venetian pronouncement of the ruling Ten as late as 1776 complained that:

> the way the times are going, together with the great and universal alteration in manners whose full effect is with us now, demonstrate, to our profound and justifiable grief, the inevitable result of the free and licentious life our women lead. This was, and ever will be, the chief cause of the decline and ruin of the Republic.
>
> (Quoted Andrieux 1972: 136)

The populationist concerns find direct expression in Florentine sumptuary legislation. A statute from 1433 grumbled that men 'avoid the bond of matrimony on account of the unaffordable expenses' (Rainey 1985). A petition from citizens of Pisa to the Signoria of Florence reveals another twist; it complained that of 900 unmarried women, 300 of them were over 24 and that this was evidence that men were refusing to marry 'on account of the great expenses that they would be required to make for the apparel and ornaments of married women, and especially because the dowries of these girls were so small' (Rainey 1985: 425). In other words the high cost of keeping a wife plus the small dowries they brought with them led to male poverty or the postponement of marriage. As Diane Hughes observes, 'throughout Italy dowries went up, and laws to restrain them multiplied' (1983: 95).

One element of the response to this petition was to renew sumptuary restrictions on women's dress and ornamentation, but the bigger issue was the pressure on the aggregate size of the dowry. It seems also that the postponement of marriage by men was directly related to a reduction in the age of brides; this in turn resulted in escalating dowry payments. At this stage sumptuary considerations became a factor because the dowry consisted of a combination of trousseau and a cash sum. Any increase in female sumptuousity would be likely to squeeze the cash element that was the husband's main concern. In general, greater expenditure on women's clothing would have further increased pressure for bigger dowries. The net effect was to shift the economic burden of marriage onto the bride's father and kin. These primary economic interests are starkly disclosed in the preamble to a Florentine sumptuary law of 1511 that contended that 'the expense of superfluous and unnecessary things has so increased that a good portion of the dowry is being consumed with little benefit to married men' (Rainey 1985: 470).

This analysis of dowry in the context of a focus on the political economy of marriage leads to two interesting conclusions. First, struggles over dowry size did not pit men against women, but rather counterposed one patrilineal line against another; in the short term a father's interests shifted depending on the sex ratio of his offspring. Second, there was a significant effect on marital relations; as men postponed marriage in the hope of securing a larger dowry it increased the financial autonomy and bargaining power of their young brides, particularly in view of the fact that the law left the dowry in the hands of the wife and on widowhood or marital breakdown the wife took her dowry with her. Once married women were perceived as having the whip hand over their husbands, since the latter depended on their dowries and consequentially had to indulge their wives' taste in fashion, that not only diminished male capital, but also signified their loss of control (Hughes 1983: 95). It should, however, be borne in mind that the positions of individuals changed over time; while a man had an interest in obtaining for himself the largest possible dowry, 15 to 20 years later he was confronted with the problem of raising inflationary dowries for his own daughters.

Another consequence of struggles over dowries had adverse consequences for women, especially in families with more than one daughter. If their fathers were unable to raise a dowry of the requisite size one or more of his daughters would be sent into nunneries and other religious institutions. The presence in these institutions of women who were there from economic circumstances rather than religious zeal was, I suspect, a significant component underlying the moral panics that flared up in many cities about the link between nunneries and prostitution. In Venice, for example, the punishment of banishment was prescribed for men having sexual relations with nuns (Gilbert 1973: 123). Evidence from Sicily attests to the fact that convents cashed in on the dowry crisis and began to charge higher entry fees and this in turn led to attempts being made to regulate these charges (Smith 1968). In Venice this practice of involuntary placement in convents of daughters for whom dowries could not be raised was outlawed in 1460 (Newett 1906: 248).

Perhaps the most significant response to the dowry crisis was that Florence actually established a dowry fund, *monte della doti*, in 1425 to provide Florentine girls with sufficient dowries (Rainey 1985: 472).[4] The capital for this fund was raised by levying compulsory loans, and this became a very significant part of Florentine public finances over the next 100 years since these long-term loans paid fixed interest. Later the proceeds from the purchase of sumptuary exemptions were also applied to the dowry fund. Thus both the dowry fund and the sumptuary laws were linked in the project of stimulating the marriage market.

The link between the political economy of marriage and sumptuary law becomes clearer when the sumptuary laws themselves dealt explicitly with dowry issues. The first episcopal ordinance in the Papal city of Perugia in 1445 prohibited married women from spending more than one third of their dowry on clothing (Kantorowitz 1970: 361). The general anxiety about the cost of marriage led to attempts to control these costs, for example by imposing limits on the amount that could be spent on the bridal dress, train, rings, etc. An expressly economic motive is clear in the provision that dowry limits did not apply to men who married women who were crippled or blind (Newett 1907: 248). In Florence the sumptuary regime generally allowed greater latitude to unmarried girls, who were exempted from many of the restrictions imposed upon married women, undoubtedly with the aim of facilitating their prospects in the competitive marriage struggles. Once a marriage had been arranged a major concern of Florentine sumptuary law was to regulate the costs of trousseau and dowry in order to avoid ruining the familial patrimony. These considerations underline the connection between sumptuary law and the shifts in women's legal personality, from daughter of one lineage, to wife in another; marriage was the moment of a major change in status.

The political economy of marriage had its effects outside Italy, although my data is less full. In Spain the inflation caused by the rapid increase in the flow of gold and silver made it increasingly difficult for poor and middling families to provide dowries for their daughters. In turn this led convents to ask for increased endowments that seem sometimes to have been referred to as 'dowries'. In these circumstances prostitution was a rational and viable alternative for many women (Perry 1978: 200). Elsewhere an ordinance from Nördlingen of 1672 forbade the daughters of artisans and labourers to squander their dowry on provocative clothing, thus revealing a mix of moral anxiety with considerations of the political economy of marriage (Friedrichs 1979: 24). France surpassed all other nations with its interventions in the political economy of marriage, making use of fiscal rather that sumptuary governance. Legislation in 1666, sponsored by Colbert, instituted inducements to marriage. Men marrying under 20 were exempted from payment of the *taille* tax until they were 25, and tax relief was granted to families with ten or more children. A decree of 1669, applying to the New France colony in Canada, imposed fines on men who did not ensure the marriage of their sons before the age of 20 and their daughters before 16 (Heckscher 1955: 160).

The role played by the institution of dowry serves to demonstrate the connection between the political economy of marriage and the sumptuary regimes that responded to the material interests affected and to the social anxieties that were stirred. However, it should be borne in mind that marriage regimes showed considerable variation and I have found that despite the wealth of information about English sumptuary laws I have not discovered any leads which allow me to make anything like the same claims for a link between English sumptuary laws and the broader panorama of the political economy of marriage.

11

Moral Regulation and Popular Culture

THE ROOTS OF MORAL REGULATION

In every epoch there has been a distinctive form of ideological critique of the existing social order which is linked with an insistence on the necessity and desirability of some regulatory intervention, captured in the pervasive idea that 'something ought to be done'. The specific object of this critique has varied over time. We have seen the persistence of the critique of luxury that stretched from the early civilizations of the Mediterranean basin down to the eighteenth century and even beyond. The focus of this chapter is on these moralizing critiques and their relationship to the projects of sumptuary regulation.

I make use of the idea of 'moral regulation' in a way that goes beyond a descriptive qualification of the object of regulation, in that it is not simply regulation in the field of morality. My usage is close to and holds out the possibility of developing Philip Corrigan's concept of moral regulation (Corrigan 1980).[1] While sharing his focus on the agency of the state I am keen to explore the way in which conflicts over antagonistic discursive formations within the field of popular culture provide the arena within which the direction and targets of moral regulation are formed and acted upon by both state and non-state agencies. In brief, it is important to avoid any suggestion that the state, conceived as some institutional personalization, is an autonomous agent that selects its targets as part of some wider strategic objective and then organizes their moralization in order to subject them to moral regulation (Muchembled 1985). It is important to avoid a polarization between state projects of the 'reform of morals' and autonomous fields of 'popular culture'. It is entirely consistent to identify the existence of such projects and also to identify fields in which popular culture exhibits elements of shared values that are also present within the dominant culture (Burke 1978; Ingram 1984). Indeed such circumstances are precisely those in which it is possible to identify the existence of hegemonic discourses.

On the borders of modernity there were two connected but never fused discursive targets, luxury and idleness, both of which episodically intersected with the shifting discourses of gender and sexuality. We have already seen how the critique of luxury expressed itself in the ubiquitous sumptuary laws. Idleness as a second focus of preoccupation was particularly significant in that while it resonates with the critique of luxury, it has its own distinctive thrust again directed against the labouring classes. It came into prominence when the regulation of labour became an increasingly significant object of governance as labour shortage and the displacement of feudalism proceeded with increasing rapidity. Luxury and idleness found common expression in fears of national degeneration and threats to public order. These critiques exhibited certain common features. They invoked some positive image of the past, a Golden Age, that is confronted by a 'present danger' (luxury and idleness) which threatens future ills of degeneration, decline and the new and disturbing element of the insubordination of the labouring classes (Thomas 1983). This discursive formation gradually came to be articulated in terms of the metaphor of disease.

In England the Reformation brought with it the triumph of the metaphor of disease. It was the Puritans, in particular, who made extensive use of the disease metaphor as a component of an organic metaphor through which society was pictured, and which generated discourses of cure and treatment. There is scope for a more extended discursive analysis of the tropes within which the regulatory projects were located. While the Anglicans invoked an image of a good old England of paternal lords and sturdy labourers who knew their place and lived in harmony, the Puritans were less preoccupied with a lost harmony, but emphasized the contemporary fact of 'disorder', evincing anxiety rather than nostalgia. The Puritan prescription involved three elements: work/discipline; congregational responsibility with voluntary submission to the community which involved what Walzer calls a system of congregational discipline; and 'a close system of collective watchfulness' (Walzer 1965: 221). The third feature is the one that is most important for present concerns; it involved a predisposition towards a general endorsement of interventionist governance focused on a need for secular regulation of widening spheres of social life. What is distinctive about these discourses is that they not only created the space for both state and congregational action, but increasingly emphasized the 'governance of the self'. The important point to be stressed is that the governance of the self should not be understood as some 'private' project, but is intimately implicated in every project of governance.

During the course of the sixteenth century emerging mercantilism exhibited a similar growing faith in the effectiveness of regulation and its targets included those of 'idleness' and 'luxury'. They came to provide an increasingly explicit critique of the canonist doctrine of charity (Johnson 1932). It is noticeable that these precursors of political economy seem to have had no curiosity about the causes of idleness, suggesting that the disparagement of the labouring classes was already a taken-for-granted truth.

The critique of idleness was especially evident in the New England colonies. One of the earliest legislative acts in Massachusetts in 1619 was a broad attack 'Against Idleness, Gaming, Drunkenness and Excess in Apparell' (Miller 1928: 94). The broadest, but probably least successful, onslaught on idleness came from Connecticut where a law was passed in 1702 stipulating that 'no person, Householder or other, shall spend their time idly, or unprofitably' (Flaherty 1972: 180–81). Indeed 'idleness' seems to have been the colonial term which subsumed that of 'vagrancy' which had roused the legislative zeal back in England. Idleness was explicitly linked to the importance of time, conceived as God's most precious resource. The hostility to time-wasting underlaid the widespread aversion to drinking and to games of chance (shuffle-board came in for much hostility), suggesting that the concern was with time-wasting rather than with gambling (North 1974). The preoccupation with the economy of time is brought out in a Massachusetts prohibition from 1639 in which the custom of drinking to the health of companions is castigated as 'a mere useless ceremony' (Fisher 1898: 190).

We see in this medieval regulation of games and pastimes the birth of one of the most persistent fields of moral regulation, one that is as alive and controversial today as it was in the late Middle Ages, namely the overlapping association of idleness, popular recreations, drinking and gambling. Over time the targeted pastimes changed. There was a shift from a preoccupation with ball games towards games whose pleasure is likely to have been that they provided an occasion for gambling. This raises the general consideration of whether the enormous regulatory effort that almost every society has made, and many continue to make, against gambling should not properly be regarded as a form of sumptuary law. Such laws, after all, involve restrictions on how individuals dispose of their leisure time and of their income. The other important similarity is that they deploy a justificatory discourse that combines moral and economic elements; gambling is, with varying intensity, morally disapproved of and is regarded as economically irrational and dysfunctional. In short, it is a harmful way for people to use their limited resources of time and money. The proximity of the regulation of consumption and of gambling is attested to by the close proximity that Blackstone gave them in his classification of public wrongs (Blackstone 1979: 180). In general the discourses surrounding gambling are marked by a persistent disingenuity; they are moralistic attacks on popular recreations while at the same time they turn a blind eye to the significant role of gambling as a form of conspicuous consumption by the wealthy.

THE MORAL REGULATION OF POPULAR CULTURE

Throughout Europe and then later in North America, the legislators exhibited a seemingly unquenchable urge to regulate the everyday life of the working population through the criminalization of many popular recreations and pastimes. We have already seen how the peasant traditions of feasting and reciprocal indulgence whenever good times came round, and the popular and pre-Christian festivities, were swept up into the ambit of the sumptuary discourses of luxury, extravagance and disorder. A fascinating snippet indicating struggle against popular beliefs and traditions is apparent in the 1509 instruction from the Coventry Leet Court to the Aldermen to search for 'all of them that keep misrule' (Baldwin 1926: 169). This presumably involved searches for costumes and regalia used in the popular festivals that were marked by a temporary reversal of hierarchy and norm. Other targets of moralizing regulation were the popular games, sports and recreations of both the urban and rural working poor.

What emerges from an examination of these regulatory incursions is that they portray a moralization of the poor and their culture in an attempt to discipline an 'unruly' and 'uncivilized' popular autonomy (Collins 1989). Popular practices, rites and festivities that had previously been tolerated, particularly those that took violent forms or exhibited characteristics of popular justice, came to be seen as a threat by rulers (Burke 1978; Davis 1975; Fletcher and Stevenson 1985; Easton and Hawkins 1988; Yeo 1981). The reform of popular culture preceded the Reformation, but was accelerated during it. It involved more or less systematic attempts by sections of the dominant classes to change the attitudes, values and cultural practices of the subordinate classes. It was epitomized by the 'triumph of lent over carnival' that aimed to bring popular culture under control and to pacify it (Burke 1978; Ladurie 1981; Scribner 1978; Hsia 1989). This reform invoked the intersecting discourses of decency, diligence, gravity, modesty, orderliness, prudence, reason, self-control, sobriety, thrift and work. Gerhard Oestreich stresses the far reaching changes implicit in the new regulatory state projects:

> The attitudes and the conduct of even the simple subject were shaped, controlled, and regulated by the process of disciplining . . . This process of disciplining produced a more or less violent change in the structure of society at all levels.
>
> (Oestreich 1982: 259–60)

This overarching moralization of popular culture goes hand in hand with a shifting combinatory articulation in which new targets and new anxieties emerge and replace earlier combinations. We encounter concern to enforce the discipline of state religion in general and Sunday observance in particular, onslaughts on gambling in the name of both economic rationality and morality, attacks on the perceived unruliness of the labouring classes whose passivity could less and less be assumed (Whitaker 1933). As anxieties over labour discipline come to the fore so do attacks on idleness that express themselves in the moralization not only of alcohol itself but, probably even more significantly, of the spaces in which communal drinking occurred, the alehouses and inns in which the poor take their pleasure away from the surveillance of the respectable classes (Wrightson 1982: 165–69). Cranmer exemplifies this moralization of idleness, drink and luxury in succinct form: 'much drinking and little working, much spending and little getting' (Cranmer 1846: II: 194). Just occasionally we encounter attempts to redirect popular culture in such a way as to promote useful and economical forms of pleasure revealing the deep conflicts between popular culture and the dominant, but still not hegemonic, culture of a new bourgeois order.

These considerations suggest some more general reflections on popular culture and moral regulation. The old order, although it was capable, if only episodically, of descending with ferocious wrath on the peasantry, in the main left the labouring classes to their own devices, and periodic acts of deference were sufficient to reassure their superiors. Popular culture in the late Middle Ages was largely autonomous and often looked down on by the landed classes with an amused tolerance. The emergence during the long transition to capitalism of what Hobsbawm has aptly called primitive rebels was not, I suggest, a one-way process of growing resistance from below, but it was as much a response to the increasingly penetrative projects of the new state formations and political projects (Hobsbawm 1965). Attempts were made to bring under control and to discipline the fairs and alehouses that had been the untroubled spaces within which popular culture was lived. In brief, state power became increasingly interfering and accordingly resented. I suggest that this stubborn resistance was reflected in and goes a long way toward explaining the revival in popularity of the Robin Hood tradition in early modern England (Hilton 1976); despite its feudal setting the 'evil' of the Sheriff of Nottingham articulated the dislike of intrusive power and explains the popularity of the Robin Hood games during fairs and carnivals that were to linger even longer in children's games (Bellamy 1985).

The trajectory of the projects to discipline popular culture can be traced through English statutes and proclamations. It is as well, however, to start with the disclaimer that I imply no suggestion that the existence of legislative intervention suggests that these incursions were successful, only that they provide evidence about the targets of such disciplinary projects.[2] For over 200 years English rulers legislated vigorously to enforce proficiency in archery upon working people. The obverse of this positive project was the attempt to eradicate many popular pastimes. A statute in 1388 required rural and urban labourers to desist from 'all playing at Tennis or Football and other Games called Coits, Dice, Casting of the Stone and other such importune Games' on Sundays and Holydays (12 Rich. II: *c.* 6; SR 2: 57), and required them to spend their restricted leisure time after the Sunday church service practising archery.[3] In a reenactment that came in 1409 (11 Hen. IV: *c.* 4; SR 2, 163) the offending games changed a little; it charged people to 'utterly leave off playing at the Balls, as well Hand-ball and Football' on Sundays.[4]

What is interesting about the list of unlawful games is that they seem to have been of two types. The first were ball games selected, I suggest, because of their unruliness since, before they succumbed to the legalist impulse to make sports into entirely rule-bound encounters that reaches its apotheosis in twentieth century baseball, these games were encounters of popular participation without very much in the way of numerical, spatial or behavioural restriction. The attempts to repress this disorderly customary style of football continue into the nineteenth century (Bushaway 1982: 250–52).[5] The second type of game, epitomized by dice and stones, was significant in providing opportunities for gambling and was also frequently associated with drinking. By the sixteenth century there emerged an interesting tension in the tactics of governance; on the one hand of maintaining the centrality of the local churchyard as the centre of village life through encouraging 'useful' recreation, epitomized by archery; on the other hand the Puritan concern to cleanse the church of traditional and recreational activities tended, albeit unintentionally, to relocate popular pastimes in and around the alehouses (Wrightson 1981). This undoubtedly explains why the alehouses, as sites of autonomous popular culture, became subject to intensified regulation and repression in the opening decades of the seventeenth century (Clark 1983).

The next statute in 1477 (17 Edw. IV: *c.* 3; SR 2: 462) repeated the list of unlawful games, adding a typical sumptuary motive by referring to the impoverishment of their devotees. It also provided an explicit rationale for the promotion of archery with the injunction that 'every Person strong and able should use his Bow, because of the defence of the land'. A tone of moral panic is added with a dramatic escalation of the perils of disobedience which are pictured as leading, in a rather implausible extrapolation, to 'Murders, Robberies and other heinous Felonies'. The other innovation was the imposition of penalties on the owners and occupiers of premises on which unlawful games were played.

The valorization of the long-bow brought together a number of themes, of which national defence was probably the least significant although the fear of invasion was to escalate during the Elizabethan era. It was of course attempted, as Spain replaced France as the national enemy. It is probably more important to understand this fixation as a component of an emerging national mythology that was to blossom into the imagery of the sturdy yeomanry of 'free-born Englishmen' whose later career E.P. Thompson has done so much to excavate as it became an oppositional spirit of a rebellious traditional culture (Thompson 1991). The long-bow was significantly a 'popular' weapon able to unhorse the feudal armies of Europe and to relocate knightly armour from the battlefield to the baronial hall.[6]

The impulse for compulsory archery was given some organizational bite by the requirement that all adult males should own a bow and that parishes should be provided with butts for Sunday afternoon practice. Efforts were made to stimulate competition, loosely modelled on the knightly tournaments, in archery and other quasi-military sports. This links up with yet another prominent feature of the Robin Hood mythology where the lowly could challenge the mighty and triumph through skill and courage.[7]

An interesting shift occurs in a statute from 1495.[8] Here for the first time a statute against unlawful games presented itself as primarily anti-gambling in its motivation when the linkage with archery was, for the first time, omitted. However, the attention to archery was soon reintroduced in 1512 with an Act whose Preamble celebrated the 'great number and multitude of good Archers that hath . . . defended this Realm and the Subjects thereof against the cruel malice and danger of their outward [foreign] enemies'.[9] This statute, in now familiar terms, went on to promote archery, the owning of bows, practice on Sundays and the provision of butts and, at the same time, prohibited 'all playing at tennis, football, coits, dice and other such importune games'.

A decisive new departure appeared in a proclamation in 1527 that not only struck a more concerned note about archery, claiming that these skills were 'almost utterly set apart and extremely decayed',[10] but more significantly it disclosed a new strand in contemporary governmentality, and presumably in the anxieties of the propertied classes, and one that was to become increasingly prominent, when the prohibited games that it listed were linked to the evils of idleness and vagrancy. Here I suggest we encounter a discursive displacement bringing into play a new configuration around the enforcement of labour discipline. One of the most morally repugnant features of those classes that have freed themselves from the necessity of physical labour is the moralization of the laziness of those classes that must work from necessity. The Tudor ruling classes were no better or worse than their successors; all of them seem to have been unable to refrain from launching themselves into transparent hypocrisy over the idleness of the labouring classes. Prohibited games and gambling are pictured as the evil that keeps the labourers from their allotted toil.

In the very next year another proclamation repeated the thematization of unlawful games, gambling, idleness and vagrancy and made the decisive move by linking these to the last piece in the jigsaw of moralization that was to remain in place down to the present – drink is added to the equation for the first time; enforcement is linked to control of disorderly inns and ale-houses.[11] Drink was thus linked to unlawful games and gambling, and to vagrancy and disorder. A further dimension was to appear with mercantilist concerns about the economic costs of the import of French wine, although it is likely that this was being consumed by the propertied classes (Baldwin 1926: 179–82).

Yet another 'unlawful games' statute in 1542 for the 'maintenance of artillery' seems to suggest an origin in commercial pressure from bow-makers (33 Hen. VIII: *c.* 9; SR 3: 837). After requiring every able-bodied man under the age of 60 to practise the longbow and to own bow and arrows, it specified that the bows be made of elm, witch hazel or ash and forbids yew. It then proceeded to complain of 'many and sundry new and crafty Games' and for the first time added a class-discriminatory clause by prohibiting all but gentlemen from playing a long list of games.[12]

The concern with archery began to fade in the middle of the sixteenth century. There was just one archery proclamation in Elizabeth's reign, in 1572 (Hughes and Larkin 1964: II: No. 587) and a final proclamation on unlawful games and archery in 1608 (Lindesiana 1886). What happens from around 1550 seems to have been that attempts to enforce archery ran out of steam, as did the endeavour to prohibit popular games; regulatory activity bifurcates in two directions that administratively, if not conceptually, separated vagrancy and drinking. The general pattern, to be explored below, reveals legislation against vagrancy becoming more repressive while the attack on drinking proceeded through the regulatory tactic of the licensing of drinking establishments. While the legislative output dried up, Parliament continued to exhibit law-making urges. Joan Kent's analysis of the bills introduced in the Elizabethan Parliament reveals that the Commons continued to have considerable appetite for moral regulation (Kent 1973). The failure to secure legislation was due, not to disagreement about the desirability of such activity, but rather to its foundering on the sticky constitutional sensitivities between the Commons and the Crown. This legislative urge remained active into the first decade of the seventeenth century. In some years the parliamentary activity verged on the obsessive; in 1601 six bills against drunkenness, in 1604 four apparel bills and 13 on drunkenness or alehouses, and in 1606 five drunkenness bills were introduced but died before enactment.

The project of regulating popular pastimes was not confined to England; elsewhere in Europe it seems to have been closely tied to the motives that imposed sumptuary restraints on weddings, christenings and funerals, namely a concern to restrict expenditure in the name of domestic economy. While the Reformation did not produce any great extension of sumptuary law, it undoubtedly extended both the range and the intensity of moral regulation. The major impact of the Reformation was the acceleration of the secularization of moral regulation (Abray 1985; Greenfield 1918). The lay Marriage Court and Morals Board in Strasbourg had, as we have seen, jurisdiction over marriage, divorce, sexual offences, blasphemy, cursing, gambling and drunkenness. Police ordinances in Strasbourg from the 1540s onward extended the range and breadth of regulation. They embraced religious issues such as Sunday observance, sorcery, blasphemy, profanity and cursing, but also addressed more secular issues such as the upbringing of children, the keeping of servants, and relations between innkeepers and guests. In addition to the general sumptuary regulations were rules governing begging and almsgiving, the status of Jews, and economic regulation of usury and of monopolies (Oestreich 1982: 158).

In Nürnberg laws concerning the consumption of alcohol went back a long way and were frequently renewed and amended. As Greenfield perceptively comments these measure do not look strange to us, as do the sumptuary rules, because we still keep the sale and consumption of liquor under close municipal supervision (Greenfield 1918: 88). Much of the motivation he argues – then as now – was concerned with social order rather than with sumptuary considerations or wider moral considerations. Here

Greenfield seems himself to fall victim to the regulatory discourses of the twentieth century for it is only under specific social conditions that alcohol comes to be associated with anxieties about social order. There is no evidence to suggest that the large quantities of beer that were normally supplied to agricultural labourers were a source of disorder; rather the regulation of drinking seems to follow upon major changes in the relationship between labourers and their employers. Similarly the general secularization processes probably explain the increased temporal regulation of drinking that Greenfield also reports from Nürnberg where drinking places were ordered to close on a wide array of religious holidays.

In Zurich there was a similar concern with general problems of social and moral order involving Sunday observance, drinking, dancing, card playing, etc. In July 1710 a meeting of the 'Triple Collegium' was held, bringing together the Reformation-Chamber, senior pastors and city officials to review the moral condition of the community. It resulted in a long list of complaints about the lax habits of the populace, non-attendance at church services, drinking, gambling and sexual immorality. Over time the court's work became increasingly preoccupied with social order offences, with increasing numbers of prosecutions for dancing, gambling and brawling (Vincent 1935: 115).

The intrusive side of Reformation moral regulation was epitomized by the attempt to control dancing. In Nürnberg an early post-Reformation ordinance gave a class character to the regulation of dancing by prohibiting artisans, apprentices and servants from dancing except on the three days before Ash Wednesday. A subsequent rule forbade anybody dancing after 7.00 p.m. This attack on dancing mixed religious anxieties with projects for the reform of popular culture; but more importantly it was a response to the unstructured contacts that the conditions of urban life allowed to the increasing numbers of unattached young men and women. Such considerations, coupled with resistance to innovation, are evident in a fifteenth century ordinance that is worth quoting:

> Since it has definitely come to the knowledge of the Honourable Council, that many unwanted shameful, immodest and novel dances are daily encouraged and practised, that is not only a sin and without doubt displeasing to Almighty God, but also may produce much dishonourable light-mindedness and scandal

> besides, among men and women, the same to prevent, our Lords of the Council earnestly and strictly command, that henceforth no player or minstrel, shall pipe, play or cause any but the customary dances that have come down from of old; also no one whoever it be, woman or man, shall dance and same, and in dancing shall not take by the neck or embrace one another.
> (Greenfield 1918: 93–94)

Another ordinance from the same period stipulates that:

> Inasmuch as it has not only been definitely made known to the Honourable Council but also is manifest to the eye and in plain sight of day in what measure at weddings and other dances where an altogether unseemly and immodest abuse prevails, in that women and maidens are excessively whirled and swung around by those who dance with them, wherefrom no small mischief and scandal proceeds, with the result that it is improperly displeasing to all modest, honour-loving persons to behold it. Therefore the Honourable Council recognizing themselves responsible by virtue of their bearing office to plant and to further whatever is conducive to modesty and honour, but on the contrary to prevent and extirpate all that is opposed to this, – they our Lords have resolved no longer to look upon this unbecoming abuse, but herewith command . . .'
> (Greenfield 1918: 94)

Interestingly I have found no evidence of attempts to police dancing in England, although there were assaults on traditional festivals such as May Day at which dancing and other forms of contact between young men and women were an important element. The nearest approach seems to have been the bills introduced by Puritan MPs in Parliament when a wide range of targets were, mainly unsuccessfully, identified; these included dancing, bear-baiting, swearing and Sunday sports (Kent 1973).

On the other hand there was little change of content in the regulation of gambling associated with the Reformation. The characteristic response took a decidedly sumptuary form with the impositions of limits on stakes indicating a concern with the sumptuary issues of extravagance and impoverishment. In addition the policy was to flush gambling out into contexts where it could be controlled and make it possible to suppress 'secret' gambling. Certain popular games and pastimes for limited stakes were exempted: 'cards, draughts, bowling, for a pfennig . . . chess, running, and shooting' (Greenfield 1918: 91).

A target of moral regulation that has made an occasional appearance in sumptuary legislation is 'youth' as a social category always capable of generating social anxiety. We have already seen that young men in general and apprentices in particular were significant targets of sumptuary laws, particularly in the Italian cities and in urban England. There are periodically more general references to measures against drunkenness and gambling by 'headstrong youth' (Jones 1970: 90) and attempts to control dancing were likely to have involved concerns about the control of youth. I suspect that inter-generational tensions were a bigger issue than my explorations have thus far revealed.

The current concern is not to provide an account of the history of sports and pastimes as a component of the regulation of popular custom save in so far as it became linked with that of sumptuary law. It is interesting to note that after the strenuous legislative activity of the Tudor period the Stuarts made some attempts at a rapprochement with popular traditions; the *Book of Sports,* issued in 1618 and reissued in 1633, lifted many earlier prohibitions on popular recreations (Gardiner 1906: 99–103).

VAGRANCY AND SUMPTUARY LAWS

The moralization of idleness was a central component in the regulatory discourses of the late Middle Ages. Idleness becomes focused on the labelling of specific social types; the labels varied but vagabond, vagrant, beggar and rogue were the most common.[13] The focus on idleness gives way to the emergence of discursive concentration around a central regulatory object – that of vagrancy. This category provides a discursive link between a number of decisive features. In the first place the vagrant is constructed as voluntarily avoiding the allotted social necessity of labour. The term, common in English legislative discourses, 'masterless men' captures not only this separation from useful labour, but it also adds the notion of social danger that occurs when a person is without a master. The other central feature of the discourses of vagrancy is that they set up a polarity between the much older category 'beggar', for whom the traditional discourses of charity and alms provided a recognized place within the social order. I have not attempted to track the shifts in theological discourses, but the terms employed in English vagrancy legislation revealed something of these shifts. The quasi-legitimate status of the beggar, the 'impotent beggar', designated by certain socially recognizable traits such as infirmity, blindness, widowhood and the orphaned mark a person as having an entitlement to community support. Moralization came increasingly to be directed against the 'sturdy beggars' who were those judged capable of work.

Histories of legislation against vagrancy have, in the main, been organized around a quest for the origins of the Poor Laws as the major precursor of social welfare systems. My concern is to pick up features of this story that have not received much attention, in order to tease out the connections with moral regulation and, in particular, the connections with sumptuary projects.

The story can be told from the English experience. It starts with the emerging problem of the mobility of labour, intensified after the Black Death as labour became scarce and its market position thus made rudimentary wage bargaining and labour mobility a fact of economic life. The other key feature was the concern over who was to bear the financial burden of the relief of the poor. The early concern was with returning indigent people to where they were born, indicating the persistence of the old principle of community obligation. While this remained the official policy it gradually became submerged by other considerations. The immediate response to the Black Death of 1348–49 was the Statute of Labourers (23 Edw. III: *c.* 1–4: SR 1: 307). It embodied three main features: prevention of labourers leaving jobs in search of higher wages; imposition of wage-fixing measures at pre-plague levels; and restriction on the giving of alms to 'able-bodied beggars'.[14] Not only was the legislation directed at keeping labourers on the land, but also at controlling the behaviour of the increasing concentrations of workers in the towns where potentially unruly populations became concentrated. With the passage of time the most numerous and unruly, the youthful apprentices, also became a target of regulation. In 1563 the Statute of Artificers (5 Eliz. I: *c.* 4; SR 4(1): 414–22) continued the attempt to control the mobility of rural labour, but also introduced a similar urban strategy with the imposition of lengthy seven-year apprenticeships. Statutes and proclamations followed over the next two centuries that rung changes within this repertoire.

One of the more significant features of the regulation of the increasing numbers of transients was that it became increasingly difficult to distinguish between those moving to obtain higher wages and itinerant beggars. The response was to employ a classic exemplification of what Foucault has called 'dividing practices', which was to become an active principle down to the present, constructing a distinction between the deserving and the undeserving poor. The traditional practices of alms giving were transformed by granting 'licences' to beg to those that 'fitted' the prevailing stereotype of the deserving poor (Tierney 1959). Another version of this strategy was the issuing of badges to licensed beggars, but the authorities undoubtedly experienced considerable difficulty with verification (Beier 1985). During the sixteenth century individual cities introduced their own schemes of badges or distinguishing marks for beggars and this was extended to the whole country in 1563 when beggars were required to wear 'some notable badge or token' on their breast or back. Badging prefigured the branding of vagabonds. Thus badging had both an evidentiary function alongside its part in the wider degradation ceremony that divided the deserving from the undeserving poor (Moore 1987).

Difficulties with verification escalated as the ranks of the itinerants swelled. Itinerants became increasingly difficult to distinguish from and indeed probably often were the same as discharged soldiers and sailors or pilgrims. The authorities responded by requiring discharge notes or authorization to undertake a pilgrimage to be carried and initiated a rudimentary system of internal passports (Hufton 1972: Slack 1974). For example, a statute in 1388 required pilgrims and scholars to carry testimonials to prove their status.[15] A more general attempt to control movement by requiring those in search of work to be provided with a passport was introduced by the Statute of Artificers in 1563 (5 Eliz. I, *c.* 4: s. 8–9; SR 4(1): 414–22) (Slack 1988b: 100). Those wanting to move in search of work were required to carry a testimonial, signed by a local official and two 'honest householders' certifying that the holder was licensed to leave the current employer and at liberty to work elsewhere. The Tudor state lacked an administration that could successfully regulate the movements of the poor through such a system of internal passports or badging; instead such measures created a fertile soil for counterfeiting and avoidance. In Exeter in 1562 two vagrants were whipped for 'wandering about and pretending to be tooth drawers and surgeons' (MacCaffrey 1958: 94). Anxieties concerning vagrancy become linked with a crisis of recognizability; more and more often people were not who they seemed to be and there was no reliable means of securing or stabilizing identity.

The nomadic life-style of gypsies posed another problem; the authorities suspected that itinerants were posing as gypsies, or 'Egyptians' as they were then known. The persecution of gypsies took legislative form from the mid-sixteenth century; a statute in 1530 (22 Hen. VIII: *c.* 10; SR 3: 327) ordered their expulsion from the kingdom and was extended in 1562 to all those consorting with gypsies and, with interesting exemplification of issues of recognizability, to those 'counterfeiting, transforming or disguising themselves by their Apparel, Speech or other Behaviour' as gypsies (Okely 1983: 3; Thompson 1923). The persecution of gypsies was linked to one of the persistent forms of moral panic that disturbed the propertied classes. The social danger of the poor was amplified by persistent stories of vagrant bands operating to ravage the countryside and spread terror, who even possessed of their own 'canting' language (McMullan 1984), but evidence suggests that the existence of such bands was greatly exaggerated (Hufton 1972; Slack 1974).

The expanding number of itinerant or displaced labourers in Tudor England, if they were not able to acquire some appropriate status, encountered an increasingly punitive set of vagrancy laws. Marx captured this period with the indictment that the displaced peasantry was 'whipped, branded, tortured by laws grotesquely terrible' (Marx 1961: I: 737). Their position was exacerbated by periodic moral panics, often associated with invasion fears, rural unrest or religious disturbances, during which attempts were made to round up vagrants as in the great vagabond searches that swept the country between 1569 and 1572 and resulted in mass whippings (Aydelotte 1967; Beier 1974). The sanctions deployed became more coercive; the use of whipping was a sixteenth century development that reached its apex with a statute in 1572.[16] Branding seems to have been used both as a punishment and as a means of imposing recognizability on repeat offenders that was discussed in Chapter 6. One commentator has aptly described similar tactics used in France as being directed at the production of 'the constraint of bodies and the submission of souls' (Muchembled 1985).

A series of statutes through the sixteenth century gradually reinforced the coercive capacity of the English state. After 1572 the felony status imposed on repeat offenders brought capital punishment into view. Tudor historians appear divided about how many vagrants were hanged; I tend to the view that the death penalty was used mainly as a threat though some accounts report that during the Tudor campaigns against vagabondage as many as 17,000 were hanged.[17]

What is significant about the legislation of 1572 is that at the same time as escalating the coercive capacity of the state it provided detailed definition of rogues, vagabonds and sturdy beggars in the course of which it also embraced the long-standing attack against popular pastimes by defining beggars as including 'idle persons . . . using subtle, crafty and unlawful Games or Plays' (Tawney and Power 1924: II: 331–32). This linkage of the attack on recreations and vagrancy was not new. An Act in 1503 (19 Hen. VII: *c.* 12; SR 2: 656) linked unlawful games and pro-archery provisions with measures against vagabonds; and in 1511 a proclamation set a trend that was to be repeated in proclamations that came with increasing frequency urging strict enforcement of a broad range of social order offences that were causing anxiety to the authorities.[18] The preamble complained, in terms familiar to modern ears attuned to the discourses of 'rising crime rates', that robberies and murders were 'more often and commonly done than ever was heretofore'. It called for dusk-to-dawn curfews and the reintroduction of the watch in every town, and also for the widening of roads and the clearing of 200 feet on either side. The proclamation called for the enforcement of the statutes against idleness and unlawful games and prescribed for a first offence one night in the stocks, and three days for a second offence; it also provided for penalties to be imposed on sheriffs and other officers for failure to enforce the specified legislation.

Time and time again the concern with public order manifested itself in increasingly strident calls for enforcement of the legislative apparatus directed at disciplining and reforming the labouring classes. Aside from political speeches and popular tracts the crescendo of royal proclamations became a vehicle for these calls. What is interesting is the way in which the proclamations discursively linked the statutes against idleness, vagrancy, unlawful games and excess apparel. The contemporary proximity between popular pastimes and the regulation of apparel emerged clearly in a case heard before the Council in 1504: in reviewing the adequacy of statutory provisions the Council considered 'the reformation of idle people and vagabonds' and, in the very next sentence, 'the great enormity of apparel, as well by great lords, as gentlemen and other persons, and the excess of meats and drinks and costly fare'. The Council decided that the Chief Justice should 'peruse the Statutes for better informacon and execucon therein' (Bayne n.d.: 40–41).[19]

The persistent moralization of customary recreation and idleness, while not being sumptuary in the narrow sense, nevertheless was directed against the cultural consumption and practices of the masses in a moralization that was given coercive inflexion through the linkage to the regulation of labour which was the root of the criminal laws against vagrancy.

THE EXPANSION OF REGULATION AND STATE FORMATION

What impact did the expansion of regulation that occurred from the late medieval period onwards have on state formation? I use the concept 'state formation' in the narrow sense pioneered by Oliver MacDonagh (1958; 1961) and developed more recently by Philip Corrigan and Derek Sayer (1985).[20] The concern is with what might be called the unintended processes of state formation when day-to-day practical problems confronting agents and institutions, both inside and outside existing state institutions, lead to the creation of sets of practices that build institutions which become absorbed into the framework of the state. A classical example is the way in which private information-gathering in the name of 'political arithmetic' grew from a concern with the size and health of populations to give rise to the institutions of censuses and the systematic statistical services that proliferate in modern states. While MacDonagh concentrated on the nineteenth century and Corrigan and Sayer insisted on the critical importance of the eighteenth century, I push the process further back.

Some important consequences follow from this attempt to think through the processes of state formation in the late medieval and early modern period. The most striking point is the importance of failure and incompleteness. The appetite for power and intervention by governments in all ages has always been larger than their capacity to affect the course of social and economic life. This was especially true when the means of conscious intervention were rudimentary and the state, unevenly separating itself from the households and courts of monarchs, could rarely lay effective claim to the exercise of territorial jurisdiction. Were it not too clumsy to do so it would be safer to insist on underlining this point by keeping the concept 'state' firmly isolated between quote marks throughout this text. The effectiveness of the state was limited to periodic, generally clumsy, and frequently oppressive forays into the world outside its literal and metaphoric court walls. For example, the English domestic state, at a time when England was already well on the way to becoming a world power, remained dependent upon the voluntary work of local gentry and burgesses. As regulatory aspirations widened new and expanded duties were added, in particular to the overburdened JPs. In one sense they understandably failed in many of these projects – they did not succeed in controlling usury or the price of food – but the Tudor governments achieved far more than could have been anticipated and secured a significant degree of influence over the economy given their limited resources (Stone 1947). This mix of success and failure points attention to how these differential results of state action are to be explained. Why was the Elizabethan state to a great extent able to secure the advancement of English overseas trade, but not apparently able to ensure the enforcement of its own sumptuary legislation?

Even with respect to the forms of intervention to which it was most suited, namely the making of war, the state laboured under severe limitations and could rarely sustain the organizational and fiscal burdens over prolonged periods. I do not intend these remarks in any way to detract from the importance of military activities in the processes of state formation that has, quite properly, been receiving renewed attention (Mann 1985; Tilly 1975, 1989). Even in this body of work some focus of attention on failure could well be productive.

I gradually came to ask questions about failure because the one thing that everyone who has stopped, however briefly, to consider the tradition of sumptuary laws is agreed upon is the contention that they were a 'failure'. Occasionally I have been beset, usually after days when I seemed to make little progress, by the anxiety that perhaps I was wasting my time. If the commentators are agreed that sumptuary laws were a failure, I might only be able to add what amounts to a footnote to a long forgotten story. However, it became increasingly clear that these doubts reflected a barely conscious acceptance of a Whig interpretation of history in which what is significant about any event or practice is the contribution it makes to a future that we already know, and thus it follows that something that makes no contribution to this future can be discounted. If we are to avoid the trap that history is only the story of the linear trajectory of the past to the present then it is important to engage with the discontinuities, and, in the sense that I now use it, with failures. In the light of the enormous energy that was invested in the dispersed projects of sumptuary regulation it will also be necessary to ask just what is meant by 'failure'.

This issue of the significance of failure became more sharply focused when I began to follow a line of inquiry that the record threw up. It became apparent that one element in the periodization of sumptuary legislation was that, in both England and Italy and possibly elsewhere, the legislative urge was often activated in response to the plagues that beset medieval Europe. In the aftermath of terrible tragedy the enactment of sumptuary legislation was a discernible reflex (Bowsky 1964). The dimension of the impact is indicated by the death rates estimated at 30 per cent for Europe as whole and running at 60 per cent of the population in Venice in 1347–48 and in Genoa in 1656–57, with 50 per cent for Milan in 1630. London alone had seventeen plague outbreaks between 1500 and the 'Great Plague of London' in 1665 (Slack 1985 and 1988a).

One element of this link between sumptuary law and plagues was undoubtedly that the impulse to legislate exemplified the well-known phenomenon of moral panics (Gottfried 1983). This aside, I became interested in the wider responses to the plagues. Without making any pretence that I offer an adequately researched study of the social history of plagues a few comments are in order. The one point that struck me was how difficult it was for the rulers, often themselves terrified both by the personal risks they experienced and by the terrible threats to the prosperity and well-being of the communities they governed, to respond effectively. For a long period, running from the fourteenth century through to the seventeenth, the rulers found themselves largely unprepared, lacking what came to be called a public health policy and the emergency powers necessary to confront the unannounced onset of the plague outbreaks. While it seems trite once stated it is nevertheless important to stress just how difficult it was to invent forms of regulation capable of addressing the problems confronted.

Italian cities seem to have learnt much more quickly than did the English rulers both about the mechanics of the plague and about appropriate responses. In Florence the city's rulers came to regard plague as a contagious disease of the poor; the result was the enactment of 'moral sanitation' legislation that lumped together prostitutes, sodomites, heretics and more generally the poor, and gave civic officials extensive powers over their movements. Restrictions were also imposed on funeral ceremonies as well as on religious processions. In Venice and other cities plague victims and contacts were required to wear the same marks of infamy, yellow badges, that were imposed on prostitutes and Jews (Carmichael 1986). Legislation against vagrants typically invoked the fear of the plague as its legitimation.

In England the succession of outbreaks of plague stimulated government activity. For example, refuse collection was initiated in Westminster after an epidemic in 1532. The tactic of using distinguishing marks, already employed with respect to such troublesome categories as beggars and prostitutes, was introduced. In Hull in 1576, immediately after a plague outbreak, civic officials launched an attack on the pride and vanity of women and were able to obtain a royal proclamation ordering the enforcement of the existing sumptuary laws (Tickell 1798). By an order made in 1590 for those living outside London the infected or exposed were required to carry a white wand; inside London the compulsory wand changed from white to red in 1583. To counter the avoidance whereby the infected often carried their wand under a gown, an order in 1583 forbade the wearing of gowns or cloaks by infected persons. From August 1592 purveyors of necessities to those confined to their houses were also required to carry white wands and penalties were imposed on those defacing or removing crosses from the doors of infected houses. In his description of London in 1598 John Stow brings together under the label 'the statutes of the streets' the mix of moral and sanitary regulation that was in force, including the provision that wife-beating was to be prohibited after 9 p.m. (Stow 1633: No. 30). During the 1603 epidemic there was much unruliness in London with crosses being removed from infected houses (Mullett 1956). There were frequent outbreaks of resistance to regulation, these often being led by clergy and priests reacting against bans on processions, festivals and pilgrimages. Such resistance confirmed governmental association of plague with disorder and prompted moral panics. For example, in Florence outbreaks of plague were associated with campaigns against prostitutes and vagrants, while in England there were frequent discursive associations between plague and vagrancy reinforcing the repression of vagrancy; a vagrant caught with plague sores could be put to death.

The interpenetration of poverty and plague was productive of major social tensions and anxieties; in many cases rulers expressed a contempt for the masses who were perceived as presenting a threat to the health and well-being of the respectable classes. The result was a sharp social dichotomy between civic rules expanding state authority and the poor who resisted these regulatory measures (Slack 1985). The response to plague provided the major impetus towards the regimes that Rosen describes as the medical police (Rosen 1974). Corbin's concept of 'hyper-regulation' catches some of the desperation of the regulatory upsurge that the plagues stimulated (Corbin 1990: 8).

The lesson that I draw from these reflections on the difficulties of governing is that the study of the history of sumptuary laws allows us to explore the problems that intervene between the developed ideological urge, linked to the moralizations of luxury, class and gender, and the securing of operative forms of governance.

I will use the next two chapters to explore these themes. The next chapter brings together a fuller account of the history of sumptuary law in England. In the following chapter, Chapter 13, I address the general question of 'failure' through an exploration of the enforcement of sumptuary laws.

12

Mapping a Sumptuary Tradition: The English Experience

THE STRUCTURE OF ENGLISH SUMPTUARY LAW

The story of English sumptuary law has been told before.[1] Most accounts are now rather elderly and come out of very different traditions from the interest in governance that motivates the present study and thus do not ask the same kinds of questions.[2] I will not so much be retelling a story already told as telling a very different story, about how both state and local legislative activity was directed towards the governance of what people ate or wore.

My account of English sumptuary law will be a legislative history and this calls for comment. Legislation should not be regarded as a formal gloss written on top of some reality that exists elsewhere. Legislation in an important sense has its own history; it tells, but not necessarily directly, about the projects of governance, the aspirations of power, how the state envisages reality and how it desires to reconstruct it. Much legislation is autopoietic or self-referential; it creates its own institutional and procedural apparatus. In the main I shall have little to say about this kind of material; instead I carve out a different slice of reality by attending to the path of sumptuary legislation in its association with other legislative projects of governance. In so doing it is important to avoid any suggestion that legislation actually produces as reality its imagined project. A significant part of the story of governance concerns the different combinations and connections within which the projects of sumptuary regulation were located. I have already discussed in some detail in the previous chapter how sumptuary matters were associated with the regulation of popular games and pastimes and how this gave way to a quasi-sumptuary regulation of alehouses. Legislative history is not remote from reality; rather it provides us not with reality, but with a particular slice into a world in which governance itself came to have a purchase upon lived experience.

Central to English sumptuary legislation is the way in which it dealt with hierarchical social categories. Table 12.1 provides a summary overview of the hierarchical categories employed in the English statutes between 1363 and 1553.

It is important to pose the question: how should we regard these legislatively defined classifications? Are they encapsulations, more or less accurate, of an already existing reality such that we can glean a picture of the structure of English social relations? Or, alternatively, were the categories invoking what might be called an imaginary social hierarchy, one desired but probably less and less corresponding to the lived social relations? These issues are complex and in addition to a few comments I propose to leave them open and to keep in mind that each legislative description may be imagined or real or some mix. They are, I suggest, boundaries that are likely to be important and to which we should attend. For example, most of the sumptuary acts make use of a distinction between Knights and the two categories, Esquire and Gentleman. These were never precise categories; knighthoods became increasingly flexible – any man with an estate to the value of £40 p.a. was expected to become a knight, but many never bothered. The upshot is likely to have been that in many communities an untitled person was the economically powerful figure and the main employer in the community while the local knight slipped quietly into obscurity even though some traditional deference may have remained. Increasingly it came to be acknowledged that status was a function of the source and level of income rather than of rank (Cornwall 1988: 11).

It may thus have been the case that the sumptuary classification clashed with the socially experienced hierarchy, although I hasten to add that I have come across no contemporary comments that support this view (Hanawalt 1975). However, Keen makes the interesting point that the sumptuary legislation of 1363 employed gradations that were pretty much the same as those specified in the graduated poll tax legislation of 1379, with the implication that these statutes more or less reflected the existing social structure (Keen 1990). Similarly the trend for sumptuary statutes to pay closer attention to the gradations within the nobility

Table 12.1 England's social hierarchy as defined in sumptuary legislation

Act:	*1363*	*1463*	*1483*	*1510*	*1514*	*1515*	*1533*	*1553*
	Knights ≥ 400 marks p.a.	Lords	Royal Family	Royal Family	Royal Family	Royal Family	Royal Family	
S			Dukes	Dukes	Dukes	Duke & Marquis	Duke & Marquis	
O			Lords	Earls	Earls	Earls	Viscount & Baron	
C				Baron	Baron	Barons	Earls	
I A	Knights ≥ 200 marks p.a.	Knights of Garter	Knights	Lords & Knights of Garter	Knights of Garter	Knights of Garter	Knights of Garter	
L	Merchants ≥ £500 goods	Esq or Gent	Esq or Gent	Knights, Esq, Gent ≥ 300 marks p.a.	Esq ≥ 300 marks p.a.	Esq, Gent ≥ 200 marks p.a.	Person ≥ £200 p.a.	
S	Esq ≥ 200 marks p.a.			Gent ≥ £100 p.a.	Gent ≥ £100 p.a.	Gent £100 p.a.		
T A	Esq, Gent ≥ £100 p.a. Yeoman	Person ≥ £40 p.a.		Person ≥ £ p.a.	Person ≥ 100 marks	Person £40 p.a.	Person ≥ £100 p.a.	
T U		Person ≤ £40 p.a.		Person ≥ £ p.a.	Person ≥ £10 p.a. *or* £100 goods	Person ≥ £10 p.a. or £100 goods	Person ≥ £40 p.a.	
S	Handicraftman Yeoman	Yeoman		Person ≥ £100 goods		Husbandmen, Shepherds, etc. ≥ £10 p.a.	Person ≥ £20 p.a.	Person ≥ £20 p.a. *or* £200 goods
	Ploughmen	Servants Husbandmen Labourers	Labourer Servants Husbandmen				Person ≥ £5 p.a.	
	Servants						Husbandmen ≥ £2	

seems to correspond to an increasing stratification of the small caste of nobles during the fourteenth and fifteenth centuries (McFarlane 1973: 123).

The history of English sumptuary law falls into two rather different and uneven parts. The first has its roots in medieval society whose consciousness, if not all of its reality, remained feudal. The second period is concentrated into the sixteenth century; in comparison to the leisurely pace of sumptuary activity in the preceding period, Tudor government was active and energetic. It was an activism that reached a crescendo only to evaporate into collapse with the repeal of all the most overtly sumptuary legislation at the very beginning of the seventeenth century. I will leave over until Chapter 14 a discussion of whether this repeal marked the end of sumptuary law in England.

PRE-MODERN ENGLISH SUMPTUARY LAW

The basic pattern of pre-modern English sumptuary law is fairly straightforward. In the fourteenth century sumptuary legislation started with a typically archaic focus on alimentary consumption; the first sumptuary statute of 1336 dealt only with food.[3] By the fifteenth century food had largely disappeared as a regulatory object and was replaced by hierarchic dress regulation. Sumptuary law emerged in a period in which there was already an established tradition of economic intervention; the regulation of the quality of production and the associated basic terms of trade such as weights and measures already existed. Also familiar were price fixing laws, one of the earliest being an enactment of 1221 imposing price control on wine, and protectionist measures, of which English shipping and the wool trade were to be among the most persistent beneficiaries.

The first true sumptuary Act of 1336 was a brief alimentary statute introduced during a period of rising trade and economic prosperity alongside sharpening conflict with France. It was universal in its form although its target was undoubtedly the landed classes. It restricted meals to a maximum of two courses and provided for an increase to three on religious festivals. Early legislative discourse was typically alarmist; the general form was to identify some undoubtedly exaggerated danger before advancing its positive prescriptions; for example, a statute barring residents of brothels south of the Thames (the stews of Southwark) adopted as its avowed motives 'to avoid Murders, Robberies and Adulteries'. One obvious lesson is that it is a mistake to take the motives invoked in statutory preambles literally.[4] The key passage in the 1336 Act is typical of such preambles:

> Whereas heretofore, through the excessive and over many sorts of costly meats which the people of this Realm have used more than elsewhere, many mischiefs have happened to the people of this Realm: for the great men by these excesses have been sore grieved, and the lesser people who only endeavour to imitate the great ones in such sorts of meats are much impoverished; whereby they are not able to aid themselves nor their liege Lord in times of need, as they ought.[5]

One interesting feature of this statute is the mix of evils invoked. Two distinguishable economic rationales are put forward. The first expressed anxiety about the possible impoverishment of the landed classes, risking loss of their patrimony through extravagant consumption. The other theme is an early invocation of imitation as a motivating force in social life bringing impoverishment to the lower orders.

Another frequently invoked economic rationale was the fear of 'dearth'. It should be borne in mind that 'dearth', food shortages and famine, were significant threats to the medieval social order; food rioting was an endemic form of social resistance until the eighteenth century. This consciousness of the vulnerability of the food supply, the memory of its past and the fear of its future occurrence, played an active part in the maintenance of social order. Famine and dearth were blamed on a wide range of social evils including gluttony, luxury, sabbath-breaking, swearing and drunkenness. These discourses existed alongside more secular traditions that blamed dearth on enclosures by landlords and on forestalling and hoarding by merchants (Walter and Wrightson 1976: 22).

The first sumptuary statute to introduce the regulation of dress occurred in 1337. It is testimony to the political and sartorial significance of furs. Its scope was restricted. It set down a prohibition on anyone under the rank of a knight or lady wearing any fur in their clothing.[6] This statute was in its conception severe and repressive since furs were widely worn against the cold and were used as rugs indoors by anyone who could trap or purchase a few skins (Cunnington and Lucas 1967). This highly restrictive distribution of furs was considerably attenuated by the 1363 Act (Veale 1966: 4); artisans and labourers were then permitted furs from lambs, rabbits, cats and foxes.

In an interesting attempt to provide an empirical study of sumptuary legislation Bell and Ruse searched for evidence of the impact of the 1337 group of sumptuary and protectionist measures (Bell and Ruse 1972). They provide some evidence that points towards a wider caution that should be borne in mind. It appears that the protection offered to the wool industry was not so much part of a 'national' project, but was more in the way of a reward for large loans advanced to facilitate the prosecution of war. This points to the importance of the effect of the rhetorical form of legislation that served to obscure the interests at play in the construction of legislative politics. They found no evidence of any prosecutions for breach of the sumptuary restrictions on furs, but they suggest that even here we have a primarily fiscal rather than sumptuary project. They claim that furs were largely imported and that this measure was largely bullionist in character, seeking to avoid depletion of the stock of gold and silver.[7] What Bell and Ruse did find was increased levels of reports and prosecutions of wool smuggling between 1337 and 1340.

The next general sumptuary statute in 1363 was titled 'A Statute Concerning Diet and Apparel', but its dietary content was minimal.[8] It specified almost as an afterthought that grooms and servants of lords were only to receive meat or fish once a day.[9]

Before leaving the regulation of food, it is interesting to note that the 1363 Act was not the end of attempts to impose alimentary restraints. Over 150 years later, in 1517, a fascinating proclamation was issued under the title of 'Sumptuary Regulations.'[10] It laid down a hierarchical ordering for the consumption of food by listing the number of dishes that could be served at each meal by each social category. Cardinals were allowed nine, archbishops seven, down to those with an annual rent of £40 or £500 in goods who might serve only three. The proclamation goes into great detail providing definition of the number and type of items that might be served in any dish. For example, only one crane, swan, bustard, peacock or other fowl was permitted per dish, whereas up to six partridge, plover, woodcock, and all other wildfowl of similar size were permitted in a dish for a cardinal, but only four in a dish for all other lords.[11] A truly delightful piece of regulatory logic followed, which expressly permitted that any person 'may have less dishes at their pleasure'. There is evidence that this proclamation was authored by Cardinal Wolsey, which probably explains the attention to clerical ranks (Youings 1984). The correspondence between Wolsey and Henry VIII indicated that they both showed a keen interest in the pursuit of sumptuary projects (Plucknett 1936: 119).

Concern with reputed indulgence in the great religious houses increased with the Reformation, which probably explains why it was that in 1541 Archbishop Cranmer and his bishops agreed upon a detailed set of alimentary rules, specifying the number of courses and dishes, for each rank within the church hierarchy. Cranmer appended a sad little memorandum 'that this order was kept for two or three months, till, by the disusing of certain wilful persons, it came again to the old excess' (Cranmer 1846: 491; Mennell 1985: 30).

One of the most enduring forms of legislation was protectionist legislation. The typical form was to forbid exports that might benefit a foreign competitor or enemy and, conversely, to prohibit importing from such a source (Carus-Wilson 1954). As part of the burst of legislative activity in 1336–7 an Act, passed in the midst of sharpening conflict with France and the opening of the Hundred Years War, introduced a protectionist measure demanding that: 'no merchant foreign or denizen [domestic] . . . shall bring or cause to be brought any woollens out of the realme . . . upon pain of forfeiture of life and of member.'[12] Another statute in the same year required that:

> No man nor woman, great or small . . . of what estate or condition he be, the King, Queen, and their children only except, shall wear no cloth . . . other than is made in England, Ireland, Wales or Scotland.
>
> (11 Edw. III: *c.* 2 (1337); SR 1: 280)

This protectionist barrage was rounded out by a third provision that prohibited the import of any foreign cloth.[13] In general during the fourteenth century there was a marked oscillation between 'free trade' and 'protectionism'. In 1350 restraints on foreign merchants were removed in response to the Black Death; yet in 1358 foreign merchants were again expelled, only to be reinstated in 1378 (Salzman 1964).

The connection between protectionist and sumptuary laws continued to play an important part in the later history of sumptuary regulation. This raises the question of whether or not such protectionist legislation should be regarded as a form of sumptuary law or as a quite different species of legislation. It is undoubtedly the case that protectionism impacts upon consumption in that it either prohibits a range of items of consumption or inflates the cost of their consumption by the imposition of duties and taxes. On the other hand, it is not consumption as such that is the target of the regulatory activity; rather the control of consumption is a means to some politico-economic objective such as protecting a particular domestic industry or starving some enemy of import revenue.[14] The similarity and dissimilarity of protectionist and sumptuary laws is not to be resolved by definitional fiat. Rather I propose to treat them as being located within distinct discursive traditions and thus able to address the same objects of regulation and frequently, as we will see in the discussion of English legislation, as forming coexisting traditions. The broad conclusion that this approach points to is that protectionist discourses, located within the emerging and expanding construct of 'the national economy', came to absorb the sumptuary discourses located within a moralizing tradition not fully compatible with the amorality of economic discourses of 'national interest'.

English sumptuary law is generally distinguished by its concentration in the form of state legislation, while during the same period the sumptuary laws of most of continental Europe took the form of local ordinances. Nevertheless, just now and again, there are traces of local law-making initiatives in England. The 'Little Red Book' of the by-laws of the Corporation of Bristol, dating from 1344, laid down expenditure limits on the furs to be worn as part of their regalia of office (Bickeley 1900; Sacks 1989: 204–08).[15] The City of London was from time to time active in sumptuary and related matters. Some time between 1338 and 1353 the Council of the City of London ordered that prostitutes were not allowed to wear even the most lowly furs like budge [lambswool] or wool (Wadmore 1902). In the meantime the London Council seems to have avoided involvement except when they were under pressure from the state to address some specific local manifestation causing concern to the Crown and its agents.

From the mid-fourteenth century the central focus of legislative activity shifted to the regulation of labour. In rapid response to the ravages of the Black Death (1348–49) the 'Statute of Labourers' had as its major project the restraint of agricultural labourers from leaving their jobs in search of higher wages:[16] 'Because a great part of the People, and especially of Workmen and Servants, late died of pestilence. . . . [M]any will not serve unless they may receive excessive wages.' This famous enactment was supported by a battery of less well-known statutes on vagrancy and the creation of the offence of petty treason 'where a servant slayeth his master, or a wife her Husband, or when a Man secular or religious slayeth his Prelate to whom he oweth Faith and obedience.'[17]

A STATUTORY SOCIAL HIERARCHY?

The distinctive form of English sumptuary legislation, the construction of a hierarchical set of dress codes, was ushered in by 'A Statute Concerning Diet and Apparel' in 1363.[18] Over the next two hundred years there followed seven further hierarchic dress codes. At first the statutes were infrequent, the next exactly one hundred years later in 1463. Thereafter the statutes came more frequently, in 1483, 1510, 1514, 1515, 1533, 1553.[19] The 1363 Act sought to put in place a general sumptuary regime for the whole population, while those that followed were predominantly concerned with the internal gradations within the landed classes and, to a lesser degree, with the urban merchant class.

Table 12.1 on page 297 sets out in simplified form the socio-economic and status categories employed in the English legislation from 1363 to 1553. It is necessary to examine in more detail the treatment of hierarchy in this legislation.

The 1363 Act originated in a petition addressed to Parliament that articulated the standard complaint against imitation that 'labourers use the apparel of craftsmen, and craftsmen the apparel of valets, and valets the apparel of squires, and squires the apparel of knights.' The Preamble attacked the 'outrageous and excessive apparel of divers people against their estate and degree' and invoked the most general economic critique that such extravagance leads to 'the great destruction and impoverishment of all the land'. The seven chapters have a very distinctive ordering in that they deal in ascending order with the different social ranks from servants, agricultural and urban workers to gentlemen, merchants, clerics and knights.[20] What is significant in comparison to the statutes that followed was that there was no attempt to differentiate within the ranks of the titled. In so far as there was differentiation it was with respect to the purely economic criterion of the annual value of the estate. For example, knights were differentiated into those worth more than £400 p.a. and those below this figure. In a society preoccupied by status it is surprising that such a 'modern' or economistic conception of the social hierarchy, measured in terms of rent values, should have been employed at this early stage (Coward 1988). Thus English apparel legislation opened with a hierarchical dress code that, in principle, applied to the whole population.

The content of the dress rules also differed from the subsequent legislation which was to become increasingly complex in designating the specific types of clothing and ornamentation that could be worn. The 1363 Act had a distinctive simplicity and was markedly 'modern', in that it designated the dress hierarchy by fixing a sliding scale of expenditure limits. Its method was to lay down an upper price limit on clothing for eight categories of citizen; in addition within these bands a number of specific restrictions were added for some categories. For example, knights with an estate with an annual value of over £400 could dress 'at their pleasure'. The only implicit reference to higher ranks was that these knights were prohibited from wearing ermine, which was presumably reserved for all or part of the nobility, although the statute does not mention any rank above knight. Knights with an income of less than £400 were restricted to a maximum of 6 marks; in addition they were forbidden garments made of cloth of gold or furred with ermine or embroidered with precious stones. The price limits went in descending steps until the lowest classification, 'Carters, Ploughmen, Drivers of the Plough, Oxherds, Cowherds, Shepherds and all other Keepers of Beasts, Threshers of Corn, and manner of people of the estate of a groom attending to husbandry and all other people that have not 40s. of goods' who were restricted to garments made from 'Blanket and Russet wool' costing not more than 12 pence per piece.[21]

The treatment of merchants in the 1363 Act is interesting.[22] They were made subject to the same dress rules as esquires and gentlemen (landowners below the rank of knight) with land to the value of £100 p.a.; however, to qualify the merchants had to own goods and chattels to the value of £500. Some commentators have suggested that this discriminated against merchants by imposing a fivefold income differential. This interpretation seems too simple since the merchants' £500 requirement refers to what must have been their total capital, whereas the landed gentry's figure of £100 related to the annual value of their income from rents. It seems likely that this differential did not discriminate in any very serious way against the urban burghers.

What is significant about this first general attempt to impose sumptuary regulation of dress was the breadth and universality of its sweep. More than any other item of legislation that I have encountered it came closest to an attempt to impose a hierarchically organized dress code for the whole population. The subsequent history of sumptuary legislation is one of increasing particularism and declining generality. Despite these universalistic attributes the 1363 Act was no sooner passed than it was repealed. There are only sketchy details of the repeal. The King was petitioned, probably from the Commons, with the complaint that all the commonalty of the realm had been greatly burdened by the 1363 law and urged that it be 'repealed and annulled'. The Crown seems to have concurred with the petition and the Act was promptly repealed (Baldwin 1926: 55; de Marly 1985: 19). The repeal statute provided 'that all People shall be as free as they were before'.[23] Some clue about the forces at work is provided by the fact that the repeal statute went on to permit merchants to trade in 'all manner of Merchandises' (although important trade items such as wool, gold and silver were excluded). It seems likely that the impulse for repeal arose most powerfully from commercial pressures about the potential damage to trade that the enforcement of the Act might occasion. The Crown's fiscal concern with military financing may have been a factor in this hasty about turn.

It was exactly one hundred years before another general dress code was enacted, in 1463. However, during the intervening period a number of significant developments took place. Interest in sumptuary law did not disappear; in 1378 Parliament petitioned the Crown for a sumptuary statute and did so again in 1402 and 1406 (Harte 1976: 158).[24] In addition there were two quasi-sumptuary pieces of legislation: no person with land valued at less than 40s. a year was allowed to own a greyhound or to own traps to catch deer, hares or 'Gentlemen's game'.[25] The other quasi-sumptuary statute prohibited the use of silver-plating for any purpose other than for knights' spurs and 'all the apparel that pertaineth to a baron and above that estate'.[26]

During the late fourteenth and early fifteenth centuries a protracted struggle over livery and the maintenance of retainers occurred. What was at stake was an attempt by the Crown to restrict the size and military capacity of regional baronial power; the key conflict was over the nobility's power to bind sections of the lesser gentry into cohesive military forces. It was always conceded that the nobility was entitled to display the magnificence of their households as a visible expression of their power through the splendour of the livery of retainers and servants (Mertes 1988). The law of livery and maintenance as it developed did not impinge upon the dressing of domestic servants although there does seem to have been a growing anxiety about the shortage of agricultural labour. While in one sense classically feudal with its oaths and ceremony, in more important respects livery marked a retreat from feudalism under which a lord's tenants were bound by obligations whereas retainers involved a form of contractual patronage (McKisak 1959). It is noteworthy that no connections were ever made subjecting the sumptuousness of the liveries to control by the sumptuary statutes; livery was viewed as a political or even constitutional question and not a matter of consumption, extravagance or luxury.[27]

When the 1463 sumptuary law was enacted it was one of a group of statutes that were part of a concerted protectionist strategy on commercial and manufacturing matters (Bellamy 1984).[28] It was initiated by petition from the Commons asking for enforcement and renewal of legislation against 'inordinant array'; the King approved the petition and also the detail of its proposed contents (Baldwin 1926: 101–04). The Preamble complained that:

> The commons of the said realm, as well Men as Women, have worn and daily do wear excessive and inordinate Array and Apparel to the great Displeasure of God, and impoverishing of this realm of England and to the enriching of other strange Realms and Countries to the final Destruction of Husbandry of this said Realm.

The specified aim was to oblige people to dress 'according to their degrees'. It regulated the clothing of a very similar range of social gradations as had been used in the 1363 Act. It should be noted that the nobility were included but as a unitary category. Whereas in 1363 merchants had occupied their own category, they disappeared in 1463 into the large and undifferentiated category of 'persons' with income of either £20 or £40 p.a. thereby grouping together a large proportion of both the urban and the rural middle classes while at the same time 'dropping' merchants from a status on a par with esquires and gentlemen to one below them. It may well be that we have here an example of the use of legislation to carry out a degradation ceremony, but again we have no evidence of the responses of any particular social groups to this statute.

The content of the 1463 sumptuary statute imposed a set of hierarchical dress restrictions. No person below the rank of Lord was to be allowed to wear cloth of gold, sables or purple silk. Nobody below the rank of knight was to wear velvet, satin, counterfeit silk or ermine. The royal family, Master of Rolls, Barons of Exchequer and the Chancellor of the Exchequer were all specifically exempted. An unusual feature of this statute was that it sought to restrict masculine exposure or at least restrict it to the upper classes; thus the conception must not only have been about 'decency' but included some element of 'appropriateness', by providing that only the nobility were allowed any item of clothing 'unless it be of such length that the same, he being upright, may cover his members and buttocks'. The statute also attacked the fashionable long-toed shoes by forbidding anyone below the rank of Lord to wear shoes with 'pykes' longer than two inches. The fashion for long pointed shoes provoked another statute two years later which ordered that no cordwainer or cobbler within three miles of the City of London be allowed to make 'any shoes, galoches, with any Pike that shall pass the length of 2 inches'.[29]

It seems evident that there are two broad classes of fashion items that attracted regulation. The first are items that retain a high status over long periods of time such as cloth of gold, silk and ermine. It was during this period in English history that the use of clothes to indicate power and domination reached its peak. This rose to quite extraordinary heights between 1500 and 1600. Unless we bear in mind the intense, almost religious significance that was attached to clothing as the expression of power and thus the aura which they acquired it is not possible to understand the intensity of the concern expressed through sumptuary law with the hierarchic order. Indeed, as J.H. Plumb points out, one would also miss the significance of the symbolism of Tudor portraiture (Plumb 1972: 191).

The second category consists of those items whose very novelty attracts the attention of the entrepreneurs of moral indignation, but which disappear from the regulatory eye either when they lose their novelty or when fashion moves on.[30] Little is known about the impact of the 1463 Act. That it did not entirely die is suggested by the fact that in 1477 Parliament petitioned the Crown for its enforcement (Harte 1976: 158).[31]

It was another petition from the Commons that initiated the next piece of dress legislation, the 'Act of Apparel' of 1483. It complained of the 'great misery and poverty' stemming from the lack of compliance with previous statutes.[32] It does seem that this move came from the Commons rather than it acting as a surrogate to the Crown; war with France was imminent and Parliament had learnt to extract commitment to approve Parliamentary statutes before voting money to the Crown for its military adventures. What is distinctive about this legislation is that it was the first to focus attention on the ranks of the nobility, dividing them into three broad categories (see Table 12.1). This feature is consistent with the increasing stratification of the nobility during this period (McFarlane 1973: 123). There is a sense in which sumptuary regulation was becoming focused upon the internal regulation of the nobility; not perhaps so much a case of self-regulation, but of the Crown setting down rules of precedence for the court and the limited circle of the nobility. A sense of this can be glimpsed from the detailed mourning edicts that were issued by Margaret Beaufort, Countess of Richmond, mother of Henry VII, between 1495 and 1510: here the gap between sumptuary legislation and rules of etiquette becomes very difficult to identify (Taylor 1983: 91; Baldwin 1926: 124–26).[33] On the other hand the whole population below the rank of esquire and gentleman is lumped under the head of labourers, husbandmen and servants. It seems likely that by this time the urban middle-classes had been absorbed under the increasingly honorific or self-designating label of gentleman. For the first time the sumptuary privileges of royalty were spelt out; only they could wear cloth of gold or purple silk.[34] There followed detailed restrictions, similar in character to those in the 1463 Act, for each of the descending social ranks.

While the characteristic form of English sumptuary law during this period was this wide-ranging imposition of dress codes there were also the occasional highly particularistic pieces of legislation. In 1487 a brief provision, without explanation, ordered that no hatter or capper should sell any hat above the price of 20d., or any cap above 2s. 8d. on pain of a 40s. fine (4 Hen. VII: *c*. 9). What was going on here? There is an element of price control as existed on many goods, though mainly food and drink; there is also a sumptuary element with an attempt to limit expenditure on the highly elaborate headwear that was in fashion for men. This provision was probably predominantly protectionist and was the forerunner of the strongly protectionist Elizabethan 'cap act', imposing what Shakespeare referred to as the 'statute cap' (Boehn 1932–35: II: 198).

As was mentioned in Chapter 9, the 1483 statute exempted all women except the wives of labourers and servants. The act of 1514 went further in exempting all women.[35] Baldwin suggests that this exemption of women might have stemmed from a male recognition of the impossibility of preventing women following fashion (Baldwin 1926: 116). Aside from its disparaging tone this explanation does not fit with the persistent moralization of luxury and fashion that was directed primarily against women. On the other hand there is no evidence that the exemption was secured by either active or passive female resistance to sumptuary restraint. It is just possible that, since the late fifteenth and early sixteenth century was a period of particularly extravagant and ostentatious male fashion, it could just have been that it was quite literally men's conspicuous consumption that was conceived of as 'the problem', but again there is no direct evidence to support this interpretation.

Early in the sixteenth century there was a flurry of sumptuary statutes in 1510, 1514 and 1515, and after a somewhat longer gap, another was enacted in 1533. These Acts continued the trend towards a greater differentiation within the nobility, the number of ranks increased and there was some alteration in their relative positions; for example, as can be seem clearly from Table 12.1 earls lost precedence within the hierarchy. The Act of 1510 against 'Costly Apparel' repealed all previous sumptuary legislation replacing it with a content modelled on that of 1463 and 1483.[36] It opens with the flamboyant assertion that:

> great and costly array and apparel . . . hath been the occasion of great impoverishing of divers of the King's subjects, and provoked many of them to rob and to do extortion and other unlawful deeds to maintain thereby their costly array.

This Preamble explicitly refers to the need to be able to distinguish 'estates, preeminence, dignities and degrees'. The content of this statute manifests what might be called an iron law of increasing complexity. The restricted items are specified in greater detail than before although the general pattern of hierarchic privileged access to material and colours remains firmly in place. In addition provisions are made for an increasing range of social categories: for example, provisions are made for graduates of the universities, municipal officers, officials of liveried companies, grooms of the King's Chamber, and other occupational categories. In addition certain new male fashions such as 'garded or pinched shirts' were prohibited to anyone under the rank of knight.

The 1514 'Act of Apparel' was very similar in content to that of 1510; although it added some marginal new details it is not clear what the reasons for this duplication of legislative effort were save perhaps in seeking to underline commitment to the sumptuary ethic.[37] The Act struck a confident tone by stipulating that it would 'last for ever'. As it turned out it was only to survive for a few months. The 1515 Apparel Act repealed all prior apparel statutes, but its content was very similar to that of the Acts of 1510 and 1514.[38] There is just a hint that some of the detailed changes conceded a little more appearential diversity down the social scale suggesting a tactical recognition of the need to bow gently in the face of the winds of fashion. It also added wider exceptions for members of the royal household and state officials and went further in recognizing the King's right to grant licences for exemption from provisions of the statute. Most noticeable was much tinkering with the enforcement provisions whose detail is considered in the next chapter. In 1522 there was another rare case of local sumptuary initiative. The Coventry Leet Court ordered the Sheriff not to wear beech-marten or 'marturnes' fur, nor velvet in doublets or jerkins unless he was a man of substance (Phythian-Adams 1979). Commoners were restricted to fox and lamb fur and were only allowed silk if they were worth £100 (Harris 1907–13). While consistent with the 1515 Act these local rules did not correspond with the current statutory provisions.

The next major piece of sumptuary legislation, the 'Act for Reformation of Excess in Apparel', came in 1533.[39] This proved to be the last of the attempts to extend a hierarchical dress regime for the whole population. There is evidence that the Bill was initiated within the executive; in a letter from Henry VIII to Thomas

Cromwell, who had replaced Wolsey, he requested that 'the bill of apparel be . . put in readiness against the beginning of the next Parliament' (Baldwin 1926: 157).

The Preamble to the Act is very explicit. After referring to earlier statutes, it states its purposes as being:

> the necessary repressing, avoiding and expelling of the inordinate excess daily more and more used in the sumptuous and costly array and apparel customarily worn in this realm, whereof hath ensued and daily do chance such sundry high and notable inconveniences as to be the great, manifest and notorious detriment of the common weal, the subversion of good and politic order in knowledge and distinction of people according to their estates, pre-eminences, dignities and degrees, and to the utter impoverishment and undoing of many inexpert and light persons inclined to pride, mother of all vices.

Aside from becoming even more detailed this statute differs in significantly lowering penalties, possibly as a contribution to a more realistic approach to enforcement. However, in other respects this Act was more restrictive in that sable furs were reserved exclusively for the royal family, lynx and black genet furs for dukes, earls and barons. Only a gentleman or above could wear an imported fur of a variety not produced within the realm. The Crown's power to grant licences was restricted to members of the royal household; this is a little surprising since there is no evidence of the widespread dispensation of exemption let alone anything approaching the use of the purchase of exemptions as a fiscal measure. However, a proclamation during the next year granted exemption to all officers and servants of the Royal Household (Feb. 1534; Hughes and Larkin 1964: I: No.143).

The Act of 1553 should probably be regarded as the last English appearential statute.[40] The 'Act for Reformation of Excess in Apparel' in the first year of the new reign was a shorter and more direct statute that related only to the wearing of silk.[41] Again it repeated the exemption of women which had been consolidated in the previous series of statutes (Miller 1928: 93). The Act contains only one substantive sumptuary provision. Whereas previous acts had allowed a limited use of silk to those with income under £20 the new Act forbade the wearing of silk to anyone below the status of 'magistrates of corporations'. It stipulated the severe restraint that 'whoever shall wear silk in or upon his hat, bonnet, or girdle, scabbard, hose, shoes or spur leather, shall be imprisoned during three months, and forfeit 10 pounds.' Hooper reports only one prosecution under this Act at Chester (Hooper 1915: 436). In addition it extended liability for breaches by servants to their masters.

PROCLAIMING A SUMPTUARY REGIME

The final stages of the English statutory regulation of apparel are intimately connected to the constitutional struggles between Crown and the Commons over legislative jurisdiction. The Elizabethan sumptuary activity was characterized by the Crown's resistance to Parliamentary involvement. As a consequence it was marked by an increasing reliance on proclamations that were issued either directly by the monarch or through the Privy Council, which during this period became a major legislative institution (Hooper 1915: 437; Heinze 1976). Parliament was by no means inactive and several bills for the reformation of apparel were introduced in both Houses of Parliament. Bills were approved by the House of Lords in 1565–66, 1575, 1588–89 and 1597, but on each occasion they failed to pass the House of Commons (Baldwin 1926: 213–16). Similarly, numerous bills were introduced in the Commons on the reform of apparel and on other forms of moral regulation. Unfortunately no drafts of these bills have survived, making it difficult to reconstruct the politics of this important era of sumptuary legislation. All this parliamentary activity gave birth to only two short appearential statutes.

One major factor was the intensification of the general opposition in the Commons to all attempts to expand governmental rule by proclamation and bills introduced in the Lords were, usually quite correctly, seen as emanating from the Crown and thus opposed, not because of their content but because they were perceived as threats to parliamentary power. On the part of the Lords they often resisted bills from the Commons because they distrusted the extension of the powers conferred in many of the bills coming from the Commons to the Justices of the Peace who were perceived as corrosive of traditional authority and lacking in deference to the peerage.

Behind these constitutional issues there was also something else.

I have glimpsed now and again the coexistence of two (or maybe more) discursive traditions that seem to agree on the desirability of regulation, but disagree in ways sufficient to lead to stalemate over the strategies of intervention. What is striking about the discourses of apparel in Elizabethan England is that almost all of those whose views we know about were agreed on the desirability and necessity of regulation, but they nevertheless found sufficient to disagree about for the result to be that the legislative output was severely limited. There was the lone voice of the MP John Bond who questioned the very desirability of moral regulation. 'Every evil in a state is not to be met with a law. And as it is in the natural, so it is in the politique body, that sometimes the remedy is worse than the disease' (quoted Kent 1973: 61). To map the different inflections in these debates about sumptuary regulation would require a major study in its own right since, aside from the constitutional dimensions, it is difficult to read from the surface what the disagreements were about. The attempt to trace the fractures and cleavages within discourses is, I suggest, a very significant component in efforts to track the histories of moral regulation; they are the other side of the important issue of alliances because they help to explain why potential alliances fail to cohere. There is a tendency for studies, such as Newburn's (1992) otherwise valuable study of recent moral regulation in England, to construct a model in which regulators confront anti-regulators; this certainly was not the situation in the Elizabethan debates over the regulation of apparel, nor I suspect, in many such battles.

The centre of gravity of sumptuary regulation swung, during this prolonged hiatus in Parliament, to the mechanism of the royal proclamation. In a matter of forty years there were 20 proclamations on matters of apparel most of which had a common and distinctive form. They invoked and reenacted the two previous sumptuary statutes of 1533 and 1553; but it should be noted that the rendition of the contents thereof departs in minor ways from the text of those statutes. Each proclamation started with a call to enforce the Acts of 1533 and 1553 and a recitation, in fluctuating levels of moral panic, of the evils consequent upon the indulgence in excess of apparel. For example, the proclamation of 1566 complained about 'the disorder and confusion of the degrees of all estates . . . and the subversion of all good order' (Dyson 1618: No. 94).

A second general feature of the Elizabethan proclamations was that the rules of apparel took the form of prohibition qualified by exemption ('No person may wear item X, except social ranks A, B, etc.'). The third standard feature of these proclamations was that they were issued accompanied by 'breviats' that gave a summary and synoptic view of the rules for the benefit of those called upon to enforce the law.[42] Figure 6.1 on pages 122–23 reproduces the tabular representation of the complex rules governing sartorial entitlements. It is easy to imagine that not only could these have been distributed in large numbers, but that they would have greatly assisted over-burdened local officials in familiarizing themselves with the details of the complex system of ranks and exceptions. We also know that considerable importance was attached to the reading of these and other proclamations from the pulpits on Sundays.

The Proclamation, 'Proclamation Against Excess in Apparel', that established the model that was to persist throughout the reign was issued in the first year of the new reign in 1559.[43] It announced the intention to enforce the existing apparel legislation of 1533 and 1553, but to do so without any 'sudden and unlooked-for extremity'; a start was to be made within the royal household and then throughout the land, giving dates for the implementation of these stages. The main content was a summary of the 1533 and 1553 statutes; they are brief enough to quote in full:

> *24 Hen. VIII: c. 13 (1533)*
> None shall wear in his apparel any:
>
>> cloth of gold, silver, or tinsel; satin, silk, or cloth mixed with gold or silver, nor any sables; except earls and all of superior degrees, and viscounts and barons in their doublets and sleeveless coats;
>> woolen cloth made out of the realm; velvet, crimson, scarlet, or blue; furs, black genets, lucerns; except dukes, marquises, earls or their children, barons, and knights of the order;
>> velvet in gowns, coats, or outermost garments; furs of leopards; embroidery, pricking or printing with gold, silver, or silk; except baron's sons, knights, or men that may dispend £200 by year;
>> taffeta, satin, damask, or silk camlet in his outermost garments; velvet, otherwise than in jackets, doublets, etc., fur whereof the kind groweth not within the Queen's dominions,

> except grey genets, bodge; except a man may dispend £100 by year.

1 & 2 Phil. and Mary: c. 2 (1553)
None shall wear any silk in:

> hat, bonnet, nightcap, girdle, scabbard, hose, shoes, spur leathers; except the son and heir or daughter of a knight, or the wife of the said son, a man that may dispend £20 by year, or is worth £200 in goods.

Issued through the Privy Council it was accompanied by the breviat in tabular form (see Fig. 6.1).

Elizabethan proclamations on apparel differed in significant respect from the statutes of the early Tudor period; their preambles typically commenced with a recital of the excess of apparel among the 'meaner sort'. It would be a mistake to treat this as evidence that the 'meaner sort' were the intended target, since preambles functioned as much as a legitimatory discourse as an actual description of existing social reality. To polemicize against the lower orders could well have been designed to elicit the support and approval of the 'better sort'. It is entirely possible that these formulations did grasp something of a new reality, particularly in the rapidly expanding metropolis where economic expansion was creating an rapid increase in the number of small traders, artisans and apprentices, many of whom seem to have been more than prepared to commit significant proportions of their income to engage in the conspicuous consumption that had previously been the prerogative of their 'betters' (Welford 1884: II: 310).

The trend was for successive proclamations dealing with apparel to become increasingly preoccupied with the specification of the officials who were to be responsible for enforcement. For example, a proclamation in 1562 provided that within the Queen's household the Lord Chamberlain and Lord Steward were to be responsible; in the City of London the Mayor and Aldermen were required to appoint 'four substantial and well-meaning men' in each ward who were to be allowed to retain a moiety [half] of the proceeds of forfeiture.[44] Similar surveillance was to be instituted at the Inns of Court and, spreading even wider, in 'all cities, towns, and villages' by mayors, bailiffs and JPs. The designated officials were ordered to report to the Lord Chancellor and to the

Justices of Assize. All officials and watchers were to be provided with breviats. The call for the appointment of watchers secured some results in London where aldermen appointed four watchers in their wards. Watchers were also utilized in the enforcement of vagrancy laws and, during plague years, to check all those entering the city (Hooper 1915: 443).

This was the basic form of the Elizabethan sumptuary proclamations. Over time this relatively simple form came to be encrusted with additional particularistic rules directed at new developments in sartorial style. Addenda, 'necessary additions', were featured in each successive proclamation adding extra provisions to combat new fashions. For example, the 1562 proclamation identified a new abuse in the hose being worn by men in London, 'the monstrous and outrageous greatness of hose' that had 'crept a late into the Realm'. This attack on male hose exhibits a classical sumptuary motif by indicting the quantity of material employed.

The 1562 proclamation instructed tailors and hosiers to limit the material used to one and a half yards of cloth, to which end tailors and hosiers were to be bound over in the sum of £40. Any who refused were to be imprisoned and deprived of their occupation. In London when attempts were made to obtain bonds from tailors and hosiers some resistance was encountered; in Blackfriars warrants had to be issued to bring tailors and hosiers before the aldermen. The same proclamation also attacked 'the outrageous double ruffs'; single ruffs only were to be worn at neck and wrist 'upon pain of forfeiture . . . and of imprisonment at the Queen's Highness' pleasure'. The Mayor of London was further instructed to organize searches of the premises of all tailors and hosiers every eight days.

Only one day after the proclamation attacking hose another proclamation identified a new and interesting target.[45] The proclamation repeats the now familiar 'monstrous abuse of apparel almost in all estates, but principally in the meaner sort'. A novel complaint linked the issue of apparel to another and apparently unrelated problem that had already elicited concern from Tudor governments, namely 'the decay and disfurniture of all horses for service within the realm'.[46] The obvious question is how do apparel and horses come to be discursively linked? Horses had become an issue of military anxiety; fears of invasion, which persisted until the defeat of the Spanish Armada in 1588, led to attempts to reinstitute a quasi-feudal responsibility on landowners to raise horses suitable for military use. This proclamation stipulated that every person with land one mile in circumference must provide two mares; those with land with a four mile compass were to provide four mares. The provision that mares must not be covered by any stallion under 14 hands was presumably to ensure horses of the desired stature for military use. The military preoccupation is confirmed by the next provision which required that all those with an annual income of £1,000 were to provide 30 sets of armour, and introduced a sliding scale down to those with an income of £20 being required to maintain one set of armour.

This does not yet explain the presence of these provisions in a proclamation also dealing with apparel. The answer is I suspect an attempt at the setting of a legislative trap. The proclamation directed special commissions in every county to conduct an inventory of the ownership of horses and to inquire 'what persons shall not have . . . horses according to the statute, by reason of their wives' apparel'. The trap is that citizens will understandably inflate their income to claim entitlement to restricted clothing and ornaments; on the other hand they will be tempted to understate their income and estate when it comes to the provision of horses and armour. The proclamation's 'trap' is to make the population's military duties match the sartorial pretensions of their wives. I have come across no evidence that bears on the success of this little bit of legislative deviousness.

A proclamation in 1566 returned to the attack on male hose. It required that the lining of hose be made from English cloth, and introduced an additional hierarchic element by restricting the use of velvet and satin to the hose of the sons of barons or above.[47]

The first Elizabethan statute on apparel did not arrive until 1563 and proved to be a very damp squib; it was styled 'An Act Against such as shall sell any Ware for Apparel Without Ready Money'.[48] It was a measure of very limited reach; it seems to have been directed against tailors and related trades. It stipulated that anyone who supplied 'any foreign wares, not first grown or first wrought within the Queen Majesties Dominions, appertaining to the clothing or adorning of the body' for credit would have no legal redress for non-payment against the customer. The wealthy with estates worth over £3,000 p.a. were exempted. It seems clear that this was intended as a protectionist measure. While disadvantaging those trading on credit, it does nothing to penalize those selling foreign goods who take the trouble to secure themselves. It is probable that the measure was emasculated after protests from commercial interests about the potential damage to trade; whatever the history of its unusual content I have found no subsequent trace of it. It is significant that in none of the subsequent proclamations of apparel is there any mention of it although they continue to refer back to earlier legislation on apparel of 1533 and 1553.

In 1571 the famous 'Cap Act' was passed.[49] There had been a tentative precursor in 1566 that banned felt or cloth caps, presumably with the implication that people would be more likely to adopt woollen headwear.[50] This statute did have a sumptuary element in that it ordered that no man under the degree of a knight or a lord's son could wear a velvet hat or cap. The Cap Act itself was significant in providing a rare instance of an attempt to impose a positive dress prescription, not from a sumptuary motive, but from unashamedly protectionist motives. It requires that every person over the age of six, with the exception of the nobility (and their maid servants, but not apparently their male servants) and all gentlemen with land worth 20 marks a year, should wear, on Sundays and holidays, 'a cap of wool knit, thicked and dressed in England, made within this realm'. The economic motive was made explicit as being 'for the relief of divers poor decayed towns and of great multitudes of her Majesty's poor subjects'.[51] The Act was reinforced by a proclamation in 1573; this required Justices of the Peace, bailiffs, and other officials to make 'searches in all churches, chapels, and other places'.[52] Given all the pressures for church attendance it could be imagined that this measure would have been relatively easy to enforce, but there is little evidence of any regular pattern of enforcement. The 'Cap Act' was finally and quietly repealed, without explanation, in 1597.[53]

The proclamatory struggle against excess in apparel quickly resumed its normal form of successive edicts invoking the authority of the legislation of 1533 and 1553. There is perhaps just a hint of a waning conviction in that after the mid-1570s the proclamations are issued with longer gaps between them. Shifts and changes, however, are most readily detectable from the evils invoked in the preambles and the 'necessary additions' that were appended to most of them. There was an increasing trend to invoke protectionist motives against 'unnecessary foreign wares' and 'anything made out of the Queen's Majesty's dominion.'[54] Occasional new anxieties emerged, as when a 1574 proclamation expressed concern about 'the wasting and undoing of a great number of young gentlemen', but one suspects that this was rhetorical ingenuity since the substantive content contains nothing that suggests any shift of regulatory target. New fashions continue to make their presence felt; while hose and ruffs continued to generate hostility, the wearing of long cloaks comes to the fore in 1579 and in 1588. The innovation that attracted attention was the new innovation of silk hose.[55]

The proclamations of the last three decades of the sixteenth century were set against a background of sharpening internal conflict alongside rising fear of external invasion. Preoccupation with rural risings in the late 1560s leads into the strenuous campaign against the rural poor through the agency of the vagrancy laws in the 1570s which were considered in the previous chapter. There is mounting concern over the general stability of the social order that expresses itself in a generalized project of disciplining both the rural and the urban poor and a predisposition favouring a variety of projects for the 'reform of manners' (Slack 1988b: 100–04). It is against this background that a decidedly unrealistic tone creeps into some of the later proclamations. They set themselves to stand against the tides of fashion by decreeing 'against the devising [of] any new forms of apparel'.[56] A more pragmatic approach is apparent in this latter proclamation that seems to tire of repetitious injunctions to local officials, and seeks to shift the burden of responsibility onto heads of households for ensuring compliance by their families and servants; but it fails to provide any mechanism whereby men are to induced to fulfil these greater patriarchal duties.[57]

The history of Elizabethan proclamations on apparel closes with one in 1597 that is the first not to invoke the authority of the sumptuary Acts of 1533 and 1553. Instead it sets out its own general dress codes of prohibitions and associated exemptions without, however, making any significant departures from the tabulations of the previous thirty years.[58] Yet the sumptuary impulse was by no means stilled. In the same year, 1597, Lords and Commons haggled long over another bill on excess of apparel that finally failed for lack of agreement between the two Houses (Baldwin 1926: 215).

GENDER IN ELIZABETHAN SUMPTUARY LAW

It will be recalled from Chapter 9 that all but working women had been exempted from English sumptuary restrictions in 1483 and that this was extended to all women in 1514.[59] Then in an apparently sudden reversal, this now traditional exemption of women from sumptuary restrictions was abandoned and a full code of sumptuary restrictions was reimposed by an Elizabethan proclamation in 1574.[60] This exemption and its reversal deserves attention because there has been little or no discussion of it, nor have I discovered any evidence of contemporary reaction.

In order to understand why sumptuary restrictions were imposed it is necessary to consider why women had been exempted. Certainly no reason was given in the legislation itself. Harte seems to think that the exemption of women does not require specific explanation since this was 'natural enough in so unquestioningly patriarchal a society' (Harte 1976: 143). My sense is that, given the mass of anti-feminine sumptuary legislation elsewhere in Europe during the same period, this feature of English sumptuary law does require a more specific explanation. However, I have failed to discover any contemporary comment or debate on the exemption of women from sumptuary restraint and in view of this absence it is difficult to offer with any confidence an explanation for this undoubtedly significant gendered dimension of English sumptuary legislation.

The 1574 Proclamation was lengthy and well organized. Its significant feature was that it provided a separate listing of the hierarchic dress restrictions for men and for women. In addition the accompanying breviats had separate tabulations for men and women.[61] This dramatic move purported to reimpose sumptuary regulation on women after nearly one hundred years of exemption and seems to have gone undetected by earlier commentators.

The proclamation makes no declaration of the change of policy. Rather it purports to derive its list of dress rules from the frequently invoked 1533 Act even though it is clear from the text of that statute that it laid down a dress code for men only. There does not appear to have been any rising tide of opinion urging the extension of sumptuary regulation to women, although the second half of the sixteenth century was marked by an increasing stridency of misogynous polemics, nor was there any wave of protest from women nor their small group of male advocates

(Anon. 1908).[62] Any attempt to explain this dramatic policy shift can at this stage only be speculative. One plausible explanation is that this attempt to reimpose restraints on women attests to the rapidly increasing prosperity of urban merchants which was allowing a flourishing of the female contribution to their conspicuous consumption. The other possibility is that the Elizabethan flurry of proclamations were a gestural or symbolic onslaught launched without any conviction that they were capable of enforcement. What counts against this view is the fact that a feature of these proclamations was that they exhibited a more and more detailed attention to the enforcement duties and procedures of both national and local officials. On the basis of available evidence it must remain undecided how we should understand this late attempt to reimpose sumptuary restraints on women after a long period of exemption.

THE END OF SUMPTUARY LAW IN ENGLAND?

According to the short version of the history of English sumptuary law it came to an abrupt end with the repeal of all the extant sumptuary legislation by the first Parliament called by James I in 1604.[63] The standard account of this repeal is that by the beginning of the seventeenth century there was general consensus as to the desirability of abandoning the attempt to impose dress codes. Elizabeth Hurlock went so far as to claim that the repeal was necessary to avoid 'open rebellion' (Hurlock 1965: 301). This I think is mere invention. There is no evidence of overt opposition to the project of sumptuary regulation; commentators continued to express themselves in favour of official dress codes as a means of restraining luxury and conspicuous consumption.

There is a longer version of the history of this period that introduces a significant question mark against the idea that the sumptuary laws were intentionally repealed. The initiating bill was introduced in the Commons on 24 March 1604, probably as a government measure; it proposed the repeal of all existing sumptuary statutes and then went on to propose that the king be empowered to regulate dress by proclamation. Exceptionally this bill was challenged on first reading, presumably because it raised all the issues over proclamatory government that had been fought out during the Elizabethan period and it was rejected by a majority of 50. On 4 April another bill was introduced 'restraining the excessive wearing of Cloth of Gold, Cloth of Silver, and Gold and Silver Lace, & Embroideries'. It passed its third reading in both Houses, but was never given the Royal Assent, presumably because it had originated in the Commons. A further bill, containing repeal provisions and empowering royal proclamations was introduced in the Lords on 14 May, passed its third reading, and went to the Commons on 19 May where it reached a third reading on 22 June. After protracted debate focused on the issue of royal proclamations, there was an adjournment until the next day. When debate resumed the Bill was passed, the *Commons' Journal* explaining that 'it repealeth all former laws touching apparel' without empowering the Crown to introduce proclamations. It seems that the government backed down and abandoned the contentious attempt to introduce rule by proclamation and had to settle for the one element, that of the repeal of all prior apparel statutes. The sudden repeal of the sumptuary laws seems attributable, therefore, solely to opposition on constitutional grounds and not to any intrinsic opposition to the sumptuary project itself (Hooper 1915: 447–49).

Aside from the constitutional issues, the disagreements that existed were about which social classes should be regulated (Shammas 1990: 217). Subsequently there were several attempts to revive sumptuary legislation; these bills never became law, but elicited extensive debate, suggesting that sumptuary regulation was still regarded as a proper field of governmental intervention. A proclamation in 1610 announced a plan for the review and simplification of many areas of statute law; it announced the intention of introducing a future measure in the light of 'the necessity of taking some politique order against excesse of Apparel', but there is no trace that this was ever acted upon.[64] In 1616 a wide-ranging sumptuary proclamation was approved prescribing the wearing of woollen clothes and prohibiting the use of cloth of gold or silver, velvet, satin and taffeta except on Sundays, holidays or festivals. However, this proclamation was never published, and seems to have been suppressed.[65]

Further sumptuary bills were introduced in the Commons in 1610, 1614, 1621, 1626 and 1628 which all made progress before failing to complete the parliamentary process without necessarily being defeated (Kent 1973: 43–45, 50–51, 56–57, 63–64). Thereafter, while the urge to introduce bills was sustained, they made less progress; bills in 1640 and 1650 failed to get a second reading (Harte 1976: 151). The last bill on excess of apparel was introduced in 1656 and similarly failed to make progress. That sumptuary motives remained a force is attested to by the fact that, for example, Blackstone continued to recognize the possible desirability of marking distinctions of rank although he was somewhat equivocal: 'it may still be a dubious question how far private luxury is a public evil' (Blackstone 1979: IV: 170). In the chapter on crime he included a paragraph on sumptuary laws as a form of economic regulation and followed it with a treatment of the laws relating to gambling.[66]

The picture that emerges is one of a failure to act because the basis of that intervention becomes more problematic. The compulsion for regulation, the sumptuary ethic, remained, but it now met not so much explicit resistance (although there was now occasional explicit opposition), but rather it wavered as it encountered indecision and lack of agreement about how the project should be pursued. One school of opinion favoured the project of imposing sumptuary restraint upon 'the meaner sort' by requiring them to wear English materials.[67] Others seemed to recognize that a hierarchic dress code would now meet resistance from below, but doubted that the upper classes would stomach more universalistic rules. It was this sentiment that came to focus its attention, to be discussed in Chapter 14, on the specific measures of economic protectionism. The cumulative effect of opposition and of tactical division resulted in the gradual attenuation of the sumptuary urge.

No sooner had the various projects for the regulation of the clothing of the living foundered than the regulation of the garb of the dead made a rather surprising appearance – a return to the very deepest origins of sumptuary rule. Funeral restrictions, which had been the earliest form of sumptuary regulation in Athens and in Rome, now made their appearance for the first time in England, but did so within an explicitly protectionist context. In 1666 an Act was passed, couched in protectionist terms, 'An Act for Burying in Woollen only'.[68] It required that everyone be buried in a wool shroud, and specifically prohibited shrouds of flax, hemp, silk, hair, gold or silver thread, or lining of coffins with these materials.[69] The Act also imposed some limited restrictions on French fashions. This statute seems to have been enforced with some enthusiasm. It provided for a fine of £5 for each offence that was to be devoted to the relief of the poor of the parish; it is likely that such tangible local benefit provided a stimulus to local clerics and churchwardens to devote energy to its enforcement. It is also possible the penalty became transformed in practice to a form of licensing allowing the well-to-do to pay the £5 and then make more lavish funeral arrangements (Harte 1976: 152).

While the traditional forms of sumptuary law gradually died out and the sumptuary spirit became confused and attenuated, we should not rush to pronounce that sumptuary law in England died, either at the beginning or even at the end of the seventeenth century. From its very earliest inception in the fourteenth century sumptuary regulation had existed in a close symbiotic relationship with protectionism. What happened in the last decades of the sixteenth century and increasingly in the seventeenth century was that the discourses of sumptuarism became integrated within and then submerged by those of protectionism. This process will be tracked in more detail in Chapter 14, but before doing that attention will be focused on the issue of the enforcement of sumptuary laws.

13

Enforcing Sumptuary Law

THE PROBLEM OF ENFORCEMENT AND EFFECTIVENESS

One thing about which there seems to be agreement is that sumptuary laws 'failed' in that their enforcement was, at best, limited. This standard attitude is exemplified by Andrieux who comments that 'in spite of the sorrowful exhortations about decadence and decline of the [Venetian] Republic, accompanied as they were by the threat of dreadful penalties, the sumptuary laws remained a dead letter' (Andrieux 1972: 51). I quote Andrieux only because he is typical of the response of so many commentators who brush aside the existence of sumptuary law on the grounds that their enforcement was inefficient or ineffective. These responses betray an unacknowledged attachment to the component of the legalist view which presumes that enforcement is related to validity and is a determining criterion of the significance and importance of whatever law is under observation. It has become a standard response from the sociological movement in law to insist that most law, most of the time, does not get enforced in the way envisaged by legalist thought. In this respect sumptuary laws are much like other laws in that enforcement is the exception rather than the rule. While the thesis that enforcement is the exception would need to be defended if the topic under consideration was some aspect of late twentieth century law, there is less need to do so in the case of the sumptuary law that inhabited the borders of the early modern period. As has been observed in other contexts the capacity for governance of the early modern state was extremely circumscribed. The reach of both the law and more generally the state was limited and it is safer to treat law as evidence about the projects of governance than it is to assume that it was a system of enforced rules and procedures.

With these strictures in mind, it is nevertheless true that sumptuary law was significantly less enforced than many other bodies of law. One possible method of grappling with the complex issue of enforcement would be to compare the patterns of enforcement in different fields of law. To undertake such work would require a much more temporally and spatially restricted study than the present. It is, however, worth commenting that the link between sumptuary law and vagrancy law in England, discussed in Chapter 11, revealed that, while the enforcement of the vagrancy laws was very patchy, the state was occasionally able to sustain an enforcement drive in a limited number of places for short periods of time. No comparable mustering and disposition of enforcement capacity can be found with respect to sumptuary laws.

The available evidence about the enforcement of sumptuary laws is at best patchy, but there are some interesting cases where the evidence available is reasonably full. This in no way detracts from the significance of the fact that in such important cases as England the existence of sumptuary law has left little or no trace in any of the documentary records generated by the courts and enforcement agencies. There is not a single reported case in any of the compilations and collections of the cases that were regarded by contemporary lawyers or judges as worthy of note. This might not be surprising because sumptuary offences are characteristically summary offences. Frances Baldwin, in her doctoral studies which provided the basis for the most comprehensive study of a sumptuary regime, found no traces that sheriffs, Justices of the Peace or any other officials devoted significant attention to their enforcement. Baldwin clearly searched hard for evidence of enforcement, both nationally and locally, and after her search comments:

> Surely, if the statutes of apparel had been executed as the legislators intended them to be, some of the cases arising under them would have been appealed to the higher courts and some reports of them would have been preserved. And yet no such reports can be found.
>
> (Baldwin 1926: 117–18)

Harte confirms Baldwin's findings that search through the main legal records of the period from Edward III to Henry VIII revealed no cases coming before the royal courts. My own investigation of sources not covered by either Baldwin or Harte confirms that the trace of sumptuary law is not writ in official black ink.

Nor does the picture look very different if one looks to other sources. Documentary sources with regard to local jurisdiction are very variable but in any case throw up scarcely the faintest whiff of the enforcement of these laws. And yet it is apparent that the legislation itself had a great deal to say about the personnel and procedures of enforcement. In the English case, the proclamations of the Elizabethan period were preoccupied with the minutiae of enforcement and sanctions. If sumptuary laws were primarily exhortations it is pertinent to inquire why it was that state officials would have committed so much energy to devising enforcement mechanisms since they must have known that little or nothing would come of their efforts.

Looking to other sources the invaluable informal record provided by diaries and correspondence reveals that sumptuary laws were rarely, if ever, to the forefront of the minds of writers, many of whom exhibited a common human interest, not to say obsession, about the dress and appearance of both themselves and others within their social sphere.[1] On the other hand there is no doubt that important elements of sumptuary discourses are present in the frequent gossip that peppers the record about others who dress above their position. This does not prove an awareness of sumptuary law since it is as likely that sumptuary law feeds off a more pervasive set of cultural sentiments linking status, recognizability and dress.

Some sumptuary tales become apocryphal such as Wolsey's personal confiscation of a prohibited item, an 'olde jacket of crymson', from one Symon Fitz Richard in 1515; Baldwin is perceptive in the suggestion that the very notoriety of this incident tends to confirm the uncommonness and infrequency of enforcement (Baldwin 1926: 152).[2] Similar repetition has followed the incident in May 1523 when a newly elected Venetian Doge, Andrea Gritti, ordered his niece to leave a party he hosted because her gown was made of the prohibited cloth of gold (Newton 1988: 182).

While most commentators have assumed as self-evident that sumptuary law was an inevitable failure, this is not true of all studies. For example, Rainey sets out to contest this conventional view and he does so by demonstrating that inhabitants of Florence, in particular women, were in fact prosecuted and, moreover, that many of them went to considerable lengths to dispute the charges (Rainey 1985). As I have commented in some detail in the context of gender and enforcement in Chapter 9, John Vincent provides very valuable statistics with regard to enforcement patterns in Swiss cities. Bell and Ruse (1972) explored a possible method for addressing another side of the issue of enforcement, namely that of compliance; did the existence of sumptuary laws affect the way people dressed? They attempted to examine evidence about changes in dress associated with the 1363 English sumptuary statute, but they found the main sources available to them, brass rubbings, were too stylized to provide reliable data of short-term shifts in dress practices. This same limitation probably applies to the portraiture which had become fashionable by the high sumptuary period of the sixteenth century.

My concerns are not so much about whether sumptuary laws were enforced. I think that there is little doubt that in general the enforcement rate measured in terms of official actions was low. The problem with this line of thought is that it assumes an identity between effective law and enforced law. One only has to think about the enforcement of modern speeding laws to realize that the connection between effectiveness and enforcement is complex. The method that I will pursue is to leave aside, for the time being at least, broad judgmental issues about the effectiveness of sumptuary laws. Instead I will attend to the more modest issue of seeing what we can learn from examining the variety of arrangements and practices that were instituted for the enforcement of sumptuary laws. Attention will be focused on the varieties of agencies and agents charged with enforcement and with the forms of prosecution and varieties of sanctions employed.

THE AGENTS OF ENFORCEMENT: HEGEMONY, PASSIVITY AND NON-ENFORCEMENT

There seems to be considerable evidence that a substantial body of both official and popular opinion accepted, with greater or lesser enthusiasm, the necessity and desirability of sumptuary legislation. Such broad ideological agreement did not ensure that there was agreement about who or what should be regulated or the extent and direction of its enforcement. Today, while there is wide agreement that effective policing is desirable, there are major differences about what this involves and requires. It is significant that the project of sumptuary regulation was not itself controversial; this I think may underlie the fact that the historical record does not reveal very much discussion or debate, or even grumbling and complaint. Kent's study of attitudes to personal regulation in the Commons reveals a concern with:

> the fear that they would be deprived of the authority and privileges commensurate with their social position and that their own conduct might thus be subject to regulation.
>
> (Kent 1973: 62)

The other side of this passive acceptance is that it elicited only a low level of motivation to compliance; it is always 'others' who should comply and against whom the sumptuary laws should be enforced. This discussion points to a wider consideration that where hegemony is constituted of passive rather than active elements it is vulnerable to more or less rapid displacements. E.P. Thompson speaks of a popular culture in eighteenth century England which 'no longer acknowledged, except in perfunctory ways, the hegemony of the Church' (1974: 397). If his historical judgment is correct then the hegemony of the church–state complex must be regarded as fragile. My point about sumptuary law is that the assent that existed was passive to such a degree that it required only the smallest ideological shift for explicit rejection to come to the fore. Yet it is important to bear in mind that within a large section of the population the moralization of luxury and the desirability of sumptuary restraint remained powerful and active. In general there remained a potentially widespread support for the regulation of personal life, but the 'vices' had to be credibly constructed as threats to social order or to an imagined social order. Sumptuary law took on some of the characteristics of those persistent invocations which are familiar today, such as 'parents no longer control their children', which are imaginary constructions of a desired past, but (and this is the important point) to which it is tacitly acknowledged there can be no return. The sumptuary ethic lived on long past its participation in an active hegemony; it survived as a component of a cultural nostalgia for a time when people knew their place and that place was recognizable from their dress and deportment.

To facilitate the exploration of the enforcement of sumptuary law let me start with an ideal typical distinction between a criminal model and a fiscal model. In the former, sumptuary laws were added to the already extensive jurisdiction of the local social control agencies and made subject to the same type of sanctions as other criminal wrongs such as imprisonment, punishments of humiliation (stocks, etc.) or financial penalties. It should be noted that criminal sanctions can themselves be deployed in a symbolic manner; it is a form of degradation of the otherwise normal activity of dressing fashionably to have it tarred by association with criminal sanctions. The fiscal strategy deploys a self-consciously pragmatic approach; regulation is secured through the bureaucratic practices of maintaining registers and extending the power of governmental paper by the issuing of certificates of exemption. While the fiscal interests of the state were no doubt paramount it would be wrong to assume that the authorities were not concerned with the prohibition of luxury. The granting of exemptions and other forms of licensing not only expanded the range and scope of governmental intervention, but also provided legitimation to the prosecution of unexempted offenders. Empirical instances of sumptuary regimes always involved some mix of the criminal and fiscal ideal typical elements.[3]

Sumptuary agents are those who are involved in the processes of surveillance, apprehension and prosecution. Three main patterns are to be found. The first was the cumulative expansion of the jurisdiction of existing officials and legal officers. The second was the creation of specialized agents. The third was seeking to locate responsibility in some other local or traditional mechanism. This latter pattern is the least significant since it was, I suspect, often a gesture of resignation, one which generally took the form of making heads of households responsible for the appearential rectitude of their household unit. In practice this meant making male householders responsible for their wives, daughters and servants. For example, in Venice the attempt was made periodically to impose enforcement upon heads of household; if they failed in their exercise of patriarchal authority they were supposed to report their family's breaches of sumptuary requirements to the magistrates (Newett 1907: 251–53).[4] Intuitively this seems to have been a strategy likely to minimize compliance. I am inclined to treat the considerable volume of talk about the responsibilities of heads of households as being rhetorical.

The response of expanding the jurisdiction of existing offices is the one with the longest-term implications, but perhaps with the least short-term success. In the processes of state formation the movement from office as a traditional burden of rank, through a system of patronage over the rewards of office (e.g. tax-farming) to the professionalization of office in which there is a separation between economic reward and the duties of office is long and tortuous. One significant feature is that the expansion of responsibility or jurisdiction tended to outstrip the capacity to perform. Most officials were at best part-time amateurs whose private concerns were often far more pressing than their public duties and who lacked effective support staff to carry out their tasks in very much more than an episodic fashion.[5]

Typical of such an office was that of the Justice of the Peace in England. While sumptuary statute also imposed responsibility for enforcement on other officers, such as mayors, bailiffs and others, it was the JP who represented both the possibility and the limits of the state's capacity to reach across the length and breadth of the country. The jurisdiction of the JPs expanded rapidly in the fifteenth century, particularly after the effective demise of the sheriffs after 1461. The JPs secured the support of the rising social forces since they had considerable local autonomy, but at the same time were not in the pockets of the feudally minded nobility. Their jurisdiction covered a wide array of summary criminal jurisdiction, and came to include sumptuary jurisdiction (Putman 1938: lvi).[6]

From the late fifteenth century onwards there was a permanent frustration at the centre with the lack of application and attention to the ever growing stream of obligations which were deposited on the shoulders of the JPs and other local officials. This is most clearly visible in the steady stream of Elizabethan proclamations concerned with the enforcement of statutes. The bulk of these on sumptuary matters are entitled 'For the Enforcement of Statutes of Apparel'. Another very important group, whose significance I have commented on in an earlier chapter, were those which called for the enforcement of a group of statutes on different matters. Calls for the enforcement of apparel statutes were most frequently linked with calls for enforcement of either vagrancy laws or laws against unlawful games, for example, in 1517 a general proclamation called for the enforcement of extant statutes on apparel, vagabonds and labourers (8 Hen. VIII: Procl. 19/2/1517; Hughes and Larkin 1964: I: No. 80), while another in 1533 contained a call for the enforcement of statutes concerning vagabonds, unlawful games and excess apparel (24 Hen. VIII: Procl. circa 1533; Hughes and Larkin 1964–69: I: No. 138).

Proclamations for the enforcement of apparel legislation move increasingly from exhortation to threats. The exhortations were sometimes quite flamboyant; one in 1595 from the Star Chamber urged JPs to use 'herculean courage' in enforcing the apparel laws (Hooper 1915: 445). Threats against officials who failed to enforce sumptuary and other legislation started from around 1495 and became more frequent and indeed were buttressed by complaints in the preambles to statutes that prior legislation had not been enforced by the officials charged with responsibility. Local judicial officials were called to account by being required to deliver information about the enforcement of specific pieces of legislation. For example, contemporary records suggest that Wolsey, on becoming Chancellor in 1515, courted much unpopularity by sending out commissions into the shires to inquire into the enforcement of the appearential regulations (Hooper 1915: 435). Alternatively officials could be fined if they failed to prosecute. The central authorities became particularly concerned by the lack of zeal in enforcement, not only of apparel rules but, in particular, of rules concerning unlawful games. Thus a proclamation in 1538 ordered a fine of 6s. 4d. for every default by mayors, sheriffs or constables (30 Hen. VIII, Procl. 13/9/1538; Hughes and Larkin 1964–69: I: No. 183). I have come across no evidence of any JPs or other local officials being presented for non-enforcement.

Scotland provides evidence of variation on some of these themes. In 1429 the confiscation of prohibited goods was entrusted to aldermen and bailies for burghs. Later Acts entrusted enforcement to sheriffs and burgh officials. An Act in 1550 provides evidence of an attempt to supervise enforcement by requiring a roll to be drawn up listing offenders for presentation to the Lord Treasurer (Shaw 1979). A significant innovation came with an 'Act Concerning Apparell' in 1672 (APS III: 71–72, *c.* 21): this shifted the responsibility for enforcement onto customs and excise officers by requiring collectors of assessment, collectors of excise and customs officials, under threat of disqualification from public office, to submit to the commissioners of excise quarterly sworn lists of offenders. In addition the Commissioners of assessment and of excise were given power to try offenders. This procedure reveals a changing consciousness of apparel regulation with a shift towards an emphasis on the fiscal and protectionist dimensions.

A variant relationship between central state and local officials is one which sought to appeal to the self-interest of officials by providing economic incentives to those reporting offences. Payments to officials from the results of their official duties has a long history. The practice of local officials sharing with the Crown fines levied and forfeitures imposed was a common feature of sumptuary legislation throughout Europe. An interesting illustration is a proclamation in 1597 (39 Eliz. 6/7/1597; Hughes and Larkin 1969: III: No. 786) which reminds officials of their self-interest by drawing attention to the fact that they 'might make great profit as well by the execution of her laws'.

The great problem in medieval and early modern societies was that the professionalization of roles and numerical expansion of state functionaries was occurring at a much slower rate than the expansion of governmental appetite or vision. The legislature then, as today, had a bigger heart for governance than the means at its disposal for putting all of those projects into effect. Two things seems clear. The first is that the state rarely slackened its resolve that the sumptuary codes should be enforced; indeed the English case provides good evidence for an increasing focus upon enforcement and related matters right up to the demise of orthodox dress legislation in the early seventeenth century. In 1561 Lord Burghley (William Cecil), principal secretary to Elizabeth, called for reports from the JPs in the south and west of the country on the enforcement of sumptuary and related laws and sent out a subordinate, one Tyldesley, on a private tour of inspection. A major enforcement proclamation in June 1562 was most probably the result of this activity at the very highest level (Hooper 1915: 438; Dyson 1618: No. 45).

It is important to grasp why it was that the central political power was so strident in invoking the necessity of a kind of regulation which they must have realized was difficult, if not impossible, to secure. Legislators persisted with projects of sumptuary controls because the economic and political doctrines from which they derived were so deeply held that the only practical response was one which blamed the non-enforcement on the officials whose duty it was to enforce them (Miskimin 1977). I am sure that this tendency to blame the administration rather than the policy was active, but I have not formed any sense of local officials wilting under the angry glare of the central authorities. When we come below to look at the statistics of enforcement it is possible to detect the kind of unevenness that occurs when officials bend under pressure to conduct a blitz on some particular offence until the pressure is removed. Or did the rising crescendo of calls for enforcement serve to vent displaced anxieties? The second conclusion to be drawn is that for local officials the enforcement of the sumptuary codes in most jurisdictions had pretty low priority when ranked against the expanding jurisdictions for which they were responsible. What we do not know is whether the local officials felt any real pressure or whether the proclamations that kept arriving from above were treated as a recognized form of ideologically necessary 'hot air' that the participants 'knew' could be ignored.

The second general style of sumptuary agency involved the creation of new regulatory agents for whom the enforcement of these rules formed the major part of their duties. The appointment of specialized agents is exemplified in the Italian cities. In Venice enforcement was entrusted to the *Signori di Notte*, the magistrates who already had jurisdiction over prostitution (Kantorowitz 1970: 359). In 1472 the Senate ordered the election of three 'serious-minded gentlemen' as *Provveditori sopra alle Pompe* [supervisors of luxury] with increased powers (Newett 1907: 253).[7] Florence from 1330 had appointed an *ufficiale delle donne'*. Note that while the sumptuary rules of that period were cast in gender-neutral terms enforcement was quite explicitly directed against women. It was prescribed that the official appointed should be a foreigner – this not only marked the seriousness of the appointment, but a desire to restrict rivalry within the patrician classes who were envisaged to be the likely offenders. In 1427 an attempt was made to create a permanent sumptuary magistracy, but this failed because the unpopularity of the job was such that there were no applications forthcoming (Rainey 1985). A statute in 1439 added an *ufficiale di notte,* who was to be concerned mainly with the prosecution of homosexual offences and the regulation of prostitution in addition to sumptuary duties.

In Siena a special sumptuary official, the *donnaio,* with exclusive responsibility for the sumptuary laws was created in the 1320s (Bowsky 1981). By 1333 this office was combined, on grounds of lack of work, with another office concerned with disputes about damage to property. In 1350 the offices were again separated because the regulations entrusted to the *donnaio* were not being enforced; the sumptuary responsibilities were assigned to the central magistracy *maggior sindaco.*[8] In general little seems to be known about these experiments with a specialized sumptuary magistracy; the fact that the office does not seem to have survived long suggests that it 'failed'; but it is not clear what the nature of that failure was; whether it failed to attract suitable occupants, generated popular hostility, or whether the subdivision of jurisdiction proved administratively unproductive.

Alongside the various experiments with a sumptuary magistracy was a more general promotion of the use of agents of surveillance who may be regarded as part of a more general expansion of surveillance. This expansion needs to be seen as part of a more general tension. On the one side is the raw inefficiency of the early modern state beset by intersecting crises of plague, famine, crime and social disorder; the limited administrative capacity led to the resort to frequently draconian legislation (as, for example, in the whipping onslaught on vagrancy in England in 1572), symbolic rule-making and a simple incapacity to enforce existing legislation (for example, the enormous difficulties throughout Europe over coinage, and weights and measures). Yet at the same time there was an increasingly dense network of surveillance and regulatory institutions. This mix of inefficiency alongside growing density is brought out well in Ian Archer's account of Elizabethan London in which state, city, guild and local courts and the traditional institutions of the 'watch' and 'wardmotes' all intersected to produce a dense regulatory net, yet one in which there remained innumerable pockets that the system could not penetrate (Archer 1991: 218).

Florence provided its magistrates with assistants to patrol the city and to keep detailed records. Their reports that have survived show that on many days there were no violations reported, but occasionally they were lodging reports at the rate of two or three a day and doing so in great detail (Rainey 1985: 320). In London the Privy Council urged the City Corporation to institute a regularized system of surveillance over compliance with dress rules. The Corporation seems to have been reluctant to get involved in the enforcement of state proclamations. They petitioned the Privy Council for a dispensation, but continuing pressure resulted in the mayor issuing a precept to city aldermen directing them to 'give a diligent eye' to the enforcement of the apparel of persons in their wards and to arrest all suspected offenders (Hooper 1915: 438). These instructions were taken a stage further in 1562 when, in response to a royal proclamation, the mayor issued a precept (14/5/1562) to the aldermen requiring them to appoint 'four substantial and well-meaning men' as watchers in their wards and to issue 'briefs' of the sumptuary regulations for their use. The watchers were to stand watch at the city's entrance gates from 7–11 in the morning and from 1–7 in the afternoon checking to ensure that no 'great and monstrous silk hose' entered the City. The watchers were to be allowed to retain half of the proceeds of any forfeiture. This system of surveillance continued on and off for the next 15 years (Hooper 1915: 443).[9] The 1562 proclamation revealed wider ambitions; similar surveillance was to be instituted in the Inns of Court and Chancery and, spreading wider, in all cities, towns and villages. Mayors, bailiffs and JPs and other designated officials were to report to the Lord Chancellor and to the local Justices of Assize. There is little evidence that this projected national system of surveillance ever got off the ground or whether any of the required reports were submitted.

We know little about the more pervasive system of informers. Some interesting work has been done on their role in the criminal process and Beresford establishes that they were important in the enforcement of economic regulation (Beresford 1957). Certainly the authorities publicly recognized their role. With the appointment of official 'watchers' in London it was carefully spelt out that these appointments did not remove the entitlement of informers to take the appointed portion of the penalty or forfeiture. We know also that informers in Florence played some role. Anonymous *tamburo* boxes were placed in communal buildings for written denunciations of violations of the sumptuary codes and other matters (Rainey 1985: 415). It can be presumed that this was an attempt to exploit rivalries between families and clans, but Rainey was unable to discover a single prosecution that was traceable to *tamburo* denunciation. Similarly in Venice the *Provveditori alle Pompe* employed informers to report infractions; these agents, *confidenti*, were appointed to report sumptuary violations, but although they seem to have submitted copious reports not much seems to have been done with them. Andrieux comments that no one was ever punished or received more than a mild rebuke (Andrieux 1972: 51).

TAXING LUXURY

An alternative enforcement strategy that was primarily a fiscal measure was the purchase of exemptions. This often involved some system of registration; for example, in Venice after 1343 women were required to register all gaudy apparel with the state notary. The most developed system of this type was to be found in Florence. From as early as 1281, in the very first sumptuary enactment, the licensing of forbidden apparel was instituted; a payment of 50 lire secured entitlement to wear head ornaments, gold or silver decoration on cloaks, and to wear pearls. The tax formed part of the *gabelle* tax, the consumption tax widely used in Europe and most frequently imposed on salt and wine. The system involved the use of fines against those who were wearing garments on which the *gabelle* had not been paid and, as was common with pecuniary penalties, half of any fine went to the informer (Kantorowitz 1970: 357). There were periodic attempts to maintain an inventory; in 1343 inspectors were sent out to examine people's clothes chests. Items in breach of the provisions of the sumptuary code might continue to be worn as long as they were taxed and marked with a special lead seal bearing the Florentine lily on one side and a cross on the other. Women had to line up to have such items listed in a register which has survived (de Marly 1985: 19). The fiscal crisis after the plague of 1363 led to a closer linking of fiscal and sumptuary motives; for a fee of 100 florins permission was obtained to wear a wider range of otherwise prohibited items. Later refinements introduced a sliding scale of *gabelle* payments for different types of items (Rainey 1985: 205).

The primacy of fiscal considerations is apparent from the wording of the Florentine ordinance of 1373:

> Considering the Commune's need for revenue to pay current expenses it is enacted that: First, all women and girls, whether married or not, whether betrothed or not, of whatever age, rank and condition . . . who wear – or who wear in future – any gold, silver, pearls, precious stones, bells, ribbons of gold or silver, or cloth of silk brocade on their bodies or heads . . . for the ornamentation of their bodies . . . will be required to pay each year . . . the sum of 50 florins . . . to the treasurer of the *gabelle* on contracts.
>
> (Brucker 1971: 180)

From the late fourteenth century the Florentine sumptuary regime alternated between a repressive mode and a fiscal mode. For example, an ordinance in 1376 extended the range of *gabelle* payments; this was enacted during a time of war with the Papacy, suggesting the primacy of fiscal considerations, but was followed only a year later by a move to a more traditional and repressive mode. The ordinance of 1377 sought to eliminate rather than to tax 'the excesses of women and youths' (Rainey 1985: 200). Then in 1384 the *gabelle* system was extended with the introduction of the sale of exemptions from funereal regulations. In the first eight years over 233 exemptions were purchased. The evidence is that the main category of exemption purchased was by husbands for the funerals of their wives (Strocchia 1989: 130–37).[10] There were subsequent fluctuations between fiscal and repressive sumptuary measures. The evidence available to me is not sufficiently detailed to explore any correlations between enforcement styles with variations in the type of political regime.

There is evidence of less elaborate systems for the purchase of exemptions from elsewhere in Europe. Some seem to have been individual requests rather than part of a regularized system, as when in 1438 the Venetian, Cristina Corner, purchased exemption from sumptuary restraints from the Pope for 4½ ducats. In Sicily so widespread was the practice that the result of the purchase of exemptions was simply to increase the cost of the 'noble way of life'; rather than serving as a restraint upon extravagance the logic of the purchase of exemptions undermined that core element of the traditional critique of luxury. In Augsburg the wealthy could and did apply for exemptions from sumptuary restrictions on the size of weddings. Lyndal Roper's evidence suggests that the considerations were not primarily fiscal since lesser citizens were often refused such exemptions (Roper 1985b: 75). But the general imperative to exploit fiscal opportunities is illustrated by the changes imposed on Jewish communities with respect to the prescribed distinguishing marks. In many cities this acquired a fiscal dimension when the Jewish community was allowed to purchase exemption, either individually or as a community, while in other cities there was a fee imposed for the purchase of the 'badge' (Rubens 1967). It seems clear that any specifically sumptuary dimension became submerged by the expanding fiscal imperative during the long history of consumption and luxury taxes that stretch down to the present. The fiscal strategy made a brief reappearance in New England. In 1676 legislation was passed in Connecticut that used general income taxation against excess apparel:

> Where excess in apparel amongst us is unbecoming a wilderness condition and the profession of the gospel . . . what person soever shall wear gold or silver lace, or gold or silver buttons, silk ribbons or other superfluous trimmings, or any bone lace above 3/- per yard, or silk scarves, shall be assessed at £150 estate.
> (Weeden 1890: 288)

A final enforcement strategy that was available was to focus attention on the producers and distributors of prohibited items. In Elizabethan England penalties were directed against tailors and other trades for producing or selling prohibited merchandise. Attempts were made to reinforce this general liability by requiring tailors and hosiers to pay bonds of £40 against breaches (4 Eliz. I: Procl. 6/5/1562; Hughes and Larkin 1969: II: No. 493). A closely related technique was to require oaths from tailors, dressmakers, cobblers, etc. to obey the law and refrain from the production of prohibited items. In Scotland during the early phase of sumptuary legislation enforcement was directed solely at the offender, but in 1641 enforcement was shifted onto those importing and selling the prohibited items; such merchants were made subject to heavier fines than consumers. Under a 1672 Act importers were subject to a fine of £1,000 while wearers could be fined 500 marks; penalizing merchants became the major strategy after this date (Shaw 1979: 110). In Nürnberg penalties were stipulated for both wearers and makers of offending articles; for example, cobblers were forbidden to make the fashionable piked shoes above a certain length and wearers could be required to disclose the name of their cobbler (Greenfield 1918: 122).

ENFORCEMENT: THE EVIDENCE

Our knowledge of the enforcement of sumptuary law is at best patchy. I regret not being able to offer any significant new evidence. With respect to England I did pursue some sources which might have been overlooked by Frances Baldwin, N.B. Harte and others who have written on English sumptuary law, but little of significance came from these inquiries. What has not been done before has been to bring together the evidence concerning the differential patterns of enforcement and to consider what can be learnt from this overview.

I want to maintain a clear separation between the discourses and the practices of enforcement. It is evident that the rulers and legislators were frequently aware of enforcement problems and, as evidenced in the Elizabethan proclamations, much effort was devoted to devising a better machinery of enforcement. All this debate, discussion and activity needs to be distinguished from the point of delivery when citizens and officials faced one another and citizens got brought before courts. Sumptuary offences were minor offences subject to courts whose record keeping was rarely complete, generally patchy and often simply non-existent. Even allowing for the accidental variation in the preservation of the record it is apparent that there was significant variation across jurisdictions in the level of enforcement. The greatest detail of long-term evidence is provided in John Vincent's study of the Swiss experience which establishes that over a long period there was systematic enforcement of the sumptuary codes (Vincent 1935). At the other extreme is the English case where there is nothing more than a handful of records of sumptuary prosecutions. Other jurisdictions fall between these cases. I will summarize the evidence of these patterns of variable enforcement and then consider whether this permits any general conclusions to be drawn about the enforcement of sumptuary laws.

The context for my discussion, and indeed the most common feature of historical work on sumptuary law, is the persistent Whiggish presumption that sumptuary law was 'doomed to failure', that it was unenforceable and indeed was not enforced. In the simplest terms the conventional view is that sumptuary laws were essentially silly and deserved to fail, and provide subsequent commentators with a means of feeling superior that today we know better and no longer try to regulate such matters. My revisionist stance draws upon the view that since the regulation of dress seems from the standpoint of the present so counter-intuitive the important question to ask is why it was that on the margins of modernity such regulation was to so many self-evidently to be desired, but at the same time enforcement was recognized to be a problem.

Enforcement in Switzerland

The most detailed evidence concerning enforcement is found in the statistics provided in John Vincent's study of Swiss sumptuary laws (1932: Appendices). His statistical data refer only to the final phase of Swiss sumptuary history in the eighteenth century, for which period the surviving records are the fullest. As we saw in Chapter 9 the most striking feature revealed is the disparity between the gender-neutral content of the substantive rules and the fact that they were so overwhelmingly enforced against women. The Reformation Chambers that exercised jurisdiction over sumptuary and related offences held sessions until the end of the eighteenth century. Some general patterns can be established that draw on data pertaining to the courts in Zurich and Basel.

Typically the courts sat for between 20 and 30 sessions each year. The number of sittings and the number of cases heard did, however, vary considerably. There were years in which few sittings occurred, and occasional years in Basel (and more rarely in Zurich) when no sessions were held. Generally the period between 1740 and 1760 saw the most active period with an average of 30 sittings each year in both cities, but thereafter the pattern became more erratic with fewer court sittings, fewer cases, sudden spurts of activity followed by increasingly long periods of inactivity. Significantly there was a decline not only in the number of prosecutions, but also in the rate of convictions. It is not possible to establish whether this indicates a greater reluctance on the part of the city fathers to convict or whether defendants made bigger efforts to defend themselves. There was also a shift of focus away from dress offences towards dancing, gambling and a new class of cases concerning servants leaving service in breach of contract.

It is particularly interesting to note that the Bern Chamber revealed a sensitivity to the increasing difficulties experienced in carrying out their work. The court wrote to the City Council in 1784 drawing attention to the difficulty experienced in enforcing the sumptuary rules and indicating that this lack of ability to enforce called the rules themselves into doubt. This is interesting, because it does suggest that they clearly perceived a link between their capacity to enforce the laws and the wider validity of the sumptuary project. It may indicate the exhaustion of the project in that, while drawing attention to the problem, they made no recommendations about what should be done. A little over a decade later, in 1796, the court was wound up and in those last few years sittings were infrequent and the number of convictions secured were negligible.

Enforcement in England

English sumptuary law was organized around a strongly hierarchical set of concerns; the detail of the legislation was much concerned with securing the separation of the gradations within the landed classes. If the law had been enforced against the landed gentry it would almost certainly have resulted in cases that were heard before higher courts and would have been expected to leave some trace in the legal records. There are records of presentment for sumptuary offences, but they are scattered and inconclusive (Emmison 1970: 30ff). One study suggests that considerable latitude was shown with respect to sumptuary laws in the fifteenth century; the authors give the example of a knight and lady wearing cloth of gold and sable fur which were reserved for lords but the offenders were only reprimanded (Mitchell and Leys 1950: 201). The same study gives examples of enforcement against the 'middling sort' as when the wife of a Sussex farmer was prosecuted in 1561, but suggests that the authorities were cautious since such prosecutions 'could lead to resentment' (1950: 355).

At least two commentators report that during the Tudor period the Court of Star Chamber exercised jurisdiction over sumptuary cases. Hooper reports that around 1559 prosecutions were entered in the Star Chamber against several gentlemen for breach of the 1553 Act of Apparel.[11] It has also been reported that offences of apparel became a normal part of the jurisdiction of the Star Chamber (Percy 1907: 61); however, the number of cases seems to have been small and few details have survived. Frederick Youngs has been more sanguine than others about the enforcement of sumptuary laws. He provides manuscript citations for offences committed at Court which were brought by the Knight Marshal who had been made responsible for sumptuary violations (Youngs 1976: 163).

Youngs also provides evidence of twelve cases in the Exchequer, at least three of which resulted in defendants agreeing to pay small fines. The most significant feature of the evidence collected by Youngs is that it suggests that the enforcement pattern during the Tudor period was marked by a shift towards local enforcement. So confident is he of this trend that he goes so far as to suggest that in the early period of the Elizabethan proclamations of apparel between 1559 and 1566 there was 'very diligent enforcement' (Youngs 1976: 163). He provides evidence of enforcement activity not only in London, but in other important centres; he lists York, Norwich, Exeter, Sandwich and Rye as hearing sumptuary cases and gives evidence of at least two cases that resulted in imprisonment, one each in London and York (1976: 165 n. 55).

The records of the Southampton Leet Court for the period 1550–80, the high-water mark of central pressure for enforcement, provide the following picture (Hearnshaw 1905). An urban leet court was primarily concerned with what today we would call 'public health' matters; the typical cases concerned keeping drains clear, the disposal of sewage into streets, animals in streets, disputes about the use of common lands, unlawful games, etc. In this particular collection there are just two batches of sumptuary cases. In 1576 there is a reference to the appearance of a group of 'dyvers women' for failure to 'weare whyte cappes, but hatts contrarie to the statute' (Hearnshaw 1905: 102). This is undoubtedly a reference to the 'Cap Act' of 1571 and it does seem that if evidence of sumptuary enforcement is to be found it will most often have been brought under this statute.[12]

Item 98 of the entries for 1577 in the Southampton Leet Court lists a set of sumptuary prosecutions: Walter Earle and his wife, he for velvet in his hose and she for wearing a 'taffeta hat lined with velvet' (Hearnshaw 1905: 239). Against John Delyll's wife the complaint was of a petticoat trimmed with velvet, and there were eight other named defendants, for the majority of whom velvet was the offending material.[13] What is significant is that there is just this one flurry of sumptuary cases and no others are reported during the thirty years covered. In February of that year a proclamation had been issued for the enforcement of apparel statutes (16/2/1577; Hughes and Larkin 1969: II: No. 624). This proclamation was one of many that had been issued during the previous 20 years. Why it should have stimulated enforcement activity, if this was the cause, remains unexplained when earlier ones had not. It does, however, suggest an important conclusion, namely that when there was enforcement of sumptuary laws this was episodic, irregular and probably unpredictable. Other local studies and leet records provide evidence of occasional sumptuary prosecutions. While it is possible that a more extensive engagement with the local records would yield a clearer picture, at present it looks as if there was indeed little enforcement that resulted in citizens appearing before courts. In England there is no record that compares to the steady, even remorseless enforcement that Vincent reports from Switzerland.

The City of London being closer to the source of the sumptuary proclamations, it was possibly under more pressure for enforcement than any other institution. Again the significant feature is that sumptuary matters came before the courts in a very erratic manner. The City Council seems to have been kept busy enforcing the proclamation of May 1562, which it will be recalled is the one which required the appointment of 'four substantial and well-meaning men' as watchers in each ward. The result was that 14 pleaders attached to the city were required to attend in rotation to assist the mayor and aldermen in dispatching the sumptuary cases that came before them. Despite these efforts the mayor and aldermen were admonished to greater diligence by the Star Chamber (Hooper 1915: 441). But by the next year enforcement activities disappear from the record.

Enforcement in Florence

It seems likely that there was much more enforcement in Florence than in England. The Florentine records contain more details of enforcement activity, but to the best of my knowledge there has been no detailed study on enforcement. Rainey's study of sumptuary laws in Florence explicitly takes issue with the 'unenforced and unenforceable' thesis, as does Catharine Kovesi-Killerby (1993). Rainey argues that records show that it was women in particular, and women from all walks of life, who were with some regularity prosecuted and that many went to considerable lengths to dispute the charges (Rainey 1985: Ch. IV). The targets of prosecutions changed; in 1349 headbands were a favourite target, as were belts and girdles. In a six-month period 18 women were reported: eight for unlawful head ornaments, six concerning length of sleeves, one for wearing multi-coloured clothes and one for wearing too many rings. Unfortunately Rainey did not undertake any detailed statistical analysis of sumptuary prosecutions. His broad generalization was that there were on average two women fined per month through the late fourteenth and early fifteenth centuries.[14] What Rainey and others provide is something of the flavour of Florentine sumptuary cases.[15]

In 1378 Nicola Frediano, aged 10, was prosecuted for wearing a dress made of two pieces of silk with tassels and bound with various pieces of black leather; she confessed and was fined 14 lire. In 1380 Monna Bice was brought before the court for wearing five rings, four with pearls and one with a stone, of which three violated the communal statutes. She also confessed and was fined, but not all were content to confess. Biago di Pace, a tailor, prosecuted in 1397 for having a woman's cloak found in his shop with sleeves over one yard in circumference, called witnesses who testified that an order had been placed by a foreigner, from Foligno, for a girl who would wear it in that town. This defence secured his acquittal. A less plausible defence was employed in 1359 by Lucia Ziraldi: she was accused of wearing a dress of prohibited cloth, being open at the neck and being pleated, all prohibited features. Her defence was one of mistaken identity. She alleged that the *ufficiale* who reported her mistook two women standing outside a church; while she was correctly dressed it was, she alleged, the other woman who wore the offending garments (Rainey 1985: 295). In 1400 Salvaza Seze was charged with prostituting herself without wearing the required distinguishing marks of gloves, a bell on her head and high-heeled slippers. Salvazza protested that she was not a prostitute but the court declared her to be a public prostitute and ordered her to wear gloves, bells and high-heeled slippers.

Enforcement in New England

The records from the New England colonies give a picture of episodic enforcement activities stimulated by some new piece of legislation or the emergence of an enthusiast as a local official. After a flurry of cases, often targeting the same fashion item, the attempts at enforcement subside, often lying dormant for long periods or disappearing entirely.

Some of the most detailed evidence comes from Essex County in Massachusetts. Between 1653 and 1654 there was a flurry of sumptuary cases. It seems likely that this activity was stimulated by the enactment by the Massachusetts Bay Court in 1651, since the prosecutions refer to the 'silver lace' which was the only occasion that this material was targeted (Shammas 1990: 218). Active enforcement seems to have taken some time to get going because the first cases do not show up until March 1653. Over the next two years a total of 34 people were prosecuted before the Essex County Court on sumptuary charges (Essex 1911). The following cases, which were heard in Ipswich on 27 July 1653, provide a flavour of these prosecutions. The wife of John Hutchings was presented for wearing a silk hood; the court was satisfied that she had been 'brought up above the ordinary rank' and she was accordingly discharged. The wife of Joseph Swett was fined 10/- for wearing a silk hood; for the same item the wives of Richard Knight and Anthony Potter avoided fines by showing that their husbands were worth more than £200. Presumably neither William Chanlour nor John Whipple were worth as much because their wives were both fined 10/- for wearing silk hoods. Tantalizingly the case against the wife of Richard Brabrooke, the only defendant that day not brought forward for a silk hood but rather for wearing a silk scarf, was not proven, but the record does not indicate the reasons for doubt or the nature of the defence. This batch of cases is typical of the whole group in that only women are proceeded against for dress offences; men only appear, as did Thomas Wheeler in April 1653, for more general moral offences, in his case that of 'profane and foolish dancing, singing and wanton speeches' for which he was fined.

In analysing the 1653–54 cases Shammas suggests that the first prosecutions were brought against socially marginal individuals predominantly already known to the authorities as drunkards, blasphemers or brawlers. But the later cases revealed a significant percentage of individuals of higher status since they appear elsewhere in the records as having served on grand juries, as constables or as clerks of the court. She suggests that while the sumptuary laws were never popular the cases were initiated by information laid by neighbours getting even on some local matter.[16] Only later did higher ranking defendants appear in the records; it is significant that 12 out of 20 cases in 1654 were dismissed because the defendants were judged by their economic or social position to be exempt from the legislation. It is not clear in these cases where the accusations of sumptuary violation originated; my suggestion is that an accusation was sufficient to initiate prosecution. That so many had charges dismissed suggests that no effort was made to check in advance on either social background or wealth before the action was initiated. This is surprising because the law had explicitly laid down these two clear criteria for exemption.

There is evidence of similar enforcement patterns from other American records. For example, Flaherty draws attention to another burst of enforcement activity during the three war years of 1675–78 in Hampshire County (Flaherty 1972: 185). William Weeden discovered significant numbers of cases; his claim that the 'town records are full of [sumptuary] prosecutions' needs some point of reference for comparison which is not provided (Weeden 1890: 285–89). Most of the cases he cites are similar in character to those found in the Essex County records. A group consisting of 25 wives and five maids from Springfield, Northampton, Daley, Hatfield and Westfield in the Connecticut Valley were presented in 1673 as 'persons of small estate who use to wear [*sic*] silk contrary to law' (Weeden 1890: 289); it looks here as if the issue of social standing had been used as a prior consideration rather than as a subsequent defence. In 1675 a grand jury threatened the selectmen of Dedham with prosecution for their failure to enforce the sumptuary laws and in 1682 the selectmen of five towns were arraigned for non-enforcement (Weeden 1890: 286). A very distinctive group of hearings was heard in 1676 when 38 women and 30 young men were presented 'some for wearing silk, some for long hair and other extravagancies' (1890: 289). This is the only occasion encountered where there was anything like gender parity. More typical was the hearing in 1676 in Northampton, Massachusetts, where 36 young women were brought as a group before the court for being 'overdressed in their hoods' (Earle 1974: 63). All 36 were fined, but when another group was rounded up in 1682 all the charges were squashed; the reason has not survived, but we might read these dismissals as evidence of a waning sumptuary ethic since there are no further unambiguously sumptuary prosecutions after this date.

It is possible that further empirical studies of enforcement records could change the picture sketched above. The essential point to be emphasized is that, with the possible exception of Switzerland, the enforcement of sumptuary laws was never routinized. Instead enforcement came in spurts occasioned by new legislation, some crisis or moral panic or new political and administrative initiative. While the substantive content of sumptuary law was often directed against the practices of the upper classes or the urban merchant classes, where there was enforcement it was almost always against the lower classes, typically the wives of artisans in towns and independent farmers in the countryside. There is one significant exception to this general pattern, namely that there is some evidence of scattered symbolic prosecutions of high-status individuals.

Symbolic enforcement

The use of periodic prosecutions for sumptuary offences of high-status individuals had potential strategic attractions for officials. Evidence of such prosecutions is limited, but a review of this evidence suggests that it played some part in the history of the enforcement of sumptuary legislation. While there is little general evidence about enforcement in Japan what is available suggests a strategic use of legal action likely to attract widespread attention among the urban elites. What the records disclose is a small number of dramatic prosecutions. For example, in 1705 for a sumptuary offence the entire wealth of the Yodoya family, one of the wealthiest Osaka merchants, was confiscated, and earlier another wealthy merchant had been banished (Shively 1964). Shively suggests that the main feature was that of symbolic severity coupled with otherwise non-coercive strategy. There are occasional references to the use of humiliation techniques such as offending items of clothing being publicly stripped from offenders. A number of commentators on Roman sumptuary law have suggested that in Rome occasional exemplary prosecutions and the general symbolic value of legislation itself was important in moderating conspicuous consumption (Miles 1987). Unfortunately I have come across no detail on any such prosecutions and it is thus safer to leave a blank against the enforcement of Roman sumptuary law.

In Geneva, for which we already have good evidence of enforcement, it is possible to identify a small number of symbolic prosecutions of the wives and daughters of magistrates and other senior officials. Monter, drawing on the same data as Vincent, suggests that there was an average of 12 cases a year that fell into this category of symbolic prosecution (Monter 1967: 217). There may be indirect evidence of a similar pattern in Scotland where a distinctive feature of this legislation is that the fines prescribed seem disproportionately high. For example, under the important 1672 Act a standard fine of 500 marks (*c.* £350) was stipulated; this was an enormous sum of money and Shaw surmises that the strategy was designed to make an example of a few prominent citizens (Shaw 1979: 93). The limited court records exclude any detailed analysis of enforcement practices, but they do suggest the possibility of the use of symbolic deterrent prosecutions. For example, shortly after the 1672 Act came into force Sir John Colquhoun of Luss was brought before the Privy Council for wearing a waistcoat decorated with prohibited lace and was fined 500 marks. An interesting line of inquiry that would make it possible to move beyond conjecture would be to consider the broader question of the enforcement of social or moral legislation as a whole in order to provide some wider framework of interpretation. For example, in reviewing the Southampton evidence it is clear that sumptuary enforcement was very infrequent in comparison to the 'public health' offences that much preoccupied a busy and expanding town. It would be interesting to have figures which made it possible to see whether the widespread Sunday observance laws were any better or worse enforced than the sumptuary laws of the same period. Until such work is available we can say little more than that the enforcement of sumptuary laws was infrequent and irregular.

If we know relatively little about the enforcement of sumptuary laws we do know rather more about the sanctions which the legislators prescribed. This evidence tells us something about the envisaged enforcement if not about the actual enforcement. That sumptuary law was conceived as being distinguishable from the regular criminal law is supported by the fact that there is little or no evidence of the application of typical criminal sanctions. Although Herbert Spencer claimed that 'in the sixteenth century women were sent to prison by scores for wearing clothes like those of their superiors' (Spencer 1879: 188) I have been unable to find any supporting evidence; indeed I have not encountered a single record of a confirmed imprisonment for a sumptuary offender. The only possible exception is with regard to French protectionist legislation which involved a mix of tax and fiscal measures along with some severe penalties for offences akin to smuggling. Freudenberger reports that in the late seventeenth century 'thousands died or were sent to the galleys for infractions of these rules' (Freudenberger 1963: 43). I have no further evidence other than that finding the means of manning the galleys was a central feature of seventeenth and early eighteenth century criminal justice in France (Bamford 1973).

The typical sanction for sumptuary offences was the monetary fine. In the earlier phases these tended to reflect the gradation of ranks but were standardly replaced over time by flat-rate fines. There was much experimentation with the level of fines. This presumably reflected the calculation that high fines, whilst symbolizing the gravity of the offence, were likely to reduce enforcement and to increase resistance. On the other hand small fines if enforced with any degree of regularity come to play the role of a tax on the prohibited luxury; for example, looked at from the standpoint of driver attitudes, modern fines for such motoring offences as parking and speeding violations are little more than one of the incidental costs of motoring, along with insurance and the cost of repairs. However, aside from the straightforward *gabelle* system nowhere did the imposition of fines achieve any administrative regularity.

There is occasional evidence of the use of sanctions of exposure and ridicule. In Tudor England sanctions aimed at shaming offenders into compliance appear occasionally. For example, Richard Walweyn, a servant, was ordered to acquire 'hose of decent and lawful fashion' and to appear before the mayor; in the meantime his 'monstrous hose' was to be exhibited for public inspection. One Thomas Bradshaw, merchant tailor, was led home through the streets with all the stuffings and linings of his prohibited hose cut out (Hooper 1915: 441). A much more regularized system seems to have been used in Venice. The sumptuary officials, the *Provveditori alle Pompe*, seem to have employed verbal admonitions as a substitute for the stipulated sanctions. The following admonition was read to one accused:

> We are astonished to hear that you have had the audacity to appear in the streets in a *tabarro* rather than the official *veste patrizia*. This scandalous conduct, made worse, as it is, by your station in life, leaves us little choice but to inflict upon you penalties in accordance with that station. For this occasion, however, being satisfied that you must be already ashamed of an action so imprudent and obnoxious, we shall administer only a well-merited rebuke; together with the warning that it is to be inscribed in the records of this court.
>
> (Andrieux 1972: 73)

AVOIDANCE AND RESISTANCE

There is one remaining way in which enforcement can be approached and that is from the standpoint of those who were its targets. There is evidence, albeit very scattered, that people sought to avoid or to resist the enforcement of sumptuary laws. Before considering this evidence it is important to recognize that perhaps the strongest evidence suggesting that the kind of systematic enforcement practices that occurred in seventeenth and eighteenth century Switzerland were exceptional is that elsewhere sumptuary laws seem to have evoked little or no response from its primary targets, the urban elites and especially urban women. So infrequent is such evidence that it is difficult to know what weight it should be accorded. For example, in 1577 the brother of the Earl of Surrey drew his sword against one of the London watchers who stopped him for wearing a prohibited ruff (Youngs 1976: 169). The breadth of the present study has not been conducive to a thorough examination of the wealth of documentary sources available in letters, diaries and other contemporary accounts which might reveal evidence, for example, of irritation at the kinds of restrictions on personal appearance which sumptuary laws sought to impose. I stress that my view is at best impressionistic, but it is nevertheless worth stating.

While there is abundant evidence that people talked and wrote extensively about their clothes and ornaments they rarely if ever even acknowledged or commented on the existence of sumptuary laws. However, David Herlihy notes that a current of humorous scepticism towards sumptuary law can be found in the popular literature of Renaissance Italy in which women are presented as successfully and ingeniously evading sumptuary restrictions (Herlihy 1990: 138).

The diverse tradition of costume studies whose major objective has been to chart what people wore and to trace the shifts in fashion has drawn extensively on contemporary accounts in which people discuss their own clothing and that of others (Brooke 1937; Cunnington 1952; Laver 1969; Ribeiro 1984). There is no trace in this material that people took any account of the existence of sumptuary rules even though they did have a great deal to say about personal restrictions in which, for example, young people were frustrated about parental restrictions or wives grumbled about the petty tyranny of their husbands in matters affecting their dress and appearance. Such contestation over dress has always embodied a male expression of hegemony and a female struggle for autonomous self-expression (Schmidt 1989: 44).

Now it may be that the absence of overt controversy over sumptuary matters proves nothing more than the fact that authors working in the costume studies tradition have not been concerned with the impact of sumptuary restrictions and, as a result, have simply ignored comments on such matters which may be present in the great mass of contemporary accounts on which they have drawn. I think this is unlikely because evidence of a consciousness of clashes between what people wanted to wear and what they were expected to wear would be significant evidence of the deep levels of the social forces governing the dynamics of shifts in the presentation of the self and its social construction.

I am content to accept the view that the existence of sumptuary restraints rarely, if ever, penetrated into the immediate experience of everyday life or significantly influenced the decisions that people made about what to buy, make or wear. Sumptuary regimes simply did not penetrate deeply enough into daily life to leave very many traces of the anger, frustration or irritation that would be necessary for such traces or marks to survive in the historical record. At best it is likely that the imprint of sumptuary laws is to be located in Christopher Hill's perceptive notion of 'occasional conformity' which he developed in a different context (Hill 1977).[17] The existence of sumptuary laws may have entered consciousness as an element in the multitude of situational compromises that go to make up the myriad of decisions that shape the self-presentation of individuals. With these considerations in mind I turn to the very dispersed and scattered traces of popular resistance to sumptuary restrictions.

Evidence of resistance by women was touched on in Chapter 9. There was the direct agitation for the repeal of the Oppian Law by Roman women in 195 BC which was opposed by Cato (Lefkowitz and Fant 1982: 177). There were a small number of subsequent instances in which sumptuary law provoked overt resistance. It is reported that an attempt in Spain during the eighteenth century to abolish the sombrero produced a rebellion that led to the banishment of the prime minister (Hurlock 1965: 301). What is interesting about this example and links it with others is that here we encounter an instance of the use of sumptuary law as part of a project of modernization. In these cases resistance revolves around dress as symbols of traditional and national identity. In Russia Peter the Great employed 'modernizing' sumptuary regulation in the early eighteenth century which prohibited men from wearing traditional Russian costume at Court and imposed a dress style based on the English suit lavishly supplemented with gold braid (Ribeiro 1984: 77–78).

In the Ottoman Empire some attempt had been made to use dress regulations to mark social estates; for example, merchants were forbidden to wear furs which were reserved for state functionaries (Karpat 1973: 86). In the periodic waves of Westernization projects dress rules were invoked as symbolic markers of breaches with tradition. For example, in Turkey Mahmud II (1809–39) introduced a general Westernization of dress; the differential dress codes and practices that had separated the social-religious communities (*millets*) were abolished. Interestingly the 'fez' itself was one of these Westernizing innovations, but it was later to become a potent symbol around which traditionalist forces rallied. The struggle over the fez erupted when, as part of a wider package of modernizing reforms of popular Turkish culture which included significant changes in the status and capacity of women, Kemal Ataturk introduced the 'Hat Law' in 1925 which provoked extensive resistance (Berkes 1964: 122–26, 473–75). Similar compulsory modernization was instituted in Iran in the 1930s which included the symbolically significant prohibition of the veil (Abrahamian 1982: 144; Akhavi 1980: 37–55). The other circumstance in which overt resistance occurs is when sumptuary rules have been imposed on defeated or subjugated populations. We have already encountered the English attack on the dress of the Irish and the use of sumptuary rules to impose subjection through degradation on Greeks and Armenians in the Ottoman Empire (Hurlock 1965: 301).

Just occasionally resistance becomes apparent in the legal record. We have already encountered the group of 36 young women who were brought before the same court sitting accused of being 'overdressed in their hoods' in 1676 in Northampton, Massachusetts. One of the accused, Hannah Lyman, had the audacity to appear before the court wearing the offending hood. She was fined and censured for 'wearing silk in a fflonting manner, in an offence [sic] way, not only before but when she stood Presented' (Earle 1974: 63).

It was avoidance rather than overt resistance which must have been the most widespread response. When the Venetian Senate in 1443 forbade women to wear dresses made from cloth of gold or silver their response was to have their detachable sleeves made from the prohibited cloth, and when this in turn was prohibited the sleeves themselves were slashed to reveal their splendid linings. By 1472 the fashion of slashed sleeves was prohibited. This was no isolated instance. The basic sequence which induces the sartorial use of slashing and layering to reveal sumptuousness of underlayers and linings was widespread in the history of European fashion. And further afield, in Japan, resistance involved the use of forbidden cloth in undergarments which resulted in a vogue for silk loin-clothes for both men and women (Shively 1964–65: 123).

The logic of sumptuary regulation tended towards a distinct legalism in which loopholes frequently needed to be plugged against tactics of avoidance or circumvention. A few examples will serve to make the point. The prominent civilian jurist Bartolus in Perugia upheld an appeal from a conviction for breach of a sumptuary provision prohibiting the wearing of pearls when the appellant established that she wore 'false pearls' and not the prohibited 'pearls' (Sheedy 1942). The complaint by the Scottish Privy Council in 1684 that women sought to evade the law by claiming that their garments were not dresses but 'only nightgouns, undresses [informal wear] or mantois [cloaks]' was discussed in Chapter 9.

Kantorowitz's discussion of the counsel's opinion written by Antonius de Rosellis in 1447 exemplifies the complex legalisms which were deployed in order to resist enforcement of sumptuary ordinances. The opinion was written to assess the validity of a special episcopal statute, *De ornatu mulierum,* that prohibited certain excesses of female toilet on pain of excommunication. Rosellis argued that both the Bible and Roman law require that married women should obey their husbands who were entitled to order the dress of their wives. Thus if married women dressed in order to please their husbands they were entitled to wear otherwise prohibited ornaments. Unmarried women might similarly use ornaments in order to acquire a husband. By the end of his *concilium* Rosellis had excluded all but unmarried women who explicitly renounce an intention to marry from the reach of sumptuary law (Kantorowitz 1970).

THE PARADOX OF ENFORCEMENT AND NON-ENFORCEMENT

While the available empirical resources are inadequate to make any final judgements about the enforcement of sumptuary laws certain provisional conclusions can be drawn. The most general aim should be to try and capture the paradox that lies at the heart of the sumptuary project. It is that while most sections of the population shared a general agreement that sumptuary laws were both desirable and necessary their existence rarely induced systematic enforcement practices from the rulers or compliance from the populace. Indeed enforcement always ran the risk of alienating the broad consensus that favoured the existence of such laws.

It seems to be the case that most people subject to sumptuary regimes paid relatively little heed to them and when they did so their conformity was only an occasional conformism. But it should also be made clear that there is a perhaps more important point to be extrapolated. The relative silence of the historical record about popular attitudes towards sumptuary law suggests that few people disliked the sumptuary restraints with the degree of strong feeling likely to have left a trace on the historical record. It needs to be stressed that there is virtually no evidence that any significant sections of the populations or influential writers held the modernist view that sumptuary legislation was undesirable in principle and unenforceable in practice. It will be recalled that even the most explicitly modernist critique by Bernard Mandeville, which evoked much more condemnation than support when it appeared, was not published until 1705. In other words the modernist critique of sumptuary law did not emerge until only the most fragile remnants of the sumptuary tradition remained. Indeed the ideological power of the critique of luxury remained active throughout the period and hardly slackened until long after the disappearance of all narrowly sumptuary legislation.

These considerations suggest that sumptuary laws should perhaps be seen as conforming quite closely to Joseph Gusfield's concept of symbolic legislation whose distinguishing feature is that it is the existence of the legislation itself rather than its enforcement that is significant (Gusfield 1963). However, on closer inspection sumptuary law does not fit comfortably into the conceptual category of symbolic legislation since Gusfield, correctly I suggest, placed significant weight on the fact that the social forces which promoted the cause of Prohibition were not, in the main, the holders of political power, but were members of social groups that were experiencing a long-running decline in their political, economic and cultural power. With respect to sumptuary laws there is no evidence of the kind of agitation from below that provided the impetus for the Prohibition movement. It is interesting to note that such movements from below, as with the social purity movements that got under way in seventeenth century England and later in the United States, appear only after the demise of sumptuary law. It should also be recalled that the social action from below during the Reformation produced continuity rather than radical transformations in European sumptuary laws. The sumptuary impulse came always from above, yet this project of governance rested on a broad social consensus. It may be useful to distinguish the Gusfield-type symbolic legislation from 'hegemonic legislation', legislation from above forming a component of a project of governance and secured by measures of active or passive popular consent. This idea shares with Gusfield's conception an emphasis that what is significant is not necessarily whether the legislation 'worked' or that enforcement occurred, but that the legislation existed and expressed elements of an ideological agenda and generated a sense that 'something was being done' about the persistent anxieties and tensions concerning class and gender relations which fuelled the sumptuary impulse.

14

Death or Transformation? The Fate of the Sumptuary Laws

WHAT BECAME OF THE SUMPTUARY LAWS?

The general pattern is clear. Between the early seventeenth century and the end of the eighteenth the 'typical' sumptuary law, regulating dress or expenditure on conspicuous consumption, disappeared from all countries, both East and West, which had during earlier periods experienced projects of sumptuary regulation. If this much is clear and uncontested, the immediate issue is: why did the sumptuary project expire? I will return below to consider whether the death certificate was as clear and unproblematic as this version suggests. I will consider the subsequent eruptions of sumptuary regulation and will discuss whether or not sumptuary law is today alive and well despite having changed its form.

The standard account of the demise of sumptuary law is disarmingly modernist. Sumptuary laws were regarded as doomed to failure; not only was enforcement so fraught with difficulties that the laws were rarely if ever enforced, but increasingly the very grounds on which they rested became undermined. The rise of a broader section of the population, most significantly the urban bourgeoisie and petty-bourgeoisie, brought conspicuous consumption within a wider reach and thus rendered attempts at restraint ever more difficult to secure. At the same time the general rise of the social, moral and economic force of individualism stripped away the very basis of the sumptuary project (Freudenberger 1963: 43). Economic realism and national interest undercut the grip of the paternalism that lay at the core of the sumptuary ethic. To invoke a more recent discourse, it simply was not the business of the law or the government what people wore. Thus the demise of the sumptuary laws was one small marker of the transition from pre-modernity. Once the transition is made the practices of the past come to be seen as vaguely foolish or ridiculous and thereby confer reflected legitimacy on the practices of the present.

There is a second variant of the modernist critique which comes down to the commonplace view that 'you can't change human nature'. This view finds expression in the widely held view that once established and on the move 'fashion' provides an unstoppable and self-sustaining force. Voltaire exemplifies this view. 'History has proved that all sumptuary laws have been everywhere, after a brief time, evaded or ignored. Vanity will always invent more ways of distinguishing itself than the laws are able to forbid' (quoted Hughes 1983: 69). Any attempt to stand in the way of vanity's materialization in fashion was inevitably doomed, but it took many centuries of frustration before the message sunk in and the rulers abandoned their pretensions. To arrive at this result it was necessary to break with the myth of legislation which Eugen Ehrlich stigmatized as the naive dilettantism that 'all that is necessary in order to abolish an existing evil is to forbid it' (Ehrlich 1962: 411).[1]

My project is self-consciously revisionist, to challenge and displace an orthodoxy. The guts of the revisionist critique is that the orthodox view grossly exaggerates the rise of economic rationalism; there was remarkably little, if any, overt criticism of sumptuary law. In general the desirability of sumptuary regulation was part of the taken-for-granted conception of the proper role of government. One risk inherent in any revisionist project is that of simply reversing the storyline; I have no interest or intention in claiming sumptuary law as an agency of modernization or of suggesting that it was widely enforced. Yet I hope to have done considerably more than question an orthodoxy. What is on offer is an alternative account of the historical trajectory of sumptuary law that not only provides an account of this specific field of law, but also offers a broader account of how particular targets came to be selected for regulation, their connection with 'state formation' (that is the expansion of the capacity of the state for governance) and the influences that affect the success and failure of different types of sumptuary regime. The thematic argument of this book which rejects the equation of sumptuary law and pre-modernity can now be taken a stage further.

The main thrust of my critique of the modernist account of the death of sumptuary law is entirely incompatible with the persistence of the sumptuary ethic and the corresponding absence of any evidence of a sustained critique of sumptuary rule. To put the point polemically: there was little or no sustained critique of the sumptuary ethic until after the sumptuary laws had been removed from the statute books. Furthermore, even after they had been removed, influential figures none of whom could be taken as advocates of conservatism or traditionalism, continued well into the eighteenth century, to speak of the need for and desirability of sumptuary law. The sumptuary ethic remained intact long after the waning of sumptuary legislation.

As we have seen, the critique of luxury exhibited remarkable tenacity and persistence. Chapter 4 demonstrated how the persistence of the critique of luxury found expression in continuing calls for the revival of sumptuary laws. The significant point is that the critique of luxury could manifest itself in three distinct directions: the call for sumptuary laws, import restrictions on luxuries, and the focus on the fiscal and not the moral significance of luxury.[2] Protectionism promoted the development of domestic manufacture for the luxury market on the 'lesser evil' principle. These tactics appeared in different combinations in different countries; for example, the French went further than others in the development of the domestic luxury trades. While the critique of luxury undoubtedly had an element of social conservatism, invoking an imagery of a golden age that was never to return, the calls for action against luxury were so persistent that they cannot all be attributed to conservative romanticism. Rather, protectionism was a significant element in the rising discourses of nationalism in which the interests of the 'national economy' became synonymous with the interests of the nation.

Certainly not everyone thought that sumptuary laws were doomed to failure. Francis Bacon was one influential figure who continued to urge the desirability of sumptuary laws upon the attentive ear of James I in 1616 and went so far as to suggest the reintroduction of the long dead alimentary rules to restrain 'excess of diet' as well as the more typical seventeenth protectionist measures. He proposed that the only silk that should be allowed was that which was mixed with wool, thereby playing on the desire to promote the flagging wool industry (Spedding 1868–90: VI: 23, 74). A major intellectual figure such as Rousseau, to take one interesting case, approved the imposition of luxury duties to inhibit an increasing inequality of wealth. 'Heavy taxes should be laid on servants in livery, on equipages, rich furniture, fine clothes, on spacious courts and gardens, on public entertainments of all kinds. . . . [and] on all that multiplicity of objects of luxury, amusements and idleness' (Rousseau 1972: II: 55). While such fiscal measures can be defended without appeal to a sumptuary ethic; it is significant that, as we have seen, he explicitly linked the potential benefit of such luxury taxes to the merits of sumptuary laws (1972: II: 56). Despite the evidence that they were ignored, not enforced, and subject to persistent reiteration, there was a continuing will and determination that viewed sumptuary regulation as the means to sustain both the economic and the moral vitality of the nation. An interesting inflection is added by a seventeenth century English commentator who, in the course of a typical anti-French polemic, reflected contemporary concerns about wage inflation when he claimed that 'for want of such a [sumptuary] Law, our Servants here are imitating their masters and mistresses, must go very gay, and to support that vanity, demand three times more wages than formerly, though they perform ten times less service, which is a great infelicity amongst us, and will lay a foundation of our ruine, if not timely prevented' (J.B. 1679: 20–21).

In the mass of writing which demanded sumptuary intervention during the second half of the seventeenth century there were three distinct strands which linked the sumptuary ethic with mercantilist preoccupations. First, luxury and extravagance can only be condoned if they involve expenditure on domestic products. Second, luxury and extravagance might even be necessary in order to furnish work for the poor. The third strand is more traditionally part of the sumptuary ethic: luxury and extravagance, whatever the immediate economic advantages, were nevertheless dangerous for the nation because they stimulated envy whereby the poor may be corrupted by the indulgences of the rich. This third element was clearly incompatible with the first and second; the very liberality that was to furnish employment for the poor might be the source of their corruption and economic downfall. It is within such composite discourses, fraught with tensions and inconsistencies, that a preponderance of writers and commentators of the period continued to support sumptuary legislation (Buck 1974: 101).[3] For example, Sir Richard Cocks, writing in 1698, found no inconsistency while urging the expansion of English trade to insist upon the necessity of sumptuary laws 'to hinder the expensive and vain way of living of our merchants and traders' (Cocks 1972: 104). The expression of the desire to reintroduce sumptuary laws was slow to wane during the course of the eighteenth century.

The summary version of my argument is that sumptuary laws did not so much 'die' as undergo a process of transfiguration or metamorphosis such that the original is barely recognizable in the resultant, just as the butterfly can barely be imagined from the chrysalis. On the visible surface there was a shift away from the distinctive selection of the objects of regulation, the clothes, jewellery, ornaments that epitomized sumptuary laws. The altered form is that of protectionist economic regulation which attaches itself to increasingly generalized regulatory objects; the targeting of French wine, Italian leather, Indian cottons increasingly became only instances of the wider category 'import' and less and less viewed as moralized objects of regulation. Yet this is a process which is never complete. In the late twentieth century under the insistent prod of recession hostility to Japanese products in the United States shares many discursive features with seventeenth century Anglo-French economic polemics.

PROTECTIONISM AND CAMERALIST GOVERNMENT

Sumptuary law had long coexisted with readily distinguishable economic protectionism; dress codes coexisted with navigation acts giving priority and protection to local ships. During an important, albeit extended, period of socio-economic development sumptuary law and protectionism became more closely intertwined. I have some difficulty in providing a suitable label for this conjuncture. I make use of the idea of 'cameralism' in order to draw a contrast with the more general category of protectionism and with mercantilism which I will later distinguish. My contention is that sumptuary law was distinctively associated with the form of cameralist government characteristic of the European cities; I do not ignore other forms of sumptuary law, for example those associated with hierarchical court societies, but I treat the laws generated by largely self-governing cities and city-states of early modern Europe as the ideal-type of sumptuary legislation.

The concept 'cameralism' derives from *Kammer*/chamber, the seat of the prince's administration, and the activities necessary for its smooth running and filling of the coffers in the prince's chamber. The focus was on a conception of 'oeconomy' conceived in terms of the metaphor of 'housekeeping' – the practical affairs of running a household – concerned to provide for the reproduction of its requirements rather than with accumulation or growth. Cameralist discourses compared the state to the family and the national economy to the family economy. Later cameralism became associated with a specific tradition in German political economy which lies outside my present concerns (Small 1900). I am not concerned with the specific economic policies that flowed from the cameralist tradition, but rather to grasp a form of governmentality that was paternalistic without being traditional. Its object was an aggregated population conceived as an integrated community, to be regulated, supervised and ordered (Tribe 1988). It was patrimonial in the sense of being concerned with the collective well-being of the community (Wegert 1981: 440).

Cameralism can be usefully distinguished from mercantilism on the following grounds: its focus was on the role of the state rather than with the interests of trade itself; public finance and the augmentation of revenue rather than private profit was the basis of economic calculation (Spengler 1960). Cameralism was part of a heightened self-consciousness of government and of a separation between government and war. Sumptuary laws were a significant component of cameralist government directed towards effecting, in the name of discipline, the securing of an economically responsible 'government of the self' that involved a whole series of breaks with pre-modern practices. The typical form of such sumptuary governance was the imposition of expenditure limits on weddings, funerals and other traditional rituals of community life. Such projects can be seen as a significant amplification of the important concept of the 'reform of popular culture' (Burke 1978). Projects of state intervention not only manifested a concern with moral regulation, but also with economic regulation, directed at encouraging useful labour and productive techniques and eliminating wasteful and uneconomic customary practices. Life barely above subsistence was punctuated with ritual indulgence (weddings, funerals, carnivals, etc.) followed by a return to the crushing rituals of survival. In the name of a new economic rationality (investment, frugality, foresight, etc.) a new level of self-discipline was promoted, and there was no contradiction in the state-city designating itself the agent of this 'self-discipline'. People, and in particular the lower classes and the rural peasantry, had to be saved from their own folly; economic waste in conspicuous consumption and loss of working time needed to be restrained, if not eliminated. Cameralist government aimed to increase foreign trade and to secure a surplus of wealth and treasure and to avoid the squandering of any hard-earned surplus. In establishing the need for sumptuary restraint, the cameralists drew heavily on the traditions of the canonists whose critique of luxury grounded all forms of sumptuary regulation. Thus the cameralist call for sumptuary laws could always trace a respectable genealogy in older discursive traditions. The important inflexion introduced by cameralism was to construct the target of 'foreign commodities' which joined hands with the critique of luxury in underpinning the codification of dress which became one of the emblematic practices of cameralist government.

Cameralist government involved the pursuit of an expanded range of 'objects' of regulation. These included the prohibition of luxury, the regulation of begging, supervision of the guilds, enforcement of Sunday observance, outlawing unlawful games, gambling and drinking in the name of labour discipline and the elimination of 'Saint Monday' or 'blue Monday'. More generally, as we have seen, cameralism set itself the task of regulating the ritual of popular culture, the annual cycle of festivities and carnivals and also the life-cycle ceremonies of betrothals, weddings, baptisms and funerals.[4] One of the central problems of cameralism was that of 'dearth': the capacity to respond to economic fluctuation and in particular to crop failures involved a notion of the responsibility of the rulers to provide and distribute grain and seed, but it also had a modernizing feature evidenced in a concern with agricultural improvements, the infrastructure of transport, grain storage and sewage. State and municipal authorities held 'buffer stocks' of grain and other necessities to hold down competition, regulate prices and to provide for periods of shortage. Indeed preparations to respond to dearth and famine played an important part in extending the time frame of governmental activities and planning throughout Europe. These concerns can be captured in the idea that cameralism focused on the conditions for the reproduction of the life of the community, to provide that which was necessary in contrast to the subsequent conception of the economy, or more accurately the 'national economy', as an object to be assessed with reference to whether it grew or not, and which had economic expansion as its primary frame of reference. A similar point can be made with respect to a subtle but important distinction between 'useful labour' and 'labour discipline'; the former implying a shared norm while the latter was increasingly concerned with the expansion of production as the key economic objective.

Marc Raeff's work on the emergence of 'the well-ordered police state' in early modern Germany captures many of these themes, but there is a significant difference between his treatment and my own that needs to be drawn out (Raeff 1983).[5] Raeff draws attention to the general expansion of governance whose primary motivation he identifies as a coherent strategy of modernization. He detects the presence of a modernizing strategy in the regulation of weddings and funerals; he suggests that the motive was anti-communitarian, a concern to make birth, marriage, death, etc. individualized and privatized: 'An essential aim of these ordinances in the area of social life was to undermine, constrict, and eventually to eliminate what may be called traditional (pre-modern) patterns of social behavior' (Raeff 1983: 85). The project was to secularize and to rationalize while depriving the traditional patterns of effective rituals and symbols:

> [T]he aim of disciplining society constituted the truly innovative aspect of the ordinances in the area of social life. . . . [T]hat is, the aim of adapting the population to the performance and attainment of the new economic and productive goals set by the state. . . . [T]his disciplining aimed at instilling a new attitude . . . establishing a closer connection between the moral realm and the life-style of the population.
>
> (Raeff 1983: 87–88)

My differences with Raeff concern the extent to which cameralist government should be characterized as modernizing, and in particular with regard to the extent to which modernization was a conscious goal of cameralism. My reinterpretation recognizes the importance of the forms of governance developed in the European city-states for long-running processes of state formation and expansion. I am less certain that this stemmed from a self-conscious strategy of modernization. My suggestion is that cameral government was concerned with the reproduction of an existing social order, rather than with changing it; but in the course of reproducing the social order the city fathers were to undertake initiatives which were to have profound long-term consequences. The city ordinances which epitomize the cameralist project were, I suggest, not some coherent legislative strategy but rather *ad hoc* responses to contemporary problems. The ordinances that Raeff discusses, although often collected together and subject to repetition and updating, were not so much codifications of a new form of government as pragmatic compilations of disparate regulations.[6]

Raeff detects a shift from the conservative and passive ordinances of the sixteenth century, designed for a world that had witnessed the collapse of its traditional and spiritual framework, to one in which legislation was deployed purposively as a tool for bringing about 'dynamic modernization as an end in itself' (1983: 171). My suggestion is that modernization was an unintended consequence of cameralist government. Raeff comes closer to this view when he concludes that the 'well-ordered police state' tried to have it both ways 'to preserve the interests of the group, the cohesion of society and the hierarchical structure of the world and at the same time encourage the active, enterprising, unfettered, and creative individual citizen or subject and promote material wealth and progress as well' (1983: 1979). I merely want to press an amendment to this view by suggesting that the most significant feature of cameralism was that it straddled the profound, but intangible, gulf between pre-modernity and modernity. Cameralism, I suggest, lacked the self-conscious projects of modernization that Raeff attributes to it. If sumptuary ordinances were one of the typical manifestations of cameralism then these, like the forms of regulation with which they were associated, stand unsteadily on the boundaries of modernity.

FROM CAMERALISM TO MERCANTILISM

While there were many elements of continuity between cameralism and the more general phenomenon of mercantilism, I am not primarily concerned to identity either the underlying economic theory or the economic policy implications. Rather I am concerned with the styles of government and the role of legal regulation and, of course, with the place of sumptuary regulation within these economic and political strategies. I employ the distinction between mercantilism and cameralism to distinguish different modalities of governmentality. I treat mercantilism as covering an extended period from the decline of feudalism to the advent of industrial capitalism. Inevitably mercantilism existed in a number of distinct forms, one of these being cameralism which I identify as an ideal-type of the governmentality of the city-states and semi-independent cities of late medieval and early modern Europe. The key difference to be drawn out of my distinction is that mercantilism embodied an escalating preoccupation with considerations of state interests calculated in narrowly economic terms, while cameralism deployed economic calculations as a measure of the social and moral well-being of the community.

The contrast I draw between cameralism and mercantilism is that they involved different conceptions of the proper sphere of government. For cameralism economic objectives subserved a more general social and moral reproduction of the social order. Mercantilism, in contrast, was an expression of a conception of the government in which 'reason of state', that may or may not be equated with private economic interests, took precedence over all other considerations. Mercantilism subordinated all economic activity to the state's interest in power; it sought to secure the state's power internally against particularistic interests and externally against competitor states.

Mercantilism was the economic policy of the period of self-conscious state formation; while it was historically associated with the conjunction of 'nation-state' and political 'absolutism' it was not confined to any particular political formation. At the heart of the processes was the 'project of unification' and elaboration of state power. Mercantilism was characterized by an increasing autonomization of 'the economic' as the primary object of state activity. At the core of mercantilism was a concern with the conditions for the expansion of national wealth and prosperity and its most distinctive regulatory technique was protectionism. The first stage was the project of unification expressed in such projects as national systems of weights and measures, the dismantling of internal trade barriers and the extension of national legal systems. These projects only slowly freed themselves from other forms of state practices, for example, the lifting of restrictive tolls on internal transportation clashed with fiscal and patronage interests.

The common form of protectionism was the imposition of restrictions upon the import and export of goods. The calculation of economic advantage employed a zero sum calculus; any benefit to one's rivals was viewed as a proportional disadvantage to the home economy. Thus exports were to be desired because they yielded revenue and imports were to be avoided because they represented an outflow of national wealth. Early mercantilist practices were frequently associated with bullionist policies directed toward maximizing the national holdings of gold and silver. However, such considerations existed alongside more complex considerations. For example, on and off through the late medieval period England imposed restrictions on the export of wool in order to provide work for the domestic labour force and to secure an enhanced trade in finished woollen products.

Protectionism has a long and complex history that lies outside my present concerns. It is sufficient to stress that it is to be found throughout medieval Europe and despite the hegemony of the discourses of free trade protectionism remains a potent force in today's economic debates and practices. The major expansion of the English textile trade during the thirteenth century was facilitated by a blanket of protection (Miller 1965; Plucknett 1949). In an early piece of English legislation in 1337 (11 Edw. III: *c.* 1–4; SR 1: 280) there was an interesting mix of protectionist and sumptuary elements. Merchants were prohibited from exporting any wool or from importing foreign manufactured clothing, while the population was prohibited from wearing any clothes made outside the King's domains. The state frequently became involved in disputes between conflicting economic interests. In 1504, for example, Henry VII's Council deliberated on a conflict between the staple merchants, favouring import restrictions, and importing merchants, seeking to have restrictions lifted on the import of foreign clothing. Having heard the representatives of the parties the Council resolved to make an examination of the sumptuary laws concerning excess apparel. 'As touching the excess of Apparrel many great reasons and long Communications were had and it was thought good to look upon Statutes [which] in times past were made for the reformation of the said excesse' (Bayne 1948: 41–42).[7] As Joan Thirsk demonstrates, the phenomenon of fashion had economic consequences that could both damage existing industries and provide momentum for new ones as exemplified in the uneven growth of the stocking knitting industry (Thirsk 1973: 51).

Not all protectionist legislation was concerned with the regulation of export and import. Much early legislation was concerned with the imposition of quality controls on domestic products. Throughout Europe legislation sought to prescribe the quality of almost every consumption good; a law from Barcelona in 1330 went perhaps the furthest in stipulating the number of rivets in breastplates (Postan 1963: 414). It is important to stress that late medieval and early modern economic regulation fluctuated significantly. In England during the fourteenth and fifteenth centuries there was an oscillation between free-trade and protectionist measures (Salzman 1964). Protectionism always brought with it the risks of reprisal by economic competitors and exacerbation of tensions between import and export trades. Smuggling was the other almost inevitable consequence of the imposition of both import and export restrictions. In the late seventeenth century silks from Northern Italy was smuggled into Britain in large quantities, whilst English painted cottons were smuggled to France (Williams 1959). The struggle against smuggling added a new dimension to the state's coercive capacity and sharpened the state's concern to extend its regulatory capacity to the most remote parts of the country thus, inadvertently, stimulating processes of state formation.

In Scotland the general claim that luxury was harming the country was commonly in use after 1600, and increasingly the complaint was against imported manufactured goods and foodstuffs. Over time there emerged a fully fledged mercantilist theory: unnecessary luxuries were being imported and the nation's stock of money was being exported to pay for them, with the result that the development of home industries was neglected. The sumptuary legislation of this period was part of a wider economic strategy that included restrictions on the export of home manufactured goods and raw materials because this damaged domestic consumption and employment interests, encouragement of foreign craftsmen to settle in Scotland and the establishment of joint-stock companies (Shaw 1979). For example, the shift from sumptuary regulation to protectionism is well captured in the case of the 1673 'Act Concerning Apparell' (APS III: 212: *c.* 3). It rescinded that part of the 1672 Act which had forbidden all but the privileged groups to wear silk fabrics, beaver hats and lace; anyone could now wear these. The result was to deprive the privileged classes of most of their hierarchic legal advantages; the lifting of the restrictions was justified in terms of the employment provided to the poor by the manufacture of these items (Shaw 1979: 88).

The battles over protectionism continue throughout the whole period of this study. Indeed one of the most violent struggles occurred at the close of the sumptuary period in the well-documented attempts to resist the importation of calico, cheap and colourful printed cotton originating in India. Strenuous efforts were made to suppress importation in both France and England with the aim of protecting domestic textile industries. In France the consequences were the introduction of dramatic penalties in the opening decades of the eighteenth century. Eli Heckscher reports that the struggle over calico cost the lives of some 16,000 people, partly through executions and partly through armed affrays, without reckoning the unknown but certainly much larger number of people who were sent to the galleys. He reports that on one occasion in Valence, '77 were sentenced to be hanged, 58 were to be broken upon the wheel, 631 were sent to the galleys, one was set free and none were pardoned' (Heckscher 1955: I: 173). In England the 'calico campaign' (1690s to 1720s) to stop the import of printed fabrics from the East illustrates the tensions generated by protectionism (Rothstein 1964). There was widespread sympathy for the displaced English weavers; there was serious rioting in 1719 and attacks on wearers of printed cottons. Shifts in consumption exhibited a decisive power as cheap and attractive materials brought fashionable clothing within the reach of the urban working classes. The end result was the stimulation of an important domestic textile industry; it is far from clear whether the sternly protectionist measures did much to smooth the economic dislocation of the transition (Mukerji 1983; Lemire 1991).

In France the economic strategy of the absolutist state became elaborated from the beginning of the sixteenth century and produced by the second half of the seventeenth century the most extensive and systematic protectionism as a national system, 'state mercantilism' (King 1949). The French system of regulation, associated with the name of Colbert and exemplified in the extensive system of *règlements*, was, in its essence, an application of medieval economic and political principles on an extended scale (Cole 1931). The major components of the scheme were taken over from elements already in place in the medieval period. This manifested itself in the detailed control of the raw materials, the methods of production and the characteristics and quality of the product. One of the major consequences was the freezing of the productive process and of the forces of production, resulting in a dampening and obstruction of innovation. There was also a developmental thrust through the conscious sponsorship and tight regulation of protected industrial development: the silk industry and, more generally, the luxury industries constituted the special form of French mercantilism.

A characteristic feature of mercantilist protectionism was the conscious promotion of domestic industries, in particular those that could provide substitutes for expensive foreign imports. The attempts to indict the importation of expensive silks was replaced in one European country after another by the promotion of domestic silk industries (Feltwell 1990). In the French case, legislation promoted by the Duc de Sully during the reign of Henry IV, with economic motives to the fore, instead a prohibition on the wearing of silk, regulation was turned to promoting a French silk industry. This policy carried forward and extended to new ventures by Colbert during the second half of the seventeenth century, laying the economic basis for French preeminence as the foremost producer of luxuries, and established its tradition of supremacy in the field of women's fashions. Silk had also been the object of protectionism in Italy; in Siena silk was still being prohibited in 1433, but by 1438 the commune began to back the local silk industry and lifted the sumptuary restrictions (Hughes 1983: 77–78).

In the context of state mercantilism the primary objective was the economic strength of the state; however, Colbert viewed sumptuary laws as a necessary component of protectionism. In a letter from Colbert to Louis XIV he made his views clear:

> We daily see Laws last but a little time, and are frequently broken as soon as made. Your Majesty must therefore lay a Tax upon all those that wear clothes beyond their Quality, and you must by an Edict declare who may wear Gold and Silver, who Silk, and so downwards; and that they who ought not to wear Gold and Silver, and yet presume to do it, shall pay so much; and they that wear silk, or any other forbidden stuff, so much.
>
> (Colbert 1695: 315)

Between 1660 and 1679 there were numerous anti-luxury ordinances which manifested a mix of hierarchic sumptuary concerns along with a fiscal dimension of luxury taxes and a firm commitment to bullionism that was one of the most persistent preoccupations of both cameralist and mercantilist economic strategy. One ordinance, prohibiting the use of gold tableware, expressed the economic doctrine that the abundance of gold and silver in commerce is one of the surest marks of the good order and prosperity of the state (Cole 1939). The system of state mercantilism involved the use of police powers of surveillance over industry and commerce with the appointment of *juges des manufactures*, and at the same time the guilds and corporations became semistate institutions (King 1949).

Despite the considerable variations in the protectionist regimes within which the economies of the European powers developed they always exhibited a tension between their developmental aspirations and the inherent conservatism of their practices. This 'conservative' dimension of protectionism has been brought out by Pirenne who employs the concept of 'urban protectionism' to stress the essentially restrictive character of protectionist regulations in the late medieval towns. One of the major consequences was to impede the economic development in the hinterland: for example, machine-breaking expeditions in the towns and villages around Ghent often resulted in the hinterland being driven into reactionary alliances with feudal interests which in turn limited expansion and imposed restraints on technical innovation (Pirenne 1956). Paradoxically the most democratic towns were the most restrictive and economically conservative. The upshot was that much truly capitalistic development took place outside the guild-dominated towns and cities.

Mercantilism exhibited a persisting faith in the effectiveness of regulation and legislation as the solution for economic and social problems. The two main targets were 'idleness' and 'luxury'. Idleness was condemned and a variety of strategies proposed for its remedy that were generally organized around a critique of the canonist doctrine of charity (Johnson 1932). The mercantilists gradually shifted the discursive context surrounding luxury from the sphere of morality to that of economics. They started from the general and persistent moralization of luxury, but a transformation occurred that involved an increasing focus on economic rather than moral dimensions. As we have seen, the most important thrust was the development of economic discourses that focused on the import of foreign luxuries.

The mercantilists came to share a general reservation, if not hostility, toward the use of sumptuary regulation; their hesitations were not on grounds of principle, but were more pragmatic (Davenant 1771). Increasingly they favoured the use of fiscal tactics, making use of luxury and import taxes. But such policies, while they might have had some restraining effect on consumption, came increasingly to be considered with respect to their productivity of state revenues. Fiscal considerations gradually became disaggregated from sumptuary motives. The *gabelle*-style taxes on luxury dress and ornaments ceased to be a tactic in the 'war against luxury' and became an end in themselves. Increasingly the selection of the objects of taxation came to be chosen exclusively in terms of their fiscal productivity, the history of the English tobacco industry being an example of this complex mix of protectionist and fiscal considerations (MacInnes 1926). Yet despite these developments the moralization of luxury continued to be a significant element of the wider economic and political discourses.

The first stage in a more radical breach with the critique of luxury occurs in those authors who begin to urge that luxury provides a stimulus to both production and trade: in seventeenth century England this view was epitomized by such disparate authors as Coke, Barbon, Petty and North (Johnson 1932; Appleby 1978). These views were to find their most dramatic presentation in Mandeville's *Fable of the Bees* (1957). Mercantilism increasingly divorced protectionist legislation from moral and social connotations. Economic debates became more concerned with the creation of an internal market. During the course of the eighteenth century the consumption capacity of wage workers did increase and this in turn stimulated industrial production of items that had previously been produced by specialized crafts. It was not until well into the eighteenth century that the Physiocrats articulated a positive endorsement of luxury (Freudenberger 1963: 46). Only then was a positive economic assessment of fashion and its vagaries possible and came to be recognized as a stimulant for economic development. More and more items, such as printed cottons, moved from exclusive wear to mass consumption. By the second half of the eighteenth century a mass consumer market existed and sumptuary laws formed no part of contemporary economic or political discourses even though they still lingered in moral discourses.

THE SILENCING OF SUMPTUARY DISCOURSES

The developments in the European economies produced a discursive shift from those which had prevailed at the opening of the early modern period; these had deployed sumptuary regulation as a central component of state policy, integral to its protectionist strategy. It is important to bear in mind the persistence of these elements even though they become increasingly tangential. Harte is quite right to draw attention to just how late protectionist measures against foreign imports retained a sumptuary element: in England this lasted well into the 1740s with France and China being the main targets (Harte 1976: 141). Not only were specific classes of imports prohibited, but these prohibitions were buttressed by rules against the wearing of the offending items. By the eighteenth century, sumptuary discourses played no part in the burgeoning political economy of the period. This shift occurred without any abrupt changes; sumptuary discourses simply faded away as new discursive formations came to the fore within which a sumptuary ethic had no place. It is now time to consider the social forces that underlay the silencing of the sumptuary discourses.

The general outline of the process was one in which the components of medieval economic discourses, within which the critique of luxury and the sumptuary ethic were tightly integrated, gradually became disaggregated. In particular the economic discourse of growth and of a national economy and the expansion of trade became separated from the anti-luxury, moral regulation discourses of the earlier period. As I have sought to demonstrate, these discourses persisted down to the present. What changed was that they continued to exist as free-floating ideological elements that sometimes coalesced with other elements to, temporally at least, play some significant role in contemporary life. For example, when rationing was introduced in war-time Britain in 1941, and not repealed until 1949, it included neo-sumptuary restrictions on conspicuous consumption. The critique of luxury took on a new lease of life. The 'utility scheme', introduced by Hugh Dalton in 1942, had fascinating resonances with early English sumptuary law. The scheme involved detailed prescriptions on both the quality and the quantity of material that went into each garment: women's skirts, for example, could not use more than a specified amount of material. In August 1943 a ban was introduced on all trimmings on women's garments (Ewing 1981).[8] These regulations became a component of the political radicalization of the period that was formed out a sense of a common cause and of national survival; it expressed itself in hostility to conspicuous consumption in many forms and in particular against those who resorted to the black market to sustain their consuming passions (Calder 1969).

The discourses within which sumptuary law had long existed became disaggregated during the course of the seventeenth century. The social forces involved reflected deep-seated changes in the relations of social power and prestige. Capitalist relations became increasingly dominant. It is important to note that aside from the command power of capital itself, the social relations in which it was enmeshed took no necessary form. From a formal point of view capitalism did not require a hierarchical form of social relations, but everywhere it developed within and even strengthened hierarchical forms. Men did not need a noble title to wield economic power: there might be added bonuses associated with a title, fashionable dress and a stylish carriage, but these things were not necessary, whereas to the feudal aristocracy their titles and castles were the very core of their social power. As has been argued the long period of the decline of feudal relations and their supersession needed its conception of a hierarchic social order whose aspiration was articulated in the form of sumptuary law. Capitalism developed within a concern to 'fix' an image of the social order that was always an imagined social order. In a society of strangers the key aspiration of the imagined social order was concerned to stabilize the recognizability of every 'walk of life' (an interesting dramaturgical image which links recognizability with occupation).

The difficult point is to explain the social reality that increasing importance came to be attached to the marks of social hierarchy, and these considerations became of central importance in the lives of wider sections of the population; in brief, fashion became more rather than less important. Yet the attempt to capture and preserve that imagined social order through sumptuary laws was abandoned. Given the obsessive concern with rank and hierarchy and its visible expressions exhibited by the upper and middle classes of seventeenth and eighteenth century Europe, it would be easy to imagine that sumptuary laws might have actually expanded and even been enforced during this period obsessed by external appearances. But this was not how it was. The immediate difficulty is to explain how it was that at a time when appearance and recognizability were becoming more important the sumptuary laws that seemed to be able to offer just that were in rapid decline. The first stage in explaining this paradox is to note that if pre-capitalist social relations were status relations which depended upon some 'mark' that rendered status as socially visible, then it follows that such forms of social relation were compatible with sumptuary laws as attempts to fix those marks. In short, the late medieval world needed sumptuary law, while the class relations that became more and more important in early modern societies simply did not need sumptuary law. It is true that sumptuary laws persisted and often became caught up in the contemporary legal and political discourses, but the bottom line was that they were not integral to the way in which social hierarchy and social differences were lived. Economic power, on the one hand, and the acquisition of cultural capital, on the other, served to structure the mechanisms of distinction.

A somewhat fuller account of the social conditions which marginalized sumptuary law starts by drawing attention to a marked bifurcation in the modes whereby hierarchical relations are generated. Capitalist social relations provide their own measure, wealth. Wealth can buy whatever is in its reach and conspicuous consumption could simply be a visible measure of the more abstract wealth of its practitioners. But the more access to economic opportunity broadens its base, the larger is the pool within which the struggle for conspicuous consumption takes place. It turned out that it was new wealth, and in the twentieth century the wealth of fame, that engaged in spiralling conspicuous consumption epitomized by gold bath-taps. Together, although they did not always realize it, older wealth and the landed classes produced another solution. The competition became focused, not on the deployment of economic capital, but rather on the use of cultural capital in the form of 'taste' and 'distinction' that was always expensive in that it required both leisure and application; indeed the possessors of economic wealth could in the longer run acquire cultural capital through such mechanisms as finishing schools, universities and inter-marriage. The preoccupation with 'good taste' was 'invented' only when the aristocracy could no longer deny access of the middle classes to conspicuous consumption (Flandrin 1989: 280). There is enormous scope for studying these processes of the 'invention' of distinction and linking them to studies of the shifting class configuration revealed in the struggles to reform popular culture. For while the 'middling' classes may have shifted into closer proximity to the landed classes and disrupted their links to the labouring classes, the dynamic of the formation of taste and distinction may have served to impede such processes by reproducing a finely graduated hierarchy that less and less corresponded to the underlying economic relations (Wrightson and Levine 1979).

The critical point about cultural capital is that its mechanisms, whilst explicit, are not capable of codification; 'dressing like a lady', 'speaking like a gentleman' can be judged by the eye and ear suffused with cultural capital, but cannot be legislated for.[9] Thus considerations of style, fashion, taste and distinction come to the fore and they have no need for the prohibitory barriers of sumptuary law. Once the criteria of social rank shift from hierarchic consumption to fashion as cultural capital, then such tests can no longer be inscribed in legislative form.

The creation of widening consumer markets had a profound impact on the significance attributed to the acquisition of what may be called 'consumption property' whose valorization takes place in the process of its conspicuous consumption. It should be noted that the mechanisms of conspicuous consumption underwent important changes. The conspicuousness of a royal procession or of parading in an open carriage is direct, but it should be borne in mind that the boundary between public and private is always shifting and that 'private' acquisitions of art, books or other collectibles, whilst being enormously important as forms of cultural capital, are less directly conspicuous in their consumption. Once items can be acquired with little or no effort, aside from having the wealth to foot the bill, then material artifacts are less and less capable of fulfilling the role of being declarations of a fixed and inherited stratification. One of the significant features of modern monarchies is that they rest on their profound anachronism: others could surely afford horse-drawn carriages, tiaras and archaic household troops, but these are reserved to set aside the monarchy as a distinctively pre-modern form of conspicuous consumption.

In recent years the advent of mass consumption has been pushed back progressively; no longer is consumption so unambiguously 'modern' and increasing attention is being paid to the earlier phases in the expansion of consumption. It is useful to keep in mind that much of this development involves 'inconspicuous consumption' (Lasch 1991: 70). The tension between conspicuous consumption and privacy has come sharply into prominence with the intrusion of the telephoto lens. The expansion of consumption in pre-industrial societies yielded easier access to the artefacts of fashion as shops able to carry substantial stock slowly replaced the travelling merchants. The upshot was that the mere fact of possession of a particular artefact, with the possible exception of the pinnacle of symbolically significant artefacts, no longer conferred or confirmed social status. Possession only came to be significant if it also provided evidence of the possession of taste, discrimination or distinction as 'interior personal attributes' (Finkelstein 1991: 114–15).

As soon as the expansion of the consumer market undermined an intrinsic capacity of artefacts themselves to confer social status then the project of regulating access to consumption goods was, if not immediately redundant, then certainly undermined. With a plentiful supply of material goods, the individual's right to possessions, be they gold adornments, furs or silk clothes, took on a different meaning. Now, the ownership and display of goods became evidence of an individual's accomplishments and attributes; ownership could make an individual appear wealthy and in possession of refined sensibilities, but it could never guarantee it and was not in itself the main examination set and marked by the entrepreneurs of cultural capital. The hierarchic dimensions of the sumptuary logic were undermined, not by an advancing individualism or democratic impulse, but by the inexorable advance of consumption which was the consequence of mercantile capitalism generating an expanded internal market, bringing wider sections of the population within the sphere of consumption.

Under these circumstances the components that made up the sumptuary discourses which, as I have argued, always involved an interplay of economic and moral discourses, now became disrupted. Increasingly the moral discourses functioned alone. As we have seen, with the rise of mercantilism there occurred a separation between the economic calculation of national interest that came to dominate the protectionist legislation and the 'interests' and 'morality' which became, if not divorced, at least estranged. The opening of this divide manifests itself in the emergence of a distinct and separate sphere of 'moral regulation' that previously had been an integral part of the general sphere of government, exemplified in sumptuary law. This separation was rendered visible by the emergence of the 'social purity' movements from below in the second half of the eighteenth century (Curtis and Speck 1976; Bristow 1977). These shifts were associated with changes in economic discourses. Economic regulation shifts its focus away from the traditional mercantilist concerns with trade and distribution towards a greater emphasis on production and its requirements, although one should not forget that in periods of serious tension, as exemplified in Edward Thompson's work on food riots in eighteenth century England, the 'moral economy' of the protectionist and paternalist interventions to guarantee supply and to smooth out market driven price fluctuations still played an important role (Thompson 1971). The trajectory of the sumptuary impulse manifested a more general fragmentation followed by the regrouping of the techniques of governance; in particular, the three key arenas of state economic regulation, moral regulation and disciplinary control became separated from each other. In general the sumptuary ethic remained vigorous, manifesting itself in association with projects of moral regulation, but now separated from the economic and hierarchic features that had earlier been dominant. This does not mean that sumptuary regulation disappeared, let alone died, rather that it changed not only its discursive emphasis but also its form. It remains a force within the projects of moral regulation and it also moved from the arena of public legislation into that of private regulation.

IS SUMPTUARY LAW STILL ALIVE?

So confident has the voice of the modernist critique of sumptuary law been that it has simply assumed that sumptuary law died a natural but belated death. On this view it is self-evident that personal consumption is not a proper target for legal regulation and that, within certain bounds prescribed by the criminal law and some general rules of decency, what individuals consume is simply not the law's business, and that this is a field of private choice which lies outside the proper sphere of law. This view is sufficiently wrong to have led to a general neglect of the extent to which consumption remains a significant target of current regulatory intervention.[10] The treatment that follows is directed towards illustrating the way in which the regulation of consumption remains active and exhibits interesting continuities and affinities with the sumptuary projects of the early modern period. I am anxious to avoid being interpreted as suggesting that the modern regulation of consumption can be equated to the sumptuary projects which have been the subject of this book. Each of the illustrations is a complex field in its own right and I make no attempt to provide a full account, for example, of the temperance movement, anti-pornography movements, prostitution regulation, or of employers' dress codes. My project requires me to say enough to draw out the consumption and appearance dimensions but to forego a wider investigation of these fields as specific sites of regulation.

Before considering whether the regulation of consumption in late modernity has any links to the earlier sumptuary tradition, I will sketch some illustrative examples of modern regulatory projects. In so doing I am anxious to draw attention to the fact that there are fields which, while not currently conceptualized under the heading of consumption, nevertheless have a significant consumption dimension. This can be illustrated by taking as the first example the regulation of prostitution. The regulation of prostitution has already played a significant part in revealing the connection between sumptuary law and the regulation of gender relations. There has been significant continuity between medieval and modern regulation in that it is precisely the visibility of prostitution, its signs, that provides the key to understanding why such enormously unproductive labour is expended waging the reciprocal dance between police and prostitutes. The prostitute conjures up disturbing 'images and perceptual schemas' inspiring deep-seated anxieties surrounding the sexualized female body (Corbin 1987). While the visibility of prostitution no longer attracts the imposition of 'marks of infamy' it has its own distinctive visibility rendered legible by the 'voluntary' dress, style and demeanour of prostitutes themselves. When the Wolfenden Committee approached 'the problem' it was defined as 'the obvious and visible presence of prostitutes in considerable numbers in the public streets' (Wolfenden 1957: 81). The attempt to suppress the visibility of prostitution is epitomized in the Wolfenden Report's preoccupation with the taken-for-granted offensiveness of city centre soliciting where prostitutes rub shoulders with 'decent citizens' going about their work and recreation. It is the explicitness of the display and commercialization of sexuality – that is its very visibility, its recognizability – which is the incitement to regulation.

It is important to stress the connection between visibility and location. It is not always specific behaviour which generates criminalization or other regulatory interventions. It is often the location of the behaviour that is significant in determining regulatory responses. Thus the discourses of prostitution have generally been constructed around such elements as its distinctive urban location, such as 'thoroughfares' and 'public places', and the pattern of behaviour in those locations. For example, the classical definition of prostitution in English law referred to a persistent presence, 'loitering', and to a temporal dimension, 'night-walker', to construct the imagery of the 'street-walker' or 'common prostitute'. This discursive construction finds practical expression in the way in which police and city government practices have led to a *de facto* zoning of prostitution. Irrespective of whether there exist licensed 'red-light' districts, they come into existence because the police act more systematically against soliciting outside the unacknowledged boundaries than within them. The modern prostitution regulation is overdetermined by a preoccupation with visibility and recognizability which is stabilized through the control of the spatial distribution of prostitution.

The practices of the regulation of social space, through such mechanisms as urban planning and zoning, have come to be an important field of governance in an increasingly urbanized world. The rise of environmental politics is significantly extending the reach of spatial regulation beyond the urban milieu. The tactic of designated land use may have a significant effect in regulating both consumption in general and appearance in particular. I will offer illustrations of both public and private forms of such regulation. The public regulation of space is well illustrated in Paul Chevigny's account of the struggles around the 'Cabaret Laws' in New York City during the inter-war period, which link the spatial regulation of racial minorities with the cultural consumption of jazz, a cultural form that generated anxieties about both the racial and the moral order (Chevigny 1991). This took the form of repressive zoning laws requiring licensing of jazz musicians, and liquor licensing and zoning restrictions on the clubs in which jazz flourished against adversity and obstruction. These events demonstrate the diverse ramifications of the governance of public space and the part that they play in institutionalizing degradation ceremonies against racial and other minorities. In particular they illustrate the way in which regulation constructs linkages between different regulatory targets; once race and social order are linked, in the United States as least, sex is never far beneath the surface. While it goes beyond Chevigny's own project, his analysis is suggestive of a more general pattern in which city ordinances play a significant role in constructing such otherwise discrete 'social problems' as race, gambling, alcohol and prostitution in such a way as not only to produce highly politicized regulatory activity, but also to generate an expansionary logic for regulatory regimes.

A very similar but distinctive mode of regulation has, more recently, been generated around the regulation of the shopping-mall as an intensive site of regulatory activity. Significantly this case exemplifies a wider privatization of regulation.[11] Shopping-malls also exemplify the instability of the public/private distinction, as places of public access and resort are increasingly subject to a private law property regime. The policing of shopping-malls has become a new form of vagrancy regulation that prods the indigent into yet another move. It is a policing that announces itself with labelling which starkly sets out the boundary between respectability and undesirability through the ever-present 'No Loitering' messages. The well-heeled shopper is, of course, encouraged and tempted to 'linger', but only because we know that the difference between 'loitering' and 'lingering' is an economic and not a behavioural question. These considerations underline my argument in Chapter 8 against Lofland's thesis that spatial regulation supersedes appearential ordering; the regulation of space and of appearance cannot be prised apart because they are the regulation of the visible and in a stronger sense the socially knowable.

It is likely that a study of city ordinances would yield a fascinating lexicon of the moral anxieties of the city governors with the feckless ways of the under classes. One city ordinance that I cite for the purpose of illustration I select because it combines so many of the features often more scattered. This is the Ordinance Code of Ann Arbor from 1957, which included the following list of offences:

> Beg in any public place. Utter vile, profane or obscene language in any public place. Engage in any indecent, insulting, immoral or obscene conduct in any public place. Make any immoral exhibition or indecent exposure of his or her person. Improperly,

> lewdly or wrongly accost, ogle, insult, annoy, follow, pursue, lay hands on, or by any gesture, movement of body or otherwise wrongfully, molest any person in any public place or public vehicle. Engage in any disturbance, fight or quarrel in a public place. Collect or stand in crowds, or arrange, encourage or abet the collection of persons in crowds for illegal or mischievous purposes in any public place. Loiter on any street or sidewalk or in any park or public building or conduct himself in any public place so as to obstruct the free and uninterrupted passage of the public. Disturb the public peace and quiet by loud, boisterous, or vulgar conduct.
>
> (Quoted Lofland 1973: 83)

What is fascinating about this passage is the interweaving of anxieties surrounding decency, propriety, public order and that pervasive sense that contact with the lower orders, unless the poor are properly respectful, always generates anxiety for the respectable citizen.

A widening range of sites of consumption seek to regulate the appearance of their customers. The requirement that men wear ties has, I suspect, spread from being a requirement in conservative clubs and restaurants to become the globalized expression of the distinction between outlets whose very expensiveness is itself a form of conspicuous consumption and all others in a world of increasing casualization. The ubiquitous interdiction of a wide variety of causal clothing, 'No Shirt, No Service', 'No Thongs', and the countless commitments to respectability that festoon the entrances to consumer establishments attests to the persistence of a concern to regulate appearance.

MODERN DRESS CODES

The project of regulating dress was the classic embodiment of sumptuary regulation. While the continued existence of some forms of control over consumption is unlikely to strike the modern citizen as particularly unusual or inappropriate, it is generally the case that such restrictions come under the cloak of strongly moralizing and/or criminalizing discourses. But the imposition of restrictions on clothing would strike most late twentieth century citizens as objectionable in principle and faintly ridiculous. Despite the self-evidence of this response my suggestion is that there is today much more regulation of dress and appearance than was ever the case when sumptuary legislation was most abundant in the fifteenth and sixteenth centuries. The legislature has retreated, the sumptuary statutes have fallen into disuse or been repealed. Today the mantle of the sumptuary ethic has been picked by employers and it is employment institutions that are now the primary sites of modern sumptuary regulation.

A significant proportion of employment institutions have dress and grooming codes, and many more have dress policies, and an even larger number have informal, unspoken managerial attitudes that impact on the employment and career prospects of employees. Any fuller study of the contemporary regulation of dress would have to address the connection between the more formalized processes of regulation (dress codes, policies, etc.) and the more pervasive processes of governances which stretch out to include more informal tactics and techniques and their interconnection with the governance of the self. I will limit myself to some comments that connect up with issues arising from the period of public sumptuary codes.

It would be difficult to quantify how many employees were affected by employer regulation of dress. There is obviously wide variation between different sectors of the economy and between different types of work, with managerial, administrative and technical staff and all those coming directly into contact with the public in service industries being the most affected. One American survey had 95 per cent of survey respondents reporting that their employers operated a dress code (Molloy 1975). Courts in many jurisdictions have upheld dress or grooming codes as a legitimate exercise of managerial prerogative, which as long as they can be shown to be reasonably connected with a business interest take priority over the liberty of employees to determine their own appearance. The usual test revolves around some construct of the 'reasonableness' that refers to a 'legitimate business interest'. This business interest has had two main dimensions; first the commercial image of the firm and, second, health and safety considerations. It may be observed that while the latter operates within the framework of technical and medical discourses such discourses are constantly permeated by extraneous elements, for example when matters of appearance, such as beards and long hair, are labelled 'dirty' and thus constructed as a sanitation hazard.

It is the 'commercial image' construct that allows the greatest latitude to employers. The dual thrust of the feminization of the labour force and the rise of feminism has ensured that many of the issues raised by the existence of dress codes have been gendered issues. From the 1960s many jurisdictions experienced controversies around two symbolically gendered issues; long hair on men and whether women could be required to wear skirts. For example, in Canada an important series of 'hair cases' established that such rules are reasonable if they further the commercial image of the firm. The objection to long hair, the moralization of appearance, becomes constructed within the discourses of health and safety. My sense is that where judges and tribunal members shared the prejudices of employers they were prepared to accept the putative 'risks' of long hair being caught in machinery, but as the length of male hair came to excite less moral anxiety this construction disappeared.[12]

There is a larger point to be made concerning the interaction between trade unionism and expansion of work uniforms. Where there is a significant trade union presence employees have treated uniform as an economic element in a wider bargaining relationship. There seems to have been considerable cooperation from trade unions in approving uniforms, particularly where some choice is offered to the individual employees. The introduction of choice brought an end to the potentially explosive issue of women and skirts.[13] In contrast, dress codes and uniforms are also common in industries with low levels of unionization, especially in financial and service sectors (banks, fast-food, etc.). Although grievances may exist few cases enter the legal record because of the absence of unions, the primary initiators of cases before industrial courts and tribunals.

One significant feature that emerges is that dress and grooming codes illustrate the significant discursive shifts that legal discourses, just as much as political discourses, exhibit. Before the 1960s the issue at stake was the extent of the employer's power over dress and appearance as one aspect of the conditions of employment. Today this issue has been completely subsumed by the problematic of discrimination that directs attention to the proportionality in the treatment of different categories of actual or potential employees. This shift is epitomized in the English case of *Schmidt* v *Austicks Bookshops Ltd* (1977): a female employee in a bookstore was required to wear a skirt when serving the public.

Her claim that this was discriminatory was rejected on appeal on the grounds that she was not treated less favourably than male employees since although the particular restriction could not be applied to men, males were subject to comparable restrictions (no jeans, no T-shirts). There are rules of clothing recognized within the community some of which apply to men and some to women. Conversely, in a Canadian case, it was held that men could be required to wear ties in the Ontario Ministry of Labour even though no equivalent restriction was imposed on female employees (*Labour Arbitration News*, April 1991). A departure from this 'equal, but different' approach is found in the recent English case of *McConomy* v *Croft Inns Ltd* (1992) with regard to discrimination in the provision of services. A young man wearing stud earrings was refused service in a Belfast pub; since a woman wearing earrings would have been served, the refusal was held to be discriminatory.

In general there is significant consistency between the approaches of English-language jurisdictions and of the European Union (Pannick 1985: 158–188). The regulation of appearance at work is seen as a legitimate prerogative of management, especially with respect to employees who come into contact with the general public. In the United States conflict over dress codes has been completely subsumed under the discrimination provisions, Title VII, of the Civil Rights Act of 1964. There is a tension in US cases. One dimension is the widely approved principle that nothing in Title VII of CRA 1964 prohibits an employer from making decisions based on grooming and dress as long as they are applied neutrally in accordance with 'community standards'.[14] This principle means that requiring female employees to wear skirts, even when there is no directly analogous rule for male employees, will generally be upheld. On the other hand there is another line of cases that holds that dress and grooming codes constitute sexual discrimination when they are applied differently to men and women. In so far as this tension is resolved the key element is the legitimate business interests of the employer. Thus in *Lanigan* v *Bartlett & Co. Grain* (1979) an employer's dress code rule that 'no women working in executive offices may wear pants' was upheld on the grounds that the decision to project a certain corporate image lies within an employer's prerogative. On the other hand in *Phillips* v *Martin Marietta Corp.* (1971) an employer's policy of refusing to hire women with pre-school children, while continuing to hire men of the same status, was held discriminatory under Title VII, even though the company hired women in other status groups (e.g. unmarried or with older children). The important test seems to be whether or not the criteria of gender differentiation are mutable or immutable, discrimination on the former grounds being legitimate. It is far from clear whether the criteria that the US courts have been striving to develop can resolve this tension. For example, in *Phillips* it is part of the social construction of gender that leads mothers to take more time off work to look after children than do fathers, and that generates a sexist stereotype linking women-with-young-children and absenteeism; there is nothing biological or immutable about this sexual division of labour.

In Australia there has long been a strong liberty principle in place. In *Australian Tramways Employers' Assoc.* v *Brisbane Tramways Co. Ltd* (1912) it was held that 'the common law right of an employee is a right to wear what he chooses, to act as he chooses, in matters not affecting his work. Prima facie a man may wear what he likes so long as he does not offend against decency.'[15] But in *Hart* v *Jacobs* (1981) the court upheld the employer's right to give directions concerning acceptable dress to a male Telecom clerical employee, not ordinarily in contact with the public, who was dismissed for wearing a kaftan and thongs. The recent shift toward the discourses of discrimination confirms, by default, the general acceptability of dress and grooming codes. This drift towards recognition of the legitimacy of dress codes is probably connected to the expansion of uniforms in employment. The link between dress codes and the return of uniforms goes way beyond my agenda but two comments are in order. First, the expansion of uniforms may attest to nothing more than the growing importance of the service sector which, in turn, establishes a pattern or style of employment which is well expressed by the uniformity and global recognizability secured by the fast-food chains. This pattern has subsequently been followed by employers outside the service sector and we may anticipate that occupational uniforms will continue to expand. My second comment is that there is perhaps a wider significance to the return of the uniform as a revival of the occupational costume that largely disappeared in the nineteenth and the first half of the twentieth century. The employer's interest in advertising promotion and the employee's interest in free or subsidized working clothes come together to produce a reinvigoration of the quest for recognizability. I have earlier suggested that the search for recognizability was closely tied to the urbanization of Europe and the rise of sumptuary laws. This new phase, marked by the return of occupational uniforms, may indicate a phase of globalization with intensification of anxieties around renewed urban alienation.

Employment institutions are not the only social institutions involved with the regulation of dress in the late twentieth century. The school is currently locked in battles around the world over the retention or abolition of school uniforms; but uniforms aside, schools continue to play a pervasive role with respect to grooming and respectability, making use of techniques of Foucauldian surveillance and what Ian Hunter calls the 'technologies of moral supervision' (Hunter 1988: 263). These forms of discipline are closely connected to one of the most distinctive manifestations of modernization, namely time discipline. It seems likely that the rediscovery of the work uniform may itself be a component in securing time-keeping (Thompson 1967; Landes 1983).

THE MEDICALIZATION OF MORAL DISCOURSES

While moralizing discourses directed towards the regulation of consumption live on, there has been a more important shift in the discursive formation within which projects for the regulation of consumption are located. Projects of simple or unexpurgated moral regulation are still active. In their most visible form they recur in instinctive responses to immediate social anxiety with the call to 'ban' some symbolically significant form of consumption. For example, public concern over drunk-driving expresses itself through calls for alcohol bans of one kind or another (Gusfield 1981). There is a continuing affinity between the United States and simple moral regulation. There is, of course, the classic case of 'Prohibition' (Gusfield 1963). Aside from alcohol other anxieties have elicited regulatory impulses, for example, changes in women's fashion excited the legislative urge in a number of states that were detailed in Chapter 9. Some part of this moralizing regulatory tradition expresses itself in the complex alliances that more recently have campaigned for anti-pornography ordinances (Downs 1989).

Medicalized regulatory discourses are not new. The spread of venereal diseases to Europe in the late medieval period initiated unremitting medicalization surrounding the regulation of prostitution. One explicit element of medical discourse entered the history of sumptuary law when an enactment in Venice in 1430 prohibited wearing *zoccoli*, a form of platform shoes. These were adopted as a practical measure to keep skirts out of the mud and dirt, but under the pressure of fashion, reached such heights that the wearers were unable to stand unless supported by one or more servants. The prohibition invoked the danger to pregnant women who might fall and abort (Newett 1907: 274), but it should be noted that the ban applied to all women and not just to their pregnant sisters. More recently the dress reform movements of the nineteenth century invoked medical danger in their campaigns against 'unnatural' styles in women's dress (Kunzle 1982).

The characteristic shift during the course of the twentieth century has been towards the medicalization of regulatory discourses. It is increasingly characteristic that regulatory projects are couched in medicalized discourses. The typical regulatory project of the twentieth century locates the logic of control by reference to physiological harm. The long-running struggles over alcohol are less focused on 'drunkenness' as behavioural deviancy, but have constructed alcoholism as a medical condition. There is a connection between the advance and expansion of medicine and the construction of conditions of addiction, dependence and allergy – categories with a sliding moral register – which are applied to an expanding range of potential regulatory objects (Sontag 1983).

Just as the sumptuary discourses of an earlier period exhibited a systematic linkage between different discursive elements, between a moralization of luxury and hierarchic recognizability, or later, between moralization of luxury and economic protectionism, so to with medicalized discourses. There is a persistent coupling of medical and moral discourses in the construction of contemporary regulatory targets. The characteristic logic is that what is immoral is harmful to the health and well-being of either the individual or society, or indeed both. Thus 'moral danger' and 'physiological harm' become coupled. The nineteenth century preoccupation with masturbation provides some wonderful descriptions of both the symptoms and the pathological consequences of this 'secret sin' (Hare 1962).

A feature that perhaps deserves more attention is the increasing burden that the concept 'harm' has been required to play. The concept 'harm' provides a key discursive connection between medical and legal harm such that the medical and jurisprudential discourses are elided, a process exemplified in Joel Feinberg's use of 'harm' as the organizing principle in a liberal jurisprudence of criminal liability (Wolfenden 1957; Feinberg 1984). Furthermore the concept 'harm' provides an expansionary potential that is exemplified in the current controversies surrounding pornography (Williams 1979; Hunter 1993).[16]

While the double-voiced medical/moral discourses are persistent and influential there is an oscillation in their internal competition. Over time a shift occurs which results in the moralization dimension becoming the sub-text behind the erstwhile neutrality of the scientific medical discourse. This is particularly evident in the rhetoric surrounding the advancing regulation directed at the consumption of alcohol, tobacco, and an expanding range of consumable psychoactive drugs.

An important and recurring linkage between moral and medical discourses is provided by the role played by the moral dimension which is persistently directed towards what Ian Hunter calls, 'the ethical discipline of the self' (Hunter 1993: 64–66). These discourses play extensively on the registers of 'dependence' and 'addiction'. Only occasionally does this moralizing dimension come to the forefront, as it did in the opening phase of the AIDS crisis. More frequently the ethical discipline summons the human objects of regulation to self-help and renunciation – to confess, to quit, to practise safe sex, etc.

FUNCTIONAL TRANSFORMATION OF REGULATORY DISCOURSES

I am tempted to conclude that sumptuary law is alive and well in all but name. Such a view has the polemical attraction of standing on its head the conventional wisdom that sumptuary law was doomed to failure and has no place in the modern world. A more cautious version would be that even if sumptuary law is no longer alive, then it has a habit of making many final curtain-calls, whether in the guise of 'Prohibition' or anti-pornography ordinances. However, I resist these polemical extravagances in order to make a more far-reaching set of conclusions.

It is necessary to insist that the liberal aspiration towards legal minimalism in the unstable and shifting realm of the private, while it has the merit of providing a platform from which to call each and every regulatory intervention to account for itself, has served to mask a more important truth. It is simply not the case that modernity has brought with it a general reduction in the regulation of some privileged sphere of the private or personal. There have, of course, been significant displacements with respect to who and what gets regulated, and by whom. These developments have taken place within a general expansion of discipline and surveillance. This expansion of regulation also applies to the field of consumption. Given the enormous expansion and diversification of the consumer market the consuming citizen experiences choice constrained only by purchasing power, and new needs are stimulated, satisfied and superseded with alarming rapidity. It is within this context that the modern regulation of consumption is a viable project only under two conditions, the first involving heavy moralization, usually backed by criminalization, exemplified by drugs control. The second strategy requires an alarmist medicalization and probably some legal intervention, alcohol and tobacco being currently the two most important cases.

I argued in Chapter 6 that while external appearance can be read for signs of deeper personal attributes, the ever-present possibility for deceit and dissimulation provided by clothes means that no regulation of appearance, outside closed institutions, can ever provide a stable regime of recognizability. The shift in the cultural capital of class and the inescapable unreliability of appearential ordering is the single most important cause of the abandonment of the widespread projects of regulating personal appearance. This is borne out by the important shift from the state to the workplace as the locus of the regulation of appearance. And it is worth adding that employment dress regulation could only exist with a sharpening of one axis of the private/public distinction, with a radical casualization of non-work dress and appearance. These inherent limitations of the project do not undermine the importance of sumptuary law and modern restraints on consumption as significant forms of symbolic regulation. As Shively expresses it, in the context of the Japanese dress and consumption codes:

> That sumptuary laws in Japan, like such laws elsewhere, would have limited effectiveness is to be expected, because they were to some extent outbursts of indignation by the ruling class against the presumptuous innovations by inferiors. They were difficult to enforce because they were directed for the most part at only

> the outward manifestations of transition – attacking as they did the symptoms rather than the causes of fundamental change in the society.
>
> (Shively 1964: 134)

However, it is important to go a step further by insisting that such laws and regulations, whether in old or modern form, provide a terrain through which these subterranean movements, rarely perceived with any precision, are fought over in the symbolic arenas of contemporary controversies. The sumptuary laws of the early modern period ceased to exist in their traditional form, epitomized by hierarchic dress codes, and became transformed without any major dislocation from a form of personal regulation to become part of a wide regulation organized around the discourses of public health and social welfare. What remains unchanged is the capacity for controversies over the regulation of consumption to be the bearer, often symbolically, of contemporary social anxieties.

15

Sumptuary Law, Regulation and Governance

A REVISIONIST HISTORY

This book starts out as a revisionist history. It is directed against the widely expressed view that sumptuary laws were an unconscionable constraint on the liberty of the individual expressing itself in the private decisions made in the market-place of consumer choice. Such views came in many forms but persistently evinced a flavour of the unquestioned sense of the superiority of the modern over the pre-modern which was so widespread in the period of high modernity exemplified by the nineteenth century view that 'the Law becomes tyrannous when it prescribes what shall be eaten and what shall be drunk; all such interference is a relapse towards the barbarism of the Middle Ages' (Pike 1968: II: 585). This rejection of the very idea of sumptuary regulation with its strong, but usually unexamined, assertion of the autonomy of a field of private consumption is buttressed by the historical generalization that sumptuary laws were in any case 'doomed to failure'. Since from this standpoint such laws played no part in the emergence of modern law and government they are simply dropped from the record or, at best, relegated to a footnote. The result has been a lack of scholarly attention to sumptuary law and to its treatment as a quaint reminder of a time now sufficiently distant to be looked back on with amusement rather than rancour.

The revisionist dimension of my project has been directed at deflating the arrogance of high modernity in order to undertake an exercise in retrieval. In the first instance retrieval involved bringing together widely dispersed material. The great volume of sumptuary projects were spread widely across the historical record. My realization of the great volume and the persistence of the sumptuary impulse allowed me to push the material beyond an interest in retrieval. It raised questions about how it was that there have been so many and such varied projects for the governance of consumption. It stimulated questions. What part did these laws play in the contemporary webs of governance? Is it true that sumptuary law simply disappeared?

In the first instance it is clear that sumptuary law has its own history. There are a number of distinct types of sumptuary law that exhibit a discernible sequence. This progression can be briefly summarized. The regulation of funerals was followed by a change of regulatory attention to focus on all the rites of passage (births, marriages, deaths, etc.) under the discursive organization of the critique of luxury. The third stage of sumptuary regulation saw a shift to the regulation of conspicuous consumption and, in particular, of dress and other manifestations of fashion. Appearential ordering existed in two main forms. The first exemplified the critique of extravagance by imposing general limits either on expenditure or on the use of particular fabrics or ornamentations. The second variant provided what I have treated as the classic form of sumptuary law, namely the hierarchic dress codes. Thereafter sumptuary regulation became entwined with protectionist economic regulation. Of course, these stages rarely followed one another sequentially and there were frequent returns, reappearances and traces of other forms, as in the final return of the regulation of the vestments of the dead in England in 1666.

The second general feature of the internal history of sumptuary laws was that the shift from one form to another was almost always associated with the emergence of a new discursive linkage or 'coupling' in which the immediate rationale of the sumptuary project became associated with some new discursive context. The most important of these shifts was the uneven and faltering transition from the theological discourses of luxury to the economic discourses of protectionism. The first stage of this transformation involved the theological discourses surrounding the sin of luxury, as a species of the major sin of pride. This gave way before distinctively secular discourses that still retained the central figure of luxury, but inflected it towards the economic wrong of 'extravagance'. Extravagance was conceived of as the wasting of resources that could be more usefully and gainfully employed: the expenditure of both income and time were the targets of the critique of extravagance.[1] In the next stage the sumptuary element came to be displaced or relegated to a minor role in a discursive formation organized around the figures of the economy and the nation and expressed itself most distinctively in economic protectionism. As a result of this process it was no longer such forms of consumption as the wearing of silk and furs that were the target, but it was the wearing of, for example, 'Italian silk' or 'imported furs' that the regulation sought to control. What is distinctive is that the shift from the discourses of luxury to protectionism moved imperceptibly; it is only at the end of the process that it is apparent that the sumptuary content has entirely disappeared from the legal norm to be replaced by the discourses of economic and national interest. Such a change is exemplified in the accomplishment of securing some state capacity for action when confronted with serious threats of famine and social disorder, a stage illustrated by the bringing together of measures of relief in the Book of Orders that provide the framework of response to dearth in England between 1587 and the 1630s.[2]

Alongside such discursive shifts (decouplings and recouplings) there were persistent, or at least repeated, combinations with other separate discourses. I have argued that the most important of these linkages were those with the discourses of gender, generation, class and population. The shifts undergone by sumptuary law can be understood as forms of functional transformation of a rather special sort.

It is in the context of teasing out the couplings between these different discourses that it becomes possible to get beneath their surface and begin to approach explanation by unravelling connections that are not apparent on the discursive surface. There is much to be explained because, at first glance, sumptuary laws often seem strange to the citizen of the late twentieth century; trying to understand the context and contemporary meaning of sumptuary regulation has itself been a challenge. To move from meaning to explanation requires a type of inquiry that starts by seeking to identify the anxieties and preoccupations that underlie the many and varied regulatory projects. For example, the central part played by gender in sumptuary projects reveals the profound social ambiguities and contradictions about the self-presentation of women in a historical period in which they were subject to the processes of privatization and vicarious consumption, were on public display but without public role. These changes and their location in the expanding urban world generated the specific forms within which patriarchal authorities directed sumptuary laws to govern the appearance of women. As I have argued, central to this was the distinctively urban problem of securing and stabilizing the distinction between 'respectable' women and prostitutes. More generally I have suggested that the construction and regulation of gender be situated in the dense and practical field that I have called the political economy of marriage. This focus is exemplified in the connection established between sumptuary laws and the dowry system.

TOWARD A HISTORICAL SOCIOLOGY OF GOVERNANCE

The significance of sumptuary law conceived in the way proposed leads to a focus on the changing configuration of projects of governance. This redirects inquiry away from the perennial question about whether it was effective. While there is much to be learnt from a study of the patterns of enforcement, there are wider considerations. In the first instance sumptuary laws have been examined for the light they throw on the kind of behaviour and excess that generated anxiety and sparked the urge to intervene. It is in the tracking of these discourses of social anxiety that the specificity of the concrete sumptuary projects emerges. The argument has been advanced that the urban sumptuary legislation of the early modern period can best be understood as a response to the quest for recognizability. The modern subject was located within a widening gulf between the individual as private being and the public social role. The former is marked by processes of individualization which are manifest, to modify Bourdieu's terms, in 'private cultural capital' deployed in the search for 'distinction' and 'taste' as a means of securing self-identity. The quest for individuality through the medium of dress and self-presentation is one dimension of this process. The other is the process of 'individuation' whose distinctive form of cultural capital takes on the form of public credentials (qualifications, skills, references and testimonials) and of the disposal of cultural capital (taste, distinction, refinement) that increasingly depends on a non-genetic sense of 'breeding'.

One consequence of this separation is that it becomes both less possible and less necessary to seek to stabilize recognizability through sumptuary law directed towards external appearance. The desire for a legible appearential ordering never entirely disappeared but it became seriously attenuated and only resurfaced in periodic and episodic form. While sumptuary laws were concerned to secure a stable connection between appearance and entitlement, the social conditions in which it did so were every day making the achievement of its goals more unrealizable.

This insight provides a more adequate understanding of the 'failure' of sumptuary laws. It was not so much that they were doomed to failure, but rather that they should be understood as attempts to grapple with a set of social and economic changes that would sooner or later swamp the idea that to secure social recognizability and stabilize it through law was an appropriate object of governance. Yet the persistence of calls for such a project echoed long after the demise of active sumptuary legislation. The sumptuary ethic lived on long past its active legislative existence as a component of a cultural nostalgia for a time when people knew their allotted social place which was recognizable by means of the semiotics of appearance.

The long-run shift of sumptuary projects was from the field of moral regulation to the field of economic policy; this process ran powerfully throughout the early modern period without ever being completed. While the targets of regulation continued to shift and their discursive expression changed accordingly, a deeply embedded and resilient preoccupation formed around a persistent moralization of appearance constructed around the two key parameters of class and gender. Class moralization involved two features: first, a degradation of the labouring classes through the almost universal preoccupation with the declared idleness of the people and, second, the concern with imitation that speaks of a desire to render social difference visible and thus legible. Gender moralization, situated within the ever-present medieval misogyny, revolved around the dichotomy of respectability and dishonour and its close associate, eroticism and its refusal. The general sumptuary phenomenon and its concrete manifestations thus occupied the central social field bounded by the three axes of urbanization, class differentiation and gender polarization.

The social concerns that stimulated the sumptuary projects exhibited surprising vitality. It is significant that the moralization of appearance continues down to the present. Appearance continues to be 'read' in much the same way as physiognomy was in the eighteenth century as a means of access to some underlying social essence. Aside from the detailed semiotics of fashion brought to a self-conscious perfection in the genre established by modern fashion magazines, appearance is still read as a means of discerning the boundary between insiders and outsiders, the virtuous and the vicious, the respectable and the immoral. Today the legibility of appearance involves both 'low' and 'high' intensity governance. Low intensity dress codes apply in the ubiquity of standard signs that 'Dress standards apply' which provide a platform for intervention. High intensity governance of appearance occurs in both the formal and informal dress codes of employment institutions. They are particularly active in senior grades of the professional and administrative classes. More generally it should be noted that low-level moralization of appearance persists, despite the individualistic self-conception of the age with regard to such judgements surrounding criteria of 'smartness', 'neatness' and 'cleanliness'. Employment tribunals still handle wrongful dismissal actions in which employers and managers continue to invoke moralizing indictments of personal appearance.

The moralization of appearance remains strongly linked to gender. The dress of women remains subject to the calculus of respectability. The length of skirts and the plunge of necklines remain active criteria in the policing of the boundary between 'good girls' and 'bad girls'. The disappearance of formal 'marks of infamy' has not eliminated the judgemental categories through which the self-presentation of women is judged. Today such governance has become increasingly more complicated and has, in particular, become an important illustration of a shift toward the governance of the self on which I will have more to say below.

More generally it is important to my case to insist on the continuing significance of projects of moral regulation. Such regulation became separated from other regulationary interventions by a discursive transformation that opened up a gap between the theological critique of luxury and the economic critique of extravagance which I have argued played such a central part in the history of sumptuary law. It should be noted that the critique of extravagance has not entirely disappeared. It lives on with considerable vitality in the moralization that underlies the complex field of the regulation of gambling (Miers 1984; Dixon 1991). More generally, moral regulation has increasingly become associated with a medicalization of the 'disciplines' and the regulatory discourses. The most active fields of contestation over moral regulation, led by the complex constituted of drugs, tobacco and alcohol, are today conducted primarily within a medicalized discursive formation. There is a general trend towards the displacement of state bureaucracies by private experts in the orchestration of the government of the self, with the aerobic trainer and dietitian joining the psychiatrist as part of the battery of experts that surround the self-governance of the metropolitan middle classes. It is important, however, to recognize the continuing role of state agencies. This is especially the case with reference to what are probably the major projects of contemporary self-governance, namely tobacco, alcohol and AIDS. In all of these the state continues to play a decisive role in the sponsorship and coordination of these medico-moral projects.

In the most recent forms of moral regulation there has been a significant shift away from a paternalistic medicalization and they have become the sites of what may be described as an intensified governance of the self. It is the cultivated preoccupation with the outer appearance and the inner health of the body that has become the focus of state sponsored interventions into the consumption of legal and illegal drugs. It is significant to note that these key current projects exemplify a very distinctive fusion of medical and moral regulation, hence my concept of medico-moral regulation. The 'heart' in its double physiological and symbolic sense has become the key target of these projects of medico-moral regulation.

Only in the field of the governance of sexuality are pure forms of moral regulation still encountered. The classic case is the continuing contestation over the regulation of pornography. The long-standing disputes of the regulation of prostitution have lost many of the characteristics of the 'purity movements' of the eighteenth and nineteenth centuries, although such discourses are often not far below the surface. Controversies over prostitution now take the form of disputes between different regulatory strategies; the voice of prohibition is now largely absent.

In each historical epoch there has been a distinctive form of ideological critique of the existing social currents which finds its own way of insisting on the desirability of regulatory intervention. The specific targets of this moral critique have changed considerably over time. We have seen the persistence of the critique of luxury that stretched from the early civilizations of the Mediterranean basin down to eighteenth century Europe. More recently we have been witness to the power that the critique of 'permissiveness' has come to have in organizing demands for intervention in the fields of sexuality and popular culture.

What interests me is whether or not there are any common or persisting patterns to these successive organizing critiques. There are a number of potential candidates. The first is the discourse of 'immorality' in which the present is stigmatized as exhibiting a lapse from some privileged moral standard that is presented as necessary for the preservation of the social fabric. Patrick Devlin's, now classic, insistence that it is the legal enforcement of the moral standards which provide the cement of core social relations is only an updated version of an enduring moralizing tradition (Devlin 1959). Another enduring organizing element of moralizing discourses closely linked to those of 'immorality' is that of 'degeneracy', importing a distinctive sense of decline.

My inclination is to think that conservative or romantic critiques, although they may change their immediate targets, for example from luxury to permissiveness, have an underlying common structure. There are a number of variants of the conservative critique, but their common core invokes some past golden age which is counterposed to the perceived 'present danger' (luxury, immorality, permissiveness, etc.) and predicts some 'future danger' generally organized around the idea of social disintegration. The second major form of such moralizing critiques employs the metaphor of disease. A past health (another way of conceiving of a golden age) comes to yield 'symptoms' (extravagance, sumptuosity, etc.) that are evidence of a deep malady (the sin of pride) which can only be treated by an appropriate regulatory intervention to effect a cure (sumptuary law, family values, etc.). Walzer, for example, draws attention to the deployment by English Puritans of a disease metaphor as an integral component of their organic analogy (Walzer 1965). As always there is an important place for an extended discursive analysis of the tropes within which projects of governance and self-governance are located as typified in my discussion of medico-moral regulation.

This study of the regulation of consumption has been organized around the emerging theoretical paradigm that I have called the sociology of governance. I am hopeful that its value has been established in the contribution it has made to my attempt to unravel the history of sumptuary law. However, there are particular characteristics of sumptuary law that should be mentioned which have made it impossible to bring into play the full potential of this theoretical framework. First, sumptuary regulation has overwhelmingly involved state-initiated projects and is thus a typical top-down form of government. Governance, however, is not primarily the work of governments; it is located within all social relations. Only occasionally did sumptuary law emerge from the interaction of state and non-state institutions and practices. In Renaissance Italy the alliance between church and state was important in generating legislation, but here the church was itself a state. In England, where the guilds played some part in both the legislation and enforcement of sumptuary rules, it seems clear that the guilds and corporations were dragged complaining into the sumptuary arena by a powerful state. In other words sumptuary law to a large extent involved 'government' rather than 'governance'.

One of the potentials offered by the sociology of governance is that of transcending the conventional external/internal distinction between 'government' and the 'government of the self', or as I have preferred to call these processes, governance and self-governance. Important though Foucault's work on the 'government of the self' undoubtedly is, there is a tendency for it to rely upon an unexplored notion of 'internalization'. Individuals are made subject to external disciplinary imperatives that they come over time to internalize and take over for themselves. Thus, for example, table manners and politeness are consciously transmitted through family socialization; similarly punctuality is learned in school and becomes internalized in a universe of time-pieces and time-watching and stands in some causal relationship to the imperatives of the factory. While there is obviously much that is useful in this type of analysis it does not differ significantly from the older tradition of social control theory with its construction of 'society' as a rarefied and brooding omnipresence bearing down up the hapless individual.

The idea of self-governance needs to capture a more active process in which the subject/person is not merely subjected to external governance, but exists in active tension and resistance to external governance. In this context it becomes important to explore the ways in which the subject is not some inert substrate on which the disciplines imprint themselves. This type of dynamic is brought out effectively in Bruce Curtis' study of the formation of the 'educational state' in Canada. The strongly disciplinary forms of organization and governance of the early schools provoked considerable local and popular resistance. This resistance was not simply oppositional, but was sustained by some alternative visions of a more participatory and relevant education. Curtis' thesis is that this resistance actually served to reinforce and strengthen the bureaucratic and centralist tendencies within the educational system (Curtis 1988). Self-governance needs to be conceptualized as an active and contradictory process – indeed, if one is still permitted to use the term, a dialectical process.

There has been relatively little opportunity to explore this interaction between governance and self-governance in the present study of sumptuary law. The most important exception is provided, as noted above, by the continuing moralization of the self-presentation of women. The ever-present tensions between display and concealment, and between eroticism and modesty discussed in earlier chapters, stem from the characteristic ambiguity that seems to be inherent in the semiotics of fashion. This ambiguity is exemplified by the co-presence of exposure and formality in the evening dress and is underlined by the choice allowed to women in the fabric, cut and colour of the evening dress when compared to the severe restraints that hark back to the 'great male renunciation' characterized in male evening dress. The implication to be teased out is that female preoccupation with dress attests, not to any essentialist notions of feminine vanity, but rather to the important sociological truth that for women their clothing is much more critically an arena of self-governance. The ambiguity of exposure and concealment, sumptuousness and simplicity are matters of everyday choice. However, such choices are never simply private, matters between the individual and her mirror; rather they are choices made in the context of a veritable battery of governance. These externalities are typified by the role of fashion magazines. Today the issue of fashion is no longer governed by a clear social hierarchy. In the first half of the present century there were class-specific fashion journals. Today choice is certainly more free from narrow class constraints, but it is also more complex. The individual has first to make some existential choice between alternative paradigms represented, for example, by *Cosmopolitan* and *Vanity Fair* and the myriad other culturally specific models of the self that are on offer on the superabundant display shelves. I do not attempt to come to any conclusions on these matters, but merely use them to underline the crucial importance to any project of the sociology of governance of grappling with the complex interaction of governance and self-governance.

For present purposes it is sufficient to note that these considerations are instructive in helping to move beyond 'internalization' to the idea that self-governance involves self-actualizing engagements with the tensions and choices of life. It is only in this way that the individual becomes a subject who is at one and the same time governed and self-governed and thus enjoins a resistance to the pervasive counterposing of freedom and governance.

THE GOVERNANCE OF CONSUMPTION

The retrieval of the history of the sumptuary laws has been the central focus of this book. In the first instance it has provided a way of making sense of projects of regulation that, at first glance, appear strange and archaic. The very distance of projects such as the imposition of hierarchic colour codes or of marks of infamy has the distinct advantage of making it easier to avoid making use of contemporary models to explain the varied projects represented by the corpus of the sumptuary laws. Simply, it makes it easier to approach the material with fewer presuppositions.

The attempt to make sense of the unfamiliar has yielded a stronger and fresher sense in which projects directed toward the governance of consumption have such a persistent place in social life that it makes it easier to attend to the place of consumption and regulation today. It should be borne in mind that 'consumption' is not simply the other face of production; nor is it simply the mechanism for the satisfaction of needs. Consumption is a process within which wants are generated whose satisfaction can induce pleasure and excitement – and of course, disappointment. It is important to take account of this link between pleasure and consumption since it underlies how it can be that consumption became and remains a major target of moralization and regulation.

The reference to the 'consuming passions' in my title is no mere rhetorical flourish. Changes in patterns of consumption produce anxieties and attest to the inherent instability of the relationship between needs and wants. It is worth repeating that I hope to have avoided falling into the trap of displacing the preoccupation of industrial societies with the mechanisms and dynamics of production by focusing on consumption. I have attempted to show the intimate connections that have existed in concrete forms between consumption and production and, more importantly, the way in which governance always acts upon everyday life. While the distinction between governance and self-governance serves a useful analytical distinction, these dimensions are always already coextensive.

The history of sumptuary laws serves to reveal the shifting preoccupations of the projects of governance. The earliest forms centred on the regulation of funerals disclose the tensions involved in the emergence of new political entities typified by both the ancient city-states and the Renaissance cities which displaced kinship or clan-based systems of social relations. The late medieval targeting of pre-modern practices of feasting, epitomized by weddings and other rites of passage, serves to highlight the emergence of new regimes of both the governance of the self and of the link between the organization of labour-time and patterns of consumption. Whereas much of the literature on the 'reform of popular culture' and of 'consumer societies' has focused on the early modern period, my conclusions add to those inquiries that have pushed back these historical boundaries. It now seems sensible to conclude that the reform of popular culture is an endemic feature of social life. Once that is said, it becomes possible to identify the shifting targets, changing tactics and varied techniques of intervention. The sumptuary laws, given the fascinating shifts in their tactical and discursive construction, provide a fruitful instance of such processes.

The identification of the sumptuary laws with endemic projects of the reform of popular culture serves to cut through the prevalent conceptual wall between the pre-modern and the modern. It is not that the profound significance of the processes exemplified by Elias's inquiries into the 'civilizing process' is to be denied, but rather that the inquiries should be extended both backwards and forwards. To pursue this objective it is imperative that we avoid the reification of such a notion as a 'civilizing process' and instead attend to the specific modality of the concrete projects of governance. It is in this light that I have tried to grapple with the location of the most intensive and extensive sumptuary governance as being on 'the margins of modernity'. In the first place this involves the revisionist refusal of the orthodox equation of sumptuary law with the pre-modern. In so doing I have been at pains to avoid a simple reversal. It is no part of my argument to contend that the sumptuary laws were a mechanism of modernization, but neither were they some residual trace of feudalism. Rather I claim that it is significant that sumptuary laws were 'around', that is they were characteristically part of the scenery during periods of decisive transitions which, despite the invectives of post-modernism, it remains useful to characterize as projects of modernity, such as urbanization, nation-state formation, discovery of national economies and the projects of the governance of populations.

To say that sumptuary laws were 'around', that is present during these processes, understates my case. In diverse respects the sumptuary laws were part and parcel of these processes. They were intimately linked to the processes of urbanization through the quest to stabilize recognizability. They were a component of the protracted contestation between the landed nobilities and the urban bourgeoisie; they intervened in the regulation of dowries and in populationist anxieties. Everywhere they were part of projects for the reform of popular culture directed at both the work and the recreations of the labouring classes. They were intimately linked with the emergence of new economic rationalities as they underwent the functional transformation that gave rise to protectionist mercantile economic strategies. They were ever-present in the shifting governance of gender and generational relations.

I suggest that a serviceable way of capturing this presence of the sumptuary laws is the formula that they straddled modernity. They had no essence that marks them as conservative or transformative projects. Once we forego any illusion that modernization involved some coherent and teleological set of strategies we can better grasp how the sumptuary laws formed an element of the tactics of governance from which the emergent strands of modernity came to penetrate the practices of everyday life. In these processes the sumptuary laws pointed in both directions: they were, at one and the same time, projects that resisted and facilitated these processes.

These considerations suggest the need to return to the question of the 'failure of sumptuary law'. It is important to avoid any simple reversal of the preoccupation with instrumental rationality that evaluates projects of governance by the extent to which they fulfil their declared objectives. To insist that governance always fails provides a necessary counterbalance to such views, but it runs the risk of sliding towards a nihilistic dismissal of the pretensions of government and governmentality. Somewhere between success and failure lies the truth of governance. The sociological tradition has one serviceable strand that contributes to overcoming the paradox of success and failure. It is provided by the theme of unintended consequences most closely associated with the name of Robert Merton and more recently systematized by Raymond Boudon (Merton 1937; Boudon 1982). Valuable though this idea is it is preoccupied with contrasting goals and outcomes. While goals or motives of social action can and should never be ignored they need to be given a more limited role in order to focus on governance and other forms of social action as sets of practices, tactics and discourses. Norbert Elias attempted to advance these considerations with his concept of 'figurations' (Elias 1970; Mennell 1989). Elias employed this concept to refer to the outcomes of the sets of social relations that arise from unplanned and unintended individual actions, and to contrast these outcomes with terms such as 'social system' that presume the unity of the social totality; social figurations intentionally do no more than identify sets or networks of social relations. While I find the term 'figuration' an unnecessary neologism, it fits well with my concern to maintain a focus upon the 'failure' of governance by insisting on the methodological tactic of 'suspending' intentions. It is not that intentions are unimportant, but rather that they should figure at the end of the inquiry so that primacy may be accorded to the aim of getting behind intentions and unintended consequences. One small indicator of this concern is a preference for paying attention to 'projects' rather that 'strategies'; the former focuses on what gets done while the later focuses on the grand design. The practically important step is to study governance as a set of practices, tactics and discourses that have no necessary unity.

A convenient summary of the approach advocated is to keep in mind the slogan that governance is always incomplete. Applied to the exploration of the history of sumptuary laws the result is the attention that has been paid to the need to understand sumptuary projects in their connection with other projects of governance in a way that views these connections as concrete conjunctures rather than the unfolding of some grand design. This leads to my contention that the sumptuary laws did not so much die or expire, but rather that the specific discursive framework in which they had existed gave way before new projects and new tactics directed toward the regulation of consumption. While the sumptuary laws faded the regulation of the consuming passions has remained down to the present an active field of governance and self-governance.

Notes

CHAPTER 1 WHY STUDY SUMPTUARY LAW?

1. Representative is the definition of sumptuary law as 'a law to prevent extravagance in private life by limiting the expenditure on clothing, food, furniture, etc.' *Webster's New International Dictionary* (1959).
2. These authors, while recognizing connections between their work, do not form a 'school', nor do many of them use the label 'sociology of governance'. The following references are not exhaustive and serve only to introduce this growing body of work: Burchell *et al.* (1991); Dean (1991); Gordon (1991); Rose and Miller (1990); Wickham (1992).
3. The other current usages of 'regulation' that I have in mind are 'regulation theory' in political economy (Boyer 1990) and the preoccupation with state agencies on the part of researchers in the field of regulatory law.
4. For a fuller theoretical discussion of the relationship between law and the forms of regulation see Hunt (1993).
5. I take as a model of this attempt to track displaced anxieties the study by Stuart Hall and his colleagues of the 'mugging crisis' in England in the 1970s where they disclose how the explosive judicial, media and popular responses to the specific 'discovery' of mugging involved deeper preoccupations about the linked realities of race, youth and inner city decline (Hall *et al.* 1978). For a recent application of the idea of displaced anxiety, see Newburn (1992: 171).

CHAPTER 2 A SHORT HISTORY OF SUMPTUARY LAW

1. For other overviews of the history of sumptuary laws see Vincent (1937), Buchner (1981) and Boehn (1932–35).
2. There has been no significant study of Greek sumptuary laws. The most interesting work is Alexiou's on the funeral lamentation, which has quite a lot to say about funereal regulations (Alexiou 1974). Mills is useful on dress rules (Mills 1984). There studies aside, details on Greek sumptuary laws are scattered and peripheral.
3. Roman sumptuary law has received little sustained attention. Devi Miles' doctoral thesis provides considerable detail, but the analysis of its place within Roman social relations is superficial (Miles 1987). Mommsen (1862–64), Astin (1989: 184–86) and Scott (1973) provide useful detail on the early period. Nörr's discussion of the Augustan marriage laws is helpful (Nörr 1981), as is Toher on funeral regulations (Toher 1986). In general there is surprisingly limited material

on Roman sumptuary law; I suspect that this is to be explained as an unconscious reflex of the modernist dismissal of sumptuary regulation as doomed to failure.

4. The ending of the military emergency produced strong pressure for repeal, the debate around which produced a report by Cato that 'Roman women whom neither counsel, nor shame, nor their husbands' orders could keep at home, blockaded every street in the city and every entrance to the Forum' (Lefkowitz and Fant 1982: 177).
5. For present purposes I define feudalism in the following terms: a system of closed hierarchic relations in which the direct producers are tied to the land, first by military force and later by religious-political authority, in such a way that the extraction of surplus is secured by the linkage between social hierarchy and the distribution of privileges over land.
6. The sources primarily relied upon concerning Japanese sumptuary law are: Hall (1906, 1908, 1909, 1979), Hearn (1904), McClain (1982), Shively (1955, 1965) and Wigmore (1969).
7. It is interesting to note that the first English statute in 1363 dealt systematically with differential alimentary rules for a set of social class and occupational categories.
8. Alimentary regulation was to persist until the end of the seventeenth century in Scotland (Shaw 1979) and into the eighteenth century in Portugal (Marques 1981).
9. I class clothing as a 'durable' luxury because, given the high cost relative to income of most clothing subject to sumptuary rules, it was made to last, as is evidenced by the fact that clothes not infrequently formed a major part of both medieval and early modern inventories and bequests (Braunstein 1988; Thrupp 1948).
10. Acts of Parliament of Scotland; hereafter APS.
11. Other alimentary legislation followed in 1581, 1584, 1621 and 1629.
12. There is a collection of 32 sumptuary edicts of remarkable detail covering the period 1650–1682 in the British Library (Venice n.d.); others report that Venice passed more than 80 sumptuary laws during the seventeenth century (Burke 1987: 144).
13. There were also sumptuary rules imposed in the French settlements in 'New France' that is now Quebec. The law imposed on the settlers was French domestic sumptuary law, and since I have little evidence beyond its existence I will focus attention on the New England colonies.
14. In 1676, Connecticut copied the 1651 Massachusetts law; earlier Connecticut laws gave town constables the general power to restrain 'all such as they judge to exceed their conditions and ranks' (Foster 1971: 29).
15. Statutes of the Realm; hereafter SR.

CHAPTER 3 TILTING AGAINST THE WINDMILLS OF FASHION?

1. APS IV: 626 *c.* 25, *c.* 1.13.
2. Evelyn reported that Charles proposed to adopt a 'Persian' style the Evelyn had himself recommended as an alternative to the dominance of French fashions; there is a strong sense here of clothing and fashion being closely linked to a sense of national identity.
3. I suspect, but do not want to push the point too strenuously, that this conception of fashion is borne out by the counter-factual example of the existence of producers in England often designated by the rubric 'By appointment to H.M. the Queen', who assiduously resist change and claim merit for their 'traditional' product. For 'traditional' products to exist presupposes a context in which change is endemic and thus conscious effort is necessary in order to preserve the traditional.
4. Sombart argued that the Papal court at Avignon was the first proper court and instituted the routinization of luxury (Sombart 1967).
5. Young's cyclical trends refer to the modern period only, but some features of her basic types are apparent in the medieval period; her three types – 'back-fullness', 'tubular' and 'bell-shaped' – refer primarily to the shape of skirts.
6. There are good reasons for resisting his contention that 'the East' did not have fashion because these societies were 'static'; it is not that variation in the rate of change is without significance: the preoccupation with fashion, although its specific content differed from that in the West, was also very much a response to socio-economic tensions.
7. In the seventeenth century small dolls dressed *à la mode* circulated among upper-class women.
8. This idea of imitation as a general principle of human sociality was advanced in a parallel development by Gabriel Tarde (1903).
9. In similar terms E.A. Ross argued that fashion is a process of 'rhythmic imitation' manifesting tension between uniformity and change.
10. It is interesting to note that there is a marked sexual dimorphism in the story of the dress of servants; the dress of female servants did not follow this law of transposed ossification, but always remained more radically distinguished from that of their mistresses.
11. Jewish communities were much concerned with the maintenance of sexual dimorphism. Mirrors came to be identified with female vanity with the result that men were prohibited the use of mirrors (Epstein 1948: 66).
12. More recently the role of conspicuous leisure has become more complex with the rise of the apparently democratic preoccupation with physical fitness and health. Absorption in the pursuit of exercise, diet and health tends to require both surplus leisure and surplus income, but significantly these are neither necessary nor sufficient conditions, hence the democratic dimension of exercise culture.
13. The concept 'imagined class' borrows from and extends Benedict Anderson's 'imagined community' that has made such a produc-

tive contribution to recent discussion of nation and nationality (Anderson 1983).

14. Such a bankruptcy was epitomized by the arrogance of Southern slaveowners who ridiculed the attempts of recently freed slaves to relocate partners and children and to solemnize their marriages as an 'imitation' of their white owners (who, of course, were responsible for ripping apart the familial relations on the 'block' as husbands, wives and children were sold apart) (Litwick 1979: 241).
15. And it seems likely that it was the opening up of such refined sports as tennis at the end of the nineteenth century that provided the immediate direction of the twentieth century revolution in women's fashion (Weibel 1977: 189).
16. Dress as eloquence is especially evident in movies; the attention to detail alongside the capacity of audiences to intuitively grasp the various genres within which the cinema operates makes possible extremely powerful statements, of which the 'entrance' of a character is used to make major claims about the identity projected. To use a familiar example, Ingrid Bergman's entrance scene in *Casablanca* creates an instant statement of virginal sensuousness, sophistication and vulnerability through the simple elegance of her clothing.
17. Hollander's point can be extended by drawing attention to the different conventions and practices operative in pornography in which items of clothing such as stockings and high-heels serve as very specific mechanisms of sexualizing the naked body.
18. For further discussion of distinguishing marks and marks of infamy see Chapters 6 and 9.
19. The earring has more recently figured in the hostility shown towards the adoption of the earring by young males in North America and Europe in which 'foreignness' and effeminacy provide the negative linkage.
20. By the early eighteenth century the masked ball had become a major commercial institution in London and was widely regarded as the occasion for sexual licence (especially for women), transvestism and homosexuality (Castle 1986: 156).
21. Marshall Sahlins (1976: 178) draws attention to other dichotomous couplets that figure in the way in which clothing terms periodize and genderize social relations: he lists public/private, work/leisure, town/country, day/evening, male/female, adult/adolescent.
22. Colour codes may have had some historical indexical aspects; for example, purple dye was originally extracted at great expense from the purpura shellfish of the Mediterranean.

CHAPTER 4 'AS IF GOD HAD NOT MADE THEM FINE ENOUGH': MORALIZING LUXURY

1. John Sekora (1977) in an extended study of the critiques of luxury argues that the moralization of luxury in England peaks in the eighteenth century. My sense is that his view is something of a flourish

since this period forms the heart of his study; what I suggest is significant is the remarkable persistence and ubiquity of the critique of luxury. Indeed it would be an interesting study to attempt to trace whether there is any discernible periodization in the assault on luxury, whether it comes in for attack more under certain social conditions than others.

2. The anthropological importance of the gift and of ritual exchange does not negate the conception of luxury as divisive, since these mechanisms are as much socially regularized ways of responding to inequalities in distribution as they are vehicles for its celebration.
3. A persistent feature in recent European opposition to US military adventures plays on this image of American 'weakness', an army unable to fight without steak, Coca-Cola and the other 'necessities' of American 'luxury'.
4. It is interesting to note that during Savonarola's dominance during the 1490s there was only one sumptuary law which did not address women's dress; it focused on the clothing of boys. But he did mobilize vigilante youth patrols searching homes for immodest dresses and wigs.
5. Sekora's inability to grapple with what we might call the 'material' historical role of luxury is an illustration of the inherent limitation of the tradition of the 'history of ideas' unless it stops to inquire about 'practices'.
6. Very similar concerns about the consequences of excess in apparel were expressed by Sir Thomas Smith in 1581 (Smith 1969: 83).
7. Similar sentiments are expressed by 'A Compassionate Conformist' in 1682 who derives a polemic against 'naked necks and shoulders' and 'painting and black patches' from the vices of luxury and vanity (Compassionate Conformist 1682).
8. One of the first social purity movements in England, the seventeenth century Societies for Reformation of Manners (SRM), were remarkably unconcerned about new legislative programmes, but used persistent campaigns of private prosecutions against drunkenness, prostitution and Sunday observance (Curtis and Speck 1976). It is interesting to notice that the ideal pursued by the SRMs was that of a self-regulating community where each citizen curbed the sins of his neighbour. It was very much this model that, briefly at least, took root in the New England Puritan community of Massachusetts Bay (Shurtleff 1968; North 1974).
9. The concern with the regulation of labour can be traced back to the Statute of Labourers of 1349, but it is only from the second half of the sixteenth century that the preoccupation with a conception that government should be concerned to stimulate employment comes to the fore. There is much scope for a Foucauldian account of the governmentality and state formation of this period to supplement the standard economic histories.
10. Note the presence of an even more marked concession to moralizing discourses in the pragmatic resignation that suggests that if you

cannot eliminate vice the best you can do is to regulate it and turn it some advantage, a position that is even more pronounced in Mandeville's case for public brothels (Mandeville 1973).

11. An issue which I have not followed up is that of nationalism. In a period in which there has been such an urgent reexamination of the question of nationalism, it is noticeable that attention is focused on the eighteenth and early nineteenth century. My impression is that an important stage occurs much earlier, in the fifteenth and sixteenth centuries, when the nation comes to be conceived not so much as a military entity engaged in conquest or subject to invasion, but increasingly as an economic entity.
12. Evidence of pronouncements within this mercantilist discourse become more frequent, but do not become common until after the passing of the sumptuary epoch: in England, for example, they do not appear regularly until the mid-seventeenth century. It was not until the mid-eighteenth century that the discursive transition was completed and the private pursuit of gratification was recognized as a major force in the stimulation of economic activity (Johnson 1932).
13. My usage has no necessary connection with Teubner's usage. I hope, however, I am engaging in a constructive borrowing rather than a misappropriation.
14. For example, Robert Williams provides a fascinating account of the theological debates associated with the Spanish colonization of the New World in which a dominant strand invoked the 'natural idleness' of the 'natives' as justifying the colonial mission of saving the natives from themselves (Williams 1990: 87).

CHAPTER 5 THE FUNDAMENTAL CONTRADICTION OF SUMPTUARY REGULATION

1. Exemptions were granted to those with incomes below £200 who held public office or had an education or employment 'above the ordinary degree'.
2. Originally in second century BC senators were seated separately at the games. In the next century the equestrian order was allocated the first 14 rows at all entertainment; later married men, bachelors and boys were segregated (Miles 1987).
3. An illustration of such a process is provided by the fact that I had for many years worn a particular brand of waterproof waxed cotton coat, a 'knowledge' accumulated from many years of outdoor pursuits. In the mid-1980s fashion took a rural turn; its devotees in England were referred to as 'Sloane Rangers'. The style was signified by four-wheel drive vehicles that never left the city, green rubber or Wellington boots that never made contact with mud, and my favourite brand of waterproof coat. My response to this intrusion of fashion into my typical intellectual's pretence of anti-fashion was that I retrieved an old and very battered specimen of the coat. I now realize

that I was, unwittingly, following the behest of fashion since what I was doing was signalling to new and intrusive wearers of the same garment an antecedent claim to priority, to an 'older' and thus superior knowledge. This fashion move is most evident in the long-running esteem accorded to faded denim.

CHAPTER 6 RECOGNIZABILITY: 'THE MINGLE-MANGLE OF APPAREL'

1. A possible snag with this generalization is that a number of the more comprehensive English sumptuary statutes do make reference to occupational categories, for example carters, ploughmen, drivers of the plough, oxherds, cowherds, shepherds and others are referred to in *c.* 15 of the 1363 Act. These categories are all occupational descriptors of a socio-economic class, for which the modern term would be agricultural wage-labourers. There was certainly no interest in separating one occupation from another, by appearance or in any other way; far from it – this section actually served to obliterate occupational distinctions.
2. It is important to avoid any modernist disparagement of ritual pageantry as trivial or a mere survival. Pageants, processions, feasts and calendar rituals were a central feature of social life over a long period of time, certainly up until the Industrial Revolution and arguably beyond (Anglo 1969; Bushway 1982; Trexler 1984). I recall moving to industrial Lancashire in the 1960s and finding the Whitsun Wakes still thriving practices.
3. However, Cunnington and Lucas are undoubtedly correct in arguing that over the centuries workwear has been more significant for its unsuitability than for its functional adaptation (Cunnington and Lucas 1967).
4. There has been a surprising expansion of occupational uniforms in post-industrial capitalism; in the expanding service sector uniforms for everyone from airline personnel to fast-food chains are endemic. Here a mix of motives is at work; most obviously trade advertising and corporate identity are significant, as are aspects of complex internal hierarchies where rank can be visually displayed. In addition I suggest that issues of internal control and discipline need to be taken into account in explaining this resurgence of the work uniform.
5. Many of these fairs lasted into the twentieth century; many became transformed into fun-fairs. I recall growing up in the 1950s in Harpenden, about 25 miles north of London, that had only recently ceased to be a rural village to become a London commuter town. The largest annual fun-fair was known locally as the 'statty fair' even though nobody seemed to have any explanation for this name.
6. It is interesting to reflect on the characteristics that led specific occupations to adopt uniforms. Two considerations suggest themselves; first, that there was probably some respect in which uniforms were manifestations of state formation (posts and police fit this type);

the second factor is with employments in which there existed strong hierarchical divisions of labour (railways and nursing fit this category).

7. This may be contrasted with the contemporary period in which the centrality of work manifests itself in that – for the middle classes, at least – their occupational clothing, typically business suits, consumes a high proportion of their clothing budget and is a very important arena of display for both men and women. It may be that occupational appearance and its regulation remains today one of the significant differences between the middle and the working class.
8. 1 & 2 Philip & Mary, *c.* 2, 1555; SR 4(1): 239 and 24 Hen. VIII, *c.* 13, 1533; SR 3:430–32.
9. Proclamation 1 Eliz. I 21/10/1559; Dyson 1618: No. 14.
10. 24 Henry VIII, *c.* 13; SR 3: 430–32.
11. 8 Eliz. I 12/2/1566; Dyson 1618: No. 94.
12. Ewing draws attention to an interesting detail when she notes that about midway through the reign of Elizabeth I portraits suddenly ceased to show her in furs (Ewing 1981).
13. Male renunciation of fur has its own history; for example, the male fur-coat persisted until more recently in North America than in Europe; climatic factors aside, this is probably to be explained by reference to the prevalent forms of national and gender mythology. The wilderness and its associations with hunting have had a special place in the formation of masculinity in both the United States and in Canada.
14. One of the factors that undoubtedly reduced the significance of fur in Europe was scarcity induced by over-trapping; over time this led to the rise of Russia and northern Scandinavia as a major source of furs. Then the massive expansion of the fur trade that resulted from the opening up of the Canadian trade produced a major surge in the deployment of furs as conspicuous consumption that reached its peak on either side of the Second World War, after which furs passed into the realm of mass consumption and created a major stimulus for the production of artificial fibres.
15. 24 Hen. VIII, *c.* 13; SR 3: 430–32. The importance of this statute was that it was to be repeated and summarized for the next 70 years.
16. In Portugal scarlet garments were reserved for the use of the royal family (Marques 1971: 90).
17. Bogatyrev (1971) illustrates a customary use of clothes as a 'code of recognizability'; he shows that folk costume produces a strong set of prescriptive dress rules (e.g. a married woman can never wear the costume of an unmarried maiden; widows have distinctive clothing, etc.).
18. 34 Edw. III, *c.* 10; SR 1: 367. The legislation, by providing for the postponement of the branding provision for first offenders, suggests that it was intended as a threat.
19. 1 Edw. VI, *c.* 3; SR 4(2): 5–8.
20. Tattooing of marks to 'record' offences against military discipline was used in the British army until the late nineteenth century (Brain 1979).

21. A similar certainty about the revelatory truth of external signs or marks was important in the searches conducted for the 'devil's marks' on the bodies of suspected witches (Perkins 1608).
22. In New England there was a veritable alphabet of distinguishing marks to be worn by offenders or branded on repeat offenders: 'A' for adultery 'B' for blasphemy, through to 'V' for venery (Miller 1966: 255–58).
23. For an extended discussion of struggles surrounding customary ceremonies and punishments see Fabre (1989).
24. Such practices found their places in colonial administrations and persisted until the 1960s in the practice of the 'disk list' system imposed on the Inuit peoples in Canada (Smith 1993).
25. A lone example of another form of distinguishing mark might be evidence of a different form of degradation or possibly the beginning of trade marks. An English statute of 1523 required that the products of alien craftsmen should carry a distinguishing mark 'by the which their wares, vessels and workmanship that they make may be known' (14 & 15 Hen. VIII, *c.* 2; SR 3, 208).
26. A preoccupation with nostalgic themes is one of the components in current debates over post-modernism (Edgar 1987; Turner 1990).
27. The phrase is harnessed to good effect as a title by Christopher Hill applying it to the seventeenth century (Hill 1972).
28. 8 Hen. VII Procl. 18/2/1493; Hughes and Larkin (1964: No. 30). That the authorities continued to be troubled is witnessed by the 1597 'Acte against lewde and wandering persons pretending themselves to be Soldiers and Marryners' (39 Eliz. I, *c.* 17; SR 4(2), 915–16).
29. 5 Eliz. I, *c.* 20; SR 4(1), 448.
30. 32 Hen. VIII, *c.* 11; SR 3, 755. Since much of this statute was directed against poaching (making the stealing of hawks' eggs and the taking of deer and rabbits a capital felony) it may be a forerunner of the *Black Acts* to which E.P. Thompson has brought such fame (Thompson 1975).
31. Veils have links with masks that have deep roots in both popular and elite culture; these links are explored further in Chapter 9.
32. A series of by-laws in London around 1400 prohibited the wearing of masks, visors and false beards. Since these by-laws refer to the Christmas period it is probable that they were concerned with combating the traditional and disorderly celebration of festivals (Riley 1868: 669).

CHAPTER 7 STYLE WARS: FASHION AND THE CLASS STRUGGLE BEFORE CLASSES

1. The term 'style wars' is borrowed from Stuart Cosgrove who uses it in connection with an account of the 1943 racist attacks on Black Americans in the US over 'zoot suits' (Cosgrove 1984).
2. Paul Veyne distinguishes between the gift relationship, epitomized by such practices as the 'potlatch' and the 'kula' (Codere 1950; Malinowski 1922), and what he calls 'euergetism' on the grounds

that the former is a form of exchange relation while the latter is not (Veyne 1990). It seems likely that some version of such a distinction might be pertinent in distinguishing different stages of sumptuary regulation.

3. A similar status elsewhere attached to elephant tails (Wilks 1980: 13).
4. The earliest enactment with anything like a sumptuary content was a decree from King John in 1188 that forbade knights to wear ermine and sable furs when going on crusade (Veale 1966: 18); I can offer no suggestions about how this provision should be understood. The first genuinely hierarchic dress statute came in 1363.
5. The case of China does not fit this model. Some form of sumptuary regulation was present throughout China's feudal period, but it intensified and became more elaborate as the bureaucratic system became consolidated. At this stage it was primarily concerned with the internal differentiation within the imperial palace and its high officials. It underwent a further expansion and became more generalized once an urban merchant class began to acquire economic power. At this stage a hierarchic concern with class competition becomes evident in order to protect the privileged status group's enjoyment of an exclusive style of life unthreatened by competition from a propertied class. Ch'ü suggests, unfortunately without supplying much detail, that there was a degree of oscillation in the extent to which Chinese sumptuary law targeted the urban merchants who were steadily becoming more powerful (Ch'ü 1957, 1961).
6. For a detailed account of the sumptuary laws of Renaissance Italy see Chapter 8.
7. This insistence on the importance of luxury trade is first associated with Sombart (1967), but receives strong support from contemporary economic historians (Le Goff 1988a; Braudel 1982).
8. The Tokugawa regime secured a centralized dominion over 25 per cent of Japanese rice production and introduced a government (Shogunate) over its own domain that also exhibited certain 'national' features superimposed on the rest of Japan which was divided between 265 feudal estates (*daimyo*) which to a greater or lesser extent were pressured into adopting many features of the 'national' laws and regulations.
9. An interesting sidelight on the regulation of the theatre was that after 1629 all females were banned from performing. The immediate result was that the *kabuki* theatre flourished with the development of female impersonation by young men. This in turn gave rise to a new regulatory target as the authorities became preoccupied with sexual morality and homosexuality in particular. This concern was manifest in a whole series of edicts designed to prohibit the social (and presumably sexual) mixing of actors with their publics. By the end of the seventeenth century there emerged a concern to prevent cross-class fraternization between actors and the samurai classes. There was an attempt to stop the type of fraternization implied by the visits of actors to the residences of lords and samurai (Shively 1955: 343).

10. This legislative trajectory runs through until 1604, as it is the acts of 1533 and 1553 that are repeated, with only minor changes, by the successive Elizabethan proclamations. For further discussion of English sumptuary law see Chapter 12.
11. It is worth bearing in mind the small size of the nobility: by 1600 there were only 61 peers in England (39 barons, 2 viscounts, 18 earls, 2 marquesses, 0 dukes); this had risen by 1676 to 156 peers (65 barons, 11 viscounts, 66 earls, 3 marquesses, 11 dukes) (Cressy 1976: 40).
12. For a more detailed discussion of the enforcement of sumptuary law see Chapter 13.
13. It is interesting to note that sumptuary laws were absent from Rhode Island whose founder, Roger Williams, did not conceive of the project of a Puritan commonwealth, but rather elevated the principle of the separation of church and state in order to protect the church, more than to save the state from religious interference. That this led to an explicit rejection of sumptuary laws suggests that these were seen as being an essentially moral matter (North 1974).
14. A similar set of disciplinary projects is identified by Ronnie Hsia as central to both the Protestant and the Catholic Reformations of the sixteenth century (Hsia 1989).
15. Raeff's account of the projects of the well-ordered police state strongly parallels the account offered by Peter Burke and others under the title 'the reform of popular culture' (Burke 1978).
16. Care must be taken with this idea of a declining class. Rarely was this explicitly recognized by the landed classes who remained arrogantly self-confident, secure in their destiny to rule until right up to, and often beyond, their loss of power. I use the term 'declining class' in an objectivist manner to describe circumstances in which their relative position was falling *vis-à-vis* some emerging class or configuration of social forces.
17. The literature on the sociology of fashion has not paid much attention to its interaction with the private/public. Fashion is displayed in the public arena, not only in the streets and squares of the urban world and in special sites of display, in the opera houses and the enclosures of race courses. Fashion is also displayed in private spaces, as in the importance of hospitality and entertainment and in the public-private world of balls, concerts, etc. where the selectivity of the invitation is itself confirmation of the distinction of the participants. Whether or not this reorganization of public and private places is manifest in the style of dress and ornamentation is a question worthy of further inquiry.

CHAPTER 8 GOVERNING THE CITY: REGULATION, STATE FORMATION AND THE COMING OF MODERNITY

1. Important issues revolved around the inclusiveness of these relations of oath swearing; they ritually excluded Jews and increasingly

came to exclude women from all but the lower order guilds. Weber was also more optimistic than was perhaps justified about the extent to which the guilds displaced relations of kinship; it is clear that the patterns of patronage were characteristic of the figuration of Italian cities that retained strong kin-based features which exhibited remarkable persistence.

2. The work of Ian Hunter, which shares much in common with the sociology of governance, lapses from agnosticism into a radical causal atheism that denies the very possibility of any causal inquiry and sees all governance as contingent (Hunter 1988; Hunter *et al.* 1993).
3. A dramatic illustration of self-governance is in the efforts, individually and collaboratively, by early Christian hermits in the Egyptian desert to devise a diet that would eliminate nocturnal ejaculations that only too readily reminded them that they had not overcome their sexuality (Rousselle 1988).
4. The term 'projects' is to be preferred to Foucault's concept 'strategies' which, despite his talk of 'strategies without strategists', is simply too close to motive and purposive action.
5. For further explorations of the implications of governmentality see Rose and Miller (1990) and Gordon (1991); and for its implications for the study of law see Hunt (1993).
6. It should be recalled that Lofland herself located this shift as occurring with the rise of industrial capitalism. I use her thesis in a more general form in order to explore the link between appearential and spatial regulation.
7. There is a very interesting story to be told (one that may already have been written) about the piazzas of Renaissance Italian cities. There was considerable competition for the use of such space which had considerable symbolic significance as a form of public beneficence by both patricians and the most successful merchants. At the same time they were significant religious sites both for regular worship and for processions and parades. They were also major sites of local trade and commerce. Tension and conflict over their use must have been an important feature of 'town planning' in early modern Italy and struggles over spatial control.
8. I rely on Raeff's own account of the content of the ordinances in making this judgment.
9. I am struck by a parallel thrown up by another project in which I am currently interested, namely the regulatory responses of governments to the crises engendered by plague. What strikes me is how pragmatic were the responses to the successive epidemics and how little cumulative regulatory strategy there was in early modern Europe that we would today recognize as a public health policy within a coherent framework of emergency legislation.
10. In one of his characteristic formulations Foucault posits that the history of sexuality involves 'two endeavors that refer back to one another. We shall try to rid ourselves of a juridical and negative representation of power, and cease to conceive of it in terms of law, prohibition, liberty and sovereignty' (1978: 90).

11. However, in 1439 the post of *ufficiale di notte,* who was to be concerned mainly with the prosecution of homosexual offences, was created.
12. A parallel linkage of 'crisis' and sumptuary law can also be seen in the case of Venice. The enactment of Venetian sumptuary laws was usually associated with some crisis or anxiety in which the city government discovered that it did not have the resources for some public project, and concluded that the city's wealth had been squandered by the guilds and the religious fraternities on ostentatious luxury, particularly on pageants (Hazlitt 1900).
13. Greenfield was somewhat timid in dating early sumptuary legislation in Nürnberg and is not forthcoming about these difficulties; no other sources that I have come across provide more specific dating for the earlier legislation.
14. Was this restriction protectionist, to ensure work for local fiddlers or was it concerned with the control of itinerant musicians whom the city fathers regarded as vagrants?
15. A moral element was evident in one of Nürnberg's more idiosyncratic quasi-sumptuary rules that designated locations at which young people could do their courting; my apologies for not recording the source of this sumptuary snippet!
16. I say this, not to disparage Greenfield, but because gender issues did not form any significant part of his agenda.

CHAPTER 9 GENDER WARS: SEX, POWER AND RESISTANCE

1. I have come across no case in which men are specifically exempted.
2. Without, I confess, expending a great deal of effort, I have not been able to discover when and where this formalized dichotomy took root.
3. The rough/smooth dichotomy has one of its primary manifestations in the male secondary sexual characteristic of facial hair that, in turn, is associated with the long-running practice of female depilation. On the grounds that sumptuary law is so predominantly concerned with dress I have not pursued the history of the regulation of beards and moustaches. I have come across passing references to sumptuary prohibitions on beards: for example, it seems to have been a symbolic element in Peter the Great's modernizing project in Russia. Their regulation has also been common in the military and in employers' dress and grooming codes; for further comment see Chapter 14.
4. Today, probably for the first time, post-industrial societies are cautiously experimenting with a more androgynous conception of gender which is characterized by a suspension of any assumption derived from knowledge of an individual's biological sex concerning their social roles or their style of dress. The adoption of unisex styles derive, as so often before, from contemporary sportswear.
5. The complexity of the eroticization of female dress is exemplified by Quentin Bell who draws attention to the fact that from the late

Middle Ages down to the present it is the most formal dress, epitomized by 'the evening dress', that has allowed the maximum exposure of neck, chest, back, etc. whilst daywear has been more 'decent'. He explains this phenomenon with great ingenuity. This fashion remained consistent with the display of a high degree of conspicuous leisure whilst it 'harmonises, both in its modesty and its particular form of outrage, with a romantic and idealistic view of women' (Bell 1976: 142).

6. 'Conspicuous leisure' Veblen identifies as involving the conspicuous abstention from labour and the non-productive consumption of time. This does not necessarily involve indolence (although conspicuous idleness has always marked an essential separation between social classes). Conspicuous leisure frequently manifests itself in time-consuming and demanding and 'labour-intensive' acquisition of skills and accomplishments; to master manners and etiquette requires the investment of conspicuous non-labour time. Thus, as Veblen puts it, 'good breeding' requires a 'substantial and patent waste of time' (1899: 51).
7. These restraints have only in the recent past been brushed aside.
8. While it does not affect the present argument it should be noted that Veblen gets himself into some difficulty trying to sustain his 'persistence of conspicuous consumption' thesis while at the same time attempting to sustain the other process that he identifies, namely the growing privatization of modern urban life, since privatization tends to undermine the conspicuousness of consumption. The late twentieth century 'rich and famous' have found one solution to this dilemma by ensuring that when consumption is undertaken in militarily defended privacy there is always a video-camera handy to record selected representations of their life-style for public dissemination.
9. For Althusser's elaboration of the concept of interpellation see Althusser 1971: 174–75.
10. A positive feature of the household economy was that it significantly displaced preoccupation with the biological reproductive function of women.
11. There is much in common between my account of the position of women in medieval Europe and that offered by Jeanne Schroeder in her study of the implications of medieval discourses about women upon contemporary debates within feminism (Schroeder 1990: 1135). While she draws attention to some of the significant shifts in the construction of femininity she comes very close to conspiracy theory in suggesting that whatever the dominant discourse has been, men always turned it to their own advantage. While she goes a long way to 'historicize feminism' she erects men into an ahistorical misogyny that detracts from her informative discussion of the primary tension between secular and sacred masculine discourses about women.
12. Freudenberger dates this shift from 1630, but without offering any reason for selecting this date (Freudenberger 1963: 39). He is un-

doubtedly wrong in two senses: first, that the significant rise of a wealthy urban merchant class occurred in the key sites much earlier and, second, that the shift of sumptuary focus had by that time long passed to women.

13. (22 Edw. IV (1483): *c.* 1; SR 2, 468–70) 'that this Act extend not nor be prejudicial to or for any Woman excepted the wives of laborers and servants' thus exempting women from the hierarchic restrictions imposed on men. The act of 1514 (6 Hen. VIII, *c.* 1; SR 3, 121–22) went further in exempting all women.
14. Procl. 16, Eliz. I: 15/6/1574; Dyson (1618: No. 154); Hughes and Larkin (1964–69: II: No. 601).
15. A classic example of the shifting locations of public and private action is the role of the 'royal bedchamber' in which what are today regarded as some of our most private routines actually formed important parts of political processes (Castan 1989: 403–45).
16. A very similar provision was included in the 1483 sumptuary law (22 Edw. IV: *c.* 1; SR2, 468–70.).
17. For further discussion of patriarchy see Chapter 10.
18. Unfortunately Burford gave no source for this ordinance and I have not been able to confirm its existence.
19. Unfortunately Karras does not indicate the source of the regulations that she reproduces.
20. The red cord had its origin in a Biblical reference to the red cord let down from her window by the harlot Rahab in the Book of Joshua.
21. While the *rouelle* or ring was the most common mark of degradation imposed on Jews as with prostitutes there was considerable local variation. The now infamous Nazi-imposed 'star' was first introduced by the local town commandant in Wloclawek, Poland, in 1939 from where it spread rapidly throughout the occupied territories (Ruben 1967: 195).

CHAPTER 10 MISOGYNY AND THE POLITICAL ECONOMY OF MARRIAGE: 'THE DETESTABLE WICKEDNESS OF WOMEN'

1. The *Codex* to *Lex Julia* (6th century AD) quoted in Lefkowitz and Fant (1982: 180).
2. All discussion of this ethic, as is so often the case, involves the male experience; I have no evidence whether it was shared by women although they did seem to have restricted the number of children they bore. It is not clear that they valorized celibacy as did the men of the Roman upper classes.
3. The historical background to the Italian dowry system involved a major shift from the early exchange of equivalents consolidating the alliance between kin groups to a one-way payment: first, from groom to bride in the early Middle Ages and second, from the late twelfth century, from the bride's family to the groom's. This reversal from bride-price to dowry, 'the triumph of the reverse dowry', may have resulted from a shifting demographic proportion of males and fe-

males (Herlihy 1978). Klapisch-Zuber (1985) suggests that the major motive underlying the dowry system in medieval Italy was to keep the patrimony intact and thus to avoid marriages resulting in women taking any land out of the male patrimony; instead women were provided with cash dowries.

4. Becker dates this development from 1434 (Becker 1989: 97).

CHAPTER 11 MORAL REGULATION AND POPULAR CULTURE

1. Corrigan's conception of state moral regulation is one in which 'the State within capitalist production, regulates and orchestrates – in short, *organizes* – in such a way that the defining material characteristics of capitalist production relations . . . are made to appear the only way those social activities could be conducted and arranged.' (1980: 15).
2. It should be noted that I have ignored the ecclesiastical or consistory courts, although they had a long history of involvement with moral regulation, since my primary interest lies with the mechanisms of secular moral regulation (Hair 1972; Hill 1969). Although there are suggestions that the English consistory courts had jurisdiction over sumptuary offences, the nearest cases I have come across concern inappropriate dress in church (Hair 1972; Wunderli 1981). In general these church courts, disparagingly labelled the 'bawdy courts', seem to have restricted themselves to a narrower realm of moral regulation concentrating on marriages and sexual offences (Ingram 1987). It should be noted that in the case of Italy Diane Hughes suggests that ecclesiastical and secular jurisdictions worked hand in hand both to legislate and to enforce more explicitly sumptuary offences where ecclesiastical legislation was much preoccupied with female modesty (Hughes 1983).
3. This statute also had a public order dimension, following as it did only a few years after the Peasants Revolt of 1381, in that husbandmen and labourers were forbidden to wear a sword or a dagger.
4. In Scotland a 1424 Act prohibited the playing of 'fut ball' on pain of a 4d. forfeit (APS II: 5: 18).
5. On occasion the military were called out to suppress street football (Delves 1981).
6. The long-bow's capacity against traditional forms of military power was another element that was celebrated and passed down over many generations through the Robin Hood legend. Growing up as a boy in suburban England after the Second World War, I recollect how the 'Tommy gun', the democratic weapon of that modern titanic struggle, after the post-war normalization was replaced in our childhood games by Sherwood green and the bow.
7. An interesting paradox of Robin Hood as a popular hero is that in many versions of the story his ancestry is a dispossessed nobility while in others he is pictured with more lowly roots as a yeoman; in his more lordly personification he could remain popular by invoking traces of Saxon hostility to 'the Norman yoke'.

8. 11 Hen. VII: *c.* 5; SR 2: 569; reenacted in 1503 as 19 Hen. VII: *c.* 12; SR 2: 656.
9. 3 Hen. VIII: *c.* 3; SR 3: 25–26: 'An Act concerning shooting on Long Bows'. Only two years later this statute was reaffirmed in 6 Hen. VIII: *c.* 2; SR 3: 123–24.
10. 18 Hen. VIII, Procl. 5/5/1526; Hughes and Larkin (1964: I: No. 108); and also in 30 Hen. VIII, Procl. 13/9/1538; Hughes and Larkin (1964: I: No. 183).
11. Procl. 12/11/1527; Hughes and Larkin (1964: I: No. 118).
12. A counter-example is provided by the suggestion that in Sicily during the eighteenth century the six laws passed against gambling were directed at saving the nobility from gambling-induced ruin; Smith (1976) claims that the nobility itself begged the king to outlaw gambling.
13. English legislation of the fifteenth century often included rather complicated differentiations between its major categories.
14. The more important detail of the provisions was as follows: *c.* 1 'Every man and woman . . . able in body and within the age of three-score years not being a merchant, a craftsman, a land-holder or a servant . . . he shall be bounden to serve him which so shall him require'; *c.* 2 imposed imprisonment for leaving employment; *c.* 3 fixed wage-rates by re-imposing the 'old rates' existing in 1346; *c.* 4 laid down penalties for any master paying over these statutory rates; *c.* 5 fixed rates for 11 named occupations 'and all other artificers and labourers' at 1346 rates; *c.* 6 forbade the giving of alms to able-bodied beggars.
15. 12 Richard II: *c.* 7–9; SR 2: 58.
16. 14 Eliz. I: *c.* 5; SR IV(1): 590–98 'An Act for the Punishment of Vacabondes'.
17. Walzer discusses the contested evidence (Walzer 1970). It should also be noted that impressment into the army or navy grew and by the end of the century transportation was added to the armament of the state (Beier 1985). In France the 'recruitment' of vagrants and those convicted of criminal offences into the galleys was a major component of the French merchant navy (Bamford 1973; Sargent 1968); in England a proclamation in 1545, 'Ordering Vagabonds to the Galleys' states that 'his royal majesty hath thought convenient and doth determine to use and employ all such ruffians, vagabonds, masterless men, common players, and evil-disposed persons to serve his majesty and his realm in these his wars in certain galleys and other like vessels' (37 Hen. VIII, Procl. 26/5/1545; Hughes and Larkin 1964: I: No. 250). I have not discovered how much use was made of the galleys in Tudor England.
18. 3 Hen. VIII: 5/7/1511 (Hughes and Larkin 1964–67: II: No. 63).
19. There is no evidence as to whether any action resulted from these deliberations.
20. MacDonagh used 'state formation' to designate the processes in which 'without the slightest spur from doctrinaires or any other *a priori* influence, experience and the brute facts of the situation forced those

who were concerned with emigration . . . towards the sort of State we recognize as modern' (MacDonagh 1958: 66).

CHAPTER 12 MAPPING A SUMPTUARY TRADITION: THE ENGLISH EXPERIENCE

1. The most significant treatments of English sumptuary law are to be found in the following. Baldwin (1926) provides the only monograph length study with a focus on the interaction of sumptuary law and fashion in the history of costume tradition. The other studies are all of chapter and article length: Bell and Ruse (1972); Harte (1976); Hooper (1915); Miller (1928).
2. Harte's (1976) study is the exception. Written from the perspective of economic history it interrogates sumptuary legislation for what it can tell us about the formation of social and economic policy in pre-industrial society.
3. 10 Edw. III: st. 3 (1336); SR 1: 278–79.
4. 11 Hen. VI: 6, *c.* 1 (1495); SR II: 279. It is a serious deficiency of Baldwin's history of English sumptuary laws that she simply accepted the preambles at face value.
5. Baldwin claims that this statute was not repealed until 1856; I think it may even have escaped that fate since the item repealed in 19 & 20 Vic., *c.* 64, The Statute of Nottingham, formed *c.* 2 of this statute while the alimentary provisions were set down in *c.* 1.
6. 11 Edw. III: *c.* 4 (1337); SR 1: 280.
7. Other studies of the English fur trade suggest that much production was local and that only the 'finer' furs were imported. This would undermine the fiscal account of the ban on furs to the whole population who would be unlikely to be importing expensive furs (Ewing 1981; Veale 1966).
8. 37 Edw. III: *cc.* 8–14, (1363); SR I: 380–81.
9. The dress regulations of the 1363 Act are discussed in the next section. In this study I have ignored the many attempts, by way of both statutes and proclamations, to impose either fasting or fish-eating that persisted well into the seventeenth century. I regard this legislation as an expression of the imposition of an established religion; but it was also mixed with protectionism for the fish industry, and additionally, as a response to famine or food shortages. In other words fasting and fish-eating had only the most generalized sumptuary dimension, namely they confirmed that the regulation of consumption was a proper object of governmental activity.
10. 8 Hen. VIII, Procl. 31/5/1517; Hughes and Larkin (1964 I: No. 81) In 1539 the attempts was made by 31 Hen. VIII: *c.* 8 – 'An Act that Proclamations made by the King shall be obeyed' – to regularize the use of proclamations; it gave authorization to the King and Council to make proclamations, but excluded enactments affecting Estates, Offices, Liberties, Goods and Liveries (Elton 1960; Heinze 1982). See also 34–35 Hen. VIII: *c.* 23 (Baldwin 1926: 165).

11. The proclamation goes on to provide interesting evidence about the hierarchical ranking and availability of birds. Eight 'quails, dotterels, snites [snipes], and all other fowls of like greatness' were allowed while only two 'pheasants, gulls, and all other fowls of like greatness' were allowed, and finally twelve 'larks and all other fowls of like greatness' were permitted in any dish.
12. 11 Edw. III: *c.* 1 (1337); SR 1: 280. This statute was repealed in 1362 (36 Edw. III: *c.* 11; SR 1: 374) probably as a result of pressure from merchants.
13. 11 Edw. III: *c.* 3 (1337); SR 1: 280. A concern with manufacturing advantage is evidenced in the fact that this statute was explicit in permitting foreign cloth workers to settle in England.
14. The question of the similarity between sumptuary and protectionist law is particularly difficult where the protection takes the form of the imposition of a luxury tax since here there is some element of attack on consumption as such. However, luxury taxes, although frequently couched in the moralizing discourses of luxury, have long been primarily fiscal measures directed to enlarging the revenues of the state.
15. The sliding scale of expenditure prescribed was as follows: the Mayor £6.13s.4d.; Sheriff £5; Recorder, Common Clerk and Bailiffs 6s.8d. (Veale 1966: 11).
16. 23 Edw. III: *c.* 1–4 (1349); SR 1: 307.
17. 23 Edw. III: *c.* 7 (1349); SR 1: 308; 25 Edw. III: St. 2, *c.* 2–5 (1350–51); SR 1: 312–13; 25 Edw. III: St. 5, *c.* 2 (1351–52); SR 1: 319–20.
18. 37 Edw. III: *cc.* 8–14 (1363); SR I: 380–81.
19. 'Act for Regulating Apparel' 3 Edw. IV: *c.* 5 (1463), SR 2: 399–402; 'Act of Apparel' 22 Edw. IV: *c.* 1 (1483), SR 2: 468–70; 'Act against wearing of costly Apparel' 1 Hen. VIII: *c.* 14 (1510), SR 3: 8–9; 'Act of Apparel' 6 Hen. VIII: *c.* 1 (1514), SR 3: 121–22; 'Act of Apparel' 7 Hen. VIII: *c.* 6 (1515), SR 3: 179–82; 'Act for Reformation of Excess in Apparel' 24 Hen. VIII: *c.* 13 (1533), SR 3: 430–32; and 'Act for Reformation of Excess in Apparel' 1 & 2 Phil. & Mary: *c.* 2–6 (1553), SR 4(1): 239.
20. *c.* 8 servants; *c.* 9 tradesmen, artificers and yeomen; *c.* 10 gentlemen under the estate of knight; *c.* 11 merchants, citizens and burgesses; *c.* 12 knights and above; *c.* 13 clergy; and finally – reversing the general order of treatment – *c.* 14 ploughmen. It should be noted that although the categories referred to male statuses and occupations the upper category is specified as being 'Knights and Ladies'; this suggests that while primarily directed at males the statute as a whole may have been intended to embrace the dress of both men and women.
21. Blanket and russet were both cloths woven from rough wool, the latter with a characteristic red-brown colour.
22. *c.* 11 referred to a surprisingly broad class composed of merchants, citizens, burgesses, artificers and handicraft men, although it is likely that few artisans and tradesmen would have capital to the value of £500.

23. 38 Edw. III: *c.* 2 (1364); SR I: 383.
24. The 1402 petition from the Commons proposed an ordinance against cloth of gold, velvet, crimson cloth and hanging sleeves for all save Bannerets or above. The Crown responded by asking Parliament to empower the Council to make ordinances, but no action resulted (Baldwin 1926: 79). Again in 1406 a similar petition was rejected with the proposal that, with the advice of the Council, the Crown would issue ordinances on sumptuary matters (Baldwin 1926: 810. As was to happen again during Elizabeth's reign and again in 1604, sumptuary legislation became entangled with constitutional disputes with respect to the legislative jurisdiction of Crown and Parliament.
25. 13 Rich. II: *c.* 13 (1389); SR 2: 65. An earlier restriction had been imposed on the hierarchic pursuit of falconry prohibiting the keeping of hawks unless the owner was 'of the estate to have a hawk' (37 Edw. III: *c.* 19 (1363); SR 1: 382). A later statute (32 Hen. VIII: *c.* 11 (1540); SR 3: 755) made the stealing of hawk's eggs a capital offence. This statue prefigured the famous eighteenth century Black Act in that it prohibited the wearing of disguises ('his face hid or covered with hood or visor or with his face painted or himself otherwise disguised such that he would not be known'); it also prohibited the taking of deer, rabbits and 'coneys' [young rabbits] from parks using nets or ferrets. More generally hunting rights were determined by reference to income from land (Holdsworth 1903: II: 466; Munsche 1981).
26. 8 Hen. V: *c.* 3 (1420); SR 2: 203.
27. The major statutes of livery were 1 Rich. II: *c.* 7 (1377); 13 Richard II: *c.* 3 (1389); 16 Rich. II: *c.* 4 (1392); 20 Rich. II: *c.* 1 (1396–97); 1 Hen. IV: *c.* 7 (1399); 2 Hen. IV: *c.* 21 (1400); 7 Hen. IV: *c.* 14 (1405); 8 Hen. VI: *c.* 4 (1429); 8 Edw. IV: *c.* 2 (1468); 12 Edw. IV: *c.* 14 (1472); 3 Hen. VII: *c.* 12 (1487); 19 Hen. VII: *c.* 4 (1503). During Henry VII's reign there were a series of proclamations aimed at enforcing early statues on livery and retainers. The campaign against livery and retainers was to persist right down through Elizabeth's reign with a series of proclamations, the last of which was in 1583 (25 Eliz. I: 19/4/1583; Hughes and Larkin 1969: II: No. 664).
28. 'Act for Regulating Apparel' 3 Edw. IV: *c.* 5; SR 2: 399–402. The first four chapters of that year's legislation (3 Edw. IV: *c.* 1–4) instituted protection for English wool, grain and silk, and the next statute (4 Edw. IV: *c.* 1–2) concerned trade standards and protectionism in the textile industry.
29. 4 Edw. IV: *c.* 7 (1465); SR 2: 414.
30. I speculate that in periods when sumptuary laws were enacted frequently, as in fifteenth century Florence or sixteenth century England, it might be possible to correlate shifts in fashion against the changing content of the sumptuary rules, but I do not have sufficient expertise in the history of costume to be able to apply this technique.
31. Baldwin went further and claimed that the petition was approved

and became law (Baldwin 1926: 113); she unfortunately gave no citation and I have been unable to trace this item.

32. 22 Edw. IV: *c.* 1 (1483); SR 2: 468–70.
33. In 1539 an Act was passed for 'Placing of the Lords in Parliament' that set down rules of precedence for the seating of lords spiritual and temporal in Parliament (31 Hen. VIII: *c.* 10 (1539); SR 3: 729–30).
34. A unique feature of the Apparel Act of 1483 was that eleven named individuals were exempted from all provisions except those relating to cloth of gold and purple cloth.
35. 6 Hen. VIII: *c.* 1 (1514); SR 3: 121–22.
36. 1 Hen. VIII: *c.* 14 (1510); SR 3: 8–9.
37. 6 Hen. VIII: *c.* 1 (1514); SR 3: 121–22.
38. 7 Hen. VIII: *c.* 6 (1515); SR 3: 179–82.
39. 24 Hen. VIII: *c.* 13 (1533); SR 3: 430–32.
40. I say 'probably' the last dress statute because subsequent enactments were either very limited in range (in particular that of 1563 (5 Eliz. I: *c.* 6; SR 4(1): 428) or should probably be regarded as protectionist, rather than sumptuary, legislation.
41. 1 & 2 Phil. & Mary: *c.* 2–6; SR 4(1): 239.
42. From 1561 breviats were used to provide summaries of current criminal law in force for local officials.
43. Procl. 21/10/1559; Dyson (1618: No. 14); Hughes and Larkin (1969: II: No. 464).
44. 4 Eliz. I, Procl. 6/5/1562; Dyson (1618: No. 45); Hughes and Larkin (1969: II: No. 493).
45. 4 Eliz. I, Procl. 7/5/1562; Dyson (1618: No. 50); Hughes and Larkin (1969: II: No. 494).
46. There had previously been upward of 20 statutes concerned with the export, breeding and keeping of horses.
47. 8 Eliz. I, Procl. 12/2/1566; Dyson (1618: No. 94); Hughes and Larkin (1969: II: No. 542).
48. 5 Eliz. I: *c.* 6; SR 4(19): 428.
49. 13 Eliz. I: *c.* 19; SR 4(1): 555.
50. 8 Eliz. I: *c.* 11; SR 4(2): 494–95.
51. Harrison suggests that the Act resulted from protectionist pressure from the Incorporated Company of Hat Makers when the wool trade was in serious difficulties (Harrison 1960: 88).
52. 15 Eliz. I, Procl. 28/4/1573; Hughes and Larkin (1969: II: No. 594).
53. 39 Eliz. I: *c.* 18; SR IV(2): 916–18.
54. 16 Eliz. I, Procl. 15/6/1574; Dyson (1618: No. 154); Hughes and Larkin (1969: II: No. 601); and 30 Eliz. I, Procl. 13/2/1588; Dyson (1618: No. 252); Hughes and Larkin (1969: III: No. 697).
55. 22 Eliz. I, Procl. 12/2/1579; Dyson (1618: No. 646); Hughes and Larkin (1969: II: No. 646); 30 Eliz. I, Procl. 13/2/1588; Dyson (1618: No. 252); Hughes and Larkin (1969: III: No. 697).
56. 19 Eliz. I Procl. 16/2/1577; Dyson (1618: No. 168); Hughes and Larkin (1969: II: No. 624).
57. 22 Eliz. I, Procl. 12/2/1579; Dyson (1618: No. 235); Hughes and Larkin (1969: II: No. 646).

58. 39 Eliz. I, Procl. 6/7/1597; Dyson (1618: No. 343); Hughes and Larkin (1969: II: No. 786). A fortnight later there was a minor proclamation (23/7/1597; Steele 1910: No. 891; Hughes and Larkin 1969: III: No. 787) granting a detailed list of exemptions for members of the royal household and named officials.
59. 22 Edw. IV: *c.* 1 (1483); SR 2: 468–70 ('that this Act extend not nor be prejudicial to or for any Woman excepted the wives of laborers and servants'); 6 Hen. VIII: *c.* 1 (1514); SR 3: 121–22. This exemption was repeated in subsequent statutes up to and including 1 & 2 Phil. & Mary: *c.* 6 (1553); SR 4(1): 239.
60. 16 Eliz. I, Procl. 15/6/1574; Dyson (1618: No. 154), Hughes and Larkin (1969: II: No. 601).
61. 16 Eliz. I, Procl. 15/6/1574; Dyson (1618: No. 154), Hughes and Larkin (1969: II: No. 601). The gender-specific regulations are repeated in the last Elizabethan sumptuary proclamation in 1579: 22 Eliz. I, Procl. 12/2/1579 'Enforcing Statutes of Apparel'; Dyson (1618: No. 235); Hughes and Larkin (1969: II: No. 646); Steele (1910: No. 745).
62. There was a rumbling debate that persisted into the seventeenth century about the social role of women, stimulated by arguments over the merits of female succession to the crown. Wright argues that despite the predominance of misogynous discourses, a distinct and novel concern with women's rights emerged among the merchant classes (Wright 1953).
63. 1 Jac. I: *c.* 25; SR 4(2): 1050–52. This repealed 24 Hen. VIII: *c.* 13 (1533) and 1 & 2 Phil. & Mary: *c.* 2–6 (1553) along with a great mass of other Elizabethan legislation.
64. Procl. 24/9/1610; Larkin and Hughes (1973: I: 113); Steele (1910: No. 161).
65. Procl. 27/12/1616; Steele (1910: No. 118).
66. Blackstone noted the repeal of most dress laws, but drew attention to the fact that the early alimentary law of 1363 (10 Edw. III, st. 3) remained unrepealed.
67. This tactic was proposed by the Privy Council Clothing Committee in 1622 (Harte 1976: 150). This sentiment was embodied in one of the first things that James I did when he urged the Commons to make laws that hunting 'be used by none but gentlemen, and that in a gentlemen-like fashion. For it is not fit that clowns should have these sports' (Morgan 1988).
68. 18 & 19 Car. II: *c.* 4; SR 5: 598.
69. This legislation was repeated in 1678 and 1680; in 1678 responsibility for enforcing the funereal sumptuary rules was placed on the clergy (30 Car. II: *c.* 3; SR 5: 885–86; 32 Car. II: *c.* 1; SR 5: 940); in some parishes the special registers were kept up until final repeal in 1814 (4 Geo. III: *c.* 108).

CHAPTER 13 ENFORCING SUMPTUARY LAW

1. I have made no attempt at a thorough coverage of even a single period in English history. I surveyed a sample of sources of informal records and came across no trace of any entry which suggested an awareness of the existence of sumptuary law. I doubt that a more intensive search would be of any great value.
2. In connection with the English legislation of 1515 it is interesting to note that Baldwin did find some evidence of exemption licences that had been granted under its provisions (Baldwin 1926: 153).
3. An example which replicates some features of these administrative alternatives can be seen in controversies over the regulation of alehouses and brewing in Elizabethan England. The Crown was in the habit of granting profitable patents as rewards to courtiers and others while the Commons favoured licensing issued by JPs. The Commons was persuaded that JPs could exercise supervision over alehouses in the public good while patentees exercised their powers for private profit. But it must be remembered that Parliament had a fiscal interest in that the patent system involved a loss of revenue since the proceeds of licensing went into the treasury rather than into private pockets (Clark 1983; Kent 1973).
4. The English sumptuary Act of 1553 (1 & 2 Phil. & Mary: *c*. 2; SR 4(1): 239) extended liability to masters for the sumptuary offences of their servants. A proclamation of 12/2/1579 laid enforcement obligation on heads of households to see that the sumptuary laws were enforced in their private households (22 Eliz. I, Procl. 12/2/1579 'Enforcing Statutes of Apparel'; Hughes and Larkin 1969: II: No. 646).
5. The system of honours moved into a post-feudal context as honours (and then the granting of patents and monopolies) became the main system of rewards available to the crown. In Elizabethan England this produced what Lawrence Stone aptly described as an 'inflation of honours' (Stone 1958).
6. The earlier sumptuary legislation had excluded JPs from jurisdiction, which attests to the initial reserve and later outright hostility of the landed nobility to the 'upstart' JPs; this probably found a particularly sensitive spot when it came to the idea of local JPs concerning themselves with the dress of their social superiors.
7. There is some dispute over the date on which the *provveditori* were created; Kantorowitz gives 1474 (1970: 359), while Hale (1973: 312) gives 1511, but he may well be referring to the creation of *Magistrato delle Pompe* which separated the investigative and prosecutorial roles (Hughes 1983: 72).
8. Sometime before 1512 Padua also acquired sumptuary magistrates (Hughes 1983: 72).
9. In a similar move a Scottish statute in 1581, 'Act Aganis Superfuus Banquetting' (APS III: 221, *c*. 19), charged court officials with appointing searchers with the right of entry into houses and power to place offenders in jail (Shaw 1979: 95).

10. This finding is inconsistent with the general thesis that funerals were subject to regulation because they embodied potentially volatile displays of the wealth and power of traditional clans. Such occasions would revolve around the burial of senior male clan members, whereas the burial of wives seem to have been more private events.
11. This suggests that the half-life of a statute was not limited to recent memory and that the modern idea that statutes live until they are actively repealed was beginning to gain ground.
12. It is interesting to note that the offence is described by reference to colour rather than to the required material, wool, prescribed by the statute; it seems unlikely that where people conformed to the Act (and it is likely that many did because the connection between church attendance and woollen cap wearing would make offenders readily visible) they would have felt constrained to limit themselves to undyed wool.
13. No cases were reported concerning the typical urban offence of prostitution, but there was one interesting item on 'masterless women'. It refers to sundry maid-servants that take rooms and 'live by themselves masterless' and are called by the name of 'charr women'; it asks their lordships to consider the desirability of this state of affairs.
14. Rainey indicates that there exists good supporting data with separate recording of offences, hearings, penalties imposed and fines collected.
15. Gene Brucker provides the most accessible source for this material (Brucker 1971: 181–85).
16. It should be noted how this explanation closely parallels John Demos' account of the initiation of witchcraft accusations as stemming from conflicts generated by the Puritan ethos of cooperation and neighbourliness and the increasing pressures of individualistic self-interest (Demos 1982: 305). While Demos' thesis is impressive it is not clear that Shammas knows where the accusations come from since the records do not reveal this information.
17. Hill used the concept of 'occasional conformity' to describe the tactical responses of many seventeenth century English non-conformists designed to ensure that they were not forced to make the potentially damaging final break from the Church of England, for example by putting in an occasional appearance at the parish church. I am suggesting that his concept can usefully have a wider applicability.

CHAPTER 14 DEATH OR TRANSFORMATION? THE FATE OF THE SUMPTUARY LAWS

1. The myth of legislation is not simply a historical controversy. The capacity or reach of law and regulation remains a key issue in the late twentieth century. It has been central to Hayek's attack on the belief in legal constructivism of both liberal and social-democratic

defenders of the welfare state and, more generally, of the neo-conservative critique of regulation that came to the surface in the Reagan–Thatcher period (Hayek 1973–79).

2. Import control was frequently associated with export restrictions, exports being restricted to ensure plentiful and cheap supply of raw materials to domestic trades and manufacturers.
3. Buck cites a full page of late seventeenth century tracts favouring sumptuary law (Buck 1974: 214–15).
4. The German city-state ordinances that Raeff discusses exhibit a concern that the dead are buried quickly; it is not clear whether this evinces an emergent public health policy or an older concern with economic waste and the loss of productive labour.
5. My differences with Raeff in no way detract from the seminal influence of his work which not only introduced me to the phenomenon of sumptuary laws, but which makes a major contribution to our understanding of the processes of state-information and the role of legal regulation in these developments.
6. Raeff's work adds an interesting dimension to the 'England problem' thrown up by Weber's work on legal rationality. England underwent the most profound and systematic transition to capitalism without, on the surface at least, undergoing some of the most important preconditions of modernization such as legal rationalization or the reform of government. Raeff argues that England did not undergo the same extensive development of the 'well-ordered police state'. He suggests that England's early economic transformation made it possible to delegate most of the functions thus fulfilled by governments elsewhere to individuals and bodies within civil society; the Crown had less need for the complex bureaucratic apparatus that was the result of cameralist government in Germany.
7. The records do not reveal whether any action followed these deliberations.
8. Although less extensive than that introduced during the Second World War, British emergency legislation in 1914–18 had sumptuary features; most prominent were the disciplinary and moralizing controls under the Defence of the Realm Acts over liquor licensing hours.
9. I want to retain the idea of the non-codification of taste and distinction, even though the writers of manuals on etiquette, taste and fashion adopted all the tropes of the legislative form; for example, the test of using the 'proper' accent is by its nature informal and thus remains invisible to those against whom it is deployed. The case of etiquette is undoubtedly analogous to the legislative form; but etiquette, while a necessary condition, is never a sufficient condition to prove acquisition of the cultural capital of taste.
10. Even more neglected is the part played by the regulation of consumption in the colonial regimes of the nineteenth century, one of the classic exemplars of which was the attempt to suppress the *potlatch*, the competitive gift-giving and feasting of the North-Western Indian tribes (Cole and Chaikin 1991).
11. The most obvious illustration of the privatization of regulation is

the expansion of 'private policing' in which more and more sectors of social space come to be regulated by private security agencies (Shearing and Stenning 1987). It is also significant that there is a blurring between the private and public regulation and surveillance institutions: vehicle licensing, police records, national insurance, consumer credit, credit cards are increasingly interactive. It is this denser mesh of regulatory practices, rather than a quantitative growth of a 'big brother' state, that characterizes the modern form of the advance of governance.

12. See, for example, the US case *Greenslade* v *Hoveringham Ltd* (1975) where the dismissal of a young male ledger-clerk for long hair and failure to wear a tie was held to be unfair since these matters had no impact on the employer's legitimate business interests.
13. The significant advance of women into more traditional male employments has brought with it some interesting issues around the appropriateness of safety and other specialist equipment for female employees.
14. *Knott* v *Missouri Pacific Railroad* 527 F.2d 1249 (8th cir. 1975); *Barker* v *Taft Broadcasting Co.* 549 F.2d 400 (6th cir. 1977).
15. CAR 35 at 41 (1912).
16. One way of approaching the ongoing controversies within feminism is to approach them as different constructions of 'harm'; while Robin Morgan, Andrea Dworkin and others find a direct equation between pornography and rape, Catharine MacKinnon explores civil libertarian constructions of harm. Anti-censorship feminists can be understood as being concerned to sustain a distinction between constructs of harm and the justifications for legal intervention (Morgan 1980; Dworkin 1981; MacKinnon 1991; Brown 1981).

CHAPTER 15 SUMPTUARY LAW, REGULATION AND GOVERNANCE

1. This link between income and time is apparent in the English usage in which both time and money are 'spent' (Thompson 1967; Harrison 1986).
2. E.P. Thompson draws attention to the long historical memory embedded in the 'moral economy' of the poor who continued to expect the governing classes to carry through measures such as corn distribution and requiring merchants to sell below the market price (Thompson 1971).

References

Where relevant the date of first publication is shown in square brackets.

Abrahamian, Ervand (1982) *Iran Between the Two Revolutions*, Princeton University Press, Princeton.

Abray, Lorna (1985) *The People's Reformation: Magistrates, Clergy and Commons in Strasbourg, 1500–1598*, Cornell University Press, Ithaca, NY.

Ackroyd, Peter (1979) *Dressing Up: Transvestism and Drag, the History of an Obsession*, Thames & Hudson, London.

Acts of Parliament of Scotland, HMSO, London, 1966.

Akhavi, Shahrough (1980) *Religion and Politics in Contemporary Iran*, SUNY Press, Albany, NY.

Alexander, Sidney (1974) *Lions and Foxes: Men and Ideas of the Italian Renaissance*, Macmillan, New York.

Alexiou, Margaret (1974) *The Ritual Lament in Greek Tradition*, Cambridge University Press, Cambridge.

Althusser, Louis (1971) *Lenin and Philosophy and Other Essays*, New Left Books, London.

Anderson, Benedict (1983) *Imagined Communities: Reflections on the Origin and Spread of Nationalism*, Verso, London.

Anderson, Ruth (1979) *Hispanic Costume 1480–1530*, Hispanic Society of America, New York.

Andrieux, Maurice (1972) *Daily Life in Venice in the Time of Casanova*, Praeger, New York.

Angeloglou, Maggie (1970) *A History of Make-Up*, Studio Vista, London.

Anglo, Sydney (1969) *Spectacle, Pageantry, and Early Tudor Policy*, Clarendon Press, Oxford.

Anon. (1908) 'Against Excess of Apparel', in *Certain Sermons or Homolies Appointed to be Read in Churches in the Time of Queen Elizabeth* [1547], Society for the Promotion of Christian Knowledge, London.

Anon. (1963) 'A Thirteenth Century Castilian Sumptuary Law', 37 *Business History Rev.*, 98–100.

Appelby, Joyce (1978) *Economic Thought and Ideology in Seventeenth Century England*, Princeton University Press, Princeton.

Archer, Ian (1991) *The Purusit of Stability: Social Relations in Elizabethan London*, Cambridge University Press, Cambridge.

Ariès, Philippe and Georges Duby (eds) (1987–91) *A History of Private Life* (5 vols), Harvard University Press, Cambridge, Mass.

Arth, Henry (1924) 'Provisions for the Poore' [1597], in Richard H. Tawney and E. Eileen Power (eds), *Tudor Economic Documents* (Vol. III), Longman, London.

Astin, Alan (1978) *Cato the Censor*, Clarendon Press, Oxford.

Astin, Alan *et al.* (eds) (1989) *The Cambridge Ancient History*, Vol. VIII: *The Rise of Rome to 220 B.C.*, Cambridge University Press, Cambridge.
Aydelotte, Frank (1967) *Elizabethan Rogues and Vagabonds* [1913], Frank Cass, London.
J.B. (1679) *Account of the French Usurpation upon the Trade of England*, London.
Baldwin, Frances (1926) *Sumptuary Legislation and Personal Regulation in England*, Johns Hopkins Press, Baltimore.
Bamford, Paul (1973) *Fighting Ships and Prisons: The Mediterranean Galley of France in the Age of Louis XIV*, University of Minnesota Press, Minneapolis.
Barber, Bernard and Lyle Loebel (1953) '"Fashion" in Women's Clothes and the American Social System', in Reinhard Bendix and Seymour Martin Lipset (eds), *Class, Status and Power*, Free Press, New York, pp. 323–32.
Barbon, Nicholas (1903) 'A Discourse on Trade' [1690], in J. Hollander (ed.), *A Reprint of Economic Tracts*, Johns Hopkins University Press, Baltimore.
Barr, Cyrilla (1989) 'A Renaissance Artist in the Service of a Singing Confraternity', in Marcel Telel, Ronald G. Witt and Rona Goffen (eds), *Life and Death in Fifteenth-Century Florence*, Duke University Press, Durham.
Barthes, Roland (1983) *The Fashion System* [1967] (trans. Matthew Ward and Richard Howard), Hill & Wang, New York.
Batterberry, Michael and Ariane (1977) *Mirror, Mirror: A Social History of Fashion*, Holt, Rinehart & Winston, New York.
Baudrillard, Jean (1975) *The Mirror of Production* (trans. Mark Poster), Telos Press, St. Louis.
Bayne, C.G. (ed.) (1958) *Select Cases in the Council of Henry VII* (Vol. 75), Selden Society, London.
Becker, Marvin (1967) *Florence in Transition*, Vol. I: *The Decline of the Commune*, Johns Hopkins University Press, Baltimore.
Becker, Marvin (1989) *Civility and Society in Western Europe, 1300–1600*, Indiana University Press, Bloomington.
Beier, A.L. (1974) 'Vagrants and the Social Order in Elizabethan England', 64 *Past & Present*, 3–29.
Beier, A.L. (1985) *Masterless Men: The Vagrancy Problem in England 1560–1640*, Methuen, London.
Bell, Clifford and Evelyn Ruse (1972) 'Sumptuary Legislation and English Costume: An Attempt to Assess the Effect of an Act of 1337', 6 *Costume: Journal of the Costume Society*, 22–31.
Bell, Quentin (1976) *On Human Finery*, Hogarth Press, London.
Bellamy, John (1984) *Criminal Law and Society in Late Medieval and Tudor England*, St. Martin's Press, New York.
Bellamy, John (1985) *Robin Hood: An Historical Enquiry*, Croom Helm, London.
Bellamy, John (1989) *Bastard Feudalism and the Law*, Routledge, London.
Bennett, Judith (1991) 'Misogyny, Popular Culture and Women's Work', 31 *History Workshop*, 166–88.

Bennett, Judith (1992) 'Conviviality and Charity in Medieval and Early Modern England', 134 *Past & Present*, 19–41.
Beresford, Maurice (1957) 'The Common Informer, the Penal Statutes and Economic Regulation', 10 *Economic History Rev.*, 221–237.
Berkes, Niyazi (1964) *The Development of Secularism in Turkey*, McGill University Press, Montreal.
Berman, Harold (1983) *Law and Revolution: The Formation of the Western Legal Tradition*, Harvard University Press, Cambridge, Mass.
Berman, Marshall (1982) *All That Is Solid Melts Into Air: The Experience of Modernity*, Simon & Schuster, New York.
Bickeley, Francis (ed.) (1900) *The Little Red Book of Bristol*, Sotheran, London.
Binder, Pearl (1958) *The Peacock's Tail*, George G. Harrap, London.
Black, Anthony (1984) *Guilds and Civil Society in European Political Thought from the Twelfth Century to the Present*, Methuen, London.
Blackstone, William (1979) *Commentaries on the Laws of England* [1765–79], University of Chicago Press, Chicago.
Blanshei, Sarah (1976) *Perugia 1260–1340: Conflict and Change in a Medieval Italian Urban Society*, American Philosophical Society, Philadelphia.
Bloch, R. Howard (1989) 'Medieval Misogyny' in R. Howard Bloch and Frances Ferguson (eds), *Misogyny, Misandry, and Misanthropy*, University of California Press, Berkeley.
Blumer, Herbert (1969) 'Fashion: From Class Differentiation to Collective Selection', 10 *Sociological Quarterly*, 275–291.
Boehn, Max von (1932–35) *Modes and Manner* (4 vols), George G. Harrap, London.
Bogatyrev, Peter (1971) *The Functions of Folk Costume in Moravian Slovakia* (trans. Richard Crum), Mouton, The Hague.
Bonawitz, Achim (1964) 'Helmbrecht's Violation of "Karles Reht"', 56 *Manatshefte*, 177–82.
Boudon, Raymond (1982) *The Unintended Consequences of Social Action*, Macmillan, London.
Bourdieu, Pierre (1980) 'The Production of Belief: Contribution to an Economy of Symbolic Goods', 2 *Media, Culture & Society*, 261–293.
Bourdieu, Pierre (1984) *Distinction: A Social Critique of the Judgement of Taste* [1979], Harvard University Press, Cambridge, Mass.
Bourdieu, Pierre (1990) *In Other Words: Essays Towards a Reflexive Sociology*, Stanford University Press, Stanford.
Bourdieu, Pierre and Jean-Claude Passeron (1977) *Reproduction in Education, Society and Culture*, Sage, London.
Bowsky, William (1964) 'The Impact of the Black Death Upon Sienese Government and Society', 39 *Speculum*, 1–34.
Bowsky, William (1981) *A Medieval Italian Commune: Siena Under the Nine, 1287–1355*, University of California Press, Berkeley.
Boyer, Robert (1990) *The Regulation School: A Critical Introduction* (trans. Craig Charney), Columbia University Press, New York.
Brain, Robert (1979) *The Decorated Body*, Harper & Row, New York.
Braudel, Fernand (1972) 'History and the Social Sciences', in Peter Burke (ed.), *Economy and Society in Early Modern Europe*, Routledge & Kegan Paul, New York.

Braudel, Fernand (1981) *The Structures of Everyday Life: The Limits of the Possible*, Harper & Row, New York.
Braudel, Fernand (1982) *Civilization and Capitalism, 15th–18th Century*, Vol. 2: *The Wheels of Commerce*, Collins, London.
Braunstein, Philippe (1988) 'Towards Intimacy: The Fourteenth and Fifteenth Centuries', in Georges Duby (ed.), *A History of Private Life*, Vol. II: *Revelations of the Medieval World*, Harvard University Press, Cambridge, Mass., pp. 535–630.
Breckman, Warren (1990–91) 'Disciplining Consumption: The Debate About Luxury in Wilhelmine Germany, 1890–1914', 24 *Jnl. of Social History*, 485–505.
Brenninkmeyer, Ingrid (1963) *The Sociology of Fashion*, Westdeutscher Verlag, Köln-Opladen.
Bristow, Edward (1977) *Vice and Vigilance: Purity Movements in Britain Since 1700*, Gill & Macmillan, Dublin.
Brooke, Christopher (1971) *Medieval Church and Society: Collected Essays*, Sidgwick & Jackson, London.
Brooke, Iris (1937) *A History of English Costume*, Methuen, London.
Brooke, Iris (1972) *Footwear: A Short History of European and American Shoes*, Pitman, London.
Brown, Beverley (1981) 'A Feminist Interest in Pornography – Some Modest Proposals', 5/6 *M/F*, 5–18.
Brucker, Gene (ed.) (1971) *The Society of Renaissance Florence: A Documentary Study*, Harper & Row, New York.
Brucker, Gene (1977) *The Civic World of the Early Renaissance Florence*, Princeton University Press, Princeton.
Brundage, James (1987) *Law, Sex and Christian Society in Medieval Europe*, University of Chicago Press, Chicago.
Buchner, Frank (1981) 'Sumptuary Laws: Stomach v. Soul', 53:4 *New York State Bar Jnl.*, 314–19.
Buck, Philip (1974) *The Politics of Mercantilism*, Octagon Books, New York.
Burchell, Graham, Colin Gordon and Peter Miller (eds) (1991) *The Foucault Effect: Studies in Governmentality*, Harvester-Wheatsheaf, Hemel Hempstead.
Burford, Ephraim (1973) *The 'Orrible Synne*, Calder & Boyers, London.
Burford, Ephraim (1976) *Bawds and Lodgings: A History of the Bankside Brothels 1000–1675*, Peter Owen, London.
Burke, Peter (1978) *Popular Culture in Early Modern Europe*, Temple Smith, London.
Burke, Peter (1987) 'Conspicuous Consumption in Seventeenth-Century Italy', in *The Historical Anthropology of Early Modern Italy: Essays on Perception and Communication*, Cambridge University Press, Cambridge, pp. 132–49.
Burton, John (ed.) (1877) *Register of the Privy Council of Scotland*, H.M. General Register House, Edinburgh.
Bushaway, Bob (1982) *By Rite: Custom, Ceremony and Community in England 1700–1800*, Junction Books, London.
J.C. (1891) 'The Sumptuary Laws of Scotland', 35 *Jnl. of Jurisprudence*, 290–97.

Calder, Angus (1969) *The People's War: Britain 1939–1945*, Jonathan Cape, London.

Cammann, Schuyler (1952) *China's Dragon Robes*, Ronald Press, New York.

Campbell, Colin (1987) *The Romantic Ethic and the Spirit of Modern Consumerism*, Basil Blackwell, Oxford.

Carmichael, A.G. (1986) *Plague and the Poor in Renaissance Florence*, Cambridge University Press, Cambridge.

Carus-Wilson, Eleanore (1954) *Medieval Merchant Venturers*, Methuen, London.

Castan, Nicole (1989) 'The Public and the Private', in Roger Chartier (ed.), *A History of Private Life*, Vol. III: *Passions of the Renaissance*, Harvard University Press, Cambridge, Mass., pp. 403–45.

Castle, Terry (1986) 'The Culture of Travesty: Sexuality and Masquerade in Eighteenth-Century England', in G.S. Rousseau and Roy Porter (eds), *Sexual Underworlds of the Enlightenment*, Manchester University Press, Manchester, pp. 156–80.

Chartier, Roger (1989) 'Forms of Privatization', in Roger Chartier (ed.), *A History of Private Life*, Vol. III: *Passions of the Renaissance*, Harvard University Press, Cambridge, Mass., pp. 163–65.

Chevalier, A. (1947) 'Medieval Dress', 57 *CIBA Rev.*, 261–75.

Chevigny, Paul (1991) *Gigs: Jazz and the Cabaret Laws in New York City*, Routledge, New York.

Ch'ü, T'ung-Tsu (1957) 'Chinese Class Structure and Its Ideology', in J.K. Fairbank (ed.), *Chinese Thought and Institutions*, University of Chicago Press, Chicago.

Ch'ü, T'ung-Tsu (1961) *Law and Society in Traditional China*, Mouton, Paris.

Cibber, Colley (1980) *The Double Gallant; or the Sick Lady's Cure*, in Rodney L. Hayley (ed.), *The Plays of Colley Cibber* (2 vols), Garland, New York.

Cicero (1879) *Pro Roscio Amerino*, Macmillan, London.

Clark, Peter (1983) *The English Alehouse: A Social History, 1200–1830*, Longman, London.

Clark, Stuart (1980) 'Inversion, Misrule and the Meaning of Witchcraft', 87 *Past & Present*, 98–127.

Cleaver, Robert (1612) *A Godly Form of Household Government*, n.p. London.

Clode, Charles (1875) *Memorials of the Guild of Merchant Taylors*, Harrison & Sons, London.

Clode, Charles (1888) *The Early History of the Guild of Merchant Taylors* (2 vols), Harrison & Sons, London.

Cocks, Sir Richard (1972) 'Views on Prices and the Economy' [1698], in Joan Thirsk and J.P. Cooper (eds), *Seventeenth Century Economic Documents*, Clarendon Press, Oxford.

Codere, Helen (1950) *Fighting With Property: A Study of Kwakiutl Potlaching and Warfare, 1792–1930*, J.J. Augustus, New York.

Cole, Charles (1931) *French Mercantilist Doctrines Before Colbert*, Richard R. Smith, New York.

Cole, Charles (1939) *Colbert and a Century of French Mercantilism* (2 vols), Columbia University Press, New York.

Cole, Douglas and Ira Chaikin (1991) *An Iron Hand Against the People: The Law Against Potlach on the Northwest Coast*, Douglas & Macintyre, Vancouver.

Collins, Stephen (1989) *From Divine Cosmos to Sovereign State: An Intellectual History of Consciousness and the Idea of Order in Renaissance England*, Oxford University Press, Oxford.

'A Compassionate Conformist' (1682) *England's Vanity, or the Voice of God Against the Monstrous Sin of Pride in Dress and Apparel*, J. Dunton, London.

Cook, S.A. *et al.* (eds) (1932) *The Cambridge Ancient History*, Cambridge University Press, Cambridge.

Corbett, Percy (1930) *The Roman Law of Marriage*, Clarendon Press, Oxford.

Corbin, Alain (1986) *The Foul and the Fragrant: Odor and the French Social Imagination*, Berg, Leamington Spa.

Corbin, Alain (1987) 'Commercial Sexuality in Nineteenth Century France: A System of Images and Regulations', in C. Gallagher and T. Laqueur (eds), *The Making of the Modern Body: Sexuality and Society in the Nineteenth Century*, University of California Press, Berkeley.

Corbin, Alain (1990) *Women For Hire: Prostitution and Sexuality in France After 1850* (trans. Alan Sheridan), Harvard University Press, Cambridge, Mass.

Cornwall, J.C.K. (1988) *Wealth and Society in Early Sixteenth Century England*, Routledge & Kegan Paul, London.

Corrigan, Philip (ed.) (1980) *Capitalism, State Formation and Marxist Theory: Historical Investigations*, Quartet Books, London.

Corrigan, Philip (1988) 'The Politics of Feeling Good: Reflections on Marxism and Cultural Production', in Richard Gruneau (ed.), *Popular Culture and Political Practices*, Garamond Press, Toronto.

Corrigan, Philip and Derek Sayer (1985) *The Great Arch: English State Formation as Cultural Revolution*, Basil Blackwell, Oxford.

Cosgrove, Stuart (1984) 'The Zoot-Suite and Style Warfare', 18 *History Workshop*, 77–91.

Coward, Barry (1988) *Social Change and Continuity in Early Modern England, 1550–1750*, Longman, London.

Cranmer, Thomas (1846) *Miscellaneous Writings and Letters* (2 vols) (ed. J.E. Cox), Parker Society and Cambridge University Press, Cambridge.

Cressy, David (1976) 'Describing the Social Order of Elizabethan and Early Stuart England', 3 *Literature and History*, 29–44.

Culler, Jonathan (1976) *Saussure*, Fontana, London.

Cunnington, C. Willett and Phillis (1952) *Handbook of English Mediaeval Costume*, Faber, London.

Cunnington, C. Willett and Phillis (1972) *Handbook of English Costume in the 18th Century*, Hogarth Press, London.

Cunnington, Phillis and Catherine Lucas (1967) *Occupational Costume in England from the Eleventh Century to 1914*, Adam & Charles Black, London.

Curtis, Bruce (1988) *Building the Educational State: Canada West, 1836–1871*, Falmer Press, Basingstoke.

Curtis, T.C. and W.A. Speck (1976) 'The Societies For the Reformation of Manners: A Case Study in the Theory and Practice of Moral Reform', 3 *Literature & History*, 45–64.

Darnton, Robert (1985) *The Great Cat Massacre*, Vintage Books, New York.

Davenant, Charles (1771) 'An essay on the probable methods of making a people gainers in the balance of trade', in *Political and Commercial Works* (5 vols) (ed. C. Whiteworth), Horsfield, London.

Davis, Fred (1985) 'Clothing and Fashion as Communication', in Michael Solomon (ed.), *The Psychology of Fashion*, Lexington Books, Lexington, Mass., pp. 15–27.

Davis, James (1962) *The Decline of the Venetian Nobility as a Ruling Class*, Johns Hopkins University Press, Baltimore.

Davis, Natalie (1971) 'The Reasons of Misrule: Youth Groups and Charivaris in Sixteenth Century France', 50 *Past & Present*, 41–75.

Davis, Natalie (1975) *Society and Culture in Early Modern France*, Duckworth, London.

Dean, Mitchell (1991) *The Constitution of Poverty: Toward a Genealogy of Liberal Governance*, Routledge, London.

De Certeau, Michel (1984) *The Practice of Everyday Life*, University of California Press, Berkeley.

Dekker, Rudolf and Lotte Van de Pol (1988) *The Tradition of Female Cross-Dressing in Early Modern Europe*, Macmillan, London.

Delves, Anthony (1981) 'Popular Recreation and Social Conflict in Derby', in Eileen Yeo and Stephen Yeo (eds) *Popular Culture and Class Conflict, 1590–1914: Exploration in the History of Labour and Leisure*, Harvester Press, Brighton, pp. 89–127.

de Marly, Diana (1985) *Fashion for Men: An Illustrated History*, Holmes & Meier, New York.

Demos, John (1970) *A Little Commonwealth: Family Life in a Plymouth Community*, Oxford University Press, New York.

Demos, John (1982) *Entertaining Satan: Witchcraft and the Culture of Early New England*, Oxford University Press, Oxford.

Dennis, John (1711) *An Essay Upon Public Spirit*, Bernard Lintott, London.

De Tocqueville, Alexis (1856) *On the State of Society in France Before the Revolution of 1789*, John Murray, London.

Devlin, Patrick (1959) *The Enforcement of Morals*, Oxford University Press, Oxford.

Dilloff, Neil (1980) 'Never on Sunday: The Blue Laws Controversy', 39:4 *Maryland Law Rev.*, 679–714.

Dixon, David (1991) *From Prohibition to Regulation: Bookmaking, Anti-Gambling and the Law*, Clarendon Press, Oxford.

Dostoyevsky, Fydor *Crime and Punishment*, Oxford University Press, Oxford, 1963.

Douglas, Mary (1966) *Purity and Danger: An Analysis of Concepts of Pollution and Taboo*, Routledge & Kegan Paul, London.

Douglas, Mary (1967) 'Primitive Rationing: A Study in Controlled Exchange', in R. Firth (ed.), *Themes in Economic Anthropology*, Tavistock, London, pp. 119–47.

Downs, Donald (1989) *The New Politics of Pornography*, University of Chicago Press, Chicago.

Duby, Georges (1983) *The Knight, the Lady and the Priest: The Making of Modern Marriage in Medieval France*, Pantheon, New York.

Dugdale, Sir William (1666) *Origines Juridiciales, or Historical Memorials of the English Laws*, Warren, London.

Dunham, William and Stanley Pargellis (1938) *Complaint and Reform in England*, Octagon Books, New York.

Dworkin, Andrea (1981) *Pornography: Men Possessing Women*, Women's Press, London, and Basic Books, New York.

Dyson, Humphrey (1618) *A Booke Contayning All Such Proclamations as Were Published During the Reign of the Late Queen Elizabeth*, Bonham, London.

Earle, Alice (1974) *Two Centuries of Costume in America* [1903] (2 vols), Corner House Publishers, Williamstown, Mass.

Easton, S. and A. Hawkins (1988) *Disorder and Discipline: Popular Culture from 1550 to the Present*, Temple Smith, London.

Eco, Umberto (1979) *A Theory of Semiotics*, Indiana University Press, Bloomington.

Edgar, David (1987) 'The New Nostalgia', 31 *Marxism Today*, 30–35.

Ehrlich, Eugen (1962) *Fundamental Principles of the Sociology of Law* [1913] (trans. W.L. Moll and intro. Roscoe Pound), Russell & Russell, New York.

Elias, Norbert (1970) *What Is Sociology?*, Hutchinson, London.

Elias, Norbert (1978) *The Civilizing Process*, Vol. I: *The History of Manners* [1939], Basil Blackwell, Oxford.

Elias, Norbert (1982) *The Civilizing Process*, Vol. II: *State Formation and Civilization* [in USA under title *Power and Civility*], Basil Blackwell, Oxford.

Elias, Norbert (1983) *The Court Society*, Basil Blackwell, Oxford.

Elton, Geoffrey (1960) 'Henry VIII's Act of Proclamations', 75 *English Historical Rev.*, 208–22.

Emmison, Frederick G. (1970) *Elizabethan Life: Disorder*, Essex County Council, Chelmsford.

Epstein, Louis (1948) *Sex Laws and Customs in Judaism*, Bloch Publishing, New York.

Essex County, Massachusetts (1911) *Records and Files of the Quarterly Courts of Essex County, Massachusetts*, Vol. I: *1636–1656*, Essex Institute, Salem.

Evans, Caroline and Minna Thornton (1989) *Women and Fashion: A New Look*, Quartet Books, London.

Evans, E.P. (1906) *The Criminal Prosecution and Capital Punishment of Animals*, William Heinemann, London.

Evans, Joan (1952) *Dress in Mediaeval France*, Clarendon Press, Oxford.

Evelyn, John (1951) *Tyrannus or The Mode: In a Discourse of Sumptuary Lawes* [1661], Basil Blackwell, Oxford.

Ewing, Elizabeth (1981) *Fur in Dress*, B.T. Batsford, London.

Fabre, Daniel (1989) 'Families: Privacy versus Custom', in Roger Chartier (ed.), *A History of Private Life*, Vol. III: *Passions of the Renaissance*, Harvard University Press, Cambridge, Mass., pp. 531–69.

Feinberg, Joel (1984) *The Moral Limits of the Criminal Law* (4 vols), Vol. I: *Harm to Others*, Oxford University Press, New York.
Feltwell, John (1990) *The History of Silk*, Alan Sutton, London.
Fielding, Henry (1988) *An Inquiry into the Cause of the Late Increase of Robbers* [1751] (ed. M.R. Zirker), Clarendon Press, Oxford.
Fiero, Gloria, Wendy Pfeffer and Mathé Allain (eds) (1989) *Three Medieval Views of Women*, Yale University Press, New Haven.
Finkelstein, Joanne (1991) *The Fashioned Self*, Polity Press, Cambridge.
Finkelstein, Louis (1972) *Jewish Self-Government in the Middle Ages* [1924], Greenwood Press, Westport.
Finley, Moses (1985) *The Ancient Economy* (2nd edn), Hogarth Press, London.
Fisher, F.J. (1948) 'The Development of London as a Centre of Conspicuous Consumption in the Sixteenth and Seventeenth Century', 30 (4th ser.) *Trans. Royal Hist. Soc.*, 37–50.
Fisher, Sydney (1898) *Men, Women, and Manners in Colonial Times*, J.P. Lippincott, Philadelphia.
Flaherty, David (1972) *Privacy in Colonial New England*, University Press of Virginia, Charlottesville.
Flandrin, Jean-Louis (1989) 'Distinction Through Taste', in Roger Chartier (ed.), *A History of Private Life*, Vol. III: *Passions of the Renaissance*, Harvard University Press, Cambridge, Mass., pp. 265–307.
Fletcher, Anthony and John Stevenson (eds) (1985) *Order and Disorder in Early Modern England*, Cambridge University Press, Cambridge.
Flugel, John (1950) *The Psychology of Clothes* [1930], Hogarth Press, London.
Foster, Stephen (1971) *Their Solitary Way: The Puritan Social Ethic in the First Century of Settlement in New England*, Yale University Press, New Haven.
Foucault, Michel (1978) *The History of Sexuality*, Vol. I: *An Introduction* [1976], Random House, New York.
Foucault, Michel (1979) 'Governmentality', 6 *Ideology & Consciousness*, 5–21.
Foucault, Michel (1980a) *Power/Knowledge: Selected Interviews and Other Writings 1972–1977* (ed. Colin Gordon), Harvester Press, Brighton.
Foucault, Michel (1980b) 'The Politics of Health in the Eighteenth Century', in *Power/Knowledge: Selected Interviews and Other Writings 1972–1977* (ed. Colin Gordon), Harvester Press, Brighton.
Foucault, Michel (1980c) 'Introduction', *Herculine Barbin, Being the Recently Discovered Memoirs of a Nineteenth-Century French Hermaphrodite* [1978], Pantheon, New York.
Foucault, Michel (1981) 'Omnes et Singulatim: Towards a Criticism of "Political Reason"', in S. McMurrin (ed.), *The Tanner Lectures on Human Values* (Vol. II), Cambridge University Press, Cambridge, pp. 223–54.
Foucault, Michel (1985) *The Care of the Self*, Vol. III: *The History of Sexuality*, Pantheon, New York.
Freud, Sigmund (1953–75) 'Instincts and Their Vicissitudes', *The Standard Edition of the Complete Psychological Works* (24 vols) (trans. and ed. James Strachey), The Hogarth Press, London, Vol. 14.

Freudenberger, Herman (1963) 'Fashion, Sumptuary Laws, and Business', 37 *Business History Rev.*, 37–48.
Friedrichs, Christopher (1979) *Urban Society in an Age of War: Nördlingen, 1580–1720*, Princeton University Press, Princeton.
Garber, Marjorie (1992) *Vested Interests: Cross-Dressing and Cultural Anxiety*, Routledge, New York.
Gardiner, Samuel R. (ed.) (1906) 'Royal Declaration of Sports' [16/10/1633], in *The Constitutional Documents of the Puritan Revolution, 1625–1660* (3rd edn), Clarendon Press, Oxford, pp. 99–103.
Geremek, Bronislaw (1987) *The Margins of Society in Late Medieval Paris*, Cambridge University Press, Cambridge.
Gies, Frances (1978) *Women in the Middle Ages*, Universe Books, New York.
Gilbert, Felix (1973) 'Venice in the Crisis of the League of Cambrai', in John R. Hale (ed.), *Renaissance Venice*, Faber, London.
Gluckman, Max (1983) 'Essays on Lozi Land and Royal Property', in George Dalton (ed.), *Research in Economic Anthropology*, Vol. III, JAI Press, Greenwich, Conn.
Goffman, Erving (1951) 'Symbols of Class Status', 2 *British Journal of Sociology*, 294–304.
Goffman, Erving (1959) *The Presentation of Self in Everyday Life*, Anchor Books, New York.
Gordon, Colin (1991) 'Governmental Rationality', in Graham Burchell, Colin Gordon and Peter Miller (eds), *The Foucault Effect: Studies in Governmentality*, Harvester-Wheatsheaf, Hemel Hempstead.
Gottfried, Robert (1983) *The Black Death: Natural and Human Disaster in Medieval Europe*, Free Press, New York.
Gramsci, Antonio (1971) Selections from the Prison Notebooks of Antonio Gramsci (ed. G. Hoare and G. Nowell-Smith) Lawrence & Wishart, London.
Great Britain (1810–28) *Statutes of the Realm* (11 vols), Dawsons, London.
Greenfield, Kent R. (1918) *Sumptuary Law in Nürnberg: A Study in Paternal Government*, Johns Hopkins University Studies in Historical and Political Science (Vol. XXXVI), Johns Hopkins Press, Baltimore.
Greven, Philip (1977) *The Protestant Temperament: Patterns of Child-rearing, Religious Experience, and the Self in Early America*, Knopf, New York.
Greyerz, Kaspar von (1984) *Religion and Society in Early Modern Europe 1500–1800*, George Allen & Unwin, London.
Gunn, Fenja (1973) *The Artificial Face*, David & Charles, Newton Abbot.
Gurevich, Aron (1985) *Categories of Medieval Culture*, Routledge & Kegan Paul, London.
Gusfield, Joseph (1963) *Symbolic Crusade: Status Politics and the American Temperance Movement*, University of Illinois Press, Urbana.
Gusfield, Joseph (1981) *The Culture of Public Problems: Drinking-Driving and the Symbolic Order*, Chicago University Press, Chicago.
Habermas, Jürgen (1986) 'Law as Medium and Law and Institution', in Gunther Teubner (ed.), *Dilemmas of Law in the Welfare State*, de Gruyter, Berlin, pp. 203–20.

Habermas, Jürgen (1987) *The Theory of Communicative Action*, Vol. II: *Lifeworld and System: A Critique of Functionalist Reason*, Beacon Press, Boston.
Hair, Paul (ed.) (1972) *Before the Bawdy Court: Selections From Church Court and Other Records Relating to the Correction of Moral Offences in England, Scotland and New England*, Elek, London.
Hale, John (1973) *Renaissance Venice*, Faber & Faber, London.
Hall, John (1906) 'Japanese Feudal Law. I: The Institutes of Judicature', 34:1 *Transactions of the Asiatic Society of Japan*, 17–44.
Hall, John (1908) 'Japanese Feudal Law. II: The Ashikaga Code (Kemmu Shikmoku AD 1336)', 36:2 *Transactions of the Asiatic Society of Japan*, 1–23.
Hall, John (1909) 'Japanese Feudal Law. III: The Tokugawa Legislation', 36:4 *Transactions of the Asiatic Society of Japan*, 683–804.
Hall, John (1979) *Japanese Feudal Law* [1906], University Publications of America, Washington, DC.
Hall, Stuart (1980) 'Reformism and the Legalisation of Consent', in National Deviancy Conference (ed.), *Permissiveness and Control: The Fate of the Sixties Legislation*, Macmillan, London.
Hall, Stuart, Chas Critcher, Tony Jefferson, John Clarke and Brian Roberts (1978) *Policing the Crisis: Mugging, the State, and Law and Order*, Macmillan, London.
Hall, Stuart and Tony Jefferson (eds) (1976) *Resistance Through Rituals*, Hutchinson, London.
Hanawalt, Barbara (1975) 'Fur-Collar Crime: The Pattern of Crime Among the Fourteenth Century English Nobility', 8 *Jnl. of Social History*, 1–17.
Hanson, Carl (1981) *Economy and Society in Baroque Portugal, 1668–1703*, University of Minnesota Press, Minneapolis.
Hare, E.H. (1962) 'Masturbatory Insanity: The History of an Idea', 108 *Jnl. of Mental Science*, 1–25.
Hargreaves-Mawdsley, W.N. (1963a) *A History of Academical Dress in Europe Until the End of the Eighteenth Century*, Oxford University Press, Oxford.
Hargreaves-Mawdsley, W.N. (1963b) *A History of Legal Dress Until the End of the Eighteenth Century*, Oxford University Press, Oxford.
Harris, Mary (ed.) (1907–13) *The Coventry Leet Book or Mayor's Register Containing the Records of the City Leet or View of Frankpledge, 1420–1555* (4 vols), Kegan Paul, Trench & Trübner, London.
Harrison, Brian (1971) *Drink and the Victorians: The Temperance Question in England 1815–1872*, Faber & Faber, London.
Harrison, Brian (1974) 'State Intervention and Moral Reform', in Patricia Hollis (ed.), *Pressure From Without in Early Victorian England*, Edward Arnold, London.
Harrison, Mark (1986) 'The Ordering of the Urban Environment: Time, Work and the Occurrence of Crowds, 1790–1835', 110 *Past & Present*, 134–68.
Harrison, Michael (1960) *The History of the Hat*, H. Jenkins, London.
Harrison, William (1968) *An Historical Description of England* [1577] (ed. Georges Edelen), Cornell University Press, Ithaca, NY.

Harsin, Jill (1985) *Policing Prostitution in Nineteenth-Century Paris*, Princeton University Press, Princeton.
Harte, N.B. (1976) 'State Control of Dress and Social Change in Pre-Industrial England', in D.C. Coleman and A.H. John (eds), *Trade, Goverment and Economy in Pre-Industrial England*, Weidenfeld & Nicolson, London, pp. 132–65.
Haug, W.F. (1986) *Critique of Commodity Aesthetics: Appearance, Sexuality and Advertising in Capitalist Society*, University of Minnesota Press, Minneapolis.
Hawthorne, Nathaniel (1981) *The Scarlet Letter* [1850], Bantham Books, New York.
Hay, Douglas (1975) 'Property, Authority and the Criminal Law' in Douglas Hay *et al.*, *Albion's Fatal Tree: Crime and Society in Eighteenth Century England*, Allen Lane, London.
Hayek, F.A. (1973–79) *Law, Legislation and Liberty* (3 vols) Vol. I: *Rules and Orders*, Vol. II: *Mirage of Social Justice*, Vol. III: *The Political Order of a Free People*, Routledge & Kegan Paul, London.
Hazlitt, W. Carew (1900) *The Venetian Republic: Its Rise, Its Growth, and Its Fall, 421–1797*, Adam & Charles, London.
Heal, Felicity (1984) 'The Idea of Hospitality in Early Modern England', 102 *Past & Present*, 66–93.
Hearn, Lafcadio (1904) *Japan: An Attempt at an Interpretation*, Macmillan, New York.
Hearnshaw, F.J.C. and D.M. (1905) *Southampton Court Leet Records*, H.M. Gilbert, Southampton.
Heckscher, Eli (1955) *Mercantilism* [1931] (2 vols) (trans. Mendel Shapiro), George Allen & Unwin, London.
Heer, Friedrich (1962) *The Medieval World: Europe 1100–1350*, Weidenfeld & Nicolson, London.
Heers, Jacques (1977) *Family Clans in the Middle Ages: A Study of Political and Social Structures in Urban Areas*, North-Holland Publishing, Amsterdam.
Heinze, Rudolph W. (1976) *The Proclamations of the Tudor Kings*, Cambridge University Press, Cambridge.
Heinze, Rudolph (1982) 'Proclamations and Parliamentary Protest, 1539–1610', in DeLloyd, Guth J. and John W. McKenna (eds) *Tudor Rule and Revolution: Essays for G.R. Elton from his American Friends*, Cambridge University Press, Cambridge.
Herlihy, David (1976) 'Land, Family and Women in Continental Europe, 701–1200', in Susan M. Stuard (ed.), *Women in Medieval Society*, University of Pennsylvania Press, Philadelphia.
Herlihy, David (1978) 'The Medieval Marriage Market', in *The Social History of Italy and Western Europe*, Variorum Reprints, London.
Herlihy, David (1980) *Cities and Societies in Medieval Italy*, Variorum Reprints, London.
Herlihy, David (1990) 'The Towns of Northern Italy', in Joel T. Rosenthal (ed.), *Medieval Women and the Sources of Medieval History*, University of Georgia Press, Athens.
Herrup, Cynthia (1985) 'Law and Morality in Seventeenth Century

England', 106 *Past & Present*, 102–23.
Hill, Christopher (1969) 'The Bawdy Courts', in *Society and Puritanism in Pre-Revolutionary England*, Panther, London, pp. 288–332.
Hill, Christopher (1972) *The World Turned Upside Down: Radical Ideas During the English Revolution*, Temple Smith, London.
Hill, Christopher (1977) 'Occasional Conformity', in R. Buick Knox (ed.), *Reformation, Conformity and Dissent*, Epworth Press, London.
Hilton, Rodney (ed.) (1976) *Peasants, Knights and Heretics*, Cambridge University Press, Cambridge.
Hilton, Rodney (1990) *Class Conflict and the Crisis of Feudalism: Essays in Medieval Social History*, Verso, London.
Hobsbawm, Eric (1965) *Primitive Rebels: Studies in Archaic Forms of Social Movement in the Nineteenth and Twentieth Centuries* [1959], W.W. Norton, New York.
Hobsbawm, Eric and Ranger Terence (1983) *The Invention of Tradition*, Cambridge University Press, Cambridge.
Holdsworth, W.S. (1903) *A History of English Law* (Vol. II), Methuen, London.
Hollander, Anne (1980) *Seeing Through Clothes*, Viking Press, New York.
Homer (1974) *The Odyssey* (trans. A. Cook), W.W. Norton, New York.
Hooper, Wilfred 1915 'The Tudor Sumptuary Laws', 30 *English Historical Rev.*, 433–49.
Horn, Marilyn (1968) *The Second Skin: An Interdisciplinary Study of Clothing*, Houghton Mifflin, Boston.
Horowitz, Tamar (1975) 'From Elite Fashion to Mass Fashion', 16 *Archives Européenne de Sociologie*, 283–95.
Hsia, Ronnie Po-Chia (1989) *Social Discipline in the Reformation: Central Europe 1550–1750*, Routledge, London.
Hufton, Oliver (1972) 'Begging, Vagrancy, Vagabonds and the Law: An Aspect of the Problem of Poverty in Eighteenth Century France', 2:2 *European Studies Rev.*, 97–123.
Hughes, Diane (1976) 'Invisible Madonnas? The Italian Historiographical Tradition and the Women of Medieval Italy', in Susan M. Stuard (ed.), *Women in Medieval Society*, University of Pennsylvania Press, Philadelphia.
Hughes, Diane (1983) 'Sumptuary Laws and Social Relations in Renaissance Italy', in John Bossy (ed.), *Disputes and Settlements: Law and Human Relations in the West*, Cambridge University Press, Cambridge.
Hughes, Diane (1986) 'Distinguishing Signs: Ear-Rings, Jews and Franciscan Rhetoric in the Italian Renaissance City', 112 *Past & Present*, 3–59.
Hughes, Paul and James Larkin (eds) (1964–69) *Tudor Royal Proclamations* (3 vols), Yale University Press, New Haven.
Huizinga, Johan (1954) *The Waning of the Middle Ages*, Anchor Press, New York.
Hume, Martin A.S. (1896) 'A Fight Against Finery', in *Ten Years After the Armada and Other Historical Studies*, T. Fisher & Unwin, London.
Hunt, Alan (1992) 'Foucault's Expulsion of Law: Towards a Retrieval', 17:1 *Law & Social Inquiry*, 1–38.

Hunt, Alan (1993) *Adventures in Law and Society: Toward a Constitutive Theory of Law*, Routledge, New York.
Hunter, Ian (1988) *Culture and Government: The Emergence of Literary Education*, Macmillan, London.
Hunter, Ian, David Saunders and Dugald Williamson (1993) *On Pornography: Literature, Sexuality and Obscenity Law*, Macmillan, Basingstoke.
Hurlock, Elizabeth (1965) 'Sumptuary Law' in Mary Roach and Joanne Eichler (eds), *Dress, Adornment and the Social Order*, John Wiley, New York, pp. 295–301.
Ingram, Martin (1984) 'Ridings, Rough Music and the "Reform of Popular Culture" in Early Modern England', 105 *Past & Present*, 79–113.
Ingram, Martin (1987) *Church Courts, Sex and Marriage in England, 1570–1640*, Cambridge University Press, Cambridge.
Jaeger, C. Stephen (1985) *The Origins of Courtliness: Civilizing Trends and the Formation of Courtly Ideals, 939–1210*, University of Pennsylvania Press, Philadelphia.
Jarrett, Devereaux (1952) 'The Autobiography of Devereux Jarratt', 9 *William & Mary Quarterly*, 361.
Johnson, E.A.J. (1932) 'Unemployment and Consumption: The Mercantilist View', 46 *Quarterly Jnl. Economics*, 698–719.
Jones, Whitney R. (1970) *The Tudor Commonwealth, 1529–1559*, Athlone Press, London.
Jonson, Ben, George Chapman and John Marston (1979) *Eastward Ho* [1605] (ed. R.W. van Fossen), Manchester University Press, Manchester.
Joseph, Nathan and Nicholas Alex (1972) 'The Uniform: A Sociological Perspective', *Am. Jnl. Sociol.*, 719–30.
Kahn Blumstein, Andrée (1977) *Misogyny and Idealization in the Courtly Romance*, Bouvier Verlag Herbert Grundmann, Bonn.
Kantorowitz, Hermann and N. Denholm-Young (1970) '*De Ornatu Mulierum*: A Consilium of Antonius de Rosellis with an Introduction on Fifteenth Century Sumptuary Legislation' [1933], in Helmut Coing and Gerhard Immel (eds), *Rechtshistorische Schriften von Dr. Hermann Kantorowicz*, Verlag C.F. Müller, Karlsruhe, pp. 341–76.
Karpat, Kemal (1973) *An Inquiry into the Social Foundations of Nationalism in the Ottoman State*, Center of International Studies, Princeton University Press, Princeton.
Karras, Ruth (1989) 'The Regulation of Brothels in Later Medieval England', 14:2 *Signs*, 399–433.
Keen, Maurice (1990) *English Society in the Later Middle Ages 1348–1500*, Allen Lane, London.
Kelso, Ruth (1956) *Doctrine for the Lady of the Renaissance*, University of Illinois Press, Urbana.
Kent, Joan (1973) 'Attitudes of Members of the House of Commons to the Regulation of "Personal Conduct" in Late Elizabethan and Early Stuart England', 46 *Bull. of Instit. of Historical Research*, 41–71.
King, James (1949) *Science and Rationalism in the Goverment of Louis XIV 1661–1683*, Johns Hopkins Press, Baltimore.
Klapisch-Zuber, Christiane (1985) *Women, Family, and Ritual in Renais-*

sance Italy (trans. Lydia Cochrane), University of Chicago Press, Chicago.
König, René (1973) *A la Mode: On the Social Psychology of Fashion*, Seabury Press, New York.
Kovesi-Killerby, Catherine (1993) 'Practical Problems in the Enforcement of Italian Sumptuary Law, 1200–1500', in K. Lowe (ed.), *Crime and Disorder in Renaissance Italy*, Cambridge University Press, Cambridge.
Kracke, E.A. (1975) 'Sung Society: Change Within Tradition', in Chun-Shu Chang (ed.), *Making of China: Main Themes in Premodern Chinese History*, Princeton University Press, Englewood Cliffs, NJ.
Krafft-Ebing, Richard von (1922) *Psychopathia Sexualis*, Physicians and Surgeons Book Co., Brooklyn.
Kroeber, A.L. (1952) 'Order in Changes in Fashion' and 'Three Centuries of Women's Dress Fashions: A Quantitative Analysis', in *The Nature of Culture*, University of Chicago Press, Chicago.
Kroeber, A.L. and J. Richardson (1940) *Three Centuries of Women's Dress Fashions*, University of California Press, Berkeley.
Kunzle, David (1982) *Fashion and Fetishism: A Social History of the Corset, Tight-Lacing and Other Forms of Body Sculpture in the West*, Rowan and Littlefield, Totowa, NJ.
Laband, David and Deborah Heinbuch (1987) *Blue Laws: The History, Economics, and Politics of Sunday Closing Laws*, Lexington Books, Lexington, Mass.
Lacroix, Paul (1931) *History of Prostitution* [1851–52] (2 vols), Covice Friede, New York.
Ladurie, Emmanuel Le Roy (1981) 'Carnivals in History', 3 *Thesis Eleven*, 52–59.
Landes, David S. (1983) *Revolutions in Time: Clocks and the Making of the Modern World*, Harvard University Press, Cambridge, Mass.
Lane, Frederic (1973) *Venice: A Maritime Republic*, Johns Hopkins University Press, Baltimore.
Larkin, James and Paul Hughes (1973) *Stuart Royal Proclamations* (2 vols), Clarendon Press, Oxford.
Lasch, Christopher (1991) *The True and Only Heaven: Progress and Its Critics*, W.W. Norton, New York.
Laslett, Peter (1965) *The World We Have Lost: England Before the Industrial Age*, Charles Scribner's Sons, New York.
Latimer, Hugh (1584) *Fruitful Sermons*, Iohn Daye, London.
Lauer, Jeanette C. and Robert H. (1981) *Fashion Power*, Prentice-Hall, Englewood Cliffs, NJ.
Laver, James (1969a) *Modesty in Dress: An Inquiry into the Fundamentals of Fashion*, Heinemann, London.
Laver, James (1969b) *A Concise History of Costume and Fashion*, Thames & Hudson, London.
Lefkowitz, Mary and Maureen Fant (1982) *Women's Life in Greece and Rome*, Duckworth, London.
Le Goff, Jacques (1988a) *Medieval Civilization 400–1500* (trans. Julia Barrow), Basil Blackwell, Oxford.
Le Goff, Jacques (1988b) *The Medieval Imagination* (trans. Arthur

Goldhammer), University of Chicago Press, Chicago.
Lemire, Beverly (1990–91) 'The Theft of Clothes and Popular Consumerism in Early Modern England', 24:2 *Jnl. of Social History*, 255–76.
Lemire, Beverly (1991) *Fashion's Favourite: The Cotton Trade and the Consumer in Britain, 1660–1800*, Oxford University Press, Oxford.
Lindesiana (1886) *Bibliotheca Lindesiana: Hand-List of a Collection of Broadside Proclamations Issued by Authority of the Kings and Queens of Great Britain and Ireland*, London.
Litwack, Leon (1979) *Been in the Storm So Long: The Aftermath of Slavery*, Alfred A. Knopf, New York.
Lofland, Lyn (1973) *The World of Strangers: Order and Action in Urban Public Space*, Basic Books, New York.
Longworth, Philip (1974) *The Rise and Fall of Venice*, Constable, London.
Lukes, Steven and Andrew Scull (1983) *Durkheim and the Law*, St. Martin's Press, New York, and Martin Robertson, Oxford.
Lurie, Alison (1983) *The Language of Clothes*, Vintage Books, New York.
MacCaffrey, Wallace (1958) *Exeter 1540–1640: The Growth of an English County Town*, Harvard University Press, Cambridge, Mass.
McClain, James (1982) *Kanazawa: A Seventeenth Century Japanese Castle Town*, Yale University Press, New Haven.
McClintock, H.F. (1943) *Old Irish and Highland Dress*, Dundalgan Press, Dundalk.
McCracken, Grant (1985) 'Dress Colour at the Court of Elizabeth I: An Essay in Historical Anthropology', 22:4 *Canad. Rev. Soc. & Anth.*, 515–33.
McCracken, Grant (1988) *Culture and Consumption: New Approaches to the Symbolic Character of Consumer Goods and Activities*, Indiana University Press, Bloomington.
MacDonagh, Oliver (1958) 'The Nineteenth Century Revolution in Government: A Reappraisal', 1 *Historical Jnl.*, 52.
MacDonagh, Oliver (1961) *A Pattern of Government Growth: The Passenger Acts and Their Enforcement*, MacGibbon & Kee, London.
McDonough, Roisin and Rachel Harrison (1978) 'Patriarchy and Relations of Production', in Annette Kuhn and Ann-Marie Wolpe (eds), *Feminism and Materialism: Women and Modes of Production*, Routledge & Kegan Paul, London, pp. 11–41.
McFarlane, Kenneth (1973) *The Nobility of Later Medieval England*, Clarendon Press, Oxford.
MacInnes, Charles (1926) *The Early English Tobacco Trade*, Paul, London.
McKendrick, Neil, John Brewer and J.H. Plumb (1982) *The Birth of a Consumer Society*, Indiana University Press, Bloomington.
MacKinnon, Catharine (1991) 'Pornography as Defamation and Discrimination', 71 *Boston Univ. Law Rev.*, 793–815.
McMullan, John (1984) *The Canting Crew: London's Criminal Underworld, 1550–1700*, Rutgers University Press, New Brunswick.
Maffesoli, Michel (1991) 'The Ethics of Aesthetics', 8 *Theory, Culture & Society*, 7–20.
Malinowski, Bronislaw (1922) *Argonauts of the Western Pacific*, Routledge, London.

Mandeville, Bernard (1957) *The Fable of the Bees, or Private Vices, Publick Benefits* [1705] (ed. F.B. Kaye), Clarendon Press, Oxford.
Mandeville, Bernard (1973) *A Modest Defence of Publick Stews* [1724], William Andrews Clark Memorial Library, Los Angeles.
Mann, Michael (1985) *The Sources of Social Power*, Vol. I: *A History of Power From the Beginning to* AD *1760*, Cambridge University Press, Cambridge.
Mann, Thomas (1947) *Buddenbrooks: The Decline of a Family* [1901], Secker & Warburg, London.
Marques, A.H. de Oliveira (1971) *Daily Life in Portugal in the Late Middle Ages*, University of Wisconsin Press, Madison.
Marsh, Robert (1961) *The Mandarins: The Circulation of Elites in China, 1600–1900*, Free Press of Glencoe, New York.
Marshall, T.H. (1963) 'Citizenship and Social Class', in *Sociology at the Crossroads*, Heinemann, London.
Marx, Karl (1961) *Capital: A Critique of Political Economy* (Vol. I), Foreign Languages Publishing House, Moscow.
Mather, Cotton (1694) *Ornaments for the Daughters of Zion*, Thomas Parkhurst, London.
Mauss, Marcel (1979) *Sociology and Psychology: Essays*, Routledge & Kegan Paul, London.
Mennell, Stephen (1985) *All Manner of Food: Eating and Taste in England and France from the Middle Ages to the Present*, Basil Blackwell, Oxford.
Mennell, Stephen (1989) *Norbert Elias: Civilization and the Human Self-Image*, Basil Blackwell, Oxford.
Merry, Sally (1990) *Getting Justice and Getting Even: Legal Consciousness Among Working-Class Americans*, University of Chicago Press, Chicago.
Mertes, Kate (1988) *The English Noble Household 1250–1600: Good Governance and Politic Rule*, Basil Blackwell, Oxford.
Merton, Robert K. (1937) 'The Unintended Consequences of Purposive Social Action', 1 *Am. Jnl. Sociology*, 894.
Miers, David (1984) 'The Regulation of Commercial Gaming', 11 *Jnl. Law & Society*, 33–66.
Miles, Devi (1987) *Forbidden Pleasures: Sumptuary Laws and the Ideology of Moral Decline in Ancient Rome*, PhD thesis, London University.
Miller, Daniel (1987) *Material Culture and Mass Communications*, Basil Blackwell, Oxford.
Miller, E. (1965) 'The Fortunes of the English Textile Industry in the Thirteenth Century', 18:1 *Econ. Hist. Rev.*, 78–82.
Miller, John (1966) *The First Frontier: Life in Colonial America*, Dell, New York.
Miller, Sylvia (1928) 'Old English Laws Regulating Dress', 20 *Jnl. of Home Economics*, 89–94.
Millett, Kate (1970) *Sexual Politics*, Doubleday, Garden City, NY.
Mills, Harrianne (1984) 'Greek Clothing Regulations: Sacred or Profane?', 55 *Zeitschrift für Papyrolgie und Epigraphik*, 255–65.
Minson, Jeff (1985) *Genealogies of Morals: Nietzsche, Foucault, Donzelot and the Eccentricity of Ethics*, Macmillan, London.
Miskimin, Harry (1969) *The Economy of Early Renaissance Europe, 1300–*

1460, Prentice-Hall, Englewood Cliffs, NJ.
Miskimin, Harry (1977) *The Economy of Later Renaissance Europe, 1460–1600*, Cambridge University Press, Cambridge.
Mitchell, Rosamund and M.D.R. Leys (1950) *A History of the English People*, Longman Freen, London.
Molloy, John T. (1975) *Dress for Success*, Wyden, New York.
Mommsen, Theodore (1862–66) *The History of Rome* (4 vols), R. Bentley, London.
Montaigne, Michel de (1958) 'Of Sumptuary Laws' [1572], in *The Complete Works of Montaigne* (trans. D.M. Frame), Hamish Hamilton, London.
Montesquieu, Baron de (1900) *The Spirit of the Laws* [1748] (trans. T Nugent), Colonial Press, New York.
Moore, Robert (1987) *The Formation of a Persecuting Society: Power and Deviance in Western Europe*, Basil Blackwell, Oxford.
Morgan, Edmund (1988) *Inventing the People: The Rise of Popular Sovereignty in England and America*, W.W. Norton, New York.
Morgan, Robin (1980) 'Theory and Practice: Pornography and Rape', in Laura Lederer (ed.), *Take Back the Night: Women on Pornography*, Morrow, New York.
Muchembled, Robert (1985) *Popular Culture and Elite Culture in France, 1400–1750*, Louisiana State University Press, Baton Rouge.
Mukerji, Chandra (1983) *From Graven Images: Patterns of Modern Materialism*, Columbia University Press, New York.
Mullett, Charles (1956) *The Bubonic Plague and England: An Essay in the History of Preventive Medicine*, University of Kentucky Press, Lexington.
Mun, Thomas (1664) *England's Treasure by Forraign Trade or the Balance of our Forraign Trade is the Rule of our Treasure*, n.p., London.
Munsche, Peter (1981) *Gentlemen and Poachers: The English Game Laws 1671–1831*, Cambridge University Press, Cambridge.
Murray, Alexander (1978) *Reason and Society in the Middle Ages*, Clarendon Press, Oxford.
Neumann, R.P. (1975) 'Masturbation, Madness, and the Modern Concepts of Childhood and Adolescence', 8 *Jnl. of Social History*, 1–27 (Spring).
Newburn, Tim (1992) *Permission and Regulation: Law and Morals in Post-War Britain*, Routledge, London.
Newett, M. Margaret (1907) 'The Sumptuary Laws of Venice in the Fourteenth and Fifteenth Centuries', in T.F. Tout and J. Tait (eds), *Historical Essays*, Manchester University Press, Manchester, pp. 245–78.
Newton, Stella (1974) *Health, Art & Reason: Dress Reformers of the 19th Century*, John Murray, London.
Newton, Stella (1988) *The Dress of the Venetians 1495–1525*, Scolar Press, Aldershot.
Nörr, Dieter (1981) 'The Matrimonial Legislation of Augustus: An Early Instance of Social Engineering', 16 *The Irish Jurist*, 350–64.
Norris, Herbert (1924) *Costume and Fashion: The Evolution of European Dress*. (Vol. I), J.M. Dent, London.
North, Gary (1974) 'The Puritan Experiment with Sumptuary Legislation', 24 *Freeman*, 341–55.

Oestreich, Gerhard (1982) *Neostoicism and the Early Modern State*, Cambridge University Press, Cambridge.
Okely, Judith (1983) *The Traveller-Gypsies*, Cambridge University Press, Cambridge.
Okey, T. (1907) *The Old Venetian Palaces and the Old Venetian Folk*, J.M. Dent, London.
O'Malley, Pat (1992) 'Containing Our Excitement: Commodity Culture and the Crisis of Discipline', in Susan Sibley and Austin Sarat (eds), *Studies in Law, Politics and Society*, Vol. 13, JAI Press, Greenwood, Conn.
Origo, Iris (1957) *The Merchant of Prato, Francesco di Marco Datini*, Cape, London.
Otis, Leah (1985) *Prostitution in Medieval Society: The History of an Urban Institution in Languedoc*, University of Chicago Press, Chicago.
Owst, Gerald (1933) *Literature and Pulpit in Medieval England*, Cambridge University Press, Cambridge.
Ozment, Steven (1975) *The Reformation in the Cities: The Appeal of Protestantism to Sixteenth Century Germany and Switzerland*, Yale University Press, New Haven.
Pagels, Elaine (1988) *Adam, Eve, and the Serpent*, Random House, New York.
Pannick, David (1985) *Sex Discrimination Law*, Clarendon Press, Oxford.
Paoletti, Jo (1987) 'Clothing and Gender in America: Children's Fashions, 1890–1920', 13 *Signs*, 136–43.
Pendarves (1656) *Endeavour for Reformation in Apparel*, London.
Pepys, Samuel (1976) *The Diary of Samuel Pepys*, (11 vols) (eds R. Latham and W. Matthews), Bell & Hyman, London.
Percy, Lord Eustace (1907) *The Privy Council under the Tudors*, B.H. Blackwell, Oxford.
Perkins, William (1608) *A Discourse of the Damnable Art of Witchcraft*, C. Legge, Cambridge.
Perry, Mary (1978) '"Lost Women" in Early Modern Seville: The Politics of Prostitution', 4:1 *Feminist Studies*, 195–214.
Perry, Mary (1990) *Gender and Disorder in Early Modern Seville*, Princeton University Press, Princeton.
Phillips, Joanna and Helen Staley (1961) 'Sumptuary Legislation in Four Centuries', 53 *Journal of Home Economics*, 673–77.
Philopoliteios (1685) *Memorials for Government of Royal Burghs in Scotland*, Forbes, Aberdeen.
Phythian-Adams, Charles (1979) *Desolation of a City: Coventry and the Urban Crisis of the Late Middle Ages*, Cambridge University Press, Cambridge.
Pike, Luke O. (1968) *A History of Crime in England*, [1873–76] (2 vols), Patterson Smith, Montclair, NJ.
Pirenne, Henri (1956) *Economic and Social History of Medieval Europe* [1937], Harcourt Brace, New York.
Pisan, Christine de (1985) *The Treasury of the City of Ladies* (trans. Sarah Lawson), Penguin Books, Harmondsworth.
Plato (1941) *The Republic of Plato* (trans. F.M. Cornford), Clarendon Press, Oxford.

Plato (1970) *The Laws* (trans. T.J. Saunders), Penguin Books, Harmondsworth.

Plucknett, T.F.T. (1936) 'Some Proposed Legislation of Henry VIII', 19 (4th Ser.) *Trans. Royal Historical Soc.*, 119–44.

Plucknett, T.F.T. (1949) *Legislation of Edward I*, Clarendon Press, Oxford.

Plumb, John H. (1972) 'Clothes', in J.H. Plumb, *In the Light of History*, Allen Lane, London, pp. 190–94.

Poggi, Gianfranco (1978) *The Development of the Modern State: A Sociological Introduction*, Hutchinson, London.

Porter, Roy (1985) 'Making Faces: Physiognomy and Fashion in Eighteenth Century England', 38 *Etudes Anglaises*, 385–96.

Posner, Richard (1990) *The Problems of Jurisprudence*, Harvard University Press, Cambridge, Mass.

Post, Robert (ed.) (1991) *Law and the Order of Culture*, University of California Press, Berkeley.

Postan, Michael *et al.* (eds) (1963) *The Cambridge Economic History of Europe*, (Vol. III), Cambridge University Press, Cambridge.

Power, Eileen (1975) *Medieval Women*, Cambridge University Press, Cambridge.

Pullan, Brian (1973) 'The Occupations and Investments of the Venetian Nobility in the Middle and Late Sixteenth Century', in John Hale (ed.), *Renaissance Venice*, Faber & Faber, London.

Pullan, Brian (1973) *A History of Early Renaissance Italy From the Mid-Thirteenth Century to the Mid-Fifteenth Century*, Allen Lane, London.

Putnam, Bertha (ed.) (1938) *Proceedings Before the Justices of the Peace in the Fourteenth Centuries: Edward III to Richard III*, Spotiswoode, Bellantyre & Co., London.

Quicherat, Jules (1875) *Histoire du Costume en France*, Libraire Hachette, Paris.

Raeff, Marc (1983) *The Well-Ordered Police State: Social and Institutional Change Through Law in the Germanies and Russia, 1600–1800*, Yale University Press, New Haven.

Rainey, Ronald (1985) *Sumptuary Legislation in Renaissance Florence*, PhD thesis, Columbia University, New York.

Redlich, Fritz (1963) 'A Needed Distinction in Fashion Study', 37:1–2 *Business History Rev.*, 3–4.

Reischauer, Edwin and John Fairbank (1958) *East Asia: The Great Tradition*, Houghton Mifflin, Boston.

Renner, Karl (1972) *The Institutions of Private Law and their Social Functions* [1949] (ed. Otto Kahn-Freund), Routledge & Kegan Paul, London.

Ribeiro, Aileen (1984) *Dress in Eighteenth Century Europe 1715–1789*, B.T. Batsford, London.

Richards, Jeffrey (1990) *Sex, Dissidence and Damnation: Minority Groups in the Middle Ages*, Routledge, London.

Richie, Donald (1973) 'The Japanese Art of Tattooing', 82 *Natural History*, 50–59.

Riley, Henry (1868) *Memorials of London and London Life in the Thirteenth, Fourteenth and Fifteenth Centuries*, Longmans, Green & Co., London.

Ritter, Abraham (1857) *History of the Moravian Church in Philadelphia*, Philadelphia.

Roach, Mary (1979) 'The Social Symbolism of Women's Clothes', in Justine Cordwell and Ronald Schwarz (eds), *The Fabrics of Culture: The Anthropology of Clothing and Adornment*, Mouton, The Hague.

Roach, Mary and Joanne Eichler (eds) (1965) *Dress, Adornment and the Social Order*, John Wiley, New York.

Roach, Mary and Joanne Eichler (1979) 'The Language of Personal Adornment', in Justine Cordwell and Ronald Schwarz (eds), *The Fabrics of Culture: The Anthropology of Clothing and Adornment*, Mouton, The Hague.

Roberts, Helene (1977) 'The Exquisite Slave: The Role of Clothes in the Making of the Victorian Woman', 2:3 *Signs*, 554–69.

Rogers, Katharine (1966) *The Troublesome Helpmate: Misogyny in Literature*, University of Washington Press, Seattle.

Roper, Lyndal (1985a) 'Discipline and Respectability: Prostitution and the Reformation in Augsburg', 19 *History Workshop*, 3–28.

Roper, Lyndal (1985b) '"Going to Church and Street": Weddings in Reformation Augsburg', 106 *Past & Present*, 62–101.

Roper, Lyndal (1989) *The Holy Household: Women and Morals in Reformation Augsburg*, Clarendon Press, Oxford.

Rose, Mary Beth (1984) 'Women in Men's Clothing: Apparel and Social Stability in "The Roaring Girl"', 14:3 *English Literary Renaissance*, 367–91.

Rose, Mary Beth (ed.) (1986) *Women in the Middle Ages and the Renaissance*, Syracuse University Press, Syracuse.

Rose, Nikolas (1992) *Towards a Critical Sociology of Freedom*, Goldsmiths' College, London.

Rose, Nikolas and Peter Miller (1990) 'Governing Economic Life', 19 *Economy & Society*, 1–31.

Rosen, George (1974) *From Medical Police to Social Medicine: Essays on the History of Health Care*, Science History Publications, New York.

Ross, Edward (1909) *Social Psychology*, Macmillan, New York.

Rossiaud, Jacques (1988) *Medieval Prostitution*, Basil Blackwell, Oxford.

Rothstein, Natalie (1964) 'The Calico Campaign of 1719–1721', 7 *East London Papers*, 3–21.

Rousseau, Jean-Jacques (1972) 'A Dissertation on Political Economy' [1767], in *The Miscellaneous Works of Mr. J.J. Rousseau* (Vol. II), Burt Franklin, New York.

Rousselle, Aline (1988) *Porneia: On Desire and the Body in Antiquity* [1983] (trans. Felicia Pheasant), Basil Blackwell, Oxford.

Rowdon, Maurice (1970) *The Fall of Venice*, Weidenfeld & Nicolson, London.

Rubens, Alfred (1967) *A History of Jewish Costume*, Peter Owen, London.

Sacks, David (1989) 'Celebrating Authority in Bristol, 1475–1640', in Susan Zimmermann and Ronald Weissman (eds), *Urban Life in the Renaissance*, University of Delaware Press, Newark.

Sahlins, Marshall (1976) *Culture and Practical Reason*, University of Chicago Press, Chicago.

Salusbury, A. (1939) *A Street Life in Medieval England*, Pen In Hand, Oxford.

Salzman, L.F. (1964) *English Trade in the Middle Ages*, H. Pordes, London.

Sargent, A.J. (1968) *The Economic Policy of Colbert*, Burt Franklin, New York.

Schama, Simon (1987) *Embarrassment of Riches: An Interpretation of Dutch Culture in the Golden Age*, Knopf, New York.

Schevill, Ferdinand (1936) *History of Florence From the Founding of the City Through the Renaissance*, G. Bell & Sons, London.

Schmidt, Leigh (1989) 'A Church-Going People Are a Dress-Loving People: Clothes, Communication, and Religious Culture in Early America', 58:1 *Church History*, 36–51.

Schneider, Robert (1989) *Public Life in Toulouse 1463–1789: From Municipal Republic to Cosmopolitan City*, Cornell University Press, Ithaca.

Schochet, Gordon (1974) *Patriarchalism in Political Thought: The Authoritarian Family, Political Speculation, Attitudes Especially in 17th Century England*, Basil Blackwell, Oxford.

Schroeder, Jeanne (1990) 'Feminism Historicized: Medieval Misogynist Stereotypes in Contemporary Feminist Jurisprudence', 75 *Iowa Law Rev.*, 1135–217.

Scott, James (1985) *The Weapons of the Weak: Everyday Forms of Peasant Resistance*, Yale University Press, New Haven.

Scott, S.P. (trans.) (1973) 'The Law of the Twelve Tables', in *The Civil Law* (2 vols), AMS Press, New York, Vol. I, pp. 58–65.

Scribner, Bob (1978) 'Reformation, Carnival, and the World Turned Upside-Down', 3:3 *Social History*, 303–29.

Sedgwick, Henry (1933) *Italy in the Thirteenth Century*, Houghton Mifflin, Boston.

Sekora, John (1977) *Luxury: The Concept in Western Thought, Eden to Smollett*, Johns Hopkins University Press, Baltimore.

Sennett, Richard (1974) *The Fall of Public Man*, Cambridge University Press, Cambridge.

Shammas, Carole (1990) *The Pre-Industrial Consumer in England and America*, Clarendon Press, Oxford.

Shapiro, Susan (1987) 'Sex, Gender, and Fashion in Medieval and Early Modern Britain', 20:4 *Jnl. of Popular Culture*, 113–28.

Sharp, Andrew (1974) 'Edward Waterhouse's View of Social Change in Seventeenth-Century England', 62 *Past & Present*, 27–46.

Shaw, Frances (1979) 'Sumptuary Legislation in Scotland', 24 *Juridical Rev.*, 81–115.

Shearing, Clifford and Phillip Stenning (1987) *Private Policing*, Sage, New York.

Sheedy, Anna (1942) *Bartolus on Social Conditions in the Fourteenth Century*, Columbia University Press, New York.

Shively, Donald (1955) 'Bakufu versus Kabuki', 18 *Harvard Jnl. of Asiatic Studies*, 326–56.

Shively, Donald (1964–65) 'Sumptuary Regulation and Status in Early Tokugawa Japan', 25 *Harvard Jnl. Asiatic Stds.*, 123–64.

Shklar, Judith (1978) 'Jean Jacques Rousseau and Equality', 107: 3 *Daedalus*, 13–25.
Shurtleff, Nathaniel (ed.) (1968) *The Records of the Govenor and Company of the Massachusetts Bay Company* [1853] (5 vols), American Medieval Society Press, New York.
Simmel, Georg (1904) 'Fashion', 10 *International Quarterly*, 130–55.
Slack, Paul (1974) 'Vagrants and Vagrancy in England, 1598–1664', 27 *Econ. Hist. Rev.*, 360–79.
Slack, Paul (1985) *The Impact of Plague in Tudor and Stuart England*, Routledge, London, 1985.
Slack, Paul (1988a) 'Responses to Plague in Early Modern Europe: The Implications of Public Health', 55: 3 *Social Research*, 433–453.
Slack, Paul (1988b) *Poverty and Policy in Tudor and Stuart England*, Longman, London.
Small, Albion (1900) *The Cameralists: The Pioneers of German Social Policy*, Franklin, New York.
Smart, Carol (ed.) (1992) *Regulating Womanhood: Historical Essays on Marriage, Motherhood and Sexuality*, Routledge, London.
Smith, Denis (1968) *Medieval Sicily, 800–1713* (2 vols), Chatto & Windus, London.
Smith, Derek (1993) 'The Emergence of "Eskimo Status": An Examination of the Eskimo Disk List System and its Social Consequences, 1925–1970', in Noel Dyck and James Waldram (eds), *Anthropology, Public Policy and Native Peoples in Canada*, McGill-Queen's University Press, Montreal.
Smith, Sir Thomas (1969) *A Discourse of the Commonweal of the This Realm of England* [1581] (ed. Mary Dewar), University Press of Virginia, Charlottesville.
Sombart, Werner (1967) *Luxury and Capitalism* [1913], University of Michigan Press, Ann Arbor.
Sontag, Susan (1983) *Illness as Metaphor*, Penguin Books, Harmondsworth.
Spedding, James (ed.) (1868–90) *The Letters and the Life of Francis Bacon* (7 vols), Longman, Green, London.
Spencer, Herbert (1876) *Principles of Sociology* (Vol. I), Williams & Norgate, London.
Spengler, Joseph (1960) 'Mercantilist and Physiocratic Growth Theory', in Bert Hoselitz (ed.), *Theories of Economic Growth*, Free Press, New York, pp. 3–64.
Steele, Robert (1910) *Bibliography of Royal Proclamations of the Tudor and Stuart Sovereigns 1485–1714* (2 vols), Clarendon Press, Oxford.
Steele, Valerie (1985) *Fashion and Eroticism: Ideals of Feminine Beauty from the Victorian Era to the Jazz Age*, Oxford University Press, New York.
Stone, Lawrence (1947) 'State Control in Sixteenth Century England', 17 *Econ. Hist. Rev.*, 103–20.
Stone, Lawrence (1958) 'The Inflation of Honours 1558–1641', 14 *Past & Present*, 45–70.
Stone, Lawrence (1967) *The Crisis of the Aristocracy, 1558–1641*, Oxford University Press, New York.
Stone, Lawrence (1977) *The Family, Sex and Marriage in England 1500–*

1800, Weidenfeld & Nicolson, London.
Stone, Lawrence (1990) *Road to Divorce: England 1530–1987*, Oxford University Press, Oxford.
Stone, Lawrence and Jeanne (1984) *An Open Elite? England 1540–1880*, Clarendon Press, Oxford.
Stow, John (1633) *The Survey of London Contayning the Original, Increase, Modern Estate, and Government of that City* [1598], J. Wolfe, London.
Strauss, Gerald (1966) *Nuremburg in the Sixteenth Century*, John Wiley, New York.
Strauss, Gerald (1986) *Law, Resistance and the State: The Opposition to Roman Law in Reformation Germany*, Princeton University Press, Princeton.
Strocchia, Sharon (1989) 'Death Rites and the Ritual Family in Renaissance Florence', in Marcel Telel, Ronald G. Witt, and Rona Goffen (eds), *Life and Death in Fifteenth-Century Florence*, Duke University Press, Durham.
Stubbes, Phillip (1972) *Anatomie of the Abuses in England* [1583], Theatrum Orbis Terrarum, Amsterdam.
Swanson, Heather (1988) 'The Illusion of Economic Structure: Craft Guilds in Late Medieval English Towns', 121 *Past & Present*, 29–48.
Swift, Jonathan (1939–74) *Prose Works of Jonathan Swift* (ed. H. Davis), Basil Blackwell, Oxford.
Tarde, Gabriel (1903) *The Laws of Imitation* [1890], Henry Holt, New York.
Tawney, Richard and Eileen Power (eds) (1924) *Tudor Economic Documents* (3 vols), Longman, London.
Taylor, Ian, Paul Walton and Jock Young (1972) *The New Criminology*, Routledge & Kegan Paul, London.
Taylor, Lou (1983) *Mourning Dress: A Costume and Social History*, Allen & Unwin, London.
Tertullian (1982) 'On the Apparel of Women' [202AD], in Alexander Roberts and James Donaldson (eds), *The Ante-Nicene Fathers*, W.B. Eerdmans Publishing, Grand Rapids.
Teubner, Gunther (1992) 'The Two Faces of Janus: Rethinking Legal Pluralism', 13:5 *Cardozo Law Rev.*, 1443–62.
Thirsk, Joan (1973) 'The Fantastical Folly of Fashion: The English Stocking Knitting Industry, 1500–1700', in N.B. Harte and K.G. Ponting (eds), *Textile History and Economic History*, Manchester University Press, Manchester, pp. 50–73.
Thomas, Keith (1983) *The Perception of the Past in Early Modern England*, Creighton Trust Lecture, University of London.
Thompson, E.P. (1967) 'Time, Work-Discipline and Industrial Capitalism', 38 *Past & Present*, 56–97.
Thompson, E.P. (1971) 'The Moral Economy of the English Crowd in the Eighteenth Century', 50 *Past & Present*, 76–136.
Thompson, E.P. (1974) 'Patrician Society, Plebeian Culture', 7:4 *Jnl. Social History*, 382–405.
Thompson, E.P. (1975) *Whigs and Hunters: The Origin of the Black Act*, Allen Lane, London.

Thompson, E.P. (1978) 'Eighteenth-Century English Society: Class Struggle Without Class', 3:2 *Social History*, 133–65.
Thompson, E.P. (1991) *Customs in Common*, Merlin Press, London.
Thompson, T.W. (1923) 'Consorting With and Counterfeiting Egyptians', 2:2 *Jnl. of Gypsy Lore Soc.*, 81–93.
Thrupp, Sylvia (1948) *The Merchant Class in Medieval London, 1300–1500*, University of Chicago Press, Chicago.
Tickell, John (1798) *The History of the Town and County of Kingston-upon-Hull*, T. Lee & Co., Hull.
Tierney, Brian (1959) *Medieval Poor Law: A Sketch of Canonical Theory and Its Application in England*, University of California Press, Berkeley.
Tilly, Charles (ed.) (1975) *The Formation of Nation States in Western Europe*, Princeton University Press, Princeton.
Tilly, Charles (1989) 'Cities and States in Europe, 1000–1800', 18 *Theory & Society*, 563–84.
Titmuss, Richard (1971) *The Gift Relationship: From Human Blood to Social Policy*, Allen & Unwin, London.
Toher, M. (1986) 'The Tenth Table and the Conflict of the Orders', in Kurt Raaflaub (ed.), *Social Struggles in Archaic Rome: New Perspectives on the Conflict of the Orders*, University of California Press, Berkeley.
Toledo, Alfonso de (1959) *Little Sermons on Sin: The Archpriest of Talavera* [1438] (trans. Lesley Simpson), University of California Press, Berkeley.
Tönnies, Ferdinand (1961) *Custom: An Essay on Social Codes*, Free Press, New York.
Trexler, Richard (1980) *Public Life in Renaissance Florence*, Academic Press, New York.
Trexler, Richard (1984) 'Follow the Flag: The Ciompi Revolt Seen From the Streets', 46 *Bibliotheque d'Humanisme et Renaissance*, 357–392.
Tribe, Keith (1988) *Governing Economy: The Reformation of German Economic Discourse 1750–1840*, Cambridge University Press, Cambridge.
Troeltsch, Ernst (1931) *The Social Teaching of the Christian Churches* (2 vols), Allen & Unwin, London.
Turkel, Gerald (1992) *Dividing Public and Private*, Praeger, New York.
Turner, Bryan (1984) *The Body and Society: Explorations in Social Theory*, Basil Blackwell, Oxford.
Turner, Bryan (ed.) (1990) *Theories of Modernity and Postmodernity*, Sage, London.
Turner, Ernest (1950) *Roads to Ruin: The Shocking History of Social Reform*, Michael Joseph, London.
Tuve, Rosemond (1966) *Allegorical Imagery: Some Medieval Books and Their Posterity*, Princeton University Press, Princeton.
Van Paasen, Pierre (1960) *A Crown of Fire: The Life and Times of Girolamo Savonarola*, Charles Scribner's Sons, New York.
Veale, Elspeth (1966) *The English Fur Trade in the Later Middle Ages*, Clarendon Press, Oxford.
Veblen, Thorstein (1967) *The Theory of the Leisure Class* [1899], Viking Press, New York.
Venice *Collection of Sumptuary Edicts* [BL 1609/1196].
Veyne, Paul (ed.) (1987) *History of Private Life*, Vol. I: *From Pagan Rome*

to Byzantium, Harvard University Press, Cambridge, Mass.
Veyne, Paul (1990) *Bread and Circuses: Historical Sociology and Political Pluralism* [1976] (trans. Brian Pearce), Allen Lane, London.
Vielle, Paul (1978) 'Iranian Women in Family Alliance and Sexual Politics', in Lois Beck and Nikki Keddie (eds), *Women in the Muslim World*, Harvard University Press, Cambridge, Mass.
Vincent, John (1897) 'European Blue Laws', *Annual Report of American Historical Assoc.*, 355–73.
Vincent, John (1935) *Costume and Conduct in the Laws of Basel, Bern and Zurich 1370–1800*, Johns Hopkins Press, Baltimore.
Vincent, John (1937) 'Sumptuary Legislation', 14 *Encyclopedia of Social Science*, Macmillan, New York, pp. 464–66.
Wadmore, James (1902) *Account of the Worshipful Company of Skinners of London*, Blades, East & Blades, London.
Waley, Daniel (1991) *Siena and the Sienese in the Thirteenth Century*, Cambridge University Press, Cambridge.
Walker, Joseph (1818) *An Historical Essay on the Dress of the Ancient and Modern Irish* [1788], J. Christie, Dublin.
Walter, John and Keith Wrightson (1976) 'Dearth and the Social Order in Early Modern England' 71 *Past & Present*, 22–42 (May).
Walzer, Michael (1965) *The Revolution of the Saints: A Study in the Origins of Radical Politics*, Harvard University Press, Cambridge, Mass.
Walzer, Michael (1970) 'The Revolutionary Use of Repression', in Melvin Richter (ed.), *Essays in Social and Political History*, Harvard University Press, Cambridge, Mass.
Warner, Frank (1921) *The Silk Industry of the United Kingdom: Its Origins and Development*, Drane, London.
Warwick, Edward *et al.* (1965) *Early American Dress: The Colonial and Revolutionary Periods*, Benjamin Blom, New York.
Weatherill, Lorna (1988) *Consumer Behavior and Material Culture in Britain, 1660–1760*, Routledge, Chapman & Hall, New York.
Weber, Max (1978) *Economy and Society: An Outline of Interpretive Sociology* (eds Guenther Roth and Claus Wittich) (2 vols), University of California Press, Berkeley.
Weeden, William (1890) *Economic and Social History of New England 1620–1789* (2 vols), Houghton Mifflin, Boston.
Wegert, Karl (1981) 'Patrimonial Rule, Popular Self-Interest, and Jacobinism in Germany, 1763–1800', 53 *Jnl. of Modern History*, 440–67.
Weibel, Kathryn 1977 *Mirror, Mirror: Images of Women in Popular Culture*, Anchor Books, Garden City, NY.
Weisner, Merry (1986) 'Women's Defense of Their Public Role', in Mary Beth Rose (ed.), *Women in the Middle Ages and the Renaissance*, Syracuse University Press, Syracuse.
Weisner, Merry (1988) 'Paternalism in Practice: The Control of Servants and Prostitutes in Early Modern German Cities', in Phillip Bebb and Serrin Marshall (eds), *The Process of Change in Early Modern Europe*, Ohio University Press, Athens, pp. 179–200.
Weisser, Michael (1979) *Crime and Punishment in Early Modern Europe*, Harvester Press, Brighton.

Weissman, Ronald (1982) *Ritual Brotherhood in Renaissance Florence*, Academic Press, New York.

Weissman, Ronald (1989) 'The Importance of Being Ambiguous: Social Relations, Individualism and Identity in Renaissance Florence', in Susan Zimmermann and Ronald Weissman (eds), *Urban Life in the Renaissance*, University of Delaware Press, Newark.

Welford, Richard (1884) *History of Newcastle and Gateshead in the Fourteenth and Fifteenth Centuries* (3 vols), W. Scott, London.

Wesley, John (1984) *The Works of John Wesley* (14 vols), Abingdon Press, Nashville.

Whately, W. (1617) *The Bride Bush*, London.

Whitaker, W.B. (1933) *Sunday in Tudor and Stuart Times*, Houghton, London.

Wickham, Gary (1992) 'Towards a Sociology of Governance', mimeo.

Wigmore, John (1969) *Law and Justice in Tokugawa Japan*, University of Toyko Press, Toyko.

Wilks, Ivor (1980) 'The Golden Stool and the Elephant Tail' in George Dalton (ed.), *Research in Economic Anthropology* (Vol. 2), JAI Press, Greenwich, Conn.

Williams, Neville (1959) *Contraband Cargo: Seven Centuries of Smuggling*, Longman, London.

Williams, Raymond (1973) *The Country and the City*, Chatto & Windus, London.

Williams, Raymond (1980) *Problems in Materialism and Culture: Selected Essays*, Verso, London.

Williams, Robert (1990) *The American Indian and Western Legal Thought: The Discourse of Conquest*, Oxford University Press, New York.

Williams Committee (1979) *Report of the Committee on Obscenity and Film Censorship*, HMSO, London.

Wilson, Elizabeth (1985) *Adorned in Dreams: Fashion and Modernity*, Virago Press, London.

Wilson, Elizabeth (1992) 'The Invisible Flâneur', 191 *New Left Rev.*, 90–110.

Wilson, Katharina and Elizabeth Makowski (1990) *Wykked Wyves and the Woes of Marriage: Misogynous Literature from Juvenal to Chaucer*, SUNY Press, Albany, NY.

Wittfogel, Karl A. and Fêng Chia-shêng (1949) *History of Chinese Society, Liao*, American Philosophical Society, Philadelphia.

Wolfenden, Sir John (1957) *Report of Committee on Homosexual Offences and Prostitution*, Cmnd. 247, HMSO, London.

Wright, Louis (1953) *Middle-Class Culture in Elizabethan England*, University of North Carolina Press, Chapel Hill.

Wrightson, Keith (1981) 'Alehouses, Order and Reformation in Rural England, 1590–1660', in Eileen Yeo and Stephen Yeo (eds), *Popular Culture and Class Conflict, 1590–1914: Exploration in the History of Labour and Leisure*, Harvester Press, Brighton, pp. 1–27.

Wrightson, Keith (1982) *English Society, 1580–1680*, Rutgers University Press, New Brunswick.

Wrightson, Keith and David Levine (1979) *Poverty and Piety in an English Village: Terling, 1525–1700*, Academic Press, New York.

Wunderli, Richard (1981) *London Church Courts and Society on the Eve of the Reformation*, Medieval Academy of America, Cambridge, Mass.
Yeo, Eileen and Stephen (eds) (1981) *Popular Culture and Class Conflict, 1590–1914: Exploration in the History of Labour and Leisure*, Harvester Press, Brighton.
Youings, Joyce (1984) *Sixteenth-Century England*, Allen Lane, London.
Young, Agnes (1937) *Recurring Cycles of Fashion: 1760–1937*, Harper, New York.
Youngs, Frederic (1976) *The Proclamations of the Tudor Queens*, Cambridge University Press, Cambridge.

CASES

Australian Tramways Employers' Assoc. v *Brisbane Tramways Co. Ltd.* (1912) CAR 35.
Greenslade v *Hoveringham Ltd.* [1975] IRLR 114.
Hart v *Jacobs* Fed. Court of Australia (General Divison) 3354 (1981).
Knott v *Missouri Pacific Railroad* 527 F.2d 1249 (8th cir. 1975).
Lanigan v *Bartlett & Co. Grain* 466 F.Supp. 1388 (1979).
McConomy v *Croft Inns Ltd* [1992] IRLR 561.
Phillips v *Martin Marietta Corp.* 400 U.S. 542 (1971).
Schmidt v *Austicks Bookshops Ltd.* [1977] IRLR 360.

Index